Read here the unthinkable. Carefully docu [illegible] a celebrated entertainer, the writer promot [illegible] boy-man sexuality. It can be, he contends, mutually positive. It can be more than sexual – caring, bonding, loving.

This very readable book is packed with extensive research on Michael Jackson's 'dangerous liaisons'. It portrays his sex partner preference, without doubt, as males – those nearly or recently pubertal. And, the author argues, such pairings need not be condemned.

Many readers will be outraged. Their convictions about the evils of any boy-man sexuality will prevail. But whether or not one is convinced, shaken, or even stirred by the author, this is a recommended read. It isn't just another book about 'Wacko Jacko'. There won't be anything written quite like it.

Richard Green, Emeritus Professor of Psychiatry, University of California, Los Angeles; Founding President, 1975, International Academy of Sex Research; Founding Editor, 1971-2001, Archives of Sexual Behavior

Michael Jackson's Dangerous Liaisons is the most engaging, informed, and generous-hearted book we have on the subject or are likely ever to have.

If it has a fault, it is the modesty which informs the intelligence and compassion controlling this study: readers (of the title alone, say) might mistake its reach and depth, both of which are enormous, ranging over our sad cultural landscape with an acuity and alertness to detail and nuance vital to this field and almost never exercised. I recommend this book strongly to anyone who feels our self-righteous egoism may have gotten in the way of our ability to see what is in front of our eyes and to act with some measure of justice and kindness.

Professor James R Kincaid, University of Southern California, author of Erotic Innocence: The culture of child molesting

MICHAEL JACKSON'S DANGEROUS LIAISONS

Arvizo, Barnes, Bhatti, Chandler, Culkin...
The A-Z of All the King's Boys

Carl Toms

Matador
5 Weir Road
Kibworth Beauchamp
Leicester LE8 0LQ, UK
Tel: (+44) 116 279 2299
Email: books@troubador.co.uk
Web: www.troubador.co.uk/matador

ISBN 978-1848763-401

A Cataloguing-in-Publication (CIP) catalogue record for this book is available from the British Library.

Printed in the UK by TJ International, Padstow, Cornwall

Matador is an imprint of Troubador Publishing Ltd

"Ever since I was born Daddy has been the best father you could ever imagine and I just wanted to say I love him so much."
Paris Katherine Michael Jackson, 11, at her father's memorial event

"Wasn't nothing strange about your Daddy. It was strange what your Daddy had to deal with."
Reverend Al Sharpton, also at the Staples Center memorial

"...even if the allegations against Michael Jackson are true, it doesn't mean all of his good deeds for children were motivated simply to seduce them. He surely has a genuine love of children that goes beyond any sexual interest."
Nicholas Groth, clinical psychologist, co-author of
Sexual Assault of Children and Adolescents
in Time *magazine, 27 December 1993*

"I wanted to believe that Michael was innocent of any wrongdoing with Jordie Chandler, of course. I hoped that was the case. But that doesn't necessarily make it so."
J Randy Taraborrelli, biographer, in
Michael Jackson: The Magic, The Madness, The Whole Story, 1958-2009

Contents

CHAPTER ONE

Introduction: Gone too Soon?

Gone too soon? Or blessed release? The sudden, tragic death of Michael Jackson in strange circumstances, on the eve of what might have been the greatest comeback in showbiz history, stunned the world – and quickly divided the soothsayers between those who believed the maestro could indeed have reclaimed his throne as the King of Pop and those who saw the superstar as a mental and physical wreck, a burnt-out shell ever since his trial on child abuse allegations four years earlier.

Like so much of Michael's life, his death was a source of mystery and intense speculation: Was it suicide? Or murder? What about the will? Who would have the children? Whose children were they anyway? What drugs was he on? Did he take them only to beat pain and insomnia? Or were libido suppressants also in the mix?

And yet such questions, mesmerising in their fascination though they were, may have been less salient for many than one overwhelming, albeit unspoken sentiment: relief. Michael's passing, after all, marked the day when it finally became possible to stop worrying whether he had been a child molester. Never again could he be arrested and dragged through the courts on some shameful and humiliating charge. It was time to celebrate the music and the moonwalks again, free from the niggling anxiety that the entertainer might once more become an embarrassment.

Gone too soon? For those who wanted to bury the bad news of his dubious sexuality death instantly changed the narrative. Like the passing of Princess Diana, it became the focus for a massive outpouring of sentiment. In the seventy two hours after the event, Michael's death generated more internet traffic than 9/11, the Iraq War, or the global financial meltdown.[1] There was grieving, there were tears, but also celebration of the legend, and a sense that it would now be bigger than ever. As the wits had it, death was the greatest career move Michael could have made. Catching the mood, the news media were flooded with special editions and commemorative supplements.[2] Jackson albums shot to the top of the charts again; Jackson impersonators were never more in demand, Jackson tribute books were rushed to the presses. And the focus was overwhelmingly positive: Jackson was big again. Bigger even than Elvis.

Ultimately, though, the questions must return. Michael had "issues" that cannot be denied, especially as regards the proper boundaries of intimacy between adults and children. Fans had always leapt to defend Michael's sleepovers with young boys. Does taboo-breaking become OK if the transgressor is seen as kind and loving, qualities so often ascribed to Michael? The fact that he was so toweringly a public figure affords us a perhaps unique opportunity to confront such questions openly – an openness which I hope will enable us better to understand the ethics not just of Michael's behaviour but our own too.

Note that I speak here of "Michael", not "Jackson". It's friendlier that way. In common with millions of his fans, I warmed to his gentle off-stage persona and his aspirations for a better world. Yes, his thoughts along these lines were vague and sentimental; and, yes, his extravagant lifestyle was always in glaring contradiction to his concern for sick and needy children, even if he did give generously to charity. But, hey, that's show business! Stars must dazzle, not just twinkle. The task I have set myself here is not to indict Michael with hypocrisy or anything else – though there will be no airbrushing of the record – but rather to look at the cards life dealt him and to ponder sympathetically how well or ill he played them.

With that aim in mind I began many years ago to research and write this book. The plan was to review fairly and thoroughly all the evidence that had come into the public domain about Michael's emotional and physical engagement with children, especially young boys. In the early days much of this information was hardly more than tabloid gossip but that changed as the years passed: legal documents came to light; detailed, credible accounts were written by investigators and insiders; and of course there was the trial.

Michael was rightly acquitted on all charges because his accusers were clearly unreliable witnesses. But, far from clearing Michael's name, some of the most credible evidence increased, rather than diminished, the suspicion that he was obsessively attracted to boys and had been involved in sexual acts with a number of them – who may or may not have included his principal accuser in court.

At the time of Michael's death these pages were fortuitously almost ready to go to press. Apart from minor revisions, and a few important additions, I have allowed the text to stand unchanged. It is a long book, so some guidance may be helpful as to its contents and where I will be taking the reader chapter by chapter. Some notes on my source material will conclude this introduction.

An account of the allegations by Michael's first accuser, thirteen-year-old Jordie Chandler, how they broke upon the world, the scandal they provoked, their impact on Michael's life, and the eventual out-of-court settlement, occupies chapters Two and Three. These chapters outline the main elements of the story largely as they unfolded at the time, so that some flavour of the initial response is retained, both in the sensational tabloids and the more temperate media. Chapters Four, Five, and Six continue with different aspects of the unfolding story, so that the narrative flow is not interrupted. Before coming to an in-depth exploration of the Chandler case, though, I have found it desirable first to delve analytically into themed chapters on research into sexual relationships between men and boys (Chapter Seven), Michael's family (Chapter Eight) and personality (Chapter Nine). Jordie's case is taken up again as the second of three chapters (Ten, Eleven, and Twelve) on "power". Using the detailed evidence now available, Chapter Eleven examines minutely the power relationships at work in the three-way dynamic between Michael and Jordie, Jordie and his father, Evan, and between Evan and Michael. Thus the early chapters about Jordie Chandler (Two and Three) are significantly separated from the third one (Chapter Eleven) in which he is once more in the spotlight. I have tried to write in a way that will not tax the reader's memory of the earlier chapters too heavily.

A further sequence of chronologically narrative chapters takes in Michael as a husband and father (Chapter Thirteen), and the trial (Chapters Fourteen, Fifteen, Sixteen, and Seventeen). Finally, Chapter Eighteen brings the story up to Michael's death and its immediate aftermath, and reviews the book's findings against its initial aims. The early chapters refer forward to later events where this is helpful, as for instance in the case of boys whose friendships with Michael were publicised in 1993-4 and who gave evidence many years later in court. This includes figures such as former child star Macaulay Culkin.

I began the original version of this introduction all those years ago with a passage intended to have emotional resonance for fans:

> Fists pound a wall in the most exclusive suite of "the world's finest hotel", the Oriental in Bangkok. "I never hurt anyone!" sobs a tortured Michael Jackson over and over again, "I never hurt anyone." No-one is about to argue. His closest aides, nervous and embarrassed, know there are times when it could be career suicide even to raise a sceptical eyebrow. Challenge Michael in mid-tantrum over the children he stands accused of abusing? Not smart. Their thoughts are on damage limitation, not moral disputation. How the hell to get out of this fix…

The dramatic scenario was an imaginative reconstruction culled from news reports of late August 1993, when the Asian leg of Jackson's *Dangerous* tour was living up to its name: the media dogs of war were snapping at his heels just after the scandal broke over his alleged sexual involvement with young Jordie Chandler. The King of Pop's fans were massing outside the hotel, clamouring for the latest news, especially anything that would prove their hero's innocence. In the air-conditioned luxury of the hotel, those aides were sweating over the crisis as surely as the fans in the tropical heat outside.

This opening scene-setter was designed to tell a story in lively terms, to show empathy with Michael's suffering and at the same time to provide a good example of a tabloid yarn that might or might not have been true: there had been no unimpeachable witnesses to what really happened in that hotel room. Many pages of my introduction were then given over to this "problem of knowledge": how can we ever really be confident we know the facts when so many of the sources have been dubious?

At that time, early in 1994, the publicly available resources could all too easily be dismissed as tittle tattle based on chequebook journalism, but that soon ceased to be the case. Even before the year was out Christopher Andersen's *Michael Jackson Unauthorized* appeared.[3] Andersen could prove nothing of significance, but his main claims have not been discredited and he builds a strong circumstantial case.

Much more substantial, though, are *Michael Jackson Was My Lover:*

The Secret Diary of Jordie Chandler, by Victor Gutierrez and *All That Glitters: The Crime and the Cover-up*, by Raymond Chandler.[4] Both books focus on the relationship between Michael and Jordan (Jordie) Chandler, whose complaint of sexual abuse (a complaint made unwillingly, at his father's behest) was what sensationally first shot Michael's love-life with boys into the public arena.

It should be said immediately that Gutierrez was successfully sued by Jackson. This was not over the book but over his claim, in a TV interview, to have seen a video in which Michael was sexually intimate with a boy. Damages of $2.7 million were awarded when he was unable to produce the video, either in court or out.[5] He fled to South America. Nevertheless, his work is to be taken very seriously indeed, for reasons I explore in Chapter Eleven. The book, which appeared in 1996, provided copious detail of an intimate social and sexual relationship between Michael and Jordie.

In many respects the extensive detail provided by Gutierrez is precisely confirmed in the account given years later in the book by Raymond Chandler, Jordie's uncle. There is no question of this family member merely plagiarising the earlier account. He had no need to. It is clear from his book that he was in the confidence of his brother Evan, Jordie's father, at the critical period, and he cites legal documents and crucial tape-recorded discussions that can only have come from his position as an insider to the case. In effect, he retrospectively validates Gutierrez' account, even though he never once so much as mentions the man's name. No commentator, so far as I am aware, has yet picked up on the forensic significance of the close concurrence between these two writers, whose styles and conclusions (to say nothing of their temperaments and motivations) are nevertheless poles apart.

The most important point about both books is that they do not shirk from boldly asserting, with powerful documentary backing (and in Gutierrez' case numerous relevant photographs, including one of Jordie's hand-written description of Michael's genitals), that the relationship between Michael and Jordie was sexual. Neither author was ever sued on account of these assertions. The authorities would dearly have loved to see Michael charged with offences against this boy but, for well rehearsed reasons, it never happened: after receiving a multi-million dollar out-of-court settlement that bound him to secrecy, Jordie never showed any inclination to take the stand in a criminal case against his former lover. He declined even to appear at Michael's trial as a witness to what became known as "prior bad acts" by the entertainer.

Those who have paid close attention to all the information available on the Chandler case in recent years – and especially from when Uncle Ray's book appeared in 2004 – can no longer reasonably doubt the sexual nature of Michael Jackson's interest in boys and the depth of his obsession with them, removing any scope for unhelpful clouds of obfuscation, denial and whitewash by writers who really ought to have known better – notably J Randy Taraborrelli, generally and rightly regarded as Michael's most significant biographer following the appearance of *Michael Jackson: The Magic and the Madness* in 1992.[6] At that time his magisterial opus of over six hundred pages seemed a model of "warts and all" biography, reporting plenty of madness along with the magic. But subsequent editions failed to keep pace with the hardening evidence of Michael's love life. It was as though the author knew the fans wanted a mad Michael and even a bad one in the street sense; but a sad and "sick" star would have been just too much.

For the most part, then, I have worked from publicly available sources, including more than two dozen books on Michael (and even a couple by him), a good many TV documentaries, numerous internet sources and literally thousands of articles in newspapers, magazines and academic journals. For the trial, I have had access to, and made extensive use of, the full 13,055-page court transcript of the case as well as leaked documents from the earlier grand jury hearing held in secret. On Michael's relations with Jordie Chandler, scholars owe a considerable debt to Raymond Chandler for putting transcripts of important tape recordings into the public domain via the internet, including long discussions between Evan Chandler and Jordie's step-father, Dave Schwarz, and Jordie's interview with psychiatrist Richard Gardner. So far, though, I seem to be the only writer apart from Chandler himself to have realised just how important this evidence is – or else others have deliberately turned a blind eye because the information does not suit their case.

In fact, it never ceases to amaze me just how purblind the champions of a "pure and innocent" Michael manage to be. The trial testimony of Brett Barnes' sister, Karlee, for instance, was that as a child Brett had slept with Michael for a total of an entire year, a claim with stunning implications coming after the young man's own evidence of an extremely close relationship. But in *The Trials of Michael Jackson* by music industry insider Lynton Guest, this testimony does not even rate a mention, except by way of the following airy dismissal: "There was also some incidental evidence concerning another boy, an Australian called Brett Barnes, but that was inconclusive." And that is it. Finito! Would he have been so insouciant, one wonders, if he found out his own son had been going to bed with Michael even for a week, never mind a year?[7] Guest is among the more sophisticated of Michael's defenders, however, and his work on Jackson's relations with Sony Music is most enlightening.

Even websites and magazines designed as vehicles for the most fanatical fandom can be sources of useful information, I have found, and occasionally they also come up with persuasive arguments for a generous interpretation of Michael's lifestyle in its various manifestations. So, with the understanding that balance and fairness are vital, I have delved quite deeply into these sources, just as I have the tabloids, and I am grateful for their contribution to my assessment. Just as with the tabloids, though, I have endeavoured to maintain caution as to matters of both fact and spin. A good example of a (presently, as I write) pro-Jackson source that is valuable but potentially misleading is Wikipedia. The entries on Michael appear to have been edited largely by committed fans. While I have found some of the information useful, and most of it sound, the bias within the entries towards down-playing or discrediting anything negative about Michael is obvious, as I shall have occasion to illustrate in due course.

This is not a book about Michael's music, but his song lyrics and – another oddly underused resource – his published poems have also been examined for clues to his character and thinking. Such scrutiny is at best an extremely inexact art, not necessarily more scientifically valid than reading tea leaves but a fascinating exercise all the same.

This might also be said of the more wildly speculative, gossipy and in some cases downright fabricated yarns spun about Michael. Falsehoods have not been confined to the tabloid press, far from it, and I place no absolute reliance on any single source, including sworn legal testimony. It is equally unwise, I suggest, to be totally disdainful of a story just because it originated with *The Sun* or TV's Fox News, or even with *The National Enquirer* or *Globe*. In the era of the Chandler allegations the British tabloids, especially *The Sun* and *Today*, led the way in breaking many Jackson stories that have stood the test of time, becoming very well substantiated as the years have passed. While it is true that a prodigious amount of colourful nonsense has been put out, not least by Michael's own publicists, there is remarkably little to suggest stories have been baselessly concocted by the media on his contacts with boys. Had they been he could always have sued, but he showed little inclination to do so. In the British courts, especially, where the libel laws are strict, Michael could very profitably have followed the well-trodden trail taken by the likes of Elton John to protect his reputation; his reluctance may be thought to speak for itself.

Detailed reference to all the more important sources I have used is to be found in the Notes and References section at the back of the book, where there is also a Bibliography.

Let us then begin to explore together whether Michael ever did say such things as "I never hurt anyone" and – of much greater moment – whether he ever really did hurt anyone.

CHAPTER TWO

Jordie, the Scandal: 'He Ate My Semen'

Jackson put "his hands under minor's shorts and began masturbating minor until minor had orgasm at which point Mr Jackson cleaned the semen with a tissue saying 'Wasn't that good?' ". He began eating "minor's" semen and then began masturbating him with his mouth. 35 yrs. old

"Minor" in question had been identified in the British press in 1993 as thirteen-year-old Jordan Chandler, son of a Beverly Hills dentist with film-making ambitions and the script of a Mel Brooks film, *Robin Hood: Men in Tights* to his credit. Almost before the ink was dry on the social worker's hand-written report about Jackson's relations with the anonymous minor, the document was reproduced in facsimile form in a world exclusive for *The Sun* on 27 August. Just as panty fetishists typically prefer *used* lingerie – the "real thing" – so the icy wording of the official report was rendered much more chillingly real in faithful facsimile: you could almost smell the fear and distress the cold authority of their pages must have engendered in Michael.

The American media generally did not name the boy in social worker Ann Rosato's report for Los Angeles Department of Children's Services, filed on 17 August 1993. By the time his complaint of sexual assault was settled out of court many months later, in a deal announced on 25 January 1994, the name was still under wraps in the US.

But "the story" was massive around the globe from just a few days after Rosato wrote her report, with the news breaking of a police raid on

Neverland. On 21 August 1993, a search warrant was issued enabling police to raid Jackson's Neverland ranch and Galaxy Way apartment in Century City, Los Angeles, which they did on that day and the 22nd. In the circumstances, all his advisors would have seen it coming. Michael's maid Adrian McManus has since related that stacks of property were removed from Neverland beforehand including numerous magazines and a lot of photos of children in their underwear – including one of child star Macaulay Culkin. Following a tip-off, the story – not yet with any allegation of sex abuse – was run on Los Angeles TV station KNBC, which broke the news of the police raids at 4pm on 23 August. The first reports of sexual allegations followed the next day. Because British time is several hours ahead of Eastern Time in the US, *The Sun* in London could trumpet a world scoop with their story, "Jacko used me as a sex toy". In a public statement, Jackson spokesman Anthony Pellicano denied allegations of sexual molestation against a minor, saying the claim arose out of an extortion attempt. The police held their own news briefing, stating they had reason to believe Michael Jackson had molested a thirteen-year-old boy.

The allegations related to a friendship that had been going on for more than a year between Michael and Jordan who, "with his delicate features and large soulful eyes", was "undoubtedly an attractive boy", in the estimation of Tina Weaver, a leading journalist on the story. Even the boy's lawyer, daringly for a man, would years later say Jordan had been good-looking and even "adorable" at that age.[8]

Michael met Jordan – or Jordie, as all of us who followed the story in the UK came to think of him, thanks to the tabloids' impertinent familiarity – in May 1992 when the star's limousine broke down and he hired a car from Rent-a-Wreck, the company owned by Jordan's stepfather, Dave Schwartz. After that meeting Michael phoned Jordie regularly while on tour abroad.

His first encounter with Jordie had actually been many years earlier in 1984 at a Los Angeles restaurant, when the boy was only four. Michael was badly burned filming a Pepsi commercial a few months later. Jordie sent him a get-well note and Michael phoned him personally from the Brotman Medical Center to thank him. Four years later, during the *Bad* tour, Jordie wrote a fan letter and sent a picture. Michael sent him free VIP tickets to one of his concerts.

These prior contacts call into question the supposedly accidental nature of the meeting at Rent-a-Wreck. Biographer Christopher Andersen asked one source if it was a coincidence:

> "Get real," said one of those who would later become involved in investigating child-abuse allegations against Michael. "First of all, Michael Jackson's car just happens to break down in LA, then instead of calling one of his hundred or so lackeys, he personally goes to a rental agency, and it just so happens to be the one where Jordie is? Pretty far-fetched."[9]

Far-fetched, but it may just have been true. It was later reported that it was not Michael who went to Rent-a-Wreck but the wife of Rent-a-Wreck employee Mel Green. She had spotted him fretting by the roadside wondering what do and phoned her husband, who then raced to the scene. Michael had used his mobile to phone the 911 emergency number, only to be told a breakdown did not qualify for assistance.[10]

After his return to the USA in February 1993, Michael invited the boy's mother, June, and younger half-sister, Lily, to his Neverland ranch, buying toys for the children and jewellery for his mother. The family visited several times, spending four days there in March. Also present were eleven-year-old Brett Barnes, ten-year-old Wade Robson, and the Cascio brothers, Eddie, nine, and Frank, thirteen, names we shall be hearing much of. Trips together came into the picture, notably five days Michael spent with the family in the gambling city of Las Vegas. It was here, at the Mirage Hotel, in March 1993, that the relationship with Jordie became a serious gamble for the star: it was here that the pair slept together for the first time. They had been watching a video of *The Exorcist* and the youngster had been so frightened that he had not wanted to sleep alone. The next night Michael wanted to sleep with him again but June was not keen. When June objected to Michael's request he burst into tears, sobbing of "love", "family" and "trust"; finally, she gave in.[11]

Michael had a reputation for tears. When his *Bad* album was less successful than *Thriller* he threw a tantrum like a spoiled kid – and he cried.[12] Tears were a factor in Jordie Chandler's formal allegations too, both in the social worker's report and the boy's later statement in his own words, filed at Santa Monica Superior Court, California. This is how Jordie related what happened after Las Vegas:

> The first step was simply Michael Jackson hugging me. The next step was for him to give me a brief kiss on the cheek. He then started kissing me on the lips, first briefly, and then for a longer period of time. He would kiss me while we were in bed together.

> The next step was when Michael Jackson put his tongue in my mouth. I told him I didn't like that. Michael Jackson started crying. He said there was nothing wrong with it. Michael told me that he had another young friend who let Michael kiss him on the mouth. He said to me: "He let me stick my tongue in his mouth."
>
> Michael Jackson said that I did not love him as much as this other friend. Then Michael did it to me. One time Michael put his tongue in my ear.[13]

The Rosato report also has Jordie saying of Michael's crying: "I guess he tried to make me feel guilty." Her supposedly confidential report was published in the tabloid *Today* with what that now defunct tabloid called "the most shocking elements" paraphrased in italics.[14] It was left to a "quality" paper, the *Sunday Times*, to publish the really "dirty bits" that begin this chapter. The *Sun* gloated over oral sex while claiming to have omitted details "too disgusting to use", thus giving readers plenty of scope for imagination.[15]

Rosato takes up the story:

> Minor said Mr Jackson also put his hand on minor's butt and his tongue in minor's ear, but minor told him to stop and he did.
>
> Minor stated that at some time in April or May, Mr Jackson took minor, mother and half-sister to Florida and "continued to rub up against me quite often". Minor said he could sometimes feel that Mr Jackson had an erection as did minor sometimes. After trip to Florida he continued to spend time with minor, primarily at minor's mother's home, but also at his father's home.
>
> At this point Mr Jackson realised he had met minor several (about eight) years previously and began to tease minor that their being together was "in the cosmos" and "meant to be".
>
> Minor said they did meet briefly when minor was five or six. Minor stated Mr Jackson also took family to Monaco which is when it really got out of hand. Minor stated Mr Jackson told him that his cousin had masturbated in front of him, and that masturbation was a wonderful thing.
>
> He coerced minor to bathe with him, and later while lying next to each other in bed, Jackson put his hand outside his shorts, saying: "This is going to be great". Then he put his hand under his shorts and masturbated until the minor had an orgasm. Mr Jackson said: "Wasn't that good?" That occurred several times.

> Jordan then told Rosato that Jackson performed one other type of sex act. But he denied he had ever been a victim of the most serious form of sexual abuse.
>
> Mr Jackson took the family to Florida once again. Minor stated: "At the end, he (Mr Jackson) had me suck on one of his nipples and twist the other one."
>
> Jackson abused himself while this was happening, Jordan told Rosato.
>
> Minor stated Mr Jackson told him that minor would go to juvenile hall (young offenders' institution) if he told, and that they'd both be in trouble. Minor also said Mr Jackson told him about other boys he had done this with, but did not go as far with them.

In addition to Rosato's encounter with Jordie, Los Angeles police interviewed the boy and, according to one account, concluded that he was telling the truth.[16] Rosato went on to say that Jackson tried to turn the boy against his parents. Once the investigation was under way Jordan wanted to be with his father. He felt his mother would "drill him with questions". She was too fond of the "glitzy life" to give it up and might allow Jackson to return to the home.

It would be understandable if Jordie did not want his mother to "drill him with questions". By this time he had been questioned for hours by a psychiatrist and before that pumped for information about his friendship with Michael by his father, who now knew all he needed to. Small wonder the boy was feeling the need for an interrogation-free zone in his life.

In his later statement for a civil suit Jordie substantially confirmed the sexual encounters described by Rosato and added to the picture, saying that before the time when he took a bath with Michael the two "would lie on top of each other with erections". Rosato's description, reproduced with her misspelling in *The Times*[17], reads "He coercieid minor to bathe with him".

Significantly, Jordie himself never used the word "coerced" in any spelling, nor did he in any way suggest reluctance to take a bath with Michael. Why should he? This was a man with whom he was used to lying in bed, both of them with erections. Jordie simply describes sharing a hotel room with Michael and goes on to say, "Next we took a bath together. Michael then masturbated in front of me. After that Michael masturbated me many times with his hand and mouth." Jordie did not say Michael "abused himself" as Rosato did in *Today*'s paraphrased version. The message peddled to its younger readers by this clumsy "family newspaper" euphemism was a throwback to the age when children were solemnly told that playing with themselves would make them go blind.

Jordie clearly said he was masturbated many times, whereas the Rosato version did not make this aspect of the allegation clear. Why would a social worker downplay the extent of the abuse? The suspicion has to be that the answer is related to the boy's age. He was thirteen at the time, not three. To play up the fact that these incidents went on and on without Jordie complaining to his mother or anyone else was to invite the possibility that he became, if not immediately then before long, a willing and perhaps even eager participant in what was going on. The statement that he had an erection and orgasm on many occasions adds support to this view: it indicates he was at some level deriving pleasure from what was going on. He also emitted semen: we are not talking here about a "little boy", though his lawyers constantly described him as such, playing up the public sense of outrage over Jackson's alleged offence. Jordie gave his father the idea for *Robin Hood: Men in Tights*. No one has suggested he lacked mental sophistication at least on a par with his physical development.[18]

Social work orthodoxy insists, rightly enough, that children should never be blamed for their abuse: what happens is the adult's responsibility. However, this often leads to the fiction that children never enjoy sexual contact with a grown-up, and that but for "coercion" they would always wish to escape from it. To think anything else raises embarrassing and difficult questions about children's sexual feelings and society's attitude towards them. A corollary of this orthodox view is that abused children are bound to resent the abusive adult, perhaps carrying hateful memories of what happened for the rest of their lives. This is an all too familiar feature of cases where abuse has gone on for a long time, particularly in father-daughter incest cases. At least one report carries hints of such resentment in Jordie's mind, quoting him as saying "I never want to see Michael again. I'm just trying to forget everything."[19]

The extent to which that quote accurately reflected his feeling will be the focus of considerable attention in Chapter Eleven. It would be surprising if Jordie did not want to forget all the recriminations arising out of his knowing Michael. The friendship was the *only* issue in a custody battle over him between his parents, whose eleven-year marriage had ended in divorce many years before, in 1985. June had allowed the friendship to develop, despite the misgivings noted already, while his father, Dr Evan Chandler, had opposed it after the end of May 1993. It was his ex-wife June's agreement, under pressure, to end all communications between her son and "a third party adult male known as Michael Jackson" that surfaced when it became part of published court papers on 24 August and, as *The Observer* put it, "unleashed the media dogs of war".[20] But the media dogs were barking up the wrong tree in one respect: the agreement did not specify ending communications with Michael. Instead, it stipulated that Jordie should not leave the county – which would, however, have been enough to prevent him seeing Michael at Neverland or going on tour with him.[21]

That media involvement, and a police investigation started just a week earlier on 17 August, piled immense pressure onto Jordie. No wonder he would want to forget everything, even if he had been quite happy with Michael before all the fuss arose. The notion that there might actually have been a period of Edenic bliss in the relationship, a time when Jordie could be emotionally attached to Michael and innocently naked with him – innocent, that is, of the trouble it would lead to – found significant support from Dr Mathis Abrams, a psychiatrist consulted by Evan Chandler. He was at first approached in mid-July for his view of the case on a hypothetical basis. Chandler told him everything he knew or suspected had been going on and how the two individuals appeared to relate to each other, though he did not at this stage reveal that the boy in question was his own son or that the pop star was Michael Jackson. By this time Chandler had seen enough with his own eyes to be able to tell Dr Abrams a great deal. After Monaco, Michael had been a guest at his house, where he had seen the star and his son in bed together. In view of his supposed anxiety over Jordie's well-being, it may be felt curious that he allowed this to go on; nevertheless he did, for reasons that will be discussed in Chapter Eleven.

Abrams produced a report based on the information gleaned in this way. Along with Jordie's other files, including Rosato's report, it was part of the deluge of confidential information splashed by the media when the story broke. He said: "The male child has had for several months an intensely emotional personal relationship with an idolised male who is more than twenty years his senior. A celebrity of some sort." Jordie's uncle would later tell how the boy copied Michael in every characteristic, from his clothes to his dance steps and his mannerisms.[22] Even Jordie's lawyer frankly admitted "Our client *loved* Michael Jackson" (my emphasis).

Abrams again: "The child spends much of his time in the company of this adult male and the relationship is described as inseparable. The child has on many occasions spent the night in the same bed as the adult male although separate beds are available. The child and the adult male have been observed in the same bed under the covers by both the child's mother and father on several occasions."

Coercion? Not a hint of it. Jordie's emotional involvement was total. There was nothing whatever in this initial Abrams report about any physical demands by Michael or psychological pressure. Other witnesses reinforced this view. Waiter Chad John, of the Mirage Hotel where Jordie and Michael first went to bed together, said of the pair that, "They talked in whispers and laughed like father and son."[23] Jackson fan Leticia Beard took the opportunity to photograph them when she happened to be staying in the same hotel. She said, "They really seemed to be enjoying themselves, just like two little kids".[24] This evident bond between Jordie and Michael proved all too much for Mary Riddell, deputy editor of *Today*, a paper which led the field in British and indeed world coverage of the emerging "scandal". Riddell went wildly over the top in calling Jordie's testimony (or rather Rosato's underplayed version of it) "one of the most chilling pieces of documentation this newspaper has ever printed".[25] Had she failed to notice the torture and mass rape that were such a feature of the war in Bosnia at the time, or the starvation in Ethiopia and Somalia?

What had "chilled" Riddell so much was Jordie's "knowingness". The disturbing feature, she said, "...was not its language, although that was harsh enough, but its fluency. How could a child so young speak with such knowingness about abusive sex?" The *child* evidently shocked and offended her far more than Michael Jackson did. Jordie's active, repeated, participation in oral sex, and his attainment of orgasm, shattered the myth of childhood innocence. Riddell and her readers desperately needed to sustain this myth. If they could not, then all manner of sexual and emotional anarchy seemed to threaten.

Why are we scared witless that this is so? Why do we make such a big deal of children's innocence? Not every society has invested emotional energy in this dubious concept and even in those that have led the way in doing so it has only become entrenched orthodoxy in relatively recent history. In our modern, "advanced" societies, so materially successful but psychically confused and ill at ease, we need to investigate how and why this emotional attachment to childhood "innocence" has come about and whether it is really doing us any good. Such questions go deep and could take us far beyond the scope of this volume, but readers can at least be assured that there is a vast literature for them to explore on the subject if they are up for it.[26]

Staying with Riddell, her own genuine discomfiture and mental turmoil were manifest in what she went on to say: "It must, even for a teenaged American sophisticate, have been the most disturbing of experiences. How to reconcile the sweet, the childish, with the unpleasant and the bizarre? How to make sense of a jumble of experiences thrown together as haphazardly as beads shaken in a kaleidoscope?" The truth of the matter, as we shall see, is that the "disturbed" party was Riddell, not Jordie. In direct contradiction of the available evidence, she was here throwing her own thoughts and feelings onto Jordie, in a classic demonstration of what Freud would have called "projection".

Even by the time, in Jordie's words, "things really got out of hand" in Monaco, there was little in his behaviour to suggest he was "disturbed" as Riddell feels he should have been. To her mind it was as though he had got hold of the wrong script in this drama. Puzzlingly, he was behaving like a happy youngster, not a disturbed one. The Monaco trip had been to attend a music awards ceremony at which Michael was being honoured. Piers Morgan, then a showbiz writer covering the awards, wrote: "I spent five days watching Jackson entertaining Jordan, his mother and five-year-old half-sister Lily in Monaco – and found the whole thing extremely uncomfortable. He could hardly take his hands off Jordan as they enjoyed a series of outings to toy shops, restaurants and parties."[27]

The giveaway is the word "enjoyed". Like Riddell, Morgan was no friend of a relationship he regarded as abnormal, and we may be certain that if Jordie had been anything other than relaxed, chatty, and apparently content in Michael's company he would have told us. But no, we had it from this impeccably hostile witness that the family "enjoyed" their outings. As for the big occasion itself, the awards ceremony, "Jordan giggled as the superstar singer hugged and cuddled him in front of a huge VIP audience and millions of TV viewers." The boy sat on Jackson's knee for over two hours. Many years later, in 2005, Jackson's publicity chief Bob Jones would write of this time in Monaco:

> Michael's wooing of the young boy from Rent-a-Wreck was embarrassing: the cooing, hugging and holding hands. Many of the hotel staff were whispering things such as: "They may as well kiss", or "Did we miss the wedding?" It was shameful, yet to Michael it was normal behaviour. I would later name the trip "The Honeymoon", because it was apparent that Michael Jackson was honeymooning with the boy.[28]

The obvious question for many would be why Michael allowed such intimacy to be so public. He must have known it would set tongues wagging, and not for the first time. Gossip about his affection for children, especially boys, had been rife for years in Hollywood, as he knew perfectly well. His biographer Randy Taraborrelli points to a confidence disclosed by Michael to his "personal videographer", Steve Howell, to the effect that he did not care about rumours that he was gay as long as the public did not know for sure. Keeping them guessing was part of his allure, part of his fascination. It would add to his fame.[29]

But this was an exceedingly dangerous game to play in connection with boys rather than men. It is doubtful that even a fanatic for fame like Michael would want to add to it in this way. *Unless it was not just a matter of fame.* Think, instead, of pride. Effectively, Michael was saying, "Look, everyone, see how this beautiful boy is fond of me. Don't you think I must be a real nice guy to win this kind of affection from him?" Pride is a perfectly natural sentiment for anyone seen with an attractive partner, especially among those for whom it is a new and heady experience. Unlike his boyfriend, Michael was hardly a teenager out with his first date, but this glitzy opportunity for publicly showing off Jordie still amounted to a rare treat.

The idea of "natural" pride in an "unnatural" kind of affection will strike some as odd. Instead of legitimate pride it may look like a two-fingered gesture to the world of decent convention: "I know what you think and I don't care. You can't get me. If you don't like it you can go to hell." There are those who complain about gay men and lesbians who "flaunt" their sexuality – people who probably never stop to think how much they "flaunt" their own heterosexuality, first as youngsters by dancing and kissing in public, and later on by visibly being couples, especially as parents. How would they like it if all their love songs were banned, if they could never send a Valentine card, if they could not be seen in the supermarket shopping with their children because it would mark them out as "breeders"? Those of us lucky enough to feel our sentiments towards our partners are good and worthy do not want to hide these feelings away as though they are shameful. There is no reason to suppose Michael was different from anyone else in this respect, whatever reservations we might have about erotic feelings for children.

The public display of affection that was there for all to see at Monte Carlo would make no sense at all if Michael had not been seriously attracted to Jordie. What sane reason could there be for going out of his way to give the world the impression of an intimate relationship, knowing the terrible danger of doing so, unless there was something in his heart that he was bursting to express? Weird as Michael has in many ways been, he had never been noted for self-destructive insanity – except perhaps to his nose, and we cannot regard that calamity as intentional.

So, if Michael felt strongly towards Jordie, were those feelings expressed in a sexual liaison? Nothing short of a criminal trial could satisfactorily resolve the issue, but the prima facie case against him is compelling – far more so than the one he faced in the 2005 trial at which he was quite properly acquitted. Even at the start of that case, before the prosecution evidence had been tested and found wanting, much of the story looked improbable. Not so the dangerous liaison with Jordan Chandler, which is why this young man will be such a key figure in these pages.

There is background circumstantial evidence, for instance, which goes much broader than what we have so far considered. We have not even touched upon the extensive intimate friendships Michael had with other children, some of whom were known to Jordie himself, and named by him. In her book published soon after the trial, Diane Dimond says the Department of Children and Family Services report on Jordie was leaked to her, plus the original report officers of the Los Angeles Police Department had written after hearing the boy's story. She noted that "RC" – the reporting child – had given names in "four other cases", saying "One is Macaulay Culkin. One lives in Australia. One is a boy named Garcia in Santa Barbara". Given brief sight of the report in a restaurant rendezvous with her source, her hurried shorthand notes did not record the fourth.[30]

It has never been disputed that Jordie spent many nights in bed with Michael, perhaps up to a hundred in a variety of locations, beginning with that first night in Las Vegas. After Michael had won over his mother, she allowed Jordie and his famous friend to share a bed for more than three months, about a month of which was almost unbroken consecutive nights under her own roof. One writer said that Michael "essentially moved in", and lived in one room of the family's "small" and "unpretentious" house in Santa Monica Canyon.[31] It would be truer to say he just overnighted there, disappearing during the day to goodness knows where, probably his "hideout" apartment in Century City, while his young friend went to school. The household was not that modest either: June had a live-in maid. And Jordie attended the exclusive St Matthew's School in Los Angeles, a private establishment patronised by the children of celebrities, such as Steven Spielberg. June had separated from her son's step-father Dave Schwartz the previous year, so he was not around to object to Michael's nocturnal visitations.

To many minds, though, the prolonged bed-sharing was evidence enough of impropriety. Surely even Michael would not be so crazy as to invite that much suspicion innocently and gratuitously. Private eye Ernie Rizzo, a rival of Jackson's investigator and fixer Anthony Pellicano, proclaimed in the first days of the scandal, "If it looks like a duck and it walks like a duck and it quacks like a duck, then it probably is a duck."[32]

"Experts" on paedophilia may not have cared for Rizzo's robust vulgarity, but their conclusions came to much the same thing. Ray Wyre, who set up the Gracewell Clinic in Birmingham, and was a well-known media pundit on the treatment of paedophiles until his death in 2008, declared himself "ninety per cent certain" that Jordie's statement was true. "I believe this boy," he said. "It is a classic case of child abuse I have come across many times."[33]

For Wyre, the pattern of behaviour described in the boy's statement was typical. "The offender starts off with non-sexual touching and then progresses, testing him out, steadily building up trust. If he went too fast the child could tell something was wrong." He cites the French-kissing allegation, and Michael's allegedly saying there was nothing wrong with this: "All very classic. From an early stage the abuser tries to groom the child to accept what's being done as normal." And of the alleged hand and oral masturbation of the boy: "A normal progression. He feels he has now won trust and developed such a relationship with the child to seriously abuse him [*sic*]."

As for Michael saying Jordie should not tell anyone what had happened: "The abuser feels wanted and loved for once – but fears he could be found out. Offenders always get the child to promise to keep their relations secret."

That word "always" should ring alarm bells. How did he know? Specialists working with sex offenders against children only become aware of offences that are discovered or confessed: their caseload is built up from sources such as court referrals or those who voluntarily seek help. But there are other cases that lie quite beyond the ken of these "experts". Many children do not want to complain against an adult who has been intimate with them; there are offences that never come to light. (We will be hearing more about such cases in Chapter Seven.) So how can Wyre or any other professional say what offenders "always" do? Wyre's perspective was restricted and distorted by dealing all the time with offenders who felt very guilt-ridden (in some cases with good reason) or who had been complained against, many of whom would have been in prison. This led him quite wrongly to assert as universal truths ("the abuser" thinks this, "the abuser" does that) things he could not possibly know.

Take his assertion on secrecy. The "offender" may not feel it necessary to say a word, much less to exact a promise of secrecy. Boys of Jordie's age and intelligence are usually well aware of society's taboos and of the need for discretion. Nor does Wyre's assertion make any allowance for the more idealistic and perhaps naive offender who simply feels it would be wrong to burden a child with secrecy. Some child-lovers believe children have a right to tell their parents or others whatever is on their minds and that it is not a lover's right to constrain them.[34]

Typically for specialists in this field, Wyre allowed his confidence in his own authority to get the better of him, knowing that other official "experts" would not argue with anything he said as long as it tended to demonise the offender in a safe, socially approved way. Likewise he knew few lay people would dare challenge him, as to do would be to demonstrate a suspicious level of interest in the subject. So there is plenty of scope for dogmatic assertions of an "All offenders do x" variety, especially when the "all" in question paints a picture of offenders who are uniformly experienced and knowing, calculating and manipulative, uniformly sinister and totally in control of a helpless child.

Putting aside these excesses, what can we take from Wyre's experience? What if anything can we rely on? As we have seen, his pronouncements made little allowance for exceptions, and there are many reasons to suppose Michael may be an extreme exception, considering his unusual upbringing and even more unusual adult circumstances, both of which we shall come to. What Wyre could have told us about, though, was the kind of cases he used to encounter all the time, some characteristics of which appear to correspond to much that is in Jordie's account.

He talked about the grown-up gradually forming a relationship with the child, building up trust. The adult would be careful not to be off-putting by jumping in at the deep end with an early attempt to go "all the way". He starts off with non-sexual touching, which might include holding hands, say, or an arm around the shoulder. When he is sure his young friend is comfortable with this he will venture a bit further, offering reassurance that there is nothing wrong with kissing, or whatever the new item in the repertoire happens to be. And provided that he is sure he has his partner's confidence, he will eventually go further; as well as becoming good friends at a social level, the pair of them will engage in extensive sexual activity together. At last the man feels not just that he loves his partner but that the feeling is mutual: in Wyre's words, he "feels loved and wanted" by the youngster.

Does this pattern sound familiar? It surely ought to. Stripped of the judgmental language, it could easily be an account of a teenage boy's progress with his same-age girlfriend, couldn't it? The teenage boy who is so desperate he tries to rush past first base too quickly is probably doomed to failure. Next time he will try to play it cool, and may succeed. It is a familiar scenario, celebrated a zillion times in rites of passage movies. We do not blame the boy for trying, or the girl for playing hard to get – if she does. This is just the game of life in action. Actually, as evolutionary psychologists attest, girls in some ways have more reason to be choosy.

Let us put this in the context of what was *not* alleged against Michael. Jordie did not suggest that anal intercourse had taken place or been attempted, nor was he asked to take Michael's penis into his mouth. There is no suggestion of any penetrative acts with Michael in an *inserter* role. In the eyes of many, including perhaps a criminal court, this would take any criminal offence out of the most serious category.[35]

No force or violence was alleged either, despite some early tabloid claims to the contrary after Ann Rosato's dubious use of the word "coerced".[36] Some reports also implied on the flimsiest of grounds that Jordie had a sense of grievance against Michael. Headlines to this effect sported bogus quotations, supposedly from the boy but in fact generated on the basis of comments from lawyers who had a stronger claim to speak for Jordie's father than the boy himself. One was "Jordie: We will see you in court"; another said "Stick your hush money".[37] Oops! There was no court battle and a hush money deal was promptly struck! There was nothing in Jordie's own statement to suggest he disliked Michael or had any sense of grievance at the time. Even his father, through Dr Abrams' report, admitted his son idolised the man and was inseparable from him – until separation was enforced.

The only negativity to be heard from Jordie in his own words was that things "really got out of hand" in Monaco. But even here there was nothing to suggest this had been his feeling at the time. With 20/20 hindsight, knowing what an issue his father (to say nothing of the entire world) would make of it, he was bound to feel uneasy about what had happened, bound to feel that what had been pleasurable and unforced at the time eventually got "out of hand" through becoming too publicly visible: remember, Monaco was where Michael made the mistake of showing off Jordie in public.

Evan Chandler was determined to break up the "inseparable" pair, though his way of going about it would prove controversial: by not going straight to the police he made it look as though money was his main concern and so he became an easy target for Jackson to accuse of extortion. Understandably, the news media saw it as highly suspicious that Evan received Michael as a guest in his home even after Monaco. At a time when many another angry father would have been more inclined to tear him limb from limb, Evan was cordially entertaining the guy and allowed him to share Jordie's bedroom. It was even claimed that after sneaking into the room in the night and seeing Michael and Jordie in bed together he had a tape recorder installed under the bed in the hope it would provide some sort of evidence of hanky-panky going on.[38] One newspaper ran a story saying a compromising "three-in-bed" tape had been made, with Jordie's six-year-old half-brother Nikki making up the trio. This tape was then supposedly destroyed by Chandler, a curious thing to do unless the results were simply dud – and that could be explained in a number of ways, such as an absence of compromising activity in the limited time the tape was running, or a lack of convincing sounds thereof. One wonders whether Evan had been expecting to hear something like the sound track of a porno movie, replete with ecstatic moaning and ejaculatory utterances.

The fact that Evan Chandler went to extraordinary lengths to prove the existence of an illicit relationship between Michael and Jordie is attested out of his own mouth in another tape recording. This was one of three phone conversations on the same day secretly recorded by Jordie's step-father Dave Schwartz. In an exchange between himself and Chandler, the latter claimed he had spent "tens of thousands of dollars" to obtain information on Michael. Many fathers, on finding their son in bed with a grown man, might have opted for a rather less roundabout procedure, such as giving him a good hiding, kicking him out of the house and calling the police. There may be little else to commend the macho style, but it would at least have avoided accusations of trying to set up Jackson for blackmail.

Of more concern here, though, is the quality of Jordie's friendship with Michael, and who was responsible for breaking it up. Was it Jordie himself, or actually his father? Did Jordie really feel things "got out of hand" or were the negative feelings essentially Evan's?

It was a murky picture at the time. When the scandal broke in the late summer of 1993 the world's media gorged with alacrity on all the sensational allegations and were in a mood to stuff themselves with every conceivable follow-up angle. But the negotiations and legal moves that had led up to the crisis over weeks and months proved a complex, obscure area of investigation, difficult to penetrate and hard to digest. Yet these had been the seismic tremors ahead of the earthquake, portents to the dangerous build-up of mighty forces, and hence an important part of the story.

What might those portents have told those with the ear to hear? What did the media miss at the time that has since been clarified? The obscure months, from late May to mid-August 1993, have been illuminated by a number of detailed accounts, principally Andersen (1994), Orth (1994), Sky (1994), Chandler (2004),Taraborrelli (2004) and Dimond (2005). Despite the complexity, there is a remarkable degree of consensus as to the facts that most concern us.

Two principal themes emerge: the tangled family dynamics of Jordie's parents and step-parents, leading to a custody dispute over the boy; and the intersection of these dynamics with a complicated tussle that developed between Evan Chandler and Jackson's representatives. This behind-the-scenes battling would provide ammunition for Jackson's chief "fixer", Anthony Pellicano, when he later publicly branded Evan an extortionist. Neither of these themes is greatly of direct significance to assessing the quality and nature of Michael's relationship with Jordie, but both of them reveal much about Evan and the key questions already raised about him above.

At the beginning of that fateful year, 1993, Jordie was living with his mother, June, and half-sister, Lily. June and her second husband, Dave Schwartz, had separated some months before. The couple remained on good terms with each other and also with June's first husband, Evan, who now lived with his second wife, Nathalie, and their little boy, Nikki. They were prosperous, well-to-do people. Dave ran a large, successful business. Evan was billed in the media as a "dentist to the stars" and his wife was a lawyer. On the surface, life looked good for them, although Maureen Orth detected "disturbing" signs in the fact that both men had left Jordie's mother, who was said to be into "hanging out". Dave, deeply immersed in his business would drop into the house irregularly. Evan would see Jordie at the weekends; however, June would complain he did not always have enough time for the boy. She was no great fan of Nathalie either but there was no acrimony among any of them. As separated and divorced couples go, the four grown-ups in this scenario rubbed along pretty well and their kids had no obvious problems. The situation was broadly satisfactory, but not robustly so.

Enter Michael Jackson, back from the European leg of his *Dangerous* tour and free by February to spend an increasing amount of time with Jordie. And he does. By the end of March, Jordie and his mother had been on three trips to Neverland. They were fast becoming a regular part of Michael's world. In April, Michael first went to bed with Jordie in Las Vegas and then talked his mother into letting it happen regularly. Perhaps motivated by bad conscience, June phoned Evan at this time to warn him about losing control over his son, though she did not go into detail about the reason for her anxieties. Only later, when he learned about the sleepovers, did Evan's concern extend to the boy's "moral" welfare. By mid-May, after Monaco, the media were talking about Michael's "new family", and Jordie would later say his relationship with the star had become sexual by this time.

Soon after Monaco, on 20 May, Evan would meet Michael for the first time when he paid a surprise visit to Jordie at June's place. That encounter is one of several discussed in detail in Chapter Eleven. Here we need only note that after a measure of momentary culture shock, Evan found himself getting on surprisingly well with Jordie's famous friend. It was Evan's younger son Nikki, with him at the time, who broke the ice. Wowed by Michael's presence, he was soon play-wrestling with him. The sense of fun was pervasive; before they knew it, all four of them were in the back yard playing with catapults.

Michael invited Evan and Nikki over to his "hideout" apartment, where the very next day he gave Nikki lots of toys and his father an expensive watch. Suspicious that this largesse might be some sort of bribe, Evan bluntly confronted the star with his anxieties, asking in the earthiest terms about the nature of the relationship between him and Jordie: Was it sexual? Avoiding a direct answer, Michael expressed astonishment the question could even be asked, but instead of reacting angrily, he merely giggled, as though the suggestion was absurd. As for the exact nature of the bond he had with Jordie, the star replied that he did not know that himself, adding, "It must be cosmic".

Michael's relaxed approach succeeded for the time being in allaying Evan's fears – so successfully that the star felt confident enough to raise for the first time what was to become a critically sensitive issue, saying he would like Jordie to accompany him in August on the next leg of the *Dangerous* tour, in Asia. Such a trip would take Jordie away from home and from the control of his parents, for months on end. In Evan's mind, such a venture would truly be "dangerous" if Michael presented any moral risk to his son. But Michael's salesmanship was good. He presented it as a great educational opportunity for the boy, who would see many different countries and meet many powerful and influential people, leading figures in music and business. Evan was seduced: the conversation ended up with him *guaranteeing* Jordie would be on the tour.

At Jordie's suggestion, Michael was invited over to Evan and Nathalie's place. Jordie was there on 21 May for Nikki's birthday, and stayed on for Michael's arrival the next day. Michael stayed for the next two nights, sharing a room with the birthday boy and his big brother. The two men discovered they had an area of common interest: film. In the course of watching and talking about several films on TV, Evan mentioned his script writing. Michael was interested. There was talk of a job for him in Michael's company, MJJ Productions. The bond between the pair had been fixed almost instantly, like the magic of superglue.

But just as superglue often fails to live up to its promise, this bond would soon come badly unstuck. Little more than a week after their great start, Evan's doubts were redoubled when Michael stayed over again for the Memorial Day weekend at the end of May. The bond between Jordie and Michael, of more convincing strength, began to alarm him. Nathalie told him the two were obviously in love: Michael couldn't take his eyes off the boy, and followed him everywhere, even the bathroom. In her firm view it was not good for Jordie. What clinched it for Evan was when he checked the boys' bedroom at 3am. Instead of being in his own bed, Jordie was in Michael's, a trundle bed that pulled out from beneath the boys' two bunks. The pair were not naked, but were intimately positioned – spooning, with Michael's arm around Jordie and his hand resting on the boy's crotch outside the covers. If, as was suggested in the press, Evan had bugged the room for evidence of sexual goings-on, this is logically when it would have happened: the previous visit had been off the cuff, at short notice; on this occasion there had been time to prepare the apparatus.

Even without conclusive evidence of "impropriety", Evan decided the relationship between his son and Michael had to end. Bringing this about would prove no simple matter though: it required June's agreement because she had custody. And she flatly refused, leading to a row and the beginning of growing acrimony within the extended family that would end up with the lawyers. Arguably, there was little Evan could do at this stage. Without good evidence it could hardly be a police matter, and Jordie was in no mood to provide that evidence by admitting anything himself: *he* was in love with Michael, not just Michael with him.

In the following month, Jordie's love and loyalty towards Michael would express itself in open defiance of his father. For one thing, he refused to give up an evening with Michael for his end-of-school dance, a traditional, heterosexual rite of passage which seemed to his father much more suitable and healthy. Evan was worried his son might be gay. Also, when Jordie and Evan met for Nikki's preschool graduation on 9 June, Jordie defied his father openly over going on tour with Michael. When Evan said he might ask Jordie not to go, he said he would go anyway. A phone conversation with June about this led to a row, with her taking her son's side. It was a day that marked a line in the sand between them.

From this point on, Evan knew he was in grave danger of losing Jordie completely. Upset and frustrated, he broke down in tears while treating one of his patients, Barry Rothman, who just happened to be a lawyer. There and then, on 13 June, Rothman heard his story and started devising a plan of action to help him. At least, that was Evan's official version for the record, though in an angry phone call the following month he said that when it came to choosing his lawyer he picked "the nastiest son of a bitch I could find" – not that he was deliberately picking a fight in the courts. On the contrary, the plan Rothman devised was a graduated one. Evan would first ask June to end the relationship between Jordie and Michael, warning her that if she refused to comply, he would file a restraining order against Michael. Only if June fought against this would phase two of the plan be triggered. This would be to start a custody suit. But it was not to be. Communications had broken down. A month went by without Evan seeing Jordie. Whenever he spoke to June there was a row. By 7 July documents had been prepared for modification of the custody agreement. They petitioned the court to forbid contact between Jordie and Michael, accusing June of "nurturing" an unhealthy relationship between them in exchange for receiving gifts and vacations.

Evan felt the only way forward was a meeting with all the key actors involved: Jordie, June and Michael himself – though why Michael's presence was essential, or even desirable, for a meeting that would inevitably humiliate him remains a mystery, unless Evan intended making demands going beyond merely ending the relationship.

That same day, 7 July, Evan made a fateful move. He left an ultimatum message on June's telephone answering machine, demanding a meeting of "all three of you" – including Michael – at June's place at 8.30am on 9 July, ending, "Take my word for it, there is nothing else any of you has to do that is more important than being at this meeting." As June later testified, it was an ominous message, menacing even. Michael's unsurprising response when he heard the tape was to call his lawyer, Bert Fields, who immediately engaged the services of renowned investigator and "fixer" Anthony Pellicano. An expert in electronic surveillance, Pellicano appears to have been busy with his dark arts the very next day.

Dave Schwartz would say that it was he, not Pellicano, who taped telephone conversations on 8 July between himself and Evan, but from the timing it looks suspiciously like Pellicano's work; furthermore, the subsequent editing of the tape for later public consumption bears the hallmarks of his craft. However that may be, the lengthy discussion that took place about Jordie's future between June's two exes proved highly revealing. But what did it reveal? Pellicano used the tape, which had been heavily doctored by the time it emerged into the public arena, as his main evidence for damning Evan as an extortionist. By dint of selective quotation and putting his own spin on Evan's words, he succeeded for a while in creating a smokescreen, shifting the focus of media attention away from Michael's questionable behaviour. A police investigation into the extortion claim later found it was baseless.

In the first days of the media explosion in August, snippets of the tape were broadcast on KCBS television, Los Angeles. Evan was heard claiming that unless he won custody of his boy, Jackson would be "humiliated beyond belief". He warned, "If I go through with this I will win big time. I will get everything I want. June is going to lose Jordan and Michael's career will be over. He will not sell one more record. He will not believe what will happen to him. This man is going to be humiliated beyond belief and I have the evidence to prove it."[39]

Getting "everything I want" and "I will win big time" were interpreted as Evan being interested mainly in money, but there was no mention on the tape of monetary demands. Evan must have known what he was saying would get back to Jackson. As an intelligent man, he would probably have suspected the conversation was being taped. But it hardly looks as though he realised the ultimate consequence would involve his words being broadcast for the whole world to hear – words that betray a vindictiveness few would want publicised:

> Jackson's an evil guy... June is harming Jordan and Jackson is harming him and I can prove it...It will be a massacre if I don't get what I want. Michael is bad for my son. I know what he has to hide. Michael is using his age and experience and money and power to take advantage of Jordan. He is greatly harming him for his own selfish reasons. He is not the altruistic human being he appears to be. What will happen to him will be beyond his worst nightmare. The facts are so overwhelming that everyone will be destroyed in the process.

Everyone would be destroyed, including his own son, a fact which seemed to have troubled him remarkably little in the whole, horribly prophetic, diatribe. Perhaps he had convinced himself his claim (at this stage a baseless one) that he had "the evidence to prove it" (whatever "it" might have been), would alarm Jackson so much he would gladly settle. He, Evan, would get custody of Jordie, the relationship with Jackson would be broken, there would be no reason to bring in the police and "destroy everyone". His own vindictive words on tape would never become public knowledge because whoever would have bugged them would not want the media to know what he had been saying.

But despite all his huffing and puffing, nobody turned up on 9 July at June's house for the meeting demanded in Evan's ultimatum. Well, not quite nobody. Dave (but not June) was there to tell him Michael and Jordie would not be coming. Dave evidently thought that Evan would have no choice but to deal directly with him. But Evan was having none of it. He and his wife Nathalie walked to their car and drove home. It was a low point for Evan, frustrating and humiliating. But had he known the full picture he need not have been so upset. Although his ultimatum meeting had been a no-show, things would soon happen, starting almost immediately with a fracas at his own house.

Only minutes after Evan and Nathalie had arrived home from June's place, Dave and June turned up in their car. When the occupants of the house made no response to loud knocking on the door, Dave kept pounding and shouting that they had to talk. When Evan reluctantly half-opened the door, Dave flung it wide open, hitting Evan's head. In his furious reaction, Evan shoved Dave off a landing outside the door, then retreated inside and slammed the door shut.[40]

End of "talks". Now that their own efforts to handle the problem on their own had so dramatically failed, Dave and June were forced to retire and re-think. There would be several highly significant huddles that day and the next, starting when Dave and June met Pellicano on the ninth and played him the secretly recorded tape. The next day Pellicano would interview Jordie and determine exactly what Michael, his paymaster, would have wished him to determine, namely that the boy had not been molested. Jordie's flat denials made it an easy task. After that, Michael's lawyer met Evan's. At this stage he was representing June, too. With a view to bringing Evan back from the brink of dangerous hysteria, it was conceded that he should be granted custody of Jordie for a week.

The decision could hardly have been more momentous. For once his son was returned to him on 11 July, Evan went straight to work on the boy's head just as systematically as he did with his dental patients. He began his mind games immediately that day, by bluffing, pretending to know everything that had happened between him and Michael. It didn't work. Jordie kept his cool and held his tongue. But there was a whole week to go and Evan would make the most of it. Also, instead of being appeased by getting his son back, he decided it was time to ratchet up the pressure on Jackson, putting him on notice that legal action would be taken if necessary. He had his lawyer draw up a modified custody agreement stating that Jordie could not be taken out of the county (which would have ruled out Neverland and the *Dangerous* tour) without Evan's consent. June signed it on the 13th, apparently on advice from Bert Fields – a concession from the Jackson camp that betrayed their anxiety: Michael had desperately wanted Jordie to go on tour with him.

It was a breakthrough for Evan, but for all his bluster on the Schwartz tape about having "the evidence to prove it" and his lies to Jordie about knowing what happened, he was still only guessing. Why would anyone believe his mere suspicions? Evan joked months later that if he had called the police in at this stage "they probably would have investigated just long enough to get Michael's autograph for their kids". The next best thing to hard evidence, he decided, was a professional opinion. If he went to a psychiatrist and posed the situation to him as a hypothetical, anonymous, case, the resulting report could be used to put further pressure on Jackson.

But pressure to what end? He could use it to force Jackson and June to accept custody conditions forbidding any *contact* with Michael (this had not been part of the agreement she had just signed), but it could also be used to squeeze a monetary settlement out of him. While it is unfair in all the circumstances to call Evan an extortionist, history would prove he hardly had a lofty disdain for money. As for the case being kept hypothetical, it was the only way to avoid triggering a mandatory report to the authorities by the psychiatrist in question. Once that happened it would inevitably explode into a big story, to everyone's detriment, including Jordie's. As long as the quiet option was on the cards it would be by far the most sensible one to pursue – and it would be conducive to a private settlement. Accordingly, on 14 July, Evan went with Barry Rothman to consult a psychiatrist recommended by the lawyer: Dr Mathis Abrams.

On the home front meanwhile, Evan was getting nowhere. Jordie was sullen and disagreeable. He said he missed Michael. Evan admitted to Dr Abrams he believed his unnamed child and the likewise nameless adult friend were in love. Abrams urged him to bring the boy in for an interview. Evan said he feared that because this would involve the authorities it would mean a traumatic separation of the pair. His son might hate him for it and he could be lost forever. Abrams' response was bleak: "You've already lost him".

Frightened and dismayed by this gloomy prognosis, Evan was more desperate than ever to prise the truth out of Jordie. If he had already lost his son, what else did he have to lose by using dirty tricks on the boy to get at the truth? Just two days after seeing Abrams, on 16 July, matters finally came to a head. Or, rather, to a tooth. It was at his dentist's chair on that day, that Evan finally succeeded in getting Jordie to talk, when the boy was his patient as well as his son. The full, appalling, story of how the "confession" was achieved will be taken up in Chapter Eleven on power and its abuses in relations between adults and children – in this case the abuse being Evan's rather than Michael's.[41] For the moment, we need only note that once Evan had heard from Jordie that Michael had touched his penis, he decided that the boy would be put at risk by returning him to his mother and thereby to Jackson's company. His resolve in the matter was also stiffened by the report he had received from Dr Abrams the same day – a report which unequivocally stated that the boy was at risk of child abuse and that there was reasonable suspicion it had already occurred.

Accordingly, when the concessionary week's custody he had been granted came to an end the following day, 17 July, he refused to give the boy back. Evan attempted to regularise the situation by securing June's agreement to new custody arrangements, but amidst distrust and acrimony over his unilateral action it came to nothing. Evan now decided to try again for a meeting involving Michael "to work out a solution", as Jordie's uncle put it in his book, or, as others might say to negotiate a pay-off. What is admitted by Raymond Chandler in his book is that Evan went to that meeting in the full knowledge that some kind of business deal would be on offer. He knew this because his lawyer Barry Rothman had phoned to tell him so. Rothman said Pellicano had phoned to tell him Michael would help Jordie and Evan "re-establish their relationship" by assisting them in setting up a screenwriting career.[42]

The precise mixture of Evan's motives as between concern for his son and the attractiveness of a business deal, or cash settlement, is not the main issue here, though we might note the comment of actress Sharon Stone once the negotiations reached the public arena: "All I know is that if a child of mine had been abused I would not have been making deals."[43] Far more important is how the parties greeted each other (especially Jordie and Michael) when that meeting took place at the Westwood Marquis Hotel on 4 August 1993, a story taken up in Chapter Eleven.

The meeting itself was short and explosive. There would be no talk of business deals or settlements. Evan began by bluntly announcing his suspicions as to Michael's sexual conduct with Jordie – though without at this stage mentioning his son's "confession". He produced the report by Dr Abrams and began citing from it. Michael calmly denied the accusations; Pellicano was furious, telling Evan to "Get the fuck out of here!" Evan obliged, but not before suggesting Michael could take a lie detector test: if he passed it, Evan said, Jordie could go on tour with him. The offer could be seen as an absurd gamble on Evan's part: what if Michael, cool and composed, as he was in this meeting, proved able to lie his way through such a test without giving the game away? In Ray Chandler's account, though, as opposed to the version in Taraborrelli, Jordie would also be asked to take such a test – and Evan already had the boy's confession up his sleeve.[44]

But the exact proposal proved immaterial. The lie detector idea just made Pellicano madder than ever. The meeting was over. As Jordie followed his father out of the room, he turned to face Michael, looking sad. It was the last time they would ever see each other. The next morning Evan made a shocking discovery. Going into Jordie's room to say goodbye before leaving for work, he found what looked like a piece of suicide art lying on the floor. Jordie had drawn a figure jumping to his death from the top of a high building. The thought of losing Michael and maybe having to testify against him had taken its toll of the boy's spirits.

Evan was not deflected from his course. If his heart missed a beat, his plans did not. That same day, 5 August, in a hand-written note to his lawyer, he outlined his intentions if Jackson refused to pay a settlement figure of $20 million. He would later claim that Pellicano had been the first to mention money, in phone calls to Rothman on 2 August. But it takes two to tango. Money, big money, was hardly the least of Evan's considerations.

Evan would later claim that in the hotel meeting he said, "I know what you've done to Jordie, he told me everything", and that Jordie had nodded affirmatively. Jackson then supposedly denied it with a smile, "like the smile you see on a serial killer or a rapist", denying everything in the face of a mountain of evidence. Evan would parlay this smile into a defining moment, an epiphany in which he suddenly realised Jackson was an evil guy, a heartless molester rather than the older partner in a mutually loving relationship. This was supposedly the moment when he decided Michael had to be punished severely and that being stung for $20 million would do the job nicely.

But if he had wanted Michael to be *really* punished, going to the police would by now have been the obvious option. At this point the truth had been wrung out of Jordie and evidence could be mounted for a criminal case. Evan's story looks like mere rationalising, an attempt to justify his mercenary machinations. As for the serial killer smile, let us just remember this guy was a Hollywood script writer: imagination was his strong suit.

For the next ten days or so the focus was on cash, not Jordie or his welfare. Lawyer-to-lawyer negotiations dominated the battlefield, or rather lawyer-to-fixer, with Rothman and Pellicano fronting the hard-nosed exchanges. On Jackson's side there would be an attempt at camouflage. A cash deal would look bad, an admission that Chandler had Jackson by the balls. The fixer needed to propose something that could be seen as a legitimate business venture. On 13 August, Pellicano offered a film-script deal, the first of two: this was for three film scripts, each valued at $350,000. Evan had no hesitation in rejecting this first bid, and the one that followed. Simply, the money was nothing like enough.

June was unhappy with all this. In a phone call with Evan, she angrily accused him of coercing Jordie into his "confession". She felt he was wrong to use his son as a bargaining tool and she wanted him back. She was represented by her own lawyer, Michael Freeman, instead of Jackson's man Bert Fields. On 16 August, Freeman gave notice that he was going to petition the court for Evan to return Jordie to his mother. It precipitated the most fateful decision not just of Jordie's life but also of Michael Jackson's.

It panicked Evan into action. He felt that if he lost custody of Jordie at this stage the boy would soon be back again with Michael, and once more fall under his influence. What does this tell us? It reveals that despite all his attempts to brainwash Jordie, to convince the boy that Michael was a bad guy doing things that would harm him, he knew that Jordie had not been fully persuaded. He knew Jordie could not be relied on to testify against Michael, whether in a civil suit or in a criminal trial, unless Evan was at his back to keep prodding him.

At the custody hearing on 17 August, Freeman won his case for Jordie to be returned to June. Evan agreed to hand the boy over at 7pm that evening but had no intention of doing so. That very evening, at that time, Jordie would be in a long interview with the psychiatrist Dr Abrams, taken there by his father. Evan knew that because Jordie would be telling Abrams about sexual episodes with Michael, Abrams would be forced to report the matter to the authorities immediately. Once that happened, there would be no chance of Jordie going back into June's custody while that offered the possibility of him resuming his friendship with Michael.

The next day, once the Los Angeles child welfare authorities, had duly heard from Dr Abrams, June lost the custody affirmed in court barely more than hours before. When the authorities told her the full extent of what Jordie had disclosed to Dr Abrams, she broke down, saying she could not believe how stupid she had been. The welfare people wanted to take Jordie into their own custody; only when Jordie settled for staying with his father did they relent from this drastic option, which would certainly have been the worst of all worlds for the boy.

The above exploration of how the relationship between Michael and Jordie reached its sorry conclusion has largely been the story of his father's role. It is clear that Evan, whether for good reasons or bad – an area of judgment to be pursued in Chapter Eleven – pushed matters to a crisis that would not have happened without him. But the theme of parental responsibility would not be complete without turning the spotlight onto the boy's mother, June.

Right from the early days of the media involvement, June Chandler was being presented as a lover of glitz and the high life, happy to exploit the Jackson connection without spoiling her own party by asking too many awkward questions. It was said that during trips to Europe she clocked up $105,000 on Michael's credit card. June Chandler had "very wide eyes", according to one source. "She dismissed the behaviour saying Jackson is eccentric, which he is. But he's also got lots of charisma and she liked being in the spotlight. June could be charged with pandering. You get $105,000 – whether a guy gives you cash or a credit card to let you fiddle the kid, if someone believes that's what's happening that's pandering."[45] A witness at Michael's trial in 2005 would say she was a "gold-digger" who wanted to be "mistress of Neverland".[46]

There could be no question of charging June, much less convicting her, without putting Michael in the dock too, and with the out-of-court settlement in the civil case some months later any prospect of this was beginning to look remote. As the pressure mounted ahead of this settlement, though, attention again turned on June, when Michael's former chauffeur, Gary Hearne gave a statement under oath in the civil case.

He said that during the five months when Michael and Jordie were close Michael spent $150,000 on gifts and travel for the family. This included $20,000 of computer equipment for Jordie and nearly $20,000 worth of jewellery for June – there was even a watch for Evan Chandler. Hearne said Michael had told him to go and "pick something nice that has large stones". Asked how much he should spend, Michael said "he didn't care". One item he picked up at Friedlander's Jewellers in Century City, California, was a ruby and diamond bracelet, described in one report as "One large carat-size ruby set in the centre...surrounded by diamond baguettes which extend down either side of the 18-carat gold bracelet so that the entire wrist is dripping in jewels." Hearne bought "an equally impressive" ruby ring and earrings at the same time.[47]

Ann Rosato reported Jordie as saying his mother was too fond of the "glitzy life" to give it up and Hearne provided graphic testimony as to just how glitzy that life had become. A source described as a friend of June Chandler and her second husband, Dave Schwartz, said that June "...was so bewitched by Michael's magic she failed to see what was staring her in the face... Because Michael was such a big buddy of Jordie's it was easy to forget he was almost thirty five years old."

At first she had not believed her ex-husband's suspicions. After a change of heart, she was "completely united" with Evan Chandler in backing Jordie's case by October 1993. "June feels guilty she didn't see what was going on earlier," a friend was quoted as saying.[48] It is interesting that this turnaround came in short order after the police and media became involved. A dose of public scrutiny and criticism can do wonders to sharpen someone's judgment. Had she suspected all along that her ex's view of Michael was right? Was her only interest in rubies and diamonds, at the expense of her son?

June testified at Michael's trial in 2005. She made the sad, embarrassing admission that Jordie had never spoken to her in all the long years since her bonanza of jewellery. In terms of her son's view, that says it all. But to suggest she had merely been cynical is too harsh. Millions of fans have been bewitched by Michael's magic. His charisma was about more than being a walking chequebook. Money talks very loud, but for many the charm of his soft voice and gentle, "innocent" manner were equally persuasive, quite irrespective of whether such attributes were genuine or just a façade. June may have loved glitz but that does not mean she did not believe in Michael.

June and Jordie could hardly help but be dazzled by everything about Michael – his fame, his charisma, and, yes, his fabulous bounty towards them. They went with him to those iconic gambling cities, Las Vegas and Monte Carlo, and must have felt they had hit the jackpot in both. But the winning streak would have been impossible to sustain by playing a cold, calculating game, pretending to like Michael and pandering to his tastes.

June could perhaps have done it, but not Jordie, unless he was a monster of precocity. In that case Michael would have been quite incapable of emotionally damaging him more than he had already been. If Jordie was anything like most youngsters he would be utterly incapable of simulating even for twenty four hours an affection for Michael he did not feel. Kids usually wear their heart on their sleeve. The bribery of presents would not work on its own to sustain months of night and day togetherness. Michael can be taken to task for "spoiling" Jordie, and it is not a light criticism, but allegations that he tried to buy his way into the boy's heart are another matter. Another mega-rich pop giant sang "Can't buy me love". We have no reason to suppose Michael thought otherwise.

The purpose of this chapter has been to review the core allegation of sexual abuse against Michael in the Chandler case, the one formal, detailed, allegation by a child that surfaced publicly in the crisis of 1993–4. We have now seen the outline of those allegations in relation to what the boy himself had to say and as regards the attitude and behaviour of both his parents. Some aspects will be looked at in more detail elsewhere. For instance, Michael's alleged threat that Jordie could go to "juvenile hall" (young offenders' institution) if he said anything, will be examined in Chapter Twelve in the context of Michael's alleged misuse of his power. The police at that time also interviewed other children who were close to Michael. None of these led to a criminal charge against him.

One case did come back to haunt Michael years later at his trial, when a young man called Jason Francia went into the witness box against him. The son of a former maid at Neverland, Jason would testify to several acts of molestation, the first when he was seven years old. His story will be taken up in Chapter Sixteen. The next chapter considers what other evidence was brought to bear on the civil claim and the implications it had for a criminal prosecution – or rather what evidence could have been brought before a multi-million-dollar out-of-court settlement effectively paralysed the criminal case.

CHAPTER THREE

Jordie, the Pay-Off: Much Tattoo About Nothing

Jordan Chandler's statement was the salient evidence against Michael. Was there anything else? We know the police were looking for child pornography and personal items such as diaries when they searched Neverland but there was no indication they found anything damning. Michael's possession of "adult" material was to feature in his trial in 2005, but not child pornography, unless two illustrated books are counted that were found by police on the 1993 raid. These books, sent to him by fans, featured photos of naked boys and were claimed as child porn by the prosecution but no charge was ever made.

By the time of the raid, Michael had known for months that trouble was brewing, and if he had possessed such material there would have been ample time to ensure its destruction or removal from his various properties and residences, including his "secret" condominium at Century City, Los Angeles, and his suite of rooms at the family home, Hayvenhurst, Encino.[49] A suitcase and a briefcase are known to have been taken away from the condo shortly before it was raided. Chauffeur Gary Hearne told lawyers he received a call from Michael and Pellicano, telling him to drive to the condo, pick up the two items and take them to Pellicano's home. Pellicano confirmed this, claiming that the "personal items" collected were of no special significance.[50]

The media made much of the Hayvenhurst raid early in November 1993 when the police were said to have seized "secret diaries", pictures and "books on babies" from the family home where Michael had lived most of his life from later childhood. Under the memorable headline "WACKO JACKO FLEES FLACKO", the *News of the World*[51] linked the raid to his dramatic abandonment of the *Dangerous* tour soon afterwards and his flight from Mexico to go into hiding in England or – for it was not then certain where he had alighted from the private flight – Switzerland. Michael's apparent panic gave every encouragement to such a reading of his motives, but the raid itself later proved inconsequential. So the diaries were "secret". Whose personal diaries are not? And what family home these days does not include "books on babies", especially one where there still lived parents who had reared nine children, among them Michael? A few days later it was revealed that the police had discovered a photo of a nude five-year-old boy in a locked briefcase in Michael's bedroom at Hayvenhurst. His lawyer pointed out that Michael had not lived in the house for over six years and claimed any such photo had no connection with his client.[52]

Pictures of children definitely interested Michael. The walls of Neverland were covered in them, as artist David Hockney remarked after his visit.[53] Leroy Thomas, a sacked security guard, made a sworn statement in a wrongful dismissal case, saying he was personally instructed by Jackson to retrieve a photo from Michael's bathroom at Hayvenhurst and destroy it. This was a Polaroid picture of a naked young boy. In order to carry out this "special assignment" he was to find a key hidden under the refrigerator to gain access to the bathroom. In the words of the statement, "Thomas did as he was ordered. The naked young male appeared to be Caucasian or possibly Asian. The photograph was a profile shot of the young male revealing his genitals and buttocks from a side view. Thomas then attempted to destroy the photo in accordance with the instructions received."[54] Exactly why that word "attempted" should appear in the statement is not explained. Having found the photo there would appear to be no difficulty in destroying it. Perhaps what is meant is that he tried, there and then, to tear it up, which would indeed have been difficult: Polaroid photos are very tough. We are not told its ultimate fate, but that one throwaway word, "attempted", may be thought to add credibility to the claim that there had indeed been a photo. In Diane Dimond's book, published in 2005, she reported an interview she did in November 1993 with Thomas and his colleague Morris Williams, two of five Hayvenhurst guards who were suing Michael. Thomas confirmed that the picture had indeed been hard to tear. He managed to destroy the image by first tearing the back off the picture, then destroying the soft front part.

Incidentally, the five guards who sued Michael – Leroy Thomas, Morris Williams, Fred Hammond, Aaron White and Donald Starkes – were inevitably dubbed "the Jackson Five" in some news reports. Confusingly, the same epithet was later applied to five Neverland staff who also sued him. These were Kassim Abdool, Ralph Chacon, Melanie Bagnall, Adrian McManus and Sandy Domz, whose allegations and grievances come into the picture later. For the sake of clarity, it is easier to think of the first group as the Hayvenhurst Five and the second as the Neverland Five.

Various staff allegations, those of the two "fives" and yet others, concern a number of children, named and unnamed. Just one point should be taken on board immediately because it relates to Jordie Chandler. This involves a figure we met a moment ago, chauffeur Gary Hearne, who confirmed the closeness and continuity of Michael's contact with Jordie by saying in sworn testimony that on thirty successive days he drove Michael to Jordie's family home so his boss could stay there overnight.[55] The regular pattern of these "sleepovers" seems hard to equate with the claim made by some on Michael's behalf that his sleeping with children was in the American "slumber party" tradition – that is to say, the custom whereby kids are occasionally allowed by their parents to stay overnight at a friend's house. Michael's rather fanciful status as "just a big kid" for this purpose in any case always made this a masterpiece of special pleading.

Jordie's own evidence contains one further item which many felt would prove decisive and damning. He talked to the police about Michael's body, in particular about distinguishing marks on his genitals and lower body area that he could only possibly have known about in an intimate context. Police sources said they were just about to serve Michael with a warrant requiring him to submit to an inspection of his naked body when he fled from Mexico.[56] Could this have been why he went into hiding? Had he been alerted to what was afoot? Was he effectively "on the run" now, fleeing from justice? The media implied as much but, for anyone interested, Michael had a perfectly good defence. Unnamed friends of his had put it about that he and Jordie had showered together, providing an intimate context in which Jordie could have seen Michael's genitals without any illegality or even impropriety. But by this time innocent explanations were well out of fashion and the excitable media relegated the possibility to a footnote if they mentioned it at all.

The *Sun*, Britain's market leader in salacious coverage, licked its lips and sucked at the story of Michael's manhood with positively gay abandon. Headed "YOU'LL HAVE TO STRIP, MY OLD COCK", their report ran: "Police plan to make Michael Jackson strip so they can see the colour of his manhood... Jackson, 35, has said he suffers from vitiligo, a disease which leaves white patches on the skin. Some patches are believed to be on his penis...One cop said: 'This whole case hinges on whether the marks on Mr Jackson's genitalia match up with what the young accuser tells us.' Last night all America was agog over the latest revelations... An insider at top-rated telly show *A Current Affair* said: 'We've been flooded with calls telling us about Michael's private parts'."[57] We were not told if these calls were all from small boys, which really would have been sensational, or, as seems more likely, from women fans indulging in wish-fulfilling fantasy, perhaps aiming also to bolster their hero's heterosexual credentials. Never mind, the paper had another angle on Michael's dangle: plastic surgery on his penis.

The reason Michael had given for abandoning the *Dangerous* tour also involved surgery, but in a completely different body zone. He said that following reconstructive surgery connected with a burn injury to his scalp, he had needed to take pain killers and had become addicted to them.[58] He had left Mexico to obtain treatment aimed at breaking this addiction, an explanation that might have been believed if it had been revealed where he was being treated, but this was kept a closely guarded secret. There was extensive speculation that he was being kept under heavy security at the Charter Nightingale Clinic, London, where he was being treated by a team including addiction therapist Beauchamp "Beechy" Colclough, a colourful character said to have cured Elton John of drug addiction and who had been recommended to Michael by him.[59]

But firm information was distinctly not forthcoming. Frustrated by endless stakeouts at half the clinics in London, and wild goose chases to country house retreats to which Michael might have been spirited away, the impatient tabloids put a price on his head: "SPOT JACKO AND WIN 10 GRANDO" offered the *Sun*, entertaining its readers with a photo of a Jackson lookalike seen reading the paper: "IS IT HIM?", asks the caption, "Reading the *Sun* from front to the backo, is it a fraud or is it Jacko?"[60] The following day lots of *Sun* readers did indeed "spot Jacko", one seeing him on the swings at a children's playground, where "All the mums thought he looked *Dangerous* and told him to *Beat It*." We are not told whether the paper coughed up 10 GRANDO for this vital information.

The secrecy surrounding Michael's whereabouts fuelled speculation far beyond the realms of comic relief. Gossip columnist Janet Charlton, writing in the *Sun*, spelt out what many were thinking: "I've heard he isn't having treatment for drug addiction at all. In fact, he's having surgery to get rid of the marks."[61] TV station KABC went one better, asserting that the mark in question was a tattoo on Michael's penis. Here was a vintage Wacko Jacko story that caught the world's imagination. Under the headline "MARKED MAN", *Today*'s Comment column cracked the riddle of Michael's mysterious movements since his dramatic arrival in England: "No wonder we can't find Michael Jackson. We've been looking in the wrong place in more ways than one. Instead of searching the world's top clinics we now realise we should have been looking at Ted's Tattoo Removers in Teddington."[62]

Whatever they thought of the tattoo story, it is evident the police took very seriously the possibility that Michael might use plastic surgery to efface the marks Jordie had identified: raids were carried out at the offices of two California-based doctors used by Michael and medical records removed. One was plastic surgeon Dr Steve Hoefflin, who had carried out surgery to rebuild Michael's chin and nose. The other was Dr Arnold Klein, a skin specialist said to have been treating him for vitiligo.[63]

A reported suicide attempt by Michael in Mexico,[64] cranked up the sense of high drama, but this turned into low farce at his expense following his clandestine, dead-of-night touchdown at Luton airport near London.[65] His hide-and-seek act, aided and abetted by Elizabeth Taylor, who had arranged the flight, and fellow pop star Elton John, became the butt of comedians and cartoonists. Perhaps the cruellest, most ghoulish aspect of how some people were taking it all was seen in a rush of punters to put bets on Michael succeeding in a suicide bid before the year was out.[66] To make matters even worse, the precipitate cancellation of his remaining tour dates had come just before he had been due to perform on American territory in Puerto Rico, serving to heighten speculation that he was now really rattled by the allegations and had no intention of returning to the USA, where he would have to face a very different kind of music to that of his famous crotch-grabbing concerts.[67]

Afraid he may have been, but return he did. And soon after his arrival back in the States early in December he submitted to the strip inspection demanded by the police, allowing his most intimate body areas to be photographed in detail. It was to be, in his own words, "the most humiliating ordeal of my life".[68] In a television statement from Neverland broadcast just before Christmas 1993 to an estimated audience of one billion people around the globe, the pain of that humiliation was plain for all to see as in his soft, quiet voice he spoke straight to camera with not a hint of presenting himself in a glamorous light. This was a stripped down Michael, looking as psychically naked, vulnerable and humiliated before the world's hard, narrow-eyed scrutiny as he had been physically naked before those police cameras. For once there was a touch of anger giving edge to his soft tones: whatever else it might have been, this riveting performance was no mere chat show pap.

The pain was surely real, but was his protestation of innocence? Protestation sums its up, for there was no attempt to respond in detail to the allegations against him in this four-minute address. As Michael said, his lawyers had advised him that this was not the right forum for that, though it has to be doubted whether it was the right forum for anything. Referring to the indignity of being inspected and photographed, he said, "It was a nightmare, a horrifying nightmare. But if this is what I have to endure to prove my innocence, my complete innocence, so be it." Reaching the emotional heart of his appeal, he went on:

> Throughout my life I have only tried to help thousands upon thousands of children to live happy lives. It brings tears to my eyes when I see any child who suffers. I am not guilty of these allegations. But if I am guilty of anything it is of giving all that I have to give to help children all over the world; it is of loving children of all races and ages; it is of gaining sheer joy from seeing children with their innocent and smiling faces. It is of enjoying through them the childhood that I missed myself. If I am guilty of anything, it is of believing what God said about children, "Suffer little children to come unto me and forbid them not, for such is the Kingdom of Heaven." In no way do I think that I am God, but I do try to be God-like in my heart. I am totally innocent of any wrong-doing and I know these terrible allegations will all be proven false.[69]

In England, patriotism is said to be the last refuge of a scoundrel; in America the scoundrels go one better and hide behind God. That, at any rate, is how the more cynical commentators reacted.[70] Others were more charitable, notably publicist Max Clifford, who felt Michael was innocent but had been made to look guilty through poor public relations.[71] Was he angling for the job? If so, by the time Michael's trial had finished in 2005 he appeared to have changed his mind, saying he had just turned down Michael's request for his services: "It would be the hardest job in PR after Saddam Hussein", he said. Roy Carr, editor of the rock weekly *New Musical Express*, thought Jackson should have returned to the USA as soon as the allegations were made and demanded that the issue be thrashed out immediately. For him that was the only convincing response an innocent man could make. Columnist Virginia Ironside sympathetically noted Michael's by now familiar claim to have lost out on childhood, but insisted, "You just can't regain a lost childhood; you can only mourn it; rage at it perhaps, and then accept it and move on."[72]

The *National Enquirer* put its faith in hi-tech, publishing the findings of "world-renowned lie-detection expert" Charles R McQuiston, who had subjected a tape of the broadcast to a computerised analysis of "voice stress levels". The Psychological Stress Evaluator method used for the analysis was said to be in use in thirty six American states and in Canada. Verdict: thumbs down. Michael Jackson lied, claimed McQuiston, a retired military intelligence officer. Of the passage where Michael says, "I am not guilty of these allegations", McQuiston comments: "That statement is an absolute lie. When Jackson says the word 'guilty', the spikes nearly leap off the page. It is clearly a tense vocal reflex caused by someone attempting to cover up the truth."[73]

So-called "lie detector" tests have been around for many years but they are known to be highly fallible. Roy Carr's innocence test is more interesting in Michael's case: there were all sorts of reasons why he should have flown back to America straight away, as Carr suggested, while the decision to go into hiding can only be seen as disastrous, making him look like a man on the run even if he was not. The Los Angeles police actually said they would have to regard the move as "a run for cover".[74] He had not been charged with a criminal offence, but in the previous month they had reportedly told journalists sufficient evidence was available to recommend charging him.[75] Also, Jordie's civil case had been filed in mid-September[76] and the court had actually ordered Michael to return to America by 1 November to answer questions, a requirement he plainly did not comply with.[77] Instead, his lawyers argued unsuccessfully that the whole matter should be delayed for up to six years, pending the prior resolution of any criminal case that might be brought.[78] The six years was significant because at that time under California's statute of limitations a criminal case could not be started once this period had elapsed. So if Jackson were to have faced a civil case in, say, the year 2000, he would not have had to worry about any evidence from the suit being used in a prosecution.

Raymond Chandler made much of Jackson's legal tactics in his book *All That Glitters*, published in 2004. He showed that Jordie's legal team thought Michael's people had made a serious mistake, a judgment in agreement with *The Wall Street Journal*, which reported that Jackson's chief attorney, Bertram Fields, had been forced off the case essentially because he had mishandled it.[79] Chandler, himself an attorney (and not to be confused with his namesake the detective writer), pointed out that for one thing the attempted six-year delay would fall foul of an absolute right accorded to minors under fourteen of a trial within 120 days. Thus Jordie's lawyers could file a motion forcing Jackson's testimony. Ironically, instead of going for the dramatic six-year delay, Jackson need only have hung on until Jordie's fourteenth birthday, on 11 January 1994, and then, if he wished, used more conventional delaying tactics.[80]

Far worse, in their answer to the Chandlers' case, Jackson's lawyers had filed a countermotion which said Jackson would take the Fifth Amendment. This meant that in court he would decline to answer questions that might incriminate him. In other words, although in public he and his PR people would always plead his total innocence, in his countermotion he was effectively admitting he had something serious to hide. If he persisted down this road it would inevitably be a disaster for public perception of the case: everyone would think he was guilty as sin. He did not. After a hearing on 23 November, Fields abruptly disappeared from the case and his tactics with him.

Not that Jackson survived these errors scot-free. The Fifth Amendment blunder escaped the spotlight, but Fields was splashed worldwide in the media thanks to yet another error, this time a comment in open court in which he sensationally suggested that a criminal indictment was imminent. In arguments before Los Angeles Superior Court, he said, "Your honour, you've got a district attorney sitting up in Santa Barbara, probably about to indict… You can't get too much closer to an indictment than to have a grand jury sitting there." Diane Dimond persuasively explained in her book that it was as if Fields was trying to convince the judge that a delay in the civil case would not take the whole of the six years, because the criminal case would be over long before that. The only thing that would soon be over was Fields' credibility: outside court, his co-counsel Howard Weitzman told the media

Fields had "misspoke himself", and that he had no idea whether a grand jury had been empanelled.[81]

As for Michael declining to return to the USA, another way of looking at it is to ask why on earth an innocent man should be expected to make himself a victim of the judicial system. Why should Michael have let himself be given the run around when he had major tour commitments to fulfil, involving multi-million dollar contractual obligations and entertaining thousands of fans who would otherwise be disappointed? Why not just carry on regardless for as long as possible? If legal matters had been the only consideration such a view might have had some force. But there was at least one other reason for Michael to return to the United States which in less fraught circumstances he might have found compelling: the funeral of his grandfather, Samuel Jackson. He had not been close to Samuel; in fact his failure to visit the old man or show any concern over his life in a nursing home in a run-down area of Phoenix, Arizona, had been the subject of criticism. Nevertheless a funeral is usually recognised as the one time respects have to be paid, not least in a family like Michael's, when it is bound to be the focus of public attention. His parents, Katherine and Joseph, attended, and it was while they were away, in early November, that the police raided their Encino home to search Michael's rooms there.[82] Katherine fainted when she was told about it.[83] God knows what turmoil of thoughts and feelings must have been churned up in the minds and hearts of this aging couple and what interpretation they put on their famous son's staying half a planet away at such a time.

For Michael Jackson, 1993 had been what the soccer commentators call a game of two halves. The first saw him quietly enjoying his hard-earned celebrity as the most successful pop singer ever. These were the months, between February and June, when he was able to be with Jordie, with little to disturb their increasingly intense friendship. Only two events attracted much public attention, both of them intentionally, and with results that must have seemed not at all bad, especially when compared with what was to come. We have already seen that the second of these, the Monte Carlo music awards in May, gave Michael the opportunity to be seen in public with Jordie, to "flaunt" the relationship as hostile eyes would see it, or maybe to take honest pride in it in a way that few would understand.

The first big public occasion had been his appearance on the Oprah Winfrey show in February, when he broke a ten-year silence during which he had become notorious among music writers for refusing to be interviewed.

This had been the period in which, alongside his achievement of unprecedented record sales, the Wacko Jacko mythology had grown, fuelled by the reluctance of the man himself to set the record straight personally. Many of the bizarre stories concerning his lifestyle had been harmless enough and some had undoubtedly been inspired by his own publicity people as well as by the fertile imagination of journalists.

Others had been less welcome, especially the suggestion that he had undergone more plastic surgery than was good for him and the allegation that he had been using chemical agents to lighten his skin colour. Michael used the Oprah interview, watched by over sixty million people, to address that question, telling the world for the first time that he used white make-up to cover skin blotches caused by the pigmentation disorder vitiligo – the disorder that was to be mentioned in a hugely more controversial context before the year was out.

There were others straws in the wind, too. Whereas in Michael's early years the Jacksons had been presented as a highly respectable family, deeply religious and squeaky clean, the image had begun to be tarnished, not least by revelations in his sister La Toya's book about their father Joseph's alleged womanising and brutality towards his children. Michael said he had not read the book, but he did say his father used to beat him and that his childhood had been blighted by a lack of contact with any children other than his siblings. He told how he would walk home from school and pass other kids out playing. He could never join them because he was always due home for a rehearsal. "You don't get to do the things that other kids do," he said. "I compensate for that now by having children around because when I was little it was always work, work, work."

Asked about his personal life, Michael was plainly on uncomfortable ground. He claimed to be dating actress Brooke Shields but said they tended to meet in their respective homes rather than go out where they would be recognised. By the end of the year it was being put about that Brooke was paid £6,500 for being seen with him.[84] Famously asked if he was a virgin, Michael replied: "I'm a gentleman. That is something that's private. Call me old-fashioned... I'm embarrassed." He was not ready to marry and have a family of his own, he said, because of his work. "I admire children, but I am married to my music."

In her book *Michael Jackson In His Own Words*, published after this interview but before the debacle, Catherine Dineen described Michael's responses to Oprah's gentle probing as "unquestionably the frankest interview Michael had given in years" – a judgment which, if correct, may be thought not to say much for the candour of the other rare occasions when he had publicly made a non-singing utterance.[85]

Those straws in the wind in the first half of 1993 can have signified little to most of Michael's adoring fans, among them many young, and not so young, women, who could still fantasise about one day marrying this highly eligible bachelor themselves. By June, Michael himself may have begun to feel seriously threatened by Evan Chandler's suspicions, and his sister La Toya was also giving cause for alarm: she seemed to have acquired a taste for juicy disclosures. Who could say what she might reveal next, or with what dreadful consequences? If he was worried, he was not showing it though. When the storm finally broke in August it came upon the world as a bolt from the blue, greeted with shock and incredulity by fans and non-fans alike.

Having followed the main strand of the case against Michael in some detail – Jordie's own written allegations, backed up by his evidence as to the appearance of Michael's unclothed body – it will be helpful here to review briefly the other main elements of the stormy second half of 1993, the better to understand the atmosphere in which a settlement of the civil case was arrived at in January 1994.

The first the world knew of any sexual allegations was on 24 August soon after the police raided Neverland and Michael's Century City condominium. In Bangkok at the time, at the start of his *Dangerous* tour, he denied the charges and indicated that the tour would go on. Nevertheless he pulled out of a concert complaining of dehydration: the pressure was taking its toll just as much as the tropical heat. On 27 August eleven-year-old Australian Brett Barnes said he had regularly shared a bed with Michael, but not for any sexual activity. Other boys' names were linked to Michael, notably those of *Home Alone* star Macaulay Culkin, who had been on holiday with him to Bermuda, Jimmy Safechuck, who had been in a Pepsi commercial with him, and Wade Robson, another young Australian who had shared his bed.

The *Today* newspaper disclosed documents suggesting Michael had paid one boy £400,000 "hush money". Another concert, in Singapore, was cancelled after the star had collapsed, causing sufficient concern for his doctors to give him a brain scan, which turned out to reveal nothing abnormal – a conclusion received with frank disbelief by some newspapers! Just days later former Neverland staffers Mark and Faye Quindoy claimed they had seen him fondling boys. Jackson was hit with a series of writs in the autumn, including the civil suit filed by Evan Chandler on 14 September (case number SC026226, filed in Los Angeles County Superior Court). Two songwriters who grew up with the Jackson family in Indiana were reaching the climax of a long legal battle in which they were suing Michael for allegedly stealing "their" songs – a battle that could cost him hundreds of millions of dollars if he lost.

On 12 November Michael fled from Mexico, where he had given videotaped evidence in connection with the "stolen" songs case. The copyright lawyers involved in the seven-hour legal stint described Michael as "normal and rational" at this time, when others have said he was suicidal and in the grip of an addiction. His own lawyer, Bert Fields, said, "The Michael I saw in Mexico was intellectually and intelligently [*sic*] impaired and I advised him not to do it."[86] Yet another concert had been cancelled in Mexico, this time through "toothache", and as Michael went into hiding in England for treatment the remainder of his world tour was cancelled.

Pepsi Cola, who had sponsored the tour and had a multi-million dollar contract with him, announced the deal was off. Five security guards (the Hayvenhurst Five) came forward seeking damages for unfair dismissal, telling of boys who came to visit their employer at night, including an "Asian" boy later identified by Michael's mother as Sean Lennon. At a time when allegations were thundering down like potatoes from a hopper, sister La Toya joined the onslaught, saying she could not remain "a silent collaborator in my brother's crimes against small, innocent children."[87]

Michael had scarcely returned to the US, on 10 December, before his maid Blanca Francia told the world on TV that she had seen him in nude romps with small boys, when he would rub his genitals against them.[88] Even after his dramatic Christmas broadcast there was to be no let up. The quiet tail end of the year, when regular folks are suffering from nothing worse than a surfeit of mince pies or brandy, carried a double legal sting for Michael. He was sued by the Children's Peace Foundation charity for £100 million, alleging theft and fraud. The second part of the double whammy was a demand for £13 million from the organisers of the world tour in compensation for lost revenue.

Today's Tina Weaver thought that if 1993 had been terrible for Michael, 1994 would be far worse, for this would be when the long arm of the law would finally catch up with him.[89] Columnist Virginia Ironside likewise suggested that this was one problem Michael could not buy his way out of.[90] But in fact January 1994 was to see the most spectacular, high-profile, case of a man buying his way out of a legal mess in the entire history of litigation.

At first no-one believed the figures when *Today* broke the story in what they dubbed a "world exclusive". The figure given for an out-of-court settlement in the Chandler case of £30 million looked so huge that it just had to be wrong.[91] Didn't it? Well, yes, but it turned out to be not so ridiculously far off. At the time, though, most of the media were all at sea. *The Guardian* followed the *Today* report five days later saying estimates of the undisclosed settlement varied widely, from $5 million to $100 million. In other words, they did not have a clue.

The fact that Michael settled for a multimillion dollar figure could only be a measure of his desperation. Jordie's lawyer Larry Feldman was claiming that new witnesses were being unearthed by the day and Tina Weaver suggested "Feldman hit on something which touched a raw nerve in the singer's camp".[92] This credibly accounted for a deal that would be bound to look like a tacit admission of guilt. Arguably, though, the continuing publicity surrounding any court case would have been damaging to Michael whatever the outcome. The case, not due to start until the March, could have dragged on for months after that, and Michael must have reckoned that even if he won many would still say his smart lawyers had got him off. It was a no-win situation. Better just to cut his losses by making a settlement while continuing to insist on his innocence, and then putting things behind him.

It was not until many years later that full details of the secret settlement were authoritatively reported. Diane Dimond, in her book *Be Careful Who You Love*, said she obtained a copy of the agreement more than ten years later. It was signed by Jackson, his lawyers, Jordie's parents and their lawyer, plus Jordie's guardian ad litem. A striking aspect of the wording is that the payout was made not for sexual molestation but for "alleged personal injuries arising out of claims of negligence". The original suit by the Chandlers had listed specific alleged sexual offences in graphic detail, but there had also been a section which included the following: "Defendant Michael Jackson negligently had offensive contacts with plaintiff which were both specifically sexual and otherwise. As a direct and proximate result of the negligence…the plaintiff has suffered…great mental, physical and nervous pain and suffering and emotional distress…" As Dimond noted, it defies logic that anyone could "negligently" have "explicitly sexual" contact, but the fact is that he paid out only on the complaint of negligence.[93] By signing the settlement, the Chandlers dropped their allegations, of seduction, sexual battery, wilful misconduct and intentional infliction of emotional distress. According to Dimond, in addition to a settlement pledge of $15,331,250, Jordie also received an extra signing bonus of about $2 million. His parents each received an additional $1.5 million up front. Larry Feldman and his team had all their legal fees paid by Michael Jackson, to the tune of around $5 million. So Michael's total payout (not counting his own legal bill) topped $25 million.

On the witness stand at Michael's trial in 2005, Feldman described the outcome of the Chandler case as an agreement that was a "confession of judgment", not a mere "contract". This abstruse legal expression could have been taken by some to support the view that Jackson was "confessing" he had done something wrong, whether "negligently" or otherwise. However, under cross-examination by Michael's lawyer Tom Mesereau, Feldman could not sustain any such impression:

> Q: You had settlement language that said neither side admits wrongdoing to the other, and you also had the confession of judgment you just described, true?
> A: True.[94]

Michael may well have felt a settlement would be better for Jordie, too, far better than dragging him through the legal process even further – a course of action we can now be certain was not the boy's own idea and which he never wanted. The idea that Michael might have been thinking of Jordie's welfare was not one that leapt to mind for media commentators. The *Daily Mirror*'s columnist Allan Hall was among legions of them crying foul over the star's money being used to buy silence. Hall wheeled on his own heavyweight witness to bolster the point, the "celebrated" American divorce lawyer Raoul Felder. He quotes Felder as saying: "The message this sends is disgusting. In other words, if you are rich, you can abuse children."[95] The point might also be made that if you are rich you can afford to buy the services of Raoul Felder, in order to screw your former marriage partner for every last penny and make sure he or she never sees the kids again. That is the sort of morally superior behaviour "celebrated" divorce lawyers are paid big bucks for.

The cynicism voiced by Hall and Felder was to be expected, and looked at in a narrow context they were right. Whichever way it was sliced it came to the same thing: Michael was indeed buying silence, buying his way out of a hole. This was patently unjust if only because we are all supposed to be equal before the law, but few of us could afford to pull such a stunt: Michael could not have given a clearer demonstration that some are more equal than others.

This blatant offence against a simple principle of justice does not mean, though, either that Michael was guilty or that justice for Jordie would have been better served by dragging matters out in the courts. The media were miffed at being cheated out of a fabulous story that they had hoped would run and run. As we will see in Chapter Eleven, Jordie never personally wanted to see Michael punished for what took place. It was a loving relationship and it pained him to see his idol brought low.

Not content with venting their spleen on Michael, some sections of the media were so upset to lose their story that they took to blaming Jordie as well. Carol Sarler in *The People* astonishingly called him a prostitute. Under the heading "YOU'RE A REAL PRO, JORDIE", she said, "I don't know what Michael Jackson thought he was doing when he paid his millions to Jordie Chandler. I do know what Jordie (or do I mean his squalid father?) was doing. It's really quite simple. Jordie has not withdrawn his allegation that Jackson sexually molested him. He simply said that he will go away and leave Jackson alone, now that a suitable financial payment has been made for the sex. A purely financial arrangement. The oldest profession in the world."[96]

That's quite an allegation. For a journalist to dump like this on a thirteen-year-old kid would normally be professional suicide. Children are supposed to be innocent. Where sex with adults is concerned they are supposed to be just passive victims, lacking any responsibility for what took place. That was the orthodoxy that made it possible for Jordie's lawyer to present the thirteen-year-old as a "little boy" without sounding ridiculous and why a social worker would feel safe in assuming the boy must have been "coerced" into sharing a bath with Michael. News reports are typically framed within socially accepted assumptions of this sort: inconvenient facts that do not easily fit into the frame are ignored or downplayed.

Opinion pieces appear to offer an opportunity to break out of this frame, but in reality the scope for commentators who wish to survive in the mainstream media is limited: it takes a brave journalist or broadcaster to challenge the more entrenched conventional wisdoms. Their task is largely not to arrive at "the truth" but to articulate what the public would have thought if they had the time and mental agility to think things through for themselves. Their task is to make the best possible fit between established values – or prejudices – and the "facts" arriving at the news desk.

The interesting thing about Carol Sarler's piece is that on the face of it she is doing nothing of the sort. To say out loud that the "victim" is no angel is to risk the wrath of the people. When a British judge did just that some years ago, describing a nine-year-old girl involved sexually with an adult as "no angel", he found himself on the end of strident calls for his resignation and complaints to his boss, the Lord Chancellor. No-one wanted to know about the girl's previous sexual encounters with other men.[97]

So how did Sarler get away with it? She had shrewdly understood that this was a case where the stereotype of "molester" and "victim" could simply no longer be made to fit the facts. This was not an obscure court story of which people knew little. The details had been blasted onto the front pages for month after month in a most unusual case of pre-trial exposure. Jordie was coming to be resented for not conforming to the way a child "ought" to behave. Never mind the orthodoxy that Michael had all the power and the money and was an adult who therefore ought to be the responsible party; it was Jordie who was now making the running and calling the shots. This presented an anarchic, frightening, topsy-turvy view of childhood, in which the power and control we in general expect to be exercised by adults seemed under threat. Jordie had gotten uppity, and Carol Sarler's role on behalf of her readers was to punish him for it, just as she was also punishing him for killing a good story. It is not just "they", the baddies, the child molesters, who sometimes forget or misunderstand what it is to be a child. "We", the general public, are perfectly capable of the same thing, giving kids a hard time when they fail to live up to our expectations – or rather when our expectations fail to measure up to reality.

That we require our children to be angels is a theme unconsciously echoed in a wistful retrospective piece by Tina Weaver in March, 1994, a couple of months after the settlement. What looked like a stolen, telephoto-lens picture, showed a "haunted unsmiling Jordie, now aged fourteen, on a skiing holiday with his father Evan, step-mother Natalie and half-brother Nikki. "This little boy with the doleful gaze is Jordie Chandler," wrote Weaver, the angel-faced youngster who was said to have bewitched pop idol Michael Jackson."[98]

Angel-faced, but by implication not the angel he should have been, and now he was being punished. "Jordie," she said, "is undergoing regular psychotherapy and the family hoped the break would help erase some of the painful memories of the last six months." Note that "the last six months" included only the period of the public scandal. The alleged sexual activity had been earlier. Weaver appeared to be tacitly admitting that it was not the relationship with Michael that had left him with painful memories. Then what had? She told us: "...he is well aware that he will always be known as the boy who plunged one of the world's top entertainers into a sensational scandal. Little wonder Jordie could not raise a smile..."

At least this poor "little boy", was now a poor little rich boy. As Weaver had nauseatingly commented at the time of the settlement, "The massive offer would guarantee the best counselling for Jordie and the finest life he could wish for".[99] Whether psychotherapy and a fine life are compatible is a moot point, but a simpler one needs to be made on the monetary aspect of the settlement: Jordie's "squalid" father had not secured a huge fortune for himself. Evan and his ex-wife June had by this time started proceedings to transfer guardianship of Jordie to a retired judge, who would administer the boy's money in a trust fund.

We have now discussed the civil settlement in January 1994 between Jordie Chandler and Michael Jackson in some detail, after a brisk run through the dramatic events of the previous year, leading up to the settlement. We must remember, though, that the civil lawsuit was only half of the picture. The other half was the distinct possibility of Jackson facing a criminal case. It is time to pick up the threads of the police investigation, and for that we must begin by backtracking a little.

In the eyes of Lauren Weiss, heading the criminal investigation for Los Angeles District Attorney's office, Michael had a great many questions to answer, but could he be made to do so? In the first month of the investigation that started on 17 August, 1993, the police investigation had Jordie's own statement to go on plus what little their raids on Michael's properties had turned up. In early October, police sources were reported as saying they had enough evidence to recommend charging Michael but higher counsels thought otherwise. The evidence of just one boy might not be enough. Tactically it would be better to wait until more witnesses came forward. Members of Jackson's former staff were beginning to talk and it must have seemed only a matter of time before other children among Michael's many young friends would do the same.

Evan Chandler, meanwhile, lost no time in consulting hotshot lawyers who had their own views on the case, and just going along with a police waiting game was not among the options they would canvass. By late August Evan had managed to rally his fractured family behind the idea of working out *together* what they wanted to achieve and needed to do. He and his wife June and Jordie's stepfather, Dave Schwarz, met as a group to thrash things out. As a result, they decided to hire the feminist lawyer Gloria Allred, who was well-known for taking on child abuse cases. As for Jordie, he too was consulted and brought in on joint discussions. No doubt the family genuinely believed they were scrupulously taking his point of view into account. But this was long after he had been thoroughly brow-beaten and brainwashed by his father into believing, or acting as if he believed, that drastic action against Michael was necessary.

Allred's strategy was to go for headlines, playing up the case in the media to put pressure on the district attorney's office to file criminal charges. She thought that by aggressively putting the case "out there" in the public arena, opinion could be turned around. Instead of buying into Michael's aura of injured innocence as polls showed the public were doing up to this point, people would come to believe in at least the possibility of his guilt by the time a trial started. She believed that as long as he stayed popular, and as long as he remained innocent in the court of public opinion, there was little prospect of a jury convicting him. A big publicity drive would also encourage other witnesses to come forward. That, at least, was her official strategy. Others saw her as a self-publicising grand-stander who wanted to use Jordie as a poster child for a feminist crusade – a crusade in which Jordie himself would be expected to fight from the witness box in a criminal trial.

Seen from the Chandler side, this was an unappealing aspect of the Allred vision. Jordie made it plain he dreaded having to take the stand against Michael. He just wanted the whole problem to go away. Even his father, who had been brutal in his determination to squeeze the truth out of Jordie about what had been going on sexually with Michael, did not want his son to suffer unnecessarily. Soon, he and the family would be pointed in the direction of another lawyer who would tell them it might be possible to hit Jackson hard without putting Jordie on the stand and – another thing the boy did not want – without sending his old friend to jail. This lawyer would play up the highly attractive possibility of winning a multi-million dollar out-of-court settlement which would bypass the criminal trial process entirely. The lawyer is question would be Larry Feldman. A past president of both the Los Angeles Trial Lawyers Association and the Los Angeles Bar Association, he had also been voted Trial Lawyer of the Year by his peers.[100]

With an attractive strategy and a highly credible track record, Feldman looked ideal for the job. By early September he had been hired, Allred had been fired, and in mid-September Jordie's civil suit against Jackson was launched. Meanwhile, police work was going on behind the scenes. On just one occasion their contribution surfaced in a big way, when they ordered Michael to strip for his naked body to be photographed. The gloves had come off against the Gloved One for the first time: he was to be humiliated like a common criminal.[101]

Apart from this one major move, the police investigation seemed to be making little progress: many children were interviewed but there were to be no more star witnesses. It was not for the want of trying. Michael's lawyer Bert Fields complained in a letter to Los Angeles police chiefs that "Your officers have told frightened youngsters outrageous lies, such as 'We have naked photos of you' to push them into making accusations."[102] Despite any such tactics the police effort, handled from the small, low-profile juvenile division, turned out to be ineffectual; it could only play second fiddle to what the Chandlers' team were achieving. It was as though the DA's office were just hoping, Micawber-like, for something to turn up. The civil case itself, scheduled for March, could have been that something. If Jordie had testified, with the case going against Michael, Weiss might at least have felt justified in recommending a criminal charge.

In the days before news of the civil settlement leaked out, Los Angeles was pre-occupied with the effects of a major earthquake. It was a time when lawyers on both sides could thrash out the details without hassle from the media, whose minds were on collapsed freeway bridges and wrecked homes. The fact that Michael was prepared to settle has been put down to the collapse and wreck of his chief means of discrediting the Chandler side just twenty four hours earlier when the police decided his extortion claim against Evan Chandler was baseless. *Today* went further, in a statement that all but accused Michael: By January, said Tina Weaver, "it was crystal clear the game was up. The singer knew that a description young Jordie Chandler had given of skin discolouration on his genitals was frighteningly accurate. Police had already photographed him naked, now the boy's lawyers were pushing relentlessly on to be allowed to do the same."[103] The police were also to show an interest in talking to Dr Arnold Klein about any plastic surgery he might have performed on Michael's penis. Years later *The Smoking Gun* revealed the findings in more detail:

> Chandler gave them a roadmap to Jackson's below-the-waist geography, which, he said, includes distinctive "splotches" on his buttocks and one on

> his penis, "which is a light colour similar to the colour of his face." The boy's information was so precise, he even pinpointed where the splotch fell while Jackson's penis was erect, the length of the performer's pubic hair, and that he was circumcised. ...In a recent sealed affidavit, [District Attorney] Tom Sneddon is quoted as saying that Chandler's pre-search description (and a drawing) "corroborated" photos taken of Jackson and observations made by officers who examined the body of evidence.

Was Jordie's description really so accurate? Diane Dimond says yes, absolutely, no question of it. She devotes an entire chapter of her book[104] to the police procedure for taking the photographs, dwelling in what can only be called malicious detail on the most intimate aspects of Michael's humiliation, and has further references to the event on no fewer than eleven other pages. She refers at first to a dark "patch", then opts for "spot", saying, "It's important to note that the dark spot was only visible when the penis was lifted – as during sexual arousal."

If true, it is a compellingly strong point. Her bias is revealed, however, by what she omits. There is no reference in her long account – which finds room for such fascinating but largely irrelevant details as the type of camera and lenses the police photographer used – to the fact that Jordie got one crucial detail wrong: Michael Jackson was not circumcised.

J Randy Taraborrelli's biography gives a more even-handed account, telling us that Jordie drew a diagram of Michael's penis on a napkin for police, and wrote on it: "Michael is circumcised. He has short pubic hair. His testicles are marked with pink and brown marks. Like a cow, not white but pink colour. He has brown patches on his ass, on his left glut." All of these descriptive points matched what the police saw – except for the circumcision. But this was not necessarily fatal to Jordie's credibility. As Taraborrelli noted, if Jordie's sexual claims were true it is likely his attention would have been drawn to Michael's penis mainly, or even entirely, at times when it was erect – and an erect penis, with the foreskin withdrawn, can look circumcised when it is not.[105]

Michael's legal team had actually said they had no objection to the Chandler side seeing the police photographs. But that was not the whole story. Jordie's lawyers wanted those photos for use in evidence and filed a court motion to this effect. *The National Enquirer* made much of the issue, claiming, "Michael's people are so worried about those photos that his attorney Howard Weitzman has filed a secret motion to keep the photos from being used as evidence in the criminal investigation. The *Enquirer* can reveal exclusively that a hearing on the motion has been set for mid-February in Santa Barbara."[106] By 12 February it was being reported that a bid by Michael to have the police photos handed over to him had failed, and that they were to be kept in "a sealed vault".[107] The battle over these photos suggests that the secrets of the vault were every bit as crucial as the tabloids suggested. And the battle was to go on and on, still unresolved, with the photos remaining in the vault after Michael's acquittal in 2005. That was of course a completely different case, at which Jordie was not a witness and the photos were not used – but as long as they existed they could have been problematic for Michael.[108]

So, we know that Michael's extortion claim against Evan Chandler had failed, he had the photos to worry about, and reportedly new witnesses were being unearthed by the day. The weight with which all this was bearing down on him may be judged by the way his legal people dealt with both the criminal and civil case threats. On the criminal side the media had been toying with the idea that he might plead temporary insanity. While Michael had been lying low in England it was suggested he could argue that the pain and distress following reconstructive surgery had made him "insane" during the months of his contact with Jordie.

This would have been a desperate recourse, an admission of guilt. The media gossips speculating along these lines knew that Michael's own behaviour – the flight into hiding, the medical attention at a secret venue, the appearance of being on the run – gave credibility to the idea, and may indeed have inspired it, but there was never any sign that the Jackson camp took it seriously. Plea bargaining was another matter. American legal practice frequently results in an accused person pleading guilty to a lesser charge in return for a prosecution agreement not to proceed with a more serious one. Such an option was technically available in the case of the alleged assault on Jordie Chandler. Instead of being made to answer a serious felony charge, Michael could have faced the lesser misdemeanour options of battery (unwanted touching) and/or child endangerment. According to the *National Enquirer*, Michael's lawyer Johnnie Cochran had discussions with Lauren Weiss, of the District Attorney's office, along these lines. The *Enquirer*'s sources suggested the Jackson camp would have considered pleading guilty to a misdemeanour and they would "have no quarrel" with facing a hefty fine and an agreement that Michael should undergo psychological counselling.[109]

If Michael was looking wobbly and ready to compromise on the criminal side – though not to the extent of admitting a specifically sexual offence – it could only mean that he recognised the potential strength of Jordie's story if it were ever to figure in a criminal trial. Many years later, just a few months ahead of Michael's 2005 trial for alleged sexual offences against another boy, Gavin Arvizo, Feldman would confirm his personal assessment of the Chandler allegations, saying there had been "a definite good case" back in 1994. He would say this in a private conversation with TV chat show host Larry King in a Beverly Hills restaurant, before making a contrast with the weakness of the Arvizo case, in which he said the accuser's mother was a "wacko" just out for money.[110]

The formidable strength of the criminal case against him gave Michael all the more reason to pull the plug on the possibility of a criminal trial. He could achieve this by buying off the Chandler side in the civil case. If the boy were to accept a cash settlement he would no longer be available as a criminal case witness. Or would he? This was the subject of considerable debate at the time. The *National Enquirer* disclosed that the Santa Barbara, California, District Attorney's office subpoenaed the Chandler camp's legal files for use in their criminal investigation.[111] At that point it looked as though Jordie might after all take the stand eventually as a criminal case witness, though the odds against it were long.

In return for the money, said the *Enquirer*, the boy and his family agreed never to discuss Michael publicly, a claim later finding authoritative support. No civil agreement could legally prevent a witness from testifying in a criminal trial. But California law at that time gave a person who claimed to be the victim of a sex crime the right to refuse to testify. It was also claimed the agreement stipulated that Jordie was to leave California, a move that would make it more difficult for prosecutors to secure his cooperation.[112]

Some of the tabloids were by now clutching at straws along with the prosecution. *The Sun* insisted that Jordie could be forced to testify: a contract of silence would be seen as illegal and a serious attempt to obstruct the course of justice, the paper claimed.[113] The *Daily Mirror* spotted another way forward for the prosecution: if Jordie were no longer available his videotaped evidence could still be used.[114] But the paper did not suggest how he could be cross-examined, or question what weight a jury would put on the word of a witness who had effectively withdrawn his complaint.

Today, by contrast, was ready to make a more frank admission that the police probe was "close to collapse" in the wake of the civil settlement. Tina Weaver's view was that the police would have "an almost impossible task".

Lauren Weiss, the woman heading the investigation, admitted as much, saying, "Everything about this case is difficult. Everything... Without the kid, we don't have a case." Weiss was also troubled by Michael's ability to handle a jury: "He's an entertainer, he's used to being in front of people and performing. When someone like that is on the witness box, a prosecutor has very little chance of getting an admission out of them, flustering and unnerving them."[115]

The utter desperation of the prosecution found further expression early the following month when legal chiefs were said to be fighting to create a new law that would force Jordie to give evidence. By this time they had plainly lost all sight of the fact that the criminal law is supposed to be there to protect people. Children especially are supposed to be protected by the law from the unwanted attentions of others. Yet here were the authorities proposing to force Jordie to testify against his will. Even Michael, with all the insults and humiliation that had been heaped upon him, was never accused of resorting to forcing a child into anything.

The fact that the police case was in trouble did not mean that Michael was innocent. We can only guess how well the case would have fared with Jordie testifying, but we have seen some indications that Michael was worried about it. Private investigator Sandra Sutherland, who worked for the Chandler side on the civil case, was said to have discovered and questioned "more than 120 witnesses" in her six months' work, and claimed to have been frustrated by alleged Jackson camp tactics in buying off some of them and scaring off others.[116] She was not saying how many of these were child complainants, or the parents of alleged victims. Plainly, though, not one of these 120 shadowy figures became available as a star witness in place of Jordie.

Over a period of many months, grand juries in Los Angeles and Santa Barbara heard many witnesses, some of them of questionable relevance, such as the film star Marlon Brando, thought to be a "father confessor" figure to Michael, and Brando's son Miko who was on Michael's security staff. The authorities could only have been praying the Neverland ne'er-do-well had 'fessed up his felonies. Neverland housekeeper Norma Staikos, who also appeared, was perhaps regarded as a better bet. Reputed to rule the staff with an iron fist, she allegedly once warned Orietta Murdoch, a top assistant at Michael's company MJJ Productions, and the mother of a ten-year-old boy, never to leave her son alone with Michael. Murdoch also testified. On the other hand, Staikos was allegedly implicated in suspect activity herself and so likely to be tight-lipped: she reportedly issued orders that the security guards at the gate should not record the arrival of "the little boyfriends", some of whom began to turn up in the early hours of the morning.[117] Other witnesses included publicist Bob Jones, dermatologist Dr Arnold Klein and security chief Bill Bray. Gary Hearne was there to testify about the suitcase we heard he had to pick up before the police raid. So were Anthony Pellicano and his wife, both called to testify about another mysterious suitcase she had been asked to hold for him. James DeBarge, Janet Jackson's ex-husband was there. As we shall hear later, he had a very interesting story to tell, as had bodyguard Charli Michaels.

But no alleged victims would appear before a grand jury. The closest they would get was Blanca Francia, mother of a boy, Jason, who would testify many years later at Jackson's trial in 2005. In these early days, though, Jason would not be talking: his mother, like Jordie's father, was negotiating a civil settlement. Several of Michael's "special friends" appeared, but not to spill any beans. When Michael's mother Katherine was subpoenaed, Michael broke what had been a long silence to protest against "the harassment of my beloved mother".[118]

This was all going nowhere. On 21 September, 1994, the district attorney's offices of Los Angeles and Santa Barbara counties issued a "statement of declination" wrapping up the work of the grand juries and what had been a joint, year-long, investigation involving the police and district attorneys of the two areas. Approximately four hundred witnesses had been contacted, the statement said, and an additional thirty witnesses were called before the grand juries. Jordan Chandler (though he was not named in the statement), fitted the bill as the "first" alleged victim. It was said he had "chosen to assert his rights under Code of Civil Procedure section 1219 and has declined to testify". It was further stated that "This decision was not communicated to either prosecutorial agency until July 6, 1994".

There was also talk of "a second boy", and that in this case the events described "occurred solely in Santa Barbara County". However, there could be no prosecution "because of the inability of law enforcement to interview the alleged victim, because that child is beyond the reach of the court process and because of the child's prior general denial of any wrongdoing". As cases go, this was as underwhelming as they come. Andersen tells us the police at this time had been particularly interested in a boy they called "the German kid", who had met Michael while he was touring in Europe. Once back in his own country, such a boy would fit the bill of being "beyond the reach of the court process". Andersen also says the boy's story, far from being underwhelming, "was supposed to have made Jordie Chandler's pale by comparison".[119] What could possibly have been meant by this? The one "German kid" who comes to mind from Michael's social diary at that time was both an aristocrat and the world's youngest billionaire. An "improper" relationship with this boy – whom we shall be hearing about in Chapter Five – would indeed have been sensational.

But wait, the DA's public statement also referred to "a third alleged victim who has been in psychological therapy since his disclosure to police in early November of 1993. He has alleged that Michael Jackson molested him on three occasions. Two of those occasions allegedly occurred in Los Angeles County beyond the statute of limitations, and the third occasion, within the statute, allegedly occurred in Santa Barbara County. In light of the primary alleged victim's decision not to testify, and because of the third alleged victim's reluctance to testify and in consideration of his psychological well-being, no charges relating to the third alleged victim will be pursued at this time". This "third alleged victim" was probably Jason Francia, who was to have a prominent role in Michael's trial in 2005.

The object of this review is not to decide the matter definitively, as though we were a jury in a criminal case. We do not have anything like enough information to be as sure as we would need to be before damning a man as only a child abuse allegation can. Acquittal might be easier, on the basis that juries are told to acquit unless they are sure beyond reasonable doubt that the accused is guilty, but we might feel uneasy about this.

No, our concern here is broader. We need to know whether we liked Michael or not, whether we can have any sympathy for what we believe on balance he was up to. Or not. This is not a matter of pleading mitigation. We are not putting ourselves in the position of a defence lawyer making excuses for a burglar: "He was out of work, your worships. Faced with a huge child maintenance bill, he simply did not know where to turn..." With a guilty client on their hands, one thing lawyers absolutely must do is confine themselves to a very limited kind of discourse, within strict limits imposed by legal considerations. We would not expect a lawyer suddenly to start pleading, "Well, what's wrong with burglary anyway? They were rich bastards living at the place. They had it coming to them." Such a lawyer might soon need to take up burglary himself – he would not make much of a living in court!

In a book, though, we can indulge in wider philosophical issues to our hearts' content. We may not agree with the 19th century radical Proudhon that all property is theft, and would hate to have our own house burgled, but that does not mean all laws are right in every respect. Some years ago male homosexuality was illegal in England. Now it is permitted, and the age of consent has been reduced in recent years, first from 21 years to 18, and then to 16. A case could be made for 14, as in Canada (until 2008). Or it may even be that children can be better protected from unwanted sexual attention by a different sort of legal framework altogether, one geared up to considering the youngster's feelings more than his or her age.

The arguments for and against particular laws are based on a complicated mixture of what is practical and publicly acceptable, as well as more fundamental matters such as whether they prevent harm to individuals or promote their well-being. Our present concern is with two particular individuals, Jordie Chandler and Michael Jackson. What we need to be doing is thinking about how the law in California, and the moral beliefs of ordinary people, including millions of fans worldwide, affected them. If Michael went against these codes does it necessarily mean he did something harmful and terrible? Or is Jordie the one who should have been deciding, without being put under pressure by his father or anyone else? If Jordie idolised Michael and was happy to share his bed, who were we to mess with his feelings?

But Jordie was not the only youngster in Michael's life. In the next chapter we shall see that he was fast friends with numerous boys, hence that frantic hunt for ones who would "talk".

CHAPTER FOUR

Boys of the Year

The music world had known about Michael's intense, personal attraction to boys for years before the Jordie Chandler scandal; but those in the know were understandably coy about what they read into it – in public at least. Michael's principal biographer, Randy Taraborrelli, whose book *Michael Jackson: The Magic and the Madness* appeared in its first edition in 1992, long shared this coyness. He discussed rumours that Michael might be gay, and pointed to the possibility of a relationship with his multi-millionaire friend David Geffen round about the beginning of the decade. Geffen, a Hollywood mogul, was very much a mature adult, so Taraborrelli was not implying Michael might be sexually interested in pre-pubertal or adolescent boys.

More recently, Darwin Porter, an aficionado of celebrity sex lives, has done much to chip away at the myth of a gay Michael attracted to adult males. He has achieved this by closely observing the star's part in the elite New York social scene to which he was introduced in early adulthood by fellow celebs. Porter gives examples of attempts to homosexually seduce Michael by Rudolph Nureyev, Mick Jagger, fashion designer Halston, Vincent Price, and Leonard Bernstein. All of them failed. I have no idea as to the truth or otherwise of Porter's detailed anecdotes. I can only suppose that if his stories are baseless he must have a very clever libel lawyer. Less controversially, Porter asserts that there appeared to be no truth in a tabloid story claiming Michael was involved in gay affairs with Boy George, George Michael and Freddie Mercury.[120]

Even more recently, in a book and newspaper articles appearing just after Michael's death, writer and self-described "undercover investigator" Ian Halperin attempted to revive the idea of a gay Michael. Halperin confided that he is gay himself – "obviously gay", as he puts it in his book. He made good use of his presumably camp style in some enterprising undercover investigations, plausibly passing himself off as a hairstylist to the stars, for instance. Eventually, in this hairdresser role, he managed to catch up with Michael himself at a Hollywood pizza parlour, where the megastar was dining in disguise with two of his children. Introduced to Jackson by "a mutual friend", the pair apparently hit it off in conversation, a triumph that seems to have gone to Halperin's head. Based on what struck this reader as mere wishful thinking, the excited author concluded that the superstar was flirting with him:

"I had visions in my mind of Michael leaning over and kissing me on the lips," he swoons.

That, for me, was a laugh out loud moment. Ha! In your dreams, honey! Hadn't a million girls yearned hopelessly for that, even his two wives? This was no investigation: it was Wacko Jacko meets Sacha Baron Cohen's even wackier Brüno!

After talking to a couple of other, similarly deluded, gay men, Halperin in all seriousness proposed the theory that Michael Jackson was not interested sexually in young boys but in adult males such as himself. The mountain of evidence for Michael's "special friendships" with boys compared to the total absence of any well attested adult gay track record tells us all we need to know about Halperin's judgment in this regard.[121]

Taraborrelli never openly speculated about Michael's interest in young boys until the whole world was doing so in 1993. Even then, he brought out what was essentially a "whitewash" second edition of his book after the 1994 pay-off in the Chandler case. A decade later, with Michael in big trouble for a second time, facing trial over allegations brought by thirteen-year-old Gavin Arvizo, Taraborrelli was still not entirely getting real, continuing to exaggerate Michael's flimsy heterosexual credentials in a further update of his book. Only after the trial did he finally, in his public utterances, abandon all attempt to make excuses for the star.

While the biographer for long avoided imputing any sexual motive to Michael's involvement with children, he did write extensively about the star's evident fondness for particular boys. He offered non-sexual explanations but cautiously indicated that an alternative, more erotic, interpretation was crossing other people's minds.

One of these youngsters was twelve-year-old actor Emmanuel Lewis, star of the TV sitcom *Webster*. Michael had seen him in commercials and, via the boy's mother, invited him to the Jackson family home at Encino, where the singer was still living in 1983 with his parents. They became firm friends, says Taraborrelli; in fact Michael "nearly" (note the caution) "became obsessed with Emmanuel". The boy was tiny for his age, only three feet four in height, and Michael enjoyed carrying him in his arms as if he were a toddler.[122]

Videographer Steve Howell later put it in stronger terms. He was commissioned to take a video of the pair together in the bedroom of the star's Los Angeles apartment. "They were face to face and Michael had this dreamy look," he said in a newspaper interview, "I thought it was all a bit too intimate." The paper's reporters saw his film and said it "shows Jackson with his eyes shut in a blissful expression as he sways from side to side, holding Emmanuel tightly in his arms."[123]

Michael and Emmanuel would play with Michael's pets, says Taraborrelli. They would run around the Encino estate like little kids playing cowboys and Indians and roll around on the lawn together. According to Vivian Greene, Emmanuel's former dialogue coach, "Manny was very taken with Michael. If you just mentioned Michael's name, Manny's eyes lit up. All he talked about, thought about, was Michael Jackson. I had heard that the Jackson family wasn't happy about Michael's friendship with Emmanuel because of the way it looked, especially when Michael began buying Manny expensive presents. But the two of them were in their own world, totally oblivious to what people around them were saying."

Taraborrelli related how a visitor to Encino watched Michael read the story of Peter Pan to Emmanuel. Then the two sat on the floor with their eyes closed and fantasised they were flying over Never Never Land: " 'Believe it and it'll be true,' Michael whispered. 'Now, are you ready? Do you believe?' 'Yes', Manny answered, his eyes shut tight, he believed. They repeated dialogue from the story. Then after a while they broke up laughing and began to wrestle on the floor like puppies."

In March 2005, with Michael's trial under way, the tabloid *In Touch Weekly* published a picture of Michael and Manny "lying in bed and sucking on the nipples of baby bottles". It has also been reported that when he turned thirteen the boy received a diamond and gold friendship bracelet said to have cost $15,000.[124]

The pair once checked in to the Four Seasons Hotel, Los Angeles, as father and son. The boy's mother, Margaret, reportedly discovered this and the friendship came to an abrupt halt. Years later, as a college student in Los Angeles, Emmanuel said, "I don't like to talk about my time with Michael because people don't and won't understand. But he's a truly nice person and there is nothing sinister about him."[125] Emmanuel's reticence makes sense: people do not understand.

Taraborrelli and an earlier Jackson biographer, Todd Gold, commented on another close friendship between the star and a child, this time ten-year-old Jonathan Spence. Michael and the blond Jonathan were working together on *Captain Eo*, a 3D movie attraction for Disneyland, directed by Francis Ford Coppola. Michael spent most of his free time entertaining this boy, said Gold. One of the film crew told him: "Jonathan was the only person allowed nearby Michael at all times. He carried a towel to wipe sweat off Michael's face, and they seemed to nuzzle and hug a lot. There was nothing sexual going on. But it was definitely a close relationship."[126]

That obligatory note of caution again: nothing sexual. Quite possibly so. But how would a member of the film crew know one way or the other? The crew could be sure only that nothing sexual went on in the studio right there in public view – which would have been quite an indiscretion even by Michael Jackson standards.

But there are other witnesses. Talking to Diane Dimond, Michael's former maid Blanca Francia confirmed that Jonathan was close to Michael for two years and called him Daddy. Asked how the boy behaved towards the star, Francia said "Like he was so close to him, he just wanted to rub against him and stay with him. He wouldn't talk. He wouldn't say nothing. He would, like, sweet talk to him, just with him." She thought he was like a little girl. Gloria Berlin, the estate agent who sold Michael his ranch, and Orietta Murdoch, an executive secretary with Michael's MJJ Productions in Los Angeles, have confirmed the picture of closeness between the pair.[127] None of these witnesses ever saw the boy's mother; Berlin said his father was a screenwriter who left Jonathan in Jackson's care so he could work in Europe. A critic might say his father had "dumped" his son, but such a judgment might be just as misplaced as similar ones against Michael: the boy was evidently happy and, as we shall see, later in life spoke well of Michael.

Having said even Michael would not dare to be deviantly indiscreet on a film set, it must be added that his capacity for bizarre surprises sometimes seemed to know no bounds, such as the time in 1984 when he was at the White House for a reception hosted by President Reagan and the First Lady. He arrived at the Diplomatic Reception Room, where he was due to meet Ron and Nancy, having being assured that the only people there would be a few children of staff members. Instead the place was packed with about seventy five adults. Michael took one look at the scene and promptly did a bunk. After running away down a hall he found a bathroom and locked himself in, with his manager Frank Dileo and the rest of his entourage left to chase after him and try to talk him out again. Taraborrelli takes up the story:

> "Hey, Mike, come on out," Frank said.
>
> "No. They said there would be kids. But those aren't kids," Michael shouted back.
>
> "But there will be children. We'll go get the children, a White House aide promised. Then he turned to an assistant.
>
> "Listen, if Mrs Reagan sees this, she's going to be mad as hell. Now you go get some kids, damn it. Get James Baker's kid. She's cute. I don't care who you get, just get some kids in here."
>
> Then he turned back to the closed bathroom door. "It's okay, Michael. We're going to get the kids." His voice was patient as though he were soothing a disturbed child. Frank stood nearby, watching with a bemused look on his face.
>
> "Well, you'll have to clear all of those adults out of there before I come out," Michael warned.
>
> The waiting senior White House staff and politicians were all unceremoniously bundled out of the reception room and the aide ran back to the bathroom door, where he conferred with one of Michael's people:
>
> "Okay. You can come out now, Michael," Michael's publicist said. "Everything is okay."
>
> "Are you sure?" came back the soft voice.
>
> Frank Dileo knocked on the door with his fist, one loud thud. "Okay, Mike, outta there."
>
> The bathroom door opened slowly. Michael appeared. He looked around, slightly embarrassed...[128]

Slightly embarrassed, but very triumphant. Back in the reception room the kids were all ready and waiting for him, without all those nasty, boring grown-ups getting in the way! It is a hilarious account, or at least it was when people first read it. Do we still find it so funny? Our response is bound to be conditioned by the interpretation we put upon the incident. If we see Michael as just a big kid himself then we cannot help but be amused by this larger than life illustration of the point. Insofar as we think the story is true (and allowing for a little dramatic licence we have no reason to suppose otherwise: there were independent witnesses), we are entitled to regard it as evidence giving strong support to the big kid hypothesis: Michael really could have been an innocent at large, a great big baby, here demonstrating in fine style the awesome power of a kid's tantrum.

It is the paradox that makes us smile: nothing could be further from our everyday notion of how power is exercised by serious, mature adults. Yet his way worked! It was exactly this childlike magic that made so many fans love Michael in his prime. They could see perfectly well that he was a ruthless exploiter of the weapons in his armoury, just as an infant has no qualms about hollering the house down until it gets its way. The charm, in his case, is that he did not appear to have any *nasty* weapons in the armoury: he did not do the adult equivalent of hollering, which would be to throw his weight around, barking orders at people. Instead he behaved as though he had no grown-up power: like a child, he would run away and hide.

As a strategy it was immensely appealing, bringing out people's tender feelings towards him as though he really were a child. There seems no reason to assign any dark, sinister meaning to such behaviour; there seems nothing wicked or evil about it. We see evil as characterised by inflicting harm on others, either intentionally, because we have malicious or sadistic impulses, or as a means to an end, such as cheating or stealing from others in order to enrich ourselves. Michael's "childish" behaviour, by contrast, seemed to be largely devoid of such negative elements, in this instance at least. On the contrary, his childishness seemed to benefit rather than harm people: everyone found it charming. It amused and delighted because it showed that the aggressive, domineering approach to life is not necessarily the only one that gets results. Even the dignitaries who found themselves surplus to requirements must surely have seen the funny side. No-one was hurt.

Michael's style even offered hope to some people that there might be a better, gentler way for everyone to do things. This was explicit in his entire "message", musical and otherwise, and a major part of his appeal to fans. Unfortunately, Michael was a tough act to imitate! And if we were all to think and behave like children there would be no psychological grown-ups left to respond to us with the indulgent tenderness on which the strategy relies. Our childlike powers would vanish before you could say Neverland! Maybe we should take it in turns to be childlike, but that also supposes an improbable set of psychodynamics.

Better, for the moment, to stick to thinking about Michael himself. Do we still see the White House episode as amusing when we think about the other forms of "childish" behaviour we have heard reported? What about Michael allegedly crying in order to get his way with Jordie? Do we begin to see sinister potential where before we saw something quite harmless? If Michael really was a child-man in some ways, was he innocently so, or must we discern a slyly manipulative, less benign aspect? It is a theme that will be taken up in more depth in later chapters. For the moment it will be helpful to stick to finding out more about his relations with children.

A third child friend mentioned by Taraborrelli was Jimmy Safechuck, who as a ten-year-old accompanied Michael on one leg of his *Bad* tour in 1988. We shall be talking about Jimmy, but the biographer's conversation with yet another young pal should not be overlooked, even though it was anonymous. This boy (if it was a boy: his interviewer just says "a young friend") said:

> I can't have my name in the book because I think Michael would be upset. But I can say that he's just like any other guy when we hang out. He never talks about himself, always what is going on with other people... He's one of the nicest people I've ever known. He's so smart. He knows a lot about everything. He's a kid. He never really had a childhood and he's having it now. The stuff I read in the papers about him, I know it's all a bunch of B.S. I just ignore it. A couple of times I've asked him about girlfriends and stuff, but we never really get into that.[129]

The "B.S." in the papers around this time was not about children but a variety of other "Wacko Jacko" themes with varying degrees of credibility, some of them put about by Michael's own publicity people. He was said to have taken to sleeping in a hyperbaric oxygen chamber in the hope of living to be 150 years old and had offered $1 million for the Elephant Man's remains. Later, he must have looked back with nostalgia to those times, when his weirdness could more easily be seen as harmless eccentricity. The view that there was really a nice guy hidden under the heap of B.S., a guy who was considerate towards children, finds further support from his voice teacher

Seth Riggs: "He's the most natural, loving person I've ever known, a very good person, as corny as that sounds. He'll see a picture of a baby, and if it's a cute kid, he will go absolutely gaga over the picture. During the tour, on his nights off, he would go into a toy store and buy ten of this and ten of that and stay up all night long putting batteries into the toys, making certain each and every one worked so that he could have them ready to give kids backstage the next day. As if he didn't have enough to worry about."[130] Riggs was still working for Michael when he said this, and knowing what B.S. the Jackson publicity machine was capable of we must take what he says with a large pinch of salt.

Few these days would doubt Michael's genuine enthusiasm for cute babies: the problem is the interpretation to be put on it. If he were a woman, such feelings would be considered natural and to her credit. A corollary of this naturalistic view is that for a man to go gaga over baby pictures is unnatural, something to be regarded with deep suspicion. We doubt a man's capacity to experience the kind of "maternal" feelings such pictures are expected to evoke in women: the nurturing, selfless, "good" love that we assign not just to mothers but potentially to all women.

There is no exact paternal equivalent even after all that once-fashionable talk about the emergence of New Man. Poor old New Man, insofar as he exists in the fantasies of liberated, career-oriented New Woman, seems to be a despised domestic drudge. He is expected to be caring, sharing and sensitive towards his partner and good for mucky stuff like changing nappies, but he is still not entirely permitted the emotional intensity towards his children that is regarded so positively in women. And many women are still jealously keen to keep men firmly off "their" emotional patch.[131]

There are many indicators of Michael's interest in children of all ages, including babies, not just boys approaching puberty. When his brother Jermaine had a baby by Margaret Maldonado in 1986 Michael took a great interest in the child, asking to spend as much time with him as possible. "Michael acted like he was the baby's father," said Jerome Howard, former business manager to Michael's father, Joe.[132] Perhaps with less charitable intent his sister La Toya recorded in her autobiography Michael's habit of saving things, including baby items: "Michael saves everything, and I do mean everything. Sweetly sentimental, he keeps family members' photographs and mementos such as all my report cards, and his young nieces' and nephews' first shoes, first outfits, even their first soiled diapers.

Among his very personal souvenirs is his own nose cartilage, extracted during surgery."[133]

La Toya's autobiography was a great deal pleasanter towards her brother in both tone and content than some of her later utterances, which stoked up the allegations started by others. It would be interesting to know if any of those early report cards had anything to say about her powers of imagination, or her capacity to tell fact from fiction. The diapers quote is irresistible, but La Toya's information is often contradictory. Credibility is not her strong suit, if indeed she has one.

In the immediate wake of Jordie Chandler's allegations and the much-publicised police raid on Michael's Neverland ranch that followed, La Toya prevaricated over her brother's likely guilt or innocence. Some of his child friends were much more supportive, including two boys who each said they had slept with him – an odd looking defensive gambit, but logical enough in the bizarre circumstances Michael needed to explain away. As we learned in the last chapter, their names were Brett Barnes and Wade Robson. What do we know about them and how did they relate to Michael?

Brett Barnes, from Melbourne, Australia, testified at Michael's trial in 2005 that as a child he had been to bed "countless" times with Michael without any sexual incident occurring; but he was extremely vague and forgetful under cross-examination about many of the details of all the time he spent with the star. We heard in his testimony that he met Jackson after his fan mail when he was five (his family helped with the letter) received a personal reply. And we know he travelled to London as a ten-year-old with Michael in 1992. The pair stayed at the Dorchester Hotel in London. Staff said they would be called up to Jackson's suite at night to deliver food, only to find the place deserted. Then they would hear muffled giggles and squeals behind the curtains and a voice would order them to leave the food and go.

Key former aide Bob Jones recalled this year in his book *Michael Jackson: The Man Behind the Mask*, saying at one point he warned his boss that the press were beginning to ask questions "about all these little white boys you keep around". The star's reply was dismissive but "back in those days, Michael did take some pains to obscure the presence of his young companions". One of those companions when Michael was touring in Africa was an Australian boy, Jones tells us, giving him the pseudonym "Damon Patrick". This can only have been a reference to Brett, while he was on the *Dangerous* tour. Jones wrote that on tour it was "part of my job to keep the kid out of the spotlight. We tucked him into a seat among the luggage. Michael got out of the car to great attention. Then the chauffeur drove the car to the other side of the plane, unloading the boy out of view of the cameras." Only later would it become clear that Brett and Michael were constant bedfellows on tour for six months.[134]

In a more forthcoming account by Darwin Porter, we learn that in the African country of Gabon, British journalist Peter Hodges witnessed just such an airport arrival and later wrote what Porter rightly calls "provocative copy" about it. Hodges reportedly wrote:

> Michael Jackson often flaunts his arrival at airports with handsome young boys. Not so in Africa. The word was out that he wanted his companion, Brett Barnes, to be kept away from the lens of carnivorous paparazzi. Even so, I got to see the kid get off the plane after the paparazzi went chasing after Michael. In London, Jackson had passed the boy off as "Brett Jackson", his cousin… He was one charismatic and gorgeous boy, fit competition for Tadzio.[135]

Tadzio, it may be recalled, was the boy in Thomas Mann's novella *Death In Venice* whose beauty bewitched an aging writer – transposed into a musician when played by Dirk Bogarde in Visconti's film version. Like Jordie Chandler's lawyer Larry Feldman, Hodges deserves congratulation, in these dangerous times, for his daring declaration that a boy could strike him as physically attractive.

In August 1993 Brett was being described in the press as Michael's closest companion: by this time the affair with Jordie had been well and truly broken up following Evan Chandler's handiwork.[136] By then eleven, Brett went property viewing with Michael just days before the star left the US for the Asian leg of the *Dangerous* tour. They were taken on a ninety-minute inspection of a Beverly Hills mansion Michael had his eye on. The two giggled a lot over private jokes, and Michael was heard to ask Brett where the two should keep their toys. And just days after Michael flew off to Bangkok for his first *Dangerous* concert, Brett was at Neverland during the police raid. He and his mother and sister had the run of the place whenever they wanted, according to a report appearing months later in *Today* and confirmed in court testimony.[137] This was part of a major two-day spread by Britain's most assiduous newshound on Jackson at the time, Tina Weaver, hailed as Reporter of the Year in the British Press Awards for her numerous world exclusives on the story.[138] Her source on this occasion was Sandra

Sutherland, a private detective whose behind-the-scenes work was credited with forcing Jackson to reach an out of court settlement in the Chandler case, as she had allegedly found new witnesses whose testimony could have proved embarrassing.

"Michael is someone who is extremely smart," she said. "He's not the helpless Peter Pan he would have many believe he is." (The lady may have been a hotshot private eye but evidently she knew nothing about Peter Pan, who is anything but helpless.) "He's organised, disciplined and runs his own affairs. He surrounds himself with the weak and the vulnerable – people without resources who come to rely on him. They're often members of fractured families. They're single mothers, foreigners struggling in a strange country."

Sutherland had a point: Janet Arvizo, Gavin's mother, would later emerge as a classic case of this kind. But the vulnerability, if we can call it that, often came primarily from being star-struck rather than economically dependent: the Barnes and Robson families had been managing perfectly well in Australia: they were not illegal immigrants from some Third World country, desperate to make it in America. In any case, when you are as rich as Michael was, when your wealth is huge beyond the imagining of most of us, it is all but impossible to find friends, lovers, anyone you can be close to, who are *not* potentially going to become reliant on your money.

There are exceptions, however, and in view of Sutherland's one-sided accusations it is important to note the ones involving children. His young friends have included Sean Lennon and Macaulay Culkin. Neither Sean, the son of John Lennon and Yoko Ono, nor *Home Alone* star Macaulay, at one time listed ahead of Robert Redford among the most powerful figures in Hollywood, could conceivably be called children from among "the weak and the vulnerable". No-one would suggest Sean's surviving parent, Yoko Ono, has no mind or will of her own, while both of Macaulay's parents were formidable characters who would have had no trouble keeping Michael at a distance from their boy if they thought it necessary. Indeed, there is evidence that his mother, Pat Culkin, did just that when the child star and the pop legend were both appearing at a concert for President Clinton's inauguration. More about that in due course. Thus the view that Michael only preyed on the vulnerable does not hold up.

And if Brett Barnes was more defenceless than Macaulay or Sean he has never shown any sign whatever of resenting Jackson for taking advantage. Michael was "naturally affectionate and caring but would never do anything to hurt a child", said Brett. This was in August 1993, when he had been a close friend of Michael's for eighteen months. He said they had slept in the same bed together but "I was on one side and he was on the other, and it's a big bed." They had kissed and hugged but "it was just like you would kiss your sister or mother, or like hugging your best friend." Michael was "a person to play with, a person to love. He's like a best friend, except big."[139] A dozen years later, well into adulthood, he would still be supporting his friend, this time from the witness box.

Another Australian boy, Wade Robson, came forward to support Michael in similar terms soon after the storm broke. He, too, would loyally back his friend in court many years later. In 1993 Wade had already known him for five years, half the lifetime of the ten-year-old. He had appeared in the star's *Black or White* video. He, too, said he had slept with Michael, but insisted, "We were both fully dressed. He wears pyjamas and so do I. He hugs me, but it's friendly. He never touched me in 'that' way." He went on: "Michael is a very, very kind person, really nice and sweet. Sure, I slept with him on dozens of occasions. But the bed we shared was huge. He sleeps on one side and I sleep on the other. Michael doesn't have a mean bone in his body. He wouldn't hurt anyone. I have never seen Michael naked."[140]

Wade's mother, in the same *Sun* report, said: "I am confident Michael has never interfered with Wade. They are great friends and I trust Michael implicitly. He is a very innocent man, so painfully shy and naive he's too embarrassed to let anyone see him naked. I don't believe he is a child abuser. I would never let my kids around someone who is dangerous. But Michael is harmless. He loves kids."

Another newspaper had her husband Dennis putting forward a similar view a few days earlier.[141] Even Wade's sister Chantal (14) joined the chorus, surprisingly saying she too went to bed with Michael: "I've slept in the same bed with Michael too. But he never laid a finger on me. The bed is very big and you don't get anywhere near each other. It's just like two buddies sleeping together." Like Brett and Wade, Chantal would repeat her story when giving witness testimony in 2005.

Can we believe her? We shall scrutinize her court performance later but it can be said immediately that the hard thing to credit is not that Michael never laid a finger on Chantal but that he let a *female* – of whatever age – anywhere near his bed. It's not exactly what he was noted for, even within marriage (as we shall see). Chantal's presence in the bedroom, one feels, would not have been welcome. He might even have taken to his heels in panic and hid somewhere, like that time at the White House. This time he would be saying, "Well, you'll have to clear that *girl* out of there before I come out."

Media comment at the time remains of interest. Reported at length in the British press, Wade's appearance on American television to talk about his relationship with Michael was commented on in the *Sunday Times*: "Wade, who looks like a typical child star in the making, or on the make, with shaved hair and a pierced left ear... talked in a relaxed way about sharing Michael's bed."[142] This is revealing in two ways. Firstly, it bolsters Wade's credibility as a witness: he was "relaxed" for an occasion that might easily be expected to tax a child, even one already used to media exposure. Would this be the case if he had been heavily coached in what to say and not to say? If he had been dreading the question that might reveal more than he was supposed to? Secondly, and of much greater significance for the themes we will be exploring, is the curious attitude displayed by the *Sunday Times* writer with that reference to a child star "on the make".

Curious, because the writer is talking here about a young child who may have been sexually abused by a grown man – a child who, in the official dogma, is necessarily an innocent victim. But like Carol Sarler, with her "oldest profession" jibe, this writer has let his guard drop. It is as though he was so shocked and appalled by the child's collusion with Michael, so unnerved by the boy's blithe disinclination to be a traumatised victim, that he was provoked to hit back by blaming the child. Instead of being innocent, Wade is now hastily recast as tainted with grubby ulterior motives: he is "on the make", a bad boy. The curiousness seems even curiouser when we remember that the rules of the sexual game are supposed to be for the child's benefit. When journalists, so often loud against the "abuse" of children, are reduced to verbally abusing the supposed victims we have to wonder who the anti-abuse campaigns are supposed to benefit. Perhaps what is being protected is not always the child. It looks as though the disguised thrust of the exercise is actually aimed at preserving in adults' minds the comforting myth of childhood innocence.

This may appear a big indictment to frame on the basis of those three words "on the make", but there was plenty more evidence where that came from. What is questionable is whether we want to put the writer in the dock. His carelessness, or bravery, in letting a taboo thought slip out into print ought instead to be accepted with gratitude. It helps us all to think the unthinkable, to slip past the hidden thought police who frame our debates. He has a point too: there are good reasons to feel uneasy about child stars "on the make", though the jibe would be more justly aimed at their parents, the world of show business and all of us who like to see talented kids perform.

To many of those parents the chance for their child to work with Michael Jackson would have seemed like a dream come true, offering untold possibilities to sprinkle their little "star" with the great child-man's stardust and for the whole family to prosper. Joy and Dennis Robson were just such parents. Their son Wade came to Michael's notice at just five years of age when he won a talent contest featuring the Gloved One's trademark moonwalk. Wade was invited to join Michael on stage.

That was just the beginning. A close relationship developed and two years on, when the family were visiting Neverland, Michael "pleaded with Joy to let him 'own' Wade for a year and keep him in California," according to Bob Graham, writing in *Today*.[143] Joy is said to have told the paper that Michael offered to coach Wade, look after him and develop his talent. Joy turned the offer down because she did not want to be parted from Wade for so long, but Michael was so upset when they returned to Brisbane that he bombarded Joy with phone calls for a year. She eventually agreed to move with Wade to California. The story came out a little differently when Joy was giving evidence on the star's behalf fifteen years later: there was to be no further reference to Michael "owning" Wade, or "bombarding" Joy with calls: it was more a matter of a stage-struck mom bursting to push her son's career forward and delighted he had found a helpful patron.

Back to Bob Graham's report. It dropped in a bombshell of a sentence. Like the *Sunday Times* writer he was suddenly caught saying something unspeakable, admitting the inadmissible: "Now, for the first time, Joy admits that Jackson and her son were in love." Sorry, what was that again? Did he say "in love"? With each other? Wade was "in love" with Michael as well as Michael with Wade? This was the reporter's admission, not just Joy's. He could have written Joy "claims" or "believes" they were in love. But no, evidently he had heard all that Joy had to say and had taken her understanding of the matter on board in his own mind. Remember, this report was about a man accused of molesting another child. When we read such stories in our local paper we generally hear about the alleged perpetrator's sexual "attack" or "assault" upon the child, strongly implying a violent, rapacious act when it may well have been an intimacy with a child or "underage" youth who was a very willing and active participant. Stories invariably and rightly describe violence, injury or threatening behaviour in those horrible cases where it has occurred, but how often do we read accounts in which the adult is described as being "in love" with his "victim" or the child "in love" with the "attacker"? Is the vanishing rarity of such accounts because no such cases ever arise? Was Michael Jackson unique in being the only alleged child molester who was not a vicious attacker? Or was it just his high-profile that influenced the coverage? Was it, perhaps, just that having millions of fans and more lawyers than you could shake a sequinned glove at meant it was harder to casually trash the superstar's reputation with the routinely misleading descriptions so typical in ordinary cases?

Graham hurried on with Joy's story, apparently unaware of the enormity of his own transgression:

> "I do know Wade idolised Michael and Michael was obsessed with Wade. Yes, they were in love in a strange way," said the raven-haired 41-year-old. She said that during the star's frantic calls to her and her son, "Michael told me Wade had called him Dad. Michael thought Wade was becoming distanced from his own father and was replacing him with Michael."
>
> At other times he was more like a mother to the young boy. Joy explained: "There were times when Wade used to wet the bed and Michael would get up, cleaning it all up and putting fresh sheets on – the sort of thing only mothers normally do." She recalled one occasion when Wade was sick while shopping with Jackson in a record store. "Immediately Michael grabbed him, rushed him out of the store and was cradling and cleaning him up like a mother."
>
> Joy spoke of how Wade was a "boy of the year" for Jackson. "It's well-known that Michael seems to have an obsession for a new boy each year. It's not unusual. Wade was the obsession for 1990, Macaulay Culkin was 1991, another Australian boy Brett Barnes was the obsession of 1992 and in 1993 it was Jordie Chandler."

Joy went on to confirm for Graham that Michael and Wade had slept together. "'But it wasn't the way ordinary people think when they hear a young boy and a 35-year-old man have shared the same bed,' said Joy, who also has two other children. 'Michael never had a childhood and when these young boys are with him he himself becomes a little boy and has the childhood he never had. When he sleeps with the boys, when he hugs and kisses them, it is not sexual, it is natural.'"

This was a statement that might send Bart Kosko, the apostle of "fuzzy logic", into ecstasies of conceptual probing and re-formulation. When are hugs and kisses sexual, and when non-sexual? We pretend for the sake of social propriety that the distinction is clear-cut, but is it? When is an apple no longer an apple? After you take one bite out of it, or two, or ten? Is an apple core still an apple? Kosko argued that in order to realise its greatest potential the computer world would have to ditch its yes/no, on/off, either this/or that, style of logic in favour of "fuzzy" thinking, which recognises that the real world consists mostly of grey areas rather than sharp black and white categories. Common sense has always told us this is so, but we are inclined to run away from the truth when the going gets tough. We prefer simple, clear-cut facts from which we can derive simple clear-cut rules to live by: we took good care to see to it that God gave us Ten Commandments not ten ifs, buts and maybes. Yet in reality nothing is more messily resistant to being put in neatly labelled boxes of separate categories than our sex and love lives.

Fortunately for Joy she was able in her own mind to pigeonhole Michael's feelings for Wade in the box marked "non-sexual" because she had a supporting piece of Jackson mythology to hang onto: the myth that Michael was trying to live through children the childhood he never had. It is a powerful, interesting myth, with roots that run genuinely deep into Michael's past. It may even be entirely true, rather than mythical, but the fact that an adult has an especially strong interest in childhood does not mean he has an especially weak interest in sex. Such a conclusion would not follow in any style of logic. If the argument is premised on the notion that Michael was asexual "like a child" it really will not do. Children have sexual feelings. They are not "innocent" in this sense.[144] In any case, however much Michael may have wanted to live the life of a child his hormones were those of an adult: he may have missed out on childhood, but not on puberty.

Joy's friendship with Michael helped drive a wedge between her and her husband, according to Graham. Differences had arisen because Michael disliked Dennis, thinking he was out for anything he could get. While Joy went to live in California with Wade, Dennis remained in Brisbane. On the slender basis that Michael helped obtain a US work permit for Joy Robson, private detective Sandra Sutherland cited her, along with Brett's mother, as a vulnerable woman who became dependent on him.

All the same, she may have been right. Soon after the Sutherland account, *Today*'s Tina Weaver revealed details of testimony contained in an eight-page statement then due to be filed with Los Angeles Superior

Court.[145] This testimony, by security guard Charli Michaels, made allegations that Michael sexually abused Wade and that his mother was kept away from him at the time in upsetting circumstances. The statement was made to lawyers acting for five security guards who were suing Michael for unfair dismissal.

The guard said:

> It was Mother's Day. Wade and his mother Joy were guests at the ranch. Joy had been given a room in one of the exterior guest units, while Wade stayed in the main house with Michael. Mrs Robson wanted to stay inside the house with her son, but she was told that there was no suitable room for her. I was working Mother's Day morning and was told to take Joy Robson on a "barn run" to see all the animals on the estate. I took her in my truck and drove her to the barn. She was crying. She hadn't seen her son all day and she appeared very nervous and concerned.

Charli Michaels was listed as a witness at Michael's trial but in the end was never called to the stand. However, Joy was asked about the Mother's Day incident in cross-examination on her own evidence. She confirmed the story in outline, and then prosecutor Tom Sneddon put it to her that she had told the security guard that Wade would rather be with Michael than herself, and she had been upset about that. Joy at first denied this but then accepted it when Sneddon confronted her with an earlier deposition she had made in which she had testified to this effect. This put matters in a very different light: instead of Michael being the villain of the piece, keeping the child away from his mother, the focus here was on Wade's own preferences.

Mother's Day. Michael made much of his love for his own mother in his autobiographical book *Moonwalk*. "One thing I know about children," he wrote, "is that if they don't get the love they need from their parents, they'll get it from someone else and cling to that person, a grandparent, anyone. We never had to look for anyone else with my mother around. The lessons she taught us were invaluable. Kindness, love, and consideration for other people headed her list. Don't hurt people..."[146]

Did Michael forget those lessons on this Mother's Day? Did he callously ignore the possibility – we might think the near certainty – that Wade's mum would be anxious to see her boy on this day of all days? Did Michael phone his own mother and send her flowers while ignoring Joy's feelings? Was he unconsciously fulfilling his own prophesy: by not allowing Joy to express her love for her son that day was he making sure Wade would seek affection elsewhere… from himself?

Possibly, but there is a quite different way of looking at this story, from an angle so unfamiliar and strange that it is most unlikely to cross the mind of anyone viewing our traditional social arrangements from a mainstream standpoint, either as parents or as younger generation people who aspire to be parents.

This different way of looking is through the eyes of non-parents, or rather the eyes of those who feel destined never to become a mum or dad. They include millions who would love to have children of their own but believe (not always correctly) they are going to miss out, perhaps because they are gay or infertile, or for whatever reason just can't believe they will attract a partner. What these people see, in ways that are often a source of pain and yearning, is a society in which parenthood is privileged. For reasons that run as deep as our animal nature, and as powerfully as our culture can emphasise and reinforce – which is to say with crushing, overwhelming might – the parent-child dyad is the prime focus of all our social arrangements and thinking, all our rituals and dramas. Nothing else matters half as much. For many, especially women but by no means only them, having children is really what life is all about. Even among the most career-oriented "high achievers", there is no shortage of men and women who regard their kids as the greatest achievement of their lives – remarkable, really, when reproduction is, so to speak, so fucking simple.

Those who are without children, and without even the hope of having any, feel all too keenly what it is to be excluded from this great universe of human meaning. They feel themselves as outsiders to society and even to humanity, standing in the cold, condemned for ever to experience the warmth and fulfilment of family life at best through stolen moments with other people's children, if at all. It may be that they rarely come nearer the real thing than seeing the idealised families of the TV commercials and sitcoms: their pain will be all the greater because they cannot see that real parenthood often has its agonies and disappointments too.

The fact that their view of what they are missing may be unrealistic is neither here nor there. It is *their* feelings that concern us for the moment, *their* pain at being left out, sidelined, on the margins of life.

Before finding his own highly improbable route to parenthood, which will be the focus of Chapter Thirteen, this was Michael's own gloomy perspective. In his own way he conquered the world with victories that put

Alexander or Napoleon to shame: he won millions of admirers without bloodshed. Familiar to a billion or more, his face at the height of his success was the most recognised on the planet, perhaps even the most famous in the history of humanity. He said then that he wanted children of his own one day at a time when he could have taken the pick of a million potential girlfriends. And yet... and yet, in this matter that was desperately important to him, he remained a nobody for decades of adult life. He was without a child of his own.

For all his wealth and power he was among the unfortunates who had to settle for stolen moments with other people's. But in his inimitable style the theft was grand larceny. No petty sneak-thief tactics for Michael. His stolen "moments" could run to months, with years a distinct possibility. But all these moments had to be fought for in the teeth of intense suspicion. Every move of a single man towards children swims against a powerful tide of convention. We were used to thinking of Michael as rich and powerful, but when we think of the all-pervasive power of the social forces he was always up against, it becomes clear that, far from finding it easy to have his own way, where children were concerned he needed all his guile, all his resources, to obtain privileged access to them. Even then, he found he could not beat the system forever.

There is no Mother's Day for childless child-lovers. You will not find a separate section in the card shops, with greetings cards for children to send to their "special" adult friend. Just imagine if there were. What might it be called? Calling a spade a spade, one might have a Paedophile's Day or (much the same thing) an Over Thirty Unpartnered Teacher's/Youth Leader's/ Church Choir Master's/Junior Football Coach's Day. Or a little more respectably there could be an Infertile Couple's Day. But can we imagine the cultural revolution this would imply, the huge shift in the ways our affections and attachments are socially privileged and sanctioned?

Can you see it? James, 42-year-old bachelor choir master, has been living with ten-year-old Oliver, his current "special" friend for the last two years. Ollie's parents generally come over for tea on Sunday, provided Jim and he do not have anything more interesting planned, which they often do. The parents try not to let their disappointment show when this happens: they are hurting like hell inside but they know they have to hide their feelings lest it upsets Jim. He is the boss after all, and if they push their luck Jim might not allow any visits at all. He is not a bad bloke, they reason. But like any child-lover he finds it hard to understand that parents feel love for their children, just as he does. Another thing they find really tough as parents is that all they can do on these visits is sit there politely making conversation with Jim, while Ollie is playing some computer game. Seldom do they find the opportunity to be physical with their son, to cuddle or play wrestle. It's not that Jim wouldn't allow it, it's just that, well, they feel a bit self-conscious, as though they are treading on his emotional territory.

And of course on Paedophile's Day they would not dream of trying to arrange a visit. That would be no time for outsiders like themselves to muscle in. They remembered reading once in the *News of the World*, or was it that American paper, *The National Enquirer*, about a couple who had spirited their child away from his grown-up lover on Paedophile's Day for the whole day, leaving the guy distressed and angry. The poor man had been reduced to tears. Jesus in heaven above, they thought, what callous bastards! How could they do such a thing!

For anyone interested in humane values, such a brave new world would be a nightmare, an appalling vision of injustice devoutly to be resisted. Yet it is not just a nightmare, an imaginary dystopia. In mirror-image form such a world is exactly the one we have now, in which sensitive, child-loving people like Michael Jackson, albeit with rather less money and power than he has, are routinely and cruelly separated from their loved ones with a total disregard for their feelings. It will rightly be objected that it is the child's feelings and future that really count, but in practice these may not be at the top of the agenda either in our society. Subjectively we value children highly, but the case has been strongly made that our means are at odds with our ends when it comes to objectively doing the best we can for them, especially as regards their sexual and emotional development. On this general theme, I highly recommend Judith Levine's book *Harmful To Minors: The Perils of Protecting Children from Sex.*[147]

For the moment let us return to Michael's relations with Wade Robson and the accusations made by Charli Michaels. As she dropped off Wade's mother Joy, following the "barn run", she received a call to take food for Michael and Wade in the private cinema at Neverland. Next to it is a studio with a mirrored wall. Michaels claimed: "As I entered the snack bar area I walked towards the dance studio. I saw in the mirror Michael Jackson draped over the back of Wade Robson, with his arms fully around the front and crotch of the little boy, holding his hand and genitals and moving them up and down, while moving to the rhythm of the music that was playing, shouting 'Whea!' repeatedly each time he pulled the boy's genitals up. I was stunned and shocked, and withdrew. I didn't know what to do or what to say."

Today knew what to say. They called it "damning new testimony".[148] And if a jury chose to believe the story, they might well feel the act amounted to "sexual battery" and other lurid offences in California law. We need be in no such rush to judgment, not least because Michaels' testimony was not used in 2005 when it easily could have been. The prosecution would ask Wade about the alleged "sex dance", though, suggesting Michael had been grabbing Wade's crotch in the same way he grabbed his own in his shows. The implication seemed to be that he was using the excuse of teaching Wade his dance routines in order to molest him.

We were not told how this incident could have happened in front of Michaels, who had on her own account actually been summoned to the room – she took no-one unawares – without any apparent embarrassment or self-consciousness on Jackson's behalf. Could it be that Michael just did not see anything wicked or shameful in it? Nor were we told how Wade was reacting during this "sex dance", as *Today* dubbed it. Why not? If he had been in obvious distress isn't it likely we would have been told? Was the boy laughing, then, enjoying himself? It seems a much more likely scenario. Why else would Michael be shouting "Whea!" in that way? Isn't that just the exuberant, daffy expression any loving parent uses when dangling his toddler, or that kids themselves burst into, when they are having fun on a slide or a swing?

As for the "sexual" element, maybe we need a reminder from more robust times that the atmosphere surrounding such horseplay has not always been hysterical. The infancy of Louis XIII of France provides a delightful example. Jean Héroard, a court physician, kept a diary from which it appears such fun was deemed fit for a future king: "He laughed uproariously when his nanny waggled his cock with her fingers," reports Héroard, which he goes on to describe as a trick the child soon copied. At one year old and in high spirits, "He made everybody kiss his cock", amusing them all. The court was later to be entertained by seeing the heir apparent's first erections: "Waking up at eight o'clock, he called Mlle Bethouzay and said to her: 'Zezai, my cock is like a drawbridge; see how it goes up and down.' And he raised and lowered it."[149]

A much more serious allegation against Michael is not that he enjoyed intimate, emotional contacts with children but that there would always come a point with each child when he *stopped* doing so. Logically, this might be thought to go in his favour: if you are doing something wrong the best thing you can do is stop it immediately. But his critics appear to want to have it both ways: he was wrong to start *and* wrong to stop. He stood accused not only of taking up with youngsters but also of "dropping" them, leaving each one in turn upset and emotionally bruised after being led to believe that they alone were the one extra-special person in his life.

This is an important charge, so we had better be clear about it. We need to be clear, first of all, that such an accusation could never be made against a "child molester" in the usual meaning of that term. The "child molester" of the court reports, the one who "attacks" his victim and "assaults" him, is perceived (though often quite wrongly) as an adult who imposes a sexual incident on an unwilling child, a child who is frightened or disgusted by what takes place. It would make no sense at all to criticise such an offender for leaving his victims alone in future. No-one would accuse him of "dropping" them.

If, then, we hear this criticism of "dropping" being made we can be sure of one thing: the finger-pointers have given up on their first line of accusation. They have thrown in the towel. They know it just will not wash to pretend that the child was "molested" or "assaulted" against his will. In these cases the facts make it obvious that the child has come to admire, idolise and, yes, even love the adult in question. This brings us onto more familiar territory. Not everyone thinks they are an expert on child sex abuse even in these times when so-called "experts" are ten-a-penny on the airwaves and in the opinion columns, but we all feel that love is an open book – a maddeningly confusing one, to be sure, but also a magical one, with a thousand stories we know by heart, for the very good reason that its language is the language of our heart. Its pages are the very stuff of our lives, its words our songs, our poems, our feelings, the music of our soul.

Love, we feel, is powerful, unstoppable, even ruthless. "Love will find a way", we say, or "Love knows no laws". When thinking about giving a rival the elbow, love licenses us to sidestep not just man's laws, but higher ethical concerns too: "All's fair in love and war," we assert, appealing to a tradition more robust than our unquiet conscience. We have so much folklore along similar lines not, however, because the sentiment it expresses contains an obvious truth, but rather because it says what we feel and what we want to believe. Love will find a way? Try telling that to Romeo and Juliet! Love knows no laws? In a hundred countries, gay Romeos and Julians could put us right. All's fair in love and war? Ask the seven-stone weakling who's just had sand kicked in his face.

When the chips are down, all but the most Quixotic romantics and the most selfish, "red in tooth and claw", survivalists are forced to accept that love is bound up in a tight web of social constraint and regulation – rules grounded in morality and economics. An example of the latter is readily apparent when we look at, say, Indian-style arranged marriages, which were once scorned in the West but now increasingly have their admirers. But there is only one rule, one moral rule, that need concern us here: the rule of fidelity. We may secretly admire and envy the free spirit of the Don Juans amongst us, the heartless "Love 'em and leave 'em" types, but we do not approve. Our culture strongly represents such figures getting their come-uppance, perhaps most unforgettably with the don's descent into hell in Mozart's *Don Giovanni*.

To people in many cultures it may seem that arranged marriages are the sensible and indeed only way of securing an advantageous future for a family in an orderly fashion. In the West there are signs of change, as already noted, but we still generally lean towards "romantic" individualism. Likewise, our moral precepts with regard to fidelity, so obviously wise to us, may not be quite so universally accepted as we suppose. We are used to thinking about men's relations with women and have a vast culture to draw upon in deciding what works and what doesn't, what's good and what isn't. Unlike the ancient Greeks, we have no tradition of thinking about sexual relations between men and boys, though in the last half century or so writers as diverse as J Z Eglinton (Walter Breen), Kenneth Dover, Michel Foucault, Thomas Hubbard and William Percy have done much to explore and re-examine the phenomenon and what the Greeks made of it.

Not that cultural relativism should be pressed into service to justify a man's callous indifference to the feelings of a boy who has come to love him. That would be monstrous. What does seem to be called for, though, if we are to have any hope of understanding Michael Jackson and his relations with children, is some information on how his kind of friendship actually works. The model of two lovers is misleading in some important respects. Let's take another model then, one that involves adult-child relations: parental love. If the parents of an only child have another baby, the older child may well be jealous, knowing he is no longer the only one his parents love; he might even feel that all the love has been transferred to the young usurper. A good mum and dad will take great care to be sensitive to the problem but there is no avoiding the fact that they cannot be one hundred per cent "faithful" in giving all their affection and attention to their "first love", and if they tried to do so it would be unfair to the new baby.

We do not agonise overmuch about it. We say it is "just life" that siblings have to share their parents. There is nothing wrong with this, far from it: children with brothers and sisters educate each other in social relations, whereas only children miss out on this early learning. It is important for children to be loved and nurtured, but they also need to grow up towards independence as the years pass, which implies a gradual weaning off a parent's loving protection. The relationship is quite unlike that of lovers who, at least in the ideal picture, grow contentedly old together as a Darby and Joan couple.

We have heard Joy Robson listing Michael's "boys of the year". What are we to make of this extraordinary information? Are we to see him as a paedophilic Don Giovanni, with Joy, his improbable aide, reading out his list of conquests, betokening a long trail of broken promises and broken little boys' hearts? It is a crazy notion, and one that only has any traction because we are accustomed to thinking of sexual love in terms of *expectations* of an exclusive, relationship, whether within marriage or not. The association of such relationships with reproduction and its burdens reinforces the significance of long-term commitment, a significance totally absent from man-boy relations, where reproduction has not been suggested as a problem by even the most potty and panicky social worker. Following the alternative model, the parental, one, we can see that a relationship does not have to be exclusive in order to be genuinely loving. Likewise we expect a teacher to care about all the children in the class; we find no fault in them spreading their attention "promiscuously" around the classroom.

Models drawn from a variety of relationships may be illuminating in making a point, but none is going to fit one-to-one. It is time to look more closely at how the fidelity factor has presented itself as a matter of concern to the parents and children in Michael's life. Joy Robson clearly considers that Michael himself found it a delicate subject, saying he did not talk much about the boys who are "just friends": "He never talks about them much and the other main boys don't know about them in case they get jealous of one another."[150]

If this makes Michael sound like a sailor with a girl in every port, we should not worry too much about him "cheating" on any of his "girls". To start with they are not girls, which is to say they are not young women hoping to marry him. Any one of Michael's young boyfriends might have been honoured and thrilled to monopolise his time and attention for a few months, or even a year or two, but no boy approaching adolescence in the western world – or indeed in practically any modern culture – is going to suffer under the delusion that he is being groomed for some sort of gay marriage. The thought would be unlikely to occur even to the few boys destined to become gay and the rest would run screaming at the idea. They may have wanted to be big pals with Michael, and share sexual and emotional feelings too, but that does not mean they wanted or expected it to be forever. If Michael avoided talking about Wade when he was with Brett, or Brett when he was with Jordie, or Jordie when he was with Macaulay, it was more a matter of diplomacy and good manners than disguising any unfaithfulness to his "steady" or his "intended".

Joy Robson put it quite well when she testified in 2005. She admitted Wade had been upset once when he heard Michael was going to spend a night with Jordie Chandler rather than himself, but she explained it was no big deal, nothing traumatic. She said there was bound to be jealousy among kids as to who would be close to Michael. She described it as being like an ordinary family having a favourite uncle all the kids wanted to be with. Being close to one of them at a particular time did not mean rejecting the others. She added that Michael referred to lots of kids as his "cousins", giving them all a secure place in his emotional "family" and so avoiding traumatic jealousy.

The question of disloyalty can only arise when there is an expectation of an exclusive, one-to-one relationship. This is usually the understanding when boy meets girl in our culture, with its pattern of dating, going steady and living together, in either informal partnership or marriages sanctioned by church or state. By no means do all cultures insist on one-to-one exclusivity: the Islamic world has its polygamous marriages, for instance, and in the West there are those who opt for "open" marriages, with the partners sharing the home but each giving the other freedom to have sex elsewhere. Such arrangements may be thought rather exotic and exceptional though. The norm in mainstream culture is that when two people of opposite sex start a loving relationship they clearly expect it to be on a one-to-one basis. Neither of them needs to be explicit about it. The rules of the game are known.

Contrast this with the boy-meets-boy world of the adult gay male and we see a different picture. Many one-to-one partnerships thrive, but there is also every appearance of much more casual sex and more fluidity and diversity of couplings and contacts. Some gay men feel a strong emotional need for a long-lasting, one-to-one relationship, but they cannot expect any particular coupling to be formed with the assumption of such a goal built into it. Such an aspiration has to be made explicit to the other man. If it is not spelt out, or implied via the subtle communications that intimacy makes possible, then the partner is under no automatic obligation to be "faithful".

Michael's situation was different from either of the above. It was not boy meets girl or even boy meets boy in the adult male gay sense. His social world had no traditional rules to operate by. Most people, wrapped up in the world of heterosexual romance, find themselves guided by the wisdom of teachers, priests and doctors, the lore of novels and popular songs, and role models drawn from a huge range of sources, from family and neighbourhood to TV and Hollywood. Michael never had any of this as he grew up into a surprisingly lonely adolescent and often even more isolated adult. Like the love between gay men until recent years, his kind of love is culturally invisible. He lived much of his life in a vacuum devoid of any social support, wise counsel or understanding that spoke directly to his feelings and how he should have related to his little friends. So he had to make up his own rules, and on the problem of jealousy and faithfulness we have already begun to see in Joy Robson's words some evidence of how he figured it out.

We are told that when he was with any particular boy he downplayed the others; it was good manners rather than unfaithfulness. This is an interpretation that finds strong support in Jordie Chandler's account, when he says Michael told him about other boys who had masturbated in front of him, in an attempt to get him to do the same. A man trying to give his girlfriend the impression that she is the only true love in his life would not be wise to say to her something like "Come on, let me lick your clit, all my other girlfriends do"! We might want to have chastised Michael over such behaviour – arguably his manners had slipped – but we surely cannot accuse him of bad faith: Jordie was plainly not being deceived. This story provides evidence that he knew there were, or had been, many other young boys in Michael's life, and by a logic that was surely not beyond him he could have seen that there might be many more to come. He must also have been well aware that the operative word was *young*, and that youth is a perishable commodity, including his own. His contact with Michael was destined to end abruptly, traumatically and against his will. But it was also against Michael's wishes: the sadness of the ending cannot be blamed on him, except in the sense that a mature adult might have been expected to know there would be social pressures on the relationship, making it possible it would all end in tears.

We say that, however, with the benefit of 20-20 hindsight, and should bear in mind that there were many other relationships that ended much more happily. Way back in 1994, I noted: "Wade Robson appears not to have reached separation point yet. He may remain close to Michael for another year or two. His mother, rightly or wrongly, still has ambitions for him in the music industry, and, using Michael's help and contacts, he was on the verge of launching a rap album by late 1993."

As I write now, we are able to see that Michael stayed loyal to Wade, and Wade to him, a dozen years later. By this time Wade's physical closeness to Michael had long since tailed off naturally. He had become interested in girls. His fiancée attended the trial with him, when, as already mentioned, he gave evidence in Michael's support. Wade's own career in the entertainment business had thrived; he was now a star in his own right. He had not been abandoned by Michael and had no reason to regret being close to him as a child. The Barnes family, too, were still hugely enthusiastic about Michael in 2005, as were the Cascios. Other close friends have also supported him since reaching adult years, including Emmanuel Lewis, Corey Feldman, Jonathan Spence and Macaulay Culkin. All this is clear testimony to the fact that it is only the calamity of public disapproval that sometimes cuts man-boy relationships brutally short, not anything intrinsic to the relationships themselves.

CHAPTER FIVE

Boys Will Be Boys – But Not For Long

The media were quick with the jibe that Michael "dumps" boys abruptly when he "has finished with them", like a puppy after Christmas or a used condom. It is an easy allegation to throw at any lover of *boys* rather than *men*, if only because boys, in the nature of things, will not be boys for long. But whether the charge sticks is another matter. Long before the Gavin Arvizo case was even a glimmer in prosecutor Tom Sneddon's eye, a dozen youngsters had been named in the media as special friends of Michael at one time or another. In all but one instance, these relationships did not show signs of abrupt or unhappy termination. Michael was accused – unfairly, as we shall see – of "dumping" just *one* of these boys. In this context his name was unfortunate: Jimmy Safechuck.

Jimmy had met Michael as a nine-year-old and the blond, blue-eyed boy appeared in a Pepsi commercial with him.[151] Soon after, as we have already seen, he accompanied Michael on the *Bad* tour. The pair had appeared on stage together in matching black leather suits. In London at the time they were seen holding hands and hugging in Michael's tour bus. Michael had to cancel two shows because he caught a cold off the boy, according to Randy Taraborrelli.[152] By late November 1993, now aged fourteen, Jimmy had spent two hours answering questions put by the grand jury at Santa Barbara about his relationship with Michael. Reporting on this, the *Sun* told its readers by way of unsourced background material, "the star bought Jimmy's parents a £110,000 Roller as a thank-you for letting him join the tour".[153]

Taraborrelli tells a similar story. In his version the Rolls Royce referred to is valued in dollars, at a much lower price tag, but the luxury limo amounts to a staggering gift either way. No politician could accept a present like that without the air being thick with allegations of bribery and corruption. People in show business are freer to give and take ostentatious gifts as they choose, without any such implication, but people were bound to wonder about the true motive for this particular generosity, its scale and circumstances being so far out of the ordinary. The *Sun*'s explanation was pure nudge, nudge, wink, wink, but can the paper be blamed? Wasn't there some explaining to be done?

Taraborrelli, perhaps wisely, declined to take on the task. He just told us that after the Rolls Royce gift, Michael's manager, Frank Dileo, thought the time had come to break off the friendship with Jimmy. He warned that rumours were going around. People were saying the relationship was perverted. Michael was hurt by what he heard and was lonely without the boy. Taraborrelli never spelt it out, but by inference Michael had taken Dileo's advice and dropped Jimmy.[154] The *Daily Express* version, in August 1993, confirmed this, adding darkly that "Jimmy has never been seen or heard of since". Pity about him turning up alive and well a few months later for the grand jury hearing: it spoiled a good story for them.[155]

The gleaming presence of a sleek new Rolls Royce in this story inevitably stands out as insistently as the top people's car itself. It is important, and we shall come back to it, but we must not allow the car to divert attention from the main question: Did Michael callously "dump" Jimmy? In Taraborrelli's version we see a totally different picture. Michael had not wanted to drop Jimmy at all. On the contrary, the relationship showed every sign of lasting intensity, rather than cooling off, and this very intensity was the cause of the rumours leading to Dileo's advice. Michael then acted under pressure rather than from some callous caprice. Doubtless it was put to him that the boy himself could suffer if all the talk got out of hand. Far from being callous, on this occasion Michael appears to have been forced into something that caused him pain and loneliness. What it amounted to was that both he and Jimmy were being sacrificed on the altar of public opinion.

But in the press Michael had to be the villain of the piece. *Today* claimed that "Jimmy Safechuck was distraught when the singer lost interest in him as he reached his teens."[156] But the *Bad* tour, the Rolls Royce present, Dileo's advice and Michael's taking it all happened in 1988 when Jimmy was just ten years old. Since when is a ten-year-old "reaching his teens"? All the evidence points to Michael being very fond of boys right up to puberty and even into it, as we have seen with Jordie. In the phrase of another child witness, the idea that Jimmy was getting too old for him is just total "B.S.".

Today piled on the agony by implying that Michael's cruel behaviour – not the cruel prejudice of an ill-informed public, of course – was responsible for Jimmy needing therapy after he had been "dumped". Jackson paid the bills, said *Today*, information given not in order to praise him for trying to help the boy, but to damn him for allegedly having caused Jimmy's mental anguish. An unnamed source is used to pinpoint the blame more precisely: "He had been put on a giant pedestal and suddenly it was snatched from under his feet. He became jealous when Jackson turned his attention to a new boy." So there is the new angle: a rival boy. It was a plausible story.

We even have a name the source might have had in mind, Brandon Adams, to whom we shall be turning shortly. As we have seen, Michael was seldom without a boy in his life in the years before the scandal over Jordie. But apart from *Today*'s allegation, there was nothing to suggest he had ditched Jimmy or any close pal in favour of another. We were told neither the new rival's name nor anything about the anonymous source nor how well placed he/she was to know what was going on. Against this we have incontrovertible evidence that *Today* was wrong about Jimmy being dropped "as he reached his teens" and an alternative explanation involving a named individual: Frank Dileo. The Dileo story was also backed in Taraborrelli's account by a comment from Jerome Howard, business manager to Michael's mother, Katherine. "Some people felt Michael was too much in the kid's life for it to be healthy for either him or the kid," said Howard. "Michael was lonely without him, though."[157]

Today was on stronger ground exploring Michael's amazing generosity to Jimmy and the Safechuck family, which visibly began with buying expensive toys for Jimmy in Hamleys, the London toyshop, and a Rolls Royce for the boy's parents, Jim and Stephanie. This, it will be recalled, was shortly before Michael and Jimmy broke up, but financial help did not stop there. Some of it was not that remarkable by Jackson standards. Michael has always spent lavishly on toys for his boys and *Today*'s claim that he paid after the split-up for Jimmy to have lessons in directing and acting, as well as the therapy already mentioned, is in line with what we might expect: even if the separation was not Michael's fault, he might well have felt he "owed" Jimmy. In any case, he has always taken pride in seeing "his" youngsters coming along in show business – witness Wade Robson.

Harder to explain without sinister overtones are both the Rolls Royce and a claim attributed to La Toya Jackson's husband Jack Gordon that the Safechucks were one of a number of families who received "hush money" from Michael.[158] The *Sunday Times* later backed this claim, saying La Toya had privately indicated that the Safechucks were among these families. More publicly she had said she saw some of the cheques herself, made out in some cases for "millions". Gordon claimed that Jimmy's father, Jim Safechuck, a former dustman, had become a millionaire since his association with Jackson. Jim was by that time the wealthy owner of a waste disposal business in the San Fernando valley, above Los Angeles. *Today* also quoted a member of Jackson's staff: "Michael picks up all the tabs for Jimmy. His parents also have all their expenses taken care of. They receive a healthy cheque each month from the Jackson organisation. I don't know the exact amount but Michael is being very generous."[159]

If these claims from staff and family sources were true – and the Rolls Royce gift has never been credibly explained – it looks even less likely that Michael ever "dumped" Jimmy of his own volition. On the contrary, we begin to get a sense of déjà vu. There was another boy, was there not, with whom Michael became very intense, another boy seen a lot in public with him until "things really began to get out of hand". Another boy, too, whose contact with him was broken off abruptly and who suddenly became a great deal richer.

The parallels marking the end of Jimmy's and Jordie's relationships with Michael are striking, and it is therefore unsurprising that Jimmy was questioned by a grand jury in the Chandler case. He answered jury questions in November 1993, very early in the grand jury proceedings. At that time he was presented in the press as a potential key witness in that case. The jury's sessions were held in secret, offering scope to the tabloids for the deployment of their dark arts: in the absence of hard facts about Jimmy's testimony they could spin his contribution as that of a freshly unearthed "victim", one who might be willing to talk, now that the spotlight was on him, even though his family had allegedly been handsomely bribed not to do so.

We now know what the media did not know at the time, or at any rate not officially: Jimmy had *not* made sexual allegations in his grand jury testimony nor said anything to support the view that improper means had secured his silence.[160] What is of passing interest is that when the *Sunday Times* phoned the family in a bid to get the lowdown, the Safechucks refused to comment, but significantly they were referring all calls not to their own lawyer but *to Michael's people*.[161] If the family's cooperation had been bought, as seems likely, the job had been done very thoroughly, on a long-term basis. It is also reasonable to infer that if Jimmy had been disillusioned with Michael and had turned against him emotionally, his family would not be making positive efforts to put the media in touch with Jackson's aides, helping them to spin Michael's side of the story.

And here's the clincher: Jimmy Safechuck would later get *married* at Neverland. Okay, admittedly, it was not Michael he was marrying, but is this a venue Jimmy would choose if the guy had brutally dumped him?[162]

Jimmy's story is one with very strong hints that the media attack on Michael for "dumping" children was a totally false picture. The bribery issue has more mileage but even this angle may pale into insignificance when – as is often the case with the tabloid Rottweilers – the criticism is generated by writers clearly bent on using every trick in the book to present an unfair picture. Such stories say far more about our willingness to demonise unpopular figures than they do about Michael: the same hateful barbarism is to be seen all the time whether the victims are asylum seekers, welfare "cheats", paedophiles or whoever else happens to be the current focus of popular bigotry and wrath.

A classic case is provided by the *Sunday People*'s onslaught against Michael's friendship with the Cohen brothers in South Africa. The story, from April 1999, drew attention to what was claimed as a two-year friendship between Michael and Dean Cohen, at this time aged thirteen, and his little (unnamed) brother, six. Jackson was said to have regularly made the fifteen-hour flight from Los Angeles to their home in Johannesburg. After referring back to other boys and their families who had been "bewitched" by Michael's fame and fortune, and "flattered by the money and attention" he lavished on them, the story positioned the Cohen brothers' *parents* – not just their children – as vulnerable and overly trusting. The family lived in a "modest" house in Johannesburg; the boys' father, Phillip Cohen, was a "humble" car mechanic. There would be no Rolls Royce for the Cohen family but Michael "took the two boys and their family on a luxury holiday to Sun City".

The implied bribery, or softening up, in this case was thus almost as modest and humble as the family itself, and would have left the story looking a tad feeble if it had been told in a brief, factual, straightforward way. But that would be to reckon without the sinister skills of tabloid presentation across a two-page spread supercharged with the language of vilification. A sidebar column headlined "SINGER'S LIST OF SHAME" made the totally false claim that "Jacko has been accused by SIX children of sexual abuse in the last six years." The boys were named as Jordan Chandler, Jason Francia, Wade Robson, Sean Lennon, Jimmy Safechuck and Brett Barnes. Only the first two ever made accusations. Far from being accusers, the others actually defended Jackson, and two of them, Robson and Barnes, would eventually do so under oath in court.

The main photo in the spread showed Michael strapped in with Dean as the pair prepared to take off on a parascending trip laid on by the star at Sun City. The headline snarled, "Would you let YOUR kids get so close to this weirdo?" The text related that Michael's hands were seen to rest on the boy's shoulders "in scenes that will horrify parents everywhere". The star, we were told, "will forever bear the label of a child sex abuser" – not even, note, an *alleged* child abuser. His friendship with the Cohen boys provided "a chilling echo" of how he got close to Jordie Chandler. A "shocked onlooker" told how Jackson's behaviour "sent shivers down the spines" of other onlookers, though we were not told how he knew, unless he witnessed his fellow shockees visibly trembling. Michael, we were told, had denied any abuse but "his sickening image as a paedophile has stuck" after his payout in 1994 to "end the shame". In another sidebar, a "top doctor" asserted that "Jackson should stay well clear of children at all times", even though he had never been convicted of anything at all, much less child abuse.[163]

That things have not always been what they seemed in the onslaught against Michael is even better illustrated by the Terry George story and its aftermath. George told the story of his contact with Michael Jackson to the *Mail on Sunday*, who ran it in late August 1993.[164] He was described as a 28-year-old disc jockey. George said that as a boy growing up in Yorkshire he had been a keen autograph hunter who would also wait about at stage doors with a camera and tape recorder to snatch a few fleeting words and a photo of any available stars.

Young Terry was thirteen in February 1979 when Michael came to perform in his home city of Leeds. After eavesdropping in the lobby of the Dragonara Hotel he found out the number of Michael's suite, slipped into the lift and knocked on the star's door. To his amazement he was invited in and given an exclusive half-hour interview. "He spoke to me like a friend," said George. "He made me feel special and at the end of it he asked if we could keep in touch and we swapped telephone numbers and addresses." Several days later Michael phoned – and kept on phoning from time to time over the following months from his California home. The chat was "easy and casual", about pop music and such like.

Then came a very different sort of call, said George. Michael began to ask young Terry in graphic terms about sexual activities. At the same time "the star described his own intimate physical actions during the conversation," as one tabloid rendering of his account put it. George takes up the story:

> He just came straight out with his questions. I felt embarrassed and awkward. I didn't really understand what he was talking about. I tried to steer him off the subject and then he asked: "Do you believe I'm doing it now?" I said, "Are you?" I felt panicky. I was shocked. I tried to talk about something else but he brought it back into the conversation. I was uncomfortable. The whole conversation lasted about fifteen minutes, but he talked about this intimate sexual act for five minutes or so. Then he said he'd phone me the next day. Looking back, I could have hung up, but he was a superstar and I was flattered and I didn't want him to stop ringing me.

Michael did stop ringing after that. The calls began to peter out. But Terry George was so far from wanting to hang up on the relationship that he then began to phone Michael, running up a bill for £340 that led to his parents' phone being cut off. "You've been phoning that Michael Jackson again, haven't you?" his mother said accusingly. Even the cutting off did not stop him, for he several times tried ringing Michael from a phone box outside his school, reversing the charges. When he got through, says the paper, "it became clear his superstar friend didn't want to know." Some years later, "as a stocky 17-year-old", he tracked Michael down in London when he came over to record with Paul McCartney. He was photographed alongside his idol, "But now the management were on hand to issue the polite brush-off".

"I felt used because he'd wanted my friendship when I was just a boy. Now I was a young man he just didn't seem to want to know," said George. "Looking back it was wrong of Michael."

The lines of the tabloid attack on Michael are clear: he shocked an innocent youngster with intimate sex talk and gave him the brush-off when he became too mature to be interesting. Simply disgraceful. Except that it is not "simply" anything. If young Terry had been all that shocked, would he really have been so desperately keen to keep up the contact? What if Michael had formed a pretty shrewd notion the lad would be turned on by his sexy chat?

These were thoughts the *Mail on Sunday* showed no enthusiasm for pursuing, especially the appalling – to a moralising tabloid – idea that innocent little Terry might have been getting his rocks off along with Michael. Which is probably why the paper made no mention of the fact that by the time it ran its story Mr George owned the rights to the Mr Gay UK competition, had become the owner of a gay news magazine, *All Points North*, and was himself, you've guessed it, gay.

Pressed by the London gay magazine *Capital Gay* to explain why he had cashed in on the anti-Jackson campaign, he said, "I was backed into a corner. I either cooperated or read my story in someone else's words." How, we might ask, could anyone else have been in a position to back him into a corner? Who would have known about a private phone call if he had not already let the cat out of the bag himself? And why not? If there really had been such a call it would have made a great yarn, especially for a gay audience. Why keep such good material to himself? Backed into a corner by *Capital Gay*, his new line is distinctly apologetic, though he did go on to say that, at the time, he did not know how to handle the call or that he was gay.[165]

It is not difficult to see that a boy of thirteen could be flustered by any encounter with a megastar like Michael, never mind a sexy phone call. The sheer surprise value would come as a shock in itself, even if the content was agreeably exciting. And there's the rub, if the expression will be excused: if Terry George's initial response was shock, we may be sure that excitement and interest soon followed. Why else persist in phoning him when there were a thousand other pop stars he could be chasing with his autograph book? If he had not known he was gay when he put the phone down there can be little serious doubt he knew before long, and certainly by the time he caught up with Michael at the age of seventeen. George has even told the press explicitly: "I do not feel like a victim and I never did feel like a victim."[166]

Clearly no shrinking violet, even when he first met Michael as a thirteen-year-old, George has lately been in the public eye again. Now a multi-millionaire, in November 2007 he presented an hour-long, prime-time TV programme for the Channel 4 series *The Secret Millionaire*. The reality show featured himself working anonymously as an assistant in a care home for the elderly, performing such menial tasks as cleaning toilets and meeting a variety of needy folk; towards the end of the hour he reveals his true identity and bounteously donates several fat cheques from his own money to hard-up people and worthy causes – public worthiness not a million miles in style, one might think, from Michael spending time with sick children in hospital and giving charitable support to such institutions. So spectacularly lacking in shyness is George that he even extends his generosity to letting the viewers see his penis, which is clearly visible when he is shown in one scene emerging from a shower cubicle. He has been bold in another way too, very commendably so, posting a defence of Michael on his website. He writes:

> Each person who is attracted to boys is different from every other, and some of these dissimilarities are important. There are some whose exclusive interest (or nearly so) is in their own gratification. They use a boy with little or no regard for the youth's well-being, satisfaction or happiness. The kidnappers, torturers, murderers, and real as opposed to statutory rapists come from this group. For boy lovers, the boy's gratification is important. The pleasure [experienced by] the boy lover derives, in no small part, from his role in the well-being, satisfaction, or happiness of the boy. Those who have long-term, loving relationships with boys come from this group. If you call a dog's leg a tail, how many legs does a dog have? The correct answer is four. Calling a dog's leg a tail doesn't make it one. The law may call it rape, but it isn't. The failure of society to make reasonable distinctions between these two groups creates gross injustices."[167]

George also said on his website that he had been approached by the Santa Barbara County Sheriff's department in connection with Michael's trial. As part of his Facebook profile he said he had indicated a willingness to testify in the case, but with views as radical as this it is easy to see why the prosecution would not have been interested – nor the defence, for that matter: in court it would be vital for Michael to distance himself from sexual boy-love, not to defend it.

At all events, the "little innocent" angle peddled by the *Mail on Sunday* really will not wash, nor is there any reason to make a federal case out of Michael's calls gradually petering out. This "relationship", after all, had amounted to a half-hour interview followed by some phone calls, one of which was sexually explicit – allegedly. Supposing, instead of a thirteen-year-old boy, we were talking about a girl of the same age. Would we think it a virtue on Michael's part to go on phoning her for years, after such a slender introduction? Would we think it right that he should encourage the girl to think she had a special place in his heart? We may think Michael unwise to excite sexual interest that could not be satisfied – if that is what happened – but no pop star can seriously be expected to live up to the amorous hopes of every fan who manages to get an autograph. Such a standard would make for some disastrously tired, washed-out concert performances!

Only the gay community, thanks to *Capital Gay*, were given the information that showed how misleadingly the Terry George story had been presented in the mainstream media. Likewise only keen Jackson fans would have known how distorted was one tabloid's exploitation of the connection with another boy, Ryan White. The media know they cannot fool all of the people all of the time, but they can certainly fool many of the people for much of the time. Only the limited circles who are "in the know" are any the wiser.

Ryan White died of AIDS at the age of eighteen, in 1990, after contracting HIV from a contaminated blood transfusion some five and a half years earlier, when he was twelve. Haemophiliac Ryan had famously been a victim of public ignorance and fear over AIDS, having been barred from school and his family forced to leave their home town of Kokomo, Indiana. A film was made of his tragic life and courageous struggle against the prejudice he was made to suffer, a struggle that saw him win a long court battle to attend a state school.

Michael had known Ryan, and wrote a song dedicated to his memory, called "Gone Too Soon". He wrote a poem too, called simply "Ryan White", that appeared in his book *Dancing the Dream*. So far so uncontroversial, it might be supposed. What scandal could possibly be provoked by paying tribute to a brave young man? That remains a puzzle even after reading the *Daily Star*'s finger-wagging front-page headline "THAT'S BAD JACKO" and a story taking Michael to task for the sleeve picture of the single, "showing him in an intimate chat" with Ryan. The photo depicted the pair walking outdoors together, well wrapped up on a presumably cold day, each with his hands in his pockets and maybe a body width apart from each other. As seen in this soft-focus shot, Ryan could be at any age in his teens, but he was plainly not a young child. "It has never been suggested that Jackson's relationship with Ryan was improper," said the *Star* correctly, while going on to quote a journalist as saying the picture was "highly inappropriate". No-one

35 yrs

said why. The "story" appeared in December 1993, when Michael had gone into hiding after quitting the *Dangerous* tour and the media frenzy was at its height.[168]

Why should such a picture have been thought "highly inappropriate", or outright "BAD"? Was the *Star* trying to suggest the very thing they said had never – up till then – been suggested? That there had been something "improper" between Michael and Ryan? Or were they saying Michael was defiantly flaunting his contact with a youngster in a way readers might find offensive? Or was something else supposed to be wrong? We were not told. Nothing was spelt out. Anyone trying to work this out is left to read between the lines in a way that can only be unfair. In courts of law it is a fundamental right of an accused person to know what he is accused of. Otherwise he is left in the Kafkaesque nightmare of having no idea how to defend himself. The principle is just the same when the news media point the finger: vague innuendo is bound to leave the reader imagining all sorts of possibilities, including the worst.

The deep injustice of this particular smear story is bound to have left many Jackson fans bitterly angry, for they knew the background to Michael's friendship with Ryan. He had not known the boy from childhood. He had never been a "boyfriend" in any sense. It was only after his story hit the headlines and Michael began to feel empathy with him in his struggle that contact was made. If he had wanted an "improper" relationship there were a thousand kids in show business he could have made friends with, and thousands more writing fan mail to him. Why on earth should he have picked on the one child with whom he knew intimacy would be dangerous? It makes no sense.

What the fans also knew was that Ryan's mother Jean had spoken movingly on the Oprah Winfrey show about Michael's concern for Ryan. At that time, early in 1993, no-one was talking about anything improper, but Jean made it clear she thought Michael was well motivated in a wider sense: "I saw a very sincere Michael and somebody that... it is strange, after Ryan died, I asked Michael, I said: 'Well, what is it that connected you and Ryan?' And he said 'You know, most people can't get over the awe of who I am. So nobody can ever act normal around me.' He said, 'Ryan knew how I wanted to be treated, because that's how he wanted to be treated.'"

The fans could understand those words, but they also knew that actions talk louder, and that Michael had spent five days with Ryan at a time when it could not have been much fun – just a short time before the young man's death, when he was gravely ill. They stayed at Neverland, just watching movies together, talking, going out shopping. Nothing spectacular, just being together, with Michael showing he cared. He had the satisfaction of knowing he did that, and he knew Jean appreciated it. Just the same, it must have been galling beyond measure for him to see such kindness perverted into something sleazy in a trashy tab like the *Daily Star*.

Some cynics might wonder whether Michael's interest in Ryan was all about generating *favourable* publicity, such as being praised on *Oprah*. Fans may see this as a mean-spirited question, but there is a better answer than indignation: proof. Michael was demonstrably generous with his time in helping many children in circumstances that enable us to discount either a sexual motive or publicity seeking.

One striking example is to be found in his long-term, low-profile friendship with a boy named David Rothenberg. Life had dealt David a really tough hand, perhaps an even harder one to play than Ryan's. He was only six years old back in 1982 when his father had "poured gasoline on him and set him on fire". The burns were severe and 90% of his body was affected. Hair would not grow afterwards on his head as scar tissue covered all the pores. Touched by his story when it came to his attention, Michael quietly paid for David's convalescence and invited him to Neverland. They remained friends over the years. With Michael's sustained help David developed a career in music. The very positive part Michael played in David's life would not be the subject of significant public attention for twenty years: no way could Michael be accused of cashing in on the relationship.

Global public awareness of the long-term friendship seemed on the cards in 2002, however, when David went to Neverland to give a speech to an invited audience, telling them what Michael had done for him and how much he appreciated it. TV documentary maker Martin Bashir was at Neverland at the time but chose to make no use of Rothenberg's story, presumably because it showed a good side to Michael's involvement with children that Bashir did not want to highlight: he turned out to be interested only in scandal. As will be seen in later chapters, David's story was to be far from the only example of Bashir editing his programme so as to dwell on the negative and suppress the positive.[169]

If the media's handling of the friendship with Ryan White was about distortion, tabloid methods sank to the abyss of outright fabrication in the case of the Newt twins in the 1980s. Robert Newt, now in his thirties, and his twin brother Ronald Jr (now deceased) were ten or eleven years old and pop star wannabes when they spent two weeks as guests in the Jackson family home in Encino, California, around 1985. Michael, Janet and La Toya were all living there at that time, as well as the Jackson parents.

Years later, in December, 1993, the *National Enquirer*, desperate to get a scoop that Jackson had abused children, heard that the Newt kids once spent time with him. The tabloid offered the Newts' father, Ronald Sr, $200,000 to say something happened between his kids and Jackson. It looks as though the father was tempted. A contract was drawn up, signed by *Enquirer* editor David Perel. *Enquirer* reporter Jim Mitteager, also now deceased, met Newt and his surviving son at a hotel in San Francisco. The Newts declined the offer when son Bobby insisted there had been no sexual involvement with Michael Jackson. Roger Friedman, then with Fox News (he later moved to *The Hollywood Reporter*), reported in 2005 that he met Bobby Newt near where he worked as a mortgage broker in Los Angeles. "Half black and half Chinese," he said, "Robert and his twin brother were likely very cute kids." All Bobby Newt remembered about the man from the *National Enquirer* was that he wanted the young man to lie:

> My dad said these dudes are offering this money to take Michael Jackson down. And the guy said, "Say he touched you. All you have to do is say it. But you might have to take the stand. You might have to go on Oprah in front of all these people. You have to be prepared for this thing. Just say it. And we'll give you money."[170]

Friedman said there were two pieces of evidence to confirm the Newts' story. One was the actual contract proffered by the *Enquirer* and signed by David Perel, who declined to comment. The contract, written as a letter, said it was an agreement between the tabloid and the Newts for their exclusive story regarding "your relationship with and knowledge of Michael Jackson, and his sexuality, your knowledge of Michael Jackson's sexual contact and attempts at sexual contact with Robert Newt and others". Mitteager expected them to sign even though it was completely untrue. The second piece of evidence is a tape recording of the conversation with Mitteager. When he died, all Mitteager's interview tapes were left to Hollywood investigator and publicist Paul Barresi, whom we shall encounter elsewhere.

Back in the mid-80s, Ron Newt Sr put his three sons together as a singing group just as Joseph Jackson had. He called them The Newtrons. After much pushing, he got the attention of Jackson Sr, who agreed to manage the group. Joe Jackson got the Newtrons a showcase at the Roxy in West Hollywood. Michael showed up and loved them. The result was a two-week stay for the boys at Hayvenhurst, Encino, where they were supposed to work on their music.

"We would see Michael in passing. We didn't see him maybe because he was working on an album. We saw him downstairs in the kitchen and we talked to him," Bobby Newt told Friedman. "He had prime time with me and my brother in the guest room for two weeks. And he didn't try anything."

The Newtrons eventually got a record contract and recorded the Jackson Five hit "I Want You Back" at Hayvenhurst. Not long before Friedman's story, Bobby Newt worked with Wade Robson on tracks for his first album, a compendium of original R&B ballads.

Another young man born around the same time as Ryan White also faced a potentially fatal problem in his teenage years, but survived to tell for himself the tale of Michael's kindness towards him. This was Corey Feldman, star of the hit movie *Stand By Me*. Like so many Hollywood talents, including his celebrated co-star in that film, River Phoenix, Corey fell prey to drug addiction. It would kill River, and Corey's fate may well have been in the balance, too. A newspaper reported him as saying that when he was sixteen he "fell under the influence of a young man who often stayed at his home and sexually abused him". He said: "I'd get real wasted, and hope that I'd pass out and not remember anything next morning. I didn't confront the man because I was afraid people would think I was a bad person. Plus I didn't want to lose him as a friend because I believed he really cared for me."[171]

Did he hope he would pass out simply because he found being fondled by another young man embarrassing and distasteful? Or was it submitting to rough violation that he could not handle? The newspaper did not quote him on that, but we can easily agree that if the story was accurate his life was in a mess. Corey gave some of the credit for his recovery from drug addiction to encouraging messages left on his phone answering machine by Michael Jackson, who had been a friend for some years. He had met Michael back in 1984 on the set of *Goonies* and said that, like Wade Robson and Brett Barnes, he had slept alone in bed with Michael, but there was nothing sexual going on. "There was no sexual connotation," he said. "Calling Michael Jackson a child molester is like calling Santa Claus a thief."

No-one, including Jordie Chandler, has suggested Michael is violent or rough, or has ever imposed himself in a bullying way as apparently happened to Corey. It is easy to believe Corey's view that Michael is not a "molester" if, for him, molesting means something like what happened to him at age sixteen. But can we be so sure this homosexually experienced young man is levelling with us when he says there was nothing sexual in his contact with Michael? In a more recent interview on TV's *20/20* he reportedly claimed that Michael tried to persuade him to look at nude magazines – the sort of invitation from a grown man to a growing boy that prosecutors do not hesitate to call sexual "grooming", and an allegation of a type that would figure prominently in Michael's trial in 2005.[172] We should not forget that these later allegations, made by the boys Gavin Arvizo and his brother Star, may have been complete lies – Michael was, after all, found not guilty on all charges – but it is not doubted that Jackson possessed a significant amount of pornography, both "straight" and gay, a fact which gives Corey's claim a measure of credibility.

Also, what adds to that credibility enormously is the very limited extent of this "accusation", which is so mild as to scarcely merit the term. After all, this was a young man who could have taken the witness stand and accused Michael of anal rape, had he chosen to do so, with no fear of being sued and with a whole world of abuse "survivors" out there ready to applaud his courage in coming forward. What he did now claim, almost as sensationally, was that Michael had not abused him but that he had been one of a group of child actors who were preyed upon and "molested by a gang of Hollywood paedophiles". Personally, I do not buy it, for the same reason I do not buy into any conspiracy theories that require us to believe in large numbers of individuals or organisations, each with their own, often conflicting interests, all being in on the plot and then contriving for years to keep it under wraps even while – as in the case of 9/11 and the "murder" of Princess Diana – the internet is buzzing with rumour and speculation. As we shall see in Chapter Ten, Hollywood has traditionally been extremely good at covering up scandals but even in the home of "the casting couch" there is a limit to what the fixers can achieve.

A related point is that the concept of a "gang" of paedophiles is largely illusory. So-called paedophile gangs, or "rings", have been investigated extensively in the US and the UK and found to be a will o' the wisp in such contexts as kindergartens (the McMartin Pre-School being the classic example and there are many others), children's homes (notably Wales, Lancashire and Cheshire), and "Satanic" sexual abuse (the Orkneys,

Rochdale, Nottingham).[173] The only truly significant exception to the rule has been the exchange of child pornography by organised groups of paedophiles on the internet, and in this case the reason for the exception is clear: the internet is the only major social context in which it has been possible to declare and act upon a sexual interest in children anonymously, without (in the early years at least) much danger of being denounced by others in the group or detected by the authorities.

"Gang" rape when perpetrated on an adult woman is typically the work of booze- or drug-fuelled young men who can assume, without danger to themselves, that their friends share their heterosexuality. They can verbally let their hair down without risk, egging each other on, talking about what they would sexually like to do. Those who are attracted to children, by contrast, usually find it very hard to so much as mention their feelings to any other adult: having paedophilic inclinations is generally a very lonely business. Even the world of internet child pornography appears to have been largely characterised not by "gangs" of paedophiles but by isolated downloaders, whose online activity turns out to be a very furtive and individual pursuit.[174]

As for Michael and Corey, whatever did or did not go on when they were in bed together, Corey showed every sign of liking him and wanting to support him under fire at the critical time. He is said to have ended his friendship with Michael in 2001, criticising him in a song called "Megalo-Man", but there is no need to read too much into this so far as the nature of their early relationship is concerned.[175] If we want to pay more than mere lip service to the child's point of view in cases of alleged sexual abuse we need to attach a lot of weight to the robust expression of loyalty Corey made at an early stage and to his continuing, steadfast denial of any sexual abuse by Michael.

Among the most publicly supportive figures towards Michael in the Chandler crisis was Brandon Adams, who was fifteen when he spoke up, straight after the allegations broke. Brandon was ten when Michael chose him to play Baby Bad, a miniature version of himself, in his *Moonwalker* video. The boy stayed at Michael's home, went with him everywhere, wore the same style clothes, and according to the *Daily Express* became his "favourite person" for almost two years.[175] It will be recalled that Jimmy Safechuck had shown every sign of fulfilling that role at the time of the *Bad* tour in 1988. If Michael had been lonely after taking Frank Dileo's advice to break off that relationship, he could not have stayed so for long because Brandon was soon on the scene.

Brandon had come a long way in five years. By this time he had become a movie actor and also had an MCA record deal. He cited "girls" as his favourite pastime. Around the time when he was publicly standing up for Michael, in 1993, it was rumoured that he had himself received a $600,000 pay-off from Jackson in the previous year, well before the settlement in the Chandler case. However, Roger Friedman more recently revealed that the story had been based on a very dubious source.[176] The teenager rejected the Chandler claims angrily:

> It's totally stupid. People who believe it are just dumb, there's nothing like that going on with Michael. He's just not interested in that sort of thing. Everybody thinks Michael's this or Michael's that but they don't know him and they don't get the chance to. He's just a big kid. He's bigger and older than other children but he thinks like them and he enjoys the same sort of things. He just likes to laugh all the time which is understandable when you think how hard he works.[177]

Brandon also explained that he had learnt a great deal from Michael:

> We worked a lot together and I enjoyed that. Now I'm older I look back and I remember the advice he used to give me. I think he really helped me with my career and I'm eternally grateful for that. He always told me that I have to practise, practise all the time. He always says practice makes perfect and that is what I do now. I want to be good at what I do, like him. At the time I was really close to him, my favourite part was the fun bit. Michael likes to have a lot of fun. We always used to have food fights, and fights with water pistols and run round all the rooms playing hide and seek. He has a great house. I used to mimic him and order pizzas in a high-pitched voice. It made him laugh. I used to beat him on his Pac-Man game too. I suppose I'm a bit old for all that stuff now. [178]

Brandon felt too old for "all that stuff", but thirty five was plainly not too old for Michael to love cavorting with kids. Even in the wake of the Chandler allegations, and in the full glare of the world's attention, he defiantly continued to surround himself with little pals, most obviously the Cascio brothers, Frank (13) and Eddie (9), sons of New Jersey restaurant owner Dominic Cascio. We shall be hearing plenty more about this family in later chapters. At first no-one knew who they were when they were seen staying with Michael at Elizabeth Taylor's Alpine resort chalet in Gstaad, Switzerland, during the *Dangerous* tour, in September 1993. The next month they surfaced again, this time standing with Michael as he waved to the crowds from a hotel balcony a world away in Buenos Aires. One woman journalist noted that the boys joined in with the waving and looked "cuter than any two boys have the right to".[179] By this time the *National Enquirer* had discovered that the boys had flown out from the US with their father to join the tour in Israel. From there they had gone to Switzerland and later to the Argentine capital. Completing a hat-trick of dramatic appearances, they were spotted running from the plane with Michael and some bodyguards, when he touched down in the US at Billings, Montana, in December, after secretly leaving England following his "addiction treatment".

If families like the Barnes and the Robsons were to be thought excessively trusting in letting their children go to bed with Michael, the Cascios could be considered excessively brave in letting their children join Michael in putting up two fingers to public opinion. There can be no doubt this is what he was doing, especially in Buenos Aires. His defiance may have been too much for the British media to stomach, for this is the one event in the whole saga they downplayed. It was left to the American *National Enquirer* to deliver a major spread with pictures of the trio on the balcony. Michael was wearing a surgical mask, an old trade mark of his, worn in parody of talk about his obsessive fear of disease and interest in medical matters. Young Eddie wore one, too.

After displaying a pillow with the words "I love you all" written on it, Michael then made a truly bizarre and brazen gesture, producing a copy of *Child Magazine*, with what reporter David Duffy calls "an adorable photo of a baby on the cover" and holding it up for the crowd and photographers to see. *Child Magazine* is aimed at parents and contains many pictures of children as well as articles about their upbringing. The issue in question was the US edition current at the time, the front page billing articles on "Your child's anger" and "46 fun baby games".

Dominic Cascio, who had been working at the Helmsley Palace Hotel, New York, when he met Michael, showed no sign of being phased by this strange publicity involving his children, nor did his wife. Interviewed later, in the US, they continued to back Michael and express their fullest confidence that they were happy for their children to be with him. We have seen that Michael was a close friend of many boys whose names were in the public arena, most of them talented youngsters in show business. While the phenomenon of ambitious parents pushing their children too hard towards stage success has often been noted with disgust – arguably it was a disastrous feature of Michael's own life – the children themselves have always been keen to praise Michael for the career help he gave them, help which was decidedly not an "all work, no play" matter, but a more benign mixture of encouragement, use of his facilities and patronage, and a lot of fun.

The dozen closest "boyfriends" or "boy friends" whose names have become familiar to us – Brandon Adams, Brett Barnes, Eddie and Frank Cascio, Jordan Chandler, Macaulay Culkin, Corey Feldman, Sean Lennon, Emmanuel Lewis, Wade Robson, Jimmy Safechuck and Jonathan Spence – make an impressive roll-call, but it is a far from complete one. The list will rival Casanova's conquest-count before this book is done.

Not that every name represents a sexual conquest, far from it. Rather, Michael's close friendship with so many boys, including being regular bedfellows with quite a few of them, puts beyond serious argument the fact that he was compulsively attracted to boys and invites examination of how such contacts impact upon the youngsters themselves – a theme at the heart of this book. This chapter, in the course of exploring Michael's friendships, has focused on those that shed light on allegations of "dumping". We would fail to explore the full range of Michael's enthusiasm for boys, though, if we did not at the same time note several of his friendships that we might call more "aspirational" rather than actualised in a major way. In other words, not even superstar status could always get him what he wanted, and in one high-society instance he could even be thought of not so much the dumper as the dumped.

So far as friendships of this kind are concerned I am indebted to Darwin Porter, author of several star biographies, whose assiduously mined gossip is colourful enough to make a rainbow look dull. While it would be crazy to swear by the complete accuracy of Porter's work, and I do not, neither does the man himself. Porter is more of a "take it or leave it", "make up your own mind" kind of guy with no discernible malice or moral axe to grind, and usually – but not always – his cheap and cheerful yarns are credibly supported. In that spirit, and with that caution, let us then turn to some of his anecdotes.

We heard in Chapter Three that Michael found it helpful during the Jordie Chandler crisis to claim he had a relationship with the actress Brooke Shields, and in Chapter Eight we shall be taking a closer look at such diversionary tactics, apparently designed to deflect attention away from his interest in boys and baselessly to bolster his heterosexual credentials. Another actress he was supposedly "in love" with was Tatum O'Neal, daughter of Ryan and child star in the film *Paper Moon*. This was claimed as his first love, many years before any boy scandal, and it is true the two were friends for a while. However, Porter has it that on the Hollywood party circuit it was rumoured that Michael had fallen not for the teenaged Tatum but "her cute little brother Griffin", a boy said to be small for his age and slightly built. Musically talented, like Michael, Griffin was skilled at playing the guitar and the piano as well as drums. The pair shared musical sessions together, with Michael "seemingly enjoying time spent with him instead of with Tatum". There is absolutely no evidence of any interest in a closer association on the boy's part, so, for Michael – if the gossip were true – Griffin could be among the ones that got away.[180]

Another of Michael's "society" connections many years ago was Jackie Onassis, widow of the assassinated US president, John Kennedy. She invited Michael to a tennis tournament where she introduced him to her children, John and Caroline. Later, Michael would invite another famous friend, writer Truman Capote, to join him at another tennis match to watch young John play. Porter reports Capote as saying that Michael was obviously "smitten" by the youngster, not least after the boy had undressed in front of them in the locker room. "He might have been just a boy at the time but that was a man's cock he was flaunting at us," according to Capote. "The kid was hung...and hung big. Michael appeared fascinated." My guess is that *Capote* was the only one getting excited: by this time, in 1977, John would have been a strapping older teenager, fully grown and well past Michael's usual age of attraction.[181]

The president's son would have made a glamorous "trophy" lover, though, and there is no shortage of evidence that Michael, like so many of the rich and famous, loved to hobnob with the social elite, those he considered to be his peers. And who could be more socially elite than a prince? Well, the King of Pop might arguably trump a certain rival artist formerly and once again known as Prince, but neither of them could boast the blue-blooded pedigree of the genuinely aristocratic Prince Albert von Thurn und Taxis. In a photograph found when Neverland was raided, Brett Barnes is seen pictured on one side of Michael and on the other is a boy who was eventually identified as the ten-year-old Bavarian prince. The photo had been taken at Euro Disney. Born on 24 June, 1983, Prince Albert featured on Forbes Rich List as the world's youngest billionaire, with a fortune of $2.1

billion. His wealth included an estate of 74,132 acres of woodland in Germany, one of the largest forestry holdings in Europe. He grew up in one of the family castles, Schloss Emmeram in Regensburg. As Porter says, "How Michael linked himself with such aristocracy and was allowed to travel with this rich and unusual child is not known. Michael certainly could not wow Prince Albert with money and toys, as the young Bavarian was obviously very wealthy in his own right."[182]

Quite. And perhaps his young highness Prince Albert von Thurn und Taxis soon tired of his "trophy" pop star and "thurned" to taxidermy instead, or (even less probably!) taxi-driving, or golf, or girls, or whatever else happened to take his noble fancy. At all events, no long-lasting "relationship" developed with Michael.

But at least the "King" got to hang out with Prince Albert for a while, which is more than he had managed a few years earlier with Prince William, England's likely future monarch – despite extraordinarily strenuous efforts to persuade his mother, Princess Diana, to let her eldest son fly over to stay at Neverland. As Porter puts it, "The more rejections he received, the more passionate he became in his campaign to entertain William for a sleepover".[183]

It had all started in July 1988 when Michael was in London on his *Bad* tour, performing at Wembley Stadium, where he met Diana and her husband Charles, Prince of Wales, backstage. He had wanted personally to present specially-made *Bad* tour jackets to both of her sons, William and Harry, and was disappointed they had been left at home. When Michael asked why the boys had not been brought along to the concert, Charles pointed out that "William is only six years old, Harry just three. There's a thing called bedtime".

Michael began to phone Diana "at least once a week" after this, according to Porter, and "most often they talked about children". Stories began to appear in the tabloids about a romantic link: Michael had supposedly at long last fallen for a woman – gossip he can only have found extremely welcome and which had quite possibly been promoted by his own publicists. There is no reason to doubt that Michael felt genuine excitement at being associated with the most glamorous woman in the world, but the tantalizing possibility of parlaying this contact into a friendship with the elder of the two little princes seems to have been the real buzz; this was the driving force behind the embarrassing, almost stalker-like persistence of his ensuing campaign to bring William into his life.

Michael became obsessed with William. One prized possession was a framed blowup of the little prince taken on his first day at Wetherby School in 1987, wearing his regulation shorts. Smiling and waving at the photographers, the prince was also dressed in a red tie with red-trimmed stockings. He carried a Postman Pat lunchbox. Michael ordered his staff to send the boy a Michael Jackson lunchbox, a gift that was to be just one of many – so many that they would soon cease to be welcome.

Note that the gifts were just for William, not for Harry, according to Porter, at least after the first one or two. Porter's understandable view is that Harry was of less interest at that time as he was only a toddler. Nevertheless, both courtesy and common sense should have alerted Michael to the need for treating the princes equally. To have an obvious favourite was to invite suspicions in the royal household that the star's highly targeted generosity was no mere token gesture just designed to impress Diana.

The danger signals appear to have been well and truly picked up. Michael sent many lavish gifts to Prince William but, just like unsolicited gifts from other sources, they were always carefully re-wrapped and returned to Neverland, and always with the same courtesy note enclosed, thanking the sender and referring to the many gifts sent from well-wishers around the world. The standard note added that, "It is our policy to return these gifts with the suggestion that they be given to other children in need. Think of the joy that would bring."

Apparently that thought did not bring much joy to Michael, or not enough to make him back off. Instead, he sent even more expensive presents and kept urging Diana to allow William to fly to Neverland.

Porter's main and probably sole source for this appears to have been Michael's former manager Bob Jones. Sacked by Michael, Jones wrote a book highly critical of his old boss. While the dismissal requires us to treat his accusations cautiously, the account as set out by Porter is highly plausible and it is possible Jones still has documentary evidence to back it. Bob Jones is quoted as saying that it had fallen to him to phone Kensington Palace on Michael's behalf, presumably after Diana had started making direct phone calls by him difficult or impossible. Instead of getting Diana to the phone, Jones could only speak to "a polite gentleman" who advised him to write down in detail the matters for proposed discussion with the assurance that the palace would get back to him. But they never did. Eventually, through this "polite gentleman", Michael was firmly told that any further presents for William would all be returned unwrapped to Neverland. Michael was also bluntly informed that William would not be available as a guest at Neverland, "not at the present time, not in the near or even distant future". At the bottom of the "carefully written note", Diana had scrawled in her own handwriting: "Michael, Please stop sending gifts! They aren't wanted. And please stop calling. Your calls will not be returned. Best wishes in your future career." In his book, Bob Jones claims that Michael spent a lot of money trying to buy friendships, including Diana's, but he does not mention William in this context.[184]

As recently as April 2005, during Michael's trial, another of Michael's alleged long-range obsessions was being reported, this time dating from over twenty years earlier, in 1984. Karina Longworth reported that a production company had optioned a film version of Victor Gutierrez's book *Michael Jackson Was My Lover: The Secret Diary of Jordie Chandler*. We shall be hearing much more about this sensational book in Chapter Eleven but for now we should note that Longworth's report drew attention to a claim made solely in the book's Spanish language edition, which contained a description of Michael's "alleged inappropriate dalliance with singer Ricky Martin". Gutierrez had said in this book that, months after the police raid on Neverland in 1993, it had been revealed that two trunks had turned up in the raid "filled", in Porter's version, with pictures of the singer Ricky Martin from when he was only around twelve years old. The photos were not pornographic. They had been taken in connection with the boy's membership of the Latin boy group Menudo, which he had joined at the age of twelve.[185]

Elsewhere in his own book, Porter cites juvenile contacts made through dozens of Los Angeles model agencies, many of them specializing in child models for TV and print advertising. Michael would order publicity photos of the boys and have them sent to Neverland. Staff (not named) reported that he would spend a lot of time carefully studying the images. What Porter calls Michael's "excuse" to the agencies, though it may at times have been a valid reason, was that he was planning to make music videos involving child actors.[186]

Porter's account of the Ricky Martin photos gives a misleading impression. Two trunks "filled" with photos of one boy would indeed seem obsessive but a careful reading suggests that although the trunks may (or may not) have been filled with photos, only *some* of them were of young Ricky. Porter duly goes on to note that a translation from the Spanish had this to say:

> Among the photographs confiscated by the police during the raid, the detectives found some of an unidentifiable Hispanic boy. Later they discovered they were of Ricky Martin, the singer and ex-member of the band Menudo…Even though the photographs of the now-actor were taken from magazines and promotional stills, they sufficiently indicate a liking towards the ex-member of Menudo.[187]

Porter adds that there is no evidence the successful solo singer of such hits as "Livin' the vida loca" ever had a relationship of any kind with Michael. In an interview, Martin was once asked about the photos found at Neverland. He said he knew Michael had taken an interest in Menudo and had always thought that "the King of Pop has a platonic liking towards me". At one point Michael had invited the Menudo boys for some photographs but Martin claimed he had not been a member of the group at that time.

So, neither the photos nor the "platonic liking" were much to get too excited over and certainly nowhere near amounted to an "inappropriate dalliance", whatever that might mean. The same might be concluded about one other "relationship" from Porter's would-be portentous pages, between Michael and actor Alfonso Ribeiro. The young Ribeiro, like Ricky Martin, had been twelve in January 1984 when the pair of them (Alfonso and Michael) were taking part together in filming a commercial for Pepsi. "Michael became enchanted with the handsome young boy," Porter claims, "and the professional relationship developed into a private friendship".[188] Ribeiro dedicated his first single, "Dance Baby", to Michael. He went on to TV sitcom fame when he played Carlton Banks in *The Fresh Prince of Bel Air*. Again, the uncovering of this friendship was hardly going to put Michael on the list of America's Most Wanted, but it does amount to yet one more indicator of his primary social enthusiasm: boys in late pre-puberty and early adolescence.

Having thus reviewed Porter's contribution to the theme of Michael's "aspirational" relationships, it may be thought the material on Prince William is especially illuminating. How many more boys, either close friends or those merely admired from a distance, can there have been? As indicated above, more names will come up in later chapters, but for the moment we can let Michael himself attest to an intriguing range of possibilities. On the sleeve notes of the *Dangerous* album, Michael recorded thanks to several families – "the Culkins, the Sandlers, the Wilkins, the Milkens, the Andrews, the Robsons and the Agajanians". We have encountered the Culkins and the

Robsons. But the Sandlers, the Milkens, the Wilkins, the Andrews and the Agajanians? *The Sun* would half-heartedly attempt to make a scandal in 1994 out of Michael's connection with a certain Jimmy Andrews, then aged sixteen and said to have been a friend of Michael's for one year. The tabloid reported that he had been flown to Budapest with his mother for a long weekend with Michael at a cost of £60,000. Even before the era of budget airlines it would have been hard to spend that kind of money just on tickets! I have no idea which Andrews family this particular Jimmy was from.[189] Many years later, Michael would also talk about his friendship with Barry Gibb and his family of five, four of whom were boys. And what of the untold thousands more he received as guests at Neverland and met as a result of fan mail or encounters at concert venues?

Any of these children, and perhaps many, may have been the object of Michael's attention and affection over the years, if in some cases only briefly. Gay men sometimes have many more or less casual encounters. Clarence Osborne, an Australian court reporter attracted to boys and young adolescents, kept meticulous records of no less than 2,500 youngsters with whom he had had a sexual encounter. None of them complained to the police. He was a mild, kind, pleasant man, who just happened to have a genius for chatting with boys and bringing out the randiness in them. As a result, one of the major problems of his life was to satisfy the sexual desires of hundreds of boys who approached him.[190] Few would be capable of such an awesome, Olympian achievement, but Michael had a known weakness for record-breaking, and was rightly proud of his place in the *Guinness Book of Records* for the sales achieved by his *Thriller* album. Could it be that his private ambitions outstripped (if that's the right term) his public ones?

Like Clarence, Michael had a decades-long track record as a meticulous, hard-working, talented individual (Clarence was rated one of Australia's best court reporters until his exposure and suicide at the age of fifty six). But it would be unfair to either of them to pursue the comparison too far: unfair to Clarence, who had neither Michael's cash nor his inclination to indulge kids outrageously with expensive presents; and unfair to Michael, who was clearly inclined towards much longer relationships than interested Clarence – unfair, that is, if we see a long (at least a few months or a year or two, rather than days), intense emotional involvement between man and boy more positively than casual sex. Not everyone would do so.

Just by looking at the publicly available facts of Michael's contacts with children, it can be seen that we are beginning to be able to infer certain things about his preferences, without any resort so far to psychological theory or surveys of offenders or clinical case studies: his young friends were generally in mid- to late-childhood, most of them in the years just before puberty. His attachment to them was highly physical, with lots of hugging and kissing, and in several cases the intimacy of a shared bed. The pattern seems to be one of "serial monogamy", a term invented to cope with what is increasingly becoming the norm in relations between men and women in western society. In Michael's case one boy at a time dominated his interest and affections, and the intensity of these contacts implies that they must have occupied a major place in his mind and emotions.

We have seen that Michael also liked babies: he would go gaga over baby pictures and behaved towards his brother Jermaine's baby as though it were his own. He did not become a father, however, until relatively recent years. And as it is all but impossible for non-fathers in our society to be accepted in a nurturing role towards infants, we need not be surprised that babies and toddlers were largely absent from the roll-call of his closest little "friends".[191]

There is in any case a limit to which even that elastic term can stretch, implying, as it does, a meeting of minds and feelings beyond pre-verbal baby talk. Michael's more "mature" relationships, with boys aged nine or more, involved him as an equal, as "a big kid", rather than an adult looking after a helpless dependent. His role had some elements of nurturance and tender care about it – remember what Joy Wade said about him changing her boy's wet bed linen? – but in other ways he was not what we expect of an adult. We hear of food fights, for instance – anarchic, "naughty" behaviour, in cheerful subversion of the disciplinary role expected of a father. Irresponsible? Shouldn't kids be solemnly reminded of the starving in Africa when they waste food? Isn't it teaching disrespect for property and the servants' labour when they are allowed to mess a room up?

Maybe. But custard pie battles in old-time slapstick comedy movies commit the same sins without upsetting anyone. Whether Michael's "big kid" behaviour was reprehensible depends on context. The trial in 2005 yielded plenty of stories of the wild goings-on at Neverland and squeamish readers should be warned they will not be spared the full horrors of all that in later chapters. For the moment, we have the opportunity to pause and reflect in a calm atmosphere, as it were. Simon Carr, in his wonderful autobiographical account of a father's "big kid" parenting style with his own two sons, shows convincingly how it is possible to have wild fun with kids *and* be responsible.

Carr's account is of particular relevance because he was a lone parent, interacting with naturally boisterous boys and, as a writer, sharing plenty of time at home with them. For Carr, it is a matter of setting the boundaries of acceptable behaviour as widely as possible but then being firm about the clearly defined boundaries you *do* set – parenting should not be a matter of saying "no" to almost everything a child wants to do. In Michael's case there is clear evidence that things truly "got out of hand" at times, to use a phrase we have heard before. But those times are by no means the whole picture: there is impressive testimony, for instance, that far from being brattish or spoilt or wild, Michael's *own* children are calm, courteous and evidently "well brought up", as will be seen in Chapter Thirteen.

We hear about love a good deal. Joy Robson was not the only one to use the word. Michael's relations with older boys in particular were especially intense, the bonding going beyond playmate or "best pal" status. Far from "dumping" his partners at this stage we have seen that twice – in the case of both Jimmy Safechuck and Jordan Chandler – he was forced to part with them in circumstances of pain and loneliness. Relations with other boys – Emmanuel Lewis, Corey Feldman, Brandon Adams – tailed off without trauma to either party, and with some very warm memories being expressed by the young men in question as they moved into adulthood. Also, more than a decade after Wade Robson and Brett Barnes went on TV to defend Michael, those boys, by that time adults, went into the witness box at his trial to do the same. They and their families were utterly united in expressing their admiration of the star, emphasising that their relationship with him had been a continuing one. Another of Michael's special friends, Frank Cascio, graduated to joining his staff as one of his most trusted aides.

Finally, on the "dumping" thesis, we may note that one of its very prominent exponents, senior FBI agent Ken Lanning, was forced to fall back onto this unsubstantiated argument against paedophilia for want of any other serious line of criticism. Michael's most doggedly persistent detractor over the years, Diane Dimond, devotes a whole chapter of her book to Lanning's work, including his profile of "the traits of a male preferential child molester". But apart from prejudicial language in which the word "victim" figures strongly, what we learn is far from terrible. Under a bullet-point listing of the traits to be discerned, he identifies "an uncanny ability to identify with and listen to children". We discover:

> Number one, they have a good ability to identify with children; they know

how to relate to children, they know what their likes and dislikes are. And maybe more important, they know how to listen to them. They learn what their interests are. So, they are very good at using these skills to, what I call, seduce children. In some ways they can be [childlike themselves]. But it would be a mistake to assume that they are going to be immature and baby-like. They just have a magical rapport [with kids]. Matter of fact, some people will describe that they are like a Pied Piper around kids; they just really know how to relate to kids so well. They have this ability to identify with children so well. It is almost as if a part of them almost never grew up. Many of these kids have never been treated so well in their entire lives as they have by a preferential molester. [Emphases all mine.][192]

How many parents can claim to be this good at listening to their kids or having a "magical" rapport with them? Not all, plainly, as Lanning implicitly admits in this revealing passage. But it is these "molesters", these nice guys, who go to jail, not neglectful, incompetent parents, and it is people like Lanning and Dimond who irrationally keep up the pressure for things to stay that way.

Another aspect of Michael's friendships with children that leaps out of all accounts is that we hear very little about girls. Michael claimed a special feeling for children in general, and wrote and spoke eloquently on the subject. He placed an enormous emphasis on children's charities in his work and at his concerts he invited children of both sexes to join him on stage. Yet in his personal, private life all we heard about was boys, boys, boys. Almost.

Some of the boys had sisters. As we have heard, Chantal Robson claimed that, like her brother Wade, she too shared a bed with Michael.[193] Brett Barnes' sister Karlee would make a similar claim at Michael's trial many years later. We hear little about the girls, though, except that Michael bought them presents: not to have done so when he was buying lavishly for their brothers would have been asking for trouble, but no-one has suggested that the level of friendship ever went beyond the purely dutiful. Asked on the witness stand why she did not spend the night in Michael's room as often as her brother, Karlee Barnes said, "Because I'm a girl, and I prefer to have a little bit of privacy." She came across in court as one of Michael's most ardent fans, appearing to all but worship the star, but the admiration seems to have been somewhat one-sided: the truth, as she sensationally admitted, was that her brother spent vastly more time than she did in Michael's bedroom.

Another girl-child said to have slept alone with Michael was his niece

35yrs

Brandi Jackson, daughter of his eldest brother, Jackie, and former sister-in-law Enid. Enid came to Michael's defence in December 1993, on his return to the US. "I allowed my little girl to spend night after night with Michael in his big bed," Enid reportedly said, "I trusted him completely. He is like a little child. I know they are saying terrible things about him, but my daughter shared his bed for years and I know absolutely nothing ever went on... She's told me he never, ever touched her. Brandi would tell me if anything bad went on...Brandi said to me the other day, 'Why are they saying all these things about Uncle Michael? He would never hurt children.'"[194]

Brandi, aged eleven at the time, had appeared in Michael's *Black or White* and *Heal the World* videos. Enid described it as a "kid sister" relationship. "When you know Michael you realise he gets on much better with children than with adults." On weekends at his ranch, "They would play in the amusement park, on the ranch, or on the video games in his bedroom." When it got late, Enid revealed, Michael would appear in a fluffy Mickey Mouse romper suit and go to bed with Brandi – he on one side, she on the other.

Enid painted a picture of wacky, charming eccentricity, and given that nobody – not the police, nor any children, nor insider gossip – has ever said anything about a weakness Michael might have had for little girls, we have no reason to suppose "anything happened". But did he ever *really* go to bed with her? Neither Enid nor Brandi testified in 2005. It looks as though Enid's story was no more than a convenient fable designed to make Michael look like an indiscriminate, "childishly innocent" bed-hopper, and hence to obscure what was in reality a single-minded obsession with boys. If he had really been going to bed with Brandi "for years", as claimed, it is hard to imagine no one else – domestic staff, for instance – would have come forward to confirm the story.

That has not happened. What we have instead from staff is an utterly damning claim by Orietta Murdoch, who was assigned to deal with letters and photographs from Michael's young fans. Porter quotes her thus:

> I felt bad seeing Michael separate the photos and reading the letters he saw with children's handwriting. Black kids and kids older than thirteen didn't interest him. And when he was reading a letter and realised that it was from a little girl, he threw it in the trash. He kept and took to his room only the photos and letters from white, Latin and Asian children. As for the rest, he

told us it was useless to answer them, so we had to fake his signature."[195]

A note of caution is once again in order here. Porter tells us Murdoch was sacked and so it is possible to dismiss her attack, like a good many others on Jackson, as the revenge taken by a disgruntled former employee. A black woman by racial origin but of fairly light skin colour, Murdoch is said to have filed a complaint on 29 January 1991 with the Equal Employment Department of California. She claimed she had been intimidated and fired for being black. Her immediate boss, housekeeper Norma Staikos, had allegedly hired her thinking she was a Latina but discovered otherwise after seeing Murdoch's much darker sister. The startling allegation that Michael not only had a preference for lighter-skinned children but was prepared to countenance discrimination against people of his own race finds a measure of support in the writings of another sacked employee, Michael's former manager Bob Jones, as we shall see. For the moment, though, we are concerned solely with what – if true – would have been a heartless form of discrimination against the little girls among his fans.[196] Even so, we should be alert to the unfairly negative spin Murdoch puts on things. She says "we had to fake his signature" while failing to point out that Michael in those days must have been getting thousands of letters from young fans, which would have made the task of answering them all personally quite impossible. Must we make a monster out of him for using staff to help in this task? The Pope has plenty of fan mail, too, and by this demanding yardstick he would never make it to heaven either.

We have now reviewed Michael's relationships with children, girls as well as boys, up until the scandal over Jordie Chandler. Next we need to look in some detail at a range of related allegations that were being made at the time, principally by members of Michael's staff and his sister La Toya.

CHAPTER SIX

Tabloid Tattlers

Children of the world, we'll do it
With song and dance and innocent bliss
And the soft caress of a loving kiss
We'll do it.

The "we'll do it" bit in Michael's poem "Children of the World" disappointingly (for scandal seekers) refers strictly to such uncontroversial stuff as making sandcastles and floating boats, plus some more ambitious tricks that might have parents worried for their kids' safety –

We'll touch the stars, embrace the moon...
Ride the rainbow the cloud the storm

but otherwise gives them little cause to be reaching for the phone to the child protection authorities.[197] All the same, the air of childlike innocence in Michael's real-life involvement with children did not always convince everyone. In the story, it took a child to see – or rather to say – that the emperor was wearing no clothes. In Michael's Neverland empire, where the children were not always wearing much either, it took a Mexican gardener to make some down-to-earth observations; a gardener not poetic enough to understand why making sandcastles and riding rainbows should so often necessitate "The soft caress of a loving kiss"; a gardener who saw a worm in the bud.

His complaint to social workers that Michael was molesting youngsters was lodged back in May 1992, over a year before the Chandler allegations, according to a press report sourced to one Mary Comstock, programme manager with Santa Barbara county department of child services. It led to the singer being put under surveillance.[198] The gardener reportedly told the authorities that Michael was engaged in "unwholesome activities with children". He said he had seen Jackson hugging, fondling and video-taping a number of youngsters who had stayed as guests. He told how some of these activities had taken place in special hidden places, such as the hot tub, which could not be overlooked – except, presumably, by the gardener himself, perhaps peering through the bushes.

On one occasion a young boy from Los Angeles who was a frequent visitor at the ranch had been invited to Michael's private theatre to watch films. The gardener told the social workers he happened to walk in because he wanted to ask Jackson something. He saw Michael fondling the boy. "As I entered the room they jumped apart and Jackson was furious with me for entering the room at all," he said. There was a showdown. He was "threatened and ordered to leave". Later he was told that what he had witnessed was "not at all what it appeared to be". The child had been upset and afraid and Michael was "just trying to comfort him".

Nothing further was heard of this Mexican gardener, but another one – yes, another Mexican gardener, of whom there are many in California – was later implicated in a quite separate Jackson boy story. Diane Dimond tells of Michael's friendship with the young son of a neighbour's Mexican gardener when he was still living with his parents at their Hayvenhurst home in Encino, California, in the mid-1980s. She says that "after receiving a generous cheque from Michael Jackson, the gardener's entire family suddenly packed up and moved back to Mexico".[199] This was one of a number of cheques Michael's sister La Toya would claim were made out in suspicious circumstances to the parents of young boys with whom he had been close.

But these gardeners' allegations are small potatoes compared to the bumper crop that sprouted up in the hothouse atmosphere that followed the Chandler story.

First of the season were produced by former Neverland estate manager, Mark Quindoy and his wife Faye, who used to cook for Michael. They had been with him for two years until 1991 and had made a new life for themselves in the Philippines after leaving because, as reported in the *Mail on Sunday*, they had not liked what they saw going on.[200] The following week the *News of the World* carried a lengthy account of the couple, who told how they saw a constant stream of young boys sleeping with Michael in his bed. On one occasion when a boy's mother turned up, an employee joked: "Well, here's Michael's mother-in-law!"[201]

Quindoy said there was one little boy staying at the ranch whose mother had one of the guest cottages on the grounds. One day she asked him to take Michael and the boy for a drive towards Solvang, a Danish-style town near Santa Barbara. One of the tourist attractions there was a massive doll's house that fascinated Michael, and he wanted to show it to the child. He and the boy sat in the back, as Quindoy drove the Chevrolet Blazer.

> As we drove in the darkness, I looked in my rear-view mirror and was astonished to see that Michael had his arms around the boy, kissing him passionately. It was just like a boy kissing a girl in the back seat. The boy wasn't protesting – but he just sat there stiffly, without moving, while Michael kissed him on the lips. Then Michael began to kiss him everywhere – his neck, head, arms, shoulders and body. I was utterly stunned. I suppose I should have expected it, knowing that they shared a bed, but it still shocked me. I was appalled that he could do that to a seven-year-old boy. I honestly think Michael didn't realise I could see. But it wasn't as if I was snooping. In traffic I had to check my mirror, and sometimes the illumination of street lamps or passing cars meant I could easily see what Michael was doing.

This particular boy spent a number of weeks at Neverland, said the Quindoys. When he went on holiday abroad another boy, aged nine, came, spending up to nineteen days at a time, staying every night in Michael's room. Michael and the boy would spend up to two days in the bedroom together without coming out. On most days they would not get out of bed until two in the afternoon. Food would be sent in, room-service style. One required item was organic mineral water. Quindoy had to drive a hundred miles to Los Angeles for supplies. The tray would be left at the door, announced by a knock, and then as Quindoy watched, the door would open and a white-gloved hand would reach out and slowly slide the tray inside.

By pure coincidence this page of the book you are now reading was drafted on April Fool's Day. Now why should such a thought come to mind? Your author is here simply reporting in an absolutely straightforward fashion, with no intention of fooling anyone, what a newspaper credited

Quindoy with saying. All the same, can we fail to be irresistibly reminded of the fine tradition in the British press of spoof April Fool's Day reports? – reports that invariably begin quite plausibly, but then become increasingly bizarre and amazing, until at last they push credulity to its hilarious breaking point.

The *News of the World* version of the Quindoys' story appeared in September, not April, but what we have heard so far follows the pattern just outlined. Like the gardener's sober account it begins with realistic detail that need not strike us as all that odd, having heard so much else about Michael. (We might pause to wonder, though, whether a gardener would ever need to ask Michael anything so urgently that he would intrude on his privacy indoors. As we shall see, Michael was "Mr Jackson" to staff, and people generally knew their place.) The really difficult stuff to swallow begins, does it not, with the bit about Michael and the boy not emerging from a bedroom for two whole days? And as for the theatrical touch about the gloved hand emerging, isn't this just a fraction over the top? Michael's famous single white glove was a stage trade mark. The thought of him wearing it to bed is like a child's vision of the Queen, forever burdened with an enormous crown! Never mind, the story is just too good to miss. This is how Quindoy continued:

> The boy and Michael never left each other's side. Michael used to gaze at him in adoring fashion, and the boy – who was really not old enough to know any better – seemed to enjoy it. He used to climb to the top of the stairs and slide down the banisters where Michael was waiting at the bottom to catch him. Sometimes they'd play on the pirate ship Michael has, or on the suspension bridge in the grounds of the house. On other occasions Michael would put the boy – and other boy guests – into a special harness contraption that swings down on a pulley across a piece of water. He'd always be waiting to catch them at the other end.
>
> I never saw Jackson or the boys naked, but frequently saw all of them in their underwear. One day Michael told me that he planned to go into the spa [Jacuzzi] with the nine-year-old. That was his coded way of saying that neither I nor any of the staff should go near the pool and barbecue areas where the spa is situated. Perhaps I shouldn't have done what I did, but my curiosity got the better of me. I watched from a position where they couldn't see me.

Question: According to the gardener there were secret places available to Michael that could not be overlooked. If on this occasion he did not want staff to see him with the boy, why didn't he go to one of these spots? Also: Why was the spa area apparently not one of these secret places? He could have had it designed and built to any specifications he liked, including being impossible to overlook. Indeed the gardener said the "hot tub" could not be overlooked. Obviously he wasn't talking about an ordinary indoor bath. But let's not spoil a good story any further:

> [Michael and the boy were both] wearing white underpants, and sat on the edge of the hot tub with their feet in the water. They were talking, and then I saw Michael lean over and put his hand down the front of the boy's underpants. He kept it there for as long as I watched. The boy didn't protest or try to stop Michael. I was utterly shocked. Michael and this boy acted like lovers. They threw food at each other, and even had screaming rows over games or toys...
>
> The boys' parents were separated, but often arrived with their son together, had a meal and then the father left. Sometimes Michael would put the woman up at a local Holiday Inn, sometimes she stayed in one of the guest cottages. I know that the mother was given a lavish gift and I was told the father got one too. It seemed to me that it was a way of paying them off.

Quindoy says staff were disturbed by the way Michael touched a boy aged three who stayed at the ranch: "...it gave us all the creeps. He would lie the kid down and stroke the whole length of his body, from top to toe, with the tips of his fingers." A woman executive assistant had a son aged two and a half who often accompanied her to work. One day other staff saw her red with rage. She claimed she had caught Michael with her son, and was so outraged that she threatened to kill him if it happened again. Quindoy said: "Once a senior executive of the Jackson organisation, who happened to be at the ranch, told one of the staff who was a parent, 'Look, do yourselves a favour – never leave a child alone with Michael, it's not a good idea.'"

The Quindoys say they kept secret journals while at Neverland, recording what happened there, saying they would reveal the contents to newspapers for £170,000. What was now being revealed, they said, was only the tip of the iceberg. Quindoy said he and his wife would sit down each night, when things had quietened down, and write in longhand an account of what had gone on. They noted the weather, who had come and gone, their feelings about the mood and atmosphere, and their reflections on what it was like working for Michael Jackson. They noted visits by guest stars such as Marlon Brando and Michael's young friends. That meant that if necessary they would be able to give the police the dates on which any named individual stayed at Neverland, in which bedroom and how long they stayed for.

The existence of the journals was confirmed in a CNN TV news report in which Mark and Faye Quindoy were filmed turning the pages and observing their hand-written entries. Quindoy said: "I'm not holding these diaries over Michael's head. In fact there are certain things that one didn't record because it would have been impossible to sleep at night, but I believe the journals would be helpful. They are a record of the strange things we witnessed at Neverland."

Some of those "strange things" fall well within the time-honoured Wacko Jacko tradition. Quindoy: "Michael said he hated it when flowers died. It made him cry. He told us that if a flower withers, he calls one of his thirty gardeners and demands they replace it immediately. He turned to me with tears in his eyes and said, 'You know I hate to see pretty things dying. I wished they lived for ever, like in the movies.'"

One day Quindoy found Michael sitting cross-legged on the floor, tearing up £50,000 in $1,000 bills and tossing them in the air like confetti. The estate manager tried to stop him but he just started laughing and giggled, saying, "Oh Mark, it's only money". To Quindoy, the superstar was like a child: "He hadn't ripped it up maliciously – he'd done it because the pieces looked pretty when he threw them in the air." Mark Quindoy claimed Michael would eat only meals named after his favourite cartoon characters, and his wife Faye said: "I made all his food and christened it – Goofy salad, Minnie Mouse milkshake and Mickey Mouse cake. When Liz Taylor visited he wanted Pluto pie and Peter Pan hot dogs."

Any readers who only "caught up with" Michael Jackson during the publicity over his trial, and with no great awareness of the Wacko Jacko background, will find these non-sexual anecdotes every bit as incredible as the April Fool's Day story about the white glove. Jacko fans know better. They heard so many weird stories about their idol down the years that even the most improbable tales became harder to resist – including ones they had flatly refused to believe at first. While some fans were resolutely sceptical, putting all "negative" stories down to the mischief-making media, the sheer quantity of Wacko yarns has meant that for many fans weirdness became an accepted part of Jacko lore, with fact and fantasy bound up inextricably together.

Randy Taraborrelli suggests in his biography that some of the early oddball stories were publicity stunts by Jackson's people, but that Michael started to worry when they went too far, especially when the media, sensing the mood, began to feel they could get away with making up their own stuff. In America, for instance, the *National Enquirer* ran a story saying Michael often saw God materialising out of a cloud of smoke while he performed onstage. *The Star* said he had fallen in love with Princess Diana and wanted her to star in his next video – an accusation Taraborrelli described with arch understatement as "unlikely".[202] As we have seen, Michael had expressed a keen interest in Diana's young sons, William and Harry, especially William, and Taraborrelli might have added that the boy princes were much more sure-fire candidates for his affection and interest. A cartoon by Griffin, in *The People* was to take up the theme when the Chandler scandal broke. A horrified Princess Diana was depicted with her hair standing on end when her sons said to her, "Well Mum, since you've offered to take us anywhere in the world, we've decided we want to visit Michael Jackson."[203]

Taraborrelli told us that Michael actually enjoyed some of the untrue stories, one being a claim that his pop rival Prince used extra-sensory perception to drive Jacko's pet chimp Bubbles crazy. The story, in the *Enquirer*, had Michael saying, "What kind of sicko would mess with a monkey? This is the final straw." Michael's reaction to the yarn? "I never saw him laugh so hard," an associate told Taraborrelli.[204]

For a long while Michael must have been just as pleased by all the other apocryphal stories generated about him: every ridiculous tale in circulation made it easier for him to point out that not all witnesses are scrupulously honest, and that they appear to be especially unscrupulous where he is concerned, either because there was money to be made from such dishonesty, or there was some other ulterior motive.

What about the Quindoys? Do we see any such motive there? They admitted, according to the *News of the World*, that they had been trying to sue Michael for more than £200,000, saying he owed them for unpaid wages and overtime.[205] This was why they left, they said, contradicting the earlier *Mail on Sunday* version which had put forward an altogether nobler motive: they were concerned solely for the moral welfare of the children.[206]

It was not to be the only contradiction. The very next day after the lengthy *News of the World* account, the *Sun* reported Quindoy backtracking. Now he was denying the detailed allegations, saying "These are creations." Yet the man was still asking £170,000 for further revelations!

Or should that be further "creative writing"! He added helpfully: "I can only say there were aberrations, some abnormalities, some things that were not normal."[207]

Evidently the enterprising Mr Quindoy had taken to marketing his work in two categories, fiction and non-fiction, without worrying too much about them getting mixed up. This was clearly a man who had missed his vocation in life: he could have been a great tabloid newspaper editor.[208]

These opportunistic machinations by Quindoy do not enable us to write him off as a witness however. Just because a man tells you he is lying does not mean you have to believe him! Two of his letters were soon to emerge which showed that he viewed Michael as a danger to children *before* the public scandal. Both were written before Jordan Chandler's allegations and two months before the police probe was revealed. In one letter, written in June 1993, Quindoy warned Michael that staff were spreading rumours about him molesting children. In another note, complaining he was owed overtime pay of £180,000, he wrote to an aide threatening to reveal the singer was a danger to children. He said he would tell the whole world about Jackson, adding: "Remember when you told us...on several occasions not to trust any male child alone with Michael in a room?"[209]

This last comment is especially interesting. The two letters, written at a time when news of Evan Chandler's manoeuvrings could well have become hot gossip around Neverland, could easily be seen as Quindoy preparing the ground for his own media coup, giving him some documentation that would look authentic. Such a view, however, demands that the aide he wrote to in the second note was a co-conspirator, for how else could his warning about Michael be discounted otherwise? It is also interesting that those warnings, if genuine, would appear to go back to well before June (the phrase "Remember when you told us..." implies something said a while back), and hence well before any gossip was in the air about Evan Chandler's intentions.

The police took the Quindoys seriously, regardless of any public backtracking. Two detectives went to the Philippines to interview them.[210] The couple told their story to the police, though doubtless not in all its colourful *News of the World* glory, and were said to have passed a lie detector test.[211] Publicly, they were now saying they never saw Michael have sex with boys, but they did find children's underwear on his bedroom floor, and they recalled one child who would stay in his bedroom for "twenty four hours or more". Mark Quindoy had seen Michael kissing a boy in the garden. "He was fondling and kissing him all around, running his hands between the kid's thighs. He was putting his hands where they normally should not be."[212] This was a much more restrained account than we heard at first. The police could not call Mark Quindoy as a witness for Jackson's trial in 2005, however: he had died by then.

A man with a much odder motive than Quindoy's for dishing the dirt on Michael was a Korean by the name of Kenneth Choi. In more than one sense he had been a man with a mission. There had been a time, beginning in 1988, when his life was dedicated to just one task, which his mission control masters had decided must be achieved at any cost: Michael Jackson had to be persuaded to perform in Korea. Choi's controllers were the Korea-based Unification Church, under the direction of the Reverend Sun Myung Moon. In other words, the "Moonies".

By the 1970s, the Moonies had gained a substantial presence in America, attracting controversy as a result of their alleged use of brainwashing techniques on recruits, and alarming parents who saw youngsters being persuaded to give up their lifestyle, move into communes and sell flowers at airports. Despite all the disapproval, the church grew and prospered, and was a rich, powerful organisation well before Choi's mission began.

Why was Michael Jackson so important to them? The reason seems laughable in view of what happened to Michael. It is almost as though God decided to have a malicious little chuckle at the expense of the manipulative Moonies, mocking their efforts to broaden the base of their appeal. For what they now needed was respectability, and a connection with Michael and his family appeared to hold out the prospect of just that. The Jacksons were then seen as a clean-living, wholesome, religious family. Michael himself was widely held up as an example to the young – a singer who had successfully resisted the temptations of drugs and casual sex. Kenneth Choi said it himself, in an interview in 1991: "In my country Michael Jackson is considered a special, unusual person. We admire his spiritual qualities. We would never, for instance, have asked Madonna to perform. To us, she does not have the same character and morals as Michael Jackson."[213]

Having failed to make headway at Michael's own office in 1988, Choi turned to the family, attempting to gain the support of Michael's parents, Katherine and Joseph. Perhaps through them a Jackson family concert could be arranged. This was to prove an extremely expensive blind alley, for what Choi failed to understand was that Michael was not at all keen on the idea of a family concert, or of any business dealings involving his family: he had encountered some dreadful experiences trying to work with them in the not far distant past and had no intention of hitting similar problems again.

After a whole year of preliminaries, including a trip to Korea by Katherine and Joseph, the Moonies embarked on a strategy of throwing money at the problem: in February 1989 $1 million was offered to anyone who could secure Michael's signature on a contract to play in Korea.[214] It didn't work, but a month later, with Jackson family help, Choi managed to contact Michael personally by phone from the family home at Encino. According to Taraborrelli, he tried a trick straight from Michael's own book: he burst into tears on the phone and threatened to kill himself if Michael did not cooperate. He just begged and begged. Michael finally agreed to meet him – but not right away.

Before that meeting was destined to take place, "a new, Moonie-induced decadence," as Taraborrelli put it, "began spreading like a cancer throughout the family".[215] Joe was given a Rolls Royce Corniche. Katherine got $35,000. Jermaine Jackson got a Range Rover, because he was felt to have great influence over his younger brother Michael. Michael himself got a Rolls. Other people were getting thousands of dollars just for knowing Michael's family and because this might have some remote bearing on matters. Security man Bill Bray got over half a million dollars "and no-one even remembers now why or how he got it".[216]

In the end this seeming madness appeared to pay off for Choi. By June 1989 Michael had been induced to sign a contract to play in Korea – but the whole deal then fell apart when the Rev Moon himself decided that the amount agreed upon for Michael's fee was too much. Michael was even sued by the Moonies' newspaper, the *Segye Times* for the return of money and gifts. Michael counter-sued. In an atmosphere of such litigious acrimony, Choi might have been expected to slink off home, head bowed, a broken and defeated man. But not a bit of it. Instead he began to befriend Jackson personally, hoping against hope that an acceptable deal could finally be struck.

But how? He had thrown millions of dollars at the problem. He had tried everything. He had even threatened to kill himself. What else could he possibly do to get through to Michael? Was there anything he had to offer that Michael really wanted? There was. His own son. Kenneth Choi does not admit that he used his own little boy, Elbert, then aged three, to entice Michael. Indeed, the thought may have appalled him, had it occurred as a conscious policy option. He did say, though, that he knew of Michael's "obsessive interest" in children. He admitted he was warned not to leave his child alone with Michael. Nevertheless he did exactly that, as he told the *News of the World* in 1992, after the relationship had finally gone sour and Michael had broken with the Choi family. The paper did not run the story at first, but decided to do so in August 1993 in the light of the other allegations that were surfacing against Michael. He said:

> I can never forgive myself for leaving my son Elbert alone with Michael all that time. Michael always insisted that little Elbert sleep in one of his secret rooms. I knew that Michael's interest with children was almost obsessive. I knew because I spent many, many days at Michael's ranch with him. During the months we spent there one of Michael's top executives, a man very close to him, warned me, "Don't leave your son alone with Michael." I've seen Michael take my little son into his private theatre to watch movies. I've seen how distressed my wife was, how she used to cry and beg me to take the family home to Korea. I wanted to kill myself because I suspected my child was in some kind of danger, and yet I left him alone at the ranch. I can only sum up Michael's sex life by saying that a nine-year-old boy does not think about sex. Michael is half genius and half nine-year-old boy. He's the loneliest person in the world, yet he hates to be alone.[217]

Choi was wrong about one thing. Plenty of nine-year-old boys *do* think about sex. If his aim here is to escape blame for leaving Elbert at risk by half-heartedly suggesting Michael did not think about sex, we are hard put to find it convincing. That Michael's interest in Elbert was intense is beyond doubt from Choi's account: he even asked Choi if he could adopt him. He gave the child gifts of clothes, antique dolls and a personal note saying, "I love you".

Choi does not say what caused the final breach with Jackson. Perhaps Michael could no longer stand the incessant harping on about performing in Korea. Once again, Choi was on the phone to him, still refusing to give up. Again there were tears. Again a suicide threat, but this time with the addition of three chillingly significant words: "Please come to Korea, or I'll kill myself *and my family*." [my emphasis]

Michael did not fall for what turned out to be a bluff, or for the threats that were to follow. Choi allegedly confessed to the paper's reporters that he asked Jackson for "huge sums of money" to hand over photographs and "secrets". He also told the paper that if Michael refused to go to Korea, "I'll expose him and the children who visit him."

It never happened. Instead he went to ground. It is said that in the days before his disappearance he had been drinking too much, using cocaine and heavily in debt. A Korean friend of Choi told the paper that Choi's wife, Mirae, Elbert and their daughter were staying secretly in California in 1993 and were worried about the possibility of being contacted by Michael's investigators. This friend spoke about Elbert: "Michael was only concerned with Elbert visiting the ranch. Kenneth wanted to go to the ranch alone and talk business, but Michael would say, 'Only if you bring Elbert. You'll bring Elbert, okay?' Kenneth's wife Mirae told me that she feared those visits, although she never said why."

It is clear that by 1992 Choi, now an embittered man, was already doing his best to put the boot into Michael by talking to the *News of the World*. He was hinting that there was more dirt to be dished, but how damaging would it have been? He allegedly tried to sell photos he claimed showed Michael dancing with a skeleton, which suggests desperation on his (Choi's) part. Michael had long been said to have an interest in medical matters: his sister La Toya said he once asked a doctor to order a full medical library for him, and another doctor presented him with a pickled brain in a glass jar.[218] Such stories are legion. Having a real skeleton in his cupboard would be nowhere near as damaging to him as a metaphorical one. The worst Choi could come up with was some half-hearted recollection of odd bedroom intimacies between himself and Michael:

> I've been in Michael's bedroom. I've been on his bed, when we've cuddled each other, laughed and cried. I told him I loved him, and he said he loved me. I never told my wife about these meetings in Michael's bedroom. As far as I know Michael has never been with a woman sexually. Michael knew what a powerful and rich figure he was worldwide, and he told me, "Only a woman can destroy me." His bedroom was off limits. When I was at the ranch I was the only person allowed in there. It was always a mess. His clothes were right there on the floor where he took them off. He wears white underwear, briefs and white socks...The bedroom itself is full of mirrors, and Michael makes sure he looks perfect before he goes out into the real world. He never leaves his bedroom without eye and face makeup.[219]

Choi also said Michael would become so lonely that he would take one of his pet chimps to bed with him – hardly the action, if true, of a man who prefers boys and has the power to summon them to his chamber at will, like an oriental potentate of old. If this was an effort to damn Michael he was scraping the barrel. What he was saying here falls well within the Wacko Jacko tradition, the kind of material that may have been a little embarrassing to the star but not particularly damaging – just the pitiful outpourings of a disappointed man.

Choi's ramblings are more interesting for what they do not say than for what they do. If he was as close to Michael as he claims, sharing laughter and tears in the intimacy of his bedroom, is it not remarkable that he did not see more going on between Michael and at least one or two boys? Wade Robson was allegedly Michael's Boy of the Year for 1990, when Choi was building up his friendship. Why do we hear not a word from him about Wade? Didn't he even know about the Australian boy? Was he always at the ranch at a different time from Wade? It appears the only real damage Choi could inflict would be for him to come right out and say he knew Michael abused Elbert – and he would find it difficult to do that without implicating himself as a "panderer", who had effectively prostituted his own son.

Wade's mother nominated Macaulay Culkin as her son's successor to the Boy of the Year title, in 1991. Did Choi have any better luck (in terms of collecting evidence to drag Michael down) by bumping into Macaulay? Well, yes and no. It is plain he was never close enough to reveal anything intimate. The best he could come up with was a video of the *Home Alone* star, showing a not-so-alone Macaulay at Michael's home. "You can see Michael as he's never been seen before," Choi is alleged to have said when trying to flog his wares to the newspaper, "Michael and Macaulay chase each other around. They play games, play with the animals and jump around on the furniture." Hot stuff, eh? Must-see scenes, perhaps, for the avid Jackson (or Macaulay) fan, but nothing to excite the tabloids. The papers did not buy.

Failures of this kind may have been what kept Choi from selling his other Jackson "souvenirs", not, as the *News of the World* suggests, "repeated requests from Jackson's legal team". It looks here as though, in order to build up their own innuendo against Michael, the paper played up the idea that Choi had some really damning material up his sleeve. But his taking to drink and drugs was more the behaviour of a man in despair than one poised to make a fortune by spilling the beans.

Macaulay Culkin was to figure much more prominently in a story told to the police by French chef Philippe LeMarque, who worked at Neverland with his wife Stella for nine months. As early as the autumn of 1991, they claimed, they had been telling friends about Michael's obsession with children, but had been too frightened to go to the police.[220] They said they were eventually sacked because they had asked too many questions about what was going on. The Jackson version was that there was a dispute involving another staff member.[221]

"We've always known what Jackson was like but no-one would believe us," said Stella. "Everyone at the ranch knew about it, but no-one spoke about it. It was crazy." She said the staff were banned from speaking to each other and were forced to sign "gagging contracts" to stop them speaking to the press. Macaulay Culkin became a regular guest in 1991 after Michael invited him over following the success of *Home Alone*. The LeMarques said the parents would sleep in a guest cottage on the estate and Michael would announce "Macaulay is sleeping with me." His parents were told their son was sleeping in a guest room adjoining Michael's bedroom, but Stella recalled: "Macaulay's mother, Pat, didn't like it. But Macaulay was Michael's big love then. He adored him, like a teenager in love."

One night, said Philippe, he saw Michael sexually "abuse" Macaulay. His lawyer Arnold Kessler takes up the story: "My client told the authorities he used a private entrance to Michael's room one day, and walked in on Michael and the Culkin kid. Michael had called him on the intercom and requested some French fries. It was late and the house was quiet. My client used the private entrance to the video room. He saw Michael sitting next to Culkin. They were playing a video game and he was groping Culkin. My client turned round and pretended not to have seen, but it made him sick. He couldn't believe his eyes."[222] In one colourful tabloid version, LeMarque was quoted as saying he was so shocked by what he saw that he nearly dropped the French fries – a claim the chef would repeat under oath from the witness box a dozen years later.

As for being made sick, some of us feel sickened by the language lawyers, police and social workers use to distance themselves from the ordinary humanity of an event and the people it involves. We heard from Jordie Chandler's social worker that "minor did this" and "minor said that". Now we have a hard-bitten, disparaging reference to "the Culkin kid", as if to say, "I wouldn't touch the little brat with a barge pole. It gives me the creeps just to mention his name." Thus is concern expressed for children who have supposedly been abused: whereas the "abuser" adored the child, "like a teenager in love", spending hours amusing him, playing with him, being interested in him and at the centre of his world, those who see it as their job to butt in and bust up such tenderness can talk about "the Culkin kid" like something they stepped in on the pavement.

The lawyerly embellishments about feeling sick failed to figure in another version of the story when LeMarque told it in his own words. This time, significantly, he described Michael as "caressing" the boy, not "groping".[223] What a difference a word makes! What a difference to the way we picture the event and judge what is going on! In everyday usage it is often a young woman who makes the distinction: she might loathe being groped at work by the boss but love going home to caresses from her boyfriend: the touching in question may be anatomically identical, but its meaning to her is hugely different. We might ask who is best placed to say which description best fits such events. Is it the woman on the receiving end of the gropes/caresses, or somebody who was not even there at the time but merely heard a third party's description of the event? If Macaulay Culkin wanted to say that Michael "groped" him, that would be one thing. For some lawyer snarling about "the Culkin kid" to do so was another.

LeMarque's own observation – as opposed to his lawyer's – does not support any claim that Macaulay felt as though he was being molested. LeMarque says nothing about the boy looking distressed or uncomfortable; nor was it apparently in any way an erotic experience for him, even if it was for Michael. In fact it was scarcely an experience at all. The important thing for him at that moment was the video game. LeMarque says he was so transfixed by it that it was as if "he didn't even notice" Michael touching him. To anyone who knows anything about young boys this is very believable: kids do get carried away with their games. Concentration can be total. Wild paedophiles couldn't drag them away from a new personal best. It is a point that also puts the entire abuse question into perspective. As adults, we are inclined these days to work ourselves into a terrible moral panic over "abuse", when what we are talking about may be a trivial matter to the children themselves. This does a disservice to children in two ways: (1) It devalues the concept of abuse. It falsely puts sexual assault (forced or coerced sexual activity) on the same level as gentle and desired touching, which need be no more traumatic than the contact children have with their own underwear; (2) insofar as they are learning about adult values, children can come to feel harmed and abused years after a friendship they had regarded positively at the time. If adults were less quick to label otherwise harmless touching as abusive, children would be less likely to feel abused.

So what did Little Mac think about all this? He was the one whose feelings ought to have counted – and not after being worked over by social workers telling him that if he had been touched he had therefore been abused. We should remember that his parents were powerful people in Hollywood. Mac never had to stay at Neverland for any reason other than that he liked it there and liked Michael's company. In public too, he has had only good things to say about Michael. Here is how, as a child, he described a typical Sunday outing to Neverland: "My parents go home. I spend the rest of the day with him watching videos and playing games. I suppose it's a bit strange that he's chosen someone like me for a friend – but I'm really happy he has."[224]

Macaulay's name turned up early in the Chandler allegations when he was cited as a "collateral witness".[225] No doubt Jordie had known Mac had been a friend of Michael's and told his inquisitors so. Not surprisingly, the police moved swiftly to interview the young actor. He told them, "Michael is one of my best friends. He is affectionate but he never touched or interfered with me."[226] As youngsters, the Jackson brothers were noted for playing tricks on each other, a family trait that lives on in the most famous of them, according to Mac. Of Michael he has said: "He has every practical joke you can think of. He's not weird – just great fun."[227] Once asked how he and Michael spent their time in each other's company he responded "Oh, you know, we just goof off together."[228] UK readers should note that this American expression does not mean what it sounds like!

In the wake of the Chandler allegations Mac's parents were highly supportive.[229] In late August '93 the *Sun* had Pat Culkin saying of Macaulay and his younger brother Kieran, who also went to Neverland: "I feel perfectly happy when they visit Michael. I know they are safe with him. He is the perfect gentleman." This was presented as a contemporary, up-to-date quote, but that did not prevent other sections of the press telling an entirely different story. The *Sunday Telegraph*, for instance, asserted that Mac and other friends had "not given Jacko a squeak of support".[230] The *Sun* even bizarrely backtracked on what it had said the day before, citing Macaulay among "silent friends" who were snubbing Michael, even though they said a spokesman told them, "Macaulay's as shocked as everyone by what has been said."[231]

Stella LeMarque said Pat Culkin had been anxious over Michael, though that had not stopped many visits to Neverland plus a holiday for Mac in Bermuda with him. On that occasion he was not so much left "home alone" as "away alone", or at least without his parents or other family.

Instead, aged around eleven, he shared a vacation with the Goldstein family, of Orlando, Florida, after becoming friends with young Brock Goldstein, whom he had met as a neighbour near the Universal lot when he was filming *My Girl*. The Goldstein parents would allegedly complain that Michael – enterprisingly invited along by Mac – spent a lot of his time solely in Mac's company, ignoring his host and going off around the island with the young film star. Brock's mother warned Mac against being alone with Michael but the boy took no notice. At all events, the trip could not have gone ahead without Mac's parents having full confidence in Michael at that time – or, at least, full confidence after taking certain precautions: Bob Jones tells us Mac had a "travelling chaperone in Bermuda" who was "quite strict and would not allow the King and Mac to sleep together in Michael's suite. This didn't sit well with the King, something Michael made a point of mentioning to me."[232]

Somewhat later, by early 1993, the confidence level appeared to have slipped a good deal lower.[233] By this time, according to *Today*, Mac's mother "went beserk" when her boy was allocated a dressing room next to Michael's for Bill Clinton's presidential inaugural concert in January. An unnamed organiser said: "We all presumed Michael and Macaulay were big buddies and put them together. But we were left in no doubt that this was certainly not the case any longer." Mac was immediately given another dressing room – nobody dared ask why such a big issue was being made of it.

By April 1994 the police were interested in talking to Macaulay again, to ask "why the relationship seemed to terminate abruptly", according to the *National Enquirer*.[234] This had not been the version previously put out. On 27 August 1993, just the day after Mac's thirteenth birthday, the *Daily Mirror* had spoken of him receiving "secret dancing lessons" from Michael, but claimed the friendship had "drifted apart" as Mac's time came to be more and more taken up by a private tutor.[235]

A question mark thus still hangs over what really happened to end things between Macaulay and Michael, and whether or not Pat Culkin's public support for the beleaguered singer truly reflected her private thoughts. If she had come to have doubts about Michael even before the Chandler crisis broke, what might have caused them? The LeMarques said that everyone at Neverland knew "what Jackson was like", so Pat could have caught some of the gossip or been given a discreet warning at any time. It is conceivable that Mac himself complained to his mother, but we now have persuasive evidence to the contrary: in his own testimony as an adult at

Michael's trial, the young Mr Culkin was the most staunch of defence witnesses: he and Michael had never been less than good friends; his most stinging barb of criticism was that Michael had not been as skilful as the kids at Neverland when it came to playing video games.

Could the alarm have been raised for Pat in a more literal sense? Philippe LeMarque said a fire alarm went off in the middle of the night once while Macaulay was staying at Neverland. "When the chief fireman arrived," he said, "Stella and I were there and Jackson came downstairs. The fireman was trying to account for everyone and he asked him where Macaulay was sleeping. Michael snapped at him, 'What does that matter. What has that got to do with you? Why are you asking me that?'"[236]

There is no need to doubt LeMarque's honesty over this particular incident but there is good reason to believe that if Mac had been in Michael's bedroom that night it would have neither surprised nor shocked his mother. Mac would later testify that right from the first times when he and his family were guests at Neverland, when he was aged nine or ten, he would sometimes sleep in Michael's room. His father, Kit, and possibly his mother on another occasion, had come up to the room and seen that the two were sharing a bed. "They never really saw it as an issue," said Mac. They had never spoken to him about it and so far as he was aware had not discussed it among themselves. The family also continued as guests at Neverland long after the Chandler scandal made serious allegations against Michael a matter of public knowledge, and Mac would still "on occasion" share a bed with him right through his thirteenth year. After that the pair remained on the best of terms but went their separate ways for some years.

Macaulay was not the only boy in whom Michael interested himself, according to LeMarque. He would invite groups of children to play in his video arcade at Neverland, and pick out ones he fancied for closer attention.[237] LeMarque, reportedly said he once saw Michael with his hand in a ten-year-old boy's pants after one of these fun days. His wife Stella said she saw Michael "groping" (this time that word is the reporter's) another young boy in his private cinema, with the boy's mother sitting a couple of rows in front. As for where child guests used to sleep, LeMarque said: "There's a stairway inside Michael's room which leads to the guest room, where he says the children sleep. But they never do. The guest bed is never disturbed."

Which children? The LeMarques did not say, but there were soon to be other witnesses who would add to the impression that Michael's interest in boys went well beyond a particular favourite Boy of the Year. I will return to that theme in a moment, but we cannot leave the LeMarques without noting that, like the Quindoys, their credibility rating was widely regarded as sub-prime, to put it politely. Gossip columnist Roger Friedman cited "tabloid story broker" Paul Barresi, who alleged that the LeMarques changed their Culkin tale, "making it exponentially worse as the bidding increased" from the newspapers.[238] So those French fries might not have been nearly dropped, after all! I offer no definitive judgment on whether or not there was a significant element of truth in this couple's version of reality. Readers can make up their own minds whether their stories were just fantasies made up to make money or whether they form part of a pattern that gains in credibility as a wealth of accounts builds up from a variety of sources.

A word of caution is in order though. Such patterns can be seriously misleading when suspicions are founded upon nothing more than a mass of dubious evidence: if each individual allegation is trash, what you end up with is a large pile of trash, not a solid case. This is essentially what happened, scandalously, in a series of late 20th century witch-hunts for paedophiles in Britain's children's homes. Investigations at that time relied disastrously on "corroboration by volume". In these cases, large sums of money available from the state as compensation for victims of abuse helped generate a formidable volume of allegations against staff at the homes. Like the tabloid dollar, this money tainted the claims in question, some of which were later shown to be false – but only after the lives of the accused had been wrecked as they were smeared in the news reports and dragged through the courts.

However, the *dissimilarities* between allegations tainted by the tabloid dollar in Michael's case and by state compensation in respect of UK children's homes, are even more striking. The two are vastly different. Like the infamous panic over abuse in American day-care centres, of which the McMartin Pre-School case was just the most well-known of many, the children's home furore in the UK involved the use of inquiry methods and evidence whole orders of magnitude less credible than anything to be seen in relation to Michael. And whereas many of the day-care and children's home staff who were accused and even wrongly convicted had previously conducted themselves in a manner utterly above reasonable suspicion, Michael could not make a similar claim: his admitted practice of bed-sharing with a large number of boys over many years just cannot be talked out of significance. Nor should we forget that in the Chandler case the formal statements of the boy in question were allegedly corroborated not by volume but by hard, if the expression will be forgiven, forensic evidence that Jordie was intimately acquainted with Michael Jackson's penis.[239]

In these circumstances, it would be wrong to automatically discount any allegation solely on account of a possible money factor. The sensible approach is to look at all such stories against the wider background of what we know about Michael and then – if we wish, and if we feel able to do so fairly – come to our conclusions after taking all relevant information into account, including tabloid sources.

Let us turn then, to another of those sources. Earlier we met Leroy Thomas, a security guard at the Jackson family home, Hayvenhurst, Encino, who claimed that Michael had ordered him to retrieve a Polaroid picture of a naked boy from his bathroom and destroy it. He had been one of five guards sacked in February 1993, because, they say, they had "seen too much". Michael's lawyer says they were laid off "for an entirely different reason".[240]

Bringing an action for wrongful dismissal, they filed a joint statement to Los Angeles Superior Court in which they said Michael would bring young boys to Hayvenhurst at all hours of the night, when his own parents were out of the way. In the words of their statement:

> During the years of the plaintiffs' employment, on many occasions, plaintiffs witnessed defendant Jackson, at all hours of the night, bring young boys, one at a time, into the compound under what can only be described as unusual circumstances. On some occasions Jackson would telephone in advance to find out if his parents were home or away or, if home, if they had retired for the night. If the parents were gone or had retired he would then arrive alone with a young boy typically appearing to be between nine and fourteen years of age. Upon arrival at the grounds he would drive to an area near his suite in the compound and disappear with the young boy into his suite sometimes for several hours, sometimes for the entire night. On at least one occasion he secreted a young Asian boy believed to be somewhere between nine and fourteen years of age in the guard shack on the premises instructing the plaintiffs there present to keep the young boy there until Jackson later called for him. After Jackson's parents left the premises, Jackson called to have the boy escorted to his room.[241]

Thomas later said he never saw Michael spend the night with an adult, man or woman, but he regularly had children staying with him.[242] Another of the five, Morris Williams, a security supervisor for Hayvenhurst, who also worked at Neverland, said Michael "maybe felt that his family was critical of him hanging around kids. Maybe he just got tired of it all. That could be one of the reasons that he would call ahead and make sure no-one was there."[243]

Interviewed on America's *Hard Copy* TV show, Leroy Thomas estimated twenty boys had stayed the night with Michael. He would sit with them in a Jacuzzi and watch TV, or entertain them in the games room. "I don't know what goes on in his room," he said. "But when you look at a grown man with a young kid sitting in a Jacuzzi, it will make you think, like, why would you want to do that?"[244]

Victor Gutierrez reckons he knows something about the fun and games that went on. He tells us that when Jordie Chandler was at Neverland on 11 March 1993, he met two other boys, Eddie and Frank Cascio. Michael had a surprise for all of them: a slot machine in his bedroom with $100 notes inside. There were two special rules: one, the game had to be played in the nude so that, according to Michael, "no one could hide trick devices in their clothing"; two, kids who played could not tell anyone.[245]

Morris Williams said: "Some parents would drop kids off at the front gate. They wanted to say their kid was with Michael, and they were so happy they don't even understand what can happen."

Once the five former security guards – the so-called new Jackson Five, or the Hayvenhurst Five – had spoken out, speculation centred on the "Asian boy" they had referred to: could this have been Sean Lennon, young son of the slain Beatles legend John Lennon? Was this the child, dark-haired and almond-eyed, his father had lovingly celebrated in the song "Beautiful Boy"?

There was good reason to think so. Michael and Sean had often been seen together in public in the 1980s, typically popping up at Broadway musicals. The pair were known to "hang out" with each other for years, pretty much exactly when Sean was between the ages of nine and fourteen, the age range identified by the security guards. Actually, the first recorded "date" they shared was when Sean was just eight, at a party put on by record company CBS in New York's Museum of Natural History (Don't ask. Maybe they thought Michael would be identified as a new species!) to celebrate the success of *Thriller*. Biographer Darwin Porter records that Michael's official date for the evening was Brooke Shields, but as the evening progressed she and Michael left for a private VIP party within an inner sanctum of the museum. Porter writes: "There, her hopes were dashed when

Brooke encountered Michael's other 'date' for the night. Looking adorable in a custom-made tuxedo, an eight-year-old Sean Lennon rushed toward Michael for a big hug." There would be another shared-date humiliation for Brooke, the second being a far more public and embarrassing one when "the competition" was Emmanuel Lewis, in an incident we shall have occasion to visit in Chapter Eight, when the spotlight turns from Michael's track record of interest in boys to his *lack* of interest in women. Let it be noted briefly here, though, that Brooke reportedly told Ivana Trump, wife of billionaire Donald, "It's all too obvious, Michael prefers the company of young boys to me."[246]

Soon, speculation would be superfluous. Rumours based on what the security guards had said received confirmation from an unexpected quarter: Katherine Jackson. Michael's mother said Sean had regularly stayed in her son's bedroom. She said: "There's no mystery about this. These guys are talking about John Lennon's son. Sean would come and stay for about a week – and he would stay in the guest bedroom. Sometimes if Michael wasn't in when Sean arrived he would ask the guards to let him stay in his room until he got there."[247]

In trying to help Michael, Katherine had unwittingly added greatly to the guards' credibility. She had confirmed what they were saying. She seems to have thought rather naively that because Sean was a bona fide guest the public reaction would be along the lines, "Oh, well, that's all right then". Instead, she had fired the starting gun in a media race to uncover the full extent of Michael's friendship with him. First across the finishing line was *Today*, with a Tina Weaver spread based on what the paper hyped as "explosive evidence" from singer James DeBarge, former husband of Michael's sister Janet.[248] The reaction must indeed have been an explosion of alarm in the Jackson household.

DeBarge was said to have lived in the Jacksons' home for three years between 1984 and 1987, during an on-off relationship with Janet, which included a two-month marriage when she was eighteen. Weaver's January 1994 account said he had made a string of allegations to a police informant who had been secretly taping a meeting that lasted several hours. Copies of the tapes had been "handed exclusively to *Today*". DeBarge said that he had seen Michael and Sean in bed together. He had watched the star's playmates come and go and reached a stage when he was unshockable.

Michael's friendship with Sean had "been noted as strange" when it had begun in the 1980s, said Weaver. When the Jacksons' *Victory* tour hit

New York he spent "every spare moment" with the boy, then aged eight. The contact was evidently not "strange" enough to worry Sean's mother Yoko Ono, however. She instructed staff at his Swiss boarding school to put through calls only from her or Michael. When the boy was in California she dropped her son off at Encino to stay for a week at a time. She assumed the youngster was being put up in a guest room. DeBarge said he shared Michael's bed. Asked on the tapes if he saw Sean and Michael together in a sexual way, DeBarge said "Yes", according to Weaver, who then continued to quote him directly: "It was John Lennon's kid. Not Julian, the little kid, Sean. The kid slept with Michael. My room was next door. I saw them when I was snooping. He knew it, too. But he didn't care...I guess he figured I was no threat."

On one occasion DeBarge found Michael running around naked with another boy. He said: "It was a rainy night. I wasn't supposed to be there and I found him running around naked with a boy. All the boys would sleep in his bed with him." He also recalled a time when Katherine found a cheque for $1 million payable to one of his playmates in Michael's drawer. He said: "His mother confronted him about it. Michael said, 'Mum, he needed help. I was just helping him'. She said, 'Michael, you can't be helping people like that'. I don't know if it was for the kid or the parents. But I do know it was some kind of pay-off. You don't just give someone a million dollars because they need it."

DeBarge also told how Michael would invite youngsters for auditions: "He had all the boys over to the house to audition for his videos, more than he needed. If you went near his room when he was with them he'd say, 'We're practising'. He didn't want anyone watching." But Michael became careless about concealing the meetings. Said DeBarge: "He got away with it so many times, he became comfortable. After doing it so many times, you feel like you don't have to hide anymore. He did it right in front of me. He knew I saw him and that I knew he was doing it, but he just kept on doing it. He trusted me."

Despite professing to be unshockable, says Weaver, DeBarge did shudder at one thing – but it had nothing to do with boys. What really freaked him out was Michael's bizarre relationship with his pet chimp Bubbles, including how he would tenderly change the animal's nappy! "The boy needs help," he said, talking about Michael, not Sean. "Michael is what he is because of what happened to him as a kid. He's living in denial. The whole family is living in denial." He claimed Katherine was aware her son had molested children. He said: "She knows. Living in that house is a nightmare."[249]

DeBarge's claims were undoubtedly colourful, like so many others we have seen. The story even lived up to its "explosive" hype, but the allegations as set out in the newspaper would not be criminally damning. They were not specific enough. DeBarge agreed that Michael and Sean were "together in a sexual way", but what does this mean? Just that they were in bed together? If he saw anything else he was being coy about it. Also, when he spoke about Michael with other boys he said, "He did it right in front of me". A jury would want to know what exactly "it" was. Why the shyness? Probably not to spare the blushes of the "police informant", if indeed there had been one. To spare his own, maybe. Most men, we can safely assume, would be uncomfortable describing their own passive acceptance of specifically sexual acts between a man and a boy.

A sort of "see no evil" passivity among staff members would be understandable: no-one wants to put their job on the line by rocking the boat. But DeBarge had no job to hang on to, and his complicity may have embarrassed him. If what he said were true, why did he just accept it as though it were a normal state of affairs? Perhaps because keeping Janet was important to him? He was a young man, only twenty one at that time, and would have been hard pushed to start behaving like a policeman as a guest of her parents. Michael was a big-shot too and, as we shall see, DeBarge was not the ideal person to start giving him lessons in good living.

There is something else though. Something easily missed: the fact that he became "unshockable". What he is saying here, in effect, is that after the initial shock – culture shock if you like – he came to accept what was going on, just as the boys themselves evidently did. What he described was not a scene out of a horror movie, with rape and mutilation and serial killings. Michael was no Bluebeard on any reckoning. DeBarge saw a series of little pals, not victims. The prancing about naked typifies the wacky innocence of it. If he thought Michael's behaviour odd, his own behavioural response – to do nothing – tells us more loudly than any words could that he did not find it gut-wrenchingly unacceptable. Far from it, he became pretty laid back about the whole thing. Michael knew that, and that is why Michael relaxed with him, too.

So what manner of man was James DeBarge? Not much of one, some might think, or he could not have stomached what he saw. La Toya Jackson tells us he was kind and generous.[250] Michael's videographer Steve Howell described him as a sort of Dr Jeckyll and Mr Hyde figure, "the nicest guy in the world" – when he isn't high on cocaine and alcohol. Katherine Jackson described him as a very comical person.[251] Michael liked his sense of humour and the two got along well together.[252] This is itself surprising, because he had reacted badly to the news that Janet had eloped with him and married against the whole family's wishes. Along with the others, especially his parents, he had felt that marrying a good-natured but immature young man with a drugs problem was a bad idea.[253]

So Michael and James DeBarge hit it off well together, at a personal level. What does this tell us about James' view of Michael's procession of little playmates? It does not indicate he approved, but even less does it reveal any sense of distaste or disgust towards Michael: there is nothing to show he thought he was anything other than friendly and kind to the kids, or that he was harming them in any way, psychologically or otherwise.

James appeared to have felt sorry for Michael though. This comes across in what we have already heard: "The boy needs help". After staying at Hayvenhurst for a month in 1984, just after his marriage, he had seen Michael as a lonely person. We hear nothing from these early days about a parade of boys in the house:

> It was while I lived there that I came to realise what a sad, lonely figure Michael Jackson is...He was a ghost, wandering around the place looking for friendship. He would come to our room late at night, tap softly on the door, and say, "Is it all right if I come in?" One time, Janet and I were making love, and he came in! He got into bed with us and poured his heart out. He said, "I envy you two, because you have each other and love each other. But I haven't got anyone." There was never a sign of a woman in Michael's life.[254]

We need not feel too sorry for Michael. He may not have dared bring boys to Hayvenhurst as early as 1984, but it was round about this time that he was working on *Captain Eo* and seeing a lot of ten-year-old Jonathan Spence, a lad we met earlier. If James was basically a good-natured guy who liked Michael and felt sorry for him, does this mean we can begin to feel he was really speaking openly and honestly on these tapes? Was it just a matter of him being caught with his guard down, his tongue loosened by a couple of drinks, innocently letting the cat out of the bag to some sharp operator he had mistakenly taken for a pal? Did he really have no inkling at all that he was being taped?

We are told the tapes were "handed to" *Today*. By whom? The "informant"? The police? Can we be sure DeBarge and the "informant" were not in collusion? James could of course have approached the newspaper directly if he had simply wanted to sell his story, but that would have put him in very bad odour with the Jackson family: his treachery would have been plain for them to see. Far better for him if it looked as though he had just been caught foolishly shooting his mouth off. Also, if he went to a newspaper directly, he would have to face embarrassing questions as to why he had known so much and done so little. Better to short circuit that hassle.

All the same, people reading the story would ask those questions for themselves. It would need a powerful motive for anyone to put themselves in line for that sort of flak. Were there any such motives? Well, cocaine is a notoriously expensive habit. The tabloids were, as ever, in the market for a Jacko jackpot. And there is evidence that James had previously been interested in striking a good price for his inside knowledge. Taraborrelli picked up his account in one of the tabloids, and rather sniffily noted: "It is difficult to ascertain the accuracy of James DeBarge's recollections about Michael Jackson, since he did not appear at the appointment he made to be interviewed for this book. Later his manager said that he had decided not to be interviewed – or even to confirm the quotes he gave Tony Castro – without first being paid for the information."[255] Nothing wrong with that in itself. It is just that anyone for whom money is a major motive is bound to be alert to the notion that the more colourful the story, the more it will be worth. James may have kept his material scrupulously accurate, but, as with others we have heard from, the money motive makes it harder to be sure.

Indeed a couple of his more rococo flourishes may be thought a shade excessive. Take the dancing naked thing. We have something very similar popping up in Taraborrelli, again from an original article by Tony Castro. This time James says it rained, and Michael stripped and danced naked around the pool. Not a boy in sight this time, it seems, but the rain is familiar.

Said DeBarge: "His mother would scream from the house, 'Put your clothes on Michael. Your father will be home soon.' "[256] That "would" is interesting, as though the scenario had been repeated a few times. In itself it is perfectly credible. Michael likes dancing and is certainly "odd" or independent-minded enough to want to do it naked. Maybe he is into rain dances! The usual thing is to dance beforehand, to induce the precipitation, but what the hell? Since when was Michael ever orthodox? He writes and talks a great deal about "communing with nature" and such, so why not dance in the rain? It would be very much in character. Could it be that James just "adapted" this earlier story a little to meet the media's need to have a boy in the plot?

Another possibility is that Michael really did dance naked with a boy as well as on his own on many earlier occasions. What a different complexion this would put on things. Instead of something akin to a bizarre, orgiastic rite, such as *Today* conjures up in our imagination, we suddenly find ourselves in a scene closer to the uncontroversial (these days) world of naturism: this is not so much *Dance with the Devil*, more *Naked as Nature Intended*.

We have to wonder about James' Bubbles story, too. Every Jacko journo back in those days tried to come up with a bizarre Bubbles line. We have seen already in this chapter that at least one was untrue. The DeBarge account made it look as though Michael was besotted with this animal to a degree many would find suspicious. But this was not the case according to Taraborrelli: "Michael liked his ape, the way he likes all of his animals, but even though the master and ape sometimes ate together at the dinner table, the relationship between star and chimp was never obsessive."[257] That idea had been put about as a publicity stunt. Bubbles' trainer, Bob Dunn, said that the chimp stayed with him most of the time, not at Michael's house.

If money added something to the flavour of James' accounts, malice might have done likewise. He blamed the Jackson family for the break-up of his marriage.[258] La Toya has gone on record to deny this,[259] but Taraborrelli had some gossip that not only confirmed his view, but in addition gave him a reason to blame one particular member of that family: Michael. The biographer had "a friend of Janet" saying, "Michael was the only person she would listen to. She and Michael had a special relationship then. He begged her to leave James. He cried on the phone with her, told her how much she was hurting Katherine. Janet was finally convinced."[260] It doesn't much matter whether the story is true or not. If James believed it, that would be a good enough reason to bear a grudge against his former brother-in-law.

Tina Weaver's sensational, "explosive" story for *Today* told us nothing of this background. It suited Weaver's purpose to present DeBarge as a credible witness, with no particular axe to grind. So we heard nothing about him being a drug addict who perhaps badly needed the tab's money, nor about Michael's antagonism to his marriage. Did she know about these things? One would have thought so. At all events, he was presented just as a regular guy telling an amazing story. Very convenient. That is how you get to be Reporter of the Year.

Weaver instead chose to emphasise what the police had to say about the tapes: they were "crucial" and "the first solid evidence" from inside the Jackson family.[261] Upbeat comments of that sort from police sources were a regular feature of the Jackson coverage as the temperature hotted up late in 1993. In November there were reports of three unnamed teenaged boys accusing Michael of molesting them. Statements were taken and the accounts were "being studied". La Toya Jackson was hinting darkly towards the end of the year that she knew more than she was saying, although what she actually said was damning enough, including a bombshell comment that she could no longer remain a "silent collaborator" in her brother's "crimes against small, innocent children."[262] Later she was reported as making a specific allegation that Michael had molested a British boy.[263]

As if all this were not trouble enough, 1993 ended for Michael with another widely reported allegation from within the Jackson household, involving the unnamed son of a former Jackson employee. Michael was said to have "fondled" the boy. Although the story was thought less damaging than the Chandler allegations, the police were soon giving another confident response: "...the testimony is strong enough to advance the Jackson investigation significantly".[264]

At the same time, Michael's former maid, Blanca Francia, from El Salvador, went on American TV's *Hard Copy* hinting her son had been abused.[265] After five years as his personal maid, she said she left in 1991 in disgust over what she saw, describing a procession of young boys who stayed for weeks, especially after Michael's move from Hayvenhurst to Neverland.

Blanca's story is among those that would be tested in court cross-examination years later. She and her son Jason would be among the most credible prosecution witnesses in 2005. As a young man, Jason would say at the trial that as a child he had been sexually abused by Michael, making him the only alleged victim to take the stand apart from Gavin Arvizo. However, Michael had been charged only with offences against Gavin, *not* against Jason, so even if the jury had been convinced that Michael had molested Jason they could not automatically find him guilty of an offence against *Gavin*. Jason's evidence had been given solely to show that Michael's behaviour was part of a pattern of "prior bad acts". As such, it was very strong.

Jason's astonishing testimony will be examined closely in Chapter Sixteen. At this point we are confining our attention to those who were coming forward with their Jackson stories during Michael's first great public boy crisis, the Chandler affair of 1993-4. Jason, unlike Jordie Chandler, was not at that stage making allegations that would surface in public, but his mother was:

"I see them taking showers together, in the Jacuzzi together, the bath together, the same bed together, the same sleeping bag together," she said, referring to various boys. She thought her own son might have been molested: "I find Michael and my son so close, and my son in a sleeping bag and my son getting closer to him in a dark room. I saw my son sitting in his lap and I said, 'What are you guys doing?' "

Later we heard that she had been even more specific in what she had told detectives.[266] Michael would call his boys "rubba" because he liked to sit them on his knee and rub them up and down his genitals, she said. She had quit her job, according to this version, because of what her own son might become involved in. She had seen him in a sleeping bag with Michael and "I didn't want what was happening to other boys to happen to my son."

"Most nights he had young boys with him," she said. "It just wasn't normal. It became a routine. In the morning there would be little boys in their underwear... One boy was with him for two years. I never saw his mother. Michael told me the poor boy had been left alone and from now on he was calling Michael daddy. They were sleeping together at night. When the boys got mature like eleven or twelve years old he'd dump them."

Remember they said he dumped Jimmy Safechuck? Not true. And Terry George? A most misleading picture. How do former little pals like Manny Lewis, Corey Feldman and Brandon Adams remember Michael? Fondly. Probably thousands of kids were once cared for in orphanages run by Mother Teresa of Calcutta. When they went out into the world was she dumping them? This particular charge made by Blanca Francia must not be allowed to gain credibility just because it is so often repeated – on this occasion, one suspects, as a result of media prompting. Certainly, Jason's own allegations would never extend to Michael casting *him* aside: his allegations were of isolated acts of molestation; he would not say there was "a relationship".

Blanca said boys' parents were given money and presents to bring their youngsters to the ranch.[267] As Jason's mother, she too benefited from Michael's sweeteners. She said Michael showered her with money to keep quiet, about £3,500 in all. She gave testimony in the Chandler case, the following being part of an exchange with Jordie Chandler's lawyer, Larry Feldman:

> *Feldman*: Did you ever have any discussion with Mr Jackson about what you saw?
> *Francia*: He said to me, "What do you think about these boys coming to my house?" I said: "It's none of my business." And he said: "Good."
> *Feldman*: Did he ever give you money?
> *Francia*: Yes.
> *Feldman*: What did he tell you? Why did he give it to you?
> *Francia*: He gave me different stories, like I was doing a good job. He would give me \$500, \$300, \$200, just like that. Altogether he gave me \$5,000.
> *Feldman*: Did he ask you to keep (the visits) secret?
> *Francia*: Yes. He says to me that what I see is none of anybody's business and that he liked me. He said if I was asked by anyone about it, not to tell anything about him.

She went on to say she had once found three \$100 notes in the trousers of one of the boys. She also said Michael kept an instant camera in his room and took photos and videotapes of children, stored in his cupboard. She did not disclose having seen anything explicitly pornographic, unless a picture of a boy naked apart from "his private parts covered with a sheet" is to count.[268] More revealing, perhaps, at least psychologically, is an apparent interest Michael had in the mouths of young boys. She found Polaroid snapshots he had taken just of close-ups of the lips of his "special friends". Several witnesses including Blanca, according to Darwin Porter, have suggested that Michael was intrigued by the mouths of young boys, especially the lips of Macaulay Culkin. Porter also tells us that Michael himself often used to speak of Sean Lennon's "rosebud mouth".[269] Asked on *Hard Copy* why she had not gone to the police, Blanca replied: "He told me I would get some rewards, and I did. I keep my mouth closed all the time to keep my job."

She said she knew about Michael's "secret hideaway", his condominium on Wilshire Boulevard, Los Angeles. "He told me if anyone asked me where the hideaway is, not to tell anyone. I said, 'What if your mother asks me?' He said, 'Tell her you don't know.'"[270]

Emma Gilbey, writing in the *Sunday Times*, felt Blanca Francia had been "convincingly tearful" when confronted by reporters.[271] Unlike the five security guards, she had not appeared to relish the spotlight, but seemed distraught in its glare. Defence lawyers, we had heard, were planning to attack her evidence because she had sold her story to a TV station.[272] Gilbey countered that she had to, in order to have enough money to pay for a lawyer in case Michael sued her for breach of a confidentiality contract she and other employees had been obliged to sign. It was an interesting bit of special pleading on her behalf. As a domestic maid and a single mother she would certainly have lacked the resources for a legal battle.[273] On the other hand Jackson could not have used the legal system to claim damages against someone going to the police as a criminal case witness – and we now know, as Gilbey did not, that her son could have been such a witness.

Blanca Francia took a TV station's money to tell her story. Fine. As long as that story was true, no-one with an ounce of charity would begrudge her the opportunity to make herself and her child a little less hard-up. But it gave the case against Michael Jackson a terrible credibility issue. With so much money swilling around from the TV stations and newspapers, it mattered little how honest the various witnesses were: their testimony was almost bound to be compromised. The Quindoys, Kenneth Choi, the LeMarques, the security guards, James DeBarge, Blanca Francia, the problem was the same with all of them, even though they appeared very different from each other: there was the possibility of big money through selling their stories. In addition, Blanca would put herself and her son out of the running as criminal witnesses by "doing a Chandler": in a deal kept secret for many years, she too accepted a pay-off from Michael. Dismissed as "tabloid tattlers" by the sceptics, most of these figures had some reason to resent Michael too, either because they had been sacked or, like Choi and DeBarge, had a more personal axe to grind. Only the anonymous Mexican gardener we met early in this chapter can claim to have spoken out purely as a matter of conscience, and he did not see enough to give compelling evidence.

Nevertheless, taken together, the consistency of all these stories was impressive: we heard so often about goings on in the Jacuzzi, or the movie theatre, about presents and bribes, about parents kept in the background and staff expected to turn a blind eye. From each witness we heard about boys, mostly of a similar age, in the years just before puberty. Michael's play with the kids and the style of his intimacy with them comes across as broadly similar in each instance, while differing – as we would expect in honest accounts – in the finer details.

And yet, and yet... all this consistency and impressiveness did not eliminate the taint of money, a taint bedevilling even the search for witnesses. One private detective hot on the trail of another boy allegedly abused by Michael said, "If I could find that kid that would be a very lucrative property for me." Quite. As Emma Gilbey remarked, the more people who were out there looking for lucrative properties, the more the evidence against Michael was devalued.[274]

We have already met the biggest of the bounty hunters: Sandra Sutherland. Acting for Jordie Chandler's lawyer, Larry Feldman, by February 1994 she was claiming to have spoken to 120 "witnesses" and had been told about "numerous" alleged victims. By this time Jordie's case had just been settled out of court, evidently to Sutherland's annoyance: she would have preferred to bust Michael's balls in a much bigger way.[275] So would *Today*'s Tina Weaver, judging by the way she and her paper covered Sutherland's story in a five-page account spread over two issues.[276] This began with a front-page picture of Michael, and beneath it a headline-size quote from Sutherland saying "I've had grown men crying on the phone telling me of experiences long ago."

Readers could have been forgiven for supposing these were men alleging they had been abused as boys *by Michael* – an impression the presentation seemed deliberately designed to provoke. Even the inside pages were laid out in a way that bolstered the implied accusation. But a careful reading would have failed to substantiate it. These guys had *not* been talking about Michael. Sutherland had been referring to men who told her they had been victims in totally separate sex abuse cases.

It is as though *Today*, cheated out of a Jackson trial by the Chandler out-of-court settlement, was trying to goad Michael into suing for libel. The rest of the copy added to this impression, with a series of unsubstantiated accusations couched in terms clearly calculated to mount the most vicious, no-holds-barred, assault on Michael's reputation ever – and by this time there had been plenty of precedents in the news media on both sides of the Atlantic. We heard from Tina Weaver, for example, that, "One little boy was said to have been picked up abroad one afternoon by Jackson only to be tossed back when he had finished with him several hours later." It's not just that the allegation was unfair, because we did not know who was making it or on what basis; it was the prejudicial, emotive language in which it was made, as though to Michael a boy is no more than a fish to an angler. It was a terrible, wounding slander for which not a shred of evidence was set out.

Much of the account hinted darkly at witnesses being bribed or intimidated into silence. “I’ve spoken to scores of people,” said Sutherland, “but it has been an uphill battle constantly to get their cooperation.” One possible reason for this went carefully unmentioned, namely that, like Emmanuel Lewis, Corey Feldman and Brandon Adams, her target witnesses may actually have liked Michael and did not want to harm him. Sutherland had a problem with this total demonisation though. She could see that it might not be entirely credible, because Michael had been seen as a kind, gentle man by the world at large. She tried to sidestep the problem by saying things were not all they seemed to be, but in doing so was forced to admit that she was talking about a real human being, not about some monstrous angler after children’s bodies. Here is what she said:

> What Michael projects on the surface is so irresistible – love, innocence, kindness and wealth – that people have difficulty believing he might really be abusing children. People envisage paedophiles as hulking, tattoed strangers. They also have difficulty in understanding that a child abuser doesn’t necessarily brutally rape his victim, he can actually fall in love with them and dote on them.[277]

Weaver was forced to agree, adding that Michael regularly fell in love with his special friends, spending endless hours just chatting to them on the phone. So how could a guy who plainly loved children, even by the account of his accusers, be suspected of abusing them? What do we mean by “abuse” anyway? Is there really a sharp dividing line between non-abusive non-sexual touching and the sexual, supposedly abusive sort? It is time to take a look at such questions.

CHAPTER SEVEN

The Neverlands

Nobody would confuse Neverland with the Netherlands. To many Americans, including perhaps Michael Jackson, most of Europe can seem like an Olde Worlde theme park, with winding cobbled streets, fairytale castles and ancient market squares, town hall clock on one side and tavern on the other. Holland is rich in such tourist delights, but it is also a busy, thriving, educated, hi-tech society, whose top companies are major-league players in the world industrial and commercial scene. It is a country whose people have their feet firmly on the ground. It is the last place on earth of which you would say the people lack common sense, are refusing to grow up, or are living in a dream world.

For these very reasons, Michael would probably not have wanted to live there. Until the trauma of his trial, at least, he looked at home in California, with its culture of Disneyland fantasy and Hollywood glitz, a lotus-eater world of fabulous lifestyles under cloudless skies. We may even feel the famously eccentric Michael was as much a product of the Sunshine State as movies, oranges, or computer software: the place has a reputation for breeding crazies of every description, from coke-head film stars to psychopathic survivalists and womanising TV evangelists. In the land of Shirley MacLaine and Charles Manson, Michael's brand of oddness hardly looks out of place.

Yet he could surely have done without the state's sexual neuroses. Remember the McMartin Pre-School saga, which generated the longest criminal trial in US history from 1983-90? It was the first and most notorious in a spate of cases that once gripped the US as kindergarten staffs were accused of sexual abuse on the basis of absurd, hysterical allegations. The McMartin case began when one mother, later diagnosed as a paranoid schizophrenic, claimed her two-year-old son had been buggered by the school principal, Raymond Buckey. Later she was to allege that Buckey wore masks, capes and other costumes, stuck the boy's head in a toilet and forced an air tube in his rectum. Within a few months she had also accused five other people of buggering the boy, including her ex-husband. McMartin teachers, she said, had run scissors into the boy's eyes, staples into his nipples and forced his fingers into a goat's anus. Peggy Buckey, Raymond's mother, had killed a baby and forced the boy to drink its blood.[278]

It was ridiculous nonsense unsupported by any corroborative evidence, and would never have gone to trial but for the lunatic willingness of police and social workers to pump little children with leading questions that common sense should have told them were bound to elicit fairy tales. By spring, 1984, Ray Buckey, his sister, mother, grandmother and three teachers had been arrested and charged with offences involving forty two children. There were never any convictions. The prosecution threw in the towel after the jury was split in Ray's case. Now acknowledged to have been entirely innocent, the poor guy spent five years in jail as a victim of collective madness.

It is instructive to note that the McMartin parents had been advised from the start by Children's Institute International, whose "experts" in child sex abuse had developed a battery of techniques which ensured that the children would "disclose" stories of molestation, along with lurid elaboration going into the realms of Satanic ritual, torture, animal sacrifice and blood-drinking.[279] We shall be hearing more about these witch-hunting zealots later on, in connection with Michael's trial. The culture in which such an ill-disciplined, unscientific approach to sexual issues could thrive, plainly a culture of particularly intense sexual anxieties, could hardly be the place for a man to take young boys to bed with him and expect nobody to be worried or upset about it.

From this point of view, if from no other, Michael might indeed have been well advised to have created his Neverland in the Netherlands. If he had moved to Holland when he left Hayvenhurst in 1988 he would have enjoyed a far more liberal climate, without the American-style threat of a draconian jail sentence. We might note that in 1984 one Luis Johnson was given a jail sentence of 527 years in the US for a sexual offence involving a child.[280] Sentencing on such a scale, calibrated for Methuselahs, cannot even be taken to imply a particularly serious case. Three-figure terms are not that unusual for offences involving neither violence nor penetration. In May 2006, the state Supreme Court of Arizona upheld a sentence of 200 years merely for downloading child pornography from the internet.[281] In August 2002 Thomas Reedy made it to four figures when he was sentenced to a total of 1,335 years for distributing child porn. All Reedy had done was to run an age verification service, which offered codes to subscribers who could then access over 5,000 adult sites. Reedy and his wife Janice had been assured by their lawyers that they were not responsible for content. Just two of the sites, located in Russia and Indonesia, turned out to be offering underage material.[282]

In the Netherlands an offence of downloading or unwitting distribution might not attract a jail sentence at all; not so long ago child pornography was on open sale in Holland and tacitly accepted by the authorities. Even "hands-on" offences often tend to attract sentences of months rather than decades. It is not that the Dutch take a relaxed view of their children being abused. They emphatically do not. Many Dutch parents, especially in rural communities, accept a moral and religious code that would satisfy the most suspicious scrutiny of church-going, God-fearing Americans. Even in the more liberally-minded cities and towns there is no mass enthusiasm or approval for "deviant" sexual lifestyles.

Why then should adult sex with children be treated so leniently? How did there come to be a climate in which, at least in the country's most liberal phase, in the 1980s, it was possible for a judge to enlist the help of paedophiles in child care? And in which a government report could speak approvingly of the "seduction" of young people into sexual relations with older ones? Most astonishingly of all, the Dutch went so far as to reduce their effective age of consent to twelve, a measure which stunned and amazed the world's media, especially when they realised it had wide-ranging support.[283] The churches, especially, and social work organisations, might have been expected to be up in arms over such an apparent coup by unseen subversive forces, yet the Dutch Ministry of Justice felt able to assure a *Newsweek* journalist that the measure had been accepted without protest throughout the country. How could such a thing possibly have come to pass?[284]

The famed Dutch spirit of toleration is often cited in explanation.

Tolerance and moderation, as one native commentator, Jan Schuijer, pointed out in the context of sexual reform, seemed almost natural ideals in a country that gained its independence fighting the Spanish Inquisition.[285] Schuijer identifies many other historical factors that have reinforced this tradition in a small country of great religious and cultural diversity, a country in which there have always been pressing reasons for people of sharply divergent views and lifestyles to find ways of getting along with each other. Broadly speaking, the attitude seems to be one of live and let live.

A key aspect of the culture has been a far greater respect for freedom of publication and debate than pertains in either the US or the UK, both of which nominally accept freedom of expression, but where, in reality, those speaking from dominant conservative standpoints are able to shout down unorthodox voices. Tabloid values did not dominate the media in the Holland of the 1980s; the papers did not scream abuse at those who made a serious effort to research and discuss sexual issues. Nor did they find funding cut off, and research topics restricted, as has happened extensively in the Anglophone world.[286] On the contrary, sexual issues across the board were widely and openly debated, leading to the provision of extensive sex education for youngsters and a society in which the teenage pregnancy rate became the lowest in Europe, with teenage abortions at only one-ninth the level of that in the US.[287] It was a society where by 1981 fully two thirds of the population agreed that children under sixteen should have access to contraceptives, with the implication that youngsters were perceived as capable of sexual self-determination.

So, rather than the Dutch people having the new legislation foisted upon them, it came about in the context of an extensive public debate and a widespread acceptance of sexually liberal attitudes. This liberalism did not extend, for most people, to an acceptance of paedophilia, and it would be a mistake to suppose the law relied on such acceptance. Instead, toleration was the watchword. There could be no prosecution for sex with consenting children aged 12-16 unless a formal complaint was made by an official child protection agency.[288]

Four relevant sections of the Penal Code were amended in December 1991, including Section 247, which retained a prohibition against sex with children under sixteen. However, in the case of a child aged twelve or over prosecution would henceforth require a formal complaint by the child, his legal representative, or an official child protection agency. Anyone could approach such an agency with a view to a formal complaint being made.

Parents, for instance, who objected to their own child's sexual contact with an adult could report the matter to a child protection agency, with a view to prosecution. While there was no guarantee the official agency would share the parents' view that the case merited prosecution, this provision appeared to allay the fears of conservatively minded Dutch parents with respect to their own children. The Dutch spirit of toleration enters the picture insofar as such parents seldom feel the need to lay down the law for *other* parents and what *their* children do, or what adults might do with them. As Schuijer put it, "That some parents might not feel the need, in a similar case, to lodge a complaint would not be relevant to the average Dutch person considering the law."[289]

A salient aspect of Dutch "live and let live" from our point of view is that the Netherlands presented an opportunity unique in the western world for detailed research into sexual relationships between adults and children – not by means of questionnaires given to adults many years after the childhood experience in question; nor through interviews with prisoners hoping to get parole by hanging their heads in shame and confessing their wickedness; nor through clinical accounts of the trauma suffered by victims of real abuse. The Anglophone countries have already undertaken a plethora of such studies. No, in Holland, and in Holland alone, it has been possible to talk to children while they were involved in an on-going sexual relationship with a grown-up partner. This is a type of study that enables us to see how such children themselves feel about what appear to be consensual sexual contacts, and to examine the wider social context and overall meaning of the relationship, both from the point of view of the child and of the adult.

Just because children of say ten or twelve years of age may be willing to have sex with a grown-up does not of course mean that they will not later regret having done so. It is sometimes argued that youngsters' feelings about such activity are likely to change as they grow older and become more aware of how powerful is the modern taboo against it; this is given as a reason why children cannot give valid consent. True consent, it is said, can only be based on a level of mature understanding they do not possess.

Nevertheless, it makes no scientific sense to pre-judge matters by refusing to consider empirical evidence. Put another way, why not take a close look at what is actually going on between adult and child in "consensual" relationships, and what children in such liaisons actually know about society's sexual mores and prohibitions? The recognised procedure in any systematic attempt to gain knowledge of a subject – whether we call it a "scientific" endeavour or not is perhaps not too important – is to begin by looking at the facts, not by refusing to face them.

What constitutes a "fact", or a relevant item for investigation, could take us into philosophically deep waters, but only an extremely authoritarian line of enquiry could rule the children's views and feelings as irrelevant, or not worth enquiring into. A major reason for research into children's contacts with adults is to ascertain what kind of public policy towards such contacts is in the best interests of the children. "Best interests", in turn, is a notion few people these days would suggest can be determined entirely without reference to the youngsters themselves, or by imposing adult standards on them in the teeth of their own contrary views and feelings. Such an approach would be coercive – the very criterion by which, without examining the facts, many conservative researchers are quite content to condemn the behaviour of all child-lovers.

One Dutch academic, Dr Theo Sandfort, of the University of Utrecht, focused his attention on just one research question designed to put the child's perception at centre stage: "Can a boy experience sex with an adult positively?" If no such positive responses could be found, even when they were being actively sought, then paedophilic activity (at least as regards contacts with boys) would be damned far more convincingly and comprehensively than had ever previously been the case. Those who have sexual relations with children often claim that they do not use force or coercion, and this finds support in the literature. But it would be a crushing blow to them if, despite the truth of this assertion, they were to discover that the children with whom they had sex reported only negative feelings about such acts.

Negative feelings, though not necessarily against the adult partner, are almost bound to be the unhappy lot of children when angry parents discover a relationship, and when a child is put through the ordeal of interviews with police and social workers. But the boys Sandfort discovered and talked to for his research had not been through the mill of legal procedures, nor had they emerged in a clinical context: they had not needed therapy. How then, it might well be wondered, did Sandfort identify his young research subjects at all? After all, even in liberally-minded Holland, it would scarcely be possible to go around primary schools asking children to put their hands up if they were having sex with a grown-up.

The answer nonetheless does reveal a remarkable feature of Dutch life, the Netherlands Association for Sexual Reform (NVSH). The early work of the NVSH was in family planning, but a wide range of sexual issues have come within its purview and it once had a membership of a quarter of a million. In the 1980s there were paedophile groups under its auspices, holding regular open meetings, to which boy- and girl-lovers were not afraid to take their child partners, despite the fact that press and police were free to attend and sometimes did.[290] These groups were the principal source through which Sandfort made his contacts. The twenty five boys involved were approached through the men with whom they were in a current sexual relationship. It was the men, the older partners, who asked the boys to participate, and in a few cases they also asked the boys' parents. The boys, aged from ten to sixteen, all took part voluntarily. The intention had been to include girls in the research as well. Some initial contacts were made but nothing came of them.

The absence of girls from the research need not worry or detain us too much. Our special concern in this book is what we are to make of Michael Jackson's close friendships with children, and we have already seen that his most intense attachments were exclusively with boys. Sandfort's work would thus seem to shine the spotlight onto exactly the area of most concern to us. This is not to imply that any of Michael's friendships were definitely sexual. Rather, it is just to suggest that if this were the case, then the comments made by the boys who talked to Sandfort could give valuable clues as to how such a sexual relationship might have been perceived by Michael's young friends. There is, to be sure, arguably a world of difference to a boy between a relationship with "the man next door" and one with a hero-worshipped superstar. Nevertheless, the Sandfort boys' comments are by far the closest form of comparison available. In order to maintain as much of this comparability as possible, particular attention will be given in what follows to the perceptions and observations of the younger boys, those aged 10-13, whose ages most exactly fit those of the boys who seem of greatest interest to Michael. Another reason for placing our emphasis at the younger end of the scale is that it is precisely such contacts, with boys who are likely to be prepubertal, or pubescent, that give rise to the greatest cause for social concern.

Eight of the twenty five boys were in fact said to be not sexually mature, while a further six were described as in a transitional phase: liquid did come out of their penises when they experienced orgasm, but it was clear and contained no sperm. Of the eleven sexually mature boys, seven were said to have achieved their first ejaculation in the course of what was then their current relationship. At the time of the interviews with Sandfort, the boys' relationships with the men had already been going on for some time, most of them for a number of years, with considerable variation in how often they met. In twelve cases the boys regularly slept overnight with their partner. The boys' men friends, aged from twenty six to sixty six (average age thirty nine), were predominantly single (two married, two divorced), and were for the most part professional people of good educational background.

This is not the place to describe Sandfort's methodology in great detail, though it may be noted that the rigour of his approach earned widespread respect even among conservative academic commentators loath to accept his conclusions – not for nothing did he later become a professor at a top American university.[291] It should perhaps be pointed out, though, that Hermans' Self-Confrontation Method was used in interviewing the boys. This is a systematic scheme whereby an individual tries, with the help of the interviewer, to define those factors that are most important in his life. These can be anything: relationships, anxieties, particular events or preoccupations. During the interview the subject is asked how often certain positive and negative feelings are experienced in connection with each of his value areas, as well as how often he experiences these feelings and would like to experience them during, say, an ordinary day in his life. These data are discussed and gone into more deeply in a second interview. During the "self-investigation" phase, the boys are asked about their older friends, the sexual contact and the pleasant and unpleasant sides of that contact.[292] Among the questions asked are: How did the men and boys come to know each other? What did the older partner mean to the boys and why did they carry on their relationships? What place did sex have in the relationships and how did the boys experience it? How did the boys handle their relationships as regards their social environment, especially in dealing with their parents and friends?

As regards the ways in which men and boys meet and become close friends, we may feel that the case of Michael Jackson is wholly exceptional. How many men, after all, have children writing to them from all over the world? How many have kids clamouring for their autograph? How many are approached by parents keen for a child to work closely with them on set together day after day making a film or a pop video? Michael was also exceptional in another way, though, which to some extent cancelled out both his advantage over others who like children's company and his difference from them: his fame meant that his relationships were always in danger of coming under intense public scrutiny, and always needed some kind of special pleading in order to justify them, by reference to, especially, "the childhood Michael never had". As Sandfort points out, the only truly accepted relationships between adults and children are ones based on parenting or education. Even in the absence of sexual connotations, simple friendship between adults and children, with no other purpose than friendship, is just not socially acceptable. At best it is thought odd, and at worst highly suspect. We are expected as grown-ups to socialise only with others in our own age bracket.

How, then, did Sandfort's twenty five boys meet their adult friends? Without Michael's special advantages, did they have to offer money to the children or give them expensive gifts? Such factors do not appear to have been a feature at all. In some cases the first encounter happened as a result of a boy's family or friends knowing the man in question. In other cases there were chance meetings on the street or at swimming pools. Often the first contact was more or less accidental, and followed up on the initiative of the adult, who would invite the boy to drop by his house. In other cases it was the boy who sought further contact, in some instances obtaining it only after surmounting considerable obstacles.

Sandfort's research includes extensive quotations from the boys on this subject. These comprise some sixteen comments taking up six printed pages.[293] What follows here is a brief selection, and as such it is bound to reflect my own feeling as to what is particularly illuminating. Even with the most honest of intentions such a procedure is bound to provide a less well-balanced picture than the research as a whole, which readers are whole-heartedly advised to consult.[294] Nevertheless, I am confident that what follows in this chapter, as regards all the questions Sandfort raises, amounts to a useful introduction.

Ton (14) would have been about ten when he met Fred (33) at a school camp:

> Yes, about four years ago, when our school went on a camp and Fred was one of the leaders. He did all the organising for our group. And of course everyone had to tell where he lived. So he said, "Oh, I live right near there," and I said, "Then you'll have to come and visit." And that's how it started. After that I dropped by every day and we'd go to the movies or something.[295]

Thijs (10) met Joop (26) on the street:

I was going to play football with my friends. I was riding a bike and the chain came off, and then Joop said, "Here, I'll put it on." I could have done that myself, but Joop wanted to do it so I let him. Then he asked, "Would you like to come inside?" So I went in, and after that I played football with him more and more often.[296]

Rob (12) was one of the boys who met his friend (Chris, 38) through a sibling connection. Evidently there was some rivalry:

Yeah, it's a long story. My brother used to go to Chris and one day they came together to our home. I thought Chris was a good-looking guy, a nice guy, with that crazy beard of his. So I went to Chris's a couple of times and liked it. I came back a second time, and a third time, and I kept on coming. Of course there was a big fight between me and my brother, over who got to stay here and who had to go. Because I didn't want my brother around when I was here – I didn't want that at all. I told Chris over and over again: "I don't want him around; I want you all to myself sometimes."

After you saw Chris that first time at your home, did you decide yourself to go to him or did Chris ask you to come visit?

No, I came here absolutely of my own accord.[297]

Jan (11) had known Sander (41) from the age of six. The contact had come about because his mother had been active in the NVSH:

Can you still remember when you got to know Sander?

On the couch at home. He asked me to sit on his lap, and then I felt him start to rub my back, and that felt so nice, and still does![298]

When asked about the friendship itself, and what it meant to them, the boys spoke about a variety of things. Sex was a pleasurable aspect of the relationship, but Sandfort concludes that it is not the most important reason for the boys' continuing interest in maintaining the contact. Doing things together was mentioned a lot: football, swimming, board games, dancing, skating, going to the movies. However, the reason they liked an adult's company for such things was less often articulated. It emerged that Lex (13) found a favourable contrast between the relatively low level of attention he could get from his parents, who were shared with brothers, and the undivided attention given him by his adult friend Richard:

> We go out a lot, we also go swimming a lot. We just do everything together. I also often do the cooking here, make macaroni or French fries. Sometimes we go to the movies or a nature park. When Richard says, "Tomorrow we'll go to the movies," I'm real glad. I think about it all the time. Or when we go to the amusement park or to Slagharen Stables.
>
> *You're pretty lucky, eh?*
>
> Yeah, that only happens if you go around with a paedophile, or you're the only child at home, of course.[299]

In such contexts trust, friendship and loyalty were built up between man and boy. Often the boys described the atmosphere in the man's house as relaxed, "different" and fun – a feeling clearly echoed in some of the comments of Michael Jackson's young friends. The boys felt at ease, and were often given more freedom and responsibility than at home. The older partner was regarded as someone the boys could talk to about anything and who was understanding:

> Theo (13): Well, he understands kids better, boys better. My mother does too, and my father. But I think he does even more.[300]
>
> Wouter (12): I feel at home at Gerard's (42). I can hide from my dad. I get a lot of support. And if I'm unhappy he understands why I'm unhappy. He is a wonderful guy, and you can do anything with him if (laughs) you don't go too far. He is considerate of me, and I'm considerate of him![301]

It will be recalled that Michael was accused of using a ruse to get Jordan Chandler in bed with him, showing a movie that would frighten Jordie and make him afraid to sleep alone. A similar suspicion could arise in the circumstances mentioned by Ben (10), but this boy shows no sign of wanting to make a federal case of it:

> I think it's wonderful to sleep together. Then I don't have to lie in bed alone. Sometimes I'm a little bit scared to go to sleep if I've seen a movie.[302]

The attention they received from their older partners was a major theme attracting the boys to the men. Were the youngsters all neglected at home then? Most of the boys in fact spoke well of their home situation, though for others the feeling was less positive. In the latter cases the relationship was particularly important to the younger party. It is easy to criticise paedophiles in such circumstances for latching onto children who are in some way emotionally deprived, but whether the criticisms make much sense is another matter. Inevitably, there will always be parents who are too busy to give as much attention to each of their children as they ought, or who are just not as interested in their kids as they might be. This is hardly the child-lover's fault, nor is it obvious that he should blamed for making good their omissions, or "filling the father gap" as another famous musician, the composer Benjamin Britten, did for his young friend Roger Duncan.

Britten was a friend of Ronald and Rose Marie Duncan and met their son Roger when the boy was eleven years old. The two soon became very close. In this case we find a benign form of parental neglect, not ideal, but a far better compromise with paternal inadequacy than Evan Chandler was able to manage. Humphrey Carpenter's biography of Britten records the following amazing conversation between Ronnie and Ben:

> "Ronnie, I've got a problem. I love children and as you know, I can't marry."
> "Yes, I know. Why don't you adopt one?"
> "That's what I want to do."
> "Then there's no problem."
> "You don't understand. It's Roger I like. I want to be as a father to him. But I don't want to put your nose out of joint. Will you allow me to give him presents, visit him at school, and let him spend part of his school holidays with me – in other words share him?"
> "Of course. He's fond of you too. And as you see, we've always got Briony."[303]

Briony felt her parents were oblivious to what might have gone on between her brother and the composer in the ten years that followed, years in which, as Ronnie says, "Ben was a second father to my son, giving him advice and affection as he grew up...I felt some shame at my own inadequacy, at my own lack that I had failed to give my son the support he had received from Ben." All the same, he let the arrangement flourish, and although Roger had indeed wanted more from Ronnie, "Ben largely filled the father gap". Rose Marie, asked if she had been worried by the friendship, said: "I don't think it occurred to me that anything would go wrong, because I remember Ronnie saying that he'd made Ben absolutely promise that he'd behave. And I suppose because we wanted to believe it, we believed it. But I'll never know."[304] Nor need she. There will always be parents who for one reason or another short-change their children by failing to give them enough attention: if at least they let a loving friend help out – a friend whose interest will inevitably be erotic to some extent, too – we have reason to believe they will be mitigating their failings, not making them worse. These parents are at least honest enough to face their limitations, and put their child's happiness before their own ego.

As Sandfort says, "It can be expected that as the bonds of the nuclear family are weakened, children will be quicker to form emotional ties with other adults. For such children a paedophile relationship can be a welcome supplement."[305]

Although the bond between man and boy is likely to be especially strong when the boy's family background is neglectful or problematic, this does not mean the relationship is of only marginal significance in other cases. The data gained through the Self-Confrontational method shed light on this. The older partner was, for all of the boys, one person for whom they had many positive feelings and few negative ones. For each of them there were people in their surroundings for whom they had fewer pleasant and more unpleasant feelings, people with whom they could not get along as well, or whom they disliked. About half the boys judged their older partners to be the most pleasant person they knew.

The boys also ranked the relative importance of the older partners to others they knew. For two boys their older friends were the most important person in their surroundings. The remaining fifteen boys found others more important, in some cases friends of their own age, but more often parents. This quite dramatic finding, in which a boy's adult lover is ranked on a par with, or even higher than, a boy's parents, indicates that we should perhaps not be too cynical about the many glowing tributes paid to Michael Jackson by Macaulay Culkin and many of his other boy friends. It is clear from Sandfort's findings that boys can respond positively to grown-ups who take an interest in them and are at ease in young company.

To speak of "responding positively" to a grown-up who "takes an interest", implies an adult in the driving seat. This in turn may suggest adult sexuality as the principal driving force, at least in terms of the older partner's motivation in seeking out a boy, and in turning the ignition key to get the friendship started. In many cases this may not be far wide of the mark.

Although a boy may have powerful reasons of his own for finding a grown-up friend, the younger he is the less likely he is to realise that such an extra-familial option is possible. Though his heart may ache over some dimly perceived sense of a gap in his life, he is unlikely to make a beeline towards a solution he does not know exists. Also, unless a boy in his pre-teen years has a strong and, some would say, precocious, sense that he is gay, he is even less likely to set his sights on a grown man because he finds men sexually attractive. The boys in Sandfort's study did not show any such tendencies. Most of them revealed heterosexual interests at some point in their interviews. Although they gained pleasure from sexual contact with their adult partner, this was not based on feelings of desire for the grown-up's body.

The idea of the adult's sexuality as the initial driving force is arguably given strong support by Sandfort's finding that in eight of the twenty five relationships sex took place at the first meeting between the partners. In another nine cases it happened soon after the first meeting, and in the remaining cases after a month or more. The first sexual contact between Rob (12) and Chris (38) gives a picture of how things can develop between an adult and a sexually inexperienced child who evidently began with no erotic expectations for the encounter whatever. Chris took photos of Rob, told him he was good-looking and asked if he could take "half-naked" shots of him. Sandfort's text says that Rob then "spontaneously got undressed". While this is slightly ambiguous, it would appear from what follows that Rob in fact stripped off completely without a specific request to do so, and would seem to have been quite relaxed and uninhibited at this point. Chris then began caressing Rob who, according to the boy himself, responded sexually:

> *Can you recall when you and Chris had sex for the first time?*
>
> Uh, a week or so after I met him. Then we had contact with each other – I mean sexual – uh, well not really, because I didn't know anything about it then, so...
>
> *What do you mean?*
>
> I'd had no education about it or anything.
>
> *Oh, you knew nothing about sex?*
>
> Nothing at all at first. Then I slowly got the hang of it, got to know how my own feelings worked, and I liked that a lot.

Sandfort does not tell us how old Chris was at the time. On the basis that the Dutch have an extensive programme of school sex education, yet Rob knew nothing of sex, it may well be that he was much younger than 12.

The phrasing of the question put to Rob also indicates that the events in question had been some considerable time earlier.

Can you still remember what happened that first time?

Yeah, I think so. We'd been making photos. Now, let's see, I think I went and lay down on the bed – that's how it began, I think. And then he started to explain things to me.

What things?

Uh, how can I say it...how you really got to jerk off and other things like that.

And those were things you didn't know about?

No, not yet.

And then you immediately got into a sort of demonstration?

You could put it that way.

Can you say now who started the sex?

Uh, I think he did, because I knew nothing about it. So it was him. Not because I didn't want it but just because I didn't have the faintest idea about any of that.

So you'd never had any sex with anybody else?

No.

Not even with yourself?

No. Okay, every so often I saw I had a hard-on, but I didn't know anything more than that. That was all I knew.[306]

Perhaps surprisingly, the number of boys who said it was the adult who had taken the initiative towards the first sex within the relationship, was slightly outweighed by the number of boys who said they themselves had made the first sexual move (4), it was a mutual thing (2), they could not remember (5), or a third party had been responsible (3). Exactly who did what first, and what counts as a sexual initiative, are difficult things to determine even between adults. Regarding his friendship with Sander (41), it would seem Jan (11) hardly regards it as a vitally important issue:

Who started it, then?

Uh, I don't remember. No, I don't remember who was the first. I've no idea.

Of course it's a long time ago, isn't it? I can understand that you no longer recall who it was.

> No, in the meantime I've had so much fun. I just don't know any more.[307]

Beyond the first sexual encounter, Sandfort discovered, most of the boys were more active in bringing about the sexual behaviour. This is how Wouter (12) described what used to happen with Gerard (42). He was asked who begins:

> Mostly I do.
> *You start it?*
> I decide if we're going to have sex or not.
> *You decide that?*
> Yes. And every day I come here it happens. I don't keep Gerard waiting around.
> *Is that a kind of rule, that it happens every time?*
> No. I like it. When I feel like it we just start. Then we first take a bath and then go to bed. Sometimes we do that the other way round.
> *But if you have to say who starts it, on average, who would that be?*
> Well, sometimes one of us, sometimes the other. Yes, and sometimes he wants it and I don't, so then we don't do it. Mostly I'm the first one to begin.[308]

It will be recalled that Michael Jackson was accused both of manually masturbating Jordie Chandler and of sucking him to orgasm, but there was never any allegation in the boy's formal statements of an attempt to secure anal intercourse, either actively or passively. This relatively limited alleged repertoire turns out to be remarkably similar to what occurred within most of the relationships described in Sandfort's work. Every one of the twenty five boys was masturbated by the grown-up, and in most cases the boy did the same to the man. Oral-genital contact with the man sucking the boy's penis was also a near universal feature, and in fourteen cases the boys reciprocated, though in no case did the man ejaculate into the boy's mouth. In seven cases the man licked the boy's anus, though in no case did the boy do this to the man. Anal intercourse was likewise not reported in many cases, and was also an infrequent occurrence for those who had done it: in five cases the boy penetrated the man, and in two the man also did it to the boy. Sandfort notes that the boy's sexual pleasure appeared to be put first in these activities, and that the men showed restraint in response to the boy's wishes.

The boys were asked what they felt about the sexual side of their friendship, in particular about both its positive and negative aspects. Most of them found the sex self-evidently pleasurable, while finding it difficult to put into words exactly what the pleasure consisted of: some referred not just to good physical feelings but also to the loving context of the intimacy, with sex as a means of both giving and receiving love.

Asked about unpleasant feelings connected with the sexual contact, most were hard-pressed to find anything negative to say, and ten could think of nothing at all. John (13), for instance:

> *What for you are the unpleasant aspects of your sexual relations with Marcel?*
>
> There's nothing unpleasant about it.
>
> *Nothing unpleasant at all?*
>
> What could there be?
>
> *I don't know. Is there maybe something you'd rather not do? You like it very much, but maybe there is still something that makes you think, well, I have a little trouble with that, or there's for me something annoying about it?*
>
> No. Marcel has always told me if you're doing something you don't like you always have to say so. But I haven't any trouble with it. I like it and he likes it, so I think why should we make problems about it?[309]

Eric (10) found something negative to say about the sexual contact: sometimes circumstances made it impossible for sex to happen! Sometimes, he said, he wasn't in the mood, "but once, twice a day is real good".[310]

By way of negative comment, some boys made remarks critical of their partner. Theo (13) for instance:

> Well, he's so prickly.
>
> *Prickly?*
>
> Yes, here. He's got stubble all over, because he shaves and he prickles so bad.
>
> *Shall we write that down?*
>
> Yes. Old porcupine![311]

Hans (13) gave voice to what might be considered a more serious problem, which sometimes made him feel angry or sad, though such feelings were very rare. He found it difficult to say no whenever his older friend wanted to do something he himself did not want to do:

Well, for example, if I'm doing something and, uh, something he likes but I, well, don't like so much. Sometimes every so often you can say no, but other times you really shouldn't. I mean, taking each other into consideration, and so on.

And when does that happen?

Well, say, he asks you, and then he asks you again, so you know he really wants it. Then you're not so quick to say no.

Why not?

Uh, I just don't think you can.

Why can't you? If you don't want to you don't want to.

Yeah, but you must be considerate of the other guy.

And he of you?

Yes, uh, of course. If I say no once in a while he'll think, well, I can ask him another time.

But sometimes it's difficult to say no?

Yes. Like when you tell him no and he gets mad. Then I think I shouldn't have said no.

You think that later?

Yeah, you think that right afterwards. If you say no you're letting the other guy down. Sometimes it's about things he really likes and I don't. So... you got to find a solution, and that's not easy.[312]

Not easy indeed, and arguably too tough a task to load onto a boy of thirteen, especially if the older partner sometimes "gets mad" at hearing what he does not want to hear. Michael's alleged solution to a similar problem with a boy of Hans's age was not to get mad but to cry. Either way, it's heavy pressure. For many this issue alone would be decisive in tipping the scales against any possibility of valid child-love relations. But at this point we still have many more weights to add to the balance trays.

Other negative feelings included embarrassment over taking part in acts of which they knew others would disapprove. Ben (10), for instance:

> Uh, embarrassed, yes, if you're just a little boy and you go to bed with a great big man; really that's bad, yeah, naughty; while your mother doesn't know anything about it; and then you do crazy things you aren't supposed to do at all.[313]

Jan (11) disliked being interrupted in sex:

Well, uh, in the middle of making love a lot of kids come in.

You find that unpleasant?

Yes. Suddenly the bell rings and we're in the middle of doing nice things, kissing and him rubbing my back, and the kids are ringing the bell and making a racket. Then we have to quickly pull everything up – well, not put on all our clothes, just get our pants up. I don't like that; I think it's awful. Being suddenly disturbed.[314]

It was suggested above that other weights needed adding to the balance of Hans's comment about finding it hard to say no. One other weight, and we may find ourselves hard-pressed to think of a heavier one, is Hans's own estimation of whether he could handle the problem. Did his dilemma trouble him so much that it all but wrecked the value of the relationship? Or was it a minor matter easily outweighed by the positive side? Was it, in other words, a problem that might look decisively important to an outside critic of such contacts, but was really nothing of the kind? The latter would in fact appear strongly to be the case. Negative feelings were heavily outweighed by positive ones for all the boys.

Data from the Self-Confrontational procedure revealed what a small influence the negative factors had on the sexual experience as a whole. Compared with other things that were important in the boys' lives (such as being weak at school maths, say), the negative aspects elicited a relatively low emotional response. These negative aspects had hardly any effect at all upon the boys' general sense of well-being.

We have already heard that Ben (10) would not want his mother to know about him going to bed with a man. Parental attitudes are a matter of particular concern to us, given the range of responses we have seen, from Evan Chandler's show of contemptuous outrage to the more laid back views of Brett Barnes' and Wade Robson's mothers. Rob (12) would probably feel Chandler père was rather old-fashioned. Here is how he conceives his parents' likely feelings over him having sex with Chris (38):

I think they wouldn't like me doing it with Chris. Yeah, if I had my own child, then of course I'd be jealous, but I'd still allow it. Why not? I think it's stupid; it's the old way of thinking, you might say. They just won't keep up with the times. Well, okay, this is sort of super-modern, isn't it?[315]

Most of the parents knew about the relationship, but not about the sex. Martin (12) comments:

> No, they don't know, but they certainly wouldn't like it. Stupid, isn't it? Just plain asinine.[316]

Jos (13) feels his father would be furious over him having sex with Bas (35):

> No, my parents don't know, but I'd guess they would think it was really bad if they did find out. Just after my first visit to Bas I told my father about it and he said, "You don't go there any more or I'll break both your legs!"[317]

Some of the parents knew or suspected something sexual was going on and, although they did not approve, avoided confronting the issue. According to Thijs (10) his mother remembered that sex had occurred in the past. When asked if he was now telling her lies he answered: "Of course: I don't want to be kept away from him." The fact that his mother thought it was dirty was "crazy stupid", he said. Why so? "Well, just because I know what it's all about. I decide myself what to do."[318]

About a third of the parents both knew about the sexual side and accepted it fully, according to the older partners. If Jordan Chandler ever reads this book, he may well ponder how differently things might have turned out had his parents been like those of Theo (13):

> My father and mother know about it. They think it's completely normal.
>
> *How do you feel about that?*
>
> I think it's great, because there are some people who would like to murder all the homosexuals and paedophiles because they don't think they're normal. My father and mother don't feel that way, and I think they're right.[319]

Regarding the boys who hid the sexual side from their parents, Sandfort points out that most young people seldom say much to their mother or father about their sexual experiences or about their doings in general. In this respect a boy-love contact is quite unexceptional. Also, the comments of the boys would seem to explode the myth put about in much of the abuse literature claiming that children are forced into secrecy through fear of the adult they are having sex with. This factor is doubtless true of many clearly non-consensual cases, including incestuous ones, but the views expressed by the boys in Sandfort's study are hard to reconcile with them being terrorised by their partner – on the contrary, in some cases they would appear to have more to fear from their parents.

Adverse peer pressure might also be expected to take some of the shine off an otherwise pleasant contact if other youngsters knew about a boy's sexual relationship with a man. We are told that Jordan Chandler was taken out of school and educated privately after the boy's sexual allegations against Michael Jackson (or, rather, allegations made at the insistence of his father) were made public: effectively, Jordie was "outed" by the media. Jordie's pals had long known about the friendship, following earlier publicity in which the Chandlers had featured as Michael's "secret family".[320] Although Jordie's name had been held back by most of the American media in the context of the sex story, the protection offered by this anonymity was effectively zero: the people who really mattered to him, the ones he shared the schoolyard with, knew perfectly well. Jordie had been a popular boy at school but, as his uncle would eventually report, "The vast majority of Jordie's schoolmates treated him with respect, but some were cruel."[321] Some taunts and humiliation would seem inevitable when such a taboo relationship is publicly alleged. And we know that some of the boys in Sandfort's research likewise found themselves running the gauntlet of peer-group jibes.

Theo (10) suspected that other kids were talking behind his back. He decided to ignore it, for tactical reasons:

> No, I don't let on I know they're talking about me. And I'm not going to say anything either – I'm not that stupid – 'cause then they'd start yelling it at me out loud.[322]

Several boys found themselves in an apparently quite embattled situation. Rather than caving in to pressure and abandoning their friendship with an adult, their response was characterised by what seems to be a remarkable independence of mind and a robust tendency to stand their ground. Although their pals might have felt sex with a grown-up was dirty, sick or such like, these boys seemed confident that their experience put them in a position to take a less ignorant view. Some will interpret this as arising not from the boys' own independence of mind so much as from the influence of their perhaps more than averagely "political" adult friends – all of whom were, after all, members of the sexual reform association, NVSH. Be that as it may, the robustness is clear enough. Jos (13), for instance, was adamant that people should not interfere in others' business. Regarding his relationship with Bas (35) he managed to face down not just other youngsters but teachers, too:

Well, once I had problems with it in the lower school, because of other boys – the same ones who always came here to Bas. My sister overheard them, and then passed it on. So...big problems.

She told your parents?

No, our class teacher and other kids. Then the headmaster came here to Bas. My mother still doesn't know about it, thank heavens.

And there are others who know you have sex with Bas?

Yes, my brother and his friends – they caught on one time when I gave Bas a kiss... in the hall. My brother said, "Hey, what are you doing?" That's how he found out. And then he told everybody, the other boys.

How did you feel about that?

Well, not nice. No, I kept on having problems at school, with teachers and other kids.

How do you feel about others making problems about it?

I think that's not normal. It all happens out of school, in the first place... and what business is it of theirs. It's my life![323]

In most cases the boys' peers did not know what was going on. Willem (13) was sure that they knew little or nothing about man-boy relationships. If they did, their outlook would change, just as his own had:

Yes, it's completely normal. But, well, the first time I thought it was sort of dirty, too.

At first you, too, found it dirty?

Yeah, at first it seemed awful strange. But now I don't find it strange at all.

But what do you think about their finding it strange?

I think it's stupid, that they think it's dirty. If they'd just do it once themselves they'd talk a whole lot different about it, I think.

What would they say about it if they did experience it themselves?

They'd say it's great! Yes, I really think they would.[324]

Rob (12) thought his pals would not understand. But his explanation would surely touch a chord with every adolescent boy who has found it tough to start scoring with girls:

They would have expected something different from me.

How do you mean, something different?

Well, that I'd go for girls and stuff, something like that. At least, that's the way you think. Yeah, not just the guys but the girls too. Chasing one girl after another. I'm really not that type. I'd like to, but, well, you don't get much.

What don't you get much of?

You don't get much from girls. With us the girls won't do practically anything. They do so little you get almost nothing out of it.

What do they do so little of?

About all they'll give you is a kiss, and nothing more, seems to me.[325]

Ah, the cruelty of girls! Boys and men alike take it as an inescapable part of the human condition that females will usually play hard to get, a lament that finds strong theoretical support from evolutionary psychology. But the experience of boys such as Rob would have been entirely different in a good many "primitive" cultures known to anthropology, cultures in which girls were *encouraged* to gain pre-marital sexual experience rather than being disparaged for doing so. Verrier Elwin, who spent most of his life among the tribal Muria people of Bastar, in central India, described in immense detail a society in which children and adolescents had a much more relaxed and fulfilled introduction to sexuality than their peers in the "developed" world.[326] Elwin's book *The Muria and their Ghotul* appeared in 1947 and it is probable that since then the old ways have been swept aside by the march of "advanced" modernity – a genuine advance in material terms, perhaps, but a costly one socially.[327]

From the age of six or seven onwards youngsters lived in their own, self-regulated communal house called a ghotul. They were free to come and go as they pleased between the ghotul and the parental home. Within the ghotul the children were free to engage in sex rehearsal play. Adolescents were able to have intercourse as they chose, able to experiment with different partners and under no pressure to make a premature commitment. It was not considered proper for adolescent boys to have coitus with prepubertal girls, but other forms of intimacy were permissible between all.

As a sexual apprenticeship, ghotul life had much going for it. Although marital breakdown was considered a misfortune rather than a shameful matter, there was very little divorce – at about 3% it was something like a tenth of the figure for Britain and the US these days. Pre-marital pregnancy was a rarity among the Muria, thanks to natural infertility in the year or so immediately following menarche. By the time full fertility was reached in Muria society a girl was old enough for married life. In western societies, with much later marriage, we cannot take such a relaxed view of teenage pregnancy, but unlike the Muria we do have birth control, and those countries with good sex education and relatively relaxed attitudes to juvenile sexual expression – Holland being a leading example – suggest it works. Teenage pregnancies in Holland are far lower than in the UK, with its poor sex education record and repressive, moralistic culture.

We have seen in this chapter some of the ways in which boys can relate to men, including sexually, in a country of the developed West. Sandfort's research, it will be recalled, set out with just one question to answer: "Can a boy experience sex with an adult positively?" His answer, backed by a far more detailed and careful analysis of the evidence than it is possible to relate here, was a resounding yes, and readers may judge for themselves whether this accords with what they have just read. How then, if at all, can such accounts be squared with the horror stories of abuse we so often hear?

The difference of tone is undoubtedly explained by a change of focus. The accent in most accounts, whether in the popular media or in academic research, is usually on child-adult sexual encounters far removed from the consensual ones studied by Sandfort. Nonetheless, conservative commentators would say we are still talking about abuse: we do not know how the Dutch boys encountered in this chapter began to feel about these early encounters once they entered adulthood. Was there regret? Did they start to feel they had been manipulated and exploited? Unfortunately, Sandfort never undertook a follow-up study. His career took him into AIDS research, in which he is now a very eminent and respected figure. It is a great pity he never found the time to go back and do a follow-up after, say, ten years when all or most of the boys would still have been easily contactable. At that point, too, in their early twenties or thereabouts, many of them would perhaps still be sufficiently uncertain about their future to ponder what effect their sexual history might have had on them – especially if, for any reason, their first one or two relationships with women did not go well. And what would these young men say about the past to their girlfriends or wives? Would they want to talk about it at all? Would they, by now fully acculturated, have grown ashamed of the past? Do they keep it as a guilty secret, a burden on them?

It is beyond the scope of this book about Michael Jackson to go into a comprehensive discussion of sexual "abuse" – or even to explore in any depth what that often misleading term means – but it would be silly just to leave the negative speculations of the foregoing paragraph hanging when at least a hint can be left that the story need not have a gloomy ending at all. Even among sexual conservatives there are, at least among those who have studied child-adult sexual relations, those who concede that they do not always have a harmful long-term outcome and that they can even be beneficial. This need hardly be so surprising, really, now that we have taken Sandfort's work into account and seen how boys can thrive on adult attention they may not otherwise have received.

Long-term outcomes have been studied indirectly through surveys, in which information is typically gained through confidential questionnaires given to selected groups of young adults, who are asked whether they experienced a sexual encounter with an adult when they were a child and how they felt it had affected them. A good many studies of this kind have been done among college students. It could be objected that those most traumatised by an early sexual encounter are precisely those most likely to miss out of getting a college education, thus distorting any figures such surveys produce. It is a strong-sounding point, but studies based on a variety of population groups, including people who have never been to college, actually tend to yield quite similar results.

The most famous student study to date was one in which all previous studies meeting appropriate academic criteria were examined together in what is known as a meta-analysis. A great advantage of this method is that the database of all the studies together is vastly greater than any single study taken on its own, and thus reveals a more representative picture. A landmark paper by Rind, Tromovitch and Bauserman in 1998 revealed the results of a meta-analysis based on fifty nine studies of college students showing the effects on those who had been involved as children in sexual encounters with adults. This provided an important corrective to the view that such encounters are always traumatic. A careful statistical analysis showed that many problems which the original researchers had uncritically assumed to be caused by sexual abuse could more plausibly be attributed to generally inadequate family environments, with which they were much more strongly correlated.[328]

This paper proved to be dynamite, provoking an unprecedented political reaction in the United States. What prompted an outraged response was not the quality of the science but the authors' highly professional and all too rare refusal to wrap their data in a moralistic package at odds with the actual findings.

The Rind study did not examine the significance of consent, whether "informed consent" or otherwise, in its impact on long-term outcomes. A subsequent study by Coxell and his colleagues fills this gap, at least with regard to consenting boys.[329] The Coxell team examined a non-clinical sample of nearly 2,500 men in Great Britain, recruited from general medical practices. They inquired about sexual activity prior to age sixteen with someone at least five years older in which they had willingly taken part, finding that 7.7% had had what the researchers termed consensual sex prior to age sixteen with persons significantly older; 5.3% of the men reported having had non-consensual sex. The men were asked whether they had reported a psychological problem of at least two weeks' duration sometime in their life. The consenting group reported no more problems than the control group but the non-consenting group had significantly more problems than either of these groups.

This raises an interesting challenge to those who say children can never give valid consent to sexual activity. If children cannot give valid consent, how come it is only the ones who do not want the sex in their encounters with adults who end up having psychological problems? Why does consent discriminate so well between good and bad outcomes if it is not valid?

Unfortunately, we cannot assume that a study like Coxell's undertaken in, say, the year 2020, would produce similar results. Anxiety over adult-child sexual contact has reached such a pitch in recent decades that children presently in such relationships, no matter how consenting they are, may later become screwed up unnecessarily over them just because of the extreme extent to which they have become ever more taboo. In other words, for society to insist ever more vehemently that children are harmed in such contacts may be a self-fulfilling prophesy. Sandfort himself recognised this:

> The fact that these twenty five boys had mainly pleasant experiences does not mean that paedosexual experiences are necessarily good for them or that adults should approve of them. What is good for the child cannot be determined quite so easily. That is dependent upon, among other things, the norms and values to which people adhere.[330]

Equally, though, it is not inevitable that society's norms and values will remain constant. Attitudes towards sex between gay men and lesbians have changed dramatically in only a few decades; there could be a similar reversal with respect to consensual child-adult sexual relations.

We have seen from the disapproval expressed by some of the boys' parents, teachers and peers in the Sandfort study that the norms and values of the Netherlands in the 1980s were not necessarily poles apart from those in Michael Jackson's home state of California. Nevertheless some differences do emerge: readers will have noticed, for instance, that a number of parents did accept and even approve of their child's sexual relationship. Even the teachers who disapproved apparently saw no compelling reason to call in the police. Such differences could be crucial to the long-term well-being of Sandfort's boys: half the battle lies in avoiding disasters like the McMartin Pre-School affair.

Sandfort also says that misuse by the older partners of their power almost never occurred, according to the boys.[331] Nevertheless, the feeling that adults have an eminently exploitable advantage over the child in terms of greater size, experience, maturity and economic strength, runs deep in many people's suspicion of adult-child sexual relations. And the problem is only compounded when the accused adult happens to be a mega-rich pop star wielding enormous power. It is a theme that will be taken up when we look more closely at Michael's world of security guards and lawyers. In fact it is already time for Michael to take centre stage again in this book. We need now to understand a little more about how his feelings and social behaviour developed from childhood onwards. The focus of many Jacksonologists has understandably been on the man's music; ours will be on his mind.

CHAPTER EIGHT

Family Values: An American Nightmare

With exquisitely ironic timing, just weeks after the Chandler allegations against Michael had broken, the TV networks were screening a mini-series titled *The Jacksons: An American Dream*, a four-hour drama documentary on the rags-to-riches rise of the world's most famous pop music family. It was the story of a model family, who had pulled themselves up by their own bootstraps. Through sheer hard work and dedication, using to the full the talents God had given them, they had stuck together in pursuit of a dream. Unlike many of their rivals in the showbiz world, their destiny was not to be destroyed by drug abuse or loose living of any kind. For they were wholesome, God-fearing folks: strict Jehovah's Witnesses. Little Michael and his elder brothers, who had comprised the Jackson Five, had been a fine example to other youngsters, not least to black teenagers searching for an escape from the mean streets of the ghetto.

That this description is a little heavy on the clichés – "rags-to-riches", "pulled up by bootstraps", "American Dream", "mean streets" – is a reflection of the stereotypical demands the public places on its heroes. It was a well-placed instinct that drove Michael's brother Jermaine and his partner Margaret Maldonado to produce a mini-series exploiting such clichés. They and their publicists know there is a powerful market for portrayals of families in which traditional, conservative values are seen to work, to yield results in terms of success and happiness. It is an image purveyed in hundreds of Hollywood movies, and can reliably be expected to have even more appeal when apparently based on real life. No matter how much the facts have to be stretched out, or chopped off, to fit the Procrustean bed of "family values" – the most important cliché of the lot – it is a product in no danger of lacking customers.

To speak of stretching the truth here, or chopping off an inconvenient fact there, may be thought an excessively restrained description of the myth-making process in the case of the Jackson family. For what are we to make of an "ideal", squeaky-clean family in which the father is more than credibly reported to have had many extra-marital affairs and even raised a second family unbeknown to his first? A father who regularly beat and bullied his children? A family in which one of the daughters (La Toya) would scandalise her "respectable" parents and siblings by appearing topless in a *Playboy* centrefold, marry a former brothel owner, accuse her father of sexually abusing her, and hint that Michael may have been a victim, too? A family most of whose children would both marry and divorce young, with the boys having a reputation for womanising and at least one of whom (Jermaine) faced allegations by his ex-wife of rape and another of beating up his spouse?[332] Or whose mother, all sweetness and light according to the official image, stands accused of being "the guiding force behind the cruelty and abuse" in the household[333] and "the most treacherous, evil person in the world"?[334] A family capable of monstrous greed and self-indulgence? One whose members were constantly squabbling and sniping at each other, parasitically dependent on its leading light? A family that hides behind the respectability of religion, yet hypocritically ignores its rules and requirements?[335]

What should we make of all this? As with the charges levelled at Michael himself, the more extreme and less well supported claims should be treated with caution. The fact that La Toya Jackson, for instance, made sexual allegations against her father, Joseph, is one about which we should be especially sceptical. In recent years it has been fashionable, positively chic, for female celebrities to parade their supposedly traumatic early life on TV chat shows. There is any number of ulterior motives for making such claims, especially in La Toya's case. Also La Toya has been an inconsistent witness, flip-flopping from support for Michael over the allegations against him to condemnation and back to support again.

Not that she ever said he was innocent. That would be an unfair suggestion. In the early stages of the scandal, she herself scandalised many loyal fans of Michael precisely because she seemed to be prevaricating, damning him with faint praise instead of proclaiming her brother's innocence loud and clear. However, that faint praise had in fact amounted to considerable support. On a TV show called *The Devil's Advocate*, for instance, she said Michael "loves children dearly", is "a very sweet and kind person" and if she had children of her own would trust them with her brother. Within a couple of months after this she was saying she could no longer remain a "silent collaborator" in Michael's "crimes against small, innocent children."[336] And before long she was piling it on much more, claiming there were boys in mental institutions as a result of Michael's "crimes", boys whose treatment was being paid for by him but who would never be normal again.[337] Can we trust anyone whose position shifts at such a rate? Michael's principal biographer, Randy Taraborrelli, thinks not, and he is a person who would appear to know a thing or two about the family, having spent years in music journalism and seen the protagonists at close quarters over a sustained period.[338]

He is not infallible. No single perspective can encompass the whole truth. But Taraborrelli's book has given us the most extensive in-depth work available on Michael's family background, and it is well documented. What follows in this chapter owes a great deal to Taraborrelli. His biography, *Michael Jackson: The Magic and the Madness*, presents a much fuller picture of Michael's background and mental development than I can encompass. The aim here is to highlight what seem to be particularly relevant factors as regards Michael's sexual and moral development and to discuss them in light of the allegations against him.

To begin with, though, a brief reprise of the Jackson legend is in order, for which I have raided Todd Gold's more concise biography, *Michael Jackson: The Man in the Mirror*.[339] Michael's mother, Katherine, "the gracious, soft-spoken, deeply religious Jackson matriarch" (well, this is the legend, remember), was born in rural Alabama in 1931 to a farming family. At the age of four, Katie, as she was known, and her family resettled in East Chicago, Indiana. She reputedly had singing talent, but would never have made a dancer, having a permanent limp following polio in her infancy.

Her husband Joseph also came from the South, having been born in 1929 in Arkansas. His father was a high school teacher who married one of his students. The marriage broke up when Joseph was eight, and he moved with his mother to Gary, Indiana, where he was later to find work in one of the local steel mills. Katherine and Joseph met soon after and wed in 1949, setting up home in Gary. He was twenty and already divorced following a brief previous marriage; she was eighteen. The next year Maureen, better known as Rebbie, was born, and the rest of what was destined to be a large family soon followed: Jackie, Tito, Jermaine, La Toya, Marlon, Michael, Randy and Janet. Michael was born on 29 August 1958.

Gary, a short haul down Route 80 from Chicago, was in those days reputedly a grim industrial town. Joe was a crane driver, sometimes moonlighting as a welder to support his many children. The family home at 2300 Jackson Street (so named long before the occupants became famous) was in a neighbourhood of modest prosperity, not a poor ghetto, though the legend plays up their early hardship. As parents, according to Gold, "Joe and Katherine fostered traditional, mid-western values of love, family unity, God, and hard work. She was generous, nurturing and kind; he was an iron-fisted disciplinarian who brooked no nonsense." Michael is presented in the legend as a composite of the two: "sensitive, gentle and pious like his mother and determined and stubborn like his dad".

Katherine was the force behind the family's upbringing as Jehovah's Witnesses, following her conversion from the Lutheran persuasion when Michael was five. Joe, himself raised as a Lutheran, found the Kingdom Hall meetings boring and soon stopped attending. Michael, by contrast, like his elder sisters Rebbie and La Toya, took the Bible teachings to heart. Michael came alive during the services and was always asking his mother questions about God. From early childhood until his break with the Witnesses in 1987, religion was to be a special bond between Michael and his mother.

Joseph had always had a dream of making a fortune and moving with the family to a grand house in California, according to the TV mini-series. Those dreams were built at first on making a musical career for himself. He gigged at weekends with a band called the Falcons. They often practised in the Jacksons' living room, where the three-year-old Michael became early acquainted with the world of show business from the inside. His elder brothers played in secret with their father's treasured guitar, an instrument strictly off-limits to them. The story has it that one day a string broke. Tito returned the instrument to the closet and tried to pretend nothing had happened. Joe got mad, discovered the culprit and "whipped Tito pretty good". But when he calmed down he asked the boy to play the guitar and show what he could do. Tito proved impressive. It was the beginning of Joe's discovery that his family had musical potential, and that they, not the Falcons, could be the key to making that dream of California a reality.

Little Michael was still only four when he joined his brothers in the Jackson Five, alternating lead vocals with Jermaine. Both as a singer and as a nimble dancer, doing James Brown impersonations, he captured hearts among the people of Gary, and won a citywide talent contest at the age of seven, with renditions of "My Girl" and "Shake it Baby". A long apprenticeship, with many hours spent rehearsing, on top of an exhausting grind performing six shows a day seven days a week by the age of nine, subjected Michael to a sweatshop regime outlawed decades earlier by child labour laws.

But the Jackson Five were making rapid strides, winning a recording contract with a local firm, making a triumphant appearance at a crucial venue for black entertainers, the Apollo Theater, Harlem, and then really hitting the big time when they were signed up by Motown Records in 1968, with Michael still only ten years old. It was to be a hugely successful arrangement. The Jackson Five released an unprecedented string of chart-topping records, the first four each soaring to *Billboard*'s number one.

Much was owed in all this to Joe Jackson's drive, the reputation and flair of Motown, and accomplished performances by Jackie, Tito, Jermaine and Marlon. The star, though, was always and undoubtedly Michael. His elder brothers may at times have felt a twinge, or more, of resentment or jealousy, but Michael's special qualities were never in question. For young girl fans, Jackie or Jermaine was often the fantasy boyfriend, the special heartthrob, but Michael was always the main attraction as a performer.

The American dream, or more specifically the Californian one, was swiftly turned into tangible reality. Joe and the Jackson Five established a bridgehead in the Golden State in 1969, Michael living for a while as a temporary measure with Diana Ross, that other Motown star who had supposedly "discovered" the Jackson Five; Katherine and the rest of the family following soon after. By 1971 the family had a mansion at 4641 Hayvenhurst, Encino, as their permanent base, a home still occupied by Joe and Katherine, and Michael's home too until he bought Neverland in 1988. Neighbours in the affluent area have included such famous names as Dick Van Dyke and Aretha Franklin.

The fame and glamour of the Jackson family was appropriately symbolised by the move west, from grey, industrial Gary to the sunshine land of Hollywood stars. By now the boys were being mobbed at airports by hysterical fans in scenes reminiscent of Beatle-mania. And as he approached adolescence Michael would become rather shy and withdrawn compared to the bubbly, outgoing child he had been. He would also begin to acquire an identity distinct from the Jackson Five. His first solo record, "Got to be there", was released in 1971 and sold over one and a half million. His first single to top the charts, though, was "Ben" the following year, a record which, even more than the California move, provides us with a symbolic landmark. A haunting, melancholy ballad about a friendship, it was the title song for a film of the same name.

While the words of the song offered no clue to Ben's identity, the film most emphatically did. For Ben turns out to be a rat, that most loathed, feared and despised of rodents. The film, and by implication the song, is about a young boy's friendship with the otherwise unloved little beast. The tone is softly plaintive, in effect telling us, with a lingering sadness, that this is a relationship only the two of them will ever understand. The adult Michael would certainly come to know a thing or two about that predicament. Indeed, in his grown-up strangeness, he was compared to E.T., an outer space alien loved by children, especially the boy who manages, improbably, to strike up an understanding with him.

In the film *Ben*, we find this rapport between child and "alien" uncannily prefigured, with the roles reversed and Michael as the young boy. This is more than just an odd coincidence. The important part of the symbolism is that this was not just any old song for Michael to sing. Its meaning seems to have touched a chord in him. He saw the movie many times. Like the film's young hero, he too was passionate about rats, keeping a cage of them in his bedroom, as Taraborrelli relates the story. Equally symbolic, we may feel, is Michael's reaction to the ghastly discovery one day that they were eating each other. "Sickened by the sight", says the biographer, Michael put the rat cage outdoors."[340]

Supposing we put this a little differently, saying instead, "Unwilling to confront this painful aspect of reality, Michael put..." etc. The new spin is not arbitrary. It reflects the latter part of the sentence: if Michael put the cage outdoors it would not stop the rats eating each other, it would just stop him having to see it. If the story is true it indicates a capacity for putting sickening things out of mind by putting them out of sight, a shallow, head-in-the-sand response. Doubtless it is an impulse most of us give way to at times and in itself gives little reason to be critical of the adolescent star, then aged fourteen. On the contrary, those attracted to Michael's abhorrence of violence may find the story reinforces his image. After all, they may say, if that is what rats do to each other, there was nothing Michael could have done about it, so why not just try to put it out of mind?

Well, to start with, he might have pondered whether keeping rats in a cage is such a good idea. Especially thirty of them. That is the number Taraborrelli gives, reporting what Katherine had discovered to her horror. Even allowing for exaggeration, it sounds like a case of overcrowding. Do we really need the benefits of controlled scientific research into animal stress to understand why rats in such conditions might attack and eat each other? If Michael had been as fond of animals, and as sensitive and empathic towards the feelings of others as his publicity people would have had us believe ("others" in the broad sense of any sentient creatures, including children), shouldn't he have sensed, even at fourteen, that he might have some responsibility for what was happening among these wretched rats?

Not necessarily. Even Taraborrelli, in his full maturity, remarks only that the rats were doing "what rats will do", as though what we are seeing is just nature red in tooth and claw, eternal, ungovernable, quite indifferent to the occasional disgust of humans, even young superstars.[341] As a society too, it is only in the last few decades that we have started to become sensitive in a major way to issues of animal welfare, and the problems for animals of being kept in unnatural conditions in zoos. While it would not be fair to Michael to lay too much emphasis on this one anecdote, even in the unlikely event of its being true to the last detail, it does mark the beginning of a real question mark over his character, a question that extended to his later friendship with (exploitation of?) Muscles the snake, Bubbles the chimp and all the animals at his Neverland zoo – and even, it may be felt, to his relations with children.

But this is to run on ahead somewhat. At any rate, the bizarre theme of the song caused a few raised eyebrows. As Michael's solo-artist career developed, there were to be ever more of those.

So much for the legend and the landmarks of Michael's early years. Now we can begin to pick out from this period some of the themes salient to our enquiry: discipline, for instance, and Joseph's role as a father. Gold's description of him as an iron-fisted disciplinarian, offered without further comment, could easily be taken as a compliment, an affirmation of his role in a family success story. Yet that same concept takes on a very different meaning in La Toya's recollections, and not just hers. She has claimed he beat her violently, brutally. He once put lighted matches to her toes, she says, and at other times delighted in pointing a gun at his terrified children, squeezing the trigger until a click told them it was not loaded.[342] Michael also publicly spoke of the beatings his father gave, telling the world Joseph could make him physically sick with fear, even into adulthood.[343]

None of the children was ever close to Joseph, who seemed quite incapable of expressing affection towards them.[344] The older boys took the full force of their father's wrath, weathering the storm as best they could, keeping out of harm's way if possible. Michael alone showed signs of fighting back. From quite early in life he knew he had a trump card to play. It could not prevent Joseph's anger, or his own fear, but he could still play the card to triumphant effect. Taraborrelli describes its use, after Joe had tried to make Michael execute a dance step in a certain way, but he had refused to listen:

> Joe smacked Michael across the face. Michael fell backward and hit the floor with a thud. "Now, you do it the way I told you to! You hear me?" Joe hollered at the nine-year-old. Michael began to cry. His right cheek turned red and sore. "I ain't doin' it that way," he said. Joe glared at him and took one step forward, his hand raised to strike again. Michael scrambled up off the floor and backed away. "Hey, don't you hit me," he told his father. "'Cause if you ever hit me again, it'll be the last time I ever sing. And I mean it." Michael must have said the magic words. Joe turned and walked away.[345]

The literature on family dysfunction, juvenile delinquency, and "mixed-up kids" growing into adulthood with all manner of social and sexual problems, overwhelmingly emphasises the chaotic effect of growing up with parents who send out mixed messages. The Jackson household could scarcely provide a better case study: the message reaching the children from each of their parents was utterly contradictory. Although our idealised view of parenting has traditionally placed a positive value on a difference of emphasis between the stern father and the caring mother, we see the two roles as complementing, not contradicting, each other. Up to a point life does seem to have worked that way at 2300 Jackson Street. Joe and Kate did complement each other and the marriage worked well enough to survive the long and rocky trail to California. They were wed when George VI was King of England and Bill Clinton was still in diapers, and have stayed together for over sixty years, which is more than can be said for most showbiz relationships, or indeed any other sort of partnership.

To their children, though, and perhaps especially to Rebbie, La Toya and Michael, who all took their religion so earnestly, the differences between their parents must have looked much deeper than that between complementary halves of a functioning whole. It must have been difficult to reconcile Joe's casual, indifferent attitude towards religion with Kate's serious, devout one. To understand the significance of this, we have to remind ourselves just what a strict and demanding sect the Jehovah's Witnesses are, and the tremendous impact the teachings would inevitably have on the minds of young children, especially those of a sensitive, serious disposition like Michael. Unless we live on a remote Hebridean island (and perhaps even then), we have all been targeted for doorstep conversion by smartly turned out smile-clones robotically peddling scripture on behalf of their cult (the term is scarcely too strong). That is how Katherine herself was recruited. Most of us prefer to decline the propaganda in some haste, shutting the door as fast as we politely can. We read newspaper stories from time to time about life and death dramas arising because the Witnesses do not approve of blood transfusions, but otherwise we don't know a lot about their faith.

A key point is their belief in the coming great battle of Armageddon, in which only a few of God's servants will survive a terrible holocaust – a few who would distinctly not be expected to include those, like Joseph, who did not even bother to go to church. It would be a tough enough matter for even the more devout and pious members of the Jackson family to win salvation and avoid hellfire. If Michael and the others wanted to be saved they would have to stick rigidly to the straight and narrow path of the church's teachings; the terrible threat of failure and eternal damnation hung over them always.

Just how straight and narrow the path is may be judged by the teaching that Christmas is a pagan holiday, hence the parties and presents associated with it are not allowed. Same for birthdays: fun is strictly a no-no. Witnesses are judged by their "good deeds", a concept which does not include giving to charities, as preaching the gospel is considered the only worthwhile charitable deed.[346] Instead witnesses are expected to witness i.e. to proselytise door-to-door. They are not supposed to interest themselves in material things such as expensive clothes or cars – or making a pile in the music business and moving to a mansion in California. Katherine herself soon became excited by the boys' growing success, but was made uneasy when they would return from gigs with their pockets full of dollar bills: she would try to tell them money was not the important thing.[347]

If the two parents taught their children rather contradictory attitudes towards money, the mixed message on sexual morality was far more striking. As might be expected, the Witnesses' teaching is full of Thou Shalt Nots. Lust, in thought or deed, is considered sinful. They emphasise 1 Corinthians 6:9. None of the unrighteous, "neither fornicators, nor idolaters, nor effeminate men, nor abusers of themselves with mankind" would inherit the kingdom of God. Sex was reserved for marriage, and even within wedlock options such as oral or anal sex were forbidden.[348] When rumours were being put about that Michael is gay, long before the Chandler allegations, his mother responded by saying "Michael is not gay. It's against his religion. It's against God. The Bible speaks against it."[349] While sophisticates might shake their heads sadly at Katherine's apparent notion that Michael would have had any choice over his orientation, the doctrine is clear enough: gayness is an abomination. And that is the thinking Michael had to grow up with.

Taraborrelli's view of Michael has understandably changed over the years, especially in the light of the 2005 trial. But the biographer appeared at one time to feel the star's religion would have been a decisive influence on his behaviour. He wrote: "Michael Jackson would never allow himself to have homosexual relationships, even if he did have feelings for other men. He is much too puritanical, a result of his religious background."[350] I am not sure Taraborrelli ever truly believed that, but if so it was a naïve notion. For one thing, as we shall see, Michael broke with the Witnesses. For decades he was not bound by the strictures of their code, and indeed we have some reason to suppose he consciously rejected them. A puritanical conscience, in a more general sense, is no doubt a harder thing to repudiate than a particular church, but the power of sexual desire should never be underestimated either.

Also, we must not forget that Michael had a father as well as a mother, and Joseph's influence was very different. Joe was keen enough on Katherine's religion in one way. God the father was revealed through the Witnesses' teachings as a tough, authoritarian figure, who believed in giving his children firm rules to live by, which they had to obey on pain of terrible penalties. God had obviously learned a thing or two from Joe about how to run a family. That God guy was one tough cookie just like himself! Joe would make the boys shift a load of bricks from one part of the yard to another and then back again, just to show them who was boss and to "toughen them up".[351] God had surely jotted down a note of that one for future use.

The idea that Joe might himself obey all the church rules was an alien concept to him. Rules were just for women and kids. And even they were exempt when Joe said so. In the early days of the Jackson Five, Joe would take the boys into dives and strip joints. "Nine-year-old Michael knew those were wicked places," says Taraborrelli. "Ordinarily strict, Joe apparently gave the boys free rein at those times, allowing Michael to stand in the wings and watch as men in packed, smelly clubs whistled at voluptuous women who took off their clothes lasciviously, piece by piece, until they were naked. They would throw their panties into the audience, and the men would sniff them."[352]

As part of the act for one of the Jackson Five's numbers, "Skinny legs and all", Joe encouraged Michael to go out into the audience, crawl under tables, lift up women's skirts and look under: "No matter how embarrassed Michael may have been, he embellished his performance by rolling his eyes and smiling wickedly because the crowds loved it enough to throw money onto the stage. The boys would scramble for the loose change, running for the halves and quarters first. "I had so much money in my pockets, I couldn't even walk," Michael recalled."[353]

Late at night Joe would come into the boys' hotel rooms with giggling girls in tow. He would say goodnight and then slip away with his lady friends. The boys, in bed in their pyjamas, would hear laughter coming from Joe's room next door. It was as if, says Taraborrelli in one of his more astute remarks, he wanted to be certain that the boys knew what was going on.[354]

Why should that be? To show the boys what a man's life should really be like, instead of all that religious crap? To let them know Joe Jackson did what the hell he liked? The biographer calls in aid a Hollywood psychiatrist to dispense a liberal dose of psychobabble on this point, culminating in a load of Oedipus schmoedipus regarding the possible effects on Michael.

The boys' actual responses are more interesting. The ones who have spoken about these episodes profess to have been shocked and hurt by Joe's infidelity to their mother, rather than amused by it. That may have been so. On the other hand the three eldest boys all grew up to have extra-marital affairs and get divorced. Rather than repudiating Joe's behaviour they have to a considerable extent copied it. We see a gap opening up between what they say is right and the way they actually behave. Taraborrelli remarks, again astutely, that at the age of eight Michael was old enough to understand what was going on, and sensitive enough to be aware that hypocrisy played a large part in his family's life, and even in his own actions.[355]

In his long bachelor years he could scarcely have extra-marital affairs or divorce problems though. For a while in his youth and early adulthood this looked fine. He was in a position to play to perfection the part of the good son, devoted to his mother and his religion. He could be a bit of a goody goody even, sermonising to other folks, not least his brothers, on how they should live their lives. Another one to get the treatment was a devoted fan called Theresa Gonsalves, who met Michael when the pair were both sixteen. Backstage after a show Jackie tried, unsuccessfully, to cajole Michael into kissing her. On another occasion Michael invited her into his dressing room. The two were alone together for the first time. Could Theresa's dream have been about to come true? Well, maybe, if she dreamed like St Theresa of Lisieux or Mother Teresa of Calcutta. For Michael started to talk about God, handing her a Bible, pointing to the scriptures and telling her how the end of the world was nigh. She was scared, but stayed talking a long while:

> He wasn't a normal kid, that's for certain. But I enjoyed being with him. I liked his innocence and was influenced by him. In fact, I stayed away from boys because of the way Michael had influenced me that night. I didn't believe in sex before marriage for a long time, because of talking to Michael about it. He was firm that premarital sex was wrong and was very convincing about it.[356]

It is easy for anyone to be firm that premarital sex is wrong if it does not happen to be a temptation for that person, if it just doesn't interest them. That thought apparently did not cross Theresa's mind. There was no reason why it should have. Our position is less innocent though. From where we stand we can see that any young pop star who is gay, or otherwise not attracted to women, is going to be plagued constantly by occasions when he is expected to kiss girls, date them, and have sex with them. Jackie and Jermaine, as youngsters, saw girl fans avid for sex as a great perk of the job. For Michael, it would probably have been a nightmare but for his religion, which offered a perfect excuse for inaction. Theresa concluded that Michael "wasn't a normal kid", but the judgment had been deflected well away from dangerous thoughts about his sexual orientation.

Michael's religion was convenient, but this is not to say it was a sham. By the age of twenty five he had scaled unprecedented heights in pop music. His *Thriller* album, just released, would soon reach record-breaking sales of forty seven million copies (by mid-2008 this had risen to an even more staggering 104 million). Yet he was still not merely attending church regularly, but also witnessing for the faith, "twice a week, maybe for an hour or two", according to Katherine, doing door-to-door work in disguise. Not a particularly effective one apparently: for some of those who recognised him, clutching a copy of *Watchtower*, it must have been like encountering God Himself on the doorstep.[357]

In themselves, such activities would prove very little beyond Michael making a show of being religious. But taken together with snatches of evidence as to what preoccupied his private thinking, plus his writing – of which we shall see something in the next chapter – a picture does clearly emerge of a sensitive, reflective individual, with sincerely held religious beliefs. His life did not always stack up too well against them, but the same could be said of half the saints in heaven. The trouble is he had no way in which to work through his problems, to get his thoughts clear. This was a young man with a busy working life, condemned to spend much of it rehearsing, or on stage, or trapped into messing about in hotel rooms with his brothers playing practical jokes on each other to relieve the boredom. What he really needed and never got, was the time and freedom to be alone, to think, and maybe to meet other people used to thinking in a more philosophical style than was available in the Jackson household: a university atmosphere would have been useful, in addition to the confused, crowded impressions gleaned from the university of life.

Instead he had to make do with chance conversations, unstructured moments, and, as regards sexuality, a random, kaleidoscopic set of impressions – the detached, voyeuristic impressions of an observer rather than a participant. He passed up the chance of making out with Theresa Gonsalves, but he did not pass up on conversation of importance to him. At first he spoke of God, and the wrongness of pre-marital sex, but that wasn't the end of matters. A later conversation with Theresa and some other girls reveals something else on his mind. Taraborrelli gives us an episode (published long before Michael was in the firing line in connection with children) recalled by Theresa. She had been with Michael at an apartment in New York. He mentioned a couple of other girl fans who had been pestering for a while, hanging about outside the building, and asked her what he should do about them. Theresa suggested inviting them up, so they would get things out of their system and leave him alone. He complied. Why? Fans hang around his hotels and homes all the time. Why invite these ones in? Was he uncomfortable being alone with Theresa, with little to keep her at a distance except by going on about God all the while? He invited them up.

> "Then we all sat around and talked about child abuse," Theresa recalled. "Michael was fascinated with child abuse. He wanted to know everything we girls had ever heard or read about it. He said he liked to read about child abuse as much as he possibly could."[358]

Michael could make good claim to having been a physically and emotionally abused child, so had every reason for a personal interest. It seems likely, however, that a conversation going into everything the participants had ever heard or read on child abuse would not have been confined to the physical side. Sexual abuse would have come into the picture too, even though at the time, in 1974, this aspect of abuse had not yet become the focus of intense public attention that it would some years later. What might Michael have had to say on the subject? It would not have been in character for him to give away much about his own feelings, and had he done so Taraborrelli might have been expected to report the fact. More likely, as Theresa implies, he listened, trying to gauge his own thoughts and feelings in relation to those of others.

The kaleidoscope of sexual impressions had been shaken in front of Michael's sometimes appalled eyes throughout his childhood. In those early years visions of his father's philandering and the naked ladies in the clubs would have made their retinal mark and been etched into his mind. As a teenager he was seldom far from witnessing his elder brothers' cheerful lechery, and is reported to have warned girls against it. On a tour of Japan in 1973, the 15-year-old Michael joined Marlon to watch pornographic movies on closed circuit TV in Jermaine's room at their Tokyo hotel.[359] No big deal for many kids, but what would the Witnesses have made of it? And how come Michael, with his strict views, didn't steer clear? There would have been social pressure to join in with the others watching the show. He had to be "one of the boys". Even if what he saw was no particular turn-on for him, he must also have been curious, and keen to make some sense of what he was seeing.

Round about this time someone in the family thought it was time Michael experienced sex for himself, and arranged for a couple of hookers to do the business, locking them in a room with him. According to Rebbie, Michael was utterly traumatised. She did not say whether he actually had sex.[360] Curiously – and revealingly, if true – he continued to see prostitutes after this time, not for sex but for company, someone to talk to. One of these women recalls meeting him after a concert in New York. On instructions from his staff she went to his dressing room:

> Michael was sitting in there alone. I walked in, and Michael told me to close the door. The first thing out of his mouth was "Why are you a prostitute?" Immediately, I was insulted – I don't know why – but I answered, "because I need the money." He said to me, "Would you like to have sex with me?" and I said, "Yes, of course I would." He asked me how much. I told him, "No charge." He seemed interested. So I undid my blouse and showed him my breasts. Immediately, he turned his head, as if my tits were the worst thing he'd ever seen. "Stop. I can't have sex with you. Please put them back," he said. When I asked him why, he told me, "Because I just can't." I thought he meant he couldn't get an erection, he looked so sad. Then he said, "Can we just talk about you and your life?" I didn't want to talk, that's not why I went there. So I gave him my telephone number.
>
> "Any time you want to get off, you call me," I said. Michael looked at me and asked, "What does that mean, to get off?" I swear he was totally sincere. "It means fuck, Michael," I told him. "Any time you want to fuck, you call me. Get it?" He said, "Oh, okay. Maybe I'll call you some day. I doubt it, though." And I left. He struck me as so pitifully lonely and naïve. Just a nice, mixed-up, good-looking guy who wanted some female companionship. No way he was about to have sex that night, though. He seemed scared to death. I wondered if he would ever call. He never did.[361]

The lack of obvious sexual interest in women was to be a continuing theme of Michael's life, unless we count his dynastic dalliance with Lisa Marie Presley, daughter of Elvis. His supposed secret marriage to her in the Dominican Republic in May 1994 was described in one early report as a cynical ploy to boost sales of his upcoming album.[362] Much the more obvious cynical motive, though, would have to be his need to boost his thin heterosexual credentials as soon as possible in the wake of the child sex allegations. It may not be without significance that the district attorneys and police heading the investigation finally met and decided to abandon their efforts to charge Jackson just one day after news of the marriage surfaced in the media.[363] The police always looked like having an uphill battle after Jordan Chandler, their main witness, had been taken out of play. Michael would be able to discredit other witnesses and explain his love of children as non-sexual – a task much easier for a married man.

Only, however, because people are so desperately keen to be fooled. By and large, people like to believe their idols are glamorous versions of themselves, not oddballs. To many, for instance, it is just not acceptable that the authors of *Alice in Wonderland* and *Peter Pan*, two of the world's most renowned classics of children's literature, had a suspiciously intense interest in children. Countless writers have scribbled at length to discount any suggestion that Lewis Carroll might have been sexually attracted to, or active with, little girls. Ditto JM Barrie and small boys. Yet Carroll, or Charles Dodgson, as he would have been called in court if he had ever been brought to justice, took nude photos of girls that would be considered child pornography by today's standards. And Barrie has described the finger-trembling excitement of undressing a six-year-old boy in terms only an idiot or wilfully blind observer could fail to recognise as intensely erotic.[364] Barrie's work was an inspiration for Michael and for that reason we shall be hearing much more about him in the next chapter.

In Michael's teenage years the fans needed only the faintest hint of a "romantic" incident of some kind to establish him in their minds as a regular guy – and one around whom millions of girl fans would build their own romantic and erotic fantasies. Just such an incident was providentially laid on, courtesy of a chance encounter between Michael, at eighteen, and Tatum O'Neal, child star in the film *Paper Moon*, and now a thirteen-year-old temptress. The two bumped into each other at the Rox club, in Los Angeles. Or rather she bumped into him. Tatum was with her father, Ryan. Michael, socialising with publicists, suddenly felt a soft hand reach over and grab his. It was Tatum. She invited him to a dinner party at the estate of *Playboy* publisher Hugh Hefner. While others were watching a show put on for the occasion, Tatum asked Michael to go in the hot tub with her. "But I don't have a bathing suit," he protested. "Who needs bathing suits?" she replied. When Michael began to blush, one of Hefner's staff was sent to produce swimsuits.[365]

It turned out to be too good a story to do the rounds unadorned. Or rather, adorned. The pair *did* bath naked together. That became the official rumour, to be enshrined in legend. Interviews were given in which it was officially denied, so the story had to be true. Michael took advantage of the situation to claim in his autobiography that Tatum was his first love. She firmly indicated, though, that the contact was strictly platonic. The two would be seen in public together from time to time, but, according to Tatum, "Sex was something Michael neither knew nor cared about."[366]

Michael would later confirm Tatum's account with astonishing and uncharacteristic candour in Martin Bashir's controversial documentary, although he would claim he had been not indifferent but scared stiff – or perhaps scared limp. He described a sexually go-getting young Tatum ringing him up and telling him to get on over to her house for love-making. Asked what she said, Michael told Bashir:

> All the sexual stuff. So I'm scared to death… scared because I'd never done anything like that. I came over there trying to be Mr Big Shot and brave, and I remember she cut out all the lights in her bedroom, opened the curtains. You could see the whole skyline of the city…It was beautiful. And she told me to go over and lie on the bed, and I did. I lay on the bed and she slowly walked over and she touched the button of my shirt to open it and I took my hands like this [He covers his face with his hands] and I wouldn't let them down. And she just walked away. She just knew I was too shy for it. That's what happened.

"Did you not feel tempted at all?" Bashir asked.

Michael shook his head, indicating that he had not. "I was frightened," he said. "I was afraid. I don't think I was ready for that."

He never would be.

Michael would later claim to have been romantically attached to Diana Ross and Brooke Shields, but both women have indicated there was never any sexual involvement.[367] In a kiss-and-tell story with a difference, Tatiana Thumbtzen, cast as a lead dancer in a Jackson video, has told of her own eighteen-month campaign to woo Michael, using all her feminine charms to seduce him into her bed.

Tatiana claims Michael flirted with her on set, but when the cameras stopped rolling he always declined to go further. "He'd go so far," she said, "but then he'd back off and say, 'See you tomorrow. Sleep well.' I'd wonder, 'Why doesn't he call? What's wrong with me?' His people would make excuses for him. He was exhausted. He had people to see." One time she plucked up courage to kiss him on stage as part of the act, despite being warned not to by staff. It was a peck on the cheek. Asked if she had gone too far, Michael reassured her she had been great. Encouraged, she went further the next night, kissing him on the lips. "I regretted it instantly, because his body went rigid," she recalls. Then when he started hanging around with a boy, whose company he obviously preferred to hers, she finally knew she had no chance.[368]

She was in good company. Madonna tried to seduce Michael shortly after the Oscars, according to her biographer Andrew Morton, later telling one of her lovers that her bedside manner failed to arouse interest. So reports Darwin Porter, along with a good many other gems illustrating Michael's less than convincing interest in women. He tells us Michael had been required to kiss supermodel Iman in a scene for a video associated with the single "Remember the time", relating that a critic wrote: "If Michael Jackson was trying to assert his heterosexual credentials in this video, he failed miserably. If Sir Winston Churchill had ever been forced to kiss Adolf Hitler, I think the British prime minister would have pulled it off with more fervour."[369]

Porter reports not one but several fake "romances" promoted by Michael in order to give himself a straight image. He claims Michael personally ordered an aide to feed a story to the *National Enquirer* about his supposed attachment to Karen Faye, who had worked as his make-up artist on the *Captain Eo* video. It was also falsely put about that he and Sheryl Crow were an item early in her career when she was a backup singer on the *Bad* tour. Once her own solo career took off she made it abundantly clear there had been no intimate relationship with the Gloved One, reportedly saying, "He never took that glove off for me". In fact Michael seems to have taken pains to make sure Sheryl kept her distance after his uncomfortable experiences with Tatiana: she was allegedly instructed by his manager not even to make eye contact with the *Bad* guy, except when performing.[370]

Shoshana Hawley, a Las Vegas showgirl, was at one time singled out as a suitable phoney "date" for Michael, according to Porter. They were spotted four times attending a pageant at the Excalibur Hotel in the city, a high-profile association which duly made it into the papers as evidence of a relationship. There were even reports the pair were spending days at a time together in Michael's hotel suite. But the press had got it completely wrong: this was at a time, in 1991, when Michael was spending his nights in "sleepovers" with Brett Barnes.[371]

Porter confirms, at least, that Liza Minnelli was genuinely a close and valued friend of Michael's, as he had declared in *Moonwalk*, but says there was never anything romantic between them. As for Sophia Loren, he escorted her to a party given by Franco Zeffirelli at his villa in Rome. Taking little interest in Loren, Michael "spent all the time playing with a gaggle of pajama-clad children".[372]

Poor Brooke Shields got by far the worst deal, though: attending the 1984 Grammy awards with Michael, she had to share the date with a boy – twelve-year-old Emmanuel Lewis. Michael, who had known Brooke for a couple of years, enjoyed her company. She was intelligent. The two had both been child stars and understood the pressures coming from demanding parents. It was something in common; they could relate to each other. She needed Michael, too: her career was flagging and the publicity value of being seen with him at a major awards ceremony would be tremendous. According to La Toya and Janet, Michael had not wanted to be with her on this occasion though. Maybe he wanted to show off Emmanuel to the world as the most important person in his life at that time, just as he would do with Jordie Chandler at another Grammy awards nearly a decade later. How could he do that? How could he tantalise and amaze the world with a bold personal statement that would have everyone whispering and speculating, if he were lumbered with Brooke? When Brooke called by to ask if she could go with him to the ceremony, Michael had to stall and escape to another room, where his sisters were. What should he do? How could he get out of it? What could he tell her? They suggested just telling her straight, but he wasn't up to that. It would hurt her feelings. So, she went. Taraborrelli describes the scene:

> Brooke seemed particularly uncomfortable about having to share her date with a twelve-year-old playmate. Earlier, photographers descended, asking them to pose for pictures. Michael held Emmanuel with one arm and hugged Brooke with his free hand. It was as if he was trying to remind Brooke that the presence of a child on the date meant that he really wasn't serious about her. "Let's get out of here," Brooke was heard saying to Michael. "People are making fun of us."[373]

Memorably, record company chief Walter Yetnikoff dubbed it "a ménage à trois to make the Marquis de Sade blush".[374] Michael would claim in *Moonwalk* that he was romantically serious about Brooke for a while, but he told a different story to Steve Howell, his video cameraman, saying there was no romance.[375] Brooke has also said the same.[376] This gap between private admission and public image is a recurring theme in the Jackson family. At various times Katherine, Marlon and Jermaine as individuals have all been publicly quoted claiming that Michael dated girls and was as sexually normal as the next guy.[377] The family as a whole (with the important exception of La Toya as the crisis deepened) also gathered at meetings, as was their wont, and issued joint statements of support for Michael when he was under fire.[378] Some such efforts had an understandable air of desperation about them, notably Jermaine's intervention early in the crisis of 1993, when he told an interviewer: "He dates all the time, but he's very, very quiet about it. He does it very secretly. And with the kind of girls who would never sell their stories."[379]

So Michael had a secret stockpile of guaranteed mute maidens? Where did he find them? And why would he want to hide behaviour that would show he was normal? Could it be that these "girls" loved water pistol fights and trips to Toys R Us? The interviewer apparently did not feel it "Jermaine" to enquire along these lines. As the crisis grew, though, and as pressure on the family mounted, Jermaine proved unable to sustain his curious line of defence. By November 1993 he was saying: "I am his biggest supporter, I love him, but yes, you have to admit you begin to wonder if there mightn't be some truth in it."[380]

Right from the early days of Motown the Jacksons had been encouraged by record promoters and personal publicists to mouth more or less any kind of B.S. considered useful to generate the right public image. Truth, commitment to honesty, had nothing to do with the matter, despite the family's religious background and the strict interpretation their church puts upon the commandment not to bear false witness. Motown boss Berry Gordy and his staff trained stars to be amiable but to reveal nothing of consequence in interviews. They were encouraged to be suspicious of reporters. While this is undoubtedly a wise precaution for anyone dealing with the media, the effect on youngsters constantly forced to put up a front was to ingrain it as a habit of mind. When distortions and lies become a matter of routine in daily life, it cannot be easy to keep a hold on the ultimate importance of truth. The inventive tongue can deploy its talent within the family, or even to deceive oneself. Motown artists were expected to lie about all manner of things. The myth that Diana Ross had discovered the Jacksons, for instance, was a Motown invention. Taraborrelli:

> From the time Michael Jackson was ten – and was told to shave two years off his age – he knew he had an "image" to cherish and guard. Michael was taught to believe that the press was out to get him and that in this media war it was every man – or boy – for himself. Motown publicists would bombard the group with sample questions and have them memorize pat answers. Michael repeated the Diana Ross discovery story so many times with such sincerity it seemed that even he believed it after a while.[381]

Michael was able to reconcile all this lying with his religion, and his conscience, by making a distinction, between lies on the one hand and public relations on the other. It was wrong to tell lies about himself but fine to be inventive about his image![382]

Anyone capable at the age of eight (or was it ten?!) of such masterly casuistry has to be regarded as a tricky character to interpret throughout his life. How can we rely on any personal statements he makes, however sincere the delivery seems, if we know that he may be seeing it purely in terms of burnishing his image? And if at times that image has become tarnished, why then the work of polishing is made that much tougher, but the process is still one of fixing the image, of public relations. It had nothing to do with truth, or the real Michael Jackson. Michael's personal writing, as we shall see, is a slightly different matter, a little more revealing, though still inhibited by image considerations.

There need be no surprise, though, that in his long reign as the King of Pop he rarely gave interviews and that even when he did he was usually considered "poor copy" because he gave so little of himself away. Some fans thought his 1993 Oprah Winfrey show appearance was an exception, but that last major interview before his fall from grace was in reality a bland affair. It was an occasion for denying, rather than revealing. It was an opportunity for Michael to deny various "Wacko Jacko" rumours, including the suggestion that he had been bleaching his skin white. He took the opportunity, as he did in *Moonwalk*, to polish up his weak heterosexual image by continuing to claim he had been in love with Brooke Shields; but his words were scarcely more concrete or convincing than anything that had gone before.

He also said he had been in love with someone else. No name offered. This was about as revealing as a distant glimpse across the desert of a veiled woman driving a tank. But it was also intriguing. Just as intriguing as that improbable veiled figure if she had slithered from her turret like a genie from its bottle and started beckoning the astonished traveller, like something in a dream or a mirage. Who was this mysterious conqueror of Michael's heart? Was she a figment of Michael's imagination? Could we even assume it was a woman? Why not a boy? Or even a number of boys? Strange as it doubtless sounds, this would make sense: several of Michael's "special friends" could thus be flattered that he alone was the one Michael had in mind as the most special of all.

Asked if he were still a virgin, Michael replied with coy embarrassment, as we saw in Chapter Three, and in the light of his discomfort the possibility just advanced loses none of its plausibility. In a book on Jackson, Catherine Dineen described it as a frank interview, but even this fan-oriented writer remarked that some commentators called it a stage-managed affair to promote exactly what Michael wanted. We may agree also with her comment: "But with his silence broken, are his fans any wiser about what motivates Michael than they were before?"[383]

Michael's family had the same problem, both with him and between themselves. Growing up in an atmosphere of duplicity, where image is one thing and truth another, could hardly have helped. Their world, as Taraborrelli copiously documents, was also peopled with more than its share of fixers, dealers and rip-off artists of every kind, anxious to siphon off some of the Jackson wealth into their own accounts, sometimes by underhand means, and sometimes, as with Motown back in the early days, simply by having so much clout in the industry that they could cut a deal that might not look too generous in retrospect. To respond, as Joe Jackson did, with anger at being financially screwed, as he saw it, by Gordy and the people at Motown, was understandable. No-one likes being taken for a sucker, least of all those who have known what it is like to sweat for every penny. It is a thin line, though, between, on the one hand, determination not to be cheated, and on the other, being mean, hard-nosed and greedy.

Sad to say, few could read Taraborrelli's account of the Jacksons' *Victory* tour in 1984 without concluding that by this time the latter unlovely qualities had come to permeate the whole family. Michael was hugely successful now. Following the success of *Thriller* he was mega. The tour was one Michael personally neither needed nor wanted. His participation was essentially a labour foisted on him by a family determined to exploit his solo success to the utmost. His brothers, who should scarcely have been short of a dollar or two, were pleading poverty and demanding the opportunity to make one or two more – one or two more millions, that is. Katherine and Joseph too were equally greedy, equally guilty. It was not a pretty sight. Interestingly, this was one occasion when Michael could genuinely take the moral high ground, expressing concern on behalf of loyal fans when ticket prices had been set outrageously high.[384] As against his holier-than-thou response to the male family members' treatment of women, this was one occasion when his own behaviour was comparatively above reproach.

The *Victory* tour was financially successful (Michael's share of the profits went to charity),[385] but a defeat in terms of its meaning for the Jackson family. It was the last time they would work together, and not just for the valid artistic reason that Michael had progressed beyond the "bubble gum pop" characterising the early Jackson Five output. Michael had spent more time on the tour with Muscles, his pet boa constrictor, than with his brothers,[386] and also annoyed them by bringing along his boy friend (or boyfriend) of the day, Emmanuel Lewis.[387]

If conviviality and cordiality within the family were at an all-time low, it was because mutual trust was sliding off the bottom of the graph too. Michael's brothers and sisters had at one time been his friends – his only friends. They were important to him in ways constantly ignored by Freudian-minded observers of the family scene, with their myopic concentration on the dynamics of the mother/child/father triad, as though every child is an only child, uninfluenced by siblings. Michael, we must never forget, had eight surviving siblings,[388] five brothers and three sisters, and they each occupied an important place in his psychological makeup, even the younger ones.[389]

Hugely significant in terms of what the Freudians would term his ego development is the fact that Michael's elder brothers were obliged to accept their junior as effectively a leader. He was always seen as the most talented of the Jackson Five, or at least the one regarded as the potential money-spinner, the really important one because of the tremendous response he could generate from an audience. There was some jealousy of the kid brother, some reluctance to cede leadership to him, but by and large they did so with remarkably good grace in the early days. He was also the only one who could stand up to Joe and get away with it, a feat his much older brother Jackie could never manage. Early on, Michael was thus able to demonstrate, both to others and to himself, a touch of steel and determination mingled in there with the sensitivity and creativity. He would be a person able to listen to others, which we can see from his serious attention to the teachings of his church; but he was also ever mindful of the value of his own thoughts. He would be an independent-minded person, not easily indoctrinated or conditioned to accept what others say. He would even, if we accept what Jordie Chandler says about him, consciously reject "conditioned" acceptance of our society's most stringent taboos.

He also needed his brothers and sisters for the simple companionship he could not obtain elsewhere. His older siblings had all enjoyed a few years of relatively pressure-free childhood before the Jackson Five, and hence some sort of life outside the home. True, their social life was always limited: their religious affiliation never encouraged too much contamination by outsiders to the faith. But life for the older kids in the family had not always been just work, work, work, within the narrow confines of the family living space, hotel rooms and the stage, as it would be for Michael. Rebbie and La Toya never became trapped in that pattern at all, though they did have problems of their own. When the family business developed, they were sidelined as unimportant, mere girls – a put-down that saw Rebbie rebel into an escape through early marriage, while La Toya became frustrated and ultimately vengeful.

Michael was ensnared by work and family more than any of them. He spoke movingly of looking across from the Motown studio at the age of eleven, watching the kids playing in a park across the street: "I'd just stare at them in wonder – I couldn't imagine such freedom, such a carefree life – and wish more than anything that I had that kind of freedom, that I could walk away and be with them. When you're young, and working, the world can seem awfully unfair."[390]

Not having had that kind of freedom, Michael needed his siblings more than most to see him through his childhood, especially Jermaine, La Toya and Marlon, those closest to him in age, respectively four years, two, and one year older than himself. Every wedding in the family came as a blow to him, a kind of betrayal, as though there was only one Jackson family; any sisters or brothers who peeled off from it to wed were guilty of desertion – a rare case in which his sentiments exactly mirrored those of his father. Marlon's desertion proved a particularly devastating blow. He married secretly at the age of eighteen without telling any of his sibs or his mother in case Joseph would get to know about it, for his father would inevitably oppose the match. Only after four months of marriage did he announce what had happened. Marlon had shown that he felt he could trust no-one with the information. Michael, especially, was deeply hurt by this because he thought he and his brother were close. "I don't understand my family at all," said Michael. "And I don't like some of the things my brothers do to their wives. I'm never going to marry. I just can't take it. It's awful, marriage. I don't trust anyone enough for that."[391]

Inability to trust anyone was a constant theme in Michael's business and social life. He always paid close personal attention to the details of his business dealings, a rare trait among successful artists and performers of any kind, who are more often content to leave such minutiae to agents and accountants, lawyers and managers. Likewise he proved reluctant to make friendships with anyone except showbiz figures such as Brooke Shields and Elizabeth Taylor, who shared his experience of having been a child star, or billionaires like Michael Milken, David Geffen and Donald Trump, people he could be sure were not after his money.

The big exception was children. It is easy to be cynical and to assume that Michael's professed attraction towards the innocence of children – innocence in the sense of their being artlessly direct, open-hearted, unsullied by ingrained habits of lying and dissimulation – was merely a cover for his attraction to their bodies. Yet we have some reason to believe the opposite. Living as he did in circumstances with trust in short supply, it made sense for him to cherish the freshness of young hearts and minds and to seek out company that promised to be honest and straightforward. Sadly, even that promise is not always delivered and Michael of all people would have been aware that some children are obliged to be early learners of cunning and devious ways. Nevertheless, there is more to be hoped for from the young. By early adulthood he was already appearing to favour idealised "child-like" qualities in his own mind, interesting himself in children's games, buying toys and withdrawing into a fantasy world, though whether this kind of interest simply corresponded with the beginnings of his actual friendships with children is a moot point.[392] As the wit Clive James remarked, "He had a child-like quality. There wasn't a child he didn't like."[393]

That sharp little shaft may not have been literally true – we know of Michael's bias towards boys, for instance – but it does remind us, having considered the important part played in his life by his older siblings, that he had younger ones, too. When Michael was entering adolescence, Randy and Janet were still children. Were they, it may both pertinently and impertinently be asked, among the children he liked?

Janet, the youngest of the nine, was born sixteen years after Rebbie, the eldest, and eight years after Michael. Randy made his debut appearance on the planet some three years after Michael's world premiere. By contrast, Michael was separated by only one year from Marlon and two from La Toya among his older sibs. Thus, although Michael was well down in the birth order, at seventh, he was at the mid-point in terms of years between youngest and oldest. And in psychological terms, his leadership qualities, musical role and closeness to Jermaine, four years his elder, effectively advanced his status above that of either Marlon or La Toya by the time he had reached late childhood. Although he was to become quiet and withdrawn in adolescence – his confidence shattered by the ravages of acne as well as sexual uncertainty – by the time the group were signing with Motown, when he was ten, he was the bright and bubbly star of his family as well as a coming star in the world beyond. In the years immediately following, until his mid-teens, Michael would have had good reason to regard both of his younger sibs, much younger and hugely less experienced in work and the ways of the world, as children rather than equals.

As such, there is every reason to ask whether they appealed to him as other children do. Were they more than just brother and sister to him? Was he especially tender towards them? Did he feel a physical, perhaps erotic, attraction towards them? His relationship with Janet certainly had its bizarre aspects. When Randy Taraborrelli interviewed Michael in 1981, for instance, he was obliged to put all the questions to Janet, then fifteen, as though Michael needed an interpreter. The star refused to do the interview any other way. Thus we have the following crazy sequence, beginning with Taraborrelli's question:

> "Janet, please ask him how he feels about the album."
> "He wants to know how you feel about the album," Janet said to her brother.
> "Tell him I'm very happy with it," Michael said. "Working with my brothers again was an incredible experience for me. It was magical."
> Janet nodded her head and turned to me. "He told me to tell you that he's very happy with the album," she said. "And that working with his brothers was an incredible experience for him."[394]

It proved an unnerving double act for the biographer to cope with, the whole thing so cumbersome and unreal he decided to cut the session short, which is perhaps what Michael had intended. If this curious interview demonstrated nothing else, though, it points to an interesting rapport between Michael, the established star, and Janet, destined to develop as the family's other major talent. And just as he had been especially shocked and hurt by Marlon's marriage, so hers to James DeBarge was later to give him special grief, almost as though she had been his wife, not his sister.

Almost. At the age of ten Janet was launching a successful acting career in a Jacksons TV series, in one sketch performing a reportedly very convincing Mae West impersonation, dressed in a pink satin hour-glass creation and a platinum-blond wig, and purring out sexy, raunchy lines like "When I'm good I'm very good. But when I'm bad I'm better."[395] While Mae West was the epitome of an excitingly adult woman, not a little Lolita, Janet's daring act doubtless stirred Humbert Humbert-like feelings in the breasts – and groins – of some male viewers. Not in Michael's case, though, we may be assured. In earlier years he would more likely have felt himself tenderly drawn towards her male partner in the Mae West act – brother Randy, three years Michael's junior. Marlon, who shared a bunk-bed with Michael in the early days at 2300 Jackson Street, said when denying that Michael was gay, "I would know, wouldn't I?" The answer to that has to be "Possibly, but not necessarily as well as Randy", for whereas Marlon had been an equal, Randy would have seemed more a child to him, with the special appeal of a child. And after the family moved from Jackson Street to Hayvenhurst the bedroom arrangements changed: Michael would now be sharing a bedroom not with Marlon but with Randy. When the family moved in, on 5 May 1971, Michael was a few months shy of being a teenager and Randy's tenth birthday lay a few days ahead.[396]

As for Michael acting upon any such attraction, in terms at least of the mild sex play common among siblings, whether that would have occurred would depend on which parental influence on both boys was the greater: the strict sexual rules of their mother's religion or the more lax example set by their father. In February 1994, it was reported in the press that La Toya was about to claim Joseph's "anything goes" approach extended to sexual abuse against herself, and that Michael, too, had been sexually abused repeatedly by "a family member" between the ages of eight and thirteen. Michael was said to be planning a lawsuit to stop her going ahead with her planned announcement.[397] A few days later, a different newspaper quoted La Toya's husband as saying she planned to sue her father for molesting her when she, too, was between eight and thirteen.[398] Court action seemed very much in the offing, but the family rift was eventually patched up. Years later, Diane Dimond brought another claim to light, this time by La Toya's elder sister, Rebbie. Dimond said Rebbie filed a sexual assault complaint against her father with the police when she was thirteen, although "all trace of this police report has long since been erased".[399] If such extensive abuse really indicated the domestic atmosphere, it would be unsurprising if sexual inhibitions were completely broken down and other couplings also took place.

Sibling sex play would not be all that surprising anyway, even in the absence of parental sexual contact with the children. It is a common occurrence.[400] Would Michael's religious background have inhibited him? Probably not. In the days of his childhood in the 1960s, grown-ups attending the Kingdom Hall doubtless had to endure many a hellfire sermon against "fornication" (perhaps another reason Joe did not like going) but such messages were hardly Sunday School material. Children in those innocent days, so close in time yet so far away from us in cultural terms, were largely spared lectures in sexual conduct aimed *at themselves*. They would have known such activity was "rude" enough to be an embarrassment, something to keep quiet about, but not that it amounted to a major crime or a mortal sin.

Sexual activity with Michael by an adult family member is much less likely. For a father (and who else would "a family member" be? Jackie? Katherine? The other candidates are just as improbable or even more so) to sexually assault both a son and daughters is quite rare in the more reliable abuse literature and vanishingly rare among men like Joseph, who had both an evident orientation towards grown women and no shortage of sexual access to them. There is the occasional spectacular case of truly pan-sexual expression, such as the sculptor and great type-face designer Eric Gill, who enjoyed sexual relations with men and women, his own small daughters and even the family dogs;[401] but do we have reason to suppose Joseph Jackson was in such an elevated league of sexual accomplishment? (or, according to taste, such a base one of sexual depravity?)

There is a hint or two, no more. Michael's publicity chief Bob Jones reports a curious conversation round about the time of his boss's marriage to Lisa Marie Presley. Jones heard of a story about to break that Joseph molested Michael when he was little. Jones succeeded in denying this story and it never ran. But he got a strange reaction when he spoke to Michael about it. Michael said to him: "How do you know that thing with Joseph never happened?" It may have been a purely philosophical point, though Michael is not noted for any such turn of mind. The fact is, though, that Jones could not possibly have known whether the story was false, only that he personally knew of no evidence to support it – a very different thing.[402]

Another hint came in an eight-page book proposal reportedly touted by Jermaine in the wake of Michael's trial. To be titled *Legacy: Surviving the Best and the Worst*, the book was said to have been written with Stacy Brown, who had also co-authored Bob Jones' book on Michael. The New York press carried claims that Jermaine was sensationally going to allege in the book not only that Rebbie and La Toya had been molested by Joe Jackson but also that Michael had suffered sexual abuse as a child by "an important businessman". There was even to be the suggestion that Joe "may have set up Michael to be somehow victimised by older men".[403]

And there was more: it was going to be claimed that Michael had once been found sitting on a bed with Tito's young sons and "holding them in a disturbing manner" following the death of their mother in the mid-1990s.[404] Jermaine had reportedly thought Michael might be guilty of child molesting but had supported him through his trial because he was worried he might kill himself in prison.

In terms of the credibility of these rumours, the most significant thing may be that the book never made it into print. Apparently HarperCollins and St Martins were among publishers who rejected the proposal. One publisher reportedly claimed most of the material was old hat, but rejection could equally have been because it was too hot to handle. Reporter Michelle Caruso claimed, "Jermaine pulled the plug after Michael got wind of it and went ballistic, threatening to sue and toss Jermaine out of the family home."[405]

Publishers also had their reputations to worry about. Appearing to give credence to patently tall stories would leave them looking either cynical or stupid. And one of Jermaine's alleged claims looks suspiciously similar to a wild rumour doing the rounds at the time of Michael's marriage to Lisa Marie. A pre-pubescent Michael, it was said, had been pimped "to paedophiles within the record industry as a means of promoting the advance of the Jackson Five". Reporting this story, writer Darwin Porter says that, "To our knowledge the only person who tried to sell such a story was a sleazy record producer... who worked the Detroit record industry for some twenty years". He approached the *National Enquirer* with a very detailed account of how a nine-year-old Michael was allegedly delivered to his hotel room in Detroit. His account did not specify who made the delivery. He was willing to tell all for a fee of $10,000.

All what, exactly? Well, impact-wise, rather a lot. Brace yourselves, tender-hearted readers, against the shocking details to come, but I trust you will not be so soft-headed as to believe a word of it. Here goes then! Giving "times, dates and places that checked out", this sleazeball said he had "sodomized young Michael" on three different occasions. The perpetrator told the tabloid: "The boy cried through the ordeal and even bled" each time. Even the *National Enquirer*, not noted as the most scrupulous of publications, rejected this story, and a moment's thought is all that is required to see why it was not credible – for who, in his right mind, would give genuinely incriminating and inevitably identifying details that could put him in jail for decades for the sake of a mere $10,000, or indeed for any amount of money? The alleged ogre could theoretically have calculated that

Michael, as an adult, would never publicly admit to having being raped with his family's connivance; and without a victim's statement there could be no viable prosecution. But the perpetrator's reputation would be trashed and he might well be subject to violent retribution by outraged members of the public. If someone really did go to the *Enquirer* with such a story, it can only have been an impostor trying to take them for a ride by fraudulently pocketing the fee. Caution, then, remains in order over Michael as a victim of childhood sexual abuse.[406]

Is there any other reason to suspect Joseph of perpetrating or facilitating such abuse? It is often suggested, especially by feminists, that sexual abuse is an expression of male power, a symbolic humiliation of those under a man's control. As a classic patriarchal tyrant (allegedly!), Joseph would definitely be a prime candidate for fears of this sort. If La Toya had stuck to allegations about herself, rather than bringing Michael into the picture as well, her story would have been much easier to believe. What her wider charge ignores is Joseph's self-image. A few decades back, before child sexual abuse became such a hot topic, it might have been possible for a man like Joseph to "fool around a little" with his daughters and still think of himself as normal.

To "fool around" with a boy child, however, would have been another matter entirely. In Gary, Indiana, in the 1960s, this would have been seen as a highly deviant thing for a grown man to do. It would have identified Joseph, in his own mind, as some sort of a "faggot", a self-image far from the one he promoted among his children, of a man who liked his women. The proposed scenario is not impossible, but the odds have to be stacked heavily against it.

By early 1994, La Toya was allegedly making over half a million dollars a week in TV appearances denouncing her brother as a paedophile, saying he had abused at least thirty boys, including an unnamed British one.[407] As ever in allegations against Michael, cash was clouding the issues and tainting the evidence. Nor was La Toya short of other ulterior motives for giving her family a hard time, as anyone who has read her autobiography will be aware. In that torrid text she castigates the "arrogance" of Jermaine, tells us Janet is one to bear a grudge and makes numerous allegations against her parents, such as their supposed anti-semitism (La Toya's husband at the time, Jack Gordon, was Jewish).[408]

Overshadowed by her more successful siblings, La Toya was plainly finding it hard to come to terms with her thwarted ambitions to be a star in her own right and her book is deeply suffused with the language of victimhood. Her bitterness is undisguised in the writing, which is also – it must be conceded – more coherent, persuasive and balanced than some of the comments made after she started "going nuclear" on TV and elsewhere with sexual abuse allegations. No such suggestions appeared in the book, though that might have been down to legal anxieties.[409] She was less inhibited when describing her father's physical violence, but her narrative was not without a patina of balance and fairness. Joseph was judged, for instance, to have encouraged the brothers' musical career "as much for their sake as his own",[410] the siblings were kind and supportive to each other in the face of Joseph's fearful dominance,[411] and above all Michael was the object of outright hero worship ("a wonderful, generous human being") to an at times absurd degree.[412] In his appearance on the *Motown 25* TV spectacular, "Michael cast a wondrous spell from which the world will probably never awaken".[413] Irony? Nope, not a hint of it.

La Toya's looks are – or were – so similar to Michael's it used to be jokingly suggested they were one and the same, like Clark Kent and Superman. The best part of the joke is that like Clark Kent and Superman they were never seen together, as Michael had not been on speaking terms with his sister for years at the time of the Chandler affair. La Toya's likeness to her famous brother had been cultivated. In the post-scandal months she publicly latched on to the waggish suggestion that Michael had plastic surgery to look like her, but the reverse hypothesis made much more sense: a videotaped conversation between Michael and his sister revealed a woman aching to emulate her brother, a woman who would give her eye teeth – or her nose – to be as celebrated as he had become.[414]

In light of the generally balanced nature of her book, her more bitter reflections there are not without plausibility. More than that, they carry psychological conviction. People do not turn against their family, as La Toya did, out of pure malice coming from nowhere. She had been badly hurt. Alone among the Jackson children, she felt her ambition for musical success had been ignored and thwarted, her talent allowed to wither on the vine. It has been suggested that she lacks real talent[415] but this misses the psychological point. In the midst of a family bursting with obvious musical ability and success, it cannot have been easy for her to accept other people's judgment – notably her father's – that she just did not have what it takes. Nobody likes to feel a failure, or insignificant, and La Toya was understandably not prepared to put up with any such writing of her life-script. She may have been better off doing something completely unmusical, an academic career perhaps. But that too isn't the point. What concerns us here is the resentment that built up inside her, partly against her father, but even more so against Katherine, to whom, like Michael, she had been very close. Her mother, she felt, had tried to trap her, to keep her at home in a state of dependency in order selfishly to satisfy her own psychological needs. It was the very closeness of the two that made for the explosive reaction of their eventual separation.

La Toya put it this way: "The older I got, the more she treated me like a little girl, tightening her grip. She'd spent her entire adult life being a mother; nothing was more important to her... The prospect of an empty nest must have gnawed at her."[416] Katherine would try to stop her dating, she says, and tried to control her life in every detail: "I now see that Mother equates love with control. Thus she especially loved me, the faithful daughter who willingly sacrificed my own needs to her happiness."[417] In these circumstances she was "miserably unhappy...a prisoner".[418]

Eventually she was to break free, marrying Jack Gordon, the man her parents had hired as her business manager. The match was deeply disapproved of by Joseph and Katherine, not least because Gordon had been a former brothel owner who had also served a prison term for trying to bribe the Nevada State Gaming Commission.[419] La Toya, for her part, said the marriage was just a stratagem to break her parents' hold over her. It remained unconsummated. (Following her sexual allegations against her father the stated reasons for this non-consummation took a more sinister turn. La Toya started saying that Joseph's alleged sexual assaults left her unable to enjoy normal sexual relations with a man.) Her parents, she and Jack claim, had gone so far as trying to kidnap her in order to wrest her from what they saw as Gordon's malign influence, to which they attributed such frowned-upon matters as her appearing in *Playboy*. She would say this was her own decision, a way of asserting her autonomy, a way of breaking free from the shackles imposed by her parents and her religion – just as, she says, Michael would assert himself in a similar outrageous manner by publicly grabbing at his crotch in his performances.[420] Unlike Michael, whose fame put him beyond criticism from the family, La Toya was scapegoated by them, especially, as she saw it, for telling difficult truths others wanted to deny.[421]

Against this background we can begin to understand the increasingly savage public exchanges between La Toya and her mother, which saw La Toya suggesting Katherine had privately branded Michael "a bloody faggot" and her mother responding that her daughter was lying, and had been stolen and brainwashed by Jack Gordon.[422]

It will be recalled that three of the Jackson children had taken their Jehovah's Witnesses faith particularly seriously: Rebbie, La Toya and Michael. At the age of eighteen, Rebbie, the eldest, had fallen in love with a devout fellow Witness and married – despite her father's opposition. She thus "fled the nest", and her parents' control, early in the Jacksons' story. The other children each found their own way to independence through marriage and, like Joseph, had never experienced religion as a binding force, as a sort of third parent from which it would become painfully necessary at some point to break free. La Toya and Michael, so alike physically, were alike psychically, too, in that they alone of the nine children were unmarried and unattached into their thirties; they alone continued to live in the family home for many adult years, fearful of their father, close to their adored mother and under the continuing influence of a profoundly controlling, spiritually dominating religion.

Crucially, though, they each did make the break, in La Toya's case through a gradual erosion of her faith, followed by all-out war with the family, while Michael's escape route was the other way around: attacked by the elders of the faith, notably in connection with the *Thriller* video, he slowly grew disillusioned. After years in which his endeavours to reconcile his work as a pop star with his religion proved unsuccessful, he formally left the Witnesses in 1987, a process paralleled by his putting physical and symbolic distance between himself and his parents with his move to Neverland the following year. Just three days after Michael quit the family home at Encino, La Toya did likewise, taking off with Jack Gordon and just a couple of suitcases.[423] La Toya suggested that Michael's final break with the Witnesses followed a demand by the elders that he should shun her, following her own failure to attend Kingdom Hall meetings. Ironically, they need not have bothered. Michael was soon to shun La Toya on his own account. He refused to speak to her for many years following her nude appearance in *Playboy* magazine in 1988 and her public claim that he approved of the pictures.[424]

The impact on Michael's psyche of discovering his father had a secret second family is made much of by Taraborrelli.[425] He was said to be desolated by the news and "would never recover from the hurt" of his mother being betrayed. Joseph's affair with Cheryl Terrell in 1973 had produced a daughter, Joh' Vonnie, whose existence he did not disclose to his wife until around 1980, when the child was six years old. But Katherine had probably known from soon after the birth. She had initiated divorce proceedings in connection with her husband's infidelities in 1973, even before Joh' Vonnie's arrival, but in the end swallowed her pride and decided to stick with Joseph and her family. La Toya relates that her father had proudly announced the new arrival to the boys when they were on tour in Senegal, as though it were a cause for their celebration and congratulations – an act, if true, of characteristic insensitivity.[426]

While the whole family were shocked by the news, the hurt felt by Michael was especially deep, according to Taraborrelli, who goes on to invoke a possible Freudian explanation: not only did he love his mother, he identified with her. When she hurt, he hurt. Crucially, such an identity of emotional response with the mother, going beyond mere sympathy, is held to be a feature in the psychological makeup of a boy who has failed to identify in a normal way with his father. Enter the ubiquitous Mr Oedipus again. Even if wildly wrong, the explanation is fundamentally important to us for two reasons: firstly, so many people still appear to find the theory persuasive; secondly, oedipal notions are constantly being invoked to explain Michael's adult love life, or lack of one. This is how Taraborrelli summarises the proposed psychodynamics:

> Freud coined the term Oedipus complex to describe a boy's undue attachment to his mother. (Oedipus unwittingly killed his father and married his mother.) Feeling attached to the opposite-sex parent is a normal stage in child development; five-year-old boys often proclaim they will marry their mothers when they grow up. However, by the time a boy is six, he usually starts to put the mother-son relationship in perspective and begins to identify with his father. If his mother remains overwhelming, however, the young son finds it difficult to detach from her. If the father is equally domineering or more so, the child may remain emotionally close to his mother because she's safer. Most psychologists agree that if a child doesn't complete the separation process from his mother and start identifying with his father by the onset of adolescence, it is unlikely that he will develop a happy relationship with any woman and may well continue to view his father as a rival for his mother's attention. An adult with an unresolved oedipal complex can place his mother on such a high pedestal that no other woman can approach her perfection.[427]

This account is weak in several respects. Firstly, there is no explanation as to why the mother should be "overwhelming". None of Michael's brothers appear to have succumbed in this way. Why should he have been the exception? Especially as we know that early in childhood he was a spirited, lively, confident child, perceived by his brothers as a natural leader, the only one of them able to stand up to their father? Secondly, in orthodox psychoanalysis, a boy's failure to identify with his father is usually ascribed to the father's long-term absence from the household, so the youngster has no father-figure on which to model his own sense of identity. Either that, or else the father is a weak personality lacking obvious characteristics of masculinity for the boy to incorporate into himself. Joseph, by contrast, could hardly have been more strongly present in little Michael's life, or more stereotypically masculine – though whether his aggressive behaviour is something with which a terrified infant would want to identify is a moot point. Again, however, we might note that Michael's brothers have grown up all too conspicuously like their father in key respects. They identified with him, so why not Michael?

Oedipal theory, on the basis of the limited facts available to us at least, is a hopelessly inadequate tool for explaining Michael's personality. Taraborrelli calls on a psychiatrist to help him out, but instead of a more sophisticated rendering of the theory, one which truly appears to account for the facts, we are merely treated to an overlay of gobbledegook that glosses over the difficulties.[428] The explanation given leans on Oedipal theory for its authority but actually bears little relation to it, straying instead into vague talk of infidelity and betrayal in ways that really belong to an adult's frame of reference, not a little child's.

This book is about Michael, not about psychoanalysis, but it does need emphasising that Freudian and neo-Freudian thinking have a hopeless track-record in terms of producing reliable psychological explanations of any sort. When Freudian hypotheses have been put to the scientific test they have not proved good predictors. For instance, it should be predictable from the psychoanalytic view of homosexuality (which is seen as caused in boys precisely by what we have been talking about: identifying with the "wrong" parent) that known homosexual men will have experienced significantly less than average positive fathering in early childhood and a high level of dominant mothers. Empirical study has not borne this out. For instance, Bell, Weinberg and Hammersmith, who interviewed 979 homosexual and 477 heterosexual men in a major Kinsey Institute study, found no such correlation. They conclude: "...the idea that homosexuality reflects a failure to resolve boys' 'Oedipal' feelings during childhood receives no support from our study."[429]

As Freud fails to account adequately for Michael's questionable gender positioning, it might be wondered whether any other theory can explain more. What about genetics, for instance? Personality, like skin colour, is said to have a strong genetic component. In Michael's case the family genes could have been shuffled in such a way that he picked up a significantly different set of personality traits from his brothers' and hence responded differently to his upbringing. But before we drown in theory we should remind ourselves that the known facts covered in this chapter already tell us a great deal. We know Michael had an exceptionally tough childhood. The familiar claim that he missed out, even more than his brothers in the Jackson Five, on the simple freedom to play with other children and just be an ordinary kid, is a strong one. He used this as an excuse for his oddly close friendships with children, but it was not *just* an excuse: it was a real factor in his upbringing, not a public relations invention. Likewise, he suffered the stresses placed on him as a result of contradictory messages: his father's promiscuous, low-life culture was totally at odds with the stern dictates and high moral tone of his mother's religion. This tension in the family lifestyle is in the domain of relatively well-established fact, not theory, and accounts more than adequately for the pervading atmosphere of hypocrisy, deceit and mutual distrust with which every one of the Jackson children was obliged to come to terms. The "facts" of the young Michael's relations (or lack of them) with girls, his attitude to his father's and brothers' sexuality and his developing moral outlook, are less transparently straightforward but are revealing nonetheless: exactly what they reveal we can each judge for ourselves.

Finally, much is said in these days of high divorce rates and social ills such as drug abuse, about the need for a return to "family values". Politicians and church leaders are constantly evoking the family as a source of strength and social stability, especially when its values are rooted in moral tenets grown in the soil of religion. The Jacksons were quintessentially such a family, and displayed sufficient strength as a family unit, under Joseph's iron discipline, to realise the American rags-to-riches dream. Yet they also provide a marvellous example of the limitations of the nuclear family, where "nuclear" is the operative word. Joseph never wanted any of the children to marry. Outsiders were a threat to his dominance and control. Katherine's religion likewise kept them all socially and psychologically somewhat apart from their neighbours. As a group they had only each other to turn to for support and friendship. It was not enough, especially when the going got tough. That's when they started turning on each other, biting as viciously as the rats in Michael's overcrowded cage.

CHAPTER NINE

Peter Pan: The Boy Who Couldn't Go Up

Long before the Jordie Chandler crisis, or his sensational marriage, Michael described himself as one of the loneliest people in the world.[430] It is not unusual for the rich and famous, egos pampered by sycophantic hangers-on, to take an excessively sensitive and self-pitying view of their condition. In Michael's case, though, in view of the evidence we have of the tensions, fear and mutual distrust within his family, and their isolation from outsiders, we may be persuaded to take his own evaluation seriously. "Even at home, I'm lonely," he was saying as a young man of twenty one, seven long years before he would find the strength to break away from living with his parents and go for his Neverland dream. "I sit in my room sometimes and cry. It's so hard to make friends, and there are some things you can't talk to your parents or family about. I sometimes walk around the neighbourhood at night, just hoping to find someone to talk to. But I just end up coming home."[431] Or, as he put it in *Moonwalk*, "I wanted to meet anybody in the neighbourhood – the neighbourhood kids, anybody."[432]

We can well imagine there were secrets he could not share with his parents: that much he had in common with most young people. But were they secrets a man could safely confide only in a mannequin? He once had a collection of fashion-store dummies and was quoted in vintage Wacko Jacko mode as saying, "I know the mannequins can be my friends. I love talking to them."[433] He was said to talk to chimps as well – in their own language. According to Rick Sky, he used to dress Bubbles the chimp in miniature versions of his own clothes, and "was even said to be learning how to speak 'chimpanzee'."[434]

Stories of Michael's "wacko" behaviour were legion: he bathed in bottled mineral water, slept in an oxygen chamber, made a bid to buy the remains of the Elephant Man, had a skeleton in his room, built a shrine to Elizabeth Taylor – the list in his heyday went on and on. Some of it was unofficial nonsense, the product of journalistic imagination; some of it was official nonsense, manufactured by the Jackson publicists; and some of it – probably most of it – was not nonsense at all. Without a real, verifiable core of wackiness the more marginal stories would have lacked all interest and would not have been generated; instead Michael would have been an ordinary superstar, generating ordinary gossip of the usual romantic or hell-raising kind.

My personal favourite, for its sheer, rollicking excess, is a story emanating from Myung-Ho Lee, Michael's financial advisor from 1998-2001, about Michael putting a voodoo curse on his enemies, complete with a spectacular blood sacrifice, presumably to give the curse potency. The story first hit the headlines in a *Vanity Fair* article by Maureen Orth.[435] This was no idle tittle-tattle either. It had been part of a sworn deposition in a lawsuit when Lee sued Jackson for $14 million in 2002, a suit eventually settled out of court. A sworn deposition hardly makes a story gospel but Bob Jones, Michael's former publicity chief, dropped a heavy hint there was some truth in the matter in his book. He wrote:

> *Already knowing the truth, the reports didn't surprise me.* The news stories were vivid, too. Michael had attended a voodoo ritual in Switzerland where a witch doctor put a voodoo curse on David Geffen, Steven Spielberg, Jeffrey Katzenberg and several others on Michael Jackson's enemy list. He paid $150,000 so that they would be cursed and hopefully killed, according to a lawsuit filed by Jackson's former business partner Myung Ho Lee. The ritual included bathing in a tub filled with animal blood. Lee was ordered to wire the money to a bank in Mali for a voodoo chief named Baba. It was said that forty-two cows were sacrificed for Michael's blood bath.[436]

The emphasis on the first sentence is mine. It appears to imply Jones knew the story was true, in part at least. But *forty-two* cows? Holy Cow, that was one big bath! Note that in this part of the story Jones is saying "it was said that" forty two cows were sacrificed, not that he personally knew the truth of the matter. As for why Geffen and the others were so massively out of favour, Jones says it was just that they "were tired of Michael Jackson's crap" and were no longer dealing with him.

Columnist Victor Lewis-Smith captured the spirit of Michael's eccentricities after the star had undergone a brain scan with "normal" results. Beneath the headline IF JACKO'S 'NORMAL' I'M AN ORANG-UTAN, he wrote:

> True, he has a plastic face, dyes his skin white, sends his Dictaphone to Press conferences, talks to chimps and orang-utans and sleeps with young boys. For all I know, he probably even has romantic, candlelit dinners for two with his gerbil. But he's normal, and that's official.[437]

Another story sourced to Myung-Ho Lee by Maureen Orth is important in the light of later allegations that Michael encouraged youngsters to drink, especially as regards the detail about the unusual type of vessel in which the drink would allegedly be offered. In February 2004 *The Abrams Report* aired an interview with college student Richard Matsuura. In this interview, Richard denied claims in a *Vanity Fair* article by Orth that back in 1988, when he was twelve, one of Jackson's people plied him with wine served in soft drinks cans until he was sick.[438] His father, Ryusaki Matsuura, had been doing business with Michael in Japan at the time and Richard had been introduced to the star. Richard admitted he was sick but claimed he had merely drunk a champagne toast under his father's supervision. He spent four days with Jackson, which he described as "a memorable time". He denied anything sexual occurred. We should perhaps not be too sceptical of the denial, including the claim that a single glass of champagne would make a twelve-year-old sick. It is well-known that some Asian populations have a low alcohol tolerance.[439]

Rick Sky wondered aloud whether much of Michael's oddness was a shield, behind which he could lead a private life without suffering intrusion.[440] The star's life was packed with the shield motif, from the sunglasses he wore to avoid meeting people's eyes,[441] to the surgical masks supposedly used to shield him from germs, to a long-term obsession with makeup, disguise and moving about incognito, to the heavy security with which he surrounded himself at Neverland and his reclusive, Howard

Hughes-like disinclination to give interviews – a sensible reclusiveness, as demonstrated by the one major departure from his usual policy, namely the disastrous decision to let TV documentary maker Martin Bashir into his life for months on end in 2002.

Lewis-Smith had his own interesting perspective on Michael's highly unusual "normality". But for the moment that "plastic face" will command our suitably awed scrutiny – surely his most impressive mask of all, it was Michael's most unique and arguably greatest artistic creation. Not his surgeons': they were the skilled craftsmen; Michael was the artist. He alone had the inspiration and courage to go through with a project that saw an utter transformation, little by little, from the broad-nosed, tubby-cheeked and fleshy-lipped African appearance of his youth to the finer-featured, paler, androgynous Michael whose face became the most recognised on the planet.

Many see it as a grotesque transformation.[442] "Monstrous", wrote *Daily Mirror* journalist Rick Sky, perhaps an aptly named newspaper for Michael to see his image reflected in. A false image? A distorting *Mirror*? Michael had sung on the *Bad* album that those with ambitions to change the world should first look in the mirror and change the man they saw facing them. Needless to say, the message was not meant to be taken literally, in terms of physical change, but it is as though that is exactly what he was doing in his own case. To many black people it amounted to a grotesque denial of his race and roots. To Michael, who professed to being "colour blind" and ambitious to promote unity and harmony among all the races and nations of the world, the symbolism was doubtless more benign, though he denied ever deliberately lightening his colour except for cosmetic reasons to hide the effects of the pigmentation defect vitiligo. Distinctions of gender and age, as well as race, were also blurred in his new appearance and style: together with his soft, whispering voice and occasional giggles he disturbingly became in the eyes of many neither black nor white, male nor female, adult nor child – and even neither gay nor straight. Riding roughshod over the ambiguities, one wag nevertheless captured the impressive scope of Michael's self-reinvention by declaring him to be the only poor black boy ever to become a rich white woman.

If the effect was a work of genius, it was also one of mutilation. Not once was the knife taken to his face, but many times – four primary rhinoplasties ("nose jobs") at least, each requiring the nose to be broken, and two secondary operations for touch-up purposes.[443] A doctor has suggested that by 1993 he had undergone at least eight cosmetic surgery procedures: the nose-bridge had been narrowed, the tip narrowed and lengthened, the nostrils narrowed. There may have been a lower eye lift, plus chin and jaw sculpting and thinning of the lower lip. A cleft had been made in the chin.[444] The first rhinoplasty, in 1979, left Michael with breathing problems.[445] For most people this would have been a warning sign not to mess about too much, a little hint that tinkering with nature has its dangers. Not for Michael. For him the pain and uncertainty of the outcome were more than made up for by the buzz of ultimately taking control of his appearance – a control almost godlike in its uniqueness: no-one before had ever physically created themselves to such a degree.

The philosopher Jean Baudrillard seemed intoxicated by the implications:

> ...Michael Jackson has had his face rebuilt, his hair straightened, his skin lightened – in short ... he has constructed himself in every tiny detail. It is this which makes him a pure, innocent child – the artificial androgyne of the fable, who, better than Christ, can reign over the world and bring reconciliation, because he is better than the child-god: he is a prosthesis-child, an embryo of all the forms of mutation we have imagined to deliver us from race and sex.[446]

Michael's annunciation as messiah and saviour is a theme to which we shall return, but his first objective was reigning over himself. The once famous gas company advertising line, "Don't you just love being in control", might have been written with him in mind: his early years had been totally controlled by his domineering father; as a teenager, acne had ravaged his face uncontrollably; the Motown moguls had left him with no artistic control over his work. Breaking with Motown and successfully creating his own musical style gave him the money and freedom to control other areas of his life, too. Michael's facial redesign enabled him to break symbolically the influence of his hated father: he now looked totally different from Joseph for the first time.

Michael's former publicity chief Bob Jones has a less charitable explanation for the change of appearance, especially the skin whitening and the loss of black African features. Jones, a black man himself, insisted his old boss was "the weirdest and most inexplicable of racists", contemptuous of his own race. In a book co-written with Stacy Brown, he writes: "His favourite word to describe blacks, his original race, was Splaboo. Yep, Splaboo. It was a word he used a lot, a word he used around people such as Macaulay Culkin." Michael spent little time with his own relatives' kids, says Jones, because they were too black, except for Tito's and Jermaine's, who were lighter.[447]

Jones, sacked by Jackson, has an axe to grind, but he does substantiate his views, drawing on medical opinion, quoting a Dr Pamela Lipkin.[448] He showed a range of photos of Jackson taken at different times in his life and cites her opinion. The first photograph showed Jackson with the Jackson Five in the early 1970s. "At that point, Michael Jackson's [a] very normal, very cute, Afro-American child, with actually very good features. You know: good lips, high cheekbones, and good bone structure. Even skin tone, I might add," Lipkin said.

As for Jackson later suffering from vitiligo, Lipkin was intrigued. When studying a photograph of Jackson taken at the time of the *Oprah* show on which he first spoke publicly about the problem, Lipkin's initial reaction was to call it "the most unusual case of vitiligo I've ever seen." Although she said it was possible that Jackson started bleaching his skin because of the disease in order to blend his natural darker tone with the lighter blotches that were appearing, she also said that a lighter skin seemed consistent with other changes she believed Jackson made to his features. "When you look at the other features, the skin bleaching sort of goes along with what I think was his quest for beauty," she said. "So I have to wonder what came first? Vitiligo or lighter skin?"

Rick Sky proposed another reason for Michael to alter his appearance, though it is one that can be seen as an extension of the control theme, an expression of his determination to dominate the world of pop, to be its number one personality: "All important is Jackson's desire to be special, to be different – no matter what it takes – and to create something the world has never seen. It is a desire which is shaped out of courage and even madness, but it is a desire that Jackson has achieved."[449]

But why such an incredible motivating force? Where was this almost insane determination to be special coming from? It is a question one could ask of many great achievers, from racing drivers to explorers, who put their bodily fate on the line in the quest for glory. Some will think in terms of a deep-seated need to fight against an insecure sense of self-worth. The biologically minded will say look no further than Joseph: Michael may have loathed the idea of being like him, but it was from his father he derived his relentless drive towards distinction. Whatever the motivation, we can be sure of one thing: it was a deep one. Much of Michael's wacko behaviour can be put down to the capriciousness we are accustomed to expect from the super rich, or publicity stunts to bolster the fortunes of a new album or concert tour. But no-one has his face slashed to ribbons on a whim. The cuts may be skin-deep but the reasons are not.

Does this fact tell us anything about Michael's sexuality? Psychiatrists have taken up the self-mutilation theme, some suggesting sexual assault in childhood as a cause.[450] There is no shortage of mental patients given to beating and slashing themselves following a violent, degraded upbringing, with or without a sexual element, but in Michael's case we are talking about a much more controlled and constructive phenomenon. It has expressed a creative ambition, not a destructive one. Most people in their early adult years do not concentrate solely on their careers, as Michael did. They are actively looking for mating possibilities, too. More often than not they experience sufficient success in their search for compatible partners to sustain the ambition, ticking away more or less consciously inside them, that before very long they will find fulfilment as parents.

This is a very big deal. It is the one occasion in life when most ordinary people have the chance to do something extraordinary and miraculous: to create another life. Michael, it seems, felt he had no such chance. Confident, always, in his artistic life, the supreme master of his craft on stage, he nevertheless appears to have thought marriage and having children of his own would be beyond him. His way of being truly creative, therefore, could only come through a most extraordinary act of sublimation, a deflection of the creative drive into the re-creation of himself. If we are to insist on finding something self-hating, or self-punishing in his self-mutilation, we might at a pinch see it as an attack on his own greatest shortcoming, the one thing about himself that must have hurt most: his self-perceived inability to create the children he loved so dearly. Later, he would have children of his own, though the manner of their begetting hardly causes us to revise this observation.

The evidence he felt this way? Not just the complete absence of any serious relationships with women throughout his adult life until his marriage, though this is remarkable enough when we consider the thousands who would swim through shark-infested waters for the chance to spend a night with him. Nor even his disinclination, in his mid-thirties, to deny being a virgin, when asked on the Oprah Winfrey show. Nor his demonstrable preference for the company of children over women, though taken together such factors in anyone but Michael would be taken to indicate a total absence of heterosexuality, or even a fear of women and a sense of revulsion towards physical contact with them. No, there was also what Michael said from time to time. We have seen the religious objections he raised against pre-marital sex, which effectively kept a physical barrier between himself and many would-be lovers. We could take this blocking device at face value given that he was genuinely religious. But what are we to make of the interview he gave to Steve Demorest for *Melody Maker*? Demorest asked him about the possibility of having children in the near future: "Michael shook his head no. He'd like to raise a child, but if he did, it would be one whom he would adopt, 'in the far future.' He would not procreate. 'I don't have to bring my own into the world,' he said uneasily."[451]

Sure, we might respond, you don't have to. But most men seem to be quite taken with the idea, whether because they like kids, or want to prove their manhood, or beget an heir, or because it's the socially done thing, or at some point they feel a need to justify their total obsession with fucking, or else a baby just happens unplanned... There are plenty of reasons men find for having their own kids, so how come none of them grabbed Michael? Concern over contributing to the world population problem? Not exactly the topic he was most noted for worrying about.

These signs that Michael really did believe he would never be able to experience an ordinary sexual relationship leading to fatherhood could be taken to indicate that he was sexually attracted to men not boys, and was thus straightforwardly gay. His feminine qualities especially, the whispering voice, the make-up, the copying of Diana Ross (which was the inspiration for his remodelled features, according to some), his rejection of tough guy, macho values, are all elements readily associated in the public mind with the stereotype of effeminate male homosexuality. The image is one of men who psychologically feel to some degree like women, and who want to take a passive "female" role in sex. The figure is that of the "size queen", voraciously on the lookout for a big, muscular, well-endowed man. Such men are not seen as interested in little boys, whose tiny tools would be the object of scornful dismissal. Taraborrelli at one time pursued this line vigorously, citing Joan Rivers' joke that Michael was so gay he "makes Liberace look like a Green Beret".[452] But despite his considerable endeavours, hinting at a possible gay relationship between Michael and the bisexual Hollywood mogul David Geffen,[453] for instance, the biographer was never even remotely convincing: his assiduous researches turned up nothing substantial. The evidence – or rather total absence of any – strongly suggests Michael was no more sexually interested in men than he was in women.

How, then, are we to account for Michael's feminine style? If we are going to veer away from the conclusion that was was a camp gay, we have to explain the "camp" – and that is not easy given that a man of conventional sexual feelings has little to gain from adopting mannerisms still stigmatised as less than manly in our society.

What causes homosexual preference, or indeed any particular sexual taste, is now known to be a matter of extreme complexity, with arguably as many "types" of homosexuality, and as many "causes" as there are homosexuals. Even the term is problematic: sex between males was customary in ancient Greece, but there were no "homosexuals", at least in the sense that such a concept had not been thought of: there was no word to match our modern notion, which has been developed in a pathologising, psychiatric context. Nevertheless, we can probably rule Michael out from one major syndrome associated with gayness: that of "gender nonconformity" in childhood. A preference in childhood for avoiding "boyish" rough and tumble games, liking to put on girls' clothes and adopting "girlish" behaviour, is a good predictor of adult male homosexuality, according to research by gender identity specialist Richard Green: the great majority of such boys he studied into adulthood became either gay or bisexual.[454] The correlation is particularly marked for those boys who grow up to be "effeminate" gays, as opposed to "straight-acting" ones.

If Michael's adult "effeminate" behaviour were an indication of this long-term developmental pattern, one would expect to find that as a little boy he had been something of a "sissy". Yet this is not what we find. As a boy Michael was a lively little rascal, not at all "girlishly" coy or timid. He was a prankster, wickedly keen on practical jokes, and the only one, in a house full of older boys, with the nerve to stand up to his father. Even in adult life he was "boyish" in most ways – unlike the super-feminine La Toya, whose living space is so neat, tidy and utterly perfect that visitors are hardly allowed to walk on the carpets,[455] Michael just slung his clothes on the floor and was happy to live in a casual dump of a bedroom.[456] What could be more blokish? Whereas she was always likely to have a fit of the vapours at the mere thought of feeding Michael's smelly animals,[457] he took a decidedly unsqueamish interest in brain surgery as a young man: he once went to the trouble of wangling invitations to highly unorthodox private attendance at operations,[458] seeing at close quarters some nifty knife work and cortical convolutions that would make supposedly tougher guys turn to jelly.

And Michael's aggressive, raunchy, crotch-grabbing stage performances were scarcely the stuff of Barbara Cartland novels: they suggested nothing feminine whatever. Even the anti-macho, anti-violence theme of the song "Beat It" puts the message across in a tough way, validating retreat as a smart stratagem for the cool, survival-minded dude. For the psychology to work, for "street cred" to be maintained, any hint of wimpishness has to be rubbed out with the ruthlessness of a mafia hit.[459]

Michael's off-stage retreat behind a mask of makeup and seeming femininity is best explained not as a deep indicator of developing gayness so much as a different kind of stratagem, an opportunistic response to the need for a different kind of credibility. It is no accident that it was in adolescence that Michael began to withdraw, developing the serious, shy, strange character which by his own admission came to set him apart from "normal" folk.[460] It all began mundanely enough with a bad case of acne which revealed him as perhaps inherently a more sensitive type than his brother Marlon (not that "sensitive" equates with feminine, but it is a teasing hint in that direction). Add to this his inhibitions with girls arising from taking to heart a religious faith that opposes pre-marital sex, and we already have the makings not only of serious hang-ups, but also of problems for Michael in how to present himself to the public. If, to top all else, he was coming to find himself drawn exclusively towards young boys, the tensions would have been desperate. No "solution" would have been apparent: there was none.

We would instead expect to find him clutching at straws, coming up with drastic and bizarre survival measures. Poor Michael must have felt all the time as precariously positioned as James Bond suspended over a pool full of piranha fish, having to resort to amazing gadgets to get him out of trouble. It was a scenario in which every Wacko Jacko story eventually became just such a gadget. Rick Sky spoke of hiding behind a "shield" of wackiness, which comes to much the same thing.[461] One such device Michael hit upon was to hint at being gay, through an increasingly feminine appearance and manner. This stood to achieve three things. Firstly, it would explain away his lack of romantic involvement with women and take off some of the pressure to "perform" with glamorous females coming his way on the showbiz circuit. At the same time, because it was only a hint, millions of girl fans would discount it as untrue, each of them preferring to cherish him as the dreamboat they would eventually marry. Secondly, it would throw the newshounds off the scent: better to have his lack of girlfriends plausibly explained away by seeming to be an effeminate, man-hunting gay, than to risk the suspicion of something far worse in the public estimation.

Thirdly – the most subtle and difficult point, but also the most revealing – to hint at gayness was for Michael to emphasise aspects of his personality that were coming to be absolutely genuine in his development as a human being. He was gradually, from within, coming to be gentle, softly spoken and "feminine". The sensitivity may well always have been there. His mother would certainly have known about that. But the entirely new factor as he grew up arose from his own reflections on life, especially his own: he was struggling towards an awkward accommodation with the world, towards a "feel" for people and a viable way of relating to them, a struggle arising directly out of the extreme oddness of his situation. As he passed through his teen years, witnessing with revulsion his brothers' coarse imitation of his equally coarse father's behaviour towards women, he was coming to be aware that his own sexual feelings were taking him in a different direction, towards young boys. Unable to express this in the simple, relaxed, animal fashion of ordinary sex at its best and worst, he began to romanticise and sentimentalise his feelings, using an unconscious survival tactic of frustrated young would-be lovers everywhere. He wrote poetry.

He started thinking about the beauty of nature, the innocence of children. His mind took him towards the magical and the mystical, towards Peter Pan and a fairy land of the imagination – a land which soon found him being associated with "fairies" of a different kind. Yet how "naturally" such thinking must have come to a young man who had lived in a fantasy world all his life, a showbiz world in which dressing up and wearing makeup were second nature not an unacceptable oddity.

The gentle, soft-spoken Michael emerging from adolescence was thus a real figure, not just a public relations creation. The "nice" thoughts and feelings he expressed were truly coming from within, thoughts and feelings based on maiden aunt sensibilities that steered him clear of unwanted grown-up sex. Just how "all my own work" his "nice" poetry is, for instance, can be judged by its quality. It is not just any old sentimental rubbish. It is plainly so dreadful it cannot possibly have been written for him by the talented ghost writers behind Hollywood stars' "autobiographies". Skilful scribes can be persuaded to do dubious things for the right money, but conning verse bad enough to ruin their reputation as writers is unlikely to be among them.

Take, for instance, "When babies smile", a fairly typical piece from the collection of poems and reflections Michael published as *Dancing the Dream*. The last verse runs as follows:

> Kingdoms topple, lose their class
> Civilisations crumble, ages pass
> Turbulent tempests ravage the seas
> Violent killings, despite our pleas
> But dewdrops sparkle when children play
> Tyrants cry, there's nothing to slay
> Fairies dance and goblins sing
> All are crowned, all are king
> In the garden we frolic awhile
> Those are moments when babies smile.[462]

Kingdoms topple, lose their class, boy can he write a verse that's crass! The point here is not to criticise Michael's poetry, even though his crime against rhyme deserved a prison sentence more than anything he may have done with boys. Not that most of us are in a position to cast the first stone. Our youthful mental couplings of William McGonagall and Patience Strong have begotten millions of equally ugly little bastards of verse. The difference in Michael's case is that he was able to publish, so his work was not left in decent obscurity. Nor did anyone apparently dare advise him he is no Byron or Wordsworth, or have the temerity to interfere editorially in any way. As detectives in search of "the real Michael", we should be delighted to stumble across such telling evidence for the existence of this illusive entity. Could it be that all is not necessarily chimerical and mere illusion?

Illusion, though, served Michael well. Magic was his favourite word. His "child-like" vision sees magic everywhere, in nature, the cosmos, a baby's smile. Magic, for Michael, is a synonym for wonder and awe. Nature is the greatest magician, he says. "When a whale plunges out of the sea like a newborn mountain, you gasp in unexpected delight. But a toddler who sees his first tadpole flashing in a mud puddle feels the same thrill."[463] Yes, we might in a charitable moment concede, he has a point here. The idea of plunging *upwards* arguably stretches linguistic flexibility to breaking point, but that "newborn mountain" image is not at all bad. We might think that with a little more discipline his writing could have been usefully expressive.

We might think that, but we would be wrong, because there is too much magic of the other kind in his writing, magic of the now-you-see-it-now-you-don't kind. He denied this. He specifically says his idea of magic does not have much to do with stage tricks and illusions.[464] Nevertheless, when Michael is telling us about all the beautiful things he finds so magical, he is saying both something real about himself (now you see him) and something illusory (now you don't). His poems, with titles like "Mother Earth", "A child is a song", "Innocence" and "Magical Child" are real: they are from the heart. But in another sense they are like the bland speech of a politician aiming to be all things to all men: they are motherhood and apple pie stuff, long on rhetoric, short on "the beef" – that is to say, short on anything that will reveal him, or commit him to any attitudes or opinions that could be considered remotely individual or controversial. There is nothing specific he can be held to. Ultimately his published poems and reflections, like his song lyrics, his autobiography and his rare interviews, are more notable for what they do not say than for what they do. La Toya hit the mark when she was asked what was missing from *Moonwalk*, Michael's autobiography. "The beginning, the middle and the end," she replied.[465]

Like Michael's many other masks, his words were used both to conceal and, tantalisingly, to reveal the fact of concealment. It is a teasing combination, most simply exemplified in his hiding behind sunglasses while wearing the unmistakable, "Here I am" trademark fedora hat, to make sure the paparazzi point their cameras the right way. We know, for instance, that Michael was "fond of" animals, had pets as unusual as snakes, giraffes and llamas, and was known to make worthy, vaguely green remarks about "pollution", and saving the planet for all its species. But where did we see the passion, the commitment, of a Brigitte Bardot prepared to fight, to make herself unpopular in some quarters if necessary, on behalf of animals? Michael, we heard, learned chimp language, presumably to talk to his pet Bubbles. But did he ever listen to what Bubbles was saying? In the hands of a Jane Goodall, or even a Desmond Morris, such an exercise would have produced results worth talking about. We would not expect a pop singer to come up with a zoologist's expert report, but why not a halfway decent poem or a song lyric?

Why is it, when we think of Michael and animals, we are stuck at the level of Disney cartoon characters? In every sense of the word we get a Mickey Mouse view of the animal world from Michael – full of "magic" and "fantasy", but totally trivial and unconnected to any real concern for other species. For Michael, his animals were just accessories, variously cuddly or amusing, but in essence little different to the stuffed toys he might find at Toys R Us for the delight of his little friends.

Was he really this shallow? Did his truly "child-like" view of nature never get beyond the merely childish? At the time of Michael's marriage to Lisa Marie Presley it seemed to some as though he was beginning to take Scientology seriously – his wife's religion. A major tenet of Scientology is a rejection of Darwinian evolution because it is a materialistic theory, one that leaves no room for "spirit". Did Michael, so close to so many exotic species over the years, never have thoughts of his own on how they may have come into being? Did he believe God just waved his magic wand? Probably he did, and he is entitled to such a view. But we could be sure that if he had more "controversial" opinions we would not be hearing about them: while Darwin is hardly controversial among the well educated there are others Michael would not have wished to offend.

Likewise we could search in vain through the pages of *Moonwalk* or *Dancing the Dream* or the song lyrics for any serious exploration either of black consciousness – a concept rejected by the officially "colour blind" Michael – or of his music's African roots, a more surprising omission. The Jackson Five had toured Senegal in 1974, when the young Michael was shown the old House of Slaves on Goree Island, from where thousands of Africans were once forcibly shipped in wretched conditions to the New World, many dying on the way. The most lasting impression the boys took away with them seems to have been of the poverty encountered in the modern African state, an impression which translated not so much into a politically radical view of the First World-Third World relationship as simply into profound relief that the slave trade had given them the opportunity to be born in relatively affluent circumstances in America.[466]

As for his musical roots, Michael appeared to have made little of them. He toured in Africa on his own account, but paid no more than lip service to the music of the continent. His greatest inspiration was not as a singer, songwriter, composer, or even as a dancer, but as a showman. Significantly, he was a great admirer of PT Barnum and Walt Disney – classic exponents of giving the punters what they want. Theirs is a philosophy of marketing, of identifying how people want to be entertained and generating the product accordingly, rather than giving what comes from within, from a deeply personal identity and set of concerns. Anything artistically produced out of personal commitment, such as black consciousness or animal rights, runs the risk of offending and alienating those who do not share a similar identity or sentiments. "Personal Statement" music is bound to be to some degree controversial and to put off some fans just as it attracts others.

Ambiguous in so many ways, Michael was at least very clear on why he avoided controversial opinions: "What a person says means so much. It can change a person's whole opinion of another person. I've seen that happen so many times – Charlie Chaplin, Paul Robeson, Jane Fonda. All people who spoke out and then world opinion started to change on them."[467] Sometimes Michael described this inhibition as a fear of being misquoted, in itself an entirely justified anxiety.[468] But it can also be a lack of courage in one's own convictions, a thought which invites a question: Was Michael hiding any significant beliefs and convictions, or did he simply lack any personal content to his life worth talking about?

Love is always deemed worth talking and singing about. Love songs dominate pop music culture, from falling in love to falling out of love, from the agony of unrequited love to the gnawing pain of having no love at all. If Michael lacked what most others would recognise as a "love life", that is no reason in itself for his not being intensely concerned in heart and mind with love and sexuality: those in search of love are sometimes among those most preoccupied with it. The claim has been made that Michael was "asexual", just not interested in any physical closeness to others. Even this rare phenomenon would be worth talking about – or worth repressing. It could be something to be shut off somewhere at the back of his mind for no-one to know about or contemplate, even himself. Either way, it would have to be considered a hugely important part of his identity, if only because it would mark him out as utterly different from most people, a truly queer fish. Love and sexuality are always special. Their social significance casts a net of importance from which even the least sexual being cannot escape.

In his music, in his stage persona, Michael was able, if not to unmesh himself, then at least to be seen as a recognisable species in the catch, singing love songs about girls just as any other male pop star would, with all the required "sincere" emotion. This came easily to him, a habit ingrained unconsciously from childhood. After he was heard recording Smokey Robinson's plaintive, bluesy "Who's loving you?" the staff at Motown were asking, "Where did he learn that kind of emotion?" He would play hide and seek around the studio like any pre-teenager, then step behind the mike "and belt a song with the emotional agility and presence of an old soul who's seen his share of heartache".[469] Maybe he had seen more heartache in his short life than people knew: adults often make the mistake of underestimating children's emotions. But insofar as "heartache" is a word we attach to love life, then Michael certainly had a facility for "faking it" – he saw many other soulful singers at work and happened to be a great little imitator. Keeping his true personal life out of his song writing was a sensitive and tricky issue for Michael, which he addressed in *Moonwalk*. He refers to his preference for writing and singing about the night life rather than going out and living it, and says:

> It always surprises me when people assume that something an artist has created is based on a true experience or reflects his or her own lifestyle. Often nothing could be further from the truth. I know I draw on my experience at times, but I also hear and read things that trigger an idea for a song. An artist's imagination is his greatest tool.[470]

This cleverly crafted comment tells us people really were taken in by what the artist presented, and that Michael knew he could fake whatever he wanted and have it taken for a genuine personal expression. Also, by saying there was some personal element in the songs he left open the possibility that this might include love experiences. As a means of pleasing millions of fans Michael's artistic strategy worked to perfection, and that in itself was a source of immense satisfaction to him: he was known in his heyday to take as much pride in his unprecedented album sales figures as in the music itself. Indeed being number one, the King of Pop, appears to have been more significant to him than the artistry that earned him the title. But was it ever enough? There were many hints in Michael's writing and music that he would have liked people to know him better, and that only the sheer danger involved in revealing himself prevented him doing so too unambiguously.

His poems, behind a discreet veil of mystical vagueness and opacity, offer tantalising glimpses of deeply personal preoccupations that emerge elsewhere in an openly sexual context. Take, for instance, the idea of "conditioned" thinking. The concept comes up time and again, but not quite in the context from which the word originates, that of Pavlov and the dogs he "conditioned" to salivate at the sound of a bell. Nor is there any evidence Michael concerned himself with psychology as a science. On the contrary, the mental universe we must enter is far removed from that of rational inquiry. Instead we must discover the mystical writings of Richard Bach, author of the cult classic *Jonathan Livingston Seagull*, known to be one of

Michael's favourite books: Bach's style finds clear echoes in poems such as "Wings Without Me" and "Dance of Life".[471]

In this world anything is possible. Walking on water, like Jesus. Flying at will, like Peter Pan. The whole of life is magical according to this way of seeing things, a way children understand but adults do not. Adults are mostly "conditioned" (by what? Society? Authority? Reality?) into setting limitations on themselves and believing there are things they cannot achieve. The trick is to understand that these limitations are an illusion: you can do anything if you believe you can. Michael allegedly convinced Jordie that the "unconditioned people" can levitate themselves right off the ground because they have not been "conditioned" to believe gravity has any power. If even the laws of physics had no authority for Michael, we might wonder what price the laws of man? Restrictive moral codes, in this view, are for merely ordinary people, who are seen as having limited spirit and imagination, talent and courage; they are the conditioned ones, the ones who blindly acquiesce to social norms only because they lack the wit and the strength to assert their own freedom and will. In another respect, Michael did recognise an authority higher than his own when he allegedly described his relationship with Jordie as "cosmic" and "meant to be", as though it conformed to some pattern of destiny beyond his knowledge or control. Significantly, though, we never found any "cosmic" indications in Michael's thinking of anything he wanted to do that was *not* "meant to be", or which ought *not* to have been done. Metaphysics were invoked only to confirm his wishes, never to deny them. Very convenient! Michael even attributed the unconditioned response to animals:

> There's a certain sense that animals and children have that gives me a certain creative juice, a certain force that later on in adulthood is kind of lost because of the conditioning that happens in the world. They are the way I wish the world really was because they are not phoney and they don't know prejudice. Prejudice is taught. If the world were full of only children it would be a much better place.[472]

Without enquiring too closely as to the nature of the "creative juice" an adolescent Jordie might have given him, we may note the ambiguity in that word "prejudice". Prejudice of what kind? These words of his, uttered before the disastrous allegations of 1993-4, would have been taken as a reference to racial prejudice – but they can equally be seen as provoked by his knowledge that sexual prejudice can be just as poisonous.

In any event, his emphasis on the conditioned, or culture-bound, nature of mainstream thinking served to set him apart, to define himself not just as more imaginative and creative than others but also as deeper and more spiritual. An enlightened one. A seer. A shaman – his feminine style echoes the native American "berdache", a revered medicine man of womanly appearance. A messiah even. The idea is not far-fetched. Millions of fans for years read their own preferred meaning into his every vague utterance. The gentleness of voice and sheer absence, in a black star, of militant commitment to black advancement, suggested a Jesus-like "turn the other cheek" aspect. His video performances, by contrast, have seen him present himself at times as a figure of positively godlike powers, a Superman saviour: after rescuing children from the clutches of a drugs baron in *Moonwalker* he transforms himself into a huge super-human robotic figure and disappears into the sky as though he had been a "god" from another planet.

Jackson fan literature sometimes served the messiah market all but explicitly, and in at least one instance in a most elaborated way. Reviewing the book *Michael Jackson: American Master* by C Mecca for fan magazine *King!*, Robin Meltzer said it is "...not a biography. It is more like a bible. It elevates Michael to a status above that of human".[473] The book was officially endorsed by the King of Pop's production company, MJJ Productions, and carried a foreword by his publicity chief Bob Jones. Meltzer continued: "Michael is portrayed more as a prophet than as a special human being. It is as if he is carrying on the work of the Creator, and that rather suggests a Messiah figure to me."[474]

Any expression by Michael of definite opinions on this or that particular issue would have opened him to charges of being misguided or wrong. His studied ambiguity presented no such Achilles' heel to the world. Instead he offered an empty set of possibilities that fans could fill according to their own imagination and tastes. He thus became all things to all men – and all women and all children. Richard Bach was immensely useful to him in this respect. In his *Illusions: The Adventures of a Reluctant Messiah*, Bach set out some good practical advice for the apprentice messiah on how to go about his messiah'ing: Don't say too much. Keep your words of wisdom mysterious and ambiguous. If the punters know exactly what you're saying straight away it won't have the necessary feel of hidden depth. Give them something they have to ponder. The handbook for messiahs is full of useful examples. Things like: "Argue for your limitations, and sure enough, they're yours."[475]

As messiahs go, Michael was never really in this class, but that did not stop him picking up a far bigger following than Bach himself. He had learnt enough. With regard to his sexuality, Michael was explicit in his wish to be teasingly ambiguous, if a reported conversation with videographer Steve Howell is to be believed. Comedian Eddie Murphy had made a TV chat show crack about Michael's effeminacy:

> "How do you feel about that, Mike," Howell asked. "I mean, this guy really made fun of you. He might as well have come out and called you a fag." Michael smiled, "I don't mind," he said softly. "I mean, the more they make fun of me, the more people are going to wonder what I really am. I don't care when people call me a fag. No one knows the truth. No one knows who or what I am."
>
> "You don't care what people say about you?"
>
> "They can say what they want to say, because the bottom line is they don't know and everybody is going to continue searching to find out whether I'm gay, straight, or whatever. It doesn't bother me. And the longer it takes them to discover this," Michael concluded, "the more famous I will be."[476]

The Chandler affair and the Presley marriage kept the guessing game going ever more famously.[477] In the end marriage, or some other spectacular gesture – a child by Madonna, say – had become an absolute necessity to keep the game in play. In earlier years the priority was different: the guessing game was better served, if dangerously so, by being seen with children. But fame was not the only spur. There was a time, I believe, when Michael genuinely wanted people to see that his was a different way of loving – different not only from the macho ways of his father and brothers, but utterly different, a cosmically "meant to be" rapport between the unconditioned spirits of a child and a child-man. Michael spoke of the courage it takes to be intimate, to reveal your true feelings, to open your heart to another. He wrote:

> When you have the courage to be intimate, you know who you are, and you're willing to let others see that. It's scary, because you feel so vulnerable, so open to rejection. But without self-acceptance, the other kind of courage, the kind heroes show in movies, seems hollow. In spite of the risk, the courage to be honest and intimate opens the way to self-discovery. It offers what we all want. The promise of love.[478]

There can be little doubt that Michael at times found the courage to be intimate with his little friends. This may sound like a cheap shot, an easy giggle, but it would be a pity if we failed to think our way past that initial reaction. Anyone in our society whose mixed-up bundle of feelings of the loving kind – erotic, tender, nurturant, playful – are oriented exclusively towards children carries a terrible burden of fear on his back. It is a grievous thing in a hostile world to have such feelings discovered by others. The shame and humiliation can be crippling, even fatal. There are those who crush their love in an iron vice of self-discipline, squeezing the spirit out of themselves in a sort of perpetual living suicide. Others tell themselves God would not have given them such feelings if they were useless, if they were not meant to be expressed for a child's benefit. Yet they too will be deeply fearful of revealing what is in their hearts, even to adult friends, lest uncomprehending revulsion and rejection should follow.

To reveal oneself in such circumstances does take courage. It takes an enormous leap of faith. You have to trust your own feelings really are "right" and good, in order to believe your fellow humans will pick up on it and believe you. Michael spoke specifically of this fear of rejection. Describing a squirrel in a park, gradually plucking up the courage to come near him to take a proffered peanut, he said:

> Trust is like that – it always seems to come down to trusting in yourself. Others can't overcome fear for you; you have to do it on your own. It's hard, because fear and doubt hold on tight. We are afraid of being rejected, of being hurt once more. So we keep a safe distance. We think separating ourselves from others will protect us, but that doesn't work, either. It leaves us feeling alone and unloved.[479]

The most terrible rejection of all for a lover of children is to be rejected by kids themselves – a real problem for those who happen to be socially awkward, introverted and shy, or else locked into the straightjacket of adult ways, like some unbending schoolmasters, who can only safely express themselves by being tough when really they ache to be tender. Michael was lucky in this respect. He always found it easy to relax with children, to behave like a kid himself. Winning their trust and confidence came easily to him. Up to a point he could play the relaxed guy on the park bench effortlessly winning cute little squirrels to his side with a bag of peanuts. Even so, the courage to be really intimate with a child, either socially or sexually, would render him just as vulnerable as anyone else. There comes a point in such a relationship when, by revealing himself to be "different", the roles are reversed. It is the grown-up who becomes the squirrel, having to trust that the little friend will not hurt him with rejection, or denounce him to his parents. Irrespective of Michael's legal innocence or guilt, his public downfall showed clearly enough how vulnerable he had allowed himself to become.

It is often suggested that child-lovers, being socially inept in adult company, seek children as a substitute. Male child-lovers are said to be afraid of women. Ironically, the complete reverse is often the case: many child-lovers are completely relaxed with adults because, so far as sexual competition is concerned, they stand emotionally outside the battle. Those child-lovers who attempt relations with women are generally motivated by the wish to become fathers, and fail not through their social ineptitude or the "faint heart" that "never won fair lady" but quite simply because they find women physically repulsive at close quarters.

The "courage to be intimate", clearly an important problem for Michael, to judge by his writing, is itself intimately related to another aspect of the same virtue: "the courage of one's convictions", which implies a willingness to be combative in pursuit of what we believe to be right, even at some personal risk. If Michael's instinct was for ambiguity, rather than for such head-on challenges to the world, it does not necessarily mean he wanted to reveal nothing of himself, or that he was unwilling to take any risks at all. There are signs that Michael would dearly have loved to be accepted for what he really was, that he would have loved to be able to trust the world with the knowledge that he was a whole-hearted lover of children rather than, as his thin "romantic" curriculum vitae implies, a hopelessly half-hearted lover of women.

The first major sign of this was tentatively, ambiguously expressed, in true Michael Jackson style, when he attended the 1984 Grammy awards accompanied by both Brooke Shields and the 12-year-old Emmanuel Lewis, as we have already seen. The autobiographical *Moonwalk* was far more circumspect, talking about dates and romance in a way seemingly designed to establish credentials of normality. Yet even here there is ambiguity, with strong hints that Michael's failure to get it together with girls was more than a minor problem (or else, though he does not say so, entirely a problem of minors). Talking about the sadness of the *Off the Wall* number "She's Out of my Life", he says the song "...is about knowing that the barriers that have separated me from others are temptingly low and seemingly easy to jump over and yet they remain standing while what I really desire disappears from my sight."[480]

"What I really desire" – Ay, there's the rub! "One day you must understand the truth of lust" he sings in a song called "In the closet", a title whose significance could scarcely be more obvious.[481] In the 1988 film *Moonwalker*, Michael's face is seen displayed on a police poster, bearing the words "Wanted for questioning". Children come along and tear the poster down. Can we seriously suppose the prophetic element here is purely coincidental? Even the egotistical (and largely justified) confidence that kids will never see any evil in him, no matter how bad things look to grown-ups, looks like consciously considered symbolism with one particular "evil" in mind.

As for the mask of normality Michael wore in his singing of conventional love songs, it was always in his adult years a studiously unconvincing disguise, mirroring precisely his many "incognito" appearances in ridiculously obvious huge false moustaches and such like, on occasions when he would have been alarmed *not* to be recognised and *not* to have a horde of press photographers jostling behind him. His love songs, for instance, were scarcely celebrations of the joys of heterosexual tenderness and togetherness. Like "She's out of my Life", they tend to be gloomy, despondent pieces, with the emphasis on failure and a flight from relationships – including one of his biggest hits, "Billie Jean". The only love Michael could sing about convincingly was love gone wrong, or else love for children or animals. As a youngster he was able to admit to a distaste for more mainstream material, and we have no reason to suppose his feelings changed:

> I just hate ordinary love songs. I'm interested in a different type of love song. I want a brand-new thought. That's what I love about Ben. There's a mystery to it... so many people come up to me and say, "Why did you create such a song about a little stinkin' rat? How'd you make it so beautiful if it's about a dumb rat?"[482]

The truth remains: Michael would rather have made a rat sound attractive than a woman. He could "fake it". He could do ordinary love songs and put on a heterosexual act, but he conspicuously preferred not to. Hesitancy and ambiguity instead were leitmotivs of his adult work. In the *Thriller* video, Michael is seen stranded in a lonely spot with a girl, after their car has run out of petrol. A classic scenario. In a 1950s Hollywood movie it would be a horny college kid in his dad's car, more interested in getting past first base than back on the road. In Michael's version the pair set off on foot to find help. "I'm not like other guys" he tells her, in words sounding more like an excuse than the warning that is their ostensible purpose. Then he begins to turn into a werewolf, prompting the girl to flee. Well, naturally. What else could a terrified Michael do to escape having to behave like a regular guy?[483]

Several times he catches up with her, reverting to his original meek self, only to undergo further horrid transformations. The climax comes when rotting corpses clamber out of their overgrown graves to take part in a dance of death. In an essay for the *Guardian*, Joan Smith adopts a Freudian interpretation:

> Jackson's sexuality has been energised by female fear, turning him from a shy, tongue-tied youth into a terrifying, sexually-aware man-beast. Jackson's character in the Thriller video copiously displays three instincts – voyeurism, exhibitionism and cruelty – which Sigmund Freud identified as frequent components of infantile sexual life.[484]

Was Michael "energised by female fear" or by his own? Steven Spielberg once vividly described him as "like a fawn in a burning forest" an image far removed from that of the predatory werewolf.[485] It was a view that saw him as vulnerable, panic-stricken, desperate to escape the encroaching flames but unsure of finding a way out. This was the Michael we could imagine banging the walls of his hotel suite in Bangkok, sobbing "I never hurt anyone!" This was the victim Michael, who fled into hiding in a drug rehab centre and was humiliatingly strip-searched and photographed by the police. The Michael of the *Thriller* video, by contrast, is in artistic control, and knows what he must do to escape the burning forest of threatening female sexuality: if he is to get away with being "not like other guys" then his difference from others must be presented in some dramatically superhuman way, rather than as wimpish failure. The bottom line, though, remains the symbolic admission of his own Otherness, his alienation from ordinary loving. Joan Smith pursues the infantile theme:

> Freud writes about two other characteristics of infantile sexuality, auto-eroticism and obsession with an erotogenic zone, which are visible in the Thriller video and which have become an increasingly significant element of Jackson's stage act. His dancing, whether live or on film, is saturated with

> images of masturbation. His much-mocked props – the oversized glove, the cod-piece which draws attention to his crotch – are a striking example of Freud's observation...that "small children are essentially without shame, and at some periods of their earliest years show an unmistakable satisfaction in exposing their bodies, with especial emphasis on the sexual parts." While it is possible that Jackson is consciously mimicking infantile sexuality, it seems just as likely that what we see on stage is an authentic expression of arrested sexual development.[486]

One wonders if Ms Smith has ever heard of Elvis "the pelvis" Presley, and whether she would interpret his raunchy, crotch-focused movements as a case of arrested sexual development, and if not, why not. Or Mick Jagger's, or those of a hundred other pop stars. Her analysis, is unfortunately typical of those given to uncritical dependence on Freudian concepts: on inspection it turns out really to tell us nothing we cannot more reliably infer from other evidence. This is not to say she is wrong, only that the evidence from Freud is weak.

La Toya Jackson's view is scarcely less open to objection and has been emphatically denied by Michael. Nonetheless it is interesting, plausible, and deserves an airing so that we can keep in mind the complexity of the situation. Reducing a life to one set of all-explanatory psychodynamics really will not do: if there is one buzz word of current psychological thinking that is more than just an empty slogan, it is the idea that life problems and situations tend to be "multi-factorial". La Toya claims to have been phoned by Michael at the time of her first *Playboy* pictures. She reported that her brother said he liked the pictures, and then went on to offer an explanation as to why she would choose to do something so controversial, citing her need to "get back" at their parents and the Jehovah's Witnesses. "I know," La Toya claims he said, "because that's why I wrote 'Bad'. And that's why I wiggle the way I do and grab myself in that video and 'The Way You Make Me Feel'. It's to get back at Joseph and the religion, and to tell them I can do what I want."[487]

Robin Hunt, in the *Daily Telegraph* had an appealingly simple and persuasive explanation of Michael's crotch-rubbing which suggests market forces call the tune in the pop world.[488] The teen market, so important to Michael, has always been predicated on the notion that "your mother wouldn't like it", he wrote. Sex and drugs and rock 'n' roll are a traditional triple act. Youngsters want something "shocking". Michael's crotch-grabbing was no odder than Madonna's sexual antics or Take That's on-stage trouser-dropping. The sting of this explanation, however, and the key to its linkage with a deeper one, was in the tail: "Michael Jackson does not simulate sex on stage but, as his a-sexual star began to wane in the early nineties, he introduced a raunchiness to his act: rubbing his crotch in time to the beat, a gesture copied by eight-year-olds worldwide."

The raunchiness in fact began earlier, but why split pubic hairs? The important thing is that prepubertal pre-teens were indeed copying Michael, in a way that could only be highly gratifying to a paedophilic pop star. In developing this particular "infantile" act, crotch-grabbing, Michael was not merely expressing his own "arrested", masturbatory sexual development, but also encouraging and validating similar self-expression by children themselves. By the time children are five or six years old they have usually taken on board the socially required standards of modesty demanded by their parents and other adults. They are no longer the shameless exhibitionists of Freud's observing. Instead their sexual feelings find more secret expression in the pre-pubertal years he (wrongly) thought were generally a time of sexual "latency".

Michael's subversive gesture offered the heady possibility of returning children's infantile freedom to them, of giving them the chance to enjoy and celebrate their sexuality rather than hiding or repressing it. "Never give up your bliss" was the message Michael allegedly gave Jordan Chandler in private:[489] it was a message he gave every child in public. It was, to be sure, a coded message, and its deciphering would not necessarily be straightforward. Children's sexuality, like that of grown-ups, is a social construct, but unpredictably, chaotically emergent in any individual. The inchoate "meaning" of Michael's gesture in terms of sexual activity and social significance was, so to speak, up for grabs. It was a truly seminal act, fertile in serving to generate a juvenile symbolic discourse of sexuality, through which children themselves might be enabled to recognise and acknowledge their desires. Freed to touch their bodies in naughty places, and to think about the implications, they would inevitably begin to negotiate the significance of it all, with themselves and others – including their peers, and perhaps a friendly grown-up or two. Possibly even, for a few lucky ones, with Michael himself.

Adult construction of the crotch gesture ranged from the scandalised (from a conservative standpoint sensibly so) to the sophisticated (but, as we shall see, with some remarkably "off the wall" and unconvincing results). A land-grab for the alluring terra incognita of Michael's gender, race and sexuality was being greedily pursued by academic cultural imperialists in the early 1990s. The big players, from the burgeoning "studies" fiefdoms – women's studies, queer studies, ethnic studies, media studies, cultural studies – carved up Michael's body and its actions as their discursive preserve. Within their ivory tower universe their word was hegemonic. And because it was in the interests of none of them that Michael should turn out to be a paedophile, their interpretations of his style and its cultural significance remained blind to all the signs, all the symbolism thereof – manifestations of which one might hope such sophisticates would be acutely sensible. On the meaning and significance of Michael's crotch-grabbing these cultural gurus were left for dead even after the Chandler affair forced the unwelcome paedophilia factor into what one might call their collective unconsciousness.[490]

Cynthia Fuchs, for example, herself from media studies, contrived to compose an academic article of which the title was daring and attention-grabbing but of which the contents entirely missed, so to speak, the point. It was called Michael Jackson's Penis and was published as a chapter in a tome brought out by a university press. The chapter ran to fifteen pages with a further six pages of notes and bibliography. Although the 1993 accusation of child molesting is introduced on the first page, not once is the word "boy" mentioned in the main text, and there is no engagement with paedophilia as an issue concerning either Michael's life in general or, more precisely on topic, the life of his penis.

Unsurprisingly, then, much of what Fuchs says is irrelevant to the present book's concerns. But her discussion of Michael's performance in the video of "In the closet" from Dangerous is revealing for what it misses. He performs in a sequence that includes model Naomi Campbell but he does not dance "with" her in the same frames. Despite scenes which Fuchs interprets as repeated "mutual masturbation", she insists that "the sex is expressly single". She writes that "He sings, passionately, 'Cause if it's aching, you gotta rub it'." The repressed meaning of "it" is clear, she says, but not "you". To Fuchs, the video suggests neither Campbell, nor the figure played by her, as the "you" being addressed, but instead:

> Jackson's lyric would seem to suggest young "men" like himself; but who would that possibly be? Masturbating men? Gay men? Black men? For that matter, could he be singing to me? As whom and for whom is Michael Jackson constructing himself, or passing in and out of this closet?

Remarkably, unless some subtle, illusive irony is intended (and the rest of the article suggests otherwise), Fuchs has managed to miss the elephant in the room or, rather, the boy watching the video in the privacy of his bedroom, where "rubbing it" becomes a possibility. The idea that Michael is addressing pre-pubescent or pubescent boys in the video fits well with Jordie Chandler's allegations and even more so with a claim that Gavin Arvizo would make at Michael's trial. The boy would say that Michael encouraged him to masturbate by telling him men needed to do it or they might end up raping a girl or having sex with animals. Arguably Gavin could have been inspired by the video to make a false allegation of this kind, but that would itself be eloquent testimony to the impact of the lyrics on its intended young audience.[491]

Returning to Robin Hunt, while he was wrong to suggest that Michael's stage raunchiness began in the early nineties, it is true to say that by this period the star was becoming more firmly linked than ever with children, to the embarrassment of his more mature fans and the dismay of music writers who likewise appreciated his talent but felt he was taking a wrong tack. For the *Dangerous* tour, begun in Europe in 1992, Michael made children, and his love of children, the key theme. Much of this was uncontentious stuff focused on his charity fund-raising for the Heal the World Foundation. Children from many countries were brought on stage in this connection. Offstage, however, he was also being seen with children, sometimes dressed as "mini-me" replicas of himself, and imitating his every gesture – with the apparent implication that they wanted to copy him in every way, including the sexual. There was coming to be a level of blatancy, of flaunting, in Michael's personal warmth towards children that reached its hubristic zenith in his public intimacy with Jordie Chandler at Monte Carlo in 1993, just three months before the debacle.

As if all the foregoing did not add up to a series of hefty hints by Michael as to his sexual makeup, we have another, perhaps the most obvious of all, at least to those familiar with the implications: Peter Pan. Michael had long identified himself with the magical world of the boy who never grew up, even naming his house Neverland after the island inhabited by the eponymous boy hero of JM Barrie's classic play for children. Part of the association in Michael's mind appeared to be a genuine enchantment with the limitless freedom at the heart of a child's fantasy. How can you fly? "You just think wonderful thoughts and they lift you up into the air", as Peter tells his new young companions in the play. The link between the spiritual (wonderful thoughts) and the physical (flying) was seized upon with child-like seriousness by Michael, and he is far from alone among adults in doing so: Richard Bach explores similar terrain (or air space) in mystical writing that seeks to reintegrate mind, body and soul in ways which positively encourage a literal belief in the possibility of transcending the laws of nature. For the many mixed up, troubled souls washed up at "self-awareness" seminars, drawn into bizarre religious cults and drawn to the feet of famous gurus, such thinking represents a flight from what they see as the harsh tyranny of modern scientific rationality.

It is not necessary to be a child-lover to be influenced by such thinking, but its child-like nature is bound to appeal to one. And anybody who doubts Michael's sincere attraction to putting the magical and fantastical at the heart of his philosophy should read his "Wings without me". Seeing a falcon in the sky, he ponders sadly why it has grown wings without him, but tells himself his thoughts are free as any bird. His heart too can soar by showing love, by singing a lullaby at a child's bedside. But then:

> "You grew wings without me," my body said. "Your flights are only of imagination." So I looked into books that I had ignored before and read about saints in every age who actually flew. In India, Persia, China, and Spain (even in Los Angeles!), the power of spirit has reached, not just into the heart but into every cell of the body. "As if carried aloft by a great eagle," Saint Teresa said, "my ecstasy lifted me into the air."[492]

Knowing Michael's attitude to narcotics, even taking his "pain-killer" experiences into account, we can safely dismiss any notion that he is here advancing a drug culture interpretation of St Teresa's words. His attraction to the magic of Peter Pan is undoubtedly quite genuine. Barrie's 1911 novel *Peter Pan* (initially released as *Peter and Wendy*), is credibly said to have been one of Michael's favourite books. And his enthusiasm could only have grown if he happened to have discovered a little background information: such as the fact that the play developed out of a privately produced text called *The Boy Castaways*, in which the prototype Captain Hook, at once Pan's sworn enemy and (covertly) kindred spirit, is a black man, "Captain Swarthy".[493] Like Michael, he later becomes a white man. Or that when the mother-figure, Wendy, emerges in the play from her new house, "She is quite surprised," in the words of Barrie's stage directions, "to find that she has nine children" – precisely the number comprised by Michael and his siblings.[494] Plainly Michael's connection with Pan was "in the cosmos". "It is meant to be".

Even if Michael's scholarly researches on the subject were restricted, as seems likely, to a frame-by-frame scrutiny of the cinematic *Peter Pan*, we would still be bound to feel the connection is one of special, magical power, perhaps even the power to mould Michael's face in Pan's image. Commenting on Andrew Birkin's TV investigation into the continuing attraction of *Peter Pan*, Craig Brown wrote in the *Evening Standard*, "I wonder if Birkin noticed what I noticed when I took my children to the Disney cartoon version of Peter Pan? Michael Jackson's face – altered over the years by the sharp knives of various surgeons – seems to be modelled on the Disney *Peter Pan*, with the same odd, upturned nose, the big eyes and the pronounced cheekbones. The similarity is so pronounced that it surely can't be coincidental..."[495]

A tongue in cheek discovery? Or a scalpel sharp one? Those who see the film may judge for themselves. What we can be sure of is that Michael identified with Peter Pan as a character, that he was content for this to be part of his public image, and that he must have known full well what people could make of his Pan-like disinclination to grow up, including its implied refusal of adult sexuality.

Let us take these points one by one. According to Randy Taraborrelli, Jane Fonda suggested way back in 1983, long before Michael's move to Neverland, that he should star in a film of *Peter Pan*:

> Tears began to well in Michael's eyes. He wanted to know why she suggested that character. She told him that, in her mind's eye, he really was Peter Pan, the symbol of youth, joy, and freedom. Michael started to cry. "You know, all over the walls of my room are pictures of Peter Pan. I totally identify with Peter Pan," he said, wiping his eyes, "the lost boy of Never-Never Land."[496]

Before long he was discussing with Steven Spielberg the possibility of his playing the title role in such a film. The idea fell by the wayside at that time over difficulties obtaining rights to the work, but his keenness to be seen as Peter Pan is nonetheless evident.[497]

Superficially the idea should have presented no problems. Pan is traditionally seen as the very archetype of sexual innocence: the little boy Peter, "who has still all his baby teeth"[498] doesn't even know what a kiss is. But a slightly older boy like Michael Jackson, who had a second set of teeth and even a second face to go with them, is less credibly presented as so comprehensively ignorant. Michael must have known – or would have been advised – that much could be made of this child-like image. While it would usefully convince many that he was indeed a true innocent, it was a double-edged sword. Yet he chose to wield it, despite the dangers. This is totally different from the situation of, say, Cliff Richard, long dubbed Britain's Peter Pan of pop. Some in the media have doubtless used the term in his case with malicious intent, as a slighting reference to his long-term bachelorhood and self-declared celibacy; others have probably intended only congratulations on his continuing youthful looks and durable popularity. Either way, it appears to have been a sobriquet thrust upon him rather than one of his own choosing. Even irritated rejection of the term would seem suspect; he had no alternative but to accept it with good grace, which, apparently, he wisely did.

Let us consider, then, what Michael's identification with Peter Pan amounts to, and why there is "much that could be made" of it. The play, first performed in 1904 (but not published until 1928), was turned into a novel by Barrie in 1911. For Joan Smith, the latter work provides fascinating insights into the preoccupations which drove him to write the former:

> ...the novel seethes with darker currents. In a key early scene, in which Peter tells Wendy why he ran away from home, it becomes clear that he is motivated as much by fear of the adult state as by his attachment to childhood. Barrie wrote: "It was because I heard father and mother," (Peter) explained in a low voice, "talking about what I was to be when I became a man." He was extraordinarily agitated now. "I don't want ever to be a man," he said with passion. "I want always to be a little boy and to have fun. So I ran away to Kensington Gardens and lived a long time among the fairies."[499]

The book's most revealing scene, in Smith's view, takes place in Peter's underground home in Neverland:

> ...when the pirate Captain Hook (educated, significantly, at "a famous public school" whose traditions "still cling to him") slides down a hollow tree and surprises him asleep.
>
> Peter has already enacted a symbolic castration on Hook, chopping off his arm and tossing it to a passing crocodile, which is how they became mortal enemies. Peter is a fitful sleeper, troubled by (wet?) dreams "more painful than the dreams of other boys", and from which he is usually rescued

> by the now-absent Wendy. At this point in the novel Barrie suddenly describes Peter's sleeping form twice on the same page, leaving the reader in no doubt that the pirate captain finds it sexually arousing: "What stayed (Hook) was Peter's impertinent appearance as he slept. The open mouth, the drooping arm, the arched knee; they were such a personification of cockiness as, taken together, will never again, one may hope, be presented to eyes so sensitive to their offensiveness."[500]

Smith goes on to say that Hook's sensitivity had been defined in terms of a fin-de-siècle decadence that was unmistakable only sixteen years after the trial of Oscar Wilde: the pirate captain "loved flowers" and "sweet music" – and he used poison, traditionally a female weapon, against Peter, rather than his (phallic) sword.

Michael's interest in the *Peter Pan* story is thus being represented by Joan Smith as an interest in a story with a paedophilic theme. Should she or we regard this as suspect? Is everyone who reads a crime novel a criminal? It is doubtful whether Michael himself ever pondered the symbolic significance of poison as against the sword, or was aware of all the fin-de-siècle nuances of Hook's style. By current standards, the sexual references are so heavily disguised they could easily have been overlooked by Michael if he had no other information to go by. But he had. Plenty. Literary and psychiatric pundits have been probing Barrie's sexuality and its contribution to *Peter Pan* for decades, just as prominently and publicly as in the case of Lewis Carroll, photographer of naked little girls and, like Barrie, creator of a children's classic. There have been books, TV documentaries, films on Barrie's life and work, many of them exploring the paedophilic theme. Michael and his image doctors cannot have been unaware of this, nor of the danger in too strong an association with anything seen as paedophilic. As for whether Barrie himself would have thought of Hook's loss of his arm as a symbolic castration, it is a virtual certainty. The figure of Captain Hook would have been taking shape in Barrie's mind after *The Boy Castaways* of 1901, with its prototype Captain Swarthy. Freud's *The Interpretation of Dreams* appeared in 1900, and heavy symbolism of the kind suggested was a fashionable intellectual concern of the time.

Joan Smith literally loses the plot, though, when she draws attention to a possible sexual meaning in Peter Pan's "painful" dreams. To interpret the pain in this way is to ignore the specific pain Peter had to come to terms with, namely that of finding the window barred against him when he flew home to his mother – but she had a new son now, and had quite forgotten him. Peter tells his tragic story to Wendy in almost identical terms in the play and the novel[501] For some commentators this is the key to Barrie's inferred paedophilia, for it symbolically re-enacts his own childhood experience of losing his mother's love following the death of his elder brother, whom she mourned to the exclusion of all else, paying more attention to the dead than the living. Having no-one else to love him, the theory goes, he turned to himself for love, a "narcissistic inversion" that fixated him for ever in his attraction to children.

Barrie's case is explored in Morris Fraser's *The Death of Narcissus*, as part of an ambitious bid to generate a general theory of the aetiology of paedophilia.[502] It is an unsuccessful one, however: the prediction of maternal deprivation as a common denominator hardly seems to square with many child-lovers' recollections of having enjoyed a perfectly secure, loving and happy home background. As for Michael's childhood, while his relationship with his father was badly flawed, few, least of all himself, would suggest he had lacked a mother's love. We might also note that Joan Smith referred to wet dreams. The only wetness produced at night by a little fellow still with his baby teeth would surely be of a kind other than sexual.[503]

Returning briefly to fresh air from the murky depths of the psycho-literary labyrinth, one thing is crystal clear. For Michael to be seen as identifying with a little boy repelled by the idea of adult contact with women was dangerous. We have seen what Joan Smith made of that. What another journalist memorably called "the grinding mills of bastard Freudian analysis" churned out similar material to hers for print and broadcast media worldwide.[504] Some have gone further, pointing out that in his own heartless way little Peter is scarcely more innocent than Hook, whose world he chooses to share. Here is Emma Gilbey, in the *Sunday Times*:

> He is described as "cunning" and "the sly one", and shows no pity as he lures the Darling children into his world. The irony is apparent: just when Jackson needs most to appear innocent, he invites comparison with a mendacious, sly predator – a thief of children, no less.[505]

The nearest available comparison with Michael would somewhat improbably cast Evan and June Chandler as Mr and Mrs Darling, opposite Michael's Peter Pan, with Jordie as the stolen child. Bearing in mind the huge publicity given to the Chandlers, and the vast sum of money secured to the family name by the civil settlement in Jordie's favour, one snippet of dialogue from the play seems astonishingly apt:

> *Mr Darling (thoughtlessly):* Ah, Mary, we should not be such celebrities if the children hadn't flown away.
> *Mrs Darling (startled)*: George, you are sure you are not enjoying it?[506]

There is even a fatally damning direct link to be made between the psychology of Pan, the child who rejects the adult world, and Hook, the adult lustfully locked into the child one. Barrie actually spells it out, in the stage directions for the scene in which Peter is required to imitate Hook's voice. Peter, says Barrie, "can imitate the captain's voice so perfectly that even the author has a dizzy feeling that at times he really was Hook".[507] The comment cannot possibly be meant to be taken literally, as a requirement that a little boy with a treble voice, or an actress taking the part, should be able to imitate Hook's voice exactly. Barrie's remark is a psychological comment, not a stage direction as ordinarily understood. All in all, we should have little difficulty in agreeing with Joan Smith's conclusion:

> What Jackson's story has in common with *Peter Pan* is not a romantic nostalgia for childhood but the fact that both are texts in which sex is the secret which insistently denies its own existence. But Jackson's games are much more dangerous than Peter's for this is a real man who has consistently flaunted his sexuality while also publicly denying it.[508]

Denial, significantly, was long uppermost in the reaction of fans to Michael's behaviour. It is a recurring feature when any famous individual, especially a well regarded one, is suspected of a crime. We hate to lose our heroes. For once, the much abused and overworked concept of being "in denial" can be seen to have a valid application.

There are also those who deny Barrie's paedophilia, despite the clearest pointers in his life and writing. In *The Little White Bird* Barrie describes a fictional boy, David, a thinly disguised version of his real-life little friend George, one of the Llewelyn Davies boys he later came to adopt. The narrator figure in the book, a stand-in for Barrie himself, describes the "tremendous adventure" of spending the night with the boy, after "at last" securing the mother's consent. He describes getting ready to undress the child for a bath:

> I produced a night light from my pocket and planted it in a saucer on the washstand. David watched my preparations with distasteful levity, but anon made a noble amend by abruptly offering me his foot as if he had no longer use for it, and I knew by intuition that he expected me to take off his boots. I took them off with all the coolness of an old hand, and then I placed him on my knee and removed his blouse. This was a delightful experience, but I think I remained wonderfully calm until I came somewhat too suddenly to his little braces, which agitated me profoundly. I cannot proceed in public with the disrobing of David.[509]

There are commentators who refuse to see the possibility of any paedophilic feeling in this, an insistence which seems to demand either extreme naivety or else a Nelsonian deployment of the telescope. Likewise Lewis Carroll's paedophilia is denied, despite his fondness for taking nude photographs of young girls which would today see him jailed for child pornography.

Kerry Mockler is among those writers who have turned a blind eye to the glaringly obvious sexual implications of the "disrobing" scene above. Her vision (or purblindness) is especially relevant to us as she has also written about Michael Jackson.[510] She sees both Jackson and Barrie as "maternal men", by which she means men with an uncommonly strong feminine side expressed through a deep yearning to care tenderly for children. She sees them as belonging to a "third sex", not quite man, not quite woman, but "betwixt and between". Mockler writes with great empathy for those who find themselves in this uncomfortable state, saying that men who love children in this way are well motivated and do not deserve to be castigated as abusers. She sensibly concedes at one point that "Barrie or Jackson, or both, may well have had paedophilic tendencies; they may even have acted on those tendencies", but devotes the rest of her seventy-page thesis to alternative, more socially acceptable accounts of their motivations. She is keen to promote a more positive valuation of a whole range of benign male involvements with children, within the family and outside, a shift in public sentiment that she acknowledges is hard to accomplish against a background of insistent suspicion and all-pervasive abuse narratives. It is as though, with this problem in mind, she has approached her focus on the "maternal male" with a firm determination that sexuality must at all costs be kept out of the story.

But can the snake be pinned down in this way; can it be kept out of sight and out of mind? Mockler's attempt to do so is a skilfully scholarly one, and illuminating even when it fails to convince. She succeeds, for instance, in getting to the heart of what *Peter Pan* meant to Barrie, a task that has eluded numerous distinguished literary commentators. It is not the story of the boy who would not grow up but the story of the man who could not mother. The true lure of Neverland *for Barrie* is not about pirates and adventure but about telling bedtime stories to little children and tucking them in at night. Wendy is given the role Barrie wishes for himself, of mothering Peter Pan and the Lost Boys. Peter tells Wendy in the novel that her inexperience as a mother does not matter: "What we need is just a nice motherly person".[511] That neuter word "person" is all important: Wendy happens to be a girl, but a man would do just as well for mothering. As for Peter not growing up, the motivation for this theme lies in Barrie's wish to forestall indefinitely the growing *away* of a child friend. His is the anxiety of the mother who dreads the empty nest when all her little birds have flown – with the added poignancy that for the outsider to the family not even filial connections will be left. We might note that the psychology outlined here is totally at odds with the accusation levelled against Michael that he "dumped" boys when they grew up beyond a sexually interesting age. We saw that this was a baseless accusation in his case and now we have a model of maternal man which – if Michael was indeed similarly motivated to Barrie – would put his feelings in an entirely different and more acceptable light.

It is often a puzzle to people that Barrie was able to write a massively successful play for children based on a child who does not want to grow up. It seems totally at odds with the fact that kids are invariably bursting to do just that: their play and fantasy life see them constantly in rehearsal for adulthood, most obviously when girls (and even the "childlike" Michael, as we shall see in Chapter Thirteen) play with dolls and boys pretend to be anything grown-up, from engine drivers to astronauts. What this puzzlement overlooks is the appeal of the play to parents, especially mothers; without their enthusiasm little children would never have been taken to theatres in huge numbers to see it. Children love the play for the adventure and the pirates and – as Barrie was painfully aware – they are sublimely indifferent to Peter's odd psychology and the authorial angst that went into its making.

Mockler examines this angst through two novels, *Peter Pan* and *The Little White Bird*, both of which take us further into Barrie's mind than the play alone. Stage and screen versions of *Peter Pan* are, indeed, positively misleading in some respects, thanks to the intrusion of technical and commercial constraints which tend to distort the original vision.

Having convincingly established the centrality of mothering in *Peter Pan*, Mockler has gone some way towards demonstrating the existence of "maternal man" and presenting him as a benign figure – "just a nice motherly person", in Peter's words. In order fully to establish her thesis, however, she is obliged to confront the seemingly unavoidable sexual implications of the disrobing scene in *The Little White Bird*. She does this by asking us to consider the scene in its original context. The novel as a whole presents a very different balance of concerns, she says. The narrator is strongly established elsewhere in the book as a person who is kind to a whole range of different people; he is a benefactor. The reader sees his loneliness as an outsider and his yearning to be a family man, not a sexual predator. The supposedly "hot" passage is from a short chapter of the book called "The Interloper", in which the little boy David spends a night at the narrator's home. Even in this controversial setting, she says, a sexual interpretation is by no means inevitable.

One scene that Mockler uses to make the point is strikingly reminiscent of Michael's benign and painstaking attention to children's needs and pleasure as encountered in Chapter Four. Remember his voice teacher Seth Riggs saying he would "...stay up all night long putting batteries into the toys, making certain each and every one worked so that he could have them ready to give kids backstage the next day"? Mockler tells us that in "The Interloper" the narrator has very carefully arranged a small bedtime snack for David with, in the narrator's words, "a tumbler of milk, with a biscuit on top of it, and a chocolate riding on the biscuit. To enter the room without seeing the tumbler at once was impossible. I had tried it several times."[512]

Mockler invites us to consider how we would react to this chapter if the narrator had been female:

> Simply put, would the narrator of The Little White Bird be so distressing if she were a woman? If roles were reversed and we had a lonely spinster with a lost love in her past, befriending and aiding a little boy and his family, would we react with alarm and suggestions of paedophilia? Would "The Interloper" chapter take on new meaning – as, perhaps, a tender scene of loving care and what can only be described as maternal feeling?[513]

My response? Nice try, but it really will not do. In our "equal opportunities" era, women themselves are no longer automatically exempt from accusations of child sexual abuse, as once they were, and in the quieter waters of feminist discussion women are also more ready to admit that their "maternal" feelings are often intensely physical and erotic.[514] If "maternal women" can experience erotic feelings towards the children they care for, so can "maternal men" – and to speak of being "profoundly agitated" while undressing a child to my mind inescapably suggests such feelings. In another passage, after the bath scene, David "timidly expresses a desire to climb into bed with the narrator", who replies, "It is what I have been wanting all the time." In Barrie's day, "innocent" interpretation of such thoughts was still possible, just about. Had that not been the case, there would have been a public scandal and he would have been the Michael Jackson of his day. Readers will have to make up their own minds whether equal innocence existed in Barrie's mind.

Our principal concern, though, is not JM Barrie's mind but Michael's, and Mockler's efforts to render his position "innocent" as a "maternal man" is even more problematic than in the case of Barrie. She cites precedents, examples of earlier figures who exhibited elements of Michael's character. There is Barrie himself, from early in the twentieth century, and also two other "maternal men", Thomas de Quincey and Hartley Coleridge, from the literary world of a century before that.

Thomas de Quincey, romantic author, journalist and poet, had "sleepovers" with a little girl, Catherine, daughter of the poet William Wordsworth. She was just a toddler and, sadly, died at the age of three. De Quincey recorded his grief over her death, writing of his love for her and saying "as it happened that little Kate Wordsworth returned my love, she in a manner lived with me at my solitary cottage; as often as I could entice her from home, [she] walked with me, slept with me, and was my sole companion." By implication the whole "affair", written about openly, was conducted with parental permission and was held to be as "innocent" as Wordsworth's famous daffodils.[515]

Hartley was an adored son of the poet Samuel Taylor Coleridge. His childhood was celebrated frequently in his father's poetry and that of Wordsworth. Whereas Michael Jackson arguably missed out on childhood, Hartley Coleridge in a sense never ceased to be a child. Small in stature as an adult, he continued to look childlike and dressed as a schoolboy. His tastes, too, were largely those of a child: he enjoyed puppet shows, sweets and nonsense verse and, like Michael, he loved animals. Crucially, he also had a maternal side to his personality, being very fond of babies, about whom he wrote in what his later biographer Earl Leslie Griggs felt was a morbid and unmanly way, taking a great interest in childbirth, suckling and weaning. Mockler notes, however, that there appears to be no evidence Hartley's contemporaries were judgmental: he may have been seen as eccentric but not sinister.[516]

Mockler invites us to be equally charitable towards Michael, a sentiment we may applaud. But a generous response needs to be grounded in reality; otherwise, it will prove ultimately to be unsustainable. Only two brief points need to be made in order to refute Mocker's claim that Michael's "maternal" feelings make a non-paedophilic interpretation of his behaviour possible. Firstly, if Michael's feelings were solely maternal, one would expect him to take just as much interest in girls as boys. This is clearly not the case. Secondly, Mockler's scholarly appreciation of the "maternal man" syndrome, especially with reference to JM Barrie, is not matched by a detailed knowledge of Michael's relations with boys, especially as regards the Chandler case. She mentions neither Gutierrez nor Raymond Chandler in her sources and baldly states that there was not sufficient evidence to bring a criminal charge in respect of Jordie's allegations, while overlooking the fact that the civil settlement effectively prevented an abundance of strong evidence being used in a criminal case.

As indicated above, attempted denial of Michael's paedophilia has not been restricted to literary commentators. In the immediate wake of the 1993 allegations against Michael, a telephone poll in the *Sun* found sixteen readers asserting his innocence for every one who thought him guilty, despite the papers' own relentless barrage of damning reports.[517] Even several weeks later, after many more revelations about his close connections with a series of boys, a clipboard poll conducted by myself suggested extreme reluctance on the streets to credit the stories: white people were just as keen as black ones to continue seeing Michael as "nice to kids" in an "innocent", non-sexual way, and committed fans were joined by non-fans in expressing similar sentiments.[518]

This is not a book about Jackson fans and what they think. We are concerned here primarily with an assessment of Michael's own mental make-up. But the influence of his huge following cannot be ignored. Michael always had to think about what the fans wanted and to shape his art accordingly. Likewise we should not overlook the fact that much of the source material for our understanding of Michael's life was written by long-time Michael-watchers with at least half an eye on appealing to Michael's loyal fans. We need to be aware of the bias involved in such writing. This caution is especially important when we consider – as any serious account must – the views of the most authoritative of these writers, notably Randy Taraborrelli.

By late 2007, some two years after Michael had been acquitted at his trial, but badly damaged in reputation, Taraborrelli was finally getting real. In an interview for a documentary broadcast on Britain's Channel 4, he had a blunt message: Michael's eventual obituary would not start with *Thriller*. The headline would be, "Child molester is dead". As for Michael's long-heard refrain that his attachment to children came from abuse in his own childhood, Taraborrelli was having none of it. Right from an early age, he said, Michael had quickly learnt that he was the real star of the Jackson Five. He used this knowledge to keep his bullying father firmly in check by threatening not to sing any more. Michael, in other words, was no mere victim and the abuse excuse would not wash.[519]

Taraborrelli has not always been so hard-bitten. Putting it charitably, his reaction to Michael's first great public fall from grace, in the Jordie Chandler debacle of 1993-4, was to give the star the benefit of the doubt. This can be seen, according to taste, as an entirely honourable response or a cynically self-serving one motivated by a need to appeal to Jackson fans among his readers.

At first glance, it may seem odd, bizarre even, to imply that Taraborrelli is a man who would toady up to Michael or his fans. The original, 625-page edition of his *Michael Jackson: The Magic and the Madness*, is an acknowledged classic of "warts and all" pop biography. Here, it seems, punches are not pulled. Madness, as well as magic, indeed stands revealed. Hard truths are courageously uncovered. Many aspects of Michael left safely obscure in the star's autobiographical *Moonwalk* are dazzlingly illuminated by Taraborrelli's work. This is distinctly unauthorised biography at its best.

Or is it? Michael and his biographer go way back. In the 1970s Taraborrelli would keep score with Michael, while brothers Jackie, Tito, Jermaine, Marlon and Randy would play basketball with more athletic members of the press. Those were the days when the Jacksons used to hold open house at Encino for the jive scribes and other assorted scribblers and snappers.[520] Taraborrelli then gained the priceless advantage of forging a relaxed acquaintance with the entire Jackson clan. It was not to last, as

Michael became more withdrawn, and the whole family became anxious over its increasingly dirty linen being aired in public. But Taraborrelli did more than just keep his ear close to the ground as a good writer should, poring over relevant documentation, too, such as a steady stream of divorce court papers and other litigation involving the Jacksons. He is also said to have maintained very close contacts with "Michael's people", including a personal association with Bob Jones, for seventeen years a key Jackson aide, rising to Vice President of Michael's company, MJJ Productions, before eventually falling out of favour, like so many of the king's loyal courtiers.

There is nothing wrong with such an association. But we do have to wonder exactly how "unauthorised" Taraborrelli's writing about Michael has at times been, especially with regard to the 1994 updated edition of *Magic and Madness*, which covered the Jordie Chandler allegations. In summary, this is what his contribution in the update seemed aimed to achieve:

- Discrediting many of the witnesses against Michael by concentrating on the cash they received, to the almost total exclusion of what those witnesses were saying.
- Shifting attention away from Michael's close friendships with boys. Things only looked bad, it is implied, because Michael's legal and public relations advisers allegedly kept fouling up.
- Ignoring testimony that was harder to discredit: Taraborrelli says not a word, for instance, about James DeBarge's revelations.
- Quoting "defence" sources as though they were gospel truth. Thus an unnamed "person close to the case" is allowed to badmouth Jordie Chandler without any querying as to his or her motives.[521] Similarly, an "associate of Michael Jackson's" puts it about that the nephew of another witness came forward to say his uncle was lying. This is put to us on a "what the public was never told" basis, as though we are being made privy to some important evidence, as opposed to desperate barrel scraping by a highly interested party.[522]
- Presenting Michael as a suffering, confused, hard-done-by victim of an attack he was too innocent-minded to understand and too emotionally battered to cope with, hence his decision to settle out of court.

In other words, Taraborrelli was making out a defence case and playing down anything that might persuade readers of his "guilt", whether in terms of a civil or a criminal case. It was not a balanced picture. It is interesting to note that his new edition hit the bookshops in July 1994, and guess who was given the world's first post-scandal interview with Michael just a few weeks later, in August? Why, surprise, surprise, Mr J Randy Taraborrelli, the man who had earned his trust![523]

All in all, the contribution by professional Jackson watchers at least until Michael was again in trouble in 2003 was disappointingly vacuous. We need not be deflected by them from the judgment that, prior to his troubles, Michael had long been simultaneously flaunting and denying a dangerous sexuality. He had always wanted to tell us something, but understandably never quite dared to do so in unequivocal fashion. If, before the Chandler debacle, he never quite found "the courage to be intimate" with his worldwide following, never quite trusted his fans to understand him, then was there even the remotest chance of him doing so afterwards? Jon Pareles, writing in the *New York Times*, gave us a refreshingly upbeat view of how Michael could have come out of his difficulties artistically strengthened. "In a way, he's free," says Pareles, whose article appeared during the trough of Michael's misfortunes:

> If his record company were to reject his next project, he could release it himself...he has less of an image to protect than ever before. He might even try to express himself...He could reveal himself – not to air dirty laundry, but to apply an artist's skill at transmuting suffering and obsession into lasting creations. He could stop trying to please the whole world; for starters, he could stop singing implausible love songs and lose the saccharine pronouncements about children... Will it happen? Probably not. But if Michael Jackson's next album were called Reality, it might just rocket up the charts.[524]

It was not to be. Instead of *Reality* we had so-called *HIStory*. Instead of Michael daring to tell us about himself, we had his silliest ever pretence, a megalomaniac presentation of himself as the saviour of Eastern Europe at the end of the Cold War. Finding himself powerless before the world's media, and humiliated by them, Michael's knee-jerk response was defiantly to insist on registering the celluloid "triumph" he could not muster in real life. A redundant insistence, it might be felt, for although Michael had been humbled, he still controlled massive personal wealth and, despite everything, industry clout. Indeed it has been Michael's great power, and his alleged abuse of that power, that lies at the heart of the distaste and distrust felt by many of his detractors. This power base is the subject of the next chapter.

CHAPTER TEN

The Power of Fame and Wealth

> I just think that when sex is used as a form of blackmail or power, it's a repugnant use of one of God's gifts.[525]

Michael's butter-wouldn't-melt-in-my-mouth use of God's name in this context will strike many as a repugnant example of his towering hypocrisy. This comment on blackmail and power, from his autobiography *Moonwalk*, was made in relation to one of his most famous songs, "Billie Jean". But if he had been writing about "The Man in the Mirror" instead, what would he have seen reflected?

The immense wealth and power of "the King of Pop" at the height of his success is beyond dispute. By the time of the 1993 allegations he had sold well in excess of a hundred million records and *Forbes* magazine put his wealth at $100 million. His authoritative biographer Randy Taraborrelli gives the much higher figure of $300 million for the beginning of the '90s. In 1992 alone he is reliably said to have earned $55 million. The *Daily Mail*, with typical tabloid disdain for understatement, claimed he was worth no less than a whopping $2 *billion* by 1993.[526]

Regardless of which figures come closest to reality, there can be no doubting that Jackson had huge resources at his disposal, evidenced most tangibly by his vast, 2,700-acre Neverland estate, complete with its own railway station, lake, fairground-style rides (Ferris wheel, merry-go-rounds and such like), amusement arcade, movie theatre, golf-course and zoo, a staff of around sixty employees and "hi-tech surveillance equipment designed to provide a level of security which would not have been out of place for an American president or indeed a cocaine baron".[527] Such was Jackson's power that he could demand – and obtain – from his employees that they should all sign a confidentiality agreement, whereby they agreed not to reveal the goings on behind the closed doors of his mansion or the security enclosed perimeter of his sprawling acres. The security system even included a bell that alerted him when anyone approached his room, and a peephole was built into the door so he could check who it was – features destined to figure prominently in his 2005 trial.

But Jackson's impressive surroundings and formal security arrangements can do no more than hint at his extraordinary influence and power over people,[528] including not just his domestic staff but also key figures in the music industry and entertainment journalism. His financial and industry clout meant that people generally were disposed to please him and do his bidding: Michael's success and continued good name for long had the power to advance the careers and boost the bank balances of his numerous lawyers, aides, music industry executives, and even supposedly independent show business writers. Likewise his prestige was such that his fans, often including the parents of children in whom he took an interest, numbered many who would have walked over hot coals just to say they had met him or even – total bliss! – entered his select social circle.

In some ways this influence and power may seem capable of benign interpretation. Take for instance Michael's admitted inclination to share his bed with young boys. Columnist Jill Parkin noted sceptically: "I bet [parents] wouldn't have allowed it with just any old Mr Jackson".[529] Of course, she was right. The fact that Michael was wealthy and prestigious made all the difference – but only because those parents bought into the idea that his fame and success were all of a piece with his unique "innocence", and that he only wanted to be with children for the purest of reasons, namely to reclaim the childhood fun he had missed out on as a hard-working child star. What this explanation left out, though, was that Michael's supposed "innocence" was itself the product of influence and power. Not the least of Jackson's resources was the ability to mount and sustain a decades-long public relations operation dedicated to burnishing his image by constantly harping on about his difficult childhood while ignoring more obvious interpretations of his behaviour.

This has enabled people – whether fans or industry insiders – to believe about Michael what it was convenient and congenial to believe. As it was put in one report:

> These days the air is thick with the chatter of Jackson's music industry associates who say they've known about his tastes for years. If true, why didn't they go to the cops?
>
> The same question should be posed to those five bodyguards who have come forward, to the maid, and to his sister: why did no one try to stop him? And why did none of his defenders tell Jackson that even if he wasn't molesting these boys, his behaviour was inappropriate, dangerous and creepy?
>
> One answer is that Hollywood is a city built on lies, and it is bad form to spill the beans on someone else's life. If Michael says he's innocently frolicking with these lads, who are we to doubt him? An even more likely answer is that Jackson was simply too big a cash cow...[530]

Jackson's public relations propaganda provided a smokescreen, a fog of unexamined possibilities in which those with an interest in his continued career success could painlessly lose their consciences. There is nothing new in this or unique to Michael Joseph Jackson. Hollywood lawyers have a long tradition of unthinkingly discounting the claims of those attacking the reputations of their star clients, reserving their polished professional skills to promote solely the version of events peddled by their powerful paymasters.

As one lawyer admitted, "The Jackson defence was a classic of its kind, a textbook example of the Hollywood use of money and power. They did it with [Marilyn] Monroe...They've done it on numerous occasions when a star has had woman trouble or man trouble or drug and alcohol trouble. They hire us to wave our magic wand and make the trouble go away." The same article examines how these lawyers are in effect corrupted by power:

> In show business a scandal to a star threatens the business interests around him like an accusation that one of their cars is defective affects an auto manufacturer. The result is a distinctive (some would say distorted) mentality among Hollywood lawyers when it comes to scandals. They refuse to see them in human terms, let alone admit the stars might have done wrong. Anyone who accuses is a blackmailer. Accusers are the enemy, the little people, to be bought off or pressured into silence.

> The *Los Angeles Times* described the process of responding to an accusation against a star as follows: "Typically, [it] involves crafting counter-attacks against the credibility of the accusers, even as the star's investigators and lawyers work behind the scenes collecting evidence and 'neutralising' unfavourable witnesses... celebrity friends are often trotted out as character witnesses...the star's reply to the allegations is carefully monitored by strategists and public access is strictly controlled."[531]

But the use of lawyers as unscrupulous fixers is a relatively civilized option for the rich and powerful. There is more, much more, they can do to secure their aims, as fans of mafia movies will know. Michael's own fascination with the criminal underworld finds expression in his song "Smooth Criminal". This sinister song is featured on the *Moonwalker* video, with Michael seen as a heroic figure saving children from being lured into drugs slavery. The real-life behaviour of some of those around him, however, suggests that his association with threatening and violent criminality was not necessarily as the good guy.

In one of the most serious incidents to surface publicly, his older brother Jackie allegedly tried to shoot one of Michael's ex-bodyguards, Fred Hammond, at a car showroom where he had joined the sales staff.[532] Bullets rained through the window at the premises. It will be recalled that five Hayvenhurst security guards had made allegations against Michael, Hammond being one of them. If the story is true, this guard was being intimidated – to put it mildly – at a time when he was a potential court witness. Four witnesses at that time, just over a month before the January 1994 civil settlement, claimed they had been threatened with death or violence. Police were also investigating another shooting, a hit and run, and a series of threatening phone calls.

In an incident reminiscent of the famous horse's head scene from *The Godfather*, one potential witness was horrified to find dead cats in his car.[533] He claimed this was the notorious Anthony Pellicano's doing – Pellicano being Jackson's number one fixer in the Jordie Chandler case. Even one of Jackson's most passionate defenders, Chandler lawyer Barry Rothman's hostile former secretary Geraldine Hughes, admits, "It is worth noting that Mr Pellicano has a reputation of being a Sicilian hardball player and accustomed to dealing with oppositional individuals".[534] She met Pellicano; she found him charming, which is no great surprise given their mutual loathing of Rothman and common interest in rescuing

Michael Jackson's reputation. But even she could not deny his "hardball" side.

Neither does the man himself. "I can't do everything by the book," he once reportedly said. "I bend the law to death in gaining information." He said he tells people he carries an aluminium baseball bat in the boot of his black Nexus. "Guys who fuck with me get to meet my buddy over there," he told a reporter, pointing towards the bat. Pellicano also tells people that he is a blackbelt in karate and a kung fu master, boasting expertise with a knife. "I can shred your face," he says. "If I use martial arts, I might really maim somebody." But revealing the gentlemanly charm Geraldine Hughes found so winning, he added, "I only use intimidation and fear when I absolutely have to."[535]

Unfortunately, if his critics in the Jackson case are to be believed, this absolute necessity seems to arise rather often. Sandra Sutherland, a private detective who claimed to have interviewed 120 "witnesses" regarding Jackson's "bizarre sexuality", to provide background in aid of the civil case against him, spoke of Pellicano leaving a trail of intimidation in his wake.[536]

Back in the days of the Jordie Chandler case, it was possible to argue the man's bark was worse than his bite. Many potential witnesses could well have been frightened off just by his brazen self-promotion as a ruthless heavy. In more recent years, though, facts have been emerging to support the awesome reputation. To start with, he has since been jailed for illegal wire tapping and possession of explosives.

The jail sentence resulted from an investigation into whether he had threatened Anita Busch, a *Los Angeles Times* reporter who was working on a story about him in 2002. Busch found a dead fish, a rose and a note reading "Stop" on her smashed windshield. When the Los Angeles police searched Pellicano's offices, they found two practice hand grenades that had been filled with flash powder, along with military explosives and detonators in his safe. He pleaded guilty in October 2003 to a one charge of possessing unregistered firearms and another of possessing C-4 explosive, resulting in a 27-month sentence. He was never charged over the dead fish incident but Busch sued him for his alleged involvement in this and other acts of harassment including the hacking of her computer and an August 2002 attempt to run her over with a Mercedes.[537]

Pellicano's methods can be summed up in the expression "whatever it takes". If the carrot would do the job better than the stick, so be it. For instance, he is said to have "made Brett Barnes and Wade Robson happy".[538] It may be recalled that these were the two boys who at the height of the Jordie Chandler crisis cheerfully admitted sharing a bed with Michael and said nothing sexual had happened. If they had instead been disposed to make trouble for the star there can be little doubt his fate would have been sealed. At the very least his career and reputation would have been damaged beyond repair. Pellicano is said to have been involved in paying off dozens of other potential witnesses, some of whom received fabulous gifts in suspicious circumstances.

Pellicano was noted chiefly for his handling of external threats to Jackson's security. But dubious means were also used to deal with internal threats in the shape of staff who knew too much, the most notorious example being in the case of the Neverland Five. In December 1994, five former Neverland employees sued Jackson and seven members of his staff for "wrongful termination". They claimed they had been harassed by Jackson's armed bodyguards and subjected to retribution for cooperating with the criminal investigation into his contacts with boys. The suit claimed each of the five, and some of their family members, had received threatening phone calls; they had been subjected to illegal eavesdropping; information in their personnel files had been used against them; and the three women among them had suffered gender discrimination and verbal sexual harassment. Before cooperating with the police investigation they had all been rated as above-average employees in their job performance appraisals and had won promotions.

Diane Dimond, who has reported on the Neverland Five in detail,[539] said that a few weeks before the settlement with the Chandlers in January 1994, "someone" in the Jackson camp decided that "widespread internal damage control" was required. The upshot was that Bill Bray, Jackson's long-time head of security, created an elite security unit at Neverland, the deadly-serious sounding "Office of Special Services" – the same name, whether Bray knew it or not, as the CIA's wartime predecessor. With specialist agents equipped with phone tapping and surveillance equipment, the OSS mission was to spy on existing staff.

For the Neverland Five, in Dimond's account, things began to get really heavy in the early spring of 1994 when subpoenas began to arrive for them to appear before a grand jury in Jackson's criminal case. Suddenly they found themselves under pressure to meet Jackson's lawyers and a private detective to divulge what they intended to testify. They refused to do so. One of the five, security guard Ralph Chacon, would eventually testify in the 2005 trial that he had personally witnessed Michael perform fellatio on

Jordan Chandler in a shower room at the ranch. According to Dimond, Chacon had been found "credible" on two polygraph ("lie detector") tests.

Others among the five also had potentially damning testimony for the grand jury hearings back in 1994. Sacking them would have looked bad and would not have helped but the five allege that this was the time when intimidation by the OSS began in earnest – a pattern of abuse that Dimond's account relates in considerable detail. By the late summer of 1994 all of the Neverland Five were jobless. They had quit, they said, because they could no longer endure the harassment. By the end of the year they had launched their suit against Jackson, Bill Bray and the OSS agents, for wrongful termination, breach of contract and sexual harassment.

It is important to reveal the allegations of hardball tactics by Bill Bray and his OSS; likewise the claims against Anthony Pellicano. But it would be wrong to leave the impression these were the work of out-of-control mavericks, doing things of which the boss knew nothing. Numerous Jackson apologists have tried to spin this line: Michael was just an innocent in a wicked world, a gentle, loving, peaceable person. He gave lavish gifts from the generosity of his heart, not as bribes, and would never have sanctioned any resort to threats and violence.

The line of apologetics is unconvincing to anyone who has studied Michael's career, in which he began to show himself as a feisty player in his own destiny even before his age hit double figures, and as an independent business negotiator by his mid-teens – in both cases in defiance of an overbearing father who totally dominated his older brothers. As we saw in Chapter Eight, smacked across the face by his father Joseph for failing to execute a dance step the right way, nine-year-old Michael knew just how to hit back. "Hit me again", he said, "it'll be the last time I ever sing."[540]

He defied his father again when, at the age of sixteen, he went behind Joe's back to negotiate privately with the legendary Motown Records mogul Berry Gordy on behalf of the Jackson Five. As biographer Taraborrelli says, it showed that the young Michael was not just a cute kid singer: "At sixteen, he was a businessman in the making...he was able to cut through the back-stabbing politics so rife in the record industry."[541] The pattern was to be maintained throughout Jackson's career. He believed in hands-on involvement in his business affairs. His bargain-basement acquisition of the Beatles back catalogue revealed him as master of the deal. He was the sole director of all his companies. He was a prolific hirer and firer. This was a man who habitually knew in detail what was going on around him, not some innocent who could have remained unaware of what a man with Pellicano's reputation might do. Indeed, it was that very reputation as a ruthless fixer that would have made him an attractive hiring for Jackson.

Make no mistake, there is plenty of evidence that the Jackson family could be unpleasant and ruthless if his chief biographer is to be believed – an account which has gone through successive editions without authoritative challenge in this regard. A string of Michael's former employees have attested to their harsher side. It is a story of staff treated like dirt, bellowed at with an endless succession of gracelessly barked commands and given no consideration. This discourtesy allegedly began with the lowly domestic servants and extended beyond them to the security staff and even technical and creative people, such as videographer Steve Howell, whose duties apparently extended to anything electrical. He once got a call when he was away on holiday, saying everything had broken down ("nothing works") and he was urgently needed. Breaking off his vacation, he grabbed a flight back to Los Angeles and then immediately made the long drive out to Neverland. He arrived to find the only thing not working was the TV, and all it needed was a cable plugging in.[542]

On that occasion the command had come from Jackson's security chief, Bill Bray. But the lack of consideration, if not the barked commands, reflected Michael's personal style, especially towards those who had fallen foul of him. Commenting on a couple of the star's many sackings, Taraborrelli said: "Once someone falls from Michael's graces, that person disappears from his thoughts – as though he or she never existed."[543] And falling from grace where Michael is concerned was not difficult, the classic example being his firing of his highly successful manager Frank Dileo, who had helped the star deliver five number one hits and one of the most successful tours in the history of show business.

Evidently Jackson thought Dileo was beginning to get too self-important and was too keen on promoting the "Wacko Jacko" image to the media. When the *Bad* album sold "only" twenty three million copies (around thirty two million by early 2008), following the even more successful *Thriller*, he decided Dileo had to go. It was not so much the fact of the sacking as its manner that showed Michael's ruthless, uncaring side. Dileo had come to feel he was Michael's buddy. The pair had worked very closely together, and although the quiet, shy star was utterly different from the loud, fat, jolly promoter he had poached from a record company, they had appeared to hit it off and complement each other very well. Taraborrelli wrote:

> Frank Dileo's firing was handled the same way Michael dismissed his previous manager, Ron Weisner (of Weisner-DeMann), in the early eighties, without notice or warning, and not personally. "I was devastated, and I am not embarrassed or ashamed to tell you," Weisner said. "I was walking flat-footed for a month because I thought Michael and I had a great relationship. I was crushed."[544]

After it was Dileo's turn for the push, the music industry got the message: you work for Michael Jackson at your peril. There would never be a shortage of ambitious characters ready to take their chance, but nobody with any sense trusted the star any more. They could see now that he was a wolf in sheep's clothing, a figure who could be more coldly monstrous than the werewolf of his *Thriller* video.

Victor Gutierrez makes the striking claim that Michael was known to cancel his own shows to spend time in bed with his boys. On one such occasion in Japan, according to Gutierrez, he cancelled a presentation where he was to cut the ribbon at a new theatre opening. He had been paid in advance for this and kept the money. The Japanese entrepreneur in charge of the event lost money, his business and his honour, as the Emperor of Japan had been invited to the ceremony and expected to see Jackson. The man committed suicide. Says Gutierrez: "Jackson didn't even bother to send his family flowers. He cares little about such things."[545]

I have no idea whether this allegation is true. Actually, I suspect it is *not*, if only because protocol would presumably not allow the Emperor of Japan to play second fiddle to anyone else as premier guest at an event in his own country. Another reason for suspicion is that a remarkably similar story, but with very different details, is to be found in Christopher Andersen's biography, *Michael Jackson Unauthorized*. The Andersen version is much fuller and more convincing. This story, sourced to entrepreneur Bob Michaelson, has a Japanese businessman offering $2.1 million for a portrait of Michael by Los Angeles artist Brett Livingston-Stone – with the proviso that Michael appear at a press conference announcing the purchase at the opening of his (the Japanese businessman's) new entertainment complex in Tokyo. Michael was reportedly thrilled, as it would land him one of many entries in *The Guinness Book of World Records*, this time the highest price ever paid for a portrait of a living person. Michael attended the unveiling in Los Angeles, but failed to turn up for the Tokyo event. The unfortunate Japanese entertainment complex owner was left "standing there in his kimono, waiting for Michael to show". When it did not happen he lost face, the business was ruined, he went bankrupt and – in this less hyped version – he *considered* suicide, then disappeared.[546]

It seems unlikely that Michael, no matter how callous, would be responsible for ruining *two* Japanese businessmen, both losing face at separate opening ceremonies. But both yarns are credible as part of a pattern. Michael's zone of emotional concern appears to have extended only to a small group of what psychologists would call "significant others" in his life. This is a group which included – but only just – his parents and siblings, because his fate and theirs were inextricably bound up together despite their many fallings out. A handful of his peers among the famous and super-rich were also among his long-term allies and soul mates, though it is doubtful he admitted his sexual interests even to these. As for his top aides and lawyers, even they are "significant others" only so long as they are in favour. An obscure Japanese businessman would not even have been a blip on Jackson's radar.

But it would not be fair to impose on him a God-like responsibility for all the thousands of people dealing with his affairs. A general in battle is not expected to rush to the aid of every injured soldier. Corporation bosses are rarely seen weeping over their down-sized workforces. Sometimes, rarely, a charismatic politician or evangelist will convince us of his "sincerity": when he says "I feel your pain" we will believe him. Some of them may even truly believe they are sincere, just as Michael doubtless did when in sentimental mood he wrote poetry about the suffering of the world's children. To his credit, unlike most of us he actually did a few things about it, one of which gives a very different impression to his seemingly mafia-like deployment of Pellicano and the OSS.

Michael had a no-guns policy at Neverland. In all the fuss over Martin Bashir's infamous documentary about him, leading ultimately to the singer's prosecution, little attention was paid to a scene in which Jackson talked about the breakdown of family life and the violence he associated with it, including youngsters going to school with guns. Because this was an interview for the media, these remarks could easily be dismissed as merely image-building, just empty words. They were not. Amongst many other tragedies, what Michael surely had in mind were the terrible high school shootings that so disfigure American society whenever some emotionally traumatised, alienated kid finally goes berserk. Perhaps believing the ready availability of guns is at least partly responsible for such disasters, Michael decided that Neverland would be a gun-free zone. The security guards, he determined, would all be unarmed. This represented a real change: at the time when Michael bought the ranch, armed guards were a feature there. He decreed that henceforth there would be no guns. On his domain, at least, thousands of children would experience a pleasant, fun place with no danger of anyone being shot and without having to experience the ugly menace of guns in holsters.

Sadly, that would change, at least for a while, with the deployment of the OSS. They were armed. The official reason for their presence was that there had been a rash of intruders at Neverland at a time of intense media focus on Michael in 1993-4, including at least one armed with a handgun; it was thus deemed necessary to bring in armed bodyguards for Jackson's protection. As for the unit's sinister-sounding title, it was *not* an official one. The guards themselves adopted OSS as a nickname. And the regular security staff remained without guns.

The general policy against guns never attracted much public attention, and so far as I can tell was never intended to do so. It was just an *implicit* message of peace to Neverland visitors, a message that would later be given to the world by Jesus – Michael's ranch manager, Jesus Salas. Salas described the no-guns policy from the witness stand at Michael's trial in response to a question about guns at Neverland by prosecution lawyer Gordon Auchincloss. Salas was a prosecution witness and it seems Auchincloss had been expecting an answer that would be damning to the celebrity defendant. When the prosecutor failed to get what he wanted he quickly passed on to other things.[547]

Another positive thing Michael actually *did* at the height of his success, as opposed to just talking and image-building, was truly to give generously of his time and money to children's causes. His unholy extravagance, however, tells us his priorities were not single-mindedly in this direction. Maureen Orth reveals, for example, that while on tour in Europe Michael arranged to be able to wake up every day and choose which form of transport would take him to his next destination – a private jet, a private railway carriage, or a convoy of buses. The railway carriage and buses had to be flown everywhere at vast expense in a cargo plane[548] – but who among us can be sure how sensible and caring we would be with a billion dollars at our disposal? A modest lifestyle is in any case incompatible with stardom. Fans want glitz, glamour and extravagance.

That Michael became monstrously egotistical is also well evidenced, though it is important to distinguish the image from the man. We have already seen how he became "a passable substitute messiah for his fans", presented both as a "gentle Jesus" in his heavily promoted concern for suffering children and world peace, and as a figure of godlike power in his video performances. His most egregious excess of self-promotion was perhaps the floating of a sixty-foot statue of himself down the river Thames in London for the launch – literally, it would seem – of the *HIStory* album.

The album, said one writer in a comment typical of many, "did little to re-establish Michael as the pop messiah he evidently thought he was, instead revealing the grotesque scale of his self-delusion...The climactic moment of this hubris was Jarvis Cocker's disruption of Jackson's performance at the 1996 Brit Awards. In the cool new world of Pulp and Oasis, the King of Pop – hoisted on to the Brits stage as a crucified pop Christ – had become the Emperor of Schlock." Jarvis Cocker himself said:

> My actions were a form of protest at the way Michael Jackson sees himself as some kind of Christ-like figure with the power of healing. The music industry allows him to indulge his fantasies because of his wealth and power. People go along with it even though they know it's a bit sick. I just couldn't go along with it anymore.[549]

Was Michael's messiah-god image truly evidence of his own "sickness", or merely that of the fans to whom he wished to appeal? According to one biographer, Michael's paternal grandfather, Samuel Jackson, went to his grave firmly believing his grandson was an archangel.[550] The décor at Neverland offers one significant clue to the "archangel's" own beliefs, and his autobiographical book *Moonwalk* offers further pointers. Soon after the Jordie Chandler crisis broke in August 1993, one tabloid was able to make us privy to what had hitherto been Michael's private world, a place where he did not need to hype himself to impress an audience. The story featured a photograph of a picture said to dominate "the secret bolt-hole of tortured idol Michael Jackson". The account continued: "He believes the characters depicted are 'his equals'. They are the Mona Lisa, George Washington, Abraham Lincoln, Einstein... and E.T.! All wear Jacko's trademark sunglasses and white glove."[551]

From *Moonwalk* we hear of his revealing response to a remark made by George Lucas. The film director told Michael his little daughter's first words were "Michael Jackson".[552] Michael reports this without a hint of recognising that Lucas must have been pulling his leg. Evidently he felt he was at the centre of everyone's universe, even that of a baby.

This egocentricity is itself very baby-like. A baby initially has no way of distinguishing the messages coming to its brain from inside its body from those coming from outside. For all the baby knows, the entire universe could be part of itself. It does not know where its own body ends and the world begins. Michael shows clear signs of having regressed to this state when in *Moonwalk* he describes his feeling on stage during the *Victory* tour:

> There was a part of the show on the Victory tour where I was doing this scatting theme and the audience was repeating what I said. I'd say "Da, de, da, de" and they'd say "Da, de, da, de". There've been times when I've done that and they would start stomping. And when the whole audience is doing that, it sounds like an earthquake. Oh! It's a great feeling to be able to do that with all those people – whole stadiums – and *they're all doing the same thing you're doing.* [My emphasis] [553]

This happy feeling is that of the baby who sees its mother imitating its own gestures. The baby feels it is controlling its mother. To the baby, the mother is a newly discovered part of itself, an exciting limb to move around and command as it wishes. For the baby at this stage, the mother and the rest of the world have no separate feelings or desires. In a more sinister manifestation we see the same egocentricity in ruthless dictators. As the psychiatrist Robin Skynner has observed:

> ...the leader will be very unclear about his own boundaries. He'll still have the idea of himself as omnipotent, with no limits of any kind – that he's god – so he'll have to control everything, everybody, every aspect of life, in an attempt to avoid every contradiction of his fantasy. To take the simplest example, every time Hitler held his arm up, he wanted everyone else to do the same.[554]

One way in which Michael demonstrated a similar need to avoid contradictions of his control fantasies was in his own personal $2 million amusement arcade. His former brother-in-law James DeBarge tells us he used to invite friends over to play there but they had to let Michael win most of the time. If they didn't, they would not be invited back.[555] It was a similar story when many of the world's top artists turned up for the charity recording of "We are the world". They were all advised in a sign outside the studio: "please check your egos at the door". Michael was the only one who apparently failed to read it: he was the only one who insisted on being filmed separately, in a way that would emphasise his own contribution.[556]

It is significant that one of the participants was Bob Geldof, organiser of Band Aid, the stunningly successful British pop music charity endeavour. Geldof's work for charity has earned him universal respect, not least because he has clearly bothered to spend a significant amount of time in famine zones; when he is interviewed it quickly becomes clear he has studied such world poverty issues as the politics of aid, trade and debt relief to the poorer countries in great detail and depth.

Jackson's knowledge and understanding were pitiful by comparison. At the Brit Awards, dressed in his "messianic" white robes, he catalogued the evils of the world, solemnly saying "Did you know that three million children die every minute?" At that rate the world would lose *all* its children in less than a day![557] Geldof had been present on that occasion too. Unlike Jarvis Cocker, he was apparently happy with Michael's mood music: for him, clearly, this was not a time for details. He even endorsed the man's deification: Jackson, he said, "sings with the voice of angels and, when his feet move, you can see God dancing".[558]

But in Michael's charity work we see feet of clay. His work for children worldwide is often now spoken of with suspicion and even outright derision. It was not always so. Before his reputation was so severely tarnished in 1993, this work was taken at face value by millions of his fans. Delving into the fan magazines of those times will quickly convince browsers that those fans believed his concern for children was genuine. Fans were impressed by his generous personal donations to children's causes: they felt that, unlike many stars, he "puts his money where his mouth is". His frequent personal visits to sick children in hospital were a source of real admiration, not cynical sniggers. His giving of both himself and his money were the main source of his immense fan loyalty. Fans truly felt Michael was different, a beautiful soul. In 1998 his support was such that he was even nominated for the Nobel Peace Prize.[559] To the end, the fan websites insisted he was special as more than just an entertainer. As recently as November 2006, at the World Music Awards, it was announced by Beyoncé that Michael Jackson had given a vast $300 million to charity, a claim added to the star's principal entry in Wikipedia and subjected to no critical challenge on that webpage up to at least January 2010.

Michael's perceived generosity in giving immense amounts of time and money to suffering and needy children was undoubtedly an engine of great power for him: the enthusiasm and loyalty of his fans continued to fill concert halls and shift records long after the music critics had begun to write him off as a has been, as long ago as the *Bad* album in 1987. If sales for *Bad* and the later *Dangerous* and *HIStory* albums were lower than those for *Thriller*, they were still respectably in the superstar league. It was they, the fans, who kept filling the coffers to pay for Michael's ever more busy lawyers, fixers and security people.

But even for a superstar whose face is perhaps the most famous on the planet, there are limits to the loyalty he can command, and to the power it generates. So far this chapter has been an exploration of the extent of Michael Jackson's power. We have seen the range of the resources that were at his disposal and the ways available to him for the use and abuse of this power. What about the limitations of that power?

It is ironic that Michael's one original album to be an undisputed financial failure is hubristically called *Invincible*. Appearing in 2001, sales were initially brisk enough to see committed fans put the record in the No. 1 slot in both the US and the UK; but a slump followed. New fans were in short supply. Even worldwide sales of around eight million units by 2005, enough to make the fortune of a new artist, were hopelessly adrift of target, given that the record had cost a whopping $50 million to make. After surviving the protracted agonies of the Jordie Chandler crisis, Michael could perhaps be excused for beginning to feel he had indeed joined the gods. He was immortal. Nothing could touch him. Even with the Chandler affair still raw, in March 1994, just a couple of months after the civil settlement, he was reportedly speaking in private about his own invincibility.

In reality, though, intimations of his mortality had long been evident. Even at the height of his success his power was never without severe constraints, especially in the one area in which that power is of ultimate concern to us in this volume: the ease or otherwise with which he could command the attention, affection and intimacy of young boys. But before turning to Michael's power in the bedroom, it is necessary to complete our survey of his power in the wider sense.

Nowhere did it become more clearly evident that the rot had set in for Michael than in the collapse of his charitable activities. Even more than his disappointing record sales, we could see this major source of his fan loyalty drying up before our eyes. Geraldine Hughes' book *Redemption*, which appeared in 2004 and aimed to shore up Michael's reputation, presented a list of his Heal the World Foundation accomplishments that ran to five solid pages. Impressive though it was, the list stopped abruptly, without explanation, at the end of 1996.[560] By 2002 Jackson specialist Roger Friedman pronounced the Foundation "pretty much dead".[561] A couple of years later an Associated Press report said that "Starved of funding and leadership, the organization has stopped donating to charitable causes and been suspended in California for failing to file yearly accounting statements."[562] The report featured Rabbi Shmuley Boteach, a one-time fashionable, publicity-conscious guru – if a rabbi can be a guru – closely associated with Jackson's charity work. Boteach is quoted making the amazing claim that Jackson stopped working with the offshoot organization Heal the Kids at the urging of friends and handlers who believed its activities were too "pedestrian" for the King of Pop. Yet Heal the World itself was apparently defunct by this time as regards any activity separate from Heal the Kids and Jackson was not visibly involved with more ambitious charity work through other channels. "He was being told this initiative was going to devalue him as a superstar. 'Overexpose' him was the word constantly used," said Boteach." If this was indeed Jackson's calculation, it was a nakedly cynical one: the message seemed to be, "Why bother to help other people if you will only be criticised for giving insufficient help?" Seen this way, the only point of charity is to improve your image. But only a stronger position financially, with further *Thriller*-level success, would have enabled Jackson to keep giving on the epic scale expected of a superstar.

The sad shambles into which his charity work slumped illustrated the fragility of Jackson's supposedly mighty empire and invincible personal power. So did other features of his crumbling world after the assault on his reputation began in 1993. For instance, the much vaunted might of his fixers, including the feared Pellicano, was unable to silence his own sister La Toya, who brought out a book packed with damaging allegations and embarrassing anecdotes. In a manoeuvre typical of La Toya, she had changed her position completely by January 2005, just ahead of Michael's trial, when she appeared on a TV programme saying – at least with regard to the more recent allegations – she felt sure of his innocence and "In my heart I truly believe he'll be vindicated."[563] Nevertheless, whatever was motivating her flip-flopping, yes-he's-guilty-no-he's-not style, she can hardly have been under Michael's control.

Indeed, when the pressure was at its most extreme, Michael was arguably in control of nothing, as reflected in the title of a *Sunday Times* analysis by Robert Sandall, titled "How superstars spin out of control". Sandall drew attention to confusion in the Jackson camp, with rival advisors and lawyers pulling in different directions:

> Unlike Elvis, who had Colonel Parker, the Beatles, who had Brian Epstein, and Bruce Springsteen, who still has Jon Landau – unlike most pop celebrities of the past thirty years whose success has partly depended on a strong partnership – Jackson does not have a manager.
>
> Or rather, he has a superfluity of them – some financial, some legal, some personal – but none in a position to guide him through disaster...
>
> They are usually referred to as advisors and for most of the past six months these highly paid flunkeys have been behaving the way courtiers have done through the ages: dithering, politicking and fighting among themselves. When the star first went into hiding in the autumn, two lawyers, John Branca and Bert Fields – both on the Jackson payroll despite representing different law firms – quarrelled over tactics.
>
> The row spread through Jackson's inner circle like a bar room brawl. When Elizabeth Taylor and Bill Bray, Jackson's longstanding aide and security man, sided against Fields late last year, he and Anthony Pellicano, a former private eye who had been elevated to the position of chief spokesman, were forced to resign. As the traumatised Jackson issued ineffectual internal memos saying how much he loved everyone, the legal baton passed to a newcomer, John Cochran. Only once the conflict had been resolved was there any likelihood of a negotiated settlement with Jackson's lawyers.[564]

Michael had been under immense pressure to keep up the appearance of business as usual in late 1993, continuing with his *Dangerous* tour under constant siege from the world's media at a time when he really needed to be focussed on his legal difficulties. For a man who liked to be in control it was all too much. Cut adrift from the calm circumstances necessary to getting on top of the legal details and strategy, it is small wonder he is said to have experienced a mental breakdown. There was talk of addiction to painkillers[565] but Taraborrelli convincingly reports that Fields and Pellicano were treating him "like an idiot kid" at this time.[566] Although they paid the price for doing so, they probably had little alternative but to take the initiative if any sort of coherent strategy was to be thrashed out.

Not that any such strategy could be agreed upon while there was division in the camp back home. His old friend Elizabeth Taylor reportedly told him at this time that he needed to get back to the US to take control. "It's time to take charge, Michael," she told him, according to Taraborrelli's source. "Then *you* be in charge," he is said to have replied. "You be in charge, Elizabeth."[567] This was desperation, the words of a man whose grip on the reins of power had by then been utterly abandoned.

The fall of powerful but tragically flawed figures can seem inevitable with the benefit of hindsight. In Jackson's case we may feel there were just too many boys in his life for scandal to be kept at bay for ever. Pellicano's darkly heroic energies were immensely successful for a while but, as we have just seen, he was eventually swept away in the storm. When Michael was at the height of his popularity it must all have seemed very different. To his servants and aides he was not a man lightly to be crossed. Likewise, the often ambitious and star-struck parents who let their kids sleep with Michael were no doubt at times influenced by him against their better judgment.

Did the same psychology apply to the boys themselves? Having now reviewed the sources of Michael's power, the material and psychological resources available to him and the limits of his might, we are at last in a position to probe the more personal and intimate aspects of his alleged dominance over boys and control of their lives.

CHAPTER ELEVEN

Power over Jordie: 'No Wenches, Bitches, Heifers or Hoes'

It will be recalled that research by Dutch academic Dr Theo Sandfort focused on just one research question, designed to put the child's perception at centre stage: "Can a boy experience sex with an adult positively?"

In Chapter Seven this work was examined in some detail. After exploring the effect on twenty five boys aged ten to sixteen involved in a current sexual relationship with a man, Sandfort was able to answer a resounding "Yes" to his own question. We saw that the investigation ranged widely: the boys were asked about their older friends, the sexual contact, and the pleasant and unpleasant sides of that contact. Also considered was how the boys were able to handle their relationships in dealing with their parents and friends.

The boys themselves in the Sandfort study said that misuse by the older partners of their power almost never occurred. Discussing this finding, the author concluded that "What is of greatest importance ...is not whether or not a power difference existed but how the person who was relatively more powerful used his power with respect to the other. Did he make use of his power at all? Did he misuse it? The latter occurs wherever the older partner takes into consideration only his own interests and does not respect the boy's feelings and right to self-determination." The boys he studied, he says, were not treated as mere objects. Their wishes and desires played an important part in the contact.[568] But what about when the adult in question happens to be a mega-rich pop star wielding enormous power? Does the Sandfort standard still apply? A fuller examination was promised once we were able to put it in the context of the special considerations applying to Michael Jackson. That will be the focus of this chapter.

Briefly, though, we must stay with abstractions, including the much vexed issue of sexual consent by children. During discussion in Chapter Seven, it was shown that well respected, morally conservative researchers have been forced to accept that children do sometimes engage willingly, even enthusiastically, in sexual contacts with adults. Opponents of such activity in earlier decades insisted on the importance of *informed* consent and focused their attention on the fact that children inevitably know little about those things of which they have little prior experience. With regard to such subjects as history, education is promoted as the answer to ignorance. Not just book learning but "hands-on" lessons too: children are encouraged to see historical artefacts, study video and film presentations, even take part in re-enactments. Of course, the hands-on sex education teacher is in for trouble! Many adults prefer to keep children in ignorance, thereby giving them an excuse to keep children sexually inactive.

Denying children the knowledge they need for a healthy sex life has become less viable in the age of AIDS. But as minimal sex education has been reluctantly and half-heartedly accepted as a necessity, the principal argument used to prevent children's engagement in sexual contact has shifted. Rather than the "informed consent" issue, these days we are rather more likely to find objections focused on the supposedly inevitable problem of adults having much greater power than children, and on the equal inevitability – allegedly – that adults will abuse that power given the opportunity. It is also an argument that is increasingly being deployed to prevent children's sexual behaviour among themselves: nearly always, the fanatical proponents of childhood "innocence" assert, if there is sex between two children then it must involve an older and more powerful child "abusing" a younger and less willing one. The fact that this is often simply not true does nothing to diminish the volubility of the claims.[569]

My return to the concept of consent is occasioned by research which shows a very revealing link to the issue of the abuse of adult power. It is a link which ought to be blindingly obvious but to which prejudice has blinded us: when children have by objective criteria been engaged willingly in a sexual encounter with an adult, they are not likely to feel the adult has abused his power. By contrast, when they are forced into such acts (by being threatened or physically over-*powered*) their feelings are very different. Likewise if their subjective assessment is that they were coerced or manipulated into doing something against their will, or which made them uncomfortable, there is a much greater likelihood they will later feel resentment: in far greater numbers these children will feel abused and victimised by the adult's misuse of his power. Put another way, the issue of the adult's abuse of power largely disappears when we are talking about contacts to which the children have consented: for them it is no big deal; it is a non-issue.

A separate study by Sandfort investigated the childhood sexual experiences of 283 young adults aged eighteen to twenty three, including those with no such experiences before age sixteen, those with experiences with age-mates and those having had experiences with adults. This study included females as well as males from a range of social class backgrounds. They were asked in detail about their early sexual contacts and their present sex life.[570]

The results revealed, not surprisingly, that differences in age and strength were a factor in non-consensual contacts. Clearly, it is easier to use force or intimidation against a person who has not yet reached adult physical strength and stature. But Sandfort also found that:

> Consensual experiences...occurred between partners with great differences in age and strength... The distribution of power in sexual experiences with adults depended upon the degree of consent: with non-consensual experiences it was more commonly reported that the adult had more power; with voluntary experiences the young persons said more often that they felt more powerful than the adult.[571]

The finding that *any* of Sandfort's subjects would report feeling *more* powerful as a child than the adult with whom they had sexual contact will seem odd to some. They will wonder, How could this possibly be so? It is a question explored in an earlier work of my own, in which I proposed the existence of a "natural law", formulated thus: *power in a relationship resides with the party that needs the relationship less*. We all know of doting parents who crave the love and approval of their child so much that the child can wrap them round its little finger. A similar phenomenon is often to be seen among "normal" adult lovers when one partner's need of the other is especially strong. And for the adult "outsiders" who love children but lack a family of their own the neediness factor is intensified.[572]

Bearing in mind the age apartheid in modern society that invisibly deters and prevents child-adult sexual contacts, we need hardly be surprised if children are sometimes set on a pedestal by those grown-ups who adore them, usually from afar. For such an adult to succeed against the odds just in making friends with a child is itself a triumph against the system of age segregation – a system in which every child-adult contact outside the nuclear family is met with suspicion and surveillance. To find in such a friendship a child who reciprocates the grown-up's physical affection is a treasure indeed. It need hardly be surprising if the child is adored beyond measure. Worshipping the ground a child walks on is a guarantee that the adult will want to please the youngster. The danger in these circumstances is not that he will be too powerful in coercing the child but that he will be too eager to please, too ready to enslave himself to the will of the little god in his life.

Does that adoration find an echo in Michael Jackson's dangerous liaisons? It is time to revisit the most famous of them all, the affair with Jordan Chandler, a liaison eclipsing by far in its long-term significance the one that would later put him in the dock. Among the star's most scathing critics is Sandra Sutherland, the private detective who claims to have interviewed 120 "witnesses" to his behaviour with boys. Even she had to concede that love played its part. While she certainly felt Jackson abused his power over boys' families, she also believed tender feelings, not coercion, were at the heart of his relationships with the boys themselves. So we need not be surprised to learn that Jordie's step-mother Nathalie came to a similar conclusion. Michael slept with the boy at her house. Seeing the pair of them at such close quarters at the height of their relationship, she and her husband Evan could hardly fail to see what was happening emotionally, even if the bedroom still held its secrets. In the account by Jordie's uncle, Raymond Chandler, Nathalie (whose real name is altered to "Monique" in this text) was the more perceptive of the two hosts:

> Monique reiterated her opinion that Michael was taking up too much of Jordie's life. But this time she offered an additional explanation. "Jordie doesn't even know you're in the room, Evan. Can't you see what's going on? They're in love!"[573]

Note the plural pronoun: *they* are in love: Michael with Jordie; Jordie with Michael. Disapproving though she clearly was, Nathalie does not complain of Michael coercing his way into bed with the boy, even though her very house was arguably being commandeered for the purpose.

Ray Chandler's book, *All That Glitters*, appeared as recently as 2004. As such, its publication could easily be dismissed as commercial opportunism related to the then forthcoming trial. This would be a pity; it is a goldmine of highly authoritative information. The author is a lawyer; his style is strongly grounded in well documented evidence. He obviously enjoyed the confidence of his brother Evan: family discussions of the Jackson crisis and their meetings with their legal team are recorded in immense and convincing detail. It was reported not long after the civil settlement in 1994 that he was working on such a book (though his name was then given as Ray Charmatz). Thus I do not think he can be accused of relying on fading memories a decade after the events: his notes were assuredly made at the time.

Michael was Jordie's hero long before the pair met in May 1993, he says, memorably telling us "to say that Michael Jackson already had some influence over the boy is like calling Niagara Falls a leak".[574] Much earlier, by the age of six, Jordie had memorised the words to half a dozen Jackson songs and taught himself many of the star's dance moves. At first even the boy's father, Evan, was charmed by him. "…you can't help becoming a kid again when you're with Michael", he said. In fact, for Evan the attraction went beyond just charm: "We were a team...I saw him as a valuable addition to Jordie's life."[575]

Amazingly, in view of Evan Chandler's later insistence that Jackson's alleged sexual misconduct had wrecked his son's life, Ray tells us that in the early "honeymoon" days Evan was not particularly worried about a sexual relationship developing between man and boy, as long as it was a "gay" affair – by which he appears to have meant mutually desired sex between two people who were both sexually oriented towards males. At this stage Jordie had shown no signs of any interest in girls, and his father thought he might be gay. He was upset by his ex-wife's seemingly casual indifference. When he mentioned it to her, she reportedly shrugged and said: "So what. So he's gay. Who cares?" Nevertheless, he described himself as a "pretty liberal" kind of guy. If Jordie had been gay he could have lived with it. He even showed no sign of the great age difference between Michael and Jordie being a problem for him. Even when he had become disillusioned with Michael, he was still able to tell Jordie's step-father Dave Schwartz, "Well, you know, age in and of itself is not a harmful thing." In the same taped telephone conversation, he went so far as to describe the age difference as positively beneficial, at least potentially. Age and power were not the problem, he insisted, but Michael's character was. Age, he said:

> ...could have been used to advantage, and in some ways Michael is using his age and experience and his money and his power to great advantage to Jordie. The problem is he's also harming him, greatly harming him, for his own selfish reasons. He's not the altruistic, kind human being that he appears to be.[576]

What we see emerging here from Evan Chandler's recorded words, and from the intimate, insider portrayal of him by his brother Raymond, is extremely apropos. Because Evan is revealed as no homophobic extremist, his developing view of Michael's use and abuse of his power takes on added credibility.

As we saw in Chapter Two, a massive effort was made to dent that credibility by portraying Evan Chandler as an extortionist. It is now clear that this picture is misleading and diverts attention from the realities of the case. The extortion claims, which had been orchestrated by Anthony Pellicano, had simply been a ploy to throw the media and the authorities off the scent. At the heart of Pellicano's accusation was the very same tape recording just cited. It is a long recording, in which Evan Chandler and Dave Schwartz exchange over 20,000 words in three separate conversations on 8 July, 1993. During the course of these exchanges, Evan returns over and over again to his reasons for attempting to set up a formal meeting between Michael, his own family including Jordie, and lawyers. Pellicano succeeded in squeezing his extortion allegation out of this tape only by the most outrageous use of brief, selective quotation. Maureen Orth, in by far the most authoritative journal article on the 1993 scandal, wrote: "Ironically, Pellicano distributed the tape to the media to bolster his side, but the tape is crudely edited, full of erasures, and at times actually seems to help the father's case."[577] No one who has read the entire transcript, as I have, would conclude from it that Evan's motive was extortion.

This is not to say Evan Chandler's growing disenchantment with Michael was unbiased and dispassionate. On the contrary, he had very questionable motives in which ambition and money played a part, but this was no case of crude extortion. As we will see, the evidence clearly points to a man driven half mad by the feeling that he was being cut out of his son's life thanks to Jackson's influence. It was not the sex that bothered him, at least initially. Rather, it was the growing feeling that he was being marginalised and ignored. From a bitter sense of humiliation grew a destructive urge towards revenge. He rationalised these feelings as an attempt to save Jordie from irreparable damage; but in reality he was quite prepared to cause more damage to the boy through his revenge than Michael had ever done by the relationship. In another ironic twist, Jordie emerged relatively unscathed whereas Evan is now, in his brother's estimation, a broken man, crazed and penniless after legal battles that continued long after the multi-million civil settlement that saw his son become rich.

Evan accused Jackson of breaking up his family, at first glance a rather strange claim given that he and his wife June had separated many years before the star's arrival on the scene. Nearly half his son's life had been spent with his mother and step-father, Dave. Evan had remarried. June and his new wife Nathalie did not get on too well, but otherwise the new arrangements were amicable enough. There was no battle over custody or child support. Dave and Evan hit it off just fine. Evan and June remained friends. He had no reason to feel Jordie was being deliberately cut out of his life, even though they lived apart. The boy spent most weekends at his father's house.

It was this that changed with Michael's arrival on the scene – not immediately, but as the relationship with Jordie developed in the spring and summer of 1993. There were trips which took the boy away with Michael, to Florida, Las Vegas, Monte Carlo, New York. Eventually he was working hard, against Evan's resistance, to have Jordie accompany him on his forthcoming *Dangerous* tour. At first these trips included June, who was seduced by Jackson's glamour and money. Evan came to believe Michael was turning both June and Jordie against him, using the power his wealth and fame gave him in order to monopolise Jordie: even June would soon have been cut out of the picture if Jordie had not been prevented from joining the *Dangerous* tour. But before that could happen, she and Evan were falling out on the issue, a result of what Evan would call Michael's policy of "divide and conquer". There was a legal battle over custody of Jordie, a case in which Michael Jackson was named.

The facts as disclosed by Ray Chandler's book convincingly support Evan's side of the story in most respects. They also match the experience of other parents whose boys have been close to Michael: so many of those who have been guests at Neverland have reported being kept away from their children for lengthy periods of time that it can only have been a deliberate policy. To my mind there is no doubt that Jackson deliberately manipulated families for his own ends, and that is no trivial charge. The primary focus of this book, however, is his effect on children, not their parents, and in this chapter the principal concern is how his exercise of power affected the boys close to him.

Disentangling these effects for the purpose of analysis is easier than doing so in real life. If you treat a child's parents badly, it is bound to have an impact on the child: Jordie was put under huge pressure from all sides thanks to Michael's disastrous manoeuvrings. But just as it takes two to make an argument, we must not overlook the easily ignored fact that parents are generally in an extremely powerful position over their own children, and that they too may misuse it. And when allegations of paedophilia are involved against an outsider to the family, that power is cranked up a thousandfold, because the parents have the whole might of the state and society behind them, from the police and the courts to the media, churches, schools, the lot. It was this power that brought Michael Jackson to his knees in January 1994 and enabled Jordie Chandler (or rather his father on the boy's behalf) to squeeze a multi-million dollar settlement out of him.

Accordingly, it is time to switch the focus briefly to Evan Chandler, rather than Michael Jackson, as a perpetrator of child abuse. Evan, as we shall see, grossly abused his own power as a parent, although, through yet another ironic twist, this abuse was initially prompted at least in part by absolutely genuine concerns for his son's welfare. We have seen that "gay" sex between Michael and Jordie was not in itself necessarily such a big deal for Evan, provided that it was something Jordie really wanted. Much more important to him was his perception that Michael was bad for the boy in other ways and was beginning to isolate him emotionally from his family.

His suspicions had been aroused even before he met Michael. The star and Jordie had been a growing "item" throughout the early months of 1993, but it was not until May that alarm bells began to ring. The *National Enquirer* ran a story about Michael's supposed new family and described Jordie as though he were the singer's adopted son.[578] This was after Jordie and his mother June had been very publicly together with Michael in Monaco. Jordie's step-father Dave Schwartz was even more outraged: he thought Michael was after his wife!

At this time Evan had no reason to believe Jordie was being turned against him. The boy phoned his dad soon after his return from Europe, inviting him over to June's house to meet Michael there. But when Evan accepted the invitation, he was shocked by what he saw. The sight of Jordie's bedroom alarmed him, packed as it was with a gross excess of expensive gifts from Michael. His first sight of the star left him equally unimpressed. Briefly, as we have seen, he softened under the spell of Michael's charm, but remained less than enchanted by the ambiguous nature of his relationship with Jordie. The next day, after being initiated in the secrets of Michael's "hideout" in Los Angeles, Evan took the bull by the horns and just came out with it: "Are you fucking my son up the ass?" Rather than getting angry, the star "giggled like a schoolgirl". Pressed by a confused Evan as to the nature of the relationship, he said, "I don't understand it myself. It must be cosmic."[579]

No boy has ever alleged he was "fucked up the ass" by Michael. Although he loved boys, there is little to suggest *fucking* them was a priority for him. He could therefore have honestly answered Evan's blunt question with a straightforward denial. Or rather the denial would have been more honest than President Clinton's famous assertion that he never had "sex" with Monica Lewinsky, though it would have been just as misleading. Not that Evan was fooled for long. Only a week later, after seeing at close quarters for the first time how Michael and Jordie monopolised each other's company – and beginning to feel excluded himself – Evan asked Jordie if the pair of them were "doin' it". Jordie's denial was plain, saying it was disgusting and he wasn't into such things. Evan tackled Michael again too, this time more obliquely. He asked Michael if he was gay, saying it wouldn't matter, he didn't care either way. He just wanted to know. "Uh-uh," he replied, "not me".[580]

The problem for Evan was that these denials were so starkly at odds with the behaviour of the odd couple. They were together all night as well as all day. They were sleeping together. One night at the end of May, when this was going on under his own roof, Evan checked up on the pair at three in the morning: "Jordie was now in Michael's bed, spooning, with Michael's arm wrapped tightly around the boy, his hand resting on the boy's crotch on the outside of the covers". He pulled back the covers. The two of them were fully clothed. The evidence was thus still tantalisingly ambiguous but highly suspicious. It was this moment, in Ray Chandler's account, that his brother Evan decided the relationship must be brought to an end:

> A picture is worth a thousand words. And the sight of his son in bed with

> Michael finally made it clear to Evan that he must end their relationship. Even if there was no sex, Jordie's personality had been seriously altered. As he morphed day by day into a pint-sized clone of Michael, he withdrew further and further from his family and friends.[581]

Unlike other fathers, he could not just throw Jackson out, or go straight to the police. His evidence was too slim at this stage for his word to count much against that of an international megastar. Besides, he had Jordie's feelings to consider and June's. She was the boy's mother, she was still on Michael's side and above all she had legal custody. At first he tried to put pressure on Jordie directly, asking him not to go on the *Dangerous* tour with Michael. What he had not bargained for was that the boy would defy him outright, saying he would go on tour even without his dad's permission. Jordie also challenged his father to give a good reason. Evan bluffed, saying it was because "you guys lied to me", and above all things he hated liars. Significantly, Jordie never asked what these lies were supposed to be. Only months later did he admit he had been freaking out at the time because he thought his dad had found out about the sexual goings-on. Never mind what the lies were about. It was clear there were things to do with Michael that Jordie did not want to discuss with his dad. As Ray's account puts it, "painful as it was to admit, Evan believed that his son's loyalty now belonged to Michael".[582]

It was this estrangement, more than any sexual shenanigans, that Evan could not abide. It was approaching mid-June by now; by this time Evan's relationship with his ex-wife had also reached an all-time low. Communications ceased between them. It was becoming increasingly clear that if Evan was going to win the battle over Jordie he would have to fight not only the pop legend but the boy himself, and his mother. To take on Michael Jackson alone would have been tough enough. To successfully take on all three, as Evan clearly began to realise, was going to require some desperate and dubious methods.

After being largely cut out of the boy's life in the weeks that followed, Evan began putting these methods into practice. He did not go nuclear immediately. Instead he worked out a plan of legal action but kept it under wraps. He would first of all warn June that he was contemplating action, giving her a final opportunity to end the relationship with Michael without a legal battle. If she refused to comply, he would file a restraining order against Michael. If she opposed the restraining order, he would fight for custody of Jordie. June was unresponsive to his overtures. Jordie later testified that Michael discouraged him from phoning his father at this time. On 7 July Evan left a message on June's answering machine giving a time and venue for a meeting, saying that as Jordie had repeatedly refused to return his phone calls this would be "my last voluntary attempt to communicate". Still Evan was ignored. Not wanting to go to law, he was by this time utterly at his wits' end over his failure to make progress any other way.

We know just how bitter and frustrated he was thanks to Anthony Pellicano, who was hired by Michael on 7 July – precisely the day of the taped answering machine message and undoubtedly in response to it. Pellicano would later claim that the 7 July message was the start of an extortion bid. He would also try to use a much longer tape, recorded on the following day, as part of the same allegation. This was the infamous tape of the phone conversations between Dave Schwartz and Evan Chandler, encountered already in this chapter. It was the tape on which Evan famously threatened to bring down Michael if he failed to get what he wanted. The extent of the malice and anger he felt was clearly revealed by quotations from the tape in Chapter Two. Pellicano claimed Evan wanted money, but the tape taken as a whole clearly suggests his interest was in wresting Jordie away from Michael.

What concerns us here is not the extensive and complex negotiations and legal to-ings and fro-ings of the following weeks, but rather the state of Evan's mind at this point and the damage he was plainly determined to cause if he could find no other way to prevail. Like the notorious trooper's comment in the Vietnam War that a village had to be "destroyed in order to save it" (from enemy hands), Evan showed himself ready to destroy his son in order to "save" him. We hear him saying his son would hate him for what he was going to do and that "everyone" would be destroyed if he was forced to bring down Michael. Dave asked him if that would be a good thing. Evan replied that it would be "great", because "June and Jordie and Michael... have forced me to take it to the extreme."

That word "great" was clearly used in exasperation with Dave's sceptical reluctance to take his side. He did not mean it literally. But the fact that he blurted it out is testimony to his impatience and emotional instability at this time. Despite protesting over and over again on the tape that he wanted to save his son from harm at Michael's hands, it was also becoming apparent that he had reached the point where he would stop at nothing. Dave put to him the common sense view that the relationship might be best left to run its course and that dramatic action to bring down Michael would only put the boy in the spotlight and make matters worse. If Evan had acted in line with his own fundamentally liberal philosophy he would have agreed with Dave, but by this time he had been ignored and humiliated so much that he was no longer being rational: the action he was about to take smacks more of concern for his own feelings than his son's.

Evan's precipitate behaviour may in part be explained by the fact that he suffers from Gaucher's disease, an inherited metabolic disorder in which harmful quantities of a fatty substance accumulate in the spleen, liver, lungs, bone marrow, and sometimes in the brain. Depending on the type of the disease, symptoms may include bruising easily and fatigue. Patients may have an enlarged liver and spleen, skeletal disorders, and, in some instances, lung and kidney impairment. Brain involvement such as seizures may be a feature.[583] The impact of the disease on Evan, now confined to a wheelchair, appears to have been serious.

Whatever the cause, Evan's reckless determination to bring Michael down no matter what the cost to Jordie was undoubtedly an abuse of his parental power – a point which even his sympathetic brother Ray appears tacitly to understand. It was also an abuse (as will be explained shortly) of society's power in a way to which apparently no one has yet drawn attention. In Ray's account, Evan only came to believe Jordie had been *molested* after Pellicano used the word. The day after the taped conversation, the private eye had phoned Evan's home and spoken to Nathalie, saying he understood Evan had a complaint of "molestation" against Michael. Until that point the idea had not occurred to Evan, who considered the word applied only to non-consensual sexual assault, whereas Jordie appeared to him at that time to be Michael's willing and enthusiastic partner. In his mind this made the sexual contact with Michael part of a "gay" relationship and – because of his liberal views – this was not so terrible that it justified "destroying everyone" to stop it in its tracks.

We know Evan had other objections to Michael: he hated the lies, the bribery (especially of his ex-wife) with expensive gifts, the "divide and conquer" tactics. These were massively important to him because they were the tactics that had cut him off from Jordie. But these things alone could not justify him in going nuclear. There had to be a big, killer argument with which to persuade both Dave and himself that total war was required.

Enter "society"! Blame society and its all-pervasive power! The obsession of modern society with child sex abuse would give Evan the excuse he needed. The killer argument would be based on "expert opinion", a form of discourse so dominant these days – so "hegemonic", in the sociological jargon – that it trumped both Evan's own liberal inclinations and Dave's pragmatic reluctance to make waves. At one point on the tape Evan says that "in the opinion of these experts" he would be a negligent father if he did not do what he was now doing; in fact in their opinion he should have acted earlier. At first he did not agree with them, he said, but his mind had been changed. A little later we hear Evan saying "Jordie and Michael are users", determined to have their own relationship; but Jordie was not old enough for such decisions. Dave asks Evan, "Do you think Jordie hates you?" Evan replies, "If he doesn't, he's gonna hate me tomorrow." He meant once Jordie was told of his intention to cut off his contact with Michael. Dave continues the theme:

> SCHWARTZ: But why would you want him to hate you, and why would you want to put him through that –
> CHANDLER: Because all I care about is what happens to him in the long run.
> SCHWARTZ: Well, the long run, is that going to be healthy in the long run?
> CHANDLER: According to the experts?
> SCHWARTZ: Yeah.
> CHANDLER: Absolutely. According to the experts, if it goes on the way it is, he's doomed. He has no chance of ever being a happy, healthy, normal human being, no [tape irregularity].
> SCHWARTZ: So what happens if you force him not to see him?
> CHANDLER: Not to see Michael?
> SCHWARTZ: Yeah.
> CHANDLER: Nobody's saying for sure what will happen. Most people's feeling is that he's gonna go on and hate me for a long time and then some day when he gets older he'll thank me.

Ever sceptical, Dave returns at a later point to his doubts:

> SCHWARTZ: You don't think it's just gonna run its course?
> CHANDLER: Dave . . .
> SCHWARTZ: I mean, you know more than I know, so I'm at a disadvantage.
> CHANDLER: Well, then, I will tell you without question. It's gone way too

far.
SCHWARTZ: Yeah.
CHANDLER: Jordie is never going to be the same person he was.
SCHWARTZ: Yeah.
CHANDLER: It's never – by the time it runs its course –
SCHWARTZ: Yeah.
CHANDLER: – if it does, he will be so damaged he'll never recover
SCHWARTZ: Yeah.
CHANDLER: – and that's not my opinion. I mean, I happen to be believe it now because my eyes have been opened –

Evan's eyes had been opened by "the experts". One can only guess that Evan had been reading up on "expert" opinion around this time. It would have been strange if he had not. Not until a week later did he receive through his lawyer a written expert opinion on Jordie's (anonymised) case. But for decades our newspapers and magazines have been full of the same dubious message: child sex "abuse" is deadlier than death itself, so no reaction to it can ever be an overreaction. Thus "society" was pulling Evan's strings: an entrenched but irrational cultural climate was about to tug those strings in a way that would walk him and his family over the edge of an abyss.

We have seen that Evan threatened to "destroy" everyone. We know that he was as good as his word: certainly Evan himself was destroyed in his brother's estimation, and Michael's reputation never recovered from his public denunciation. What about the impact of his actions on Jordie? How did the father's reckless use of parental power express itself to the son, behind closed doors? His own words on the subject, as reported by his brother, are shocking in their candour. By 16 July, when Jordie was about to go on tour with Michael for five months, Evan was telling himself the boy would be "totally screwed up" as a result. That meant, he said: "I could be as tough on him as I wanted. I had nothing to lose."[584]

The scene of the torture, appropriately enough, was the surgery where Evan practised as a dentist. Jordie needed an extraction, which was performed under sedation. After he had come round, his father began to get to work on a more painful operation, for which there could be no sedative. He told his son he knew everything that had happened between Michael and him, "so you might as well admit it". When Jordie remained silent he changed tack:

"Look, Jordie, lots of famous people are bisexual and nobody gives a shit. They're not embarrassed. It's sorta cool, in a way."

After ten minutes of meandering monologue Evan had elicited nothing from his son but a blank stare. Frustrated, he switched back to his original approach. "I'm going to give you one last chance to save Michael. If you lie to me, then I'm going to take him down in front of the whole world, and it'll be all your fault because you're the one person who could have saved him."

Nothing.

In his heart, Evan already knew the truth; he didn't need Jordie to confirm it. But he believed if his son could just hear himself say it, if he could just spurt it out quickly and painlessly like the tooth, it would release him from the prison in his mind. Without a plan, Evan began babbling away again, saying whatever came to mind in the hope of eventually hitting on something that would push a button in his son and free him.

"I know about the kissing and the jerking off, so you're not telling me anything I don't already know," Evan lied. "This isn't about me finding anything out. It's about lying. And you know what's going to happen if you lie. So I'm going to make it very easy for you. I'm going to ask you one question. All you have to do is say yes, or no. That's it. Lie and Michael goes down. Tell me the truth and you save him."

Jordie remained silent for what seemed to Evan a hopeless amount of time. Then, "Promise?"

"Have I ever lied to you?"

"No."

"And I never will."

"You won't hurt Michael, right?"

"Right."

"And I don't want anyone to know. Promise me you won't ever tell anyone."

"I swear, no one."

"Okay. What's the question?"

"Did Michael touch your penis?"

Jordie hesitated. Then, almost inaudibly, he whispered "Yes."[585]

That was it. The truth was out. After extracting the tooth, Evan had extracted a "confession". But at what price? Evan had always impressed on Jordie the importance of truthfulness but here he was lying through his doubtless perfectly maintained dentist's teeth to his own son. He claimed he knew for certain about the sexual side when in fact he was only guessing. But that was not the wicked lie. That was not the lie that should be a stain on his conscience for ever. By far the worst of it was the lie that would turn out to be a betrayal of Jordie's trust. He had promised – he had sworn – not to hurt Michael. Even as he uttered that solemn oath he knew full well he would break it if that was the only way to prevail. Just one month later, by taking action that would inevitably explode into the public arena, he would hurt Michael with a far deeper and more lasting pain than even the most sadistic dentist could inflict in his chair.

And what about the hurt to Jordie? How are we to weigh the damage to his sense of trust, especially trust of his own father, in the scale of evils? To my mind, nothing that Michael would have done on tour – very probably just more kissing, masturbation and expensive gifts – would have been remotely as corrupting as this one terrible deed of his father's. It may be that to this very day he feels there is absolutely no one in the world he can trust. After all, if children cannot trust their own parents, who can they be sure of?

We know that Jordie did not want to hurt Michael. More specifically, we know he did not want to testify against him. Evan himself later spoke of "Jordie's heart-wrenching pleas not to make him go to court". Fortunately, the boy was blessed with a less neurotic character than his highly-strung father. Legal secretary Geraldine Hughes saw him at close quarters during the crisis period that followed the "confession", and describes him as "a perfectly normal child". She said:

> I understood why Michael Jackson was fond of the boy. He was ...warm spirited and cute....he was very kind and had a gentle personality. He did not act or appear as though he had been harmed in any way...Although I do not have enough psychological experience to know how a child would act who had been sexually abused, I can say that there was nothing abnormal about his behaviour, personality or attitude. In fact, he was the one who kept calming and consoling his father, who was a nervous wreck. It appeared as if the boy was protecting his father instead of vice-versa. He was more concerned about his father's well-being than his own.[586]

A curious feature of this case is that no one close to it has had anything but good to say about Jordie with the exception of his father. We saw above that Evan referred to Jordie and Michael as both being "users", in a statement of moral equivalence between the two that many will find shocking. He also said "Michael was so slick he made Jordie slick" and that the boy had betrayed him. For many, the most shocking aspect of these anguished denunciations will not be their undoubted unfairness (Evan palpably betrayed Jordie, not the reverse) but the fact that they deny Jordie his victim status. Victims of child sexual abuse are not supposed to be agents with minds and intentions of their own; it is only their adult abusers who are capable of being "slick" and "using" or "betraying" others.

Evan, in his moral confusion, declared on the famous Schwartz-Chandler tape that Jordie was not old enough to decide he wanted to be with Michael, but nonetheless credits his son with some remarkably grown-up-sounding moral actions and responsibilities. What could have squared the circle for him was his claim that one day Jordie would thank him for his actions. If he turned out to be right about this we might be able to conclude that his seemingly reckless and ruthless use of parental power was justified by a happy ending. So a key issue to be explored below is whether such an outcome was ever achieved.

While Evan was plainly wrong to accuse his son of betrayal, he was absolutely on target in seeing Jordie as more than just a passive victim. As we have just seen from Geraldine Hughes, he was capable of showing a rather grown-up level of real concern for his anxious father. At school he was both popular and well regarded. People loved his humour. They would fall about laughing, including Michael. Especially Michael: the boy's charm and sense of fun was a vital part of the chemistry between them. This was no timid little boy just doing sexually what a grown-up told him. He was lively, witty, a real character in the fullest sense. It was his comedy ideas that his father later wrote up for the screenplay of the Mel Brooks movie *Robin Hood: Men In Tights.*

Remember, too, that he was thirteen years old, not three. Before his next birthday he would have a beautiful and very thoughtful young lady by the name of Sonnet Simmons as his girlfriend. Her elegantly composed letters to him are touchingly tender. The text of one of them is reproduced (there are also photos of Sonnet) in full in a book by a highly controversial Jackson commentator, journalist Victor M Gutierrez.[587] This diligent investigator is to be congratulated on securing many "hot" documents and artefacts. Arguably his utter disregard for the personal privacy of any of the participants in the drama is in the public interest, as well as merely interesting to the public, but in this instance I believe he went a little too far. Ms Simmons had nothing to say that would have satisfied a salacious appetite but some things are simply private. What interests us here – I doubt she would mind me saying it – is that her letters reveal how deeply impressed she was by Jordie's level of understanding, of not just herself but also her mother and siblings.

Jordie, then, was a young man of considerable intellect and discernment. Emotionally too, he was quite definitely mature beyond his years – probably more so than a good many older teenagers who have reached the age of consent. Even Evan admitted it in his saner moments. On one occasion in May 1993, Jordie's half-brother Nikki was coming up to his fifth birthday. As Ray's account put it, "...what better present, than to have Michael Jackson at your party? Michael was all for it, but Jordie knew better. The other kids would pay no attention to [Nikki] once The King of Pop showed up." Jordie was here showing his characteristic thoughtfulness and "Evan was pleased that he had his priorities right". A few weeks later, Jordie was away with Michael and not keeping in touch by phone with either Nikki or Evan. The latter put it down to Michael's bad influence.

How bad that influence was, at its worst, emerges in colourful fashion from Gutierrez' pages, if they are to be believed. It is a big "if". In the wake of the civil settlement of January 1994, Gutierrez was for a while regarded as the hottest journalist covering the Jackson case. Unlike the others, he had been researching Jackson's relations with boys for three years before the Chandler case hit the headlines. In May 1994 he secured a major scoop for the *Daily Mirror*, revealing a wealth of detail claimed to be from Jordie's "secret diary" – information which could only have come from the family.[588] Even more sensationally, by the following year he was claiming he had seen a videotape made in December 1994, showing Michael engaged in sexual activity with a boy. Michael's response was to sue Gutierrez for slander, saying the claim was a monstrous lie. No such tape existed. The star won the court case in April 1998 and was awarded $2.7 million. The video was never produced, either in court or out. Damages were awarded against the journalist, who fled to South America, from where little was heard of him for years until the more recent allegations against Michael in 2003.[589]

A fascinating footnote to this episode can be written thanks to the appearance of a book by Margaret Maldonado Jackson, former partner of Michael's brother Jermaine. In *Jackson Family Values: Memories of Madness*, she mentions the videotape allegation in order vigorously to deny a rumour that the boy who had supposedly been filmed – allegedly being masturbated by Michael – was one of her own two sons by Jermaine. Her first-born by him, Jeremy, was born in December 1986, thus at the alleged time of the tape being made he would have been almost exactly eight years old. Her second son, Jourdynn (pronounced Jordan) would have being coming up for five, as he was born in January 1989. The thought that Michael may have been "scoring" with a second "Jordan" in the same year as his public disgrace over the first may seem far-fetched, especially in view of this boy's very tender years. Where Michael is concerned, though, nothing is too bizarre to be beyond the bounds of possibility.[590]

In fact, the allegation appears to relate to Jeremy, who was accordingly interviewed in December 2004, by this time aged eighteen, by Santa Barbara County police as part of their investigations ahead of Michael's 2005 trial. Clearly, the young man made no allegations and in June 2005 his mother was still maintaining her confidence in Michael's innocence in a conversation with Roger Friedman.[591]

Gutierrez could have been just a straightforward liar in pursuit of a quick buck. God knows his trade is full of them. Or he could have been a victim of Pellicano-style dirty tricks: the tape, on which Jackson was allegedly filmed by his own security cameras, may have existed before (possibly) being stolen and destroyed. Those who could testify to its existence may have been bought off. Gutierrez' own explanation at the time was feeble. He said another boy's mother had shown him the tape. But he kept silent on who this was, invoking a California law allowing reporters to protect their sources. There may have been a less lofty reason for his refusal to reveal the full truth of the matter. Years after the event, in 2003, he was tracked down in Chile by Maureen Orth, the journalist who had been the first to produce a near-definitive account of the Chandler affair. In her 10,000-word report for *Vanity Fair*, Gutierrez reportedly said he had been beaten up by three men under Pellicano's direction.[592]

Jackson's legal onslaught had also extended to suing Paramount Pictures for allowing their TV news programme *Hard Copy* to carry a report about the videotape. Paramount won. Diane Dimond, presenter of the TV programme, said she had believed in Gutierrez' integrity: he had been a long-time reliable source on Jackson. By 2003, with further allegations being made against Michael, Guttierez had sufficiently regained his credibility to be back in business. As the trial hove into view at the start of 2005 he was assigned to cover the case for *Dateline NBC*. Pro-Jackson conspiracy theorists pointed excitedly to the fact that Maureen Orth was married to leading political journalist Tim Russert, who was the senior vice president of NBC News, which also engaged the services of Diane Dimond.[593]

Do such connections between some of Jackson's key accusers automatically invalidate their claims? To my mind those who rely on such ad hominem denunciations are clutching at straws.

Another key point adding hugely to Gutierrez' credibility is the fact that Michael never sued him over the many explicit, highly graphic claims he makes in his book about the star's sexual exploits with boys. Nor did he sue Ray Chandler, whose later account of the Jordie Chandler affair confirms the Gutierrez version in practically every detail. Gutteriez could not possibly have just been making things up about Jordie and Evan: he must have had access to "insider" details that would only later be publicly revealed by Jordie's uncle, the ultimate insider.

What, then, is so hot in Gutierrez' pages that such a fanfare is required? For many, the most damning anecdote in the book will be one which appears to show that Jackson was "a bender": a man who deliberately attempts to turn boys away from a heterosexual to a homosexual life course. Boy-lovers generally have no interest in doing any such thing. JZ Eglinton's cult 1970s book on the subject, *Greek Love*, emphasised the lover's potential role in educating youngsters on their future role as husbands and fathers.[594] A good many boy-lovers see themselves as mentors in one way or another, depending on their own range of knowledge, skills and enthusiasm. Few these days would see it as a duty to educate a boy for marriage or feel themselves qualified to do so. But neither would they try to influence a boy's future sexuality – at Jordie's age it would probably be futile anyway. Jackson, though, does appear to have made the attempt. Gutierrrez tells us Jordie learned from him to repeat six wishes three times a day, so they would come true:

1. No wenches, bitches, heifers or hoes.
2. Never give up your "bliss" (sex acts).
3. Live with me in Neverland forever.
4. No conditioning.
5. Never grow up.
6. Be better than best friends (lovers).[595]

No wenches, bitches, heifers or hoes! What purer example could there be of misogynistic bender-speak? For the tabloid Jackson-baiters this was a quote to die for, the ultimate proof of Jackson's corrupting influence. But wait a minute, what about the other wishes, especially number five? Is Jordie seriously being expected to wish never to grow up? The tabloid hacks, in their own "bliss" over the wenches revelation, failed to consider the full context. They made much of Michael as a Peter Pan figure who had himself refused to grow up. But because of their determination to cast Jordie as his innocent victim, they played down the boy's sophistication and above all his terrific sense of humour. He and Michael were forever giggling together over all sorts of things. If the first wish had said "No women", it might have been possible to take it seriously. But wenches, bitches, heifers or hoes? How could they fail to laugh? Not that the list was entirely a joke. Number four, "No conditioning" was a principle of great importance to Jackson. Social conditioning, he believed, was a great evil. There was nothing wrong with boy-love except the "conditioning" that dogmatically condemned it.

As we have seen from earlier chapters in this book, Jackson was on remarkably solid ground on this point, just as adult-attracted gay people were right when *they* began to rebel against *their* feelings being dismissed as evil or sick. Evan Chandler accused Michael Jackson of "brainwashing" his son. Insofar as this comment related to "seducing" Jordie into believing sex between man and boy was okay, we can now begin to see there were two sides to this story: what Evan condemned as "brainwashing" was merely Michael's attempt to combat social "conditioning" – a valid strategy of resistance in face of society's monstrously unjust suppression of boy-love.

Consider the terms in which Ray Chandler writes about Michael's supposedly sinister seduction techniques. He begins here in April 1993, referring to a three-day stay at Disney World hotel, before the relationship had reached its most sexually advanced stage:

> At night in their hotel room Michael grabbed Jordie's butt and stuck his tongue in the boy's ear. When Jordie protested, Michael began to cry and said that other boys… must love him more because they let him do those things. But Michael did not want to drive the boy away, so he refrained from doing the specific things Jordie didn't like. Instead, he continued to do whatever else he could to engage the boy in a sexual relationship. And by the end of April his slow but steady seduction had progressed to the point where a peck on the cheek had become a lingering kiss on the lips, and a quick, goodnight hug in bed was now a loin-tight embrace.[596]

When there were things Jordie did not like, or was not ready for,

Michael backed off. He used persuasion – moral (or immoral) blackmail, some would say – but not force. Was this non-consensual? Was it near rape? Was it an abuse of his power? The only person who could convincingly deliver such a verdict is Jordie himself, and he has never done so. Remember that a few weeks after this hotel "seduction" Jordie was enthusiastically introducing Michael to Evan. This is when the three of them, father, son and lover, were "a team", as Evan put it, having fun together. Complaining about Michael coming on strong was not on Jordie's agenda. Evan had no suspicion anything was wrong from the boy's point of view simply because there was indeed nothing wrong. As he put it: "Jordie looked great and acted the same as always."[597]

Did Jordie later change his mind and turn against Jackson? With so many people around to tell him he was a "victim" of Michael's evil ways it would be surprising if the boy did not go through a phase of reassessment. At one stage, in a rare direct conversation Ray Chandler reports with his nephew, Jordie said he had come to understand that all that glitters is not gold. The star, it seemed, had lost his lustre in the boy's eyes. This talk with Jordie was pure gold for Ray at least. It gave him the title of his book, *All That Glitters*, and it enabled him to entrench more deeply the view that Jordie was a victim of an adult's abuse of his power to manipulate. In the public arena, too, Jordie was at an early stage quoted as saying he never wanted to see Michael again. This was in his official statement to the authorities.

But this is only a small and misleading part of the story. Evidence emerges from Gutierrez' account showing that Jordie was an active participant in the sexual activity. He truly enjoyed Jackson's company, including the sexual side, and missed him long after the relationship was terminated by his father. Crucially, Jordie never told the authorities that he masturbated Michael:

> He did not want to appear to be a homosexual in front of the police. He did, though, reveal this fact to his father. Upon consulting his attorney, his father recommended that he did not tell the police or anyone else. It was convenient for Jordie's legal advisors that he remain a victim. It sounded better in front of society and the law. Nevertheless, the sentence in the diary written by Jordie appears as: 'I masturbated Michael', a phrase which his father crossed out and wrote a question mark.[598]

Like the elusive videotape over which Gutierrez was successfully sued, the existence of a diary in which Jordie personally recorded his encounters with Michael at the time has never been convincingly demonstrated. The full title of Gutierrez' book is *Michael Jackson Was My Lover: The Secret Diary Of Jordie Chandler*. The book features a wealth of photographs and facsimile documents, both legal and highly personal, which look as though they must have been obtained with the cooperation of the Chandler family. Indeed there are legal documents relating to Jordie's funds after the teenager obtained financial independence from his father. Short of an unauthorised leak from a lawyer's office, these must have come from the young man himself. They cannot have been leaked from grand jury testimony and documentation – which internet rumours were proposing as Gutierrez' main source of information on Chandler – because these financial documents were produced at a later date.

In view of what appears to be full cooperation between Jordie and Gutierrez, it seems very strange that we are not treated to facsimile pages from the diary itself. We see a note, part printed, with additional notes in Jordie's own hand-writing, plus his signature. But this is not part of a diary as usually understood. There is no book with printed dates in it. There is no reference to a diary kept in a computer file, though we do know he had a computer. There is not even a school exercise book. If Jordie had actually written things down, or keyed them into a computer, at the time of his affair with Michael, we would need to know how he found the time to write it, and how he managed to keep it secret from Michael himself. When they were away in hotels together they sometimes went whole days barely leaving each other's sight for a moment.

The author claims Jackson decided to settle in the civil court once he learned of the existence of Jordie's diary and knew it was in enemy hands. He says the diary became "the pillar" of his investigation and that the diary "is presented within this book". But throughout its pages there is no reference to specific diary entries. It is my belief that there never was any such diary and Guttierez does his credibility no favours when he pretends there was one. He had an immense amount of genuine insider information to impart in his book but decided to gild the lily. No doubt he thought calling his information a "secret diary" would be a powerful selling point: it *sounds* like a hot document.

This does *not* mean the man is a charlatan. There really was a hot document, but it was not a diary as such. He gives the game away by giving us facsimiles of a printed (or typewritten) document called "The original chronology", which gives sequential dates and accounts of the sexual encounters, along with information about meetings with lawyers and a great deal else.[599] This is clearly the work of Evan Chandler, as the writer refers in the first person to his work as a dentist, and his conversations with Michael. At least part of it must have been compiled after Jordie's "confession", because not until then would Evan have known the sexual details wrung out of his reluctant son. Remember the tell-tale question mark:

> … the sentence in the diary written by Jordie appears as: 'I masturbated Michael', a phrase which his father crossed out and wrote a question mark.

What we in fact get is not a sentence in the first person ("I masturbated Michael"), but a third person report of this event appearing in a facsimile page of "the original chronology" written by Evan. It is part of a list of points Evan noted from what Jordie had told him. The points are written in sequence thus:

1. [A long point, not relevant]
2. Michael came over and stayed for the Memorial Day Weekend.
3. Michael masturbated Jordie at night while in bed.
4. Michael had fellacio [sic] with Jordie from this point until the end of the relationship.
5. Jordie masturbated Michael.
6. At Michael's request, Jordie twisted Michael's nipple while Michael masturbated himself.

So what we see here is not "I masturbated Michael" but, in point five, "Jordie masturbated Michael". *This sentence, in Evan's chronology, is followed by a hand-written question mark*. In other words, it looks very much as though Evan wrote up the details after hearing Jordie's oral "confession", keying them into a computer file. He then went through those details to review them. At this point he thought about the implications of Jordie telling the authorities his son had been engaged *actively* in a sexual act with Michael. Deciding it would be unwise for this to come out, he hand-wrote a question mark by this item. *There is no crossing out*. If Evan had planned to use a genuine diary by Jordie as evidence in court, he could not possibly have contemplated crossing anything out. Such a clumsy attempt to alter the evidence would stick out like a sore thumb. This reference to crossing out was a careless error by Gutierrez which reveals the true story: there was no diary as such. Perhaps he thought the implications of showing the page with the tell-tale hand-written question mark in his book would escape readers' notice because the facsimiles are reproduced in a very small size. It is only possible to read the small print when the pages are magnified – which is what I did. Once they are blown up, however, the facsimiles are crystal clear.

The significance of the document here called "the original chronology" was confirmed in 2005 with the publication of Diane Dimond's book *Be Careful Who You Love*, in which she says:

> Some time after his son revealed what had been going on between him and his famous friend, Dr Chandler began to write things down. He spent hours painstakingly trying to reconstruct a chronology of events. A copy of that 42-page typed document would ultimately find its way to me.[600]

Dimond quotes liberally from this document, though she does not note that Jordie actively masturbated Michael. Indeed, she clearly did not have access to the sexually explicit part of the chronology. She says "Evan Chandler did not want to press his son for details of the sexual abuse; he wanted Jordie to offer them voluntarily, when he was ready to do so. Ironically, that never happened." She added that "Chandler wrote in his chronology that he learned the specific details of the molestation only when he heard them quoted from the police report on national television about a month and a half later." Ray Chandler, in his book, also says that Evan never spoke to Jordie about sex between Michael and the boy after the single word "yes" had been wrenched from him in the dentist's room confession. But it is clear from the photographs of the "chronology" appearing in Gutierrez' book that Evan *must* have heard about the relationship in all its physical detail – unless those photos are of a completely bogus document. As there are good reasons for supposing it is genuine, this in turn implies lengthy confessionals which would have given Evan the opportunity of doing everything in his power to turn Jordie against Michael.

Diary or no diary, Gutierrez plainly knows his stuff about this. We know that following Jordie's brief, initial confession to his father, after which Michael was taken out of his life, Evan had time alone with his son. It was time in which he could have turned his son decisively against Michael had there been anything for him to work on psychologically. If Jordie's loyalty to

Jackson had been shallow all along, any "brainwashing" by the star could soon have been reversed. It did not happen. In August 1993, when Evan was angling for a settlement with Michael, the parties met at the Westwood Marquis Hotel. Gutierrez describes the encounter:

> Upon arriving at the hotel, Jordie calmly walked in, but when he saw Jackson, he jumped into his arms as they both hugged and kissed each other on the cheeks. Jordie rested his head on Jackson's chest. Jackson stroked his hair and asked him:
>
> "Are you okay, Jordie?"
>
> "Yes, but I miss you," responded the boy.
>
> The pleasantries ended when Evan told Jordie to sit down next to him.[601]

Ray Chandler's account of this meeting is very different. In his version it was Evan who embraced Jackson, "with a big, happy-to-see-you hug, patting him on the back like an old friend". Jordie wouldn't go near him, according to his uncle, because he was embarrassed over having given away what happened between them.[602] Both scenarios have their bizarre, improbable elements, You pays your money and you takes your choice. But let's stick with Gutierrez for a while. He gets very interesting.

We learn that Jordie resented these negotiations, in which the money factor inevitably brought another question mark into play. It must have made Jordie wonder how pure his father's motives were. Was he really worried Michael would wreck his son's life, or was he mainly interested in squeezing a big payoff out of the star? Gutierrez tells us Jordie had a way of rebelling:

> In a way to rebel against what was happening, Jordie decided to keep wearing the Calvin Klein underwear that were Jackson's favourite. The underwear was size 34, very large for the skinny boy. Jackson asked him to wear this size so that his genitals would hang down, and Jackson could see them through the spaces. Another garment that Jackson liked to see his friend wear were his blue gym shorts with the school logo from Saint Matthew school. These shorts had "Jordan Chandler" printed on the left leg, next to the school logo. They were also among Jackson's favourite to take off.[603]

It is the detail of Gutierrez' account that is so compelling. We see photos of the inside of the boy's bedroom, photos of Jordie and his half-brother in earlier years, a photo of Michael in pyjamas ready for bed in Jordie's bedroom, even photos of Jordie's underwear. We have not heard Michael's lawyers or aides rushing to say all these photos are fakes. Even when Jordie was taken to Dr Abrams, Gutierrez tells us, he told the doctor about how much fun he had had with Jackson, and that he did not feel abused since he had of his own free will participated in all their sexual relations. He said that on many occasions he initiated the sex himself. To characterise the relationship as merely sexual would also be misleading. It went deeper than just fun and games too, as Jordie told a friend three years later:

> "It wasn't the games we played or the expensive presents. It was the attention and love we received from Jackson," declared Jordie to a close friend. "On many occasions I tried to tell the therapist and the authorities that Michael never made me do anything I didn't want to but the authorities had told me that Michael had seduced me by buying toys and expensive presents. Michael did more than buy me presents. The attention and love he gave me was amazing. He always worried with details. He spent time with me. I was an important part of his life, a man that was so busy."
>
> "Why is it so difficult for the people to understand that I like Michael. If one is in love with a school girl or a friend, everyone is happy and says it's so wonderful, but when I say I like Michael, people don't want to listen. I am sixteen years old and I know what has happened. I think people are bothered by homosexual relationships but I'm not a homosexual. I just feel an attraction towards Michael and I had sex with him. My friends and professors have told me that it's normal for a boy to be attracted to other children or adults. It happened to me. But if people don't want to listen it is another thing."[604]

So, even three years after the affair, at age sixteen, it appears Jordie was still not saying how right his father was to end things. That bold prediction of Evan's, "One day you'll thank me", could not have been more mistaken. As for "making" Jordie homosexual, it is clearly not what he is saying here. Also, his relationship with Sonnet Simmons proved more enduring than a good many marriages. Described as his "long-term girlfriend", Sonnet spent Easter 2005 on a skiing holiday with Jordie in the Californian resort of Tahoe.[605] Another of Michael's boys, Jonathan Spence, talked to Gutierrez. He said the singer had been a profoundly positive influence in his life. Jonathan too has well established heterosexual credentials: he was living with his girlfriend when Gutierrez interviewed him.

The Gutierrez account, as we have seen, is fiercely contested. We know he has immense detail and documentation to support his case but the niggling possibility remains that the man is a chancer, ready to peddle a line spun for a particular market. In the introduction to his book he said that what he was discovering was confusing to him. Having approached the case as a crime he found himself "not knowing whether to refer to the boys as victims or ex-lovers". His eventual title, *Michael Jackson Was My Lover* shows how the cookie finally crumbled. His information would make a hot book, but who would want to hear about Michael as a "lover" of boys? Why, other boy-lovers of course. His book concludes with sympathetic information on boy-love, including material garnered from the North American Man Boy Love Association (NAMBLA). While this has my enthusiastic approval – minority voices in this field such as NAMBLA deserve a fair media airing but seldom get one – I am conscious of the need to take account of *all* informed sources.

The books by Ray Chandler and Victor Gutierrez are by far the most important. But there is one further account that arguably trumps both. This is a tape recording of an interview with Jordie in October 1993, two months after his official allegations hit the headlines. The interview was with a psychiatrist, Dr Richard Gardner, who had been consulted on the advice of Larry Feldman, Jordie's lawyer in the civil case against Jackson. Feldman had seen Gardner as the ideal figure to buttress Jordie's claims in court because he was a noted expert in false sexual abuse claims: if even this professional sceptic failed to smell a rat, it was reasoned, a jury could hardly fail to believe the boy.[606]

The case was in particular need of an expert in false abuse claims because of a story that Evan had "planted" sexual molestation in Jordie's subconscious while the boy was under the influence of anaesthesia. An article in *GQ* magazine by Mary Fischer in October 1994 claimed "the controversial drug sodium Amytal" had been administered to Jordie before his confession following a tooth extraction.[607] Amytal is a trade name; the generic name is amobarbital. This drug is known to induce suggestibility.[608] The article was hugely influential among Michael Jackson fans desperate to believe their idol was innocent. However, in her book *Be Careful Who You Love*, Diane Dimond attests to information from several sources that Amytal was *not* used. Anaesthetist Dr Mark Torbiner had been present that day (but had left before Jordie's confession). According to his own records from 16 July 1993, says Dimond, Torbiner gave the boy a combination of Robinul and Vistaril; he made no reference to Amytal. Even more significantly,

Fischer later had "a change of heart" about her own article, according to information supplied in 2004 by Ray Chandler.[609]

Dimond also cites Ray Chandler: "If my brother or someone put this story in my nephew's head, then where did all the details come from? Evan didn't know what Michael Jackson's penis looked like – but Jordie did."

As with the Schwartz-Chandler tape, the full text of the Gardner tape was presented not in Ray Chandler's book but as part of a package of documents he made available over the internet. Not unnaturally, I read Chandler's book first and looked at the supporting documents later. It would have been easy to have fallen into the trap of concluding that the Gardner tape was merely an unimportant rehash of the key interview with the first psychiatrist in Jordie's life, Dr Mathis Abrams.

The first half of the interview is indeed pretty much a rehash of Jordie's official complaint, with the addition that on about ten occasions Michael "had me masturbate him". Note the "had me". Significantly, he indicates that this was at Michael's request, not his own. It is a straw in the wind. The second part of the interview is much more revealing with regard to the issue that concerns us in this chapter: Michael's proper or improper use of his power. At first sight what Jordie has to say is utterly damning. We pick up the threads just after Jordie has admitted he was defiant towards his father. The boy wanted to go on tour with Michael when Evan was opposed to the idea:

> GARDNER: You still wanted to go on the tour?
> JORDAN: Yes, at the time.
> GARDNER: Why is that?
> JORDAN: Because I was having fun. At the time, the things Michael was doing to me, they didn't affect me. Like, I didn't think anything was totally wrong with what he was doing since he was my friend, and he kept on telling me that he would never hurt me. But presently I see that he was obviously lying.
> GARDNER: You're saying you didn't realize it could hurt you? Is that what you're –
> JORDAN: I didn't see anything wrong with it.
> GARDNER: Do you see the wrong in it now?
> JORDAN: Of course.
> GARDNER: What is wrong as you see it?
> JORDAN: Because he's a grown-up and he's using his experience, of his age

in manipulating and coercing younger people who don't have as much experience as him, and don't have the ability to say no to someone powerful like that. He's using his power, his experience, his age – his overwhelmingness – to get what he wants.

Bad enough? It gets worse.

GARDNER: Did he say he loved you?
JORDAN: Mmm-hmm.
GARDNER: You know how you look at a romantic movie sometimes and you see the man and the woman, and the man says how much he loves the woman, how much he adores her and praises her. You know about that?
JORDAN: Yeah.
GARDNER: Would you say that was the way Michael was with you?
JORDAN: Like, it was sort of like a weird kind of love. Like, it was like that but he, he loved me selfishly. Like, regardless of the fact that what he was doing might hurt me, he continued.
GARDNER: When you say it could have hurt you, how could it have hurt you?"
JORDAN: Everybody thinks what he was doing could hurt; otherwise, it wouldn't be a crime.
GARDNER: Okay, how could it hurt? As you see it, how could it hurt you?
JORDAN: Because – that's a touchy subject, I guess. It separates you from any other people.
GARDNER: How?
JORDAN: I don't know.
GARDNER: Just your own guess.
JORDAN: It could make me depressed or something, I don't know.
GARDNER: Well, this is important. You say it's a crime. Why is it a crime?
JORDAN: Because, like I said before, he's using his experience, power, age–
GARDNER: How could this have left you? If this had gone on and not been interrupted, how could you have ended up?
JORDAN: According to his pattern, I believe he would have left me and, sort of dumped me, I guess you could call it. And I would be, sort of, a vegetable.
GARDNER: Why a vegetable?
JORDAN: Because he would continue to do those things and I would have no knowing of what else is out there.
GARDNER: Say that again. You wouldn't know what else is out there?

JORDAN: Right. Like, he didn't like it if I would want to call a girl or something. You know, I wouldn't know, like, there were other options.
GARDNER: Are you saying that he would pull you off the track of going out with girls.
JORDAN: Right.
GARDNER: What would you say is the best thing that ever happened to you in your whole life?
JORDAN: When I told my dad what Michael was doing to me.
GARDNER: Why do you say that?
JORDAN: Because once I told him, I knew that Michael would never be able to do that to me again.

For most followers of Fox News or Britain's *Sun* newspaper, this would be all they need to know. For them, it would now be crystal clear from the Gardner tape not just that there had been sex between man and boy, but also that Michael had grossly abused his power in a potentially devastating way. Readers of this book may be a little less certain. Those who have patiently followed me this far will know that first appearances can be deceptive and that texts need careful consideration.

The first snippet above ends with a speech from Jordan so articulate, eloquent and damning it could have come from the mouth of a prosecuting lawyer – or a lawyer aiming for a multi-million dollar payoff such as Jordie would win before the next month was over. We do not need to be particularly cynical to suspect that Jordie had been hearing a lot from his father and his lawyer in the weeks before this interview about Jackson "manipulating and coercing younger people". Smart as Jordie undoubtedly was, one has to doubt that such vocabulary would have tripped off his tongue so readily without coaching. He knew what he needed to say in order to win the civil case.

The second snippet is far more revealing, though, because Gardner's probing questions push Jordie onto the ropes. We now see him hard put to deliver the words his coach would have liked. When Gardner asked what harm Michael's actions were doing he replies, "Everybody thinks what he was doing could hurt, otherwise it wouldn't be a crime." In other words, Jordie is hard pressed to come up with any harm that Michael's behaviour had *actually* done to *him*. Instead he is forced to surmise that "everybody" must be right – especially his father and lawyer, who were doubtless not slow to tell him what "everybody" thinks.

Pressed further on how he personally could have been hurt, Jordie says it is "a touchy subject, I guess. It separates you from any other people". Jordie had good reason to feel it was a touchy subject: it had been the focus of a battle with his father, running for many weeks throughout the summer, a battle his dad won, as we have seen, by threats, lies and betraying his son's friend. The irony of the situation comes out in that word "touchy": it is ironic indeed that Jordie has been manoeuvred into complaining that Michael's behaviour "separates you from any other people", when Evan's actions had forcibly separated him from his grown-up friend and lover. When Gardner presses him even further, Jordie says the relationship *could have* made him depressed or "a vegetable". *Could have*. It had not actually done so, but it *could have*. He also says it could have turned him away from girls. This too was no more than speculative. Far from saying his interest in girls had waned since meeting Jackson, in another part of the interview he unequivocally expresses enthusiasm for the opposite sex. This does not preclude some homosexual interest, about which he may understandably have been less than frank, but what we definitely do not hear is any claim that Michael has made him gay. The anxieties he expresses are all mere speculations based on what he would have been hearing from his father and lawyer. There is nothing at all in this part of Jordie's interview to show that he had *actually* been harmed or to demonstrate convincingly that Michael's alleged abuse of his power presented definite dangers. Does this mean Michael is off the hook? Not entirely, as this final snippet illustrates:

> GARDNER: But are you saying through all of this, although you enjoyed it, you felt a sense of pressure?
> JORDAN: Yeah.
> GARDNER: Was it a big heavy on you? Do you know what –
> JORDAN: Yeah.
> GARDNER: Could you describe –
> JORDAN: Like, I couldn't be open with how I felt. Like if I didn't want to do something I couldn't just say "I don't want to do that" because he would start crying or whatever. He wouldn't just say '"Okay, whatever, we'll just be friends and play video games.'" He'd start crying and do everything in his power to convince me that –
> GARDNER: But you voluntarily went back there. You could have said, I don't want to go up to Neverland again, right?
> JORDAN: Yeah.
> GARDNER: So why did you go back?

> JORDAN: Because regardless of the fact that I went to Neverland, he would be with me. No matter what, he was always with me. It was like, I couldn't just say I don't want to hang out with you today.
> GARDNER: Why not?
> JORDAN: It's not that easy. He would cry. He would say "You don't love me anymore." It would be, like a whole deal, you know, it was hard.

It's a slippery concept, isn't it, this "adult power" business? In this passage Jordie's complaint is clearly a genuine one. When he says he was under pressure from Michael the allegation rings true. It is not just some vague possibility of future harm that has been dinned into him by his minders. But the power Jackson used to control Jordie is quite unlike the dominance we usually associate with adults over children. His "power" as described by Jordie is not that of a stern pater familias. It is not a power rooted in physical strength and the potential for exercising disciplinary sanctions. On the contrary, his "power", if we can call it that, is expressed through tears and pleading. It is the kind of "power" more usually associated with women, or indeed children. It is the "power" of the ostensibly powerless.

Unlike the tears of the truly powerless, however, Michael's appeared seldom to be shed in vain. He would get his way. He used tears to his advantage in his business dealings. In that world his lachrymose leanings delivered the goods – or used to at the height of his musical success – because big money turned on keeping him happy. When he was happy, contracts would get signed, records produced, people employed, money made. In his dealings with boys and their families there was also an acquisitive dimension. For the children and their parents alike there was the prospect of exotic travel and expensive gifts. For the boys, especially, keeping Michael sweet was once (until scandal struck) a passport to glamour and esteem among their peers that could scarcely have been achieved in any other way.

There was pressure, certainly. Jordie's complaint that he was never given any breathing space in the relationship, that Michael was in his face the whole time, is horribly likely to be entirely true. Michael appeared to be a serial offender in this respect. Even those who make no allegation of sexual abuse bear witness to the fact that his social relationships tended to be overwhelming in their intensity. A typical complaint was from a family featured in a British TV documentary in January 2005 called *Michael Jackson's Boys*[610] Introduced only as "Damien", the young man in question was said to have been "Michael's boy" from 1985-90. When aged nine, he had met Michael after sending him a poem.

Damien said Michael used to stay in the spare room at the family's home in Orange County, California. He said bedtimes had to be organised around Michael's preferences. Also: "Our whole family catered to him...He had his breathing exercises. He has to take a certain pill at a certain time...I mean, the whole thing, it was the Michael Jackson show." Michael spent endless hours offloading the troubles of his early life in long phone calls night and day to his mother. When his father became suspicious he started taping the calls, extracts of which were played. Then Michael suddenly stopped calling. Damien found it "difficult to accept that", as though the family suddenly counted for nothing.

The bottom line, though, is that parents did not lack the power to tell Michael where to get off; nor did the boys. Nobody was going to be drowned in the lake at Neverland for failing to obey him. The worst that could happen was falling from favour. If parents – or boys – wanted to go on seeing him despite the pressure, that was a matter for them. They were entirely free to choose whether on balance the benefits of being Michael's friend were outweighed by the downside.

We should also remember that long-lasting positive feelings about Michael have been voiced by many of his young friends after they have passed into adulthood. These include well-known figures such as actors Emmanuel Lewis and Macaulay Culkin, people in no way dependent on the star's favours. It is absurd to paint these men, stars in their own right, as victims of an adult's abuse of his power. Talk of manipulation, coercion and power abuse just evaporates in the face of their long-term loyalty.

In the Chandler case, it is a moot point who was the more manipulative and abusive, Michael or the boy's father, Evan. As we have seen, Evan had reason to feel humiliated and excluded from his son's life. Jackson abused his power by gross manipulation of the Chandler and Schwarz families, a fact which would have made any self-respecting parent angry. Gutierrez does not accuse Evan of extortion but we may agree with this author, rather than with Ray Chandler, as to his less than squeaky clean motives.

> Jackson's sexual conduct with Jordie was not the error that brought Jackson down. His error was underestimating Evan, who turned out to be a vocal and aggressive negotiator, in contrast to the other parents who acquiesced, exchanging silence for houses, luxury vehicles and a few hundred thousand

dollars. If only early on he had offered Evan a small project, plus a few thousand dollars, Evan would have given in, and he would have overlooked the sex between Jackson and his son... [611]

Almost exactly a year after the civil settlement with Jackson, it was being reported that Jordie wanted to see Michael again, to talk things through. It was suggested that friends and relatives were astounded by how unscathed Jordie had been as a result of his time with Michael. Wrote Millicent Brown, "...the reality is that he probably enjoyed the attention lavished upon him by the superstar. He is thought to have been extremely fond of the man who transported him into a fantasy world but whose behaviour eventually overstepped the mark". Jordie reportedly said: "People don't understand how it was".[612]

Just a couple of months after this, in March 1995, we were to hear that Jordie had been "dumped by his dad in a bizarre divorce deal". Under the terms of the deal, Evan would live alone but would be able to claim for income tax purposes that Jordie was living with him. As the report puts it, Jordie now knows how his father views him: "As a handy tax perk".[613] His separation from his father hardly suggests a young man who was in the end grateful for having been forcibly parted from his friend Michael. Jordie would instead live with his step-mother, who would send Evan the bills for his upkeep. But: "It has already been revealed that all he does with these expenses is forward the receipts to Jackson for reimbursement".

A few months later, in July, news surfaced of a move by Jordie to "divorce" his family! He wanted a parting of the ways because "they only love him for his money". Diane Albright's story for *Globe* said that the boy told a friend his father and stepmother were blowing his cash on lavish vacations and home renovations. Jordie was said to have asked his lawyers to prepare papers for a Petition for Emancipation. Shortly after the settlement with Jackson, Evan quit his dental practice. Jordie's stepmother also resigned from her job as a lawyer. According to this version it was Jordie, not Jackson, who was picking up the tab for the family expenses:

> Besides their trips, his stepmother is renovating her home and charging it to his trust account. But the only part of the house that isn't being redone is the boy's bedroom! If he wants a haircut, he has to ask his stepmom or his dad for money. But his father, who lives in an apartment a few blocks away, says he cuts his son's hair himself to save money. There are times when the boy

wants to buy some clothes, like Beavis and Butthead shirts or shorts. He's been told he'll have to take that out of his pocket money, but he says he doesn't have any money of his own – it's all in his trust account.

For his birthday, he wasn't even allowed to invite anyone over to celebrate. He was told they didn't want to invite strangers into the house for his own protection. His father stopped in for a short visit and gave him a pocket knife. Instead of a cake, he was given five special cookies on a paper plate with a few candles on top. No party, no friends, no family gathering, no happy birthday song. He said it was one of the saddest days of his life.

In the time since charges were filed against Michael Jackson, the boy's life has been hell. He suffers from depression and spends hours on end in his bedroom with the door closed, the curtains closed and the lights off. He sits there alone and no-one comes in to ask him if he's all right, how he's doing or if he wants to talk. He says he misses Michael. He says he was supposed to undergo therapy after the molestation charges were filed, but now he says leaving his family might be the best therapy. Then maybe he could find a family who would love him just for himself – instead of for his money.[614]

Now it has to be said that *Globe* is not the most authoritative of sources, even among tabloids, but the Petition for Emancipation was no fantasy. It is mentioned, in precisely those terms, in a letter to Jordie dated 13 June 1995 from Patricia Phillips of the law firm Morrison & Foerster, Los Angeles: a facsimile appears in Guttierez' book.

A rather different slant made its way into the 16 June cover story of *Entertainment Weekly*. The magazine featured an interview with Evan Chandler's brother Raymond, under the earlier version of his name, Ray Charmatz. He is quoted in a way that gives the impression of a *united* family. And if that seems strange in view of strong evidence to the contrary, he was also claiming the Chandlers were united in their feelings about Michael Jackson. Now they had stopped *fighting* him they were all *for* him! The family harboured no resentment, quite the reverse. Says Ray: "They – Evan, Jordie and family – all loved him. That was why it was so hard to come to grips with what was going on. It's too bad to see his career take the hit it did and we hope he gets it back. They don't hold any malice in their hearts toward Michael. I think they understand what's happened in his life, and how he's an even bigger victim of abuse."[615]

While there is a strong case for saying that Jordie held no malice towards Michael, the claim for family unity is quite another matter. The rift between Jordie and his family reportedly remained as wide as ever many years later. In February 2003, when Michael was again at the centre of a media storm, over his close friendship with another boy, the *Sunday Mirror* ran a story saying Jordie was by now living alone in New York. In a story quoting Victor Gutierrez and another of Jordie's uncles, Lawrence Charmatz, who was also said to live in New York, it was claimed that the family had lost contact with Jordie years ago. He had "lost touch" with his father as well as having no contact with his mother or step-father.[616]

By March 2005, Michael's new boy troubles were no longer just a media storm. By this time the star was on trial for sexual molestation. It was an opportunity for Jordie to seek "justice" against Michael had he wished to do so. The terms of the multi-million dollar pay-off he had received from Michael prevented him from speaking publicly about his abuse allegations but a court subpoena to appear as a prosecution witness to Jackson's past behaviour with boys would have been the perfect excuse to do so: as a witness, Jordie would have been able to speak openly. It is inconceivable that any court would have supported Jackson if he had sued for breach of contract in such circumstances. But when the prospect of being served with just such a subpoena drew near, young Mr Chandler showed himself absolutely determined *not* to go into the witness box against his old friend: he made himself scarce by going to live abroad for the duration of the trial.[617]

According to Diane Dimond, "several sources close to him" told her, "He believed it was the adults around him who had created this particular hell so many years ago. Now that the matter had finally made it into court, he felt it was those same adults who should speak – not him." So much for Jordie thanking his dad one day for betraying his friend, Michael.[618]

All this softens the case against Michael. The most relevant charge against him so far as this volume is concerned is not how he may have abused his power over his staff, or boys' parents, or in any other way except one: his effect on any children with whom he had sexual liaisons. The boy's judgment, as we have seen, is more complex than first meets the eye. In the immediate wake of the affair, under heavy pressure from his father to portray Michael in a bad light, he says things to Dr Gardner which appear to be utterly damning. But reading between the lines, we can see he is "spinning" his account to fit in with typical child abuse preconceptions being force-fed to him at the time. Even the facts may have been subtly adjusted to look good. Thus instead of "I masturbated Michael" (the item in his father's notes against which he placed a question mark), in the Gardner interview we hear that Michael "had me masturbate him".

Jordie also said in the Gardner interview that until he met Michael he had never masturbated. There is no particular reason to disbelieve him, except that the overwhelming majority of boys his age do masturbate. Much less credibly, Jordie claims that despite the good feeling he learned he could get from masturbation, he stopped doing it soon after the affair with Michael stopped. Why? It is not as though his father was giving him heavy messages over this. Nobody was telling him masturbation is a sin or it would make him go blind. Jordie was just beginning at this time to take an interest in girls but he had not yet been anywhere near to "scoring" in bed. In such circumstances, stimulated by sexual interests but having no outlet for them, it seems extremely unlikely a teenage boy would stop masturbating, just like that. He does not even offer Gardner any explanation. He says nothing about believing masturbation is unhealthy or wrong. It is unlikely, to put it mildly, that he is telling the truth at this point – another small indication that although we have no reason to doubt his candour in general, there are specifics where his account may not be the gospel truth.

Bearing in mind the evidence that Jordie later missed Michael, it is far from clear his long-term view is antagonistic. By 2003, as we have seen, Jordie was reported to be living alone in New York. He was said to be living in a 35th-floor high-security apartment in a luxury block near Broadway and had graduated from New York University's Stern School of Business.[619] Significantly, we heard that he was no longer in contact with his parents. He had not seen for years the father who "saved" him from Michael Jackson. Evan, remember, once said "some day when he gets older he'll thank me". But how thankful could Jordie be, if he cut his father right out of his life?

The story turned out to be only partly true, however. It would be testified in court in 2005 that Jordie was indeed estranged from his mother but the position concerning his father is more complicated, as will shortly become plain as a pikestaff – or, rather, as plain as certain other weapons.

It would, of course, be helpful if writers could ask Jordie directly as to how he feels now about his father, Michael and the whole affair. This is not as easy as it might sound. The authorities could not persuade or coerce him into the witness box and he has been silent as a Trappist monk at other times. An interview with Jordan Chandler has become the Holy Grail of Jacksonology. Dimond, as we have just seen, managed only to get "several sources close to him", rather than Jordie himself – and whether these were any closer than his lawyer's second cousin is anybody's guess. Even Jordie's uncle, Raymond Chandler, has not spoken to him for years.

While this book is essentially a work of analysis and interpretation, and makes no pretence to insider knowledge or investigative foot slogging, I did find myself sufficiently curious and frustrated over this one key matter as to pursue it a little way beyond the publicly available texts. To this end, I wrote to Jordan Chandler through Patricia Phillips, of Morrison & Foerster. She claimed to be unable to forward my letter as he was no longer a client. I also engaged in a substantial series of emails with Ray Chandler and a shorter exchange with Victor Gutierrez.

These were interesting "conversations" even though they both ended acrimoniously. While conceding my approach appeared "intelligent, and I respect that", Ray became increasingly annoyed by my sceptical disinclination to accept his answers at face value. In the absence of any killer evidence as to his nephew's present views, he was reduced to saying "I bet you" Jordie would agree his father had done the right thing. When I replied, "Why do we need to bet? Why can't you just pick up a phone and talk to Jordie?" he declined – or was unable – to take up the challenge. At that point he refused to take our emails any further, complaining that for any answer he could give I would just shoot back more questions. He had a point.

As for Victor, I told him about my book and offered him the opportunity to put the record straight over the disastrous "video sex" episode. He could only do that, of course, if he had a plausible explanation, perhaps along the lines I have already suggested above. If I could make progress in that direction, it seemed within the bounds of possibility to tease out of him how close he had been to Jordie, and whether the pair of them still had lines of communication. At first he blustered, saying "I don't need to set any record straight. I have no concerns about a law suit. I got several of those, for me lawsuits are medals". He asked how he could help, but after a couple more exchanges it looked as though no explanation of the video would be forthcoming. At this point I thanked him but warned that "Your silence makes it impossible for me, and by extension my readers, to sustain the belief that the infamous video ever existed. Inevitably, therefore, you are making it impossible for me to cite you as a reliable source on the Chandler affair or anything else." This provoked an angry diatribe accusing me of threatening him – but still giving no explanation whatever for the video. Was my warning really a threat? Does Gutierrez have any credibility? Readers may draw their own conclusions.

Unfortunately, therefore, neither of these contacts took me any nearer to Jordie Chandler. Some time after these exchanges of mine with Ray Chandler and Victor Gutierrez, Evan and Jordie were briefly in the spotlight again for an intriguing reason that served to thicken the plot rather than resolve it.

They were in court again in 2006 – this time against each other, after Evan had allegedly physically attacked his son the previous year. Jordan had filed a restraining order against his father on 5 August, 2005. The reason for the order was that Evan had allegedly hit Jordan over the head from behind with a twelve and a half pound weight. He had also allegedly sprayed him in the face with mace and tried to choke him.

According to a report by Roger Friedman, court papers indicated that, far from not having seen each other in years, the two were living together in a luxury apartment in New Jersey with panoramic views of Manhattan. Friedman said the case had been remanded to trial by a pair of appellate judges on 8 June 2006. This followed a reversal of the restraining order by another judge who felt that Evan Chandler's actions did not represent a pattern of abuse and did not qualify as domestic abuse. The appellate judges disagreed, reinstated the restraining order, and sent the case to trial. At the present time of writing no further developments in the case appear to have surfaced publicly.[620]

Expressing surprise that the restraining order had ever been lifted, the appellate judges noted that the heavy weight, mentioned in some reports as a dumbbell, could have caused serious bodily injury or death, and that it looked as though Evan Chandler had truly intended to harm his son.

Before taking the New Jersey apartment, father and son had owned a beach house in Westhampton, New York, and had had an apartment in New York. According to Friedman, public records showed that Jordie sold the beach house for $2.9 million in 2003. He bought a condo for $775,000 in West Harlem in June 2005, one week after Michael was acquitted of child molestation and about six weeks before he accused his father of attacking him. At the time he purchased the condo, Jordie gave a PO Box in Jersey City as his address. "It's only conjecture," wrote Friedman, "but it's likely that Evan Chandler – whom his brother Raymond had said in interviews was seriously ill in 2005 – didn't want his son to leave him." It will be recalled that Evan suffers from Gaucher's Disease.

Jordan Chandler's Wikipedia entry opines that Evan got mad with his son when the young man "bought the wrong bread".[621] At all events, it does not look as though their odd-couple relationship has improved much over the years. I find myself surmising that Jordie only ever stayed with his pop purely from a sense of duty in view of his illness. As Jordie is much wealthier than his father it can hardly be the prospect of inheriting his dad's money that has kept him under the same roof in difficult and dangerous circumstances. Perhaps one day we will be afforded deeper insights, possibly as a result of further revelations in court. For the moment, though, we have only conjecture, opinion and surmise.

This chapter began with just one question. In his ground-breaking research, Dr Theo Sandfort put the child's perception at centre stage. He asked: "Can a boy experience sex with an adult positively?" In addressing that question he studied the effects on twenty five boys aged ten to sixteen involved in a current sexual relationship with a man. The results he came up with were astonishingly positive. Even the supposedly damning issue of adults abusing their power evaporated in the face of the evidence. We have confined our attention to a detailed study of Michael's relationship with just one boy in his life, Jordie Chandler. There can be little doubt that if Jordie had been interviewed by Sandfort in May 1993, before the boy's father had intervened to break up the relationship, Jordie too would have had nothing but good to say about Michael. He was enjoying life, the sex was fun, everyone around Jordie – even his father – saw a boy sparkling with wit, popular at school, not in the least troubled or traumatised. This being the case, how fair can it really be to speak of Jackson abusing his power? The more nuanced and in some ways negative view that emerges later appears largely to have come about – as is so often the case – as a result of matters reaching the authorities following the precipitate behaviour of a parent.

It is time now to shift our focus, but to remain with "power". The analysis of Jackson's "abuse" of power is not exhausted. We have dealt with the supremely important child's point of view in the case of Jordie Chandler from many angles, using all the key sources available. What remains to be considered is our own feelings: why parents like Evan, and district attorneys like Tom Sneddon, feel the need to go charging in like the proverbial bull in a china shop, causing trauma instead of preventing it. We need to look at Michael's supposed abuse of power as it is refracted through our own sentiments, to see whether those strongly felt emotions are really justified. This will be the subject of the next chapter.

CHAPTER TWELVE

Society's Power: The Rage of the Lynch Mob

The two preceding chapters have each separately examined a single major aspect of the power Michael Jackson potentially wielded in relation to his contacts with boys. The first of these focused on his power to control other adults through his wealth and fame, including the ability to silence parents and staff who might have wanted to blow the whistle on him. The second examined in detail the power dynamics of one particular relationship with a boy, Jordan Chandler. Theoretical concerns were introduced, notably Theo Sandfort's studies of how power makes itself felt at the personal level between adults and children in sexual contacts. But for the most part these chapters were about probing the relevant facts of Jackson's life. It is now time, in this third and concluding chapter on the power theme, to stand back a little so we can see the bigger picture – one in which our own attitudes come into the frame and are brought under critical scrutiny.

Those attitudes are widely reflected in the news media. One detail of the Chandler case seized on throughout the media, from trashy supermarket tabloids to posh broadsheets and sober broadcasting corporations, was the pressure Michael had allegedly put on Jordie to keep silent about their sexual relationship. He was said to have threatened Jordie that letting the cat out of the bag could have dire consequences: he might end up in juvenile hall (young offenders' institution). Typically, this was presented as a news item in stark, unexamined terms, as though the "threat" to Jordie spoke for itself. What it said by implication was that Jackson had used improper pressure on Jordie to keep silent. He had lied to him by suggesting that in the event of disclosure Jordie would be regarded by the authorities as a joint participant in a crime and would be punished accordingly.

Much is made, these days, of the view that children involved in sexual acts with adults are always to be regarded as victims of a crime, not criminals themselves. And it is true that there was never any question of Jordie being sent to juvenile hall. If Michael said that, he was either mistaken or telling a deliberate untruth.[622] But what went unexamined in the media was that this was a lie with a great deal of truth in it: youngsters who refuse to complain in circumstances of suspicion tend to be treated like offenders by police and social workers. They are questioned and questioned until they stop giving "dumb" answers, a horror perpetrated on even very young children in the notorious McMartin pre-school case. Older minors, such as Jordie, are routinely treated as corrupted participants who must be coerced to "confess". In the US it is not unknown for juveniles to find themselves facing criminal charges for entirely consensual sex with each other, as in the 2002 Pensacola, Florida, case, when two boys and two girls all aged eleven and twelve found themselves charged with "committing a lewd and lascivious act on a child", despite all being children themselves.[623]

What the news media and the public at large never stopped to consider (judging by the absence of any debate I have been able to detect), was that Michael's warning could be considered an entirely sensible precaution, not just for himself but for Jordie too. Let's illustrate this from a different context, that of a French resistance fighter under the Nazi occupation. What would we expect such a fighter to tell his son if the boy discovered guns or explosives secreted in the house? He would be crazy not to warn the boy how vital it was not to mention these armaments to anyone, and certainly not to German soldiers. Alter the context slightly and the moral judgment shifts again: what if the "freedom fighter" is a Palestinian or Iraqi "terrorist", and the soldiers are Israeli or American? My point here is not to defend terrorist acts but to establish that the moral status of many acts depends critically on context.

To those who believe there is nothing intrinsically wrong in loving intimacy between partners of any age, being careful to keep their relationship from the harm a hostile outside world could inflict simply makes sense. Another analogy would be with religion in times of persecution. In the era of the Spanish Inquisition, Jews were forced to convert to Christianity but often kept up their Jewish faith and rituals in private – practices which made it vital to ensure their children could keep a secret. No one today would accuse such parents of "threatening" their children with being tortured by the Inquisition or being burned at the stake. The fear that any indiscretion could have terrible consequences was all too real, but we would think it absurd to blame the parents. To us it is clear the moral responsibility lay with the Catholic Church.

Those who allege misuse of power in situations such as Michael's see children as typically under the adult's thumb, but the "juvenile hall" incident illustrates no such thing. Jordie's interview with psychiatrist Dr Richard Gardner shows that only a few months after his initial statement to the authorities his recollections were already somewhat foggy. Here is how the discussion went:

> GARDNER: By the way, going back, did he say, "It's a secret"?
> JORDAN: Michael?
> GARDNER: Yeah. In terms of did he make any threats?
> JORDAN: I think he may have said, like, if you tell – if people say "Don't worry, just tell us, Michael will go to jail and nothing will happen to you." He said that wasn't true, and I could, like, go to juvenile hall or something.
> GARDNER: That he could go to jail but you'd go to juvenile hall?
> JORDAN: Something like that.
> GARDNER: That he himself could go to jail?
> JORDAN: I don't specifically remember. I'm almost positive though, that he said about juvenile hall. I'm almost positive he said that, but I do indeed remember that he said that he would go to jail, and that, like, I wouldn't get off scot-free.
> GARDNER: Did you believe that?
> JORDAN: Well, I didn't really believe it at the time, and I definitely don't now. But at the time I didn't really believe it but I said, okay, whatever, and just went along with it.

Thus we see that it was Gardner, not Jordie, who raised the issue of secrecy. It was plainly not an issue that had been troubling the boy. Contrary to the sensational way the alleged "threat" played in the media, Michael had not given him a heavy trip and he had not even found the warnings particularly persuasive or memorable. The whole thing was no big deal.

From Juvenile Hall to Liberty Hall. We have heard that a number of boys were left with happy memories of Michael because he gave them a lot of time and attention they did not get at home, as well as physical affection. Neverland was also a place where the strict rules of conduct insisted on by many parents were suspended. As Jordie told Dr Gardner, Michael liked kids to feel they were the ones in charge at his home: "Neverland was a place where kids had the right-of-way, on the roads, had the dominance, sort of. Could have what you want when you want it." Such an atmosphere of freedom, fun, and having "the dominance" could hardly fail to appeal to kids. Just as predictably, grown-ups everywhere would be bound to disapprove. Their instinctive reaction is that kids need to keep kept on a tight rein, not taking part in Michael's famous food fights and generally being allowed to "run wild".

In the 2005 trial we heard much of boys being plied with alcohol to soften them up for sex and left to run wild on the ranch. This was never part of Jordie's allegations but Gutierrez has plenty to say on the subject of drink. Kassim Abdool, one of Michael's security guards, is reported as saying a bar was put at the disposal of kids. Three guards, including Abdool, remembered one day when this resulted in a fire:

> The boys were extremely drunk that afternoon, and were throwing lit matches into the room's fireplace. The gas was turned on full force, but was not lit. The boys were having a contest to see who could light it first. As they were drunk, they of course did not realize the consequences of their little game. An explosion caused the room to go ablaze. One of the firefighters, who was also a guard at the ranch, received third degree burns on his body. When Jackson later saw what had occurred, as he was in another part of the ranch with another minor, he asked who was to blame. When the boys told him that it had been them because they were playing the game out of boredom, Michael never said a harsh word to them. "I won't accuse you, and you don't accuse me." It was a "gentlemen's agreement".[624]

If it is true, it is terrible. People die in gas explosions and fires. In this case a firefighter was seriously hurt. Third degree burns are the worst kind. This means the skin is burnt through all its layers; typically in such cases a skin graft is required. To allow such a thing to happen through kids being drunk would be criminally irresponsible. This is not a sexual offence but it is an issue which touches upon Jackson's power and his abuse thereof. As such it represents a curious inversion of the usual case of the power argument made against paedophiles. The classic argument derived from the feminist critique of "patriarchy" is that adult male control over society and all its institutions, including the family, allows them to dominate and abuse women and children.

But in Neverland we see a place where, in Jordie's words, children have "the dominance". The problem was not that Michael threatened any of the boys. Far from ruling over them with an iron fist, he appears to have allowed anarchy to reign. Rather than being *too* controlling, he was not *sufficiently* in control. By all means, if the facts turn out to be true, we should be content to let this stand as a very severe criticism of Michael. My purpose in this book is not to praise him but to illuminate the moral issues engaged by paedophilia through his very public life. All I would say here is that those whose knee-jerk reaction is to blast paedophiles as domineering control freaks and power abusers are just plain wrong. What anarchy in Neverland illustrates is that adult authority can itself be subverted when the grown-up in question is too desperate to be popular with kids. In a society more accepting of child-love there would be less desperation and a more sensible balance could be struck. In ancient Greece, the adult male at his best was able to be a lover *and* a mentor, a role model who set proper standards of behaviour through his own example. At his worst he may well have been the domineering swine of feminist orthodoxy. We should seek not an impossible return to those days but rather a society in which (socially and sexually) loving adults are respected to the extent which they play a positive role in a child's life.

The fact that Michael's power did not make him a coercive bully towards boys should be obvious by now to readers of this book. Only the flat-earthers of last-generation, bra-burning, feminist dogma could fail to take the point. For me, it is established beyond doubt by an incident captured on a store's security camera tape when Michael was shopping with a boy after closing hours at New York's FAO Schwartz toy shop two days before Christmas 1989. The scene is described in Christopher Andersen's biography, *Michael Jackson Unauthorized*:

> That night, an unidentified boy in a baseball cap was being shown a $1-million-solid-gold Monopoly set by an assistant when Michael put his arm around him to leave. The boy shoved Michael away roughly and continued looking at the Monopoly set. After viewing the tape, psychologist Joyce

Brothers observed that in that outburst of temper, they were displaying a significant degree of intimacy – "Here's a little boy with real power in the relationship," she said. "He is not in awe of the superstar. There is more on the scale than meets the eye."[625]

What appears to have happened in Michael's case is that he was carried away by a romantic dream of childhood freedom. His own famously harsh upbringing, with its constant regimen of musical practising and performing, genuinely appears to have left him with the strong feeling that kids – or at least the boys for whom he felt such a strong affinity – need a measure of freedom to thrive. It is a widely held belief. Hardly a week passes without a columnist somewhere bemoaning the restraints that beset modern childhood.[626] It's not just the endless round of school homework and tests. It's the fact that kids are penned into their homes for security reasons. The anti-paedophile hysteria is such that children are seldom allowed to walk to school or explore the countryside without adult company. Their hobbies are all strictly monitored; even in the privacy of their own bedrooms their internet use is subject to control and surveillance. Not since they were forced to work long hours in dark Victorian mills have children been less free.

Even the very parents who impose tight restrictions on their children often look back to the freer days of their own childhood with nostalgia. They know something is wrong but feel it would be irresponsible to expose their kids to the dangers that freedom implies. When it comes to drunken youngsters messing with fire it is easy to see their point. But that does not mean all today's perceived risks are as real or harmful as is believed. We need to sort out the genuine risks from the hysterically manufactured ones. I have written extensively elsewhere in favour of children's rights and freedoms. That does not mean I favour abandoning kids to predators or the kind of mayhem seen at Neverland.[627]

A key point strongly illustrated by the above discussion is that whether children have "the dominance", or whether they are under adult control, it makes no sense whatever to single out sex as the sole line of analysis, or even the most important one. Drink is more important; ditto drugs. Parents have enormous power over their children: they control what their kids eat, where they live, whom they meet and talk to, which religion they are taught, everything. Across the whole range of issues parents are presumed to know what's best for their kids and to exercise their power sensibly. In some communities, notably extreme religious cults, parental authority has been set aside in favour of blind obedience to the dictates of a strong charismatic leader. Some communist regimes have also tried to bypass the authority of the family. These experiments tend to end in tears. Parents, it is widely agreed, must in general be trusted with authority over their children even though some parents are violently abusive, criminally neglectful, or simply foolish and incapable. Modern states in the developed world aim to deal with these exceptions by intervening in cases of parental abuse, neglect and inadequacy, sometimes by taking children "into care".

In order to be fair and balanced, criticism of Michael Jackson's failure to use his adult authority in the interests of his boys (and of staff who suffer third degree burns) needs to be considered in this wider context – a context in which parents, too, sometimes fail to live up to the high standards required. Approaching the issues in this way, it will be seen that some points of theoretical importance may be discerned. Firstly, we need to take account of the fact that whoever is effectively in charge of children – whether we mean the state, or a cult leader, parents, teachers, a child-lover outside the family, such as Michael, or even a teenage baby sitter – will probably be in a position of some power over them. Even when this is not the case, as when a teacher cannot keep discipline in class, issues of power are engaged: we have a sense that in any circumstance there is a *proper*, or optimum, level of control that ought to prevail. Secondly, whatever level of power is exerted (and in whichever direction it flows, because the older party is not necessarily the one in control), there is always potential for abuse. This holds good for all issues, not just sex. Thirdly, and following from my observation about the *flow* of power, in order for power to be an issue at all there must be some level of inequality. Human power, just like its equivalent in electric power cables, "flows", or makes its impact, from a higher energy state to a lower one.

It follows from the above that what needs to be addressed is not solely power in a sexual context and certainly not "power" itself, which is an inevitable and generally useful feature of human relations: we speak of the power to do good as much as ill. Nor will our concerns exclude the family hearth from scrutiny. If abuse is potentially everywhere, then measures to prevent or minimise it should be everywhere too. My view, shared by a range of children's rights advocates, is that children should be equipped with the knowledge and facilities (together forming a species of power) to counteract abuse in any context, whether at home, or school, or anywhere else in their social world.

A full description of how children's rights can work in practice without undermining adults' legitimate authority lies beyond the scope of this volume, but I can give one pertinent example. In the UK an organisation called ChildLine has for many years operated a phone number which children can call to report abuse of any kind. Staff members are trained to take the details and alert the appropriate intervention agencies where necessary. It is a great idea. It empowers kids to stand up for themselves. A range of problems, from school bullying to parental neglect and real sexual abuse have been addressed by this means. My only quarrel with ChildLine – albeit a huge one – is with its implicit anti-sexual agenda. It was set up by TV personality Esther Rantzen, a woman with a bee in her bonnet about child-adult sex. To her *all* adult-child sexual contacts are abusive, even when the child has no such negative feelings, or puts a strong positive value on their intimacy with a grown-up friend. This has meant in practice that ChildLine's wonderful *potential* for empowering children has been hamstrung. It has only been *half* realised. It does a vital job in terms of enabling children to escape from bad, unwanted sexual contacts but would never support them in a good, desired sexual relationship. Any child who asked ChildLine to intervene with their parents to stop them breaking up an intimate friendship with a loved grown-up would soon find the service does not work that way. They would quickly discover that ChildLine would take the parents' side, not theirs. The unfortunate young person would probably be made to undergo "counselling" (i.e. subjected to propaganda against their adult friend) to make them "understand" that the relationship was abusive.

One-sided "empowerment" of this sort scarcely deserves the term. If children have the "power" to say No but not to say Yes then what choice do they have? This is not power but a mere illusion of power, in which adults such as Esther Rantzen are not supporting free choice but instead imposing their own values and prejudices on the young. Children's empowerment does not have to be like this. ChildLine could evolve towards more genuinely choice-based support for children, or a rival service could head in that direction.

Feminists, inspired by the fundamentally socialist perception that equality in personal relations is the indispensable foundation of fairness and justice, often try to suggest that adult-child sexual relations are doomed to be abusive because – as they see it – such relations are necessarily unequal. It is a grossly blinkered view, which utterly ignores the inequality inherent in relations between parents and their children. These relations are often denounced *only* when sexual expression takes place. This is illogical because

(a) as discussed earlier, especially in Chapter Seven, sexual contacts are not inherently harmful and (b) bad parents are capable of misusing their power in a variety of harmful ways.

Good parenting is a *nurturant* form of inequality. So is good teaching. So is a good cross-generational relationship that has no raison d'être beyond its social and erotic content. The language we use to describe these things often fails us. We resort to metaphors of conflict, describing situations in which the adult has "the upper hand", the implication being that a struggle is in progress and that the child will inevitably be the loser. While it is true that even the best families or child-love relations involve some tussles with each other, our language too often turns gentle verbal sparring into all-but murderous assault by the "powerful" adult.

I have much sympathy with both feminist and socialist ideology. I applaud the progress women have made towards social equality and equal opportunities. Likewise I deplore the grotesque inequalities of wealth and incomes between rich and poor, especially as regards the gap between the prosperity of the developed world and the poorer regions. These inequalities are hugely important; they cannot coexist with fairness and justice. But that does not mean equality per se should be fetishised as a universal good. An equilateral triangle in not the only good one; other triangles are not "unfair" to their shorter sides. If a mother was no more than equal to her baby in size and strength, knowledge and maturity, she wouldn't be a mother at all, still less a good one. To demand equality in inappropriate places is both futile and foolish.

Bruce Rind, contributing to a debate in the prestigious *Archives of Sexual Behavior*, challenged the notion that inequality in sexual relations is necessarily unacceptable or deleterious. Such an assumption, he points out, is not made in relation to other adult-child interactions, such as wrestling, tickling, hugging, mentoring, disciplining or preaching, which clearly involve power imbalances. Elaborating his point, Rind articulates a key logical weakness pervading the argument of leading opponents of adult-child sexual contacts:

> The assumption of the overpowering of sexual self-determination deserves further elaboration. Finkelhor (1979, 1984) many years ago already articulated the positions Schmidt is currently espousing. [Dr Gunter Schmidt, another contributor to the Archives debate.] But the weakness of his articulation is instructive, as it points to the problem of trying to be a

> scientist and a moralist simultaneously. Like Schmidt, Finkelhor argued that harm is not needed to establish the immorality and unacceptability of adult-child sex. Instead, Finkelhor continued, the unacceptability is based on the child's inability to consent, because he does not know what he is getting into and he cannot say no. A critic then complained that, if it is true that children cannot make judgments about sex, how can they judge among rival claims of the various religious sects (e.g., agree with an adult to be taken to one church rather than another or none at all)? Finkelhor responded that it is different with sex, because sex is more likely to be harmful. His argument is circular – the issue falls back to harm, even though harm is claimed to be unessential to the point.[628]

As Rind goes on to point out, whether particular acts are harmful is open to empirical investigation, such as we saw in Sandfort's research. In other words, we should look at the facts rather than determining in advance that something *must* be harmful because our moral intuition (which, like our religion, in most cases largely boils down to our specific cultural upbringing) tells us it is wrong.

Gut feelings will probably have left us in little doubt that the facts revealed in the first of these three chapters on the theme of "power" disclose an inevitably harmful situation. In Chapter Ten, "The Power of Fame and Wealth", we visited the dubious world of Anthony Pellicano, with his sinister underworld methods of witness intimidation and bribery. I like to think that if I were in the same position as Michael – extremely rich, with things to hide – I would draw the line at beating people up and shooting at them. However, no analysis of his great power can be complete without also considering the ultimately even greater power of society: power which in 2005 brought him to trial, confronted by witnesses whom it had proved beyond his power to intimidate or bribe out of the picture. In the face of the overwhelming hostility of the state to adult-child sexual relations, it seems to me no more than a sensible precaution that Michael should have used his legal and financial muscle to defend himself – through such means, for example, as the "gagging contracts" his staff were required to sign. Without such measures he would have been a ridiculously easy target, brought to his knees years ago by dozens of blackmail bandits, totally irrespective of the type or quality of his relations with children.

After the scandal of 1993 the balance of power moved significantly against him. The tabloids and TV channels had plenty of loot of their own to splash around, while his own finances dried up. Michael was no longer in control of his image. Fortunes were made out of his misfortune. Quite a few people, as a result, made allegations as to his sexual conduct – security guards, domestic staff, his sister La Toya, writers Victor Gutierrez and Raymond Chandler, all in addition to several boys – yet none of them conclusively revealed a deeply unpleasant figure who ought never to be near children. On the contrary, their descriptions fit the view that he was socially attractive to children and related well to them.

One recent Jackson insider to join his detractors was his sacked (and vengeful) publicity chief Bob Jones, who wrote in a book with Stacy Brown:

> Michael had a sinister gift for identifying these boys; it was as if he had some sort of radar. I was continually amazed by how he could determine which of the many children he came into contact with might be "woo-able", whose parents could be bought off and counted on to keep quiet about what was going on. I came to understand that Michael manipulated people and events with a great deal of finesse.[629]

But what do we learn from this condemnation apart from the power of prejudicial words such as "sinister" and "manipulated"? Should we really be so quick to condemn Michael's secrecy contracts and pay-offs, along with the more obviously objectionable methods of Pellicano? Significantly, such tactics were handled through his lawyers. They belong to the world of formal deals and binding contracts, and as such they have a status similar to the exceedingly unromantic Hollywood phenomenon of pre-nuptial agreements, and even to the marriage contract, with its implication of binding people into arrangements that purely personal attachment might leave in doubt.

The most personal of contracts can be remarkably cold-blooded: arranged marriages, for instance, serve the interests of dynasties, including the secure transference of property across generations. Michael Jackson's personnel contracts served him personally insofar as the silence of his staff helped him stay out of jail, but the necessity for the existence of gagging contracts need have no relation whatever to the quality of any sexual/social contacts with his boyfriends. Any sexual contact with a minor is illicit. Therefore his personal and property interests had to be defended against any intrusions into the private domain, intrusions which inevitably risked disastrous exposure of the illicit element. He might have the most beautiful, mutual, tender – pick your own adjective – relationship with a child imaginable, but this cold-blooded apparatus would still be necessary for anyone of his wealth. It is no different to protecting copyright interests. Like any other pop star, he had to deploy heavy legal artillery to fend off people claiming he had stolen their songs. Such measures are simply par for the course.

The right to use all means within the law to protect one's personal space and privacy is not particularly controversial in most circumstances. It has always been a proud boast that "an Englishman's home is his castle" – a bastion against the insolence of official intrusion. The US has an even more rugged tradition of "stay off my land" individualism. Feminists, with their emphasis on the personal as the political, have reason to view such customs with suspicion. It is no accident that an Englishman's home is *his* castle not *hers*. One of the earliest targets of the late 20th century feminist revival was incest, a crime that required patriarchal power and privacy in order for it to thrive behind closed doors.

Feminists are also among those likely to be sceptical and suspicious of a conclusion I drew in the last chapter in response to Jordie's criticism of Michael. It will be recalled that in the interview with Dr Gardner he had complained his grown-up friend could be "overwhelming" in his relentless attentions. He gave the boy no breathing space. My defence was that although this was true, Jordie was entirely free to say enough is enough. He could at any time have decided the benefits of the friendship were outweighed by the downside and turned away from the star. It is not as though he would have been without support: his father was desperate for just such a result. But instead of breaking with Jackson, Jordie held out for many weeks in defiance of his father, determined to go on tour for months with this man he found so "overwhelming".

As one who holds feminist analysis to be – at its best – extremely insightful and worthy of the highest respect, I feel the need to pursue feminist concerns a little further in this chapter. In fact I have already done so: what follows is from a letter I wrote in 1994 to a feminist friend who had once been a colleague of mine on the staff of the Open University:

> Here in Yorkshire hardly a week goes by without the *Wakefield Express* publishing some dreadful court story about a man battering his wife or girlfriend. The woman almost invariably speaks up for the man in mitigation: "We're back together now," she'll say, "We have made it up. I still love him." Some of these women, one imagines, are locked into the situation

through sheer terror. These are people who can be helped by the provision of women's refuges and by the social support needed to make a clean break.

As you would be the first to say, though, these things are not simple. "Claudia", in a contribution to the Alison Assiter & Avedon Carol book I showed you, suggests:[630] "...most women are beaten, raped and murdered by the men with whom they are 'in love'. Economic constraints, although highly important, are not the main reasons why women stay with or return to violent men. Women tolerate ill-treatment because they want to believe in the prevailing social fantasy of love as a recipe for earthly happiness. They are conditioned to reject any alternative prospects. My best friend declared at the age of sixteen that 'Life's not worth living if you don't get married.'"

Entrenched socialisation of this sort is not easy to tackle. It is even questionable whether and to what extent one should try. My view, as hinted above, is that lifestyle and life-goal choices should be the subject of reflection and debate infusing society at all levels, including children. Everyone should have access to the idea that there is more than one way of doing things and to information on how alternatives might be achieved in the practical context of ordinary lives.

What we should not do, however, is to be prescriptive and coercive. This seems to me to be the mistake made by Adrienne Rich... The emphasis of her political lesbianism – "heterosexual women are collaborators with the enemy" – is striking for the lack of sisterly solidarity which is otherwise supposed to be her big theme. I view such authoritarianism as a threat to a free and just society. Ultimately women (and men) must be free to pursue "the prevailing fantasy of love" and free to reject, if they wish, the bossy boots who claim to know better. The dangers of allowing prescriptive "correctness" to prevail are splendidly advanced in Assiter and Carol...

"The prevailing fantasy of love" is not, mercifully, a social construct that traps many small boys. A pop star may be idolised, but no boy is ever going to suppose his life is not worth living unless he marries one, especially not a male one. In any case, children usually wear their hearts on their sleeves much more than adults: they have not yet learnt to dissemble their feelings. Many children over the years have been seen apparently having fun with MJ in public. The consistency of these reports, and the consistency of reports coming from staff members and others now denouncing him, none of them describing aggressive or domineering behaviour by MJ, leads me to suppose that the children's smiles do not switch off like a light as soon as the bedroom door is closed.

I can imagine Michael being as powerless to make someone want him as most of us have on occasion been. It hurts. It's sad. At moments like that you have no power at all. You are a supplicant. You are on bended knees. You are vulnerable. A beggar merely. And if you are lucky, if your child takes pity on you, you may be thrown a crumb of comfort. He may give you the gift it is only his to give, the gift that it is quite impossible for you to take without his giving it: his warmth, his approval, his love. He, your child, is the custodian of that, and at such a time there is no-one richer or more powerful than he.

A three-year-old child would have no such gift to give. Or a sevenling, usually. As JM Barrie put it, at that age they are pitiless, merciless creatures, utterly heartless. If they want you they'll take you, and they often do, smothering you in kisses and affection. But if they don't, you are wasting your time. Tears will not move them! You might as well plead your case before a stone! The bodies of such little children are easy prey to an adult, nobody would dispute that. Incestuous fathers know it and may, with a range of feelings from brutal indifference to trembling self-hatred, simply take.

Yet what they cannot take may be what they most desire, call it mutuality, love, whatever. That must be given. Some of us settle for less. We are weak. We cajole, we plead, we coerce. The degree to which we simply take is the degree to which we hurt ourselves, as well as our children. We see our failure written in their eyes and we curse ourselves.

If pleading is a waste of time with a threeling, thirteen is a different matter. That was Jordan's age. Emotional blackmail is now an available option at last. We are approaching – ah, what liberation! – the wicked power plays available to the world of grown-ups, beginning with the teenage Lotharios. "If you really love me you'll let me do it." When we arrive at this stage exploitation is only possible if the boy, or more usually girl, being addressed does indeed feel herself in love and does indeed want to show it. Given the safeguards we want to make about safe sex, contraception etc, that option should be open. As I have said in my book, if there is the possibility of being bruised in what turns out to be a casual encounter, there is also the hope of something better: it is not for outsiders to second-guess people's feelings about each other.

...if the "love gambit" was a non-starter, what chink in Jordie's armour was available to Michael? How could he secure that French kiss he wanted? Simply an appeal to the boy's good nature. An appeal to put MJ out of his misery! No power on earth that I can see, certainly not all of MJ's wealth, could guarantee the success of such an appeal. The response was in Jordie's heart. He would have given, or not given, according to what was in him. The power was all on his side.

It may be said that he had certain things to lose by not playing along. Gifts especially. Jacko is rightly notorious for buying his way to popularity with kids. It is utterly disgraceful to do this, as all of us without the resources to commit that particular sin will agree! Children are in any case not that good at "playing along". An adult gold-digger might succeed in doing so for quite a while, but if Jordie had not liked MJ I doubt whether the "relationship" could have been sustained for more than a day, never mind the months of intensive togetherness we know occurred. It is no surprise to me that he is described as having a "deep emotional attachment" to MJ...

Have you ever considered what the inserter role in oral sex might be like for a boy? To have this great giant of an adult kneeling in front of you? Some boys report it as a tremendous role reversal. For maybe the very first time in their life they are the big shot for whom the gods bow down. They are the master!

I realise of course that this will sound very un-PC. That word "master", especially, what a dangerous button to press! It could just as well have been "mistress". The gender of the actors in this regard is quite beside the point and so is the sexual content of the action. Children love role reversal games, especially when they are perceived as something excitingly, dangerously, half-real. Slave games are great. If a child (boy or girl) senses you will be his/her slave, they will take up the game with the utmost alacrity, bossing you around like crazy and marvelling at the results. It is headily subversive of the usual state of things, liberating for both slave and master alike. All good parents know this through playing "horse" with their kids.

It is also a learning-process in responsibility. Some little slave masters are extremely bossy but they soon learn to distinguish the pleasure of being in control from the capacity to hurt: most people do not like being on the receiving end of sadistic orders and if that happens will very quickly revert to their socially assigned role! In fact such games tend to be highly scripted, or rather moded: it is possible for either side to move in and out of game mode at will, according to the needs of the moment.[631]

Another extraordinary but generally unacknowledged power children can wield in our society is that of the accusatory word. Far from being too easily silenced these days, children have been positioned as infallible accusers, who supposedly never lie about sexual abuse. Try telling that to teachers, who know that disruptive pupils have nuclear strike capability tucked down their pants. UK statistics collected by the National Association of Schoolmasters and Union of Women Teachers (NASUWT) showed that from 1991 to 2002 only 62 out of 1,557 sexual abuse allegations were substantiated. They pointed to teachers' wrecked careers, sometimes resulting in suicide, as a result of publicity following false allegations.[632] Faced with the threat of malicious allegations, it is arguable the balance of power has these days shifted too far away from teachers in favour of their pupils.

This is one of many cases in which crude considerations of comparative age utterly fail to reflect the realities of power. In any case, arguments based on the balance of power are bedevilled by the fact that in personal relationships the balance is multidimensional and in a constant state of flux. Paul Okami, contributing to the *Archives of Sexual Behavior* debate mentioned earlier, points this out very neatly:

> Who has the greater power in a relationship? A black man or his white wife? A smart, beautiful, well-heeled female medical student or her somewhat dim-witted, cab-driver boyfriend (who is built like Arnold Schwarzenegger?)? A teacher who is desperately in love with her fifteen-year-old former student or the fifteen-year-old who doesn't much care one way or the other and could imprison the teacher for a hefty stretch with a few words?[633]

The race issue raised by Okami is of course also a feature of the Jackson case, albeit in a very muted way because, as noted earlier, Michael morphed over the years from "a poor black boy to a rich white woman". If that doesn't confuse the balance of power issue, nothing will! These subtleties did nothing to stop the black civil rights organisation, the National Association for the Advancement of Colored People (NAACP), from taking up the cudgels on Michael's behalf as a supposedly oppressed black man. This is not a road I propose to go down because I believe it will be obvious to most readers, black and white alike, that age barriers, not racial discrimination, are at the heart of the case against him. Geraldine Hughes is totally wrong when in her book she makes much of the theme that the Jordie Chandler case "involved the word of a thirteen-year-old white boy against an adult black male".[634] Hughes, herself a black woman, is clearly sensitised to racial issues. But despite spending time in Jordie's company she appeared not to notice that Jordie is not actually a "white" boy. As his uncle Raymond points out, he has "a considerable amount of 'black blood' flowing through his veins", and his olive complexion is probably darker than Michael's.[635]

Race was not an issue in Michael Jackson's contacts with boys, or at least not in terms of the "balance of power" within his relationships. However, racial barriers do offer an interesting analogy with those based on age. I often talk about the "age apartheid" that forbids unauthorised social contact between adults and children. The comparison with the racial separation enforced in the old South Africa is explicit in this phrase. Another writer, Bill Andriette, also sees points of similarity between racial and age divisions in society, in his case focusing on inter-racial sexual relations in the old American Deep South. With this comparison, Andriette illuminates a vital element of the "balance of power" discussion untouched upon so far in my three chapters on power. His analysis clearly reveals the immense power of society to re-shape – or distort – the feelings and even the memories of those who risk breaking racial or age taboos:

> A white woman might consensually have sex with a black man, enjoy the relationship (in part perhaps because it was forbidden), yet feel troubled and conflicted afterwards. Her emotions might include shame at having had illicit sex, guilt at having enjoyed it, anxiety at having to keep the relationship secret, and a sense of having been tainted and ruined, not only by compromising her womanly virtue but by intimacy with a racial "inferior". If the relationship were found out, these conflicts could come to a head.
>
> Yet a white woman's culture would offer a ready interpretive schema to resolve these powerful conflicts. Simply by saying she was raped, the woman would be absolved of all responsibility for what happened and allowed to return to good grace, something she would resolutely lose were she to, say, escape to Canada with her black paramour. Quite possibly, the woman wouldn't even have to say she was raped because it would be the automatic conclusion of the white authorities when faced with evidence of sex between a black man and a white woman – a sort of union so unnatural and barbaric that it had to be coerced by the only party who stood to gain by it.
>
> With her relationships with the family and community at stake, the woman would be under enormous pressure to play along. Circumstances would now encourage her to portray a sexual encounter that was voluntary and enjoyable at the same time it was devastating. That portrayal would not necessarily be dishonest, since in the pressure cooker of racial and sexual bigotry, even the memory of the experience could imaginably

transubstantiate into something monstrous. Anything the woman said bolstering a monstrous image of the sex would be readily accepted because it would retell a deep cultural myth serving to justify racial boundaries, into which extraordinary cultural energy was invested. Toward the preservation of those boundaries the black man would likely be executed or lynched.

The ideological pressures that tended to transform consensual interracial sex into rape in the South parallel contemporary society's ideology around intergenerational sex. The blind rage of the lynch mob closely resembles that expressed today toward men who have sex with children or adolescents; indeed, calls for the killing of such men are a staple of the contemporary rhetoric. Just as with interracial sex in the old South, intergenerational sex today is seen as intrinsically evil because it violates socially constructed boundaries across which sex is taboo. Those who violate these boundaries are severely punished and "victims" themselves face ostracism if they fail to embrace a role carefully laid out by therapists, media, and the rhetoric of police and prosecutors.

This is not to say that sexual coercion of children is not widespread, any more than it is to say that black men did not sometimes really rape white southern women. Moreover, one has to consider how in the above scenario the ideological baggage that each person carried into the interracial relationship could have poisoned it. One can imagine the relationship going badly because the black man couldn't help thinking about the lynching he risked, and the white woman the loss of her social status. I think that the corresponding pressures make many non-coercive intergenerational relationships problematic. But thanks to the political struggles of black people, most readers today will have no trouble seeing that it is racial bigotry that is the root of the problem in the above scenario, not interracial relationships, which in a non-bigoted society are as difficult and fraught with ambiguity as relationships between straight-haired and curly-haired people.

Anyone wanting seriously to deal with the problem of rape in 19th century southern culture would have had to deal first with racism and the myth of the black rapist. Dealing with the real problem of rape in southern culture would have meant making the South safe for interracial sex. Likewise, if we are seriously to deal with the problem of the sexual coercion of children, we will have to make the world safe for consensual intergenerational sex.[636]

Andriette's analysis once again shakes up our understanding of Jordie Chandler's feelings in the wake of his enforced break with his adult lover.

Michael is now cast as the taboo-breaking "nigger" not because he is black but because he has transgressed the age laws. And we can see that just like those white women in the South who had a black lover, Jordie was at first portrayed as an innocent victim who must have been "raped". When it became clear this story could no longer be sustained in the face of the facts, there were those who turned against him. I don't mean the "deniers" among Jackson's fans, who were hostile from the start because for them Michael was innocent. The Chandler family received death threats from this quarter. One wrote: "We're coming to Los Angeles to take your blood. Your blood, your fucking whore of an ex-wife's blood, and your shitty little son's blood."[637]

Shocking as these crazy fans showed themselves to be, they can at least be dismissed as a lunatic fringe. It is not an excuse available to those writing in the mainstream media, such as Carol Sarler. As noted in Chapter Three, when it emerged that Jordie had accepted a financial settlement from Jackson she wrote:

> Jordie has not withdrawn his allegation that Jackson sexually molested him. He simply said that he will go away and leave Jackson alone, now that a suitable financial payment has been made for the sex. A purely professional arrangement. The oldest profession in the world.

There could hardly be a clearer indication of Andriette's point that "victims" themselves "face ostracism if they fail to embrace a role carefully laid out by therapists". Here we see the participant "victim" branded as a prostitute.

This chapter promised that in contrast to the factual specifics of the first two chapters on Jackson's possible abuses of power, this third one would take in the bigger picture. As such it has led us to examine the questionable assumptions we bring to key power-related issues, such as enjoining secrecy on children, letting them "run wild", equality in relationships, "manipulative" love, and the validity of fiercely enforced taboos. In the next chapter we see Michael Jackson's emergence as a family man – an astonishing transformation which exposes "questionable assumptions" we make about the very essence of family life.

CHAPTER THIRTEEN

Husband and Father

There was a time, back in the 1980s, when seven-times married screen legend Elizabeth Taylor jokingly suggested to Michael Jackson that the pair of them should get married. Michael was alarmed. "But will we have to have sex?" he wanted to know. "Oh, of course not, you silly boy," said Elizabeth reassuringly. "Why, I don't know *any* married couples who have sex!"[638]

But Randy Taraborrelli, to whom I owe this jewel of an anecdote, thinks he knows at least one married couple who did have sex: none other than Michael Jackson and his first wife, Lisa Marie Presley. Taraborrelli, as I have stated elsewhere, is a fine biographer, except that his admirable generosity of spirit towards his subject's foibles sometimes went too far, at least until reality finally caught up with him after the 2005 trial. In the second edition of *Michael Jackson: The Magic and the Madness*, which appeared in the wake of the Jordie Chandler crisis, his positive spin for Jackson amounted to whitewash in ways I specified in Chapter Nine. In the third edition, brought out in 2004, after Michael's two marriages, to Lisa Marie Presley and Debbie Rowe, and with a criminal investigation under way against the entertainer in relation to yet another young boy, Taraborrelli again painted a rosy picture. Michael, he assured us, did not marry Elvis Presley's daughter Lisa Marie out of any ulterior motive. It was, he insists, a genuine romance:

> ... it was the first time he had ever experienced such chemistry with a woman, or with anyone, for that matter...

Who knows why it became so intense for Michael with Lisa. However, it was this surprising – some may think of it as astonishing – sexual component that most cemented the relationship between Michael and Lisa.

The "first time" for them was in Florida, during a weekend stay at Donald Trump's Mar-A-Lago estate in Palm Beach. Donald recalls seeing Michael and Lisa walking hand in hand on his estate, seeming lost in a mutual dream. In a photograph taken that day, Lisa was elegantly dressed in a severely tailored, black silk dress that fell in fluid lines around her shapely figure. Michael was wearing a sharp, black suit, scarlet-coloured shirt and matching tie. At one point, he dropped to one knee and kissed her hand. She urged him to his feet; the two embraced. Michael gazed at her intensely, mesmerized by her face. They kissed. He pulled from his vest pocket a small, wrapped box. When she opened it, Lisa's face lit up. Pearls.

"It was romantic," Donald Trump recalled. "Later, I asked Michael how things were going and he said, 'Great. I just got to kiss the most beautiful girl in the world. I hope I'm worthy of her. I think I might marry her.'

"They made love at the Trump estate," said another one of Lisa's confidantes. "She said it was intense, it took her breath away. I have no idea what they were doing, or what he was doing to her, but since she gravitates toward the unconventional, she was out of her mind over this guy. Maybe it's hard for some to believe," she concluded, "but true, just the same."[639]

Sexual chemistry, romantic courtship, making love – Lisa's friend is right when she says it is hard to believe. Michael, after all, was by this time into his mid-thirties and had never previously shown the slightest romantic interest in any woman. Even when "dating" Brooke Shields he felt it necessary to have a little boy with him. And it is not as though women had been unavailable in his teens and twenties: as his brothers had soon discovered to their delight in the Jackson Five era, there's nothing to beat being a young male pop star for getting a girl's attention. Come to think of it, even aging rockers don't have much to complain about in that department.

So there is plenty of cause for cynicism but that does not mean Taraborrelli is necessarily completely wrong. It is time to look in more detail at the circumstances of Michael's marriages with the aim of assessing the man both as a husband and, as in due course he became, a father.

Michael first met Lisa Marie Presley in Las Vegas when she was just six years old and he was sixteen. She was already a fan of the Jackson Five and her father Elvis treated her to seeing one of their shows. In fact the King of

Rock was always treating his adored little girl to something. When she was only six he bought her a fur coat, a diamond brooch and her own little golf cart. A year later he gave her a blue and white passenger jet he dubbed *The Lisa Marie*.[640] Small wonder her mother Priscilla thought she was spoilt; Lisa Marie has candidly referred to her child self as a "fucking little tyrant".[641]

But for Michael, despite his fondness for children, romance did not flourish with her at that stage. Nearly twenty years later they were both mature adults – in years at least – when they were again brought together. This was in February 1993, at a private dinner in the Los Angeles home of artist Brett Livingston-Stone, a mutual friend. They hit it off, according to the artist. As Taraborrelli says: "They realized that they shared the same kinds of backgrounds, both had been sheltered and protected from the real world, both felt they had missed out on their childhoods, both were mistrustful of outsiders after having spent most of their lives feeling exploited by outsiders."[642] It is a questionable interpretation. One could equally argue they had little in common: whereas Lisa's every whim had been monstrously indulged, Michael had been equally monstrously deprived – even Christmas presents were denied in his strict Jehovah's Witnesses upbringing. Undoubtedly, though, they had both been brought up in highly unusual ways, framed by the aura of their celebrity.

Writing for the *Daily Telegraph*, Susannah Herbert agreed they were "a couple made for each other". She disapprovingly noted that Lisa Marie had pursued Michael despite being already married. In the words of her mother, Priscilla Presley, Lisa as a child had been showered with "everything a two- or three-year-old shouldn't have and wouldn't appreciate". When Priscilla had confronted Elvis over the abysmal values he was imparting to his beloved little girl, his response had been "To hell with values".[643]

In patching together the thin case for Michael's sexual normality, Taraborrelli quotes Lisa Marie's efforts in the same direction. So we hear that in private he is a regular guy, who uses swear words and drops to a lower voice pitch than the falsetto familiar to his fans. But only a page later one cannot help feeling a hint of contradiction when Lisa says, "I'm not a woman who goes for the norm, anyway."[644]

We hear that, as the relationship begins, Michael was "kissing her *fairly* passionately". *Fairly*? Has a phrase more damning in its ambivalence ever been penned? I felt more than fairly sorry for Michael as regards the excruciatingly detailed scrutiny to which his rare intimacies with women were subjected. On one famous occasion, though, he set himself up for such scrutiny. In September 1994, soon after the official announcement of the marriage, the couple appeared at the MTV Music Video Awards, and millions of viewers saw Michael locked in a protracted kiss with his wife. According to one merciless press story, the smacker was a "made-for-TV phony!" Maxine Fiel, described as a "world authority on body language" gave an analysis of the kiss that ran for paragraphs. She concluded: "The newlyweds' lip-lock was obviously rehearsed and completely empty of any real passion...Judging from this kiss these are not two people in love. Their body language doesn't reveal one sign of real tenderness."[645]

The problem on this occasion was not so much Michael as Lisa. Whereas he was clearly desperate to establish his heterosexual credentials with a sceptical public, she had been all but ambushed into the performance, and appeared to be pulling her body away from her husband. She had pursed her lips "as if she were kissing an uncle, not a lover". Later she said: "I hated it. I felt used, like a prop. It was awful."[646]

The *Hello!* magazine photo spread of the previous month, however, had offered no such camouflage to Michael. Commenting on this showing by the two "honeylooners", the *Sun*'s story also deployed a "top body language expert", psychologist Jane Firbank. Of one particular photograph, she said:

> Lovers want to touch each other and will lay their hands flatly on their partner's body. This picture indicates they have not taken pleasure in each other's flesh. Couples who have made love look comfortable when they touch each other. These two look awkward about it. Michael Jackson's body is in no way moulding itself to hers and his arms are very stiff. He looks like he is placing his hands on a hot plate rather than the woman he loves.[647]

Reading body language has a stronger scientific basis than reading tea leaves, but it remains primarily an art not a science. Having seen for myself the full *Hello!* feature, though, I can say that I find Firbank's interpretation highly convincing.[648] Nor does she necessarily go too far in pronouncing, with a positively biblical flourish, that the couple "have not taken pleasure in each other's flesh". Note that she carefully does *not* say the couple have never had sex – only that if they have done so they have not enjoyed it. Countless couples have had sex without pleasure in the hope of having children: could this pair have been among them? It is a point to which we will return.

First, we need to explore the circumstances in which Michael's supposed "romance" with Lisa Marie developed after they were brought together in February 1993. The timing is hugely significant. The month and year are the very same in which Michael returned from tour and his "romance" with Jordie Chandler began in earnest. Was Michael two-timing? In characteristic style, Randy Taraborrelli attempts to suggest that Michael's serious relationship was with Lisa Marie: "Throughout 1993, during the time Michael seemed obsessed with Jordie Chandler, he was dating Lisa, intermittently." Ah, so Michael only *seemed* obsessed with Jordie, while his heart *really* lay elsewhere! But even Michael's loyal biographer finds it impossible to sustain this farcical ambivalence. In the very next sentence he finds he has to get real:

> When the molestation allegations surfaced in his life, however, Michael's relationship with Lisa became a more urgent matter to him. Ironically, if not for Jordie's accusations and the ensuing scandal, he and Lisa may never have become anything more than just friends...[649]

Quite so! But Taraborrelli is probably right in a less ironical sense when he says Michael came to depend on Lisa Marie emotionally during the crisis, phoning his woes from overseas. Using a woman's shoulder to cry on was nothing new to him and did not imply anything more than friendship. The shoulder up to this point had been Elizabeth Taylor's, a woman in her sixties. Despite the joke about marriage, there had never been any credible sign of Michael having a romantic interest in Elizabeth. But this does not preclude a woman discovering such an interest in *him*. His insistence in those phone calls that he had been wrongly accused seems to have brought out Lisa Marie's sympathies – and more. "I started falling for him," she declared. "I wanted to save him. I felt that I could do it."[650]

One day Michael phoned and "posed a question that surprised them both", saying, "If I asked you to marry me, would you do it?" Put that way it could have been a purely hypothetical question as indeed it should have been, for at this time she was married to another musician, bass player Danny Keough. But without hesitation she replied that she would.

Did Michael and Lisa Marie ever make love? Lisa's friends, according to Taraborrelli, say she is a woman who enjoys physical intimacy and would not become involved in a relationship that was not physical. There is no reason to doubt this: the heiress of the Elvis Presley estate had no need of a sham marriage. But the biographer goes too far when he says: "In truth, Lisa and Michael had an intense and active sex life..."[651] The seasoned sceptic will respond, "Beware of assertions beginning with phrases such as 'in truth'." Such statements demand the question: How does the writer know? We are not told.

We have every reason to doubt that Michael would have wanted an "intense" sex life with this rare woman in his life. But he may well have forced himself to have an active one, at least for a while. The motive would not have been passion for a woman's body but the desire to have children. Taraborrelli:

> To say that Michael wanted children is to understate the way he felt about procreation. He craved offspring. When Lisa didn't become immediately pregnant, even before they were married, he began to express his disappointment. 'I want children,' he said, 'and I thought we would be expecting one within a couple of weeks of making love. But Lisa says it takes time. I don't have time,' he said. 'I want it to happen, now. I want children so badly.'[652]

The urgency is suspicious, making it look as though Michael is finding the sex a total nightmare. It is as though he is desperate for her to be pregnant so that going to bed with her will no longer be necessary. Many gay men, especially, will recognise the feeling, or rather men who have deluded themselves into believing they are bisexual. The struggle to convince a woman and themselves that their passion is real can be extremely stressful.

We are told that Lisa felt Michael truly loved her. How did she arrive at this judgment? He had told her so, and she felt she had no choice but to take him at his word! Her mother Priscilla was far more sceptical, and so should we be. The fact that Lisa had only Michael's *word* to tell her of Michael's love is revealing. Time and again, throughout his life, we have seen that false words came easily to Michael, right from the time when he agreed to lie about his age: to little Michael and the Jackson Five's promoters, it wasn't telling a lie, it was "public relations". He told countless lies about the plastic surgery he underwent: obvious, palpable lies. He would say one thing one minute and contradict himself another, within the same interview – and we are not talking about the occasional innocent slip of the tongue. What we nowhere hear from Lisa is a ringing endorsement of his love: there is nothing about him worshipping the ground she walks on, nor any sense that he hungered for her body in ways that would be obvious to her beyond mere words. There are no songs about her in his next album. *HIStory*, billed as a highly personal compilation, as the name implies, was largely a bitter reflection on the tragic ending of his affair with Jordie; poor Lisa doesn't even rate a mention, except as an afterthought on the sleeve notes.

It is just possible that Lisa Marie's sympathy for Michael was made all the greater by the knowledge that he was at heart a boy-lover, not a lady's man. We have already heard that she thought she could "save" him and I do not think she meant just rescuing his image so that the police would back off, though this is precisely what did happen: within days of the announcement of their marriage, the criminal investigation against him arising from the Chandler case was dropped. It makes more sense to interpret that word "save" in another way. What Lisa meant was that she believed she could change Michael. As an attractive woman, she flattered herself that by sympathetic encouragement she could wean him away from boys and change his sexual orientation.

She already had reason to believe deeply in the power of personal transformation. She had been heavily into drugs but overcame the problem through a rehabilitation programme. When a desperate Michael was admitted to the Charter Nightingale Clinic at the height of the Chandler crisis, allegedly suffering from addiction to painkillers, she must have felt she had much to offer him by way of sympathy and advice about getting drugs out of his life. Her own rehab had been at the Scientology Centre in Hollywood. She has said she would be either "insane or dead" but for Scientology. Having become a committed follower of the controversial cult, she is quoted on its official website. She said that L Ron Hubbard, the cult's founder, had "precisely mapped a route out of the madness, misery and unwanted conditions one can encounter in life".[653] She may have felt Michael's behaviour with boys was exactly one such form of madness and that through her own personal commitment to him, with the help of Scientology, she could lead him in another direction. It was a delusion, but a very understandable one.

Her own childhood also gave her some grounds for empathy as regards his penchant for children. By her own account, her first sex was at fifteen, but she had been the subject of erotic interest considerably earlier. With admirable candour, her mother's boyfriend Michael Edwards has admitted his lust for Lisa when she was only twelve. Edwards, a former marine who later found fame as a model, wrote in his book *Priscilla, Elvis and Me*:

> I'd had to put an end to our swimming together after one disturbing afternoon in the pool. Lisa had innocently thrown her arms around me, and we were jumping up and down. I became aroused. A sick feeling crept slowly into the pit of my stomach. I was craving Lisa sexually.[654]

Finally, after nearly seven years, he decided he had to move out, saying his feelings for Lisa were so strong "I needed to get away from her before I went nuts." Lisa has since described him as sick, saying he made attempts at coming into her room and "being inappropriate while drunk". She has dismissed him contemptuously as a "sorry-ass motherfucker".[655] Edwards pretty much pleads guilty as charged. He wrote that after a quarrel with Priscilla he lurched drunkenly into Lisa's room:

> I wanted someone to talk to, but Lisa was asleep. I lifted a corner of the sheets and gazed at her. She was lying on her back, and her honey-coloured hair was spread out over the pillow. She was my beloved, and I couldn't even tell her...[656]

Edwards is clearly a figure straight out of Nabokov, but what about Lisa? Did she actively do anything to play the seductive Lolita to his smitten Humbert? Her angry repudiation of the man in recent years would suggest quite the opposite, but methinks the lady doth protest too much. She had, after all, thrown her arms around Edwards in that swimming pool incident. While she may have been "innocent" as to the sexual aspect of his passion for her, she must have been aware of his deep fondness, which would not have emerged overnight. He had been around in the house for years, and it is clear she was not steering clear of his company, as she would if his presence had been hateful to her.

At the time of Michael Edwards' aquatic arousal, Lisa was much the same age as Jordie Chandler had been when he was in the arms of another Michael. Lisa surely understood the intensity of both Michaels' feelings – and may have felt compassion, rather than contempt, for these men, cursed as they were with such a dangerous, impossible love.

It is said we admire people for their strengths and love them for their weaknesses, but mere empathy is not generally regarded as a good basis for marriage. No one wants to marry a pathetic partner. Yet, by the end of 1993, in the depths of his Jordie Chandler woes, Michael Jackson was cutting a very sorry figure indeed. He still had the wealth and glamour that would have made him an attractive match for millions of female fans, but for the already wealthy and glamorous daughter of Elvis Presley there had to be something more. Some commentators saw it as a business affair, an old-fashioned dynastic merger, uniting "the two great pop houses of Graceland and Neverland". The July 1994 announcement of the wedding was timed, it was said, to generate publicity in the lead up to the release of the *HIStory* album, scheduled for November of that year. The very week of the wedding announcement also saw the release of news of a Jackson video shoot in Budapest. But why should Lisa be so keen to act as a prop for Michael's commercial interests? Because she had her own musical ambitions. Until now she had been seen – with considerable justification – as just a screwed up rich kid. Now she wanted to use the marriage as a springboard to advancing her own career in music, working partly in collaboration with her new husband. If he was seen to take a serious interest in her talent, others would surely follow.

In typical Wacko Jacko style, the wedding itself was as odd as a talking turnip. Instead of the grand occasion associated with dynastic marriages, it was a tiny affair conducted in secret. There were no limousines to escort the wedding party to the ceremony, just a couple of Toyota minibuses – and the drive to the wedding venue was a tedious eighty five miles. The official performing the civil rite was a judge, but his garb was far from sober. He sported a ridiculously loud tie, featuring the cartoon caveman Fred Flintstone. Michael told the judge he was a great fan of the Flintstones and just loved the tie – but the judge never heard him say he loved Lisa Marie.[657]

To complete the Mickey Mouse tone, there were doubts over the validity of the wedding, conducted at the home of Judge Hugo Francisco Alvarez in the Dominican Republic on 26 May, 1994. The secrecy of the arrangements had the tabloids (when they later caught up with events) in a blizzard of speculation over supposed immigration and passport irregularities which could have rendered the union invalid. Also, more seriously, the alarm was raised over whether Lisa Marie was still married to Danny Keough, whom she had married in 1988 and who was the father of her two children.[658]

These concerns later evaporated, but the words of Judge Alvarez were more telling. Acting rather as though he were sitting in court handing down a stern judgment, the judge gave his own damning (and no doubt lucrative) verdict in tabloid interviews. He said, "There were no tears of happiness, no joy, no laughter. The ceremony had a sombre tone. It was bizarre." He was particularly concerned that Michael was reluctant to kiss his bride: "She had to reach out and pull his face to hers to kiss him on the lips." Even more revealingly, Michael was staying at the resort of Casa de Campo, but Lisa Marie was billeted in Villa 11, five miles away! TV comedian Jay Leno's quip sums it up nicely: "Lisa bought Michael a beautiful wedding gift: the Vienna Boys Choir".

Why, it may reasonably be asked, had the pair married secretly, delaying the announcement of their wedding in May until July? Taraborrelli has the most convincing answer to this one. It was simply in Michael's nature to create intrigue. He wanted to generate a big, worldwide controversy about his relationship with Lisa: "He just couldn't help himself".[659] The strategy worked. For the next two months the press ran with speculations as to whether they were or were not married. Meanwhile, the couple took an apartment in Trump Tower in New York, while Michael began working on his *HIStory* album.

For the next year, the couple divided their time between Neverland and Lisa's home at Hidden Hills, a hundred miles away. Michael wanted her to move into Neverland permanently, but Lisa is said to have wanted to keep her independence. Of particular interest for this volume, though, are Michael's relations with her children. The pair were Danielle Riley, born in May 1989, and her younger brother, Benjamin Storm, born in October 1992 (not 1993, as Taraborrelli has it). Thus, by the autumn of 1994 when the couple were settling down – though that is hardly the right expression – to married life, Danielle would have been five and Benjamin two.

Little Benjamin kept his opinions of Michael a closely guarded secret but not so Danielle. She never took to him "no matter how hard he tried with her", according to Taraborrelli.[660] She would take one look at him, squeal and run away. Catching the mood, the tabloids ran a story (probably fanciful) which had Michael sporting a toupé and getting mad at one of the kids (not identified) for tugging it off.[661] At least Danny Keough had faith in Jackson as a step-father. In a remarkably generous comment for an abandoned husband, he professed to be friends with Michael and said he thought the children were in good hands. Talking to Rabbi Shmuley Boteach, in taped conversations published as the present work was going to press, Michael made no mention of problems in relating to Danielle. Perhaps her reported reaction to him was no more than the typical reaction of a small, shy, child introduced to someone new. Michael claimed, "I was really good to her two children [Lisa Marie's]. Every day I'd bring them home something and they'd be waiting by the window for me and hug me. I love them. I miss them so much."[662]

Another tribute around this time came from someone who ought to have known him reasonably well, Margaret Maldonado, who styles herself Margaret Maldonado Jackson. She is his brother Jermaine's ex-girlfriend and the mother of two of his children, Jeremy and Jourdynn (About Jeremy, it will be recalled, there had been speculation as regards an alleged video showing Michael in sex acts with the boy). In November these two boys accompanied Michael on a photo shoot for his new album and stayed alone with him for a while after three of his other nephews left (those being his brother Tito's three boys). In her book about life with the Jacksons, Maldonado is scathing about her ex and the Jackson clan in general, but for Michael she has only praise. She said she knew her boys would be safe and well taken care of. While he was "meditating", she said, Michael would keep the boys *out* of his cabin. She then referred to what she called the most "incredible" aspect of their trip: Michael had checked the boys' homework and it was "perfect". Incredible indeed: Michael's spelling was so erratic it is hard to imagine the homework would have been perfect *after* his checking.[663]

The marriage was put under the spotlight when the couple were interviewed by Diane Sawyer on 14 June 1995 on ABC television's *PrimeTime Live*. Things were going well until Sawyer asked: "What is a thirty-six-year-old man doing sleeping with a twelve-year-old boy, or a series of them?" Lisa spiritedly leapt in to say she had seen these kids: "They don't let him to the bathroom without running in there with him... *They* jump into bed with *him*," she asserted.

Sawyer's follow-up put Lisa on the ropes: "But isn't part of being an adult and loving children keeping them from ambiguous situations? And again, we're talking about over an intense period of time here. Would you let your son, when he grows up and is twelve years old, do that?" After battling on for a while, saying she knew Michael, she found herself admitting "I know he has a thing for children..." Faltering, as she realised she was going nowhere, she finally just said "Sorry..."

Turning to Michael, Sawyer pressed as to whether there would be any more sleepovers with kids.

"Of course," he answered. "If they want. It's on the level of purity and love and just innocence, complete innocence," he concluded. "If you're talking about sex then that's a nut. It's not me. Go to the guy down the street, 'cause it's not Michael Jackson. It's not what I'm interested in."

The easy answer would have been to say the sleepovers had been a mistake and they would not happen again. But given Michael's addiction to children – or rather boys – where would that have left him the next time he was caught in bed with one? Any public renunciation of sleepovers would have been shoved in his face. Challenged with why he had gone back on his word, it is hard to see what excuse would have been available. His weakness would be plain for all to see. At least by sticking gamely to his "It's innocent, so why not?" story, he was keeping his future line of defence intact – a defence that proved to be his only option in the 2005 trial. As for the claim that he was not interested in sex with boys, it could well have been entirely true, albeit in a Clintonesque way. After all, masturbating boys, or sucking their penises, well, that's not really sex, is it? Even Lisa Maria might have been hard pressed to see it in such terms. Judging by an interview she gave in *Playboy* in 2003, only the most raunchy hard screwing would count as sex with her. Asked about her taste in sex, she replied: "Probably 'porn style'. [Laughs] I am a little dark on the subject. I like it rough, the way they do things in porn movies."[664]

In several other respects Michael's level of candour fell below even the Clintonesque. To put it bluntly, he told outright lies. One was in response to a question as to whether police photographs of his genital area matched the description provided by Jordie Chandler. He said, "There was nothing that matched me to those charges…Nothing." Asked whether there was a marking of some kind he flatly denied it: "No marking". This is absolutely at odds with police eyewitness evidence and a statement by Santa Barbara District Attorney Tom Sneddon.

Visual evidence of the kind in question is of course open to interpretation and the authorities would not be unbiased in their assessment. Michael more definitely told a lie, however, when he was asked about photographs and "books of young boys who were undressed" that had been found on a police raid at Neverland. At first he replied, "Not young boys, it was children, all kinds of children". When Sawyer added, "…they found photographs, books of young boys who were undressed", he said, "No. Not that I know of. Unless people sent me things that I haven't opened…" At Michael's trial in 2005 it was revealed that Michael had two books in his possession which each contained a number of photos of nude boys. One of them, as we shall see in more detail in Chapter Sixteen, was inscribed with a note that appeared to be in Michael's own handwriting expressing his approval of the pictures.

Michael was also asked whether settlements with other young boys were likely. He answered: "No, that's not true. No, no, no that's not true..." What Sawyer doubtless had in mind was the settlement with Jason Francia, rumoured to have been in negotiation in 1994, but which his lawyer, Kris Kallman, testified at Michael's trial in 2005 may not have been finalised until as late as 1996. If the deal had in fact been sewn up by the time of the Sawyer interview in June 1995, then of course it would strictly have been true that there was no deal in the offing. If it had *not* been sewn up by June 1995 then it *must* have been just around the corner, making Michael's injured protestations look a lot less than honest.

Only weeks after the Sawyer interview, cracks began to appear in the marriage. According to Lisa's friend Monica Pastelle the problem was not sexual incompatibility:

> Lisa started to wonder if she'd made a mistake in choosing him as a life partner. The great sex continued, though. It was the thing that made it difficult for her to see straight where he was concerned. What was going on in the privacy of their bedroom was enough to keep her hooked into the relationship. However, things were getting strained. When they weren't in bed making love, they were fighting.

Great sex, eh? Porn style? It is what Taraborrelli seemingly wants us to believe, because he quotes this witness uncritically.[665] Lisa insisted on the Sawyer show that she and Michael did indeed have sex, but she said nothing to endorse her husband as a wild stud. In fact her music suggests otherwise. In a lyric for one of her own songs, she describes a "masturbative" Michael. Interviewing Lisa for *Rolling Stone* in 2003, Chris Heath said he had been sent the lyrics to her new album. There was one more lyric than there were songs on the advance CD. It was called "Disciple", of which this was the first verse:

> You will flourish in your disciples bringing you pleasure.
> In so many masturbative ways
> Until you've simply no use for them anymore
> And then they will remain and suffer in your concentrated haze

Probed on the point, Lisa did not attempt to deny that the song was about Michael. She told Heath:

> I'm not into Michael-bashing at all. I have no interest in doing that. He is

who he is. I know people want to know what that was about, and I'm trying to say it without making him a bad guy, you know... It's hard to do, because it was such a bad situation and it was so fucked up.[666]

Quite. Time, the great healer, had clearly tempered any anger she may have felt when the marriage was "under strain" and the couple were always "fighting". Looking back after a number of years, as she is here, Lisa is reflecting calmly on events, and her assessment is honest and fair. The subject of their quarrels would certainly have included those "disciples". Only weeks after the Sawyer interview, he went off with them again. This time it was the Cascio boys. When she heard about Michael's plans for a vacation with them she was stunned:

> "How did you get to be this way?" she demanded, her eyes hard and condemning. "Do you care how that makes me look, you going on vacation with two kids? Don't you care about me, at all?"
>
> "Me? Selfish?" Michael asked, seeming dismayed. "But look at the money I give to charities. Why, Lisa! I love all the little children of the world." According to witnesses, Lisa stared at him, her mouth agape. "What does that have to do with anything?" she countered. She was furious and getting more so by the second. "I'm talking about you and me, Michael. Not, all the little children of the world. In fact," she concluded, "you are the most selfish person I have ever known."[667]

Even Michael would have been hard pressed to fit "all the little children of the world" into his vacation plans, but in July 1995 he did go away to France with Eddie and Frank Cascio – and without Lisa. Evidently Michael felt the marriage was to be on the basis "love me, love my boy-love", and if Lisa did not like it, too bad. Unsurprisingly, marital bliss did not prevail. Michael continued to hope he would become a father by Lisa but by this time she was in no mood to oblige. As she later confirmed, with the marriage in trouble she began to worry what would happen to the child in the event of a divorce, saying, "all I could ever see was a custody battle nightmare". For the next few months Michael hardly saw Lisa. He was constantly away from Neverland. When he finally returned in December 1995, Lisa's mother Priscilla decided to pay him a visit to see what was going on. According to Monica Pastelle:

When she arrived she saw Michael in the living room playing with about a

> dozen babies, all crawling about, some laughing, some crying. It was like a big nursery, with a grown man in the middle of it all, seeming in a state of bliss. Though nothing wrong was going on, she was flabbergasted. It was so unsettling. Priscilla left immediately.[668]

By January in the new year, 1996, Lisa filed for divorce. In her petition she gave the Date of Separation as 10 December 1995. Years later she told *Newsweek*:

> He is not stupid. He's very charming when he wants to be, and when you go into his world you step into this whole other realm. I could tell you all about the craziness – all these things that were odd, different, evil or not cool – but it still took me two and a half years to get my head out of it.[669]

"Evil" is a strong word, all the more ominous for being left unspecific. What on earth could she have being talking about? And why would "not cool" spring to mind? Who would use that expression to describe, say, the evil activities of a sadistic serial killer? Could we imagine the killer's wife using it? – "All this torturing people to death, honey, it's so not cool". Some forms of evil *are* considered cool in some quarters, notably gang violence. There is only one thing I can think of that is widely seen to invite both the descriptions "evil" and "not cool": an adult being "masturbative" with "disciples".

Porter provides some support for such a view He reports that the Rev. Rick Stanley, evangelist stepbrother of Elvis, claimed Lisa told him that she had discovered some videotapes at Neverland that caused her great distress. She had refused to talk about their exact nature but she learned, as Stanley reportedly put it, "the sick truth about Michael" and knew her husband had "an unusual interest in young boys".[670]

Lisa's belief that she could "save" Michael must have been shattered by his decision to go on holiday with the Cascio brothers, but it was several months later before she filed for divorce, citing irreconcilable differences. What finally precipitated the breakdown of the marriage is uncertain. In December, just before the cited Day of Separation, she was heard shouting at her husband behind closed doors at the unlikeliest of times: when she was visiting him in the Beth Israel Hospital in New York, where he was being treated for heart arrhythmia. The row was so public that when finally she burst out of the door and marched towards the elevator, she was taken to task by both a doctor and Michael's mother Katherine for upsetting the patient. Taraborrelli's explanation for the incident – that Michael had been caught out in sexual infidelity with the woman who was to be his next wife – is to put it mildly unconvincing.[671] More to the point may have been that the Cascio boys had left Michael's hospital bedside just before she walked in.

As for Lisa Marie's apparently callous behaviour towards a man in peril of his life, it was probably nothing of the kind. It seems she was instead justifiably angry not just over the Cascio boys but also because her husband was not ill at all: he was faking it. In his book *Michael Jackson: The Man Behind The Mask*, Jackson's former communications chief Bob Jones explains that Michael had a penchant for staging illness to get out of commitments. He even tells of his own part in arranging such a deception in 1990 when Michael was admitted to St John's Hospital in Santa Monica, California. Regarding the admission to the Beth Israel Hospital, he said this came after Jackson had collapsed on stage during a rehearsal for an HBO concert special – a collapse that had more to do with wanting to get out of the show than with heart arrhythmia.[672]

If Lisa Marie's bedside manner and idea of how to treat a heart patient were somewhat unorthodox, the same criticism could not be levelled at the next woman in his life. Debbie Rowe, destined to be his bride in the same year as his divorce from Lisa, is a nurse. Just as with Lisa, he had met her many years before there was to be the faintest hint of matrimony. This was in the early 1980s and the circumstances had been strictly professional. Michael had consulted Dr Arnold Klein about the appearance of mysterious blotches on his skin, marks that would later be announced to the world as vitiligo. Debbie was on Klein's staff, and he told Michael to call her at any time about his condition if he felt the need. Phone calls duly followed, and Michael also saw Debbie when he needed to attend further consultations with Klein. He took her copies of his CDs and she became a Michael Jackson fan in a big way. She cared about him. There were even long night-time phone calls. She said he was best on the telephone. "All of his defences break down when he doesn't have to look at you, face to face," she said. She felt that he was sweet and misunderstood and also a rebel.[673]

Many people have testified to Michael's love of the telephone. The stories are legion of his hours-long calls, not least at night-time. It is hardly a unique trait and would not merit comment but for the revealing point hinted at by Debbie. Putting physical distance between himself and Debbie allowed him psychological closeness without the threat of that closeness turning into bodily intimacy. Without being face to face, he did not have to worry about any awkward moment when a woman might be thinking of going lips to lips. He could talk freely on the phone without being vulnerable.

Some writers, including Taraborrelli, have tried to paint a different picture, discerning a budding romance even while Michael was still married to Lisa. It is amusing the lengths to which some scribes would go in order to give the King of Pop some desperately needed heterosexual credentials. The *National Enquirer* provides a classic case in point. In a story appearing soon after Michael's second marriage, a "friend" has Debbie supposedly saying "Sleeping with Michael was the weirdest experience of my life". Why? Because "his idea of foreplay was to put on a horse's head or a suit of armour", but "he was an incredible lover who left her exhausted". The story is credited to Tony Brenna, John South and Alan Butterfield – apparently it takes *three* guys, perhaps "brainstorming" together while inhaling dubious substances, to come up with such banal Wacko Jacko nonsense.[674]

If anyone was going to dress up in such bizarre gear it would have been Debbie, not Michael. Off duty, she used to fling off her demure white nurse's uniform in favour of Hell's Angel-style black leathers and roar around Los Angeles on a 1000cc Harley-Davidson covered in dents from all her smashes. She painted arrows pointing to the damaged bits and painted the words "Shit happens" on the fuel tank. Her biker friend Mario Pikus said she swore like a sailor (she had that much in common with Lisa Marie) and drank gallons of beer. After a few drinks this large-framed, robustly-built woman would punctuate her raucous conversation with friendly punches that would sometimes knock the wind out of her macho companions.[675]

Rough, tough women may have their attractions for some men but it is hard to see Michael being among them. The thought of her towering bulk crashing into bed with him would have been terrifying. He would rather have been laid by her Harley. Mario and his wife Rebecca were in no doubt that Debbie's relationship with Michael was non-sexual. Rebecca felt Debbie was not a very sexual person anyway. She was star-struck as a great fan of Michael's, but there was no romance. Even Lisa Marie never regarded her as a rival, laughingly referring to her as "nursie". The closest the pair ever came to intimacy is a classic of Wacko Jacko lore: Debbie was the ministering angel who treated his burnt scrotum after he had inadvisedly tried to bleach it![676]

"Nursie" turned out to have more uses than nursing though. It could even be said that he experienced an intense desire for her body – a desire to use it *without* sexual intercourse as a means of begetting his own children. A pregnancy brought about by artificial insemination would avoid all the heifer-humping he so abhorred, and who better for the task than a highly sympathetic nurse he had come to know well and felt he could trust? Once Lisa Marie had made it plain she did not want his children, it must have seemed the only option. It appears he even put this to Lisa as an ultimatum. He told her straight that having kids was his chief goal and that Debbie had agreed to get pregnant. He said: "If you won't do it, then she will. How about that?" Lisa said, "Fine, go ahead and do it."[677]

September 1996 saw the start of Michael's *HIStory* tour. A few weeks later he was in the headlines with the news that a woman was carrying his baby. Debbie was five months pregnant. Her existence in his life was finally sprung upon the world after she had been tricked into talking to a "friend" who had been taping the conversation. The story ended up on the front page of the *News of the World* on 3 November 1996. Debbie was quoted as saying that Michael Jackson was the father and he would be raising the child without her. She also reportedly said they had had sex, but that when she did not immediately become pregnant they decided to try what Michael called "a foolproof way of doing it": artificial insemination. She said the process took place at the Los Angeles Fertility Institute, on Brighton Way in Beverly Hills. She also disclosed she would receive about $500,000 on delivery. Debbie's father, Gordon Rowe, a retired cargo pilot who lived in Cyprus, went on record to say the baby was conceived by artificial means. He retracted this statement, however, after Jackson expressed his displeasure.

Steve Schmerier, an ex-boyfriend of Debbie, insists she had agreed to try artificial insemination to get a baby for "a friend". Debbie did not tell him the name, but Schmerier said she is not the maternal type. She would only have agreed to do it on the basis of not being a traditional wife.[678] This found support in 2004 when Debbie spoke to Paramount TV's *Entertainment Tonight*, giving the show a tour of her home. MSNBC's Dan Abrams observed that "noticeably absent from the home were any photos of the children she bore for Jackson – a disturbing sight for any parent who may have watched the interview. The truth is that Rowe really wants more to be in Jackson's company than anything else".

Taraborrelli said Jackson could insist there was no artificial insemination, but he went too far in claiming there was no economic relationship with Debbie. As a surrogate mother, he pointed out, it was just not credible she would give a rich man a baby for nothing. The biographer said she had had millions of dollars worth of "gifts" over the year. When Jackson's former business manager Myung Ho Lee sued him in 2002, among the court papers was Michael's monthly budget, which included "payment to Debbie Rowe" for $1.5 million. This figure would not have been on every month's statement but she certainly did well financially. He bought her a $1.3 million home in Beverly Hills in autumn 1997. The pair never lived together.[679] Earlier, Caroline Graham, writing in the *Sun*, had reported the artificial insemination element as hard fact, citing a £1 million pre-nuptial deal with Debbie, signing over her custody rights. In this version the contract was for more than one child, but no source for the information was given.[680] Graham's story appeared to be borne out later in Martin Bashir's famous documentary *Living With Michael Jackson*, when Michael not only admitted to using a surrogate mother for his third child but also hinted at the use of artificial insemination to beget the first two, saying it involved "my own sperm cells" – a strange expression to use if he was talking about ordinary sex.

Also, just after the Bashir programme aired, *Entertainment Tonight* showed interview footage in which Debbie Rowe was asked if she and Michael ever slept together. Rowe answered with what seemed like evasive irony, saying, "Yeah…There's been times when there's been five people in our bed". Pressed on whether the couple had actually had sex she avoided the question, saying, "I don't want to go there."[681]

By January 2004 Debbie had given Michael two children, a son, Prince Michael, and a daughter, Paris. She was in a custody dispute over them and it was being reported she was about to file a legal dossier claiming Michael was not their father and that they were born after she was artificially inseminated with anonymously donated sperm. Debbie claimed she entered into a surrogacy agreement with Jackson in 1996, some nine months before the couple wed. The agreement reportedly stipulated that she should not have sex for six months before she was inseminated. She said she received (according to the report, which gave the details in British currency figures) a £6 million pay-off, a £1.6 million Beverly Hills home, a car, clothes, furs and jewels as part of the agreement. Michael was said to be paying her £35,000 a month. In the agreement, she reportedly agreed to "knowingly and voluntarily waive my right to contest Michael's paternity of either child" and "consent to Michael being declared the father".[682]

The financial figures in this report are not identical to those featured earlier, but further support for the key claim – that Michael was not the father – emerged near the end of Michael's trial in 2005. This came up when the lawyers were debating the jury rules in connection with what became known in court as the "Outtakes Tape", on which the jury had heard Jackson claim that all his children were biologically his own, and that the elder two had been conceived in the usual way with Debbie. Michael's lawyer Robert Sanger said that evidence "as to the circumstances of the birth of his children would not be offered for the truth of the matter". It looked as though Sanger thought the claims might well be false. At the very least, it appeared his client had not mentioned the existence of any evidence that could have proved his claims.

After Michael's death in 2009 a newspaper would say they had seen legal documents confirming that Debbie had entered a surrogacy agreement with Michael on 23 January 1996, before artificial insemination conducted by Dr Hal C Danzer with anonymously donated semen from a semen bank. They repeated the procedure in June 1997.[683] Also after Michael's death, Debbie was quoted as saying she knew she would never see the children again, adding colourfully, "I was never cut out to be a mother – I was no good. It's just like I impregnate my mares for breeding. It was very technical. Just like I stick the sperm up my horse, this is what they did to me. I was his thoroughbred. I don't want these children in my life."[684]

Going back to when Debbie was pregnant for the first time, in 1996, she was frantic for a while after the *News of the World* broke the artificial insemination story. She thought Michael would blame her for being indiscreet. But in fact he was sympathetic, being well aware of tabloid trickery and how anyone can easily fall into traps. Said Debbie's friend Tanya Boyd: "She was so relieved, she decided that she would be loyal to him, and once you have Debbie Rowe's loyalty, you have it for life – unless you screw up royally."[685] One might add that she proved capable of stupendous loyalty even *after* Michael had indeed screwed up royally. She stood by him at his trial in 2005, confounding commentators such as Diane Dimond, who predicted she would let all hell loose on the witness stand. This was despite the fact that by this time Debbie was in a "bitter" custody dispute over the children and Michael had cut her totally out of his life despite all she had done for him. It must be supposed that he saw her simply as a gold digger.[686]

The impact on his image of Michael paying someone to have a baby for him by artificial insemination was of course immense. It would confirm his inability or unwillingness to do what usually "comes naturally" through being in a steady relationship with a woman and "making love" frequently. His publicity people had spun his marriage to Lisa Marie as just such a relationship. The formal break-up of the marriage clubbed that idea on the head with all the media-friendly warmth and humanity of a seal cull. The only way Michael could hope to keep alive any faint plausibility as to his sexual normality was by marrying again. Why not, after all? In the show business world the most rampantly "normal" stars often seem to marry and divorce on a whim, and then – like Michael's friend Elizabeth Taylor – even re-marry the same partner.

So, for the sake of appearances if nothing else, marrying Debbie Rowe logically had to be Michael's next career move. Not that we hear much of this in the "authorised" version. Taraborrelli's spin, sourced to a Jackson "associate" emphasises the role of his mother. In this version, Katherine thought Debbie was a "nice girl" and that for her sake she told Michael to "give your child a name".[687] It is just the sort of family values sentiment one would expect to hear from a conventional church-going Christian such as Katherine. Doubtless this is exactly how she felt but it totally misses the vital point that Debbie's agreement, as would later become clear, effectively excluded her from a continuing role in the life of any child or children she might bear for Michael. Far from giving *her* child a name, the child would cease to be *hers* in any meaningful way. It would be almost as though she had sold the child to strangers. Thus Katherine's rationale for the marriage did not stack up.

Bob Jones described the idea of Michael marrying Debbie in order to placate his disapproving mother as "laughable". Jones identifies the real reason as the need to placate the Saudi prince with whom Michael was a business partner at the time, Prince Alwaleed. Jones felt that the prince, as a Muslim, would not have approved of having children outside marriage. As for the marriage itself, Jones calls it a sham: "Michael Jackson wasn't the least bit interested in Debbie Rowe. He was only interested in her churning out those blond-haired, blue-eyed babies."[688]

The *HIStory* tour was into its Australian leg when the news of Debbie's pregnancy broke. When she flew to Australia to meet Michael, she had no idea he planned to marry her. Her friend Tanya Boyd got a call from her on 12 November 1996, and Debbie said she would be getting married the next day. Asked if she loved him, Debbie thought for a moment and said: "Yes, I do, sort of." Tanya pressed further: "Romantically?" Another pause, then Debbie said: "The kind of love I have with Michael is bigger, more important than that. It's not the kind that most people can understand. Simple love affairs end. This relationship will never end."[689]

The whirlwind "romance" brought an immediate wedding, on 13 November 1996, conducted in Michael's suite at the Sheraton on the Park Hotel, Sydney, in front of fifteen friends. The couple were dressed in black. Michael's best man was a new friend of his named Anthony – who was eight years old. Taraborrelli says Michael identified him as a nephew but the long-time Jackson watcher could discover no nephew of that name. After being pronounced man and wife, the couple exchanged "an affectionate look and a brief, tentative kiss".

A day or two after the wedding, Michael and Anthony – *not*, as scheduled, Michael and his bride – attended the Australian premiere of Michael's video *Ghosts*. Anthony, observers agreed, was a dead ringer for Jordie Chandler. Anthony was one of a small group of children who were later all invited back up to his hotel room for "a little party with games, dress-ups (in Michael's own stage clothes) and food and pillow fights," according to an article in a Jackson fan magazine.[690] Only the previous month, commentators had been noting the presence in Michael's life of yet another playmate: eleven-year-old Omer Bhatti, a boy of mixed Norwegian and Pakistani parentage. Years later, Omer was cited by former Neverland housekeeper Kiki Fournier, in evidence at Jackson's trial, as having once been one of his "special" boys. By this time, in 2005 and now aged twenty, Omer was living at Neverland and, according to one columnist, Michael had for some time been passing him off as his son![691]

This story of convenience was revived as a major news angle (but none the less spurious on that account) after the Staples Center, Los Angeles, memorial event following Michael's death. Omer had been allocated a seat in the front row alongside the Jacksons, giving rise to speculation that he might actually be part of the family. But his place of honour was unsurprising given that he had been close to Michael for many years at Neverland, starting in 1996. One of the young man's friends, Ricky Harlow, revealed that Omer, like so many of Michael's favourite boys, used to share the star's bed – while his parents stayed in a cottage in a different part of Neverland. They were given jobs in Michael's employ. Pia, Omer's Norwegian mother, was a nanny to Michael's son Blanket, and Huayoun (named in many reports as Riz), his Pakistani father – his *real* father – was a chauffeur. Omer himself denied that he is Michael's son, describing him instead as "my best friend".[692]

Marsha Devlin, a neighbour of Debbie's, was in touch with her by phone after the wedding. When Marsha asked, Debbie said Michael did not stay with her in her suite at the Sheraton the night before they wed, nor on their wedding night. He stayed with "an assistant" in another room.[693] She returned to Los Angeles less than a week later, never having slept with Michael. The day before the wedding, Michael phoned Lisa Marie to tell her. She gave him her blessing.

Three months later, in February 1997, Debbie gave birth to a baby boy at Cedars Sinai Medical Center, Los Angeles. Michael's first child was named Prince Michael. Later, with the birth of his second son, the first would become known as Prince Michael I and the second Prince Michael II. A streak of grandiosity may run in the family: Michael's maternal grandfather and great grandfather both bore the same "royal" title. A deeper explanation, though, is to be found in the response of black Americans to the appalling history of their enslavement and, until very recent times, their continuing enforced subservience: many of them understandably reacted by choosing names that proudly and justifiably asserted their dignity and significance.

When Michael and Debbie posed for photos with the baby in March at the Four Seasons Hotel, it was the first time Debbie had seen the infant since she had given birth six weeks earlier: "She was smuggled into the hotel room, given the infant to hold, told to smile for the camera with Michael...and then, her work done, thanked profusely by Michael and sent on her way."[694] Macaulay Culkin and Elizabeth Taylor were announced as godparents. The child was light-skinned with black hair and dark brown eyes. Six years later, though, when he was seen in the Bashir documentary (albeit wearing a face mask), Prince Michael was strikingly blond. Had his hair changed colour naturally, as sometimes happens with children? The roots of the child's hair were dark. It looked as though the hair had been dyed and the blondness was beginning to grow out. Had Michael dyed Prince's hair on a whim? When they appeared at the Staples Center, Los Angeles, public memorial ceremony in July 2009, shortly after Michael's death, the hair of all three of his children was dark, especially that of his youngest, Prince Michael II ("Blanket"), which was black. The urge to alter his own appearance over the years was such a disaster that one might suppose he would steer well clear of any such tendency towards his children. Hair dyeing is hardly in the same league as plastic surgery but it was a worrying sign. Ahmad Elatab, one of the many boys who shared a bed with Michael, has spoken of the star's preference for blonds, saying he liked them to look like the young Macaulay Culkin. In a newspaper interview, he also confirmed that Michael bleached Prince's hair.[695]

There would have been good reason for young Prince Michael to look like little Mac if bloggers' rumours were true: it was being claimed that Macaulay was not only the baby's godfather but had provided the semen for the artificial insemination as well. Michael's death saw the tabloids and even the "quality" press join in the rumour-mongering with gusto, this time saying Mac was Blanket's father.[696] One paper quoted Mr Culkin as saying that out of loyalty to the singer he would not comment on the claims. That in itself could be taken as a comment, though: to have denied the story would surely not have been taken as disloyal; but confirming it might indeed be thought so. Therefore, we can conclude... Or maybe not!

But Macaulay Culkin was far from the only potential pop in this protracted paternity puzzle. Nigel Pauley, writing for the *Daily Star*, was particularly industrious in supplying alternative candidates. He reported that so-called "Mafia heir-apparent" Al Malnik was claiming to be Blanket's father, adding that "sources" had speculated he might be the father of all three of Michael's children. Pauley opined that "Paris bears an incredible resemblance to Malnik's own daughter by his wife Nancy", adding that Jackson gave "special thanks" to Malnik on the cover credits of his *Greatest Hits* album.[697] But less than two weeks later this same writer, in the same paper, was touting another name, this time implicating Dr Arnold Klein, Debbie Rowe's boss, as the father of the two children she bore! A friend of Rowe's reportedly laughed at the idea, telling gossip columnist Roger Friedman, "When Debbie heard that, she said it made her skin crawl."[698] But Pauley insisted his paper's photo "shows the children are dead-ringers for Debbie, 48, and her ex-boss. Both Paris and Prince Michael I have bachelor Dr Klein's dark skin and eyes." The story went on to say Dr Klein had told TV chat show host Larry King that he had once donated sperm; but Klein had none too helpfully added he was not the father, "to the best of my knowledge".[699] Within a week, though, Klein had become far more knowledgeable. Now he was "telling friends" he was the father of Michael's two children by Debbie Rowe and could prove it; he was even said to be planning to claim custody of the kids, who knew him as "Uncle Arnie".[700]

The good doctor seemed to have been telling people a great many things, if the hearsay is true. The most sensational story came from Paul Gohranson, described as a former live-in masseur and lover of Dr Klein.

From this source we heard that Michael was infertile, hence physically incapable of fathering his own children. Gohranson claimed to have heard from Klein that Michael's testicles had been damaged in childhood during beatings by his father. In a video interview, Gohranson says Klein told him Michael had spoken of at least two occasions, maybe more, when Joe Jackson had hit him in the privates. The first was when he was very young. On that occasion his father had not deliberately targeted the genital zone, but a blow landed there in the course of a beating when he was being held by one leg. The second time was more serious, when he was considerably older. This came after a solo album did not do very well. Joe told Michael he was losing his voice and his looks; he was shaming the Jackson family. Michael had started to cry. Joe said, "You're a sissy. If you're a sissy you don't need balls." He then allegedly kicked Michael in the privates causing one testicle to swell badly, becoming permanently enlarged and painful.

We need to bear in mind that Gohranson heard it from Klein who heard it from Michael. Allegedly. Triple-removed hearsay should be treated with caution. Klein also allegedly told Gohranson that he knew "for a fact" that Michael had never molested children. But how could he know such a thing unless he had been at Michael's side every day of the star's life, watching his every move?[701] For good measure, Gohranson also said Klein had claimed to be the father of all three of Michael's children.[702] Joe Jackson took to the airwaves soon after Gohranson's video went online. Talking to Larry King on CNN, he denied ever abusing his son, saying, "A lot of people in America spank their kids. But Michael was never beaten by me."[703]

Whatever the truth or otherwise as to the beatings, it would emerge from the autopsy that Michael's body had been "actively producing sperm" at the time of his death, according to a report carried by the Associated Press.[704]

Even if Michael had been fertile, though, there was strong reason, as we have already heard, to believe his two children from Debbie were not from his own sperm. Further confirmation of this emerged after Michael's death. In a defamation lawsuit brought by Debbie in July 2009, the complaint included a summary for the judge which included the following wording: "Ms Rowe is the mother of two children born during her marriage (dissolved 2000) to the internationally renowned performer Michael Joseph Jackson." Intriguingly, Rowe's attorney did not cite Michael Jackson as the childrens' father. According to Roger Friedman, who drew attention to this wording in one of his columns, the word "father" does not appear at all in the fifteen-page document. Lawyers are paid to be careful about such matters: the fact that Jackson was not mentioned as the father is unlikely to be accidental.[705]

So, how many fathers are we up to now, apart from Michael himself, that is? Let's see: Culkin, Malnik, Klein, and er... oh, yes, former child star Mark Lester. He had incontestably fathered all of Michael's three children in a way, having been added to the list of their godparents at a ceremony in Las Vegas in 2003. Famed for his lead role in the 1968 movie *Oliver!*, he was born in the same year as Michael and enjoyed a close friendship with him. Also, Michael was godfather to Lester's own four children, three girls and a boy.[706]

Soon after Michael's death, Lester gave an interview to the *News of the World*, in which he spoke about his own and his family's relationship with Michael, claiming he had secretly donated sperm to help the singer have children. He went into detail about how the arrangement had been made, and the procedures at the London clinic where the donation had taken place. After seeing over the years what he took to be a striking physical likeness between his daughter Harriet and Michael's daughter Paris, he became convinced he was the father of both, and he said he was prepared to take a paternity test. The paper carried photos of the two girls. I could see his point. It all seemed very convincing.[707]

Just one week later, though, Mark's ex-wife Jane claimed he had not even been in contact with Michael at the time he claimed to have been donating sperm. More damning still, it emerged that in a newspaper interview six weeks earlier, with rival paper the *Sunday Mirror*, Lester had confirmed Jane's point out of his own mouth, saying contact between him and Michael amounted to just "a few phone calls" between the early 1980s and 2001. According to Jane, Lester lost touch with Michael in the 1980s and did not pick up the friendship again until after their youngest child, Felix – their first boy – was born in 1999. She said Mark took Felix with him to Neverland. In view of the allegations against the star she had urged her husband not to let the child sleep in a bed with him.

Intriguingly, though, this newspaper story trashing Lester's claims ends with a quote from Jackson family lawyer Brian Oxman commending the former child star as "honest and decent" and said he was not making anything up. Thus he could indeed have donated sperm but would this would not necessarily mean he was father to Paris.[708]

That is quite enough about fathers, especially fantasy ones. Let's get back to Debbie. Despite the lucrative financial deal Debbie Rowe, now

Jackson, had struck with her improbable husband, she reportedly felt uneasy over the way things had gone. It was said that, "She has this sickening feeling that she has become a bit player in Jackson's whole world of make-believe and forever changing moods." Her ex-boyfriend, computer executive Steve Schmerier, said she agreed to help Michael on the understanding that she would not become a traditional wife. She had succumbed to the argument that the child should not be born out of wedlock but had belatedly realised that the wedding had really been more for the sake of Michael's image than the baby's future.[709]

Not that the wedding helped him once the baby was in the spotlight. Instead he became a figure of fun, especially in America, where TV wits battled for supremacy in the wisecrack league. "Michael is amazing," said one. "He was married for two years, has a son and is still a virgin." Said chat-show host David Letterman: "While the baby was being delivered, Michael was pacing nervously up and down the hall – just like he did during the conception." And: "The birth made medical history. It's the first time doctors knew the sex of the baby before they knew the sex of the father."

But one aspect of the story was rather more serious. For no amount of photos of "the couple" holding the infant could disguise the sensational fact that they would not be living together as a couple and that Prince Michael would have no mother. Surrogacy is itself controversial, even when commissioned by parents with all the conventional credentials of a loving home to offer. For Michael to go a giant step further and deliberately engineer an experiment in motherless childhood was more than sensational. To many, it was unambiguously scandalous. There turned out to be no laws against it, however, so the media simply goggled in amazement, reporting with a mixture of fascination and horror on the childcare arrangements for the baby:

> He lives in an antiseptic world where even the air he breathes is checked every hour. No one is allowed to kiss or cuddle him. And every toy he plays with is thrown in the bin as soon as he puts it down…
>
> …his mother has been replaced by a team of **SIX** nannies and **SIX** nurses who work around the clock…The day team do all these drills with him to build up his strength. They are kept under video surveillance to make sure they do it.
>
> One of his first nannies explained: "When we fed him, all the utensils had to be boiled first and could only be used for one type of food. They were

all thrown away after a single use. He's not even allowed to mix with other kids so he has a chance to feel normal."[710]

This was part of a typical British tabloid report coming out one year after the birth. Every detail cited is designed to crank up the idea of horrific abnormality. But is it fair? The last sentence is a giveaway. The poor little mite has no playmates. What seems to have escaped the writer is that the child is still only twelve months old at this point, not twelve years. How many first-borns in a family have playmates before they can walk or talk? How many need one? As for his mother being replaced by nannies, it is an especially ironic comment to appear in a British paper: not so long ago the entire British upper class were raised by nannies, including many of its most celebrated figures, such as Winston Churchill. All the love and affection he received came from his nanny, Mrs Everest. His mother was too busy with her social round to bother with him. While not all nannies end up being as loved as Elizabeth Everest, neither do all mothers.[711]

Michael's own contribution as a parent was also downplayed in the story, referred to only deep into the text of a long report. But it is interesting once we get there. Again, one of the nannies reports:

> Michael gets a kind of faraway look in his eye whenever he holds Prince. He seems to have a very protective streak in him. He likes to feed his son and change the nappies. They often take naps together and Prince gets grizzly when Michael has to be away. If Prince cries, Michael will sing and dance for him which the baby seems to love…Whenever the baby is awake, Michael is with Prince the whole time unless he is on tour. When the baby is sleeping he will lie with him for a while and then steal away to work. Michael puts his voice on tape for Prince. There are little stories or poems. When he's out at concerts, the nurses play it for him.[712]

By the spring of 1997, when the baby was just a few months old, it was being put about from the Jackson camp that the star was "still besotted with his ex-wife" Lisa Marie Presley.[713] What is certainly true is that the pair retained a degree of friendship and Lisa was seen with him on tour in the UK and South Africa. But in July, the very month a "besotted" Michael was preoccupied with his beloved Lisa in London, Debbie was becoming pregnant by him again in Paris! In the Fox Channel documentary *The Michael Jackson Interview: The Footage You Were Never Meant to See*, Jackson is shown in outtakes from the Martin Bashir documentary claiming he slept with his ex-wife Debbie Rowe, and their four-year-old daughter Paris was conceived in the French capital. In this intriguing tale of two cities we have several possibilities. Michael was (a) extremely good at the most perilous kind of diary management, which also had to include his busy concert schedule; (b) for an encore to his moonwalk, he had perfected the even more dazzling art of being in two places at once; (c) Debbie's second pregnancy, like the first, was achieved by artificial insemination. I know which my money is on.

By October, Lisa and her children had joined Michael and his parents in South Africa. But she began to be uncomfortable with the new Michael, whose earlier sense of doom at the time of his 1993 troubles "...had now been replaced with a kind of bravado. It appeared that Michael felt invincible," says Taraborrelli, who then mentions a boy he does not identify but who was almost certainly one we have already met, Omer Bhatti: "A particularly troubling fact for Lisa was the appearance of a thirteen-year-old Norwegian boy. He was a cute kid who wore a red baseball cap all the time, given to him by Michael. Did Michael still not realise how dangerous it was for him, in terms of his public image, to have young boys with him on tour?" Lisa tried to raise this point with Michael. He just did not want to know. She felt powerless, and like an outsider. As Lisa later said to Katherine: "I did love him. That I know. But, face it, Katherine, your son is one big mystery. "Katherine laughed: "Girl, tell me about it!"[714]

Did Lisa think Michael had ever loved *her*? On *The Oprah Winfrey Show* in March 2005, she was asked whether he had loved her "as much as he could". She replied, "Yes, as much as he was capable of loving somebody." Had he used her? "All the signs point to yes on that. I can't answer for him."

Debbie's second baby, a girl, arrived on schedule in April 1998, nine months after the "conception" in Paris, the event being memorialised in her name: Paris Katherine Michael Jackson. It is an odd name in more than one way. The inclusion of Michael's mother's name is an understandable tribute to her, but the obsessive replication of his own name in that of all three of his children is another matter. In his daughter's case it leaves the strange feature that two out of her three monikers are "officially" boys' names, not that Paris has been used much since classical times. Had he given much thought to the Paris of Greek myth, son of Priam, King of Troy, Michael might have changed his mind – a dream about the child's birth had been interpreted as an evil portent. On arrival into the world Paris was expelled from the family, exposed to the elements and left for dead.

Curiously enough, Pope John Paul II, no less, seemed to detect something of an evil portent about the arrival of Debbie's Paris. Michael's people had contacted the Vatican with a view to having the pope baptise the baby. The request was declined on the eminently sensible grounds that it might be perceived as a publicity stunt. In the event, the birth and infancy of Michael's second child attracted relatively little publicity compared to the first. Likewise, when her unusual arrangement with Michael no longer felt right for Debbie (it was later suggested she had medical complications following Paris's birth which forced Michael to look elsewhere for a mother),[715] the divorce in October 1999 passed without much comment. Debbie received around $10 million in the settlement. She was destined in 2005 to re-emerge dramatically into the spotlight during her ex-husband's trial. But from the divorce onwards the star's publicists were unable to conjure up any credible "romantic" interest for him.

Even the resourceful J Randy Taraborrelli was stumped – and being, as ever, unable to resist a juicy anecdote, he contributed to the contrary view, that Michael did not like being around women unless he knew he was "safe". He tells the story of how, round about 2002, Michael wanted to meet the young pop superstar Justin Timberlake. A meeting was duly arranged through his former "boy of the year" Wade Robson, who had become a choreographer and was now a friend of Timberlake. Wade showed up with his girlfriend Mayte Garcia, ex-wife of rock star Prince. Justin arrived with his then girlfriend Britney Spears. "Oh no," Michael said when told that Justin had brought Britney. "I didn't invite her. Why'd he have to bring her?" Dismayed, Michael wondered whether she could wait downstairs. He had wanted to see Justin, not her. As Taraborrelli wryly remarks: "The notion that Britney Spears might wait in the lobby while Michael entertained Justin, Wade and Mayte was not an idea his associates felt they could suggest." In the end, Michael was forced to "put up with" the company of the sexiest young woman in the world.[716]

What a waste! If only he had muscled in on Justin's scene for a while, by "borrowing" Britney for a couple of very public dates, it would have done wonders for his image. But for once Michael had a better idea, a more subtle public relations strategy that would draw its strengths from truths, or at least half-truths. Outrageous misrepresentations, such as his "romance" with Brooke Shields, had been good for a quick PR fix in the past, but they had proved unsustainable. Now, having chalked up two marriages and two children, he at last had the more sensible option of presenting his interest in children in a favourable light, by showing the world he was a good father.

For a while, around the turn of the millennium, there was some reason to suppose he might succeed. The Jordie Chandler affair was ancient history, and his later *HIStory*, both album and tour, had seen a triumphant return to megastar status. The Presley marriage had added glamour, despite its typically Wacko Jacko aspects, and the children – never mind how they had arrived – were now part of his acceptable family-man image. In September 2001, just ahead of the 9/11 terrorist attacks, Michael was in New York for two special concerts in Madison Square Garden in celebration of his thirty-year career as a solo artist. Nearly fifty million would watch one of those concerts when it was broadcast a little later as a CBS special on 13 November. Those paying tribute at the event included Ray Charles, Gloria Estefan, Ricky Martin, Liza Minnelli and Britney Spears. He was even entertained by a 13-year-old boy – rising star Billy Gilman, who sang Michael's early solo chart-topper "Ben". Michael was well and truly back. There were, to be sure, dark clouds on the horizon financially, thanks to expenditure that consistently exceeded his enormous income, but his assets would keep him creditworthy well into the future and his musical talent would always be able to generate cash to sustain his megastar lifestyle – or so he had good grounds to believe. For a brief interlude of a couple of years, he appeared to be in control of his destiny in general and his publicity in particular.

One publicity initiative of his stands out in this period: an appearance he made in March 2001 at the Oxford Union (the Oxford University student debating society) in connection with his latest charity project, Heal The Kids, aimed at "bringing parents closer to their children". Michael gave a lecture on what parents could learn from their offspring. A website statement about the charity said, "Major studies show that children who experience no tactility, no tenderness or hugging in their formative years, bear emotional scars that will not heal later in life. However, parents nowadays have often been replaced by television, computers, and home video games."

It took chutzpah for Michael, once accused of child molesting, to be seen promoting "tactility" with children – but then he had a rabbi to help him. The occasion had been set up in collaboration with Shmuley Boteach, a controversial Oxford rabbi introduced to Michael through their mutual friend the magician Uri Geller. Rabbi Boteach had raised a few eyebrows with the publication of his book *Kosher Sex*, and its serialisation in *Playboy* magazine. His six children were said to be "close" to Michael. One commentator astutely detected the rabbi's hand in the text of the speech:

> When Jackson said every child deserves "the right to be thought of as adorable (even if you have a face that only a mother could love)" it had the rhythm of a Jewish joke rather than one from Neverland.[717]

Other critics sniped from a variety of angles, memorably so in the case of John Walsh for the *Independent*:

> Dressed in that self-designed black frock coat with matching coat-of-arms, he looked like one of the playing card courtiers in Tenniel's illustrations for Alice In Wonderland...the lipstick was some obscure homage to Joan Crawford...and the nose – well, the nose is so sharp and snub these days, you could open bottles of beer with it.[718]

It will come as no surprise to learn that Walsh did not think much of the speech either. In general the upmarket British papers dismissed it as sentimental and – in a sign that Michael's rehabilitation had yet to reach the sober columnists outside the music press – inappropriate coming from a figure dubiously qualified as a child care expert.

Perhaps he would have done better to talk in a simple, anecdotal way about his own children, as the advertised theme suggested he might. Instead, he went in for grand generalisations: "Ours is a generation that has witnessed the abrogation of the parent-child covenant..."[719] You can almost hear the parents in the audience grinding their teeth. He also played the victim card yet again: "I am the product of a lack of a childhood, an absence of that precious and wondrous age when we frolic playfully without a care in the world." He did, however, attempt to strike a forgiving posture towards his harsh father. He wondered rhetorically whether his own children would grow up to resent him, as he had resented Joseph, for not having a normal childhood. He said he prayed they would take into account the "unique circumstances" he faced, concentrating on the sacrifices he made for them, not the things they had to give up, or the errors he made.

But did we learn much about what Michael is actually like as a parent? No, we did not. Long before he had children of his own, Michael once said about his mother, "Because of Katherine's gentleness, warmth and attention, I cannot imagine what it must be like to grow up without a mother's love."

He did not return to *that* point in his Oxford lecture, nor say anything about how Prince and Paris were faring without a mother's love.

Nevertheless, Michael's speech was much more substantial and, to all appearances, more sincere and heartfelt than some of the news coverage would have had us believe. Appropriately for an academic audience, there was a heavyweight statistical paragraph on youth crime in America and parent-child interaction in Britain. Like the element of Jewish humour this was surely not all Michael's own work: he was never noted for poring over government figures and sociological research papers. But there was also a good deal of personal anecdote that was revealing, moving, and mostly *not* about his own victimhood but pointed to a real concern reaching out beyond his own narrow self-interest. The complete speech was to have been included as an appendix so you could judge for yourself as to the accuracy and fairness of the more critical news reports. Unfortunately, the executors of Michael's estate refused permission for use of this copyright material.

Less than a year after Oxford, in about February 2002 – the exact date was never announced – Michael became a father for the third time with the birth of Prince Michael II. Not only was the birth kept quiet but so was the name of the mother. "She doesn't know me and I don't know her," Michael said later.[720] All he knew was that the mother in this new surrogacy arrangement was healthy, with good vision and intellect. He first claimed the mother was black, then later changed the story and said he did not know her identity. Debbie Rowe confirmed the child was not hers.

After Michael's death it was claimed in a *Daily Mirror* story that the surrogate mother was a Mexican nurse named Helena. And despite all those rumours of Michael's supposed sterility, and alternative fathers, the paper plumps for Jackson as the biological dad. Prince Michael Jackson II, aka Blanket, was born on 21 February 2002 at the Sharp Grossmont Hospital in La Mesa, near San Diego in Southern California, according to the *Mirror*'s very detailed story. Helena was paid a $20,000 surrogacy fee. On the baby's birth certificate Michael Joseph Jackson was identified as the father but the line for "Name of Mother" was left blank. The child was conceived through IVF, supposedly using Michael's sperm.

The *Mirror* relates that Michael had taken great care in his choice of "pretty" Helena. She struck him as attractive, stable and intelligent. But Blanket would not inherit looks, personality or brains from her. This is because *another* woman, identity still unknown, was an egg donor for the conception, thus making her, not Helena, genetically Blanket's mother.

Confused? We would have to be as wacko as Jacko *not* to find our heads spinning at the implications. This unknown woman was paid $3,500 for her contribution and signed legal papers handing over all rights to the child. The *Mirror* thought it unlikely she was even told that her eggs were involved in Blanket's birth.

The medic who had delivered Blanket was named as Dr Maria Castillo. She reportedly said Michael was not present at the time and the baby had been taken away from the hospital by an attorney. She later heard from a nurse that the mother had named the baby Prince Michael Jackson; Dr Castillo assumed the mother was a fan of both Michael Jackson and Prince, one of his rivals for superstar supremacy.[721]

Shortly before the *Mirror* story appeared, Michael's sister La Toya had spoken about Blanket's mysterious provenance, telling another newspaper he had come from a donor egg and *donated* sperm. She was quoted as saying: "Michael didn't want to know who the biological parents were. They took eggs from a donor and I believe the sperm came from one of five donors picked from a book."[722] One plausible bit of gossip was that the egg had been donated by Pia Bhatti, mother of Michael's long-time "special friend" Omer Bhatti. As we have heard already, Pia became Blanket's nanny at Neverland, and the source of the story is quoted as saying: "...you only had to see her with Blanket. She treated him as her own for one very good reason – he is."[723]

Michael had a nickname for the little boy: "Blanket". He "explained" that this was an expression he used with his family and employees. People were urged "to blanket" those they love and care for, "meaning like a blanket is a blessing".

"Blanket" may have been a blessing to Michael, but his infancy was not to be blessed with good fortune in terms of the star's public image as a good father. At only eleven months old Blanket burst into fame, putting the un-Jacksonian obscurity of his first months firmly into the past. Suddenly, he was very high-profile indeed – about sixty-feet high, according to press estimates. That was reckoned to be the height of the railed window in Michael's suite at the Adlon hotel in Berlin from which Michael dangled the child in one moment of madness in November 2002. He had simply come to the window to wave to his fans, massed in the street below – a totally routine occurrence for him, except for the fact that he would not usually be holding a baby. For a heart-stopping second or two when Blanket wriggled in his one-armed grasp, it looked as though tragedy was at hand. There is no doubt in my mind that the widespread unease expressed over this incident was thoroughly justified. Having seen the footage along with millions of others, I have no reservation in saying this was an act of child endangerment.[724]

A witness would later testify at Michael's trial to further serious irresponsibility affecting his children. Staff member Jesus Salas would say he saw Jackson drunk in front of his own children no fewer than three times. Michael had been so far gone, Salas, said, he thought the children were unsafe.

Two days after the Berlin incident Dr Carole Lieberman, a prominent Beverly Hills psychiatrist and child welfare advocate, lodged a formal complaint with California's Department of Social Services charging that Jackson was "not emotionally stable enough" to care for his children. Los Angeles attorney Gloria Allred (whom we have already met) made a similar complaint. Each of these ladies had an axe to grind. Typically, complaints such as theirs were exaggerated, and fancifully linked to the subject of their primary agenda: sex. They sought to imply from this one act of thoughtlessness that Michael was self-centred and inconsiderate of children's needs in a wider context – especially as regards his presumed sexual behaviour with them.

Unfortunately, Michael gave such critics all too much to talk about. Blanket was again a significant focus of their chatter in the infamous documentary by Martin Bashir, *Living With Michael Jackson*, which aired on British television's ITV 1 channel in February 2003. The allegations arising from this programme of sexual misconduct with the boy Gavin Arvizo will be taken up in the following chapter. But for the moment, our concern is with the light cast by the programme on Michael's behaviour towards his own children. Wrote Rupert Smith:

> Jackson's...parenting style was unique. His treatment of Prince Michael I, Paris and Prince Michael II (known as "Blanket") was distressing to observe. After the famous Berlin baby-dangling episode, Jackson strove to prove to Bashir what a good father he was by bottle-feeding little Blanket, fretfully wrapping the baby's face in a green chiffon scarf then whisking him away from the camera's glare. He snatched Paris from the maternity ward while she was still covered in afterbirth, and took her right home. Older brother Prince (nearly six) believes that "I haven't got a mother"; he also appears to have bleached hair. The kids never went out without masks on, and, when Daddy took them to the Berlin Zoo, were stuck in a terrifying scrum of overwrought adults.[725]

Bashir had said Prince had told him he did not have a mother. He had asked Michael what he thought that meant. Michael just shrugged it off, saying there are plenty of one-parent families. Speaking of Debbie, he claimed, "She can't handle it. She prefers the kids to be with me." He said the children were a gift from her.

"I used to go around holding baby dolls," Michael revealed.

"Really?" said an astonished Bashir.

"Yes, because I wanted children so badly."

Coming from a young woman, such an admission would have won sympathy. From Michael it was sensational confirmation of his oddness.[726] Mere words, though, however strange, paled into insignificance compared to the barrage of visible eccentricity Michael was displaying right there on screen, so powerful that Rupert Smith's "distress" would surely have been widely shared by the audience. But the "fretful" behaviour Smith complains of was understandable: while Blanket was being fed, Bashir was putting the infant's father under immense pressure with a barrage of questions over the dangling incident. Small wonder Michael seemed almost comically manic, his leg nervously jiggling at great speed, so that poor Blanket, precariously positioned thereon, was vibrating like a pneumatic drill. Just as understandably, the baby itself started to fret over the ridiculous transparent mask, which was totally ineffective in disguising his face but momentarily threatened to smother him.

One commentator said it looked as though Michael was playing with a doll: he did not appear to realise this was a person. This reaction made sense. To my mind the bizarre scene had a quality of cartoon-like violence about it. I mean the kids' cartoons like *Tom and Jerry*, in which an unfortunate mouse will be dismembered one minute but just fine the next. Or maybe Punch and Judy, the traditional British glove-puppet show for children featuring a deformed, child-murdering, wife-beating psychopath who commits appalling acts of violence and cruelty upon all those around him and escapes scot-free – and which it is greatly enjoyed by small children.

While Michael certainly cannot be accused of wanton violence and cruelty towards Blanket, he did appear to share Mr Punch's recklessness. It was indeed as though, just like a child playing with a doll, he was happy to "play" at being loving and tender one minute then ready to cast the toy aside when his attention was caught by something else. This impression was confirmed for me by the zoo incident. Michael later made the excuse that he had thought the zoo would be closed to the public, so there would be no fans or paparazzi to overwhelm Prince and Paris. But that does not explain his behaviour during the crisis: instead of worrying about the kids being crushed, and struggling to get them out of danger, he spent his time apparently unconcerned, "basking in the adulation of his fans", in Bashir's words. Footage from the scene showed not fans but a mêlée of photographers and reporters. So far as it was possible to tell, Jackson, Bashir and the two children were trapped in the middle, the kids completely lost to view beneath the barging grown-ups like a rugby ball in a scrum. We could hear Bashir calling to Michael in a nervous voice that he had got hold of Prince's hand. Michael later acknowledged that things had been difficult, even using the word "pandemonium". But astonishingly he showed no real concern, adding, "as long as I get to see the gorillas I'm satisfied. I love the gorillas."

Bashir put to him that Prince had been poked in the eye. At last, Michael sounded alarmed. "Did Prince get poked in the eye?" he asked anxiously. It was as though this was something no one had told him about. But then, after seeming to turn it over in his mind, he said no, that had not happened. Prince was okay.

Asked by Bashir why he could not have left his bodyguards or nannies to take the children to the zoo, Michael's response was unconvincing. He said he could not "take that chance", but he would not, or could not, explain what he meant by that. If he was implying Prince and Paris might have been kidnapped, it says little for his faith in his security staff. But in the middle of that scrum in the zoo he seemed entirely relaxed about leaving the kids in their hands or those of Bashir himself, who was at the scene.

Astonishingly, it was not to be the last episode of its kind. An official Jackson fan website, of all places, reported a similar incident in London in October, in 2005.[727] Hundreds of Michael Jackson fans turned up outside a theatre to catch a glimpse of the pop star as he arrived to see the stage version of the hit movie *Billy Elliot*. Security staff forced a path for Jackson through a crowd of admirers and photographers standing outside the Victoria Palace theatre so he could reach the front door. But, as the website for MJJ Source reported, "the singer fell to the ground in the commotion. Jackson's children accompanied him to the show but had their faces covered by clothing as they entered the theatre".

The idea that "faces covered by clothing" would somehow have kept the children safe is preposterous, though that seems to be the suggestion. Masking the children, or otherwise hiding their faces, was bound to strengthen the suspicion they must be Jackson's, not weaken it. I saw no report claiming the children were in any difficulty, but that may have owed more to the restraint of the fans on this occasion than Michael's care over their safety.

These are serious criticisms, but are they decisive in terms of judging Jackson to have been a bad parent, so incompetent or neglectful that he should have lost his parental rights? The verdict of the commentocracy, of which Rupert Smith's views were typical, appeared to set a standard few parents would meet if subjected to a similar level of intense scrutiny over a period of eight months, in the company of a reporter bent on discovering scandal. Parents are generally deemed unfit in the courts only in cases of sustained neglect or horrific cruelty. Mere incompetence, by contrast, tends to be regarded with indulgent amusement – witness the popularity of TV parenting programmes, in which a child psychologist or a "super nanny" are powered in to sort out kiddies' tantrums and disobedience, problems invariably caused by poor parenting. The sympathy accorded to the parents is reflected in the fact that there is no shortage of volunteer mums and dads willing to have their shortcomings publicly exposed. No one suggests they should have their children taken away from them.

Nor should we exaggerate the level of Michael's incompetence exposed by Bashir. We should remember, to start with, that as a child he was routinely exposed to unruly fans, and there were times when their behaviour threatened to get dangerously out of control. He survived, and rightly or wrongly he may have taken the view that some of the hazards of a star lifestyle could not always be avoided. Compared to the risks accepted as an inevitable part of growing up in every generation before our own, the dangers occasionally faced by Jackson's children have not been that great. The time is not long past when even quite small children were left free to roam and encounter serious adventure: from my own childhood a few decades back I well recall "scrumping" expeditions which ran the risk of ending with a beating from a farmer, or even being shot at by him, while the misadventures to be encountered by kids at loose in the urban jungle hardly need rehearsing. In our present risk-averse society – too tame, some would say – it is all too easy to get child protection issues out of proportion.

Of greater interest and significance is the rapport Michael had with his kids. The appearance he gave of treating his baby like a mere doll does not, I believe, survive close scrutiny. The manic Michael we saw, wildly jiggling, as he fielded Bashir's awkward questions, was also interacting with Blanket more effectively than was immediately obvious. Phased for a moment by the unwonted face mask, Blanket started to protest, but began to settle when the reassuring bottle was in place and Michael started cooing to him lovingly. However improbable it may seem to conventional observers, Michael's strange behaviour could not be taken to imply a deficient relationship with his children.

And testimony to his excellent parenting, of Blanket in particular, emerged on the *Ebony* website, when the magazine ran an online background piece to an interview and photoshoot with Michael, carried in December 2007 in its printed edition. A question and answer session between *Ebony*'s readers and senior staff who had been working on the project included questions about Blanket. Harriette Cole, *Ebony* creative director, replied:

> We didn't meet Michael's two other children. His daughter, Paris, is nine and he has another son, Michael Joseph [sic], ten. Blanket was incredibly well-behaved while he was in our company, which is saying a lot for a five-year-old. He is obviously very close to his dad. They walked into the fitting holding hands and only separated when both of them became at ease. Michael's parenting skills were to be commended. Without many words, with very subtle gestures he offered discipline, guidance and support. Michael also obviously wants Blanket to learn good manners, so when the Ebony team came into the room for the interview, Michael coached Blanket on the proper way to shake hands and say hello. Small things, but isn't it the small things that show the measure of one's true self?

On the question of his biological relationship with the children, Michael at first claimed he had had a relationship with Blanket's mother. Interviewed again some time later, but for the same programme, he admitted to Bashir he had never known her and that she had been a surrogate mother on an anonymous basis. He said he had merely ascertained she was intelligent and healthy. Bashir did not point out the discrepancy between Michael's two stories, perhaps because nailing down the earlier untruth was not the biggest fish he had to fry. Instead, he pointed out that none of Michael's children is black. Would he ever have a child by a black mother? To Bashir's astonishment and apparent disbelief, Michael claimed Blanket's mother was indeed black. He added he was also thinking of adopting two kids from every continent, one boy and one girl.

While filming of *Living With Michael Jackson* was taking place, Jackson's videographer, Hamid Moslehi, had also been shooting footage of the same scenes, for the star's own record. This was a wise move. When

Bashir betrayed him through biased editing and a hostile voiceover, Jackson was able to demonstrate the dirty tricks he had been up to. He released his own footage, which showed many points favourable to him that Bashir had edited out. The Fox network used this Moslehi-shot material as part of a documentary presented by Maury Povich and titled *The Michael Jackson Interview: The Footage You Were Never Meant To See*. The show was in effect a rebuttal of Bashir, but it should not be confused with the so-called "rebuttal video" in which the Arvizo family took part, and which did not receive its first public showing until Michael's trial in 2005. This was shot by Moslehi with the specific purpose of rebuttal *after* Bashir had aired.

One of the most telling points in what I shall dub the Fox riposte was the glowing terms in which Bashir had spoken to Michael about his qualities as a parent, terms totally at odds with the footage that made it to air in his programme. In his own show, he professed to have been "saddened and deeply disturbed" by Jackson as a father. But the Fox riposte shows that even after the Berlin zoo episode he felt able to tell the star: "Your relationship with your children is spectacular. It almost makes me weep when I see them with you because your interaction with them is just so natural, so loving, so caring." This tells us much about Bashir but little about Jackson: the flattery may or may not have been empty. However, what he says next is rather more revealing. He says he must have heard "a million times" a little ritual in which one or other of the kids tells Michael "I love you", and just as predictably Michael replies "I love you more". While sugary endearments of this kind are not for all of us, they are hardly the mark of an emotionally neglectful or unloving parent. Nor was Bashir alone among Michael's adversaries in noting the star's good points as a parent. Former business associate Marc Schaffel, even after suing Michael over money he claimed was owed to him, admitted: "I have to say, with his own children, he absolutely shows to be one hundred percent a wonderful father. He has full-time care of the children, spends a lot of time with his children."[728]

In the wake of Bashir, the papers and the chat shows were full of judgmental accounts like Rupert Smith's; the scribblers and the chatterboxes were universally aghast. The Queen of Mean against Michael was psychiatrist Carole Lieberman, who issued a complaint to the Santa Barbara Child Protective Services. Her "psychological analysis" of the programme listed no fewer than eighteen reasons "why Michael Jackson's children should be removed from his care until he gets psychiatric treatment and takes parenting lessons". Her response to Michael's policy of keeping his children's faces covered in public is particularly interesting. Michael had claimed the children had needed to wear masks in order to protect them from potential kidnappers and to maintain their privacy. Lieberman's response invoked the way the children themselves would see it:

> Surely, they don't believe Michael's explanation of it being to protect them – since they experience his lack of protection of them when they are out in public. For example, when he took them to the Berlin zoo he was oblivious of their fears of being crushed by the crowd. Michael's children experience having to wear the mask as an indication of his believing that they are too ugly and monstrous for him to want the public to see. They would believe that Michael is ashamed of them and wants to hide their face. Add to that the rejection that they must feel from their mother's abandonment, and they would be more convinced that she rejected them because they are ugly lepers.[729]

Lieberman's colourful alarmism later found a new source of inspiration. She began to tout herself as "The psychiatrist America turns to for help coping with terrorism".

Did Michael's children ever really think they were ugly lepers? Taraborrelli criticises the masks policy in a more subtle manner, questioning whether such costumes were really for the children's sake, or rather a tool of his image building. Were the masks, he wonders, a way for Michael to distinguish himself as the most prominent, sought-after man in the world, by making it look as though his offspring were the most prominent, sought-after progeny?[730]

One trouble with Lieberman and large elements of the empire-building child abuse lobby is a tendency to shoot from the hip, firing off fierce and damaging accusations based on a superficial and one-sided acquaintance with the facts. Those who went to Neverland, or otherwise encountered Michael's family in private, reported a very different impression. Michael's parents might of course have been expected to support their son, but their views were echoed by others. Taraborrelli tells us that when they visited Neverland Joseph and Katherine found that:

> Prince Michael I and Paris are bright, confident, affectionate and considerate. They pray before meals. They are polite, thoughtful and funny. Michael becomes angry when they swear, as they sometimes do since most

of their friends are adults. He never spanks them, however; he would never lay a hand on them, but as he puts it, 'No means no.' He doesn't raise his voice in anger, and doesn't seem to have to do so – they are generally well behaved. If one does act up, he or she has to endure a 'time out', which means standing in a corner, alone, to cool off.[731]

Michael explained to his biographer that he rationed the youngsters' toys and sent presents they received as Christmas gifts from his fans to orphanages. Rabbi Boteach confirmed that he was not indulgent but firm. He would read to the kids. He had discipline but never raised his voice. Taraborrelli sees it as significant that Michael did not like seeing his children stare into a mirror for too long when getting ready for the day. "I look great," young Prince once said, as he combed his hair. "No, you look okay," Michael said, correcting him. Prince Michael, at least, seems in little danger of thinking he is an "ugly leper".[732]

Surprisingly, even long-time Jackson baiter Diane Dimond came up with information revealing him as a good parent with delightful children. She interviewed air stewardess Lauren Wallace shortly after she stepped out of the witness box at Michael's trial in 2005. As a prosecution witness, she had said she saw Jackson cuddle with an eleven- or twelve-year-old child on a cross-country flight in a private plane the same year he allegedly sexually abused another boy. Nevertheless, she told Dimond, most of her contact with Jackson was very positive.

"He was salt of the earth. He was wonderful," she said. "I loved flying with him even though weird things did happen. He was so polite to me all the time."

Wallace worked for Jackson on fifteen to twenty five flights and said she was consistently impressed with him, especially in the way he raised his children. She said the two boys and a girl were "cuter than a bucket of baby ducks," had large vocabularies, a respectful demeanour, and seemed happy and healthy.[733] Macaulay Culkin, godfather to two of the children, has been similarly effusive. He said he was regularly in touch with Michael: "His kids are beautiful. I love them so much. They're so great."[734]

Strong public support for Michael as a parent also came from another famous source, veteran movie actor Gregory Peck, until his death in June 2003. Darwin Porter tells us he had been a friend of Michael's for a quarter of a century, the singer having been a particular fan of his film *To Kill A Mockingbird*, in which Peck's character is a lawyer who bravely defends an innocent black man charged with raping a white girl in the old Deep South. As a black man – well, at one time anyway – Michael might have been expected to warm to the theme, but the prominent role of child characters in the film may have been an additional factor drawing him back to watching it time and time again.

The film would also have been important to him for the character of Boo Radley. Kept indoors by his stern, "mean" father following a minor infraction in his youth, Boo was rarely glimpsed by anyone in the small community for years and years. Rumours thrived that he came out at night, up to no good; unsolved crimes in the town were said to be his doing. Echoes of the story are to be found in the answer Michael gave when an interviewer for *Ebony* asked what he thought about all the bad things people were saying about him following his trial in 2005. He said he paid no attention because "...it's ignorance. It's usually not based on fact. It's based on, you know, myth. The guy who you don't get to see, so you gossip about him. Every neighbourhood has the guy you don't see."[735]

When charges of child molestation were laid against Michael, Peck defended him. He called Michael a model parent and posted a letter of support on his fellow star's website. Porter relates that Peck visited Neverland many times and saw for himself how well Michael got on with his children.[736]

For the last, and longest, word on Michael Jackson as a parent I turn to the British journalist and biographer Jonathan Margolis. Unlike all but a handful even of his numerous biographers, Margolis actually knew Michael at close quarters. In the wake of the Bashir documentary, his defence of the star in a newspaper interview was robust. He said he spent several months working with Michael and Rabbi Boteach on a book about the importance of adults retaining their childlike qualities. The book was never finished but he came to like Michael and his children. Michael, he said, was "sweet, charming, intelligent... and highly eccentric." He was also deeply sad, not in the sense of being inadequate but "melancholic, unhappy and damaged". As for Prince and Paris, they were "bright, well mannered, unspoilt and unaffected".

What about the masks the children were made to wear in public? Wasn't that a bit weird? Margolis answered that one by talking about when he first saw Michael cover his own face with a mask as the pair of them were about to leave a London hotel that was surrounded by fans. Explaining to his friend what he was up to, Michael had lifted the corner of the mask and whispered:

"Razzle-dazzle 'em." Whether he was covering himself or his kids it was all about glamour and mystique. He also taught his children to get used to the inevitable attention that goes with fame.

Far from being weird, said Margolis, Michael was more level-headed than a good many celebrities, such as those gullibly taken in by cults such as Kabbalah or Scientology. He also had his own views on what was weird, regarding it as disgusting, for instance, that Princess Diana's children were encouraged by their father to witness the bloody aftermath of a fox hunt.

"I saw Michael's amazing empathy with kids many times," he said. "He talks to them as though they are adults. He will not tolerate them interrupting an adult conversation, but is unusually attuned to young voices asking questions or requesting a drink, when most of us choose to pretend slight deafness.

Abused children inevitably advertise their suffering with introversion, aggression, shyness, sullenness, distrustfulness and depression. But, neurotic, eccentric and downright flaky as their famous father is, I don't see any of the above in Prince and Paris."[737]

To my mind Margolis went over the top at some points, determined as he was to defend every aspect of Michael's behaviour as presented by Bashir, even the notorious dangling incident. On balance, though, we have no good reason to believe that he was far from the mark on Michael's qualities as a parent. In the full version of Margolis' testimony he also made it clear he believed absolutely that Michael was not a child molester. It is to that contention, and to the criminal trial of 2005 arising in the wake of Bashir, that we must now turn.

CHAPTER FOURTEEN

The Trial, Part One: Wacko Jacko v Trasho Basho

Famed for an interview with Princess Diana in which the tragic royal sensationally poured her heart out to the world, Martin Bashir must have struck Michael Jackson as the ideal conduit for his own bid to "set the record straight", especially over his love of children and qualities as a parent. Bashir had come across as a sympathetic listener, someone who truly understood that glamour and fame can mask untold sorrows and heartache. He had allowed Diana to accuse her husband of adultery and confess to her own – theoretically an offence of high treason against an heir to the throne and one which still carried the death penalty at that time – without questioning her aggressively or adding a judgmental voiceover. Bashir, at least in Diana's case, had given his subject free rein, rather than attacking like a tabloid Rottweiler.

With the considerable advantage of 20-20 hindsight, we know that rather than free rein, what Bashir gave Michael was enough rope to hang himself. The idea that the journalist would present a sympathetic and uncritical view of his relations with young boys, proved hopelessly deluded. The all but universal response among the commentocracy was what on earth could Michael have been thinking of? How could anyone with such long and bitter experience of media manipulation and malice have expected any better?

Such astonished incredulity can be seen as premised, consciously or otherwise, on the differences between Michael's situation and Diana's. There had to be a reason why Bashir was willing to give her a break but not him. To many this reason will be utterly obvious: adultery, even in circumstances quaintly amounting to treason, is these days nothing like as devastating to anyone's reputation as paedophilia – suspicions of which were bound to be revived in view of the amazingly candid footage Jackson would serve up to Bashir on a platter.

Yet Jackson must have thought otherwise, and his optimism was not as totally off the wall as it now appears. As was reviewed in the previous chapter, since the Jordie Chandler scandal of a decade earlier Michael had done much to rehabilitate himself in the public eye *without ever downplaying his interest in children in general or even being discreet over his continuing close friendships with young boys in particular*. As we have seen, his first wife, Lisa Marie Presley, had to share her marriage with the Cascio brothers while the second, Debbie Rowe, found that even her honeymoon was usurped by an eight-year-old boy.

Somehow, he got away with it. His *HIStory* album and tour were successful. In 2001 he was even able to lecture on parenthood at Oxford University. People listened – not all of them with cynical derision – as he promoted his vision of a better world for children, with less child abuse. He must have felt he was making headway at this time. Insulated in his bubble of fame from a world in which ordinary Joes perceived as paedophiles were being coerced more ferociously by ever more repressive legislation in terms of sex offender registration, longer sentences and life-long control and supervision, to say nothing of the growing panic over child pornography and internet child abuse, Jackson must have thought his celebrity truly made him "invincible" – had it not been for the commercial failure of his album of that name his Heal The Kids initiative, launched at Oxford, might have become a success instead of a damp squib. If Jackson had had the funds to put serious money into Heal The Kids, Bashir's documentary might have taken a very different turn. Instead of trashing Wacko Jacko, the man the *Sun* newspaper would dub Trasho Basho might have felt obliged to take a more charitable view not just of Jackson's charity work but also of his whole personality and relationships with children. He might even have begun to persuade people that there is nothing horrific about going to bed with kids, even if – whisper it gently – bodies happen to touch beneath the sheets.

The alternative thesis is that Jackson agreed to the Bashir interview not out of optimism but out of desperation. In this interpretation, disappointing sales of *Invincible* and mounting financial problems drove Michael into accepting the risky project. He needed a boost to his flagging public profile at this time. His friend Uri Geller, the self-proclaimed "psychic", persuaded him Bashir could be trusted – itself a telling commentary not only on the limits of Geller's visionary powers but also of the flaky characters Michael sometimes relied on in preference to taking sound professional advice.[738] The outcome was that Michael's desperate hope, if that is what it was, proved forlorn: Bashir did his worst. It is now time to examine what that worst entailed and how it led inexorably to the great drama of Jackson's trial in 2005.

Living with Michael Jackson, a Granada Television documentary screened first in the UK by ITV 1 on 3 February 2003, and then three days later by ABC news magazine *20/20* in the US, was watched by a total of over 40 million people in those two countries. It was the outcome of a project in which Jackson allowed Martin Bashir complete access to his life for eight months, including living at Neverland. In the previous chapter, we saw how this meant that Bashir would see the star interacting with his children at some very revealing moments

The documentary also shows a boy named as Gavin who was Jackson's friend at the time, and later became his accuser. Born in December 1989, he was twelve years old at the time of the filming in 2002. Gavin is seen holding hands with Jackson, his head nuzzling against the star's shoulder. The pair of them told about how they had slept in the same room, though not in the same bed: Michael had slept on the floor.

Gavin's body language proclaimed utter devotion to his hero, who had befriended him two years earlier when he had been told the boy was suffering from incurable cancer. Gavin's brother and sister also appeared on the show. The sister related that her parents had been told to prepare for Gavin's funeral. Bashir's voiceover said Gavin believed it was Michael's friendship and support that helped him beat the cancer, from which he had made a complete recovery.

But the thrust of Bashir's questions was not about this strikingly benign, inspirational aspect of the relationship, which was surely worth following up in some detail, even for a cynic wary of attributing a "miracle" to Jackson. Instead, he homed in on the bedroom factor, professing astonishment that after the allegations of 1993-4 Michael would still be allowing young boys to stay with him overnight. Of course, if Bashir had done his research he would have known the score long before getting anywhere near Michael – and as he had reportedly been angling for the project over a five-year period, he was probably better briefed on Michael's ways than Lisa Marie had been on her wedding day.[739] Bashir also knew his audience, and how thrillingly shocked they would be to hear the troubled star was still up to his old tricks.

What may have genuinely taken Bashir by surprise, though, was the degree of Jackson's candour: he seemed happy for his obvious affection towards Gavin to be known to the world. Just as with Jordie Chandler at Monaco a decade earlier, he clearly took pride in the relationship and wanted to show off his rapport with the boy. The years had not dimmed his belief that he could sell such friendships as benign and innocent.

Gavin's verbal contribution to the interview was actually quite consistent with such a view. Bashir asked him what made Michael connect so well with children, and he replied it was because Michael is a child at heart. He also said sharing a bedroom had been his own suggestion, not Michael's. It was only when Bashir turned his attention to Jackson that the wheels started to come off. He said:

"Michael, you are a 44-year-old man now. What do you get out of this?"

Maintaining his "child at heart" theme, Gavin gamely shot back "he's four."

"Yeh," said Michael, "I'm four. What they get from me is what I get from them…. My greatest inspiration comes from kids." Then we had the usual Jacksonian spiel about innocence and purity and God ("I see God in the face of children.") before Bashir pulled him abruptly back down to earth, asking whether it was appropriate to share his bedroom with children.

Instead of retreating from the issue, or downplaying it, Michael boldly advanced into more dangerous terrain: he had been asked about sharing his bedroom but answered about sharing his bed:

"Why can't you share your bed? That's the most loving thing you can do is share your bed with someone." Taxed further on the subject in a later interview, without Gavin present, he said: "When you say 'bed', you're thinking sexual. They make that sexual; it's not sexual. We're going to sleep, I tuck them in and I put a little music on, and when it's story time I read a book…I give them hot milk, you know, we have cookies. It's very charming, it's very sweet; it's what the whole world should do."

In this later interview, Bashir also pressed Jackson as to whether he had shared a bed with Gavin or his siblings: "No," said Michael, "but I have slept in a bed with many children. I sleep in a bed with all of them. When Macaulay Culkin was little, Kieran Culkin would sleep on this side, Macaulay Culkin on this side. His sister was in there. We all just crammed in the bed."

It didn't help. Bashir continued to probe his position relentlessly with a barrage of sceptical, hostile questions. Michael kept talking about love, Bashir kept refusing to believe it. Eventually, the star's distress was apparent, but in a trembling voice he quietly and gently, but resolutely, stuck to his theme, drawing on some of the thoughts behind his Oxford lecture. Speaking of kids in general in modern society, he said:

> They don't even eat with their father any more, or their mothers. The family bond has been broken. There's an outcry for attention. It's why kids are going to school with guns. They want love, they want to be touched; they want to be held. But they're busy off on their day job and maybe at home on their computer and they do all kinds of crazy stuff, and that's destroying our world. We need to bond again. It's very important, Martin.

In cold print it doesn't look the greatest speech. There are none of his usual vacuous but poetic excesses here, of the "I see God in the face of children" variety, and his theme is not expressed with the greatest eloquence. None of the commentators appeared even to notice this faltering, seemingly feeble rhetoric, which is a pity. Because unlike the flowery God-talk that tends to be his first resort under pressure, and which can be seen as narcissistic in its inward focus on his own emotions, this modest little sequence of utterances shows Michael connecting his feelings to the needs of society and of children beyond those in his immediate social circle. It demonstrates a sincere belief that his personal insights are of universal relevance – not such a foolish and self-regarding apprehension when we consider his strange personal odyssey through life. Sometimes it is possible for the outsider, the one who is different, to see what others cannot, bound up in their busy, ordinary lives. That is why, when we try to imagine how absurd some of our customs may be in reality, we often evoke the image of the bemused Martian, scratching his little green head over our peculiar, irrational ways. It is why the words of the prophets of the desert, scorned in their own day, have resonated down the millennia.

The *Guardian*'s Rupert Smith was among those unconvinced, referring uncharitably to Gavin as Jackson's "current minion", and pointedly asking why, if he wanted to share love, he "imported other people's children when he had three of his own".[740] Tom Utley of the *Sunday Telegraph*, by contrast, felt short-changed by Bashir as regards Michael's music: "It was as if Mr Bashir had been given eight months' unfettered access to Napoleon, and could think of nothing to ask him about except his relationship with Josephine."[741] Bashir in fact looked at considerably more than just the "Josephine" angle, also dwelling on Michael's plastic surgery, his extravagance, his eccentricities, the violent abuse to which he and his brothers were allegedly subjected by his father, and, as we saw in the last chapter, parenting issues. Small wonder the music made it no further than snippets of the sound track. All these issues have been covered elsewhere in this volume and need not detain us here.

Of greater concern is the reaction the programme provoked, including Michael's own. Unsurprisingly, he issued a statement accusing Bashir of bad faith, especially in terms of leaving out footage at odds with the criticisms made in his voiceover. This was soon followed up, as we saw in the last chapter, by the release of simultaneously shot footage from Jackson's own videographer Hamid Moslehi, featured in the editorially independent, but remarkably sympathetic, Fox riposte – the documentary *The Michael Jackson Interview: The Footage You Were Never Meant To See*. As we saw, this succeeded in demonstrating Michael's point, especially with regard to his qualities as a parent: what Bashir said to Jackson and what he said in his voiceover were significantly at odds, and at some points totally contradictory. Unfortunately for Michael this was not hugely helpful. It revealed Bashir as oleaginous and ingratiating but did nothing to allay the concerns he had raised about the star's relations with young boys.

But the Fox riposte contained other material too. We see Debbie Rowe stoutly defending her husband. She claimed it was she who made their children wear face masks in public. "That was my request not his. I'm the one who is terrified." She wept as she told how happy Jackson was when their first baby was born and said if he asked her to have more children she would do it "in a heartbeat". Michael's parents and his brother Jermaine make an appearance in the riposte; his make-up artist Karen Faye is also in the interview line-up. Was all this of any greater help? Not really. The only significant new information on the key issue of young boys was provided by Jamie Masada, the comedian and club owner through whom Gavin had been able to meet Michael when the boy was at death's door. Masada protested that Gavin had not known the Bashir programme would be broadcast to millions. He said the boy had called him in tears to say how he had been taunted at school over his relationship with Jackson – a fact which hardly helped Michael, as arguably he too should have given some thought to that possibility. Bashing Bashir's lack of sensitivity on the subject really doesn't cut it, except to expose the hypocrisy of child protection blowhards, many of whom couldn't care less about children's feelings except when it comes to denying kids any "inappropriate" friendships or sexual expression.

What the Fox riposte did not show is of some interest too. Michael's videographer had shot further material which did not merely duplicate Bashir's out-takes. Some of it was shot with the specific aim of rebuttal, after Bashir's show had aired, hence this footage came to be known as the "rebuttal video". This comprised Gavin's family praising the star, and figured extensively in Jackson's subsequent trial. Filmed on the night of 19 February 2003 in Moslehi's home, it failed to make the deadline for the Fox riposte, which aired only the following day. Moslehi later said that even as he shot it he knew the production deadline had passed. According to another account, though, he withheld the footage because of a financial dispute with Jackson.[742] It was later recovered by police during the course of their investigation.

Back to those blowhards. We met one of them, Carole Lieberman, in the last chapter, when we heard that following the Bashir programme she issued a complaint to the Santa Barbara Child Protective Services, listing eighteen "reasons" why Jackson's children should be taken away from him. Others were to blow ever harder and more lethally, initiating proceedings that would eventually see revived criminal charges. But this was by no means immediately apparent. A US child protection charity called for the singer to be investigated, but Santa Barbara County District Attorney Tom Sneddon reacted cautiously. He said that under California law, merely sleeping with a child without "affirmative, offensive conduct" is not a criminal offence. Police would require co-operation from a victim before any charges could be brought. "Sleeping in bed with a kid is not a crime that I know of," he told the *Santa Barbara News-Press*. Sneddon had reason to be wary.[743] As Jackson's local D.A., it was he who had led the bid in 1993-4 to mount a criminal case against Jackson, without success. Sneddon had been publicly frustrated and humiliated. If he was going to get Jackson – and he would try – the last thing he needed was to wet his pants with premature excitement.

Despite this caution, Sneddon made it clear he had not entirely given up on the Chandler case of a decade earlier. His press release of 6 February 2003 in response to the Bashir programme said the case could be reactivated if credible new evidence emerged or witnesses were willing to cooperate. Thus the investigation remained "open, but inactive." Back in 1993, Jackson had reason to suppose he would be safe if there was no prosecution within six years, the time limit then set under California's statute of limitations for the alleged offences in question. Thus by 1999 he should have been totally immune. But that reckoned without changes in the law. By 2003 the relevant provision, set out in California Penal Code Section 803(g), apparently enabled old cases to be revived just as Sneddon claimed. I say "apparently" because the new provision was to a limited degree successfully challenged in the US Supreme Court in the case of *Stogner v. California* later in the same year. Whether Sneddon could still have validly claimed the Chandler case was "open, but inactive" up to the time of Michael's death is a moot point. An article published the following year in the *Journal of Criminal Law and Criminology* showed that the battle over Section 803(g) was a work in progress.[744]

Sneddon's caution over Jackson's sleeping arrangements, which seems well justified in the light of the star's later acquittal, contrasts interestingly with the gung-ho style for which he is better known, and in which he appeared to have been matched by another key player in the events of 1993, Dr Mathis Abrams, the psychiatrist consulted by Evan Chandler, father of Jackson's reluctant accuser in that year. Chandler, it may be recalled, at first put the case to Abrams on a hypothetical basis, without indicating his son's involvement and without naming Michael Jackson. In his book, Evan's brother Ray Chandler, himself an attorney, described Abrams' response to the scenario sketched by Evan: "From a legal standpoint, Dr Abrams believed that a thirty-four-year-old man consistently sleeping in the same bed with a minor when other sleeping accommodations are available is a violation of the law regarding lewd and lascivious conduct towards children."[745]

Sneddon would certainly have been thinking in the coming months of 2003 about the consistent pattern of Jackson's behaviour. Eventually, he would get wind of an interestingly "consistent" episode that summer at the party for the star's forty fifth birthday, and would investigate accordingly. In one superheated newspaper account when the story surfaced the following year, "Teen pop singer Aaron Carter spent a wild unsupervised night with his 'idol' Michael Jackson… and Carter's mom is still haunted by fears of what may have happened..." Aaron was fifteen when his elder brother, former Backstreet Boys star Nick Carter, left him at the Neverland birthday bash, "triggering a night of sheer panic for Aaron's mom, Jane Carter", according to the *New York Daily News*.[746]

When TV show *Access Hollywood* interviewed her, she revealed that when Aaron finally came home it was with a gift from Michael of a sequined jacket. But that was just a modest part of his largesse. She said the boy told her the star also gave him a Bentley, at an estimated value of $350,000. She said when prosecutors in Jackson's case heard about the luxury car they questioned her and she, in turn, quizzed Michael, who denied there had been any such gift. Aaron was also grilled by the authorities. He told his mother he spent time in Jackson's bedroom and that he had "a crystal bedspread", but mostly described "innocent fun" like dance lessons and riding around the ranch.

The boy himself later spoke to *People* magazine, criticising his mother and defending Michael, saying nothing sexual had happened – but suspicions may have been intensified, rather than the reverse, when he said he and Michael had been friends for three years, which would have meant he was only twelve at the start of the friendship. As for the Bentley, Aaron explained much later, when Michael's trial was getting under way in February 2005, it was one of five the pop superstar intended auctioning off for charity. He told *Contact Music* Michael offered him the car for his sixteenth birthday, which would have been on 7 December 2003, but that was "before all this stuff happened" (the child molestation accusations).[747] Small wonder Aaron never got the gift: his birthday happened to fall in the middle of an earthquake in Jackson's life, as we shall soon see: to have given the boy a suspicious gift at this time would have been utter madness even by Michael's standards.

He was crazy enough to have more than one boy in his life that year, though, after those first months monopolised by Gavin Arvizo. With his departure, Aaron was back on the scene, but even the famously cute, blond little pop star did not entirely fill out Michael's social diary, for there would be another claimant to the title Boy of the Year, 2003. Then aged nine, and the son of Jawad and Hanadi Fattouh, he was interviewed on *Michael Jackson's Boys* on 26 January 2005, a TV documentary for Channel 4. His name was said to be "Juju", like the West African word for a magical thing, a charm to be worshipped, a word said to come from the French joujou, a toy. In a soft and husky voice that might be described as sexy if it belonged to a woman, this tiny joujou said Michael was "the best person I ever met". He said he once went to sleep on Michael's lap but denied his "parts" were ever touched. He said some of his friends claimed Michael was gay. Juju had told them this was not true, and if they kept saying it he would not be friends with them any more. The words were as childlike and "innocent" as any doting parent could wish.

Juju's elder brother Ahmed also appears in the programme. He is dubbed "Michael's boy 1995-2003". If true, it would put him right up there among the all time greats, a contender for longest reign in the title. Corroboration that a boy called Ahmed was among Michael's circle at this time, and then aged seventeen, is to be found in a number of newspaper reports, but with the family name Elatab, not Fattouh. This Ahmed (or Ahmad) was reportedly a regular visitor to Neverland only from October 2002, which makes his title claim look no more than, so to speak, retrospectively aspirational. Reports also say he had a younger brother about the same age as Juju but called Jawad. It seems likely the "Elatabs" and the "Fattouhs" are the same family.

Ahmed told one paper how Michael would pretend he slept in a normal room, when he actually went to bed with youngsters in a hidden bedroom above his home cinema: "It is his secret room. Anyone is welcome to stay the night or even a few days," he said. *Anyone*? Well, perhaps not girls or grown-ups, otherwise it would hardly qualify as secret. Jackson usually slept on a pullout couch in the room with six other kids, Ahmed continued. But the star asked children to call their parents before staying overnight. Ahmed revealed that the only time he saw Michael angry was when Martin Bashir's name was mentioned.[748]

If Sneddon managed to avoid creaming his jeans over the Bashir programme in February 2003, it is now clear his self-containment was tenuous; by November, with big news to handle, he was like a dog humping the media's leg. Indeed, once nick-named "mad dog" in the courtroom, he would be living up to his reputation. The occasion for all the hullabaloo was a police swoop, with a search warrant, on Michael's Neverland ranch as part of an unspecified criminal investigation. Court TV, whose reporter was on the scene on 18 November, quoted sources saying it stemmed from a new allegation of sexual abuse brought by a twelve-year-old boy. One exciting item thrown into the mix was the tabloid revelation by Jackson's former head of security Robert Wegner that more than a hundred children slept in the singer's Neverland bedroom over the three years he worked there, which would appear to have amply met the criterion of "consistency" mentioned above.

Michael was not at Neverland at the time of the raid, otherwise he would have been arrested. This gave Sneddon the opportunity to announce to the world that Jackson would have to give himself up. "Get over here and get checked in," the D.A. reportedly said. Sneddon offered his words of advice to Jackson after law enforcement officials announced that they had issued an arrest warrant on suspicion of child molesting.[749]

Sneddon denied he wanted revenge, or the limelight, saying he was only interested in justice. But his cock-a-hoop manner suggested otherwise, as exemplified by his exquisite sarcasm when Jackson protested in a statement that the allegations surfaced on the release day of his new greatest hits CD, *Number Ones*. Sneddon dismissed any connection to the album's release. "Jackson himself, I believe, has said that this was all done to try to ruin his new CD that was coming out or whatever it is he's doing. Like the sheriff and I really are into that kind of music," he said. He also confidently told a news conference this case was different because he had a cooperative victim and because of a change in state law "specifically because of the 1993-94 Michael Jackson investigation". The D.A.'s long-time friend, former Santa Barbara Mayor Hal Conklin, said Jackson's comments, and the song from his 1995 *HIStory* album in which Jackson sings "Sneddon is a cold man," never bothered the D.A. "Tom Sneddon's all business," Conklin said. (The printed lyrics refer to "Dom Sheldon" but no one was fooled.)[750]

On 20 November, Jackson flew in a leased jet to Santa Barbara and surrendered to the police, who arrested him at the airport. Driven by them to the Santa Barbara County Jail, he emerged from the police vehicle in handcuffs. The rest of the world disappeared from television news networks. For more than two hours, CNN, Fox News Channel, MSNBC and Court TV covered nothing but the pop star's appearance at the Santa Barbara jail, where he was charged with "lewd or lascivious acts" with a child younger than fourteen. Over and over, they repeated "the money shot" – Jackson walking into the sheriff's office in handcuffs.

He would later allege police brutality, saying his shoulder had been dislocated during rough handling at the jail. But in the end he blew apart his own claims. In an interview with Ed Bradley on the CBS show *60 Minutes*[751] (itself an extraordinary media opportunity for an accused person) he said he could not raise his arms above the shoulder, but minutes after this supposed manhandling he was seen scratching his head. And even as he exited the police station he waved to fans, with both arms above his head. The damage to his credibility from the obvious falsity of his police brutality charges would have made him a dubious witness in his own defence. California State Attorney General Bill Lockyer ordered an independent investigation into Jackson's complaints. After interviewing 163 witnesses the complaints were rejected, in August 2004.

When images of a handcuffed Jackson were first broadcast, though, his humiliation brought a measure of public sympathy: some saw the cuffing as a calculated police attempt to convince the public of his guilt; fans around the world were outraged. To them the measure was viewed as unnecessary considering Michael had voluntarily presented himself to the police.

In the same Bradley interview, Michael gave what was widely interpreted as a bold answer to a key question, especially for a man now facing criminal trial. Asked whether he *still* thought it acceptable to share his bed with children, he answered:

> Of course. Of course. Why not? If you're gonna be a pedophile, if you're gonna be Jack the Ripper, if you're gonna be a murderer, it's not a good idea. That I'm not. That's how we were raised. And I met – I didn't sleep in the bed with the child. Even if I did, it's okay. I slept on the floor. I give the bed to the child.

At this point he was admitting only to sharing his bedroom, not his bed, but many commentators thought he was reckless to defend the practice. What he should have done, it was asserted, was to give a firm indication that his intentions had been innocent but that he now realised he had left his motives open to misinterpretation and knew it would be unwise to do the same thing again. There would be no such indication. Not that he forgot the innocence bit, far from it. There would be familiar protestations of a pure heart: "When I see children, I see the face of God", he declared again, in a mutation of a memorable soundbite from his confrontation with Martin Bashir. Emboldened, perhaps, by the uplifting tone of his own sentimental piety, he evidently felt strong enough to re-assert his point that it would be okay even if he did sleep in bed with a child, not just share the bedroom, because, "I am not going to do anything sexual to a child. It's not where my heart is."

His answers were thus pretty much the same as those he gave on the "sleepover" issue in his and Lisa Marie's interview with Diane Sawyer back in 1995.[752] Another point common to both interviews is that, as a tactic to emphasise his own innocence, he sought to distance himself from those who *do* have sexual contact with children. Asked by Sawyer what he thought of such people he said they needed help, they were nuts. With Bradley, he cited murderers, including Jack the Ripper, as people utterly unlike himself. Mad, bad, sad, it made little difference: in the popular imagination they were all bad guys – perverts, evil, paedophiles.

As we have just seen above, Jackson actually uttered the poisoned and poisonous P word, setting up paedophiles as the dreaded Other, the Not Michael. In recent times the tabloids, and increasingly, in their wake, the more up-market media, have taken "paedophilia" away from its original, morally neutral (in theory, at least) medical meaning and turned it into a term of vilification. "Paedophilia", which started life as a psychiatric term primarily to describe sexual *attraction* to children, not sexual *acts* of any kind, either with children or against them, has come to be presented as a synonym for sexual "attacks" or "abuse", no matter how loving and kind the contacts in question may have been – no matter how much, indeed, they were like Michael's relationships with boys.

This tabloid appropriation of the language makes it very difficult for Michael (or anyone) to communicate the positive value of physical attraction to children – including sexual feelings – within a loving relationship: to admit to being a paedophile, even one who never acts upon their feelings, is to call oneself a monster. At one time Michael bravely tried to *demonstrate* this positive value, rather than use words, most notably in his very public display of affection towards Jordie in Monaco. Pinned to the wall by Bradley, it is understandable, but regrettable, that he felt forced, in effect, to denounce not just murderous criminals like Jack the Ripper, but also gentle, well-meaning child-lovers like himself. It was a St Peter moment. In panic, the rock upon which the Church was built thrice denied Jesus. Now Michael was denying not Jesus but *himself*, and denying thereby the cause of others, ordinary people who would keep on being unjustly persecuted because Michael lacked the strength to be himself and say honestly what he was. To have done so might have made a martyr of him but ultimately it would have increased public understanding of paedophilia immeasurably.

Not that Michael is alone in having missed his moment for glory. Other famous figures in recent years, brought low by accusations of under-age affairs or downloading child pornography, have sought ignoble refuge in denying their own feelings and have been reduced to betrayal of their own cause.

The star was directed to give up his passport and he was released on bail of $3 million. Coincidentally, another legendary figure in the music business, record producer Phil Spector, was at that time on $1 million bail on a charge of murdering an actress (he was eventually convicted), prompting the question as to whether killing a woman is only one third as serious as sexual misconduct with a boy.

Details of Michael's alleged offence were not revealed, nor the name of the alleged victim; but the media were able to get their teeth into the relevant law, introducing Dr Abrams' "lewd or lascivious" conduct to a wider audience. Side-bar stories in the papers and on the websites informed readers about California Penal Code Section 288(a):

> Any person who wilfully and lewdly commits any lewd or lascivious act, including any of the acts constituting other crimes provided for in Part 1, upon or with the body, or any part or member thereof, of a child who is under the age of 14 years, with the intent of arousing, appealing to, or gratifying the lust, passions, or sexual desires of that person or the child, is guilty of a felony and shall be punished by imprisonment in the state prison for three, six, or eight years.

Jackson's lawyer, Mark Geragos, told reporters his client had come "to confront these charges head-on. He is greatly outraged by the bringing of these charges. He considers this to be a big lie."[753]

The ritual of the post-arrest procedure included the taking of a police mugshot, plus the recording of personal details which revealed the singer to be five feet eleven inches tall, pretty much average for an American male of his age, while at eight stone eight pounds (120 lbs) he was alarmingly slim – as were his chances of acquittal, to judge by much of the media reaction. NBC contributor Michael Ventre advised him to rent some prison movies, because "in all the films and television shows I have seen that deal with the milieu of the maximum-security penitentiary, there are no stuffed animals, video games, swing sets, cotton candy machines or choo-choo trains. In the yard, they don't play 'Ring Around the Rosey,' they play 'Garrote the Squealer.' In the shower, when somebody passes you the soap, it's not just a gesture of courtesy, it's the beginning of a relationship." Comfortingly, he added: "I bring this up because I sense that Michael doesn't get it. I don't think he believes he is destined to do hard time. My guess is …he figures he's headed to some sort of home for wayward children in a bucolic setting run by Bing Crosby..."[754]

Joining in the schadenfreude, Mark Lawson decided a drastic line of defence was called for, based on precisely the lack of touch with reality discerned by Ventre: "So warped by his fame as a child that the only adult companions with whom he feels at ease are Elizabeth Taylor and a chimpanzee, the singer constructed a fantasy world in which a theme park could be a home and 45-year-old men could have 12-year-old friends for sleepovers…Permitted for four decades by money and fame to behave any way he wanted, Jackson has become a man so bizarre that there must be serious doubts about his fitness to stand trial. A pre-trial plea bargain of insanity by virtue of celebrity might be legally unconventional, but it would be honest."[755]

Within a few weeks, the background to the investigation into Jackson's conduct would be revealed through the leaking of an official memo. The case had begun with a call to the child abuse hotline of the Los Angeles Department of Children and Family Services (DCFS). According to the memo, a "Child Abuse Referral" was phoned in on 14 February 2003 by a "school official" from the Los Angeles Unified School District. Citing the prior week's ABC broadcast of *Living with Michael Jackson*, the official lodged allegations of "general neglect by mother and sexual abuse by 'an entertainer' ". The school official identified a boy and his younger brother as the "referred children." The older brother aged, thirteen at the time of the memo, was said to be a cancer victim.

The memo also summarized the results of a confidential investigation into these allegations that had been conducted in February 2003, in the immediate wake of the Bashir broadcast, by the Los Angeles Police Department and child welfare officials. They had interviewed the alleged victim, his twelve-year-old brother, his sixteen-year-old sister and his mother. All of them denied any form of sexual abuse. The child said he never slept in the same bed as the entertainer. The L.A. investigation dismissed the allegations as "unfounded". Santa Barbara D.A. Tom Sneddon angrily dismissed the dismissal, saying the probe had been based on a single interview. "To call that an investigation is a misnomer," Sneddon said. "It was an interview, plain and simple, and we are not concerned about it."[756]

With the benefit of hindsight, however, this embarrassment for Sneddon proved to be a significant straw in the wind, as did a claim by the producer of American TV's *Celebrity Justice* that young Gavin was not the willing witness the prosecution would have wished for, saying: "This boy told a therapist that Michael Jackson fondled him in his private parts, but he's a very reluctant witness. He did not come out and spill his guts about what allegedly happened between him and Michael Jackson. We're told it literally had to be pulled out of him, first by attorney Larry Feldman and then by a therapist, who ultimately got the story from the boy."[757] The truth is that even the therapist did not get *the* story out of the boy but, as we shall see later, he did get *a* story.

Following further charges made on 18 December, Jackson attended his arraignment in the case on 16 January 2004. He formally pleaded not guilty to seven felony counts of lewd or lascivious acts with a child under fourteen and two counts of giving the child an intoxicating agent. But, being the celebrity he is, that hardly seemed the point of the occasion judging by his "performance" and the intense media reaction it provoked. Leaving the court, this was the famous occasion when he stood on top of his chauffeur-driven SUV, waved to hundreds of his waiting fans and invited them all to a party. He gave a little dance atop the vehicle and flashed victory signs. The spectacle came after he had arrived twenty minutes late: not the best way of making friends with the judge, who blasted his tardiness as an "insult".[758]

Not to be outdone, Michael's sister Janet provoked even more controversy the following month when, in what was unconvincingly excused as a "wardrobe malfunction", her right breast became exposed to millions during her televised performance at the Superbowl halftime. Being certain this would "cause great outrage among the American people", the Bush administration launched a full-scale enquiry within hours, whereas the decision to investigate intelligence failures ahead of the Iraq war was nearly a year in the making.[759] Hurricane Katrina would later expose the president's dubious priorities even more glaringly than Janet's offending boob, but public reaction to the escaped mammary – which became the most searched-for image in the history of the internet – was in its own modest (or immodest) way not without serious cultural significance. It reminded the world that the United States was a place in which it is fine dozens of times a day to show people being shot dead on TV but where the mere glimpse of naked flesh on the box freaks folks out. Bearing this in mind, Michael's willingness on the Bashir programme to confront such prudishness, and to propose loving physicality as an antidote to gun culture, begins to look like the courageous stand of a prophet. If American society thinks Jacko is wacko it should take a look in the mirror.

A whole year of pre-trial skirmishes would pass between Michael's sensational opening courthouse "gig" and the altogether more sober date with destiny he kept when the main event opened. There were to be numerous legal pleadings and rulings. There would even be a further police raid on Neverland in December 2004 – another straw in the wind, this, suggesting the prosecution still lacked the killer evidence they needed and were desperately hoping to find something decisive. Also in this vein, it was reported that in the months before the trial, prosecutors were hunting other "victims" who might testify. One was said to be living in El Salvador, another in South Africa. Police quizzed the son "of a professional athlete in England". Jeremy Jackson, son of Jermaine, was questioned too.[760] Significantly, the new Neverland raid came well after the prosecution had given their case a full dummy run before a grand jury which resulted in the issuing of an indictment on 21 April of that year. This marked the culmination of closed-door hearings at which the prosecution had presented a case going far beyond child molestation. The indictment handed up by the grand jury included charges of conspiring to commit child abduction, extortion and false imprisonment.

These extra charges came as a bolt from the blue because the grand jury hearings had been held in secret – a move justified by Judge Rodney Melville on the grounds that Michael's celebrity made him especially vulnerable to trial by media and also to protect the identity of the young accuser. The ruling was only partially successful, as the 1903-page transcript of the grand jury hearings, including the evidence of forty one witnesses, was sensationally leaked via the website The Smoking Gun less than two weeks before the first evidence was heard in the trial proper.[761]

But on 30 April 2004 when the indictment was unsealed, the kidnapping and other new charges were truly a mystery, and one which on the face of things made Jackson's position look even more serious than the world had supposed. Even the indictment itself was heavily redacted, so that little was made clear about the evidence beyond the bare facts of the charges. Jackson, present in court for what was effectively a second arraignment, pleaded not guilty to the new charges.[762]

That was no surprise, but the lawyer representing him was: he had sacked hot-shot celebrity lawyer Mark Geragos for refusing to give the case his undivided attention. Instead Thomas Mesereau made his first court appearance on behalf of the singer. Outside court Mesereau took a swipe at "celebrity lawyers", saying: "This case is about one thing only. It's about the dignity, the integrity, the decency, the honour, the charity, the innocence and the complete vindication of a wonderful human being named Michael Jackson." Some of us might count that not as "one thing only" but half a dozen. No matter. It was clear from the outset that Mesereau was not a man to understate his belief in his client.[763]

Three months later, in July, Mesereau would be in court again, this time dismissing the indictment as "absurd", predicting it would be "laughed out of court" by a jury. He had been applying to have the indictment dismissed after the prosecution had publicly outlined the case for the first time. This was when Deputy District Attorney Gordon Auchincloss spelt out the astonishing theory that Michael Jackson had held the recovered cancer victim and his family virtual prisoners at Neverland as the pop star conducted a bizarre campaign to both save his image from ruin and seduce the boy.[764]

While the long gestation of the great drama would last a further six months, most of the main elements of the plot – including the alleged literal plot to kidnap – had now taken shape. In the end there were to be three major elements. The first was the issue of Jackson's sexual conduct towards the boy Gavin; the second was the alleged plot to kidnap the youngster's family; the third and most controversial would bring in alleged so-called "prior bad acts" of child abuse by the defendant, including his relationship with Jordan Chandler more than a decade earlier.

As readers of this volume will be aware, Michael had never been tried in a court over the Chandler affair, or over any other child abuse allegations. Having never been tried, it followed that he had never been found guilty of abuse, and in such a position would ordinarily be regarded as an innocent man without any stain on his character. The traditional supposition would be that if credible evidence of abuse existed, charges would have been made and tested in court. But that had never happened. By January 2005 Michael's lawyers were petitioning Judge Melville to bar such "flimsy" evidence as the prosecution now proposed to put to the court – evidence which would not stand up on its own but was clearly aimed at smearing Jackson's name through "corroboration by volume", allowing several prior dubious allegations to be loaded onto the scales of justice along with the current ones. The fact that the prosecution needed to resort to such a tactic also implied that the current allegations might be as weakly supported as the earlier ones that had never made it to court.

Interestingly, in view of the decision Judge Melville would later make, his first words on the subject were conservative and cautious, citing a case early in his career where the prosecution first presented "prior bad acts" of alleged abuse in a similar case. The primary case that the prosecution then put forward was so weak that the defendant was convicted on the alleged "prior bad acts". Judge Melville called this a "miscarriage of justice" and stated that he would not allow something like that to happen in the Jackson case.[765]

Commenting on the issue, Roger Friedman was an early sceptic over the prosecution's tactics and viability, earthily cutting to the chase over the implications:

> Sneddon seems to not have much of a case with the current kid, so his plan is to bolster it with the gossip about other cases that never came to fruition. But he's not going to get very far with Culkin or Safechuck. Additionally, the young man who got a large payout from the 1993 child-molestation case now also has the financial resources to block testimony. What's Sneddon going to do? Jail all these kids for contempt of court?[766]

Sneddon was so desperate to nail Jackson he might have considered doing exactly that if by so doing he could force other former young friends of Michael into the witness box. To victimise Michael's "victims" by bullying them into court would of course expose the rationale of the prosecution for what it was: an utter sham. Dropping the veil in this way would be to expose the fact that the case was all about the enforcement of sexual and social conformity, rather than the protection of children. In no case, past or present, had any of Sneddon's would-be "accusers" shown any sign of real grievance against Jackson. They were Michael's friends, not victims in any sense they would recognise themselves. If Jackson had been a true victimiser in the "prior bad acts" cases surely at least one boy could be found, now a young man, who would relish the opportunity to seek justice by coming forward. Some might be reluctant to take the stand but it could be argued – and they might be persuaded – they had a public duty to do so in order to prevent other children from being victimised. But right up to the start of the trial in 2005 absolutely nothing had emerged in public to suggest anyone believed himself to be a victim of Jackson. That situation would change, but in the pre-trial period any attempt to *coerce* potential witnesses would have been a public relations disaster.[767]

Yet Sneddon had long ago appeared willing to move towards coercive measures. After the civil settlement won by Evan Chandler on his son Jordan's behalf, Sneddon had worked hard behind the scenes to get Jordan into the witness box in a criminal prosecution. When his efforts failed, it was no coincidence that California law was altered with the objective of preventing victims from refusing to give criminal testimony in such cases. In 2005 Jordan was subpoenaed by the prosecution to testify to "prior bad acts". His mother June took the stand but Jordie reportedly got out of doing so by absenting himself from the United States for the duration.[768]

Sneddon's dilemma over what to do about reluctant victims of alleged abuse – either lose them entirely or coerce them into the box with disastrous PR effects – was evident in several press releases he put out in 2003. We have already heard a bit about the first of them, issued on 6 February. Another point he made in that release was that a child victim "must voluntarily cooperate with law enforcement". By 19 November, when Neverland had been raided, he said the law "no longer allows child victim who obtains civil settlement to refuse to testify". The very next day he was forced to backtrack, saying "my use of the word 'compel' to describe the effect of the new legislation was unfortunate and not legally correct".

As he then explained, what he had actually meant was that a child who had made money out of a civil case could be hit in the bank balance if he refused to testify in a criminal one: refusal meant the settlement money could be forfeit. Sneddon cited a legislative change which he said had been enacted in direct response to his 1993-94 investigation of the Chandler case. This was section 1669.5 of the California Civil Code, which he said was "calculated to remove from the victim of an unlawful sex act the financial incentive not to cooperate". Whether, in 2005, this could have been retroactively applied to the Chandler case is another matter, but there was no sign of Sneddon trying to go down this road.

Michael, meanwhile, in the month when the third of the three main elements of the case against him – "prior bad acts" – hove into view, kept himself in the headlines in extraordinary style. In the aftermath of the great tsunami disaster he issued a statement of the sort we might expect from the Queen of England or the Pope, sending sympathy for the victims and prayers for the success of the relief efforts. In his straitened circumstances the statement understandably said nothing about him sending money.[769] While I have no reason to suppose the sentiments expressed by Michael were less than entirely sincere, one does not have to be much of a cynic to note the self-serving nature of a statement that positioned him so magisterially above the sordid concerns of a criminal court hearing.

But whatever he did, that hearing was ultimately not to be denied or evaded. On the very first day of the next month, February 2005, Michael Jackson's motorcade drove the short distance down from Neverland, in the hills over Santa Maria, and arrived at the courthouse in that modest Californian town, where he was cheered by hundreds of fans and surrounded by bodyguards; one of them held a large black umbrella over him as a sun shield. He then took his seat in court as the trial officially got under way with the task of selecting a jury.[770] The superstar was dressed totally in white – a symbol of innocence – with a jewel-encrusted belt and gold braided arm band. A Reuters correspondent reported that "He looked upbeat, smiled and joked with his lawyers, shook hands with the court clerk and occasionally dabbed at the pink lipstick he was wearing with a tissue. When jurors were being questioned, Jackson sat completely still." The next day Michael wore black, presumably for razzle-dazzle variety, rather than to symbolise guilt. This time his suit bore a badge emblazoned with the British royal arms, including the famous motto of the Order of the Garter, "Honi soit qui mal y pense", officially interpreted as "Shame on him who thinks this evil."

The star, it seemed, would be cutting a dignified and proper figure in court – and also one which, like the tsunami statement, would underline the regal status of the King of Pop. It was a status that prompted one eminent writer on legal affairs, Marcel Berlins, to ponder a TV reporter's casual assertion that Michael Jackson was the most famous person ever to have been brought before the criminal courts. Berlins decided that any contender for such a title would have to be someone from the modern age. Before the arrival of the mass media few people had fame or notoriety that would have spread very far – and one might add that there were far fewer people for that fame to reach compared to the billions on the planet today. The trial of King Charles I had been huge in England, but few Japanese would have been aware even of His Majesty's existence. Hitler was never put on trial. In recent times Slobodan Milosovic is well up there among modern political leaders who have been in the dock, while Saddam Hussein and Augusto Pinochet were both expected to share that dubious privilege at the time when Berlins was writing.

But Berlins pointed out that to be known universally, not just by those interested in current affairs but by society as a whole, is very rare. He felt such fame was limited to two classifications, sport and popular entertainment. This brought the boxer Mike Tyson into consideration but Berlins judged Jackson to be even more well-known everywhere, including China and Russia, which were both unaware of Mick Jagger when he was charged with possessing drugs in the 1960s. Jackson, concluded Berlins, "is a truly universal star, worthy of the accolade conferred on him by the television reporter".[771]

Also in keeping with his star status, when Michael caught a touch of flu (if that is what it really was) in the jury-picking stage of the trial, he did not just sit snuffling miserably in the dock with only a box of tissues for his comfort as a lesser mortal might. Instead he had himself hospitalised for thirty three hours and the trial was delayed for a week as he recovered. Said to be "overcome by vomiting", he was put on an intravenous drip for a while at Santa Maria's Marian Medical Center. It was widely speculated that Michael was just being his usual drama queen self but you cannot argue with a doctor's note, and he had one. On his return to court, Judge Melville was obliged to assure jurors that the defendant really had been ill. There was in any case a disruption to the proceedings as Michael's top lawyer, Tom Mesereau, also had to take time out after a death in his family.

The jury selection stage of the trial passed remarkably quickly, despite interruptions, compared to the norm for high-profile trials in the US. By far the most significant feature of this smoothness arose from the fact that Jackson, on good advice from Tom Mesereau, chose not to play the race card. The jury would not include a single black face. Jackson's namesake, the Rev. Jesse Jackson, veteran campaigner against racial discrimination, made a valid point when he said, "...the lack of inclusion of even one African American on the jury casts a cloud of reasonable doubt on the fundamental promise and purpose of the courts: to provide a fair trial by a jury of one's peers."

Yet Mesereau made no big deal of the issue, and in letting it slip past without attempting to hold up the jury selection until the panel took on a darker hue, or blasting the injustice of the system, he quietly signalled contentment that his client would be tried simply as a human being, not as an "African-American" victim of racial oppression. The race prejudice claim was always going to be an absurd hypothesis given that Michael had effectively long been white not just in appearance but also in status: he was no poor ghetto kid, easy for the police to kick around. If his lawyer pressed hard and succeeded in getting two or three black jurors empanelled, what would it really achieve? At best a split jury and a re-trial if the panel divided on racial lines. And a split of that kind would be achieved only by harping on about race throughout the trial, which would do nothing but irritate the non-black jurors and convince them of the insincerity of the defence. When Mesereau replaced Geragos as Michael's key lawyer, it was not just a matter of the former committing more time to the job. That was a big part of it, but Geragos had shown signs of allowing race into the trial as a major issue. It was on his watch that the militantly race-conscious Nation of Islam organisation was seen to be gaining influence within the Jackson camp. Sacking him was probably Jackson's smartest move in the whole case, with the possible exception of his decision not to take the stand.

The absence of black jurors was suspicious, given the huge jury pool available to the court, but it also reflected the racial composition of the court district in question, central to which was the small town of Santa Maria, inhabited mainly by whites and Hispanics. And Mesereau appears to have judged there were more salient issues than race as a basis for prejudice among the candidate jurors: many questions would be put to these candidates in a bid to weed out the more obviously unsympathetic among them.

Race was among those questions. They were asked in writing about their feelings towards people of different races, but there was much else besides, such as whether they knew about past or current accusations of child sex abuse against Jackson. In all, no fewer than forty one questions were set out in a seven-page questionnaire. The form, written by the judge, reflected concerns raised by both the prosecution and defence.

A number of the questions covered such basic background information as age, gender, marital status and occupation. The jury pool were also asked if their feelings about people of different races might affect their ability to be fair or if they had ever worked for a group dealing with child safety, abuse or mistreatment. They were asked to inform the court if they or a friend or relative had ever been accused of "inappropriate sexual behaviour" or had been the victim of such acts. They were asked if they had ever had cancer.

Only five questions referred directly to Jackson, one asking: "Have you ever known anyone who has met Michael Jackson or spent any time at Neverland?" A second question asked for knowledge of the current case. Another asked if they knew of child abuse accusations levelled against Jackson in the past. It said, "Do you know or have you read, seen or heard ANYTHING about the publicity regarding the 1993-1994 investigation against Michael Jackson?"

In many jurisdictions intensive jury vetting is not a luxury open to the defendant, who is more or less stuck with the dozen or so people with whom he is confronted. In England, for instance, twelve jurors are brought before the court for swearing in, and that's it. At one time it used to be possible to exclude one or more jurors on the basis of their appearance – the clothes they wore or the newspaper they carried might be clues to an unsympathetic disposition – but these days the rules are tighter and successful challenges are rare. As for questionnaires, quite out of the question!

The scope of the information available about the jurors in the US is astonishing to a UK reader. Yet from an American perspective that information was relatively restricted in the Jackson case. While the questionnaire touched on a variety of issues, it did not go into the kind of detail that would help attorneys eliminate jurors they saw as sympathetic to the other side, according to law professor Laurie Levenson, who reckoned it was the skimpiest questionnaire she had ever seen: "It's very superficial. The judge obviously did not want a sociology study, but this will make it more difficult for the defence to find the kind of jurors they want."

Nevertheless, compared to other countries the American system allows vastly more scope for the defence to get the right panel – but the prosecution are also allowed to be choosy. In these circumstances jury selection becomes a hugely important part of the trial, indeed the most important part. Asked about this in the Jackson case, another legal expert, Stan Goldman, opined: "It's the whole ball of wax. It's going to decide if he wins or loses."

Goldman said prosecutors in a case like this would be looking for older, more conservative jurors, less enamoured of celebrity, willing to accept authority and appalled by child molestation. Jurors with their own children would be a natural choice. The prosecution would be wise to avoid anyone who was a devoted fan of Jackson, as well as jurors who might want to "overly" analyse the case or second-guess authorities. The best sort of juror would be someone who was going to say, "Yeah, I think he did it. Bang!"

Jackson's attorneys should have been keen on those with advanced degrees, critical thinkers who question authority. The perfect defence juror might be "a left-winger who just moved from San Francisco with a lot of education and who is willing to forgive Michael Jackson his idiosyncrasies," Goldman said.

So much for the theory. How did it work out in practice? A record four thousand prospective jurors were summoned in the case. These were brought into the court in batches of 150 for screening by the judge. Most were excused when they pleaded the trial would cause them undue financial hardship by depriving them of their incomes for months on end. Legal commentators noted there had been no shortage of willing and even enthusiastic candidates, and interpreted this as a favourable omen for Jackson. A pool of 242 people remained who were willing to serve, only about half a dozen of whom were black. This remainder were given the questionnaire. Those whose answers did not indicate they should immediately be disqualified were called back to be grilled in court by rival lawyers, backed by specialised jury consultants. Each side was allowed to dismiss up to ten potential jurors without citing a reason and was able to challenge others they felt could be biased. Almost nine in ten potential jurors said they had read or watched at least some news about the case. About 60% said they knew something about the 1993 investigation of Jackson on similar molestation accusations.

A jury of four men and eight women was eventually chosen, plus eight alternates. Seven jury members were white, four Hispanic and one Asian. Eight were parents. No juror was black. The prosecution team vetoed two black women, including one who criticized the jury pool's composition. Only five of the twelve said they were aware of 1993 child molestation allegations against Jackson; one said they or a family member personally knew Jackson.

The panel also included a widowed 79-year-old great grandmother whose grandson was registered with police as a sex offender, and a 42-year-old school aide whose sister had been raped at age twelve. The second woman also said she had two nieces who had been sexually molested. Ages ranged from twenty to seventy nine, averaging at forty five; occupations included a civil engineer, a horse trainer, a physical therapy aide, a wheelchair-bound student and a student nurse whose aunt had visited Neverland. Most of the panel said they had read or watched a little news about the case.

One good sign for Jackson was that most of them said they enjoyed his music and were impressed by his career. Most also said they distrusted what they heard in the media. Perhaps less promisingly, one juror's ex-husband was a police officer. The youngest juror, aged twenty, told the court his sister and her boyfriend had visited Neverland. The second youngest, a 21-year-old student, was a paraplegic. He said he visited Neverland with a United Cerebral Palsy group when he was at school.

It was hardly surprising that a jury from in and around Santa Maria would include several members who had visited Neverland, or whose close relatives had, nor that there would be fans of his music and career, given his immense popularity. If the exclusion of blacks was a reason for Michael to worry, these more positive aspects of the jury composition gave a strong indication there was no need to despair.

So at last, with the jury in place, and over a thousand print and broadcast journalists in attendance, the stage was finally set for the great court drama just over two years after Bashir's exercise in "trial by television", which had set the ball rolling. There would be no place on this stage for television, however. Trial by Judge Melville would prove very different to that by "Judge" Bashir. Melville made a number of controversial legal rulings against Michael, but his handling of the media consistently favoured the defendant. The domination of the criminal trial by the media circus in the OJ Simpson murder case had convinced him of the need to keep control, and so he banned TV cameras from the court. The potential audience of well over a billion would thus have to be content with re-enactments of the trial played by actors, plus shots of comings and goings outside the courtroom. The squawks of protest by the media were loud, long, and utterly without success.

It is time now to go where the cameras could not, but not before one final glimpse into the mind of America afforded by a media expert's reflections on the TV ban. Tim Rutten, media critic for the *Los Angeles Times* and a veteran of the OJ Simpson trial, said the O J case had been altogether more satisfactory to the American public. The absence of TV cameras was not the only reason for this. In words which uncannily echo Michael's own lament on the Bashir programme for the sickness of American society, he said:

> Murder, even a double murder with a knife that left two people bleeding to death on the pavement, is somehow not so far out of the American mainstream. Look at the video games our kids play: we are inured to violence. Murder is easy to talk about, but this is different. Child molestation is distasteful. You can't have a loud conversation in a restaurant about what Michael Jackson is accused of doing to some little boy's penis. It's taboo.[772]

CHAPTER FIFTEEN

The Trial, Part Two: The 'Bashir Boy' Accuses

Even the media were not entirely immune from the taboo on graphic descriptions of "child sexual abuse" at the outset of the Jackson trial. An online report by CNN coyly avoided the details of Michael's alleged misdeeds as set out by district attorney Tom Sneddon in his opening statement. In a positively Victorian circumlocution, the report delicately hinted that Michael had "allegedly sought to alter a teenager's morals".[773] So this was the great sensation that had gripped the world's attention? That Jackson had *sought to alter* a teenager's morals? Note the fastidious choice of the word "alter", rather than, say, "corrupt". Why, if parents caught their children reading this story, they could explain that Michael had merely being trying to *improve* the youngster's morals!

The coverage on Court TV and Fox News, two of the top US players in celebrity court dramas, was also somewhat muted on the opening day, ironically bringing a heightened sense of distaste and horror to the court of public opinion: for what could be worse than deeds deemed appalling beyond words? In the courtroom itself, the ears of the jury could not be spared these horrors; theirs was the solemn and very adult duty of squarely confronting the abominable facts. Nor would the district attorney shirk his task of detailed revelation and thunderous denunciation.

What all this solemnity disguised – aided and abetted by the intense atmosphere of expectation built up over months of pre-trial hype – was that the sexual allegations were downright trivial compared to others seen every day in the courts: no rape or violence would be claimed; the alleged acts were few in number and of the mildest type. The presence of a famous figure in the dock, and the fact that in the US he could end up serving a maximum fifty six years in jail if found guilty, gave substance to the notion that this was a "sensational" occasion; the sexual charges themselves did not.[774] The kidnap allegations were far more dramatic, but soon proved insubstantial. The case in many respects, but not all, turned out to be much ado about nothing.

My principal task in this chapter is to sort the wheat from the chaff, to distinguish the substantial from the insubstantial, and having done so to explore what, if anything, the evidence in the trial has to tell us about Michael and the quality of his relations with children. This evidence, from both prosecution and defence witnesses, had been marshalled with a view to addressing narrow questions of the defendant's legal innocence or guilt in relation to specific charges. Those charges are in themselves of no great concern to us in this volume; we have been exploring ethical issues in ways that call into question the validity of current laws on adult-child sexual behaviour, and we hardly need accord them undue reverence in this chapter. But the evidence, given on oath and tested under often intense interrogation, may nonetheless have yielded a few revealing secrets.

In searching for such secrets, and examining, as it were, the entrails of the trial, I will not be seeking to second-guess the verdict of the jury, with which I have no reason to disagree in any way. I am content that Michael Jackson may have been truly innocent of all the charges, including innocent of furnishing a minor with alcohol, which apparently split the jury right up until the last hour or two of their long deliberations. It is important to note that four such "furnishing" charges were offered to the jury as lesser alternatives if they were unable to find the defendant guilty of the four more serious felony charges of plying minors with alcohol *for the purpose of facilitating a sexual offence*. As the defence pointed out, these felony charges were not the same as a charge against a bartender of serving drinks to minors in the ordinary course of his work: that is where the misdemeanour of mere "furnishing" would come in. Several of the jurors said after the trial that their verdicts were a response to the charges as laid. It did not mean Jackson had never had sexual relations with boys, and he may have done so with the boy Gavin. I share their position.

The trial went on for four months; the official transcript ran to 13,055 pages. This account is comparatively short; necessarily it is selective. The issues are best approached with an overview of the case, and at this point I see no reason to depart from a summary of the facts and issues as presented by the prosecution and the defence lawyers. Thereafter our priorities will take a more specialised course. Bearing in mind what we distinguished in the previous chapter as the three main elements of the case – the sexual allegations involving the boy Gavin, the claim that his family had been kidnapped, and the alleged "prior bad acts" – this narrative will focus on what matters for our purposes. The kidnap issues, being absurd and baseless, need not detain us long.

So, to the great event itself. Opening the prosecution's case, Tom Sneddon said that Michael Jackson had abused a thirteen-year-old boy who suffered from cancer, plying him with alcohol and sexually molesting him, and that Jackson had conspired with his aides to silence the boy and his family by warning that they could be killed. The conspiracy would involve kidnapping the family, holding them captive at Neverland to keep them under control. Judge Rodney Melville permitted the boy's name to be revealed: the "Gavin" familiar to the world from the Bashir documentary turned out to be one Gavin-Anton Arvizo, whose family, especially his eccentric mother, Janet, would soon become almost as high-profile as himself. The day had begun with Judge Melville reading the indictment to the jury, revealing the names of five unindicted alleged co-conspirators. These were Jackson's aides Frank Tyson and Vincent Amen, business managers Dieter Wiesner and Ronald Konitzer, and video producer Marc Schaffel. Tyson had changed his name from Cascio. Now twenty four, he had graduated from being one of Michael's boys to joining his team. The judge also read twenty eight overt acts allegedly committed in the conspiracy.

Responding later for the defence, Tom Mesereau said his client was the victim of a con artist who repeatedly used her cancer-stricken son to prey on celebrities for cash. She had fraudulently claimed to many people that she was destitute and that her son needed money for chemotherapy. In truth, he said, the boy's father, David Arvizo, was a member of the Teamsters union, through which he had medical insurance for the family.

Mesereau said Janet Arvizo went to comedian Jay Leno for money and Leno was so suspicious he called Santa Barbara police. The mother also approached comedian George Lopez and a Los Angeles TV weatherman,

Fritz Coleman, who staged a fund-raiser for the child at a comedy club called Laugh Factory. Said Mesereau: "As you entered the Laugh Factory for the fund-raiser, there was Gavin with his hand out in the lobby, with Janet prodding him on." It later emerged that David Arvizo, not Janet, was at the Laugh Factory fund-raiser.

In any case, Sneddon's version had put it the other way round: instead of being a victim of exploitation, Jackson was a perpetrator of it. The singer had tried to boost his career by using Gavin, posing as his saviour in his battle against cancer. The D.A. told how the background to the case began when the boy's cancer was diagnosed, by which time his condition was already desperate. He had a medicine-ball-size tumour, weighing sixteen pounds, removed from his abdomen. Lesions were removed from his lungs. His gall bladder was removed, and a kidney. He was put in touch with Jackson by comedian Jamie Masada, owner of Laugh Factory. As a result, he was invited to Neverland, where he and his family met the star and stayed for several days.

Born in December 1989, Gavin had been aged ten at the time of this first Neverland visit, in August 2000. There were to be a couple more trips to the ranch that year for Gavin and his younger brother, Star, but thereafter the Arvizo family lost contact with Michael for a long while even though (as Mesereau pointed out) Janet continued to write to him. Then, in September 2002, over two years after that first visit to see Michael and with Gavin now twelve, Jackson again invited the boy to Neverland. This time he would be accompanied by his older sister Davellin as well as Star. The idea, said Sneddon, was to use Gavin and his siblings in the Bashir documentary, which was then in production. The aim was to boost Jackson's image by getting the kids to tell the world how Michael helped Gavin through his cancer.

Sneddon said their mother had not been invited, and Jackson told Gavin what to say on the show. He had taken the boy on one side on his arrival at Neverland and told him privately that the filming would be like an audition. He knew this would appeal to Gavin, who wanted to be an entertainer, but he did not reveal that the film would be on international TV. Jackson left the ranch immediately after the filming and had no further contact with the Arvizo family, not even a phone call.

This was a curious feature for the prosecution to emphasise: it ran counter to the claim – which we will come to – that Jackson began "grooming" Gavin for sexual "abuse" right from the time of his first Neverland visit. If that had been true, why did he not keep up the friendship, making it ever closer? In the event – and this is something even quite close followers of the trial's media coverage may have overlooked, because the time sequencing of events was rarely a feature of news reports – the only period in which Jackson would take the opportunity to be close to Gavin after 2000 was in February-March 2003, when the boy was thirteen. Would Gavin have been too young to excite Michael's interest at an earlier age? Hardly: as we have seen in earlier chapters, some of his most intense relationships have been with pre-teen boys, notably Brett Barnes at age ten. What would emerge later was testimony that Michael had been warned that the Arvizo family could be dangerous to him. Bringing them back into his life via the Bashir programme appears to have been intended as a "one off", but this policy broke down when they were needed for further filming just a few months later.

The Bashir programme, as we know, did not meet its objective of boosting Jackson's image. On the contrary, in the words of one of Jackson's aides at the time, it was "a train wreck". Continuing his opening statement in the trial, Sneddon said "Jackson's world was rocked" when the documentary aired in February 2003 creating negative publicity. At that point, he said, Jackson's team tried to get the boy and his family to rebut it, in what would become known as "the rebuttal video". The prosecutor said the molestation occurred in February or March 2003, after Bashir had aired. He described two specific incidents of molestation, including one when Jackson reached into Gavin's underpants and masturbated the boy and himself.

Sneddon said that after Gavin's surgery, when the prognosis was bleak, the boy made a dying wish. Having met Jamie Masada through the comedian's comedy camp for underprivileged children, Gavin said he wanted to meet film stars Chris Tucker and Adam Sandler – and also Michael Jackson. He actually did meet all three of them. When Gavin came to Neverland for that first visit in 2000, Jackson told him over dinner to ask his mother if he could sleep in Michael's bedroom, and the boy did. That night, said Sneddon, Jackson took Gavin and Star to his bedroom along with his elder son, Prince Michael, and one of his aides, Frank Tyson – already known to readers of this book as Frank Cascio, one of Michael's former little friends, now a young adult.

On that night, said the prosecutor, Jackson took the boys on a 45-minute tour of sexually explicit websites with naked bodies. When an image of a woman with bare breasts came on the screen, Jackson allegedly turned to the group and said: "Got milk?" It was later revealed that this could have been a humorous reference to a commercial current at the time. Sneddon said Jackson also turned at one point to his little son lying asleep on the bed, saying "Prince, you're missing a lot of pussy." It would later be suggested by the prosecution that this internet tour was part of a grooming process, through which Jackson made it obvious that his household was a place without too many inhibitions, where kids could safely let their hair down – and their pants.

Sneddon even seemed to indict Neverland itself. While conceding the ranch was a "beautiful thing", used for "beautiful causes", such as hosting deprived inner-city kids on day trips, he contended its influence on young visitors staying for longer periods (which applied to the Arvizo children in February-March 2003) was less benign. They would begin to change, he said, "because of the personality of the ranch". Basically, he was saying they were allowed the run of the place, with no rules, and had more fun than was good for them.

The Arvizo boys, he said, had free rein at Neverland. They had a vast amusement arcade, a driving circuit, a park with rides and a big wheel; they had Michael Jackson's undivided attention, slept in his bed, enjoyed his wine and also – a major prosecution theme – viewed his extensive collection of pornographic magazines, a number of which, seized when the ranch was raided, bore their fingerprints and Jackson's. For boys of that age, said Sneddon, "it just doesn't get much better than that". For someone supposed to be condemning such terrible corrupting influences, it was an almost wistful comment, as though somewhere within this stern conservative lawyer a fun-loving youngster was struggling to get out, and maybe one who dimly recollected that kids are not always sexual innocents.

But we do not need to psychoanalyse Sneddon to know he understood that Gavin was no victim of crudely coerced molestation, for he openly conceded that the boy genuinely became fond of Jackson and wanted to be with him *after* the sexual incidents. He even pointed out that when the family finally left Neverland for the last time in March 2003, the boy was distraught. When they got back to their grandparents' house he threw a tantrum, said the D.A., raging that he wanted to be back at the ranch with Michael. That was quite an admission for a prosecutor in a molestation case to be forced to make. After all, the kids are supposed to be traumatised by the sex, not angry at being torn from the "abuser".

As for the downside of Neverland, the sinister "personality" of the ranch, Sneddon did have a serious point. The behaviour of the Arvizo boys deteriorated there, he said. They became rude to staff; they got drunk. And, Sneddon claimed, not only were the boys able to get hold of drink at Neverland, Jackson deliberately plied them with it to reduce their sexual inhibitions, a tactic coupled with showing them pornography and encouraging them to masturbate. This was a very serious charge but, as it related to Gavin, even the lesser charge of simply giving the boy alcohol without necessarily any sexual intent (offered as an alternative later in the trial) was damning in moral terms: the boy was recovering from cancer; he had only one kidney. Letting him drink would have been near murderous irresponsibility.

Turning to the alleged conspiracy, Sneddon reminded the jury of the indictment, saying "the objectives of the conspiracy were to extort, to falsely imprison, and to abduct the children". We have heard about the abduction and imprisonment side already – under the shorthand term "kidnapping" – but not the extortion. Sneddon understandably said very little about it in his opening, having bigger fish to fry at this stage. What would be alleged in more detail later was that Jackson's perilous financial position after years of over-spending and a faltering career meant that at the time to which the indictment related he was desperate for money. He had needed the Arvizo family to take part in the "rebuttal video" not only to bolster his image but also to generate funds by selling the broadcasting rights to the Fox Channel for a multi-million dollar figure. In doing so, he had allegedly forced the family to take part while depriving them of a just financial return for their contribution. What the allegation overlooked was that the money on offer from Fox, impressive though it had been, was peanuts in relation to the massive scale of Jackson's debts. Extorting from the family would have been to take a huge risk for little financial gain: as a motive, it failed to stack up.

Sneddon referred to an item in the indictment which stated that between February and March 2003, Tyson threatened Gavin, telling him that "Michael could make the family disappear" and that he also said, "I could have your mother killed." The indictment alleged a series of bizarre activities including a panicky effort by Jackson employees and associates to get the family of his accuser ready for a trip to Brazil. It alleged that Tyson told the family they were in danger and "this is not the time to be out there alone. This is not the time to turn your back on Michael." It also alleged that in February 2003, Jackson's staff were instructed in writing not to let the boy leave Neverland.

Even before the defence rose to speak, a glaring improbability could not have escaped the attention of close Jackson-watchers in the court. Why would Jackson have become sexually involved with Gavin at such a crazily dangerous time, in the middle of a damage-limitation crisis? His intimate friendships with boys had just been given massive world-wide attention in the Bashir programme. It was no secret that complainants were out to get him and that Sneddon would leap on such a golden opportunity to investigate and bring a prosecution. If, as claimed, he and his aides were holding the family captive and forcing them to contribute to the rebuttal video, he could only fear their resentment and what they might later tell the police.

It was not alleged that Michael had sexually attacked Gavin against his will, only that he had seduced him and lowered his resistance with alcohol. But if the family was being held prisoner, with people in fear of their lives – as was claimed – the atmosphere would hardly have been conducive to seduction. And Michael must have known that even if he had managed to grope Gavin while the boy was drunk, the family would soon have the perfect chance to take revenge: in the wake of Bashir, their complaints would not be ignored. As for the idea that all this was to be hushed up by putting the family on a plane to Brazil, it can only be called a wild flight of fancy – as the jury eventually decided. What was *not* alleged was also striking. There would be no claim of any sexual involvement between Michael and Gavin *before* the Bashir documentary was aired, even though, as we have seen, the boy had stayed at Neverland years earlier, when he was ten.

Mesereau's first priority in his opening statement for the defence was to paint a glowing picture of his client and – even more vitally – damn his accusers as liars and scam artists. On the praise side, he had a vivid anecdote:

> ...[Michael] asked Gavin to envision he's playing Pac-Man, and the cancer cells are being gobbled up by the good people. He had gotten that from studies of visualization techniques that were perfected in England years ago for cancer patients. The theory is that if you will visualize and imagine in your mind a way to beat a disease, if you will visualize the good cells going after the bad cells – they're sometimes described as fish, the good fish eating the bad fish – if you will visualize healing, if you will visualize through imagery how you can beat a disease, the studies show it sometimes succeeds. And he taught that to Gavin.[775]

If the story played well with the jury, its success owed little to the truth of the matter, which is that "visualisation techniques", far from having being "perfected", are not even recognised as a form of therapy in mainstream medical practice.[776] It seems Mesereau, with his talk of "studies" and "techniques", was trying to invest Michael's efforts with some sort of bogus scientific authority. It was an early hint that the smooth lawyer could be a bit of a snake-oil salesman.

This is not to criticise Michael, far from it. No doubt he did tell Gavin he could use his mind to beat cancer, and really did believe it might help. He may even have been right: mental attitude is thought to play an important part in combating disease, even if talk of "perfected" techniques in this instance was hogwash. At the very least, Gavin would have got the message that Michael cared about him and was willing his recovery. That would surely have been a great comfort.

Mesereau was at it again with his dodgy claims when he said, "Michael is a voracious reader. He loves to read books on all subject matters. He has close to a million books at Neverland." A *million*? This was an assertion to set off any thinking person's pork pie alarm and that included the prosecution. They would later say that, apart from the pornography, most of the books in the Neverland library looked as though they had never been opened and had probably come with the house. Mesereau himself was later forced to backtrack, and talked about "thousands" of books at Neverland, saying the rest were in storage. But where? We were never told. And judging by Michael's level of conversation in interviews no one would ever mistake him for a bookish intellectual.

Jackson's top lawyer was on much stronger ground once he stopped defending his client and started attacking the Arvizo family. Janet Arvizo, he said, was a shakedown artist who used her sick son as bait, a woman who coached her kids to lie in connection with an assault lawsuit the family once brought against the clothing and home furnishing retail chain JC Penney. Janet claimed in the suit that she and Gavin had been attacked and she had been sexually assaulted by store security guards. Significantly, she had since admitted to lying in that case, in which – just as in the present one – she had made an allegation of false imprisonment.

In documents filed with the court it had been claimed the case stemmed from a 1998 incident in which the family had been detained for alleged shoplifting. Defence attorney Robert Sanger had written: "Rather than admit to their culpability in using their children to shoplift, [Janet Arvizo] concocted an outrageous story that the security guards responsible for detaining the family assaulted them by using excessive force and she eventually claimed that they sexually assaulted her." The store settled the case, said Sanger, in order to avoid a trial in which jurors may have decided in the family's favour since Gavin, then aged nine, was suffering from cancer.

In court, Mesereau referred to Mary Holzer, a newly-surfaced defence witness who worked as a paralegal for the lawyer representing the family in the JC Penney case. She would claim the mother had confided that she had lied under oath about the incident and then threatened to kill Holzer and her nine-year-old daughter if Holzer told. To back up the threat, the mother had said she had relatives in the Mexican mafia. As a result, the paralegal had hesitated to come forward.

Along with the alleged JC Penney scam, Janet Arvizo illegally obtained welfare benefits, Mesereau said, adding that she never bothered to mention her six-figure settlement from the department store when applying for those benefits. In other instances, Mesereau said Janet "undertook a programme to use her son to raise money." This involved the family targeting Jay Leno, who spoke with Gavin on the telephone at one point. Leno had rebuffed the financial pitch and later told Santa Barbara police that the family was looking for a "mark". Leno had said to the police, "Something was wrong. They were looking for a mark. It sounded scripted. The mother was in the background, and I terminated the conversation."

Reeling off one alleged financial deceit after another, Mesereau remarked, "It goes on and on."

Addressing the mother's claim that she and her children had been held against their will at Neverland, Mesereau said Janet had numerous chances to alert law enforcement authorities to their plight but never said a thing. He told jurors that the guest unit in which she was allegedly held captive was the suite that Elizabeth Taylor requested when she stayed at Jackson's estate. He also mentioned that during this same period the Jackson camp paid more than $3,300 for Janet's beauty treatments, including cosmetics, aromatherapy and leg waxing. She had received the leg waxing treatment at a local salon to which she had been driven at her own request, and had been left alone there while it was carried out. This was at a time when she had supposedly been kidnapped and prevented from communicating with anyone.

And as for prosecution claims that the family had never considered filing a lawsuit against Jackson, Mesereau pointed out that Janet, in conversations with law enforcement officials, mentioned that her children would have until they were eighteen to file a civil claim against the performer. Countering Sneddon's claim that Janet was not seeking money from Jackson, Mesereau said that he would prove otherwise. He told jurors that after the Bashir documentary aired, Janet was expecting a payday in return for her children's participation in the Jackson rebuttal video. However, when an opportunity to cash in never materialized, the molestation accusations emerged – and the family went first to lawyers, rather than the police.

Turning his fire from Janet to her children, Mesereau said they went "out of control" at Neverland when Michael was not around. The two boys, he said, broke into the estate's wine cellar and a fridge; they stole alcoholic drinks their host had ordered for adult guests; they were found drunk by ranch employees; they were discovered at the top of a Ferris wheel, where they threw things at elephants and people.

Mesereau even managed to turn the tricky issue of Jackson's pornographic magazines into an accusation against the boys. In this version, Gavin and Star had somehow managed to raid his locked briefcase, from which they took magazines such as *Playboy* and *Hustler*. When Michael caught the kids going through these magazines he grabbed them back. The prosecution had not suggested that any of Michael's magazines were illegal, but they were undoubtedly an embarrassment. How would Mesereau deal with this? By using the "adult" material to bolster Michael's thin credentials as a normal heterosexual guy. "Mr Jackson will freely admit that he does read girly magazines from time to time," said the defender. For "admit", the prosecution would substitute "claim". Sneddon and his team would suggest that magazines of this sort were there solely to stimulate his young male guests and that Jackson had no personal interest in them. Homosexual erotica would emerge as a feature later in the trial and the prosecution would say this was more to Michael's taste.

Towards the end of his opening, Mesereau turned to Michael's feelings about the family, saying that one time at Neverland he got a "bad feeling and intuition" about them, after Janet had been overly familiar, grabbing his hand and getting the children to hold hands in a circle, saying, "Let's all kneel down and pray with our Daddy Michael." He felt something was wrong and he had to get away from the family.

Mesereau's wording had seemed to hint that Michael would take the witness stand to testify about this and other matters himself. As we have just seen, he told the jury Michael "will freely admit" reading girlie magazines.

In the end, though, he never did tell, and so the accuracy or otherwise of Mesereau's claims on his behalf were never put to the test of cross-examination. As we shall see, the prosecution's star witnesses failed to come up to scratch. In legal terms, that was rightly the end of the story, for it was up to the prosecution to prove its case, not for the defendant to prove his innocence. In terms of the broader assessment essayed by this work, however, it is striking that the most compelling possible defence witness – Michael himself – never uttered a single word on oath. Under California law the prosecution could not demand his presence on the stand. And most commentators on the case were in agreement after the prosecution witnesses had been heard – and largely discredited – that Jackson had little to gain (and possibly much to lose) by giving evidence of his own accord.

Had he ever been put under direct, detailed, sceptical and doubtless sarcastic scrutiny by his old enemy Tom Sneddon – or more likely by attorney Ron Zonen, who would prove to be the sharpest tool in the prosecution's box – would Michael's testimony have fared any better than that of the Arvizo boys or their mother? While we shall never know the answer to that one, we can imagine the kind of questions he might have wished to avoid. Bearing in mind the wide scope of the trial as regards "prior bad acts", how would he have explained his persistent bed sharing with a whole succession of boys, sometimes (as with Brett Barnes or Jordie Chandler) for weeks or months on end? How come, if there were nothing sexual in his motivation, his love for children was so strongly biased towards boys, not girls? Could he really have convinced a jury that only pure generosity was in his heart when the parents of these boys received huge gifts, such as a Rolls Royce, or expensive jewellery, or a new house? Successful objections could perhaps have fended off certain other embarrassing questions, about Michael's long-time lack of any women in his life, and his apparent lack of conjugal relations even to beget his own children, but it is doubtful such merciless intrusion into his "private" life (or lack of one) could have been avoided altogether. No wonder he kept schtum.

So as the trial settled down to its core business over the long weeks and months ahead, testing the evidence of witness after witness in a seemingly endless prosecution parade of characters, from the bizarre and seemingly deranged Janet Arvizo to the sober but deadly tedious finger-print expert, Michael's role in court was to be what he had always been: not the star witness, but simply the star. The media would concern themselves with his (occasionally dramatic) comings and goings from the courtroom and with his ever-changing sartorial statements. It would be like acting in a movie where everyone else had speaking parts but he was still trapped in the silent era – a devastating disadvantage, one might suppose, except that his unspeaking features would be constantly under scrutiny, and his every gesture threatened to upstage the official script.

So it was when the very first witness took the stand, none other than Martin Bashir, the man whose treacherous TV programme had precipitated the investigation that led to the trial. It was believed to be the first time he and Jackson had been in the same room together since the filming. "The second Michael Jackson spotted Martin Bashir, Jacko's demeanour changed in an instant," according to Britain's downmarket tabloid the *Sun*. "And his reported hatred for the British journalist could not have been more obvious. He glowered ferociously at Bashir…"[777] Or at least, that's how it *would* have been had Jackson been a macho mafioso type like his menacing one-time fixer Anthony Pellicano. *Sky News* had a gentler version, saying that as Bashir entered the courtroom, Jackson pointed at him, smiled and mouthed: "It's Martin, it's Martin."[778]

What the journalists in attendance could agree on was that Michael was reduced to tears – or at least to dabbing his eyes with a handkerchief – by parts of Bashir's film, which was screened for the jury in court. The press remarked on his evident distress when confronted with the footage in which he talked about being abused by his father as a child, and also when his own children were shown on screen. But his greatest agitation reportedly came when the subject turned to his relations with Gavin Arvizo, with Bashir asking what it was that Jackson got out of sharing his bedroom with a boy. The *Sun* again: "He began to twist a handkerchief between his fingers before blowing his nose and dabbing at his eyes."

Bashir himself was given a tough time in the witness box, subjected to a hail of questions he was loath to deal with, such as whether he got Jackson to sign documents without lawyers present, how many hours of footage were cut from his documentary and whether he was being paid as a correspondent at the trial. These were among around thirty questions he refused to answer, pleading protection under California's Shield Law, designed to allow journalists to protect their sources. His tried to get a ruling that would have blocked questions about all aspects of the news gathering process. The judge ruled against him and when he still refused to answer the questions he was cited for contempt of court. The judge promised to make a ruling on the contempt issue at a later date. No news of Bashir suffering any judicial wrath has since come to my attention – not that the fate of this dubious character need detain us further.

Next up was Ann Marie Kite (professional surname Gabriel), a PR advisor hired by Michael as a specialist in crisis management on 9 February, 2003, immediately after Bashir's documentary was shown in the US. She testified to the panic gripping the Jackson camp at that time, panic which the prosecution claimed would lead to the Arvizo family being held against their will at Neverland and coerced into making a "rebuttal video" praising the star. This would be filmed on the night of 19 February, going on until the small hours of the next day.

Only one feature of her testimony need concern us. The crisis, she said, was not about the Bashir programme alone. Some documents newly released on a website had made things even worse. A courtroom skirmish ensued in which Tom Mesereau battled to prevent further details being mentioned. He failed. And so it was that Ann Kite revealed that the documents, posted at *www.thesmokinggun.com*, were about what she initially described as a public relations issue for Michael Jackson in 1993. After a flurry of objections, she was allowed to answer a question by deputy D.A. Gordon Auchincloss, for the prosecution, as to what the contents of that PR issue had been:

> A. They involved Mr Jackson having inappropriate actions with a young boy.
>
> Q. Okay. The '93 case?

With this short, oblique exchange the jury heard the first reference in the case to the Jordie Chandler affair. Up to this point the sexual allegations in the trial had been solely about Gavin Arvizo. It would be much deeper into the proceedings before Judge Melville would rule on the admissibility of alleged "prior bad acts", including the Chandler case, which is why such acts were not mentioned in either the prosecution or defence opening statements. This passing allusion marked the beginning of Michael's past coming back to haunt him. Did any of the jury log on to The Smoking Gun website back at home that evening? They had been instructed to concentrate on the evidence in the court, not on media accounts. But they were not a sequestered jury. Nothing physically prevented them from reading and seeing whatever media coverage they wished, including internet coverage. In any case, as we saw in the last chapter, five of the jury admitted already knowing about the 1993 allegations – and it is hard to believe the remainder of a panel drawn from Jackson's own neck of the woods could truly have known nothing of the stories.

The first Arvizo family witness was Gavin's older sister, Davellin, now an eighteen-year-old college student. During her testimony, the now famous rebuttal video would be played in full for the jury, in which all three Arvizo children and their mother Janet fulsomely praised Michael – allegedly coerced into doing so by his aides and acting out a script supplied by them. Janet is seen calling Michael "...an ideal family man", saying "I appreciate him with all my heart." The children all lauded him as a kind father figure. Unlike the Fox riposte to Bashir, this tape had never before been seen in public. It failed to make the deadline for that broadcast and the Arvizo family never in the end gave permission for it to be shown. Watching the uncut video in court, Jackson sat motionless. Behind him, in the public gallery, his sister La Toya, his brother Jermaine and his mother Katherine, also watched attentively.

Davellin's testimony offered jurors the first direct account of the events at Neverland around the time in early 2003 when prosecutors claimed Jackson's aides moved to intimidate her family and the entertainer molested Gavin. She described how she had seen Michael hugging her brother and kissing him repeatedly on the head and the cheek. "He would constantly be hugging, kissing him," she said. "Anytime I saw them, really."

She became emotional as she told of the changes she said came over Gavin following his time alone with Jackson, when the family had left Neverland. Sneddon had already told the court the boy became angry and inconsolable after being torn away from Michael. Tearfully, Davellin said: "He didn't want to be hugged. He didn't want to be kissed. It just hurt because I'm his older sister."

She claimed she saw the singer give alcohol to both her brothers, saying she saw him give the boys booze in a wine cellar. She also backed the prosecution case that the family – except at least for Gavin – had felt intimidated and imprisoned at Neverland.

Under cross-examination, though, she admitted that her praise for Michael on the rebuttal video had been sincere – as she had also testified to the grand jury. Mesereau pointed out inconsistencies in her story about the wine cellar incident. When she had first spoken to investigators she had mentioned being in the wine cellar, but had not said she saw Jackson pour wine for the children, as she was now claiming. She also displayed an apparent inability to remember key facts, suggesting she had been coached by the prosecution.

It was not a convincing endorsement of the prosecution's case, and her younger brother Star's would be even less so. The hapless youngster would be caught out in innumerable inconsistencies. And at a massive 225 lb (just over sixteen stone), the fourteen-year-old in court did not even *look* the part of a boy who could be the *younger* brother of a recent child sex abuse victim.

Star's accusations were right at the heart of the case though. He told jurors he twice saw Michael masturbating himself and groping his sleeping brother, the first testimony directly implicating the singer in sex abuse. Star said he witnessed the scene on two nights in February or March of 2003, while climbing stairs to Michael's bedroom. He said that on both occasions Michael and Gavin were lying on the bed; Gavin, then thirteen, was asleep. Jackson was not aware that he was on the stairs and peering through a railing, the boy testified. "Michael's left hand was in my brother's pants and his right hand was in his [own] pants," the boy said in describing the first night. "He was masturbating. He was rubbing himself."

Star, who was twelve at the time, said he watched for only a few seconds before leaving to spend the night with his sister in a guest cottage at the ranch. He did not tell his sister or his mother what happened, nor did he tell his brother what he had seen. "I didn't know what to do," he said. "I went back to my guest room." Star said the first person he told about the incident was a psychologist who interviewed him and then notified the authorities. On most nights, he said, he and his brother both slept in Jackson's room. He testified that once when the pair of them were watching a movie, "Michael walked up naked and picked up something. Me and my brother were grossed out. He told us it was natural." Asked if there was anything unusual about Jackson's genitals, the boy replied, "He had a hard-on." He said that on one occasion Jackson brought up the subject of masturbation and asked if he ever did it. Star said he answered no. "Then he said to me, 'Everyone does it. You should try it. It's OK.' "

The boy also described an incident in which Jackson grabbed a mannequin that he kept in his bedroom and "he pretended like he was having intercourse with it" on the bed while fully clothed and laughing. Jurors were shown a photo of a mannequin that had been at Neverland, depicting an Afro-American girl with braids. Mesereau would later suggest it was a custom-made mannequin depicting a cousin of Michael's. The vaginal portion had been defaced with a magic marker, he revealed when cross-examining Gavin. Nothing to do with me, the boy replied. The mannequin was one of dozens at the ranch when the police raided, including many child-size ones. The jury had earlier been shown pictures from inside the ranch.

The police "video tour" also included hundreds of dolls, and in his private quarters the walls were covered with pictures of small children.

Star confirmed Sneddon's claim that Michael had shown him and his brother internet porn during the family's first visit to Neverland in 2000. He also said Jackson had a suitcase full of pornographic magazines that he would show the boys. He identified the black case when Tom Sneddon showed it to him in court. Shown pictures of several magazines inside, Star said they were among the magazines Jackson had in the case.

He said he and his brother drank wine with Jackson several times, and that Michael called it "Jesus Juice". Star said the singer nicknamed him "Blow Hole" and called his brother either "Apple Head" or "Doo Doo". Gavin called Jackson "Daddy". The prosecution suggested "Blow Hole" had a sexual connotation. Mesereau later countered with a question: "Blow hole is a nickname for a fish, right?" Star responded: "I made it up. I was going to give it to Michael. We did rock, paper, scissors and I lost and got stuck with the name."

Star claimed that during one visit to Neverland, their host made obscene nuisance calls to women. He said Jackson told them: "He was having a census and he wanted to know how big her pussy was." He added: "If the phone number didn't exist he would have us drink wine."

After a long session on the stand Star appeared fatigued at the end of the day, yawning widely and rubbing his eyes with his hands. But by far the toughest part still lay ahead of him. The next morning he testified that Michael told him and his brother to keep their activities at the ranch secret "even if they put a gun to your head". It was to be his last colourful claim before Tom Mesereau's cross-examination began to take him apart. Jackson's lead defence attorney accused him of lying, breaking into the singer's suitcase full of adult magazines and wine cellar and "snooping" around his bedroom. And he hammered at the boy's testimony that he twice stumbled on Jackson groping his sleeping brother.

Star agreed with Mesereau that a bell sounds in a hallway whenever visitors approach Jackson's bedroom door. But he refused to concede that Jackson would have heard the alarm, saying that it was only audible from the bed area if a second door was open. Mesereau also homed in on inconsistencies in the boy's account, saying that his testimony about the two incidents conflicted with what he had previously told a psychologist. The attorney also pointed out that a copy of the "adult" magazine *Barely Legal*, presented by prosecutors as among those that Jackson showed the boy, was dated August 2003 – six months after the family left Neverland for the last time. Star said he never claimed to have seen that issue.

Mesereau pointed out that, in an earlier account to police, Star claimed to have been resting on a couch pretending to be asleep when he witnessed the second alleged incident of abuse, not on the stairs and peering through a railing as he had testified in court. Star now changed his story again, saying he had in fact witnessed three incidents, not two.

The boy responded to numerous questions about inconsistencies from his previous accounts in the case by saying, "I don't know exactly what I said." In one instance he had an unusual explanation. In direct testimony he said there was a red ring around a 7Up can he saw his older brother drinking from when the family were with Jackson briefly in Miami, implying there was wine in it. Mesereau pointed out that in the past Star had testified there was white wine in the can. The boy said the court reporter must have got it wrong.

If exposing inconsistencies was useful to the defence, squeezing damaging admissions was pure gold. It panned out well for Mesereau. Crucially, Star had claimed he saw Michael masturbating Gavin. But under cross-examination it turned out Michael had only been masturbating himself. Asked to explain why he had changed his story, Star claimed nerves got the better of him. Mesereau asked: "So because you were nervous you didn't get the facts right?" The teenager replied, "Yes."

But it was a revelation about another case that scored the most palpable hit against Star's credibility. Mesereau wrung out of him an admission that he had lied under oath in a deposition for the JC Penney suit, in which he had sworn that his mother and father never fought and that his father never hit him. When Mesereau asked him to tell the jury why he lied under oath, he said, "I don't remember. It was five years ago. I don't remember nothing." It might even have been true: five years is a long time, especially in the life of a fourteen-year-old. But Mesereau had done more than enough to sow the seeds of doubt.

As a witness, Star had hardly lived up to his name. What of his elder brother, allegedly the victim and carrying a huge burden of expectation on his young shoulders? Would Gavin be the true star witness the prosecution so badly needed? So far, we have seen him only in ways reflecting the vulnerability attendant on his victim status. We have seen the seemingly doomed cancer sufferer and the hero-worshiping Michael Jackson fan of the Bashir documentary, snuggling up to the star with love in his eyes; we have heard how Jackson allegedly groomed and manoeuvred him into a sexual situation, softened up by porn and booze. Would he be a soft touch for Mesereau when it came to the hard questions?

Even before the trial, there were to be strong hints that if Gavin had indeed been a victim, then he was not to be defined by victimhood. Cancer had not beaten him; he was a survivor in the truest sense. As for being a "survivor" of sexual abuse, the early signs were of a boy for whom sexual "survival" was a piece of cake. Far from being a tender innocent, it astonishingly emerged that he had seen Jackson as the sexually naïve one.

The surprising appraisal came during an interview with Santa Barbara Sheriff's Department officials on 19 January 2004, as revealed by the seemingly omniscient website The Smoking Gun. At the end of the interview, a detective asked Gavin about conversations he had with Jackson about girls and any related guidance offered by the performer. The boy, who was thirteen at the time of the alleged molestation, replied that Jackson would "always, like, try to give me advice" about "the birds and the bees." But Gavin had known more than Michael!

The audiotaped interview came about two months prior to Gavin's grand jury appearance. During his testimony, the boy occasionally appeared flippant while discussing the alleged sexual assaults and Jackson's provision of alcoholic drinks to him and his two siblings. When Sneddon asked if he had ceased drinking alcohol after leaving Neverland for the last time, the boy responded, "That period of my life, I went to AA. That period of my life is over." To "make sure the record is clear," Sneddon asked the boy whether he was kidding about attending Alcoholics Anonymous. "I'm just joking," replied the accuser.

At another point during his testimony, Gavin was asked to describe the alleged molestation incidents in Jackson's bedroom, which he did in graphic detail. The boy, who had been in the US Navy's Sea Cadets programme, was then asked by Sneddon if anyone else had been present during the assaults. "No," he answered, adding, "not unless a Navy SEAL dropped down." At the close of his first day of testimony, the boy received Sneddon's standard witness admonition that a judicial gag order barred him from talking to the media about his confidential testimony. "Oh, man," he replied, "I was going to have a press conference."

The wise-cracking showed a side of Gavin the public had not seen – a smart, street-wise, tough-cookie aspect to his character. We have seen the family had connections with a comedy club called Laugh Factory. He had his own ambitions to be a comedian. If he sticks with it, he might well be famous one day as something more than the kid in the Jackson case. Mesereau would not find him such easy meat as his sister and brother.

But first it was Sneddon's turn. At the start of one session when the District Attorney said "Good morning" the boy replied "Morning, Tom", adding "Mr Sneddon" as an afterthought. Overawed he was not. Indeed he sometimes seemed so underawed and bored he might drop off to sleep. He yawned repeatedly, prompting even Sneddon to ask him: "I'm keeping you awake, am I?" To which the boy replied: "All I need is a pillow." The image was hardly that of a traumatised child victim; the prosecution had an uphill task.

Gavin calmly told jurors the singer had foisted wine and hard liquor on him at Neverland and twice molested him under the guise of showing him how to masturbate, which Jackson said was a necessary and natural act. He said he thought there had been other incidents he could not clearly remember. "In my memory it was only twice that I know for sure," he said. "I feel it was more than twice but it was only solid in my mind twice."

"Michael started talking to me about masturbation," he said. "He told me that if men don't masturbate they might get to a level where they might rape a girl... He said that once he was looking over a balcony and he saw a boy who didn't masturbate who had sex with a dog."

Gavin said Jackson then said he would show him how to masturbate. "He put his hands in my pants and he started masturbating me," the boy said, adding that he "felt weird" about it but that Jackson told him it was "OK and natural". The boy said the second molestation followed a day or so later, when they were watching television. That incident followed a similar pattern except that about midway through Jackson tried to get him to reciprocate. "He kind of grabbed my hand to do it to him and I pulled my hand away, I didn't want to do it to him," he said. Gavin claimed he ejaculated in both incidents and felt embarrassed but that Jackson tried to "comfort me".

Earlier, the boy testified that Jackson first gave him wine, concealed in a Diet Coke can and called "Jesus juice" by the singer, in a Miami hotel room on the night the Bashir documentary was broadcast in the United States. Pulling him into a separate room in his hotel suite, Jackson "gave me another little audition, like he was the principal of the school and if a girl said I had done something bad. I was the student who got in trouble." The boy said Jackson had him drink more wine in a soft drinks can on the plane ride back to California, asking him not to tell anyone about the alcohol, and gave him a jacket and a watch that the entertainer said was worth $75,000. At Neverland, Gavin said, Jackson showed him pornography and served him wine, rum, vodka and bourbon, even though he had lost a kidney to cancer and told the singer at least three times that alcohol was bad for him.

Towards the end of his time at Neverland, Gavin had a problem. In connection with his recovery from cancer, he needed to provide a urine sample for medical analysis. But he had been drinking, and worried that alcohol would be revealed in the sample. He asked Michael what he should do. Gavin testified that Michael replied, "Doo, Doo, just don't take the test." In the end, Gavin gave a sample but it was "spilt" while being taken in a car driven to the hospital by one of Jackson's aides.

The accusations of criminal sexual conduct astonishingly occupied only the last ten minutes of Gavin's direct testimony, coming at the end of three hours of questioning by Sneddon – and the testimony on the molestation was notably vaguer than that on other matters. As Tina Brown remarked in the *Washington Post*, "in his first appearance, the kid's testimony was all about being a participant in Jackson's media charade for Martin Bashir".[779] Gavin said Michael had wanted him to embellish their relationship on camera: "He told me he wanted me to say certain things, to say that he helped me and pretty much cured me of cancer." The boy said this had not been true; much of the time when he had cancer Jackson had not been around. He added that he was willing to say the things Jackson had asked him to say because at that point "I thought he was the coolest guy in the world, my best friend ever, if you know what I mean."

Gavin said he returned to Neverland at least seven times during his cancer treatment but had rarely seen Jackson and had often found that phone numbers the entertainer had given him were disconnected. He testified that as he went through his chemotherapy, he had "twenty calls, maybe" from Jackson – some of them lengthy – both when he was at the hospital and while recuperating at his grandmother's house. But he also said there were times when Jackson seemed to be trying to avoid him, dodging his phone calls and pretending to be away from the ranch during the boy's visits, when he was actually there. Sometimes he would be told by Neverland staff that Jackson was not home, and then spot him on the grounds. On one of those occasions, he said, "I walked into the house and I saw Michael walking toward me and then he acted as if, 'Oh, crap!'"

Regardless of what inroads Mesereau would later make into Gavin's testimony, this was clearly damaging and embarrassing to Jackson. So veteran Jacksonologists were hardly surprised when the cunning old magician upstaged the boy's performance with an even more dramatic and colourful one of his own by failing to turn up at court, risking jail and the forfeit of his $3 million bail. His lawyer said he was in hospital with a back problem. The judge was not impressed, ordering that Jackson's bail be revoked and the entertainer jailed if he did not appear within an hour.

Jackson, finally turned up a few minutes after the deadline – wearing pyjama bottoms under his jacket and with his hair in a mess. Taking the arm of an aide, he hobbled slowly into the courtroom, apparently in pain. A hospital spokeswoman confirmed he had spent forty five minutes in the emergency room at Santa Ynez Valley Cottage Hospital.

Media speculation was rife that it was nothing but a stunt, a diversionary tactic. One report noted that in 2002 he hobbled into a California courtroom on crutches for a contract lawsuit, saying a spider had bitten his foot. And one commentator claimed that although his hair was ostentatiously uncombed, he had found time to "put on all his facial makeup, do his eyes, and put on lipstick." It looked as though the pyjamas, the hobbling and the bad hair day were a bid for sympathy. It did not go unnoticed that although Jackson had been at the hospital he had not been seen by a doctor. A statement issued by the hospital said, "We don't know why he was here." But he got away with it: Judge Melville took no punitive action. In fairness, it should be added that opinion was divided on the makeup. The *Guardian*'s Dan Glaister said "Jackson had left home without fixing his face. His skin, lacking the usual white pancake, had an orange hue. Unexpectedly, it made him look more normal than usual." Glaister added that he did indeed enter the courtroom that day with his face made up – but not until the afternoon session.[780]

With the sideshow over (though an "ill" Jackson would turn up late again just a few days later) and the spotlight once more on Gavin, Mesereau confronted the boy with a police interview in which Gavin had said it was his *grandmother* who told him that if men do not masturbate they end up raping someone – not Jackson, as he had testified in court. Standing firm, the boy told Mesereau he discussed masturbation with both Jackson and his grandmother. "Michael tried to explain to me first. He was more pushing it on me... I guess my grandmother saw I was very confused about sexuality. She didn't make the identical quote."

Mesereau also claimed the boy had changed his story about when

Jackson allegedly fondled him. He said the teenager had told the court it happened after the rebuttal video was filmed on 20 February 2003. But Mesereau said the boy had previously told the police he was molested *before* the video was filmed. Jackson's attorney tried chipping away at other seeming contradictions in the boy's account, notably the fact that he had originally claimed to have been molested five times. Gavin held his ground, but the gruelling cross-examination provoked a surly and argumentative response that may not have gone down well with the jury. Focussing on the boy's disciplinary record at school, Mesereau drew an admission from Gavin that he had a long history of being disruptive in class and getting into trouble with many teachers – trouble that led to two interviews with the principal in the weeks after the alleged molestations. He admitted to trouble with Mr Geraldt, Mr Murphy, Mr Parker, Mr Collins, Miss Shapiro, Mr Finkelstein, Mr Moon, Miss Bender, Mr Martinez – young master Gavin was clearly no angel at this time. Miss Bender, however, had written a note referring to his "good acting skills", a point exploited by Mesereau, especially in relation to the boy's apparent distress in a police interview.

Then, with his own theatrical touch, Mesereau dramatically struck to deadly effect when it emerged that the principal had asked Gavin whether there was any truth in all the rumours about possible sexual abuse by Jackson. The defender read from an interview record, quoting Jeffrey Alpert, principal of the John Burroughs Middle School in Los Angeles as saying, "Look at me, look at me ... I can't help you unless you tell me the truth – did any of this happen?" The boy acknowledged from the witness stand that his answer was "No." Mesereau again asked: "You told Mr Alpert twice that Mr Jackson had never done anything to you of a sexual nature, is that true?" The boy said: "Yes."

Recalled to the stand later by Sneddon, Gavin explained that he had been taunted by schoolmates over being "raped" by Jackson, and had got into fights as a result. He was then sent to see Mr Alpert, who asked him whether Jackson had molested him. "I told him that it didn't happen," the boy said. "All the kids were already making fun of me at the school and I didn't want anyone to think it had really happened." The story made sense, but the fact remained that if the molestation had really happened, then Gavin had lied to the principal – and any clear evidence of important untruths spoken by the boy and his family had to be good for the defence.

Little mentioned by courtside analysts was the fact that Mesereau only delved briefly into the two alleged incidents of molestation. Jurors might have wondered why, if Jackson were innocent, more time was not spent examining those charges, and less time on the accuser's school record. A few other significant points were also overlooked in the media, at a time when the focus was understandably on the most sensational allegations. Gavin's honesty was tested and found wanting on another matter. Trying to play down Michael's role in helping him during his cancer, the boy at first tried to deny talking to Michael on the phone a lot while he had been in hospital. But then it emerged under cross-examination that he and Michael had been engaged in a great many lengthy phone calls at that time, often lasting for hours at a stretch. Yes, Gavin admitted, but *Michael* had been doing most of the talking!

Not that Gavin came over simply as unpleasantly devious. He just seemed angry over what he took to be Michael's eventual rejection of him – a distancing which may have owed a lot to early anxieties on Michael's behalf that the boy's parents could become a problem. Asked whether he was upset about being "inappropriately touched", he said, yes, and gave a reason: "Because, I mean, something happened to where, like, it's not like I can go back and change it. It's like something that I have, like, no control of." One has to wonder whose reasoning that really was: was it truly Gavin's, or that of the lawyers, cops and shrinks who had prepared him for the occasion?

A pleasanter side of the boy's character – a side Michael had no doubt found attractive – emerged when he was talking about the star's elder children, Paris and Prince. Sometimes, he said, he would go and visit the little ones in their rooms, and he spoke fondly of a session spent with them in the company of Grace, the nanny, when he was helping the kids do drawing and solving puzzles. Did he think of them as his brother and sister? He was asked: "Yeah…I would always play with them, and we would go look at stuff together…" He spoke of going around Neverland hand-in-hand with these little kids, one at either side. It was a far cry from the picture of drunken wildness and disruptive school behaviour heard at other times in the case.

One utterly surreal moment that went unremarked in what was often a surreal trial, was an answer given by Gavin: "No, I travelled in a Rolls Royce when I was escaping from Neverland with Jesus." It was not a religious experience and the answer did make some sort of sense – but let's not spoil it with explanations!

At the end of a total twelve hours on the stand over four days, Gavin faced his final question. Sneddon asked the boy's current opinion of Jackson. Gavin hesitated and then replied, "I don't really like him anymore. I don't really think he deserves the respect I gave him as the coolest guy in the world." It may have been his true considered opinion. In the course of his testimony, Gavin had given his account of the alleged molestations in an unemotional, matter-of-fact way. Whether they had happened or not, there was nothing to suggest he had been traumatised by any sexual events. But he had another reason to be upset. The one topic in his long testimony that roused him to evident sadness and anger was when he spoke of how Jackson began to avoid him and then – as he saw it – abandoned his family in the long months before the Bashir project found them in favour again.

Gavin's emotional detachment from the alleged sexual abuse was not lost on the media, and after hearing all three of the Arvizo children commentators began to wonder out loud and in print whether the accusations might all be a put up job, just as the defence suggested. Mesereau's strategy, of painting these witnesses as dishonest pawns of their cunning mother was beginning to pay off. In his opening statement he had been prevented from asserting that the criminal case was a setup for a lucrative civil one. But in his questions to the Arvizo siblings he had battled to link the charges of molestation to the hiring by the family of a lawyer who had won massive compensation in an earlier case against Jackson, namely Larry Feldman, who had secured a multi-million dollar settlement in the Chandler case. As one report put it "the jurors were surely catching on to that sentiment, as the timing was suspect".

The prosecution attempted to explain away the brothers' inconsistencies and lies. All three of the children had testified that they had been frequently subjected to physical abuse at the hands of their father, David Arvizo, with Davellin saying she had suffered attacks almost daily; her mother claimed her eldest child had been sexually abused by him as well, when she was little. The prosecution would claim the backdrop of domestic abuse was crucial to understanding the essential truth of the children's testimony, despite some lies. When Mesereau had wrung from Star Arvizo the admission that he had lied in a deposition when he denied his father ever beat anyone in the family, he had cast the boy as a hardened liar from an early age. The prosecution would counter by saying the answer was typical of many abused children trying to protect someone they loved. It did not mean they would conjure up allegations out of thin air. But if anything about this assertion was typical it was the child abuse industry's dogma that children never lie – never lie, that is, when they are making allegations, only when they say nothing happened. Fortunately, the jury didn't buy it.

The abuse industry's salesman in the witness box was Anthony Urquiza, a child psychologist who was called by the prosecution to talk not about Gavin but about child sex abuse more generally. He told the jury about "child sexual assault accommodation syndrome," in which youngsters are said to become secretive, feel helpless and trapped, delay reporting acts of abuse, and finally learn to cope with the situation, accommodating to it. The syndrome had first been described – or invented – by one Roland Summit, a child abuse specialist. Summit had also been a prominent defender of the notorious interrogation methods used in the McMartin Pre-School "abuse" case, discussed in earlier chapters.[781]

Under cross-examination, Urquiza was asked about that case, Mesereau wringing from him the admission that he knew false allegations of sexual abuse had been made. No one in court pointed out Summit's dubious role in McMartin, but the admission was still damaging to the prosecution case: it was one of several ways in which Mesereau made the psychologist retreat from his claim that children seldom make false allegations of sexual abuse. Urquiza would also concede that children may be manipulated into making false abuse claims by their parents.

One interesting indicator of the psychologist's own mindset emerged when he was attempting to deal with Mesereau's insistence on talking about an "alleged" victim. The accommodation syndrome, he said, relates to *actual* victims and "makes as its presumption that the child has been sexually abused". Taxed by his interlocutor, he had to admit there is no scientific way of knowing in a particular case whether a child is telling the truth:

> Q: "Nobody can determine that a child has been abused just based on what the child says, right?"
> A: "I don't think I've ever been asked that question before. I don't know how to answer that. I mean, I can only say that that would be a difficult thing to do."

In the self-interested world of the child abuse industry, participants such as Urquiza are not used to scepticism. They would far rather proceed on the basis of convenient presumptions, such as this key one just admitted by the witness, a foundational presumption underlying the accommodation syndrome. The reason he had never been asked such a fundamental question is that the question was not in the interests of sustaining careers such as his own, which depend on providing "therapy" to "traumatised" children. Even more staggering is that he had apparently never even asked *himself* the question in the privacy of his own head.

Urquiza told of relationships in which a child likes or loves the person who is abusing him. "The need they have for affection and someone who cares about them helps to sustain the relationship," Urquiza said. We need have no quarrel with this: it was an important concession from the prosecution side. But then he added that children often undergo changes in behaviour because of the abuse, including "acting out, becoming defiant, name-calling". Under questioning from the prosecution, he agreed this could include talking back to teachers and getting into fights – the kind of misbehaviour seen in Jackson's accuser. In cross-examination, Mesereau simply asked what if the pattern of bad behaviour had been established *before* the alleged sex abuse? How could it be an indication of abuse that had not yet happened? Urquiza had no effective answer. They were talking purely hypothetically. Gavin was never mentioned. But the implications were there for the jury to ponder.

If Urquiza was a damp squib for the prosecution, their other psychological witness was a loose cannon. Whereas Sneddon and his legal team were out to portray Jackson as a paedophile, psychologist Stanley Katz had pronounced even before the trial that he was not. His "off the record" view of the subject is best described as idiosyncratic. In a taped telephone interview revealed on The Smoking Gun, Katz gave a sheriff's investigator his opinion of the entertainer. Katz told detective Paul Zelis that Michael "is a guy that's like a ten-year-old child. And, you know, he's doing what a ten-year-old would do with his little buddies. You know, they're gonna jack off, watch movies, drink wine, you know. And, you know, he doesn't even really qualify as a paedophile. He's really just this regressed ten-year-old." Just as astonishingly, Zelis replied, "Yeah, yeah, I agree".

Quite possibly Zelis was simply overawed by Katz, who is something of a celebrity in the US, having made numerous TV appearances on high-profile shows such as *Larry King Live*, *Oprah*, *The Today Show* and *20/20*. He was also the consulting psychologist on the reality series *Starting Over*, for which he won an EMMY as co-host.[782]

Celebrity or not, if the statement attributed to Katz is an accurate transcription of what he actually said on tape, he appeared to be ignorant of the fact that most of his profession would certainly describe such behaviour as that of a paedophile. A common distinction in psychiatry is between "fixated" and "regressed" paedophiles. The former have an enduring primary preference for children as sexual partners; the latter show "normal" sexual interests but "regress" to sexual involvement with children in some circumstances. The evidence based on Michael's long social involvement with children and apparent lack of sexual engagement with adults, would suggest that if he was a paedophile he was a fixated rather than a regressed one. But, regressed or not, a lifestyle of "jacking off" with kids would undoubtedly merit a diagnosis of paedophilia – and more to the point it was illegal no matter what you called it.

Unfortunately for the prosecution, they had little alternative but to call Katz as a witness: he had been the psychologist who interviewed Gavin and Star at the request of the family's lawyers. He interviewed the brothers twice, once in May 2003 and again the following month. Katz told Zelis in the taped phone interview that it took a lot of time to get Gavin to trust him before the boy was ready to disclose any sexual abuse. Indeed, he never did tell Katz the full story he later gave to police. Katz noted that he was helped by the boy's mother, who "had to really spell out" that the psychologist was "helping us, working for us". Katz told Zelis that he assured the child he was doing the right thing by relating his experiences at Neverland. "We talked all about how courageous this was," Katz told Zelis, "and I said to him, 'You know, you don't want Jackson to do these things to kids again, do you?' "

Katz recalled that the boy responded, "Well, Jordie Chandler did not stop him." The fact that Gavin knew about the Chandler case was of vital significance. He had been only four years old when the Chandler case was settled. Except in the vanishingly unlikely event of Michael himself talking about the case to Gavin, it meant the boy had probably learned of it from his mother or his lawyers. This would later be seized upon by Mesereau as evidence that the family had spun a yarn about molestation just to get a big pay-off – and Mesereau's hand would be massively strengthened by the Arvizo family's choice of lawyer.

As we have seen, the family had engaged Larry Feldman, the lawyer who represented Chandler and filed a sexual battery lawsuit against Jackson in September 1993. Testifying before the Jackson grand jury in 2004, Feldman said he had a "sixth sense" that Gavin was not telling him what "really happened" with Jackson. The boy at this stage had not made any allegation of sexual abuse. So he had sent Gavin and his family to Katz, a child abuse specialist, for further interviews. Feldman also testified that he had retained Katz during the 1993 case.

In the Katz-Zelis phone interview, Katz gave a clear indication that the family were contemplating a civil action for damages, rather than just going to the police to start a prosecution. He said: "Mr Feldman actually referred these kids to me because they had come to him in this lawsuit." He said he thought the boys' stories about sexual abuse were true, but what about the motive for a lawsuit? Was the mother out for money? He said: "Whether mother's motive is to do it for money, I can't tell you. I mean, certainly they're...kind of a poor family." In Katz's view, though, Gavin was definitely not after money. Talking about the two brothers, he said:

"I don't think they see the financial motive here because when I sat down with Gavin I said, 'Look, if you go ahead with the civil lawsuit your family will get money if you win.' " When he told the boy that his identity could become public via such a legal proceeding, Katz said, "He sat there and started crying. So I don't feel like, you know, from Gavin's point of view at all, this is something he wants to do. I think he feels really caught."

By going to lawyers before police, it looked as though Gavin's mother, if not the boy himself, was giving priority to running a civil case. Unlike the Chandlers in 1993-4, though, they could not have kept the alleged child victim out of the witness box if the police had later brought a criminal prosecution. As mentioned in the last chapter, this is because the law had changed. By this time, if the Arvizos had won a civil case, any agreed financial settlement could be made forfeit if the victim refused to take the stand in a criminal case. It is unlikely the family would have known this before consulting a specialist lawyer, so from their point of view it would have made sense to get someone like Feldman involved at an early stage.

Ahead of the trial, then, the prosecution would have known through the Zelis interview that Stan Katz would have to be handled with kid gloves on the witness stand. Not only did he have strange views on paedophilia, he also knew too much. He knew Gavin was a reluctant witness, trapped into an embarrassingly public legal confrontation with the man his family could barely drag him away from only a couple of months before – a man whom he would probably still have regarded as his friend but for a whole bunch of adults working on his head (his mother, her lawyer, the psychologist and later the police). Katz also knew that Gavin's mother, Janet Arvizo, was interested in suing Jackson, and that her interest in the case looked suspiciously financial.

All this was dangerous to prosecutor Sneddon and his team. This is why their questions to Katz in the witness box shocked the media by their extreme caution and brevity. Reporters had been expecting a key witness: they thought Katz had been the first person on the planet to hear the boys' sensational allegations. One news report spoke of a "stunning twist", in which the psychologist failed even to reveal to the court what Gavin told him of the alleged abuse.

"It was an astoundingly short examination, conducted with great fear," said legal expert Ann Bremner. Prosecutor Ron Zonen "was worried about cross-examination," she said, explaining that rules limit the scope of cross-examination of a witness to the extent of their earlier testimony before the jury. Nevertheless, Katz revealed under cross-examination that he had discussed the possibility of the Arvizos suing Jackson during his interviews with them. Yet more points were being scored for the defence before they had even started to present their own case.

As for the alleged abuse, what might Katz have revealed if he had not been closed down so tightly by his own side? We know from his leaked grand jury testimony he might have confirmed some of what the boys said in the witness box, though the details varied considerably. He might also have added to the allegations. Before the grand jury, he said that "James" (the name assigned to Star before his real name was disclosed) indicated that one time when Michael was in bed with "John" (Gavin), he saw Michael "rubbing his penis against John's buttocks". "John" had also alleged an offence against "James" with which he was never charged. "John" said: "Michael had touched James on his butt. And that one time while they were in the golf cart he put his hand on his penis, and James moved away and it was never discussed again".

Note, however, that Gavin never disclosed a sexual offence against *himself*. Katz later told the police Gavin had been "very emotional and scared," during their interview session of 3 June, noting that he deliberately did not press the boy too hard. Gavin would always maintain that the first time he spoke to anyone about what allegedly happened to him was in a police interview some weeks later in July 2003. It was yet another reason for the prosecution to find the psychologist's testimony a problem.

It also emerged under cross-examination that Stan Katz had been another member of the psychological cabal driving the McMartin case, along with Roland Summit, the child abuse guru relied on by Anthony Urquiza. Katz had been the director of training and professional education at Children's Institute International, which had conducted the interviews with the McMartin children. This was important for the defence, not least because the Jackson case was being tried by a Californian jury, and the McMartin trial had received massive exposure in the state. Many jurors would surely have remembered the scandalous travesty of justice involved.

"Are you aware that was the longest and largest criminal case in the history of Los Angeles County?" Mesereau asked, for the defence. The witness confirmed he was aware. Not only that: it also came out that Katz had written a book after the case in which he conceded that therapists and parents are often capable of making children believe they had been molested when no abuse occurred. So the McMartin sinner had repented!

This in itself was of only limited help to the defence because Katz maintained that an older child such as Gavin could not be talked into false memories in the same way as the very young pre-schoolers of McMartin. Overall, though, neither Urquiza nor Katz had been able to deliver convincingly what the prosecution needed from its experts on the psychology and behaviour of child sex victims. Urquiza's "accommodation syndrome" failed to accommodate contradictions in the boys' stories; Katz, already castrated by his own side, had been put down by Mesereau. The taint of McMartin had undermined the clinician but even more important had been probing by the defence on Larry Feldman's involvement in the case – and hence the smell of a financial motive on the Arvizo family's behalf.

So far, neither the boys themselves, nor the psychologists, had made an impregnable case for the prosecution. And now, if we discount police and forensic figures (who would not play a major role) there were only a few significant witnesses left on the sex 'n' booze side of the Arvizo case. Would they fare any better?

One was Jackson's former housekeeper, Kiki Fournier. She said children stayed at Neverland from just a few days to months at a time; sometimes they would stay in Jackson's room. She described kids running wild without parental supervision and little discipline from her boss, being permitted to stay up late, eat candy, watch movies and play games. She denied criticising Michael for the lack of discipline but felt more staff were needed – and parents were sometimes at fault for failing to keep their own children under control. She said she had been worried about kids falling in the lake.

"They would get in candy-throwing fights in the theatre," she said. "Sometimes they would get pretty rowdy... He did let them have a free hand, so to say. They could get pretty rambunctious." It was on account of the wildness at Neverland, she said, that she called the place "Pinocchio's Pleasure Island".

Was this also a reflection on the truthfulness of her employer? No one asked. At all events, stern-minded students of *Pinocchio*, Carlo Collodi's classic morality tale for children, should find the housekeeper's analogy rather apt: in the original version, the character Pinocchio is hanged for his innumerable faults. Taken merely at face value, Fournier's comparison is no less interesting. In the Disney version, boys are tempted to Pleasure Island by the prospect of endless games and fun, freed from tiresome obedience to their parents. No Disney film would ever show kids involved in sex, but the forbidden pleasures of the flesh are symbolically represented by smoking. Being a morality story, there is a price to pay: the boys are turned into donkeys for their follies. Their Neverland counterparts were turned by today's moralists into "victims".[783]

Gavin and Star were among the children who became wilder the longer they stayed at Neverland, Fournier said. She noticed the room they shared was getting increasingly untidy and dirty. Towards the end of the boys' stay it had become so messy she had to tell her boss. This was highly significant in terms of the time-line of the alleged molestations. Gavin said these sexual incidents had occurred towards the end of his stay at Neverland, when he had been staying overnight in Michael's bed. But the housekeeper made it clear that the beds in the boys' guest bedroom appeared to have been slept in by both boys during this period.

Asked by prosecutor Gordon Auchincloss if she had ever seen children who appeared to be intoxicated, she said she had seen three or four such incidents. She said she once served dinner to Jackson and about four children, three of whom appeared to be drunk. Another time she saw him at an outbuilding with local children, including some who appeared under the influence. But she never saw him give alcohol to a minor. She described him as an indulgent host and suggested that children took advantage of him.

Fournier admitted Jackson liked to spend time with boys aged ten to thirteen, including Gavin. She named a string of boys, including the child actor Macaulay Culkin, who became close friends of Jackson and spent lots of time at the ranch during her intermittent tenure from 1991 until she left in September 2003. Those she named as Michael's special young friends were: Brett Barnes; Omer Bhatti; Frank Cascio; Aldo Cascio; Dominick Cascio; Jimmy Safechuck; Jordie Chandler; "Elijah", said to be a relative, who would have been eight years old in about 1995; Gavin Arvizo; Macaulay Culkin; and "four or five" local boys from Los Olivos. Those who had stayed at Neverland without their parents were: Brett; Elijah; Omer Bhatti; Frank and Aldo Cascio; Los Olivos boys; and possibly Wade Robson.[784]

Elijah and Levon Jackson, it turned out, were Michael's cousins. Real ones, that is, as opposed to a number of boys whose "cousin" or "nephew" status was purely honorific or a matter of convenience. Both would be briefly named in Brett Barnes' testimony as children who had shared Michael's bedroom. They were featured in *Michael Jackson's Private Home Movies*, a two-hour Fox TV programme aired in April 2003 with footage of Michael's home videos and a commentary by him. A number of kids are shown cavorting at Neverland, including Michael's nephews Taj and Auggie[785] and Macaulay Culkin plus his older brother Shane. The show ends with clips of Prince and Paris. This was one of two specials put out in response to what Michael felt was the distorted picture given by the Bashir documentary. When "Lee and Eli" were older, they would become well-known to Michael's fans, serving as a liaison between them and the star.

Fournier's lists were an embarrassment to the defence, but they proved absolutely nothing. In general, the jury could easily have mistaken Kiki Fournier for a defence witness. She criticised parents, rather than Michael, for the bad behaviour of the children, gave important evidence suggesting her boss had not been sleeping with Gavin at the time of the alleged offences and declined to say he had ever given the kids booze. As if all that was not enough to make Sneddon weep, she even appeared to laugh off the idea that Gavin and his family were kept prisoners at Neverland. She had thus been a brilliant witness, but not for the prosecution.[786]

The parents' failure to supervise their kids, noted by Fournier, has been commented upon by Paul Barresi. Remember him? He was introduced in Chapter Five as a "Hollywood investigator and publicist" and mentioned again in the following chapter as a "tabloid story broker". Now we meet this colourful character once again in the guise of ex-legman for Michael's jailed fixer Anthony Pellicano. He was not a witness at the trial but Porter has him saying this about Michael's tactics at Neverland:

> First, he wins the parents over. They become just as mesmerized as the kids. Then he puts the parents in separate buildings. He naps all day intermittently with the kids in the tepee or different places so the kids are well rested. Then he frolics and plays with the kids all through the night while the parents are sleeping.[787]

Flight attendant Cynthia Ann Bell said she had served wine to Jackson in a soft drinks can during a private jet trip, but denied she ever saw him serve alcohol to Gavin or other children. She also did the prosecution no favours by saying she had never witnessed any improper behaviour by Jackson towards his future accuser. Gavin had testified that Michael had offered him wine in a can, dubbed "Jesus Juice", on a February 2003 flight from Florida to California.

Bell was clearly no friend of the boy, saying he was rude and obnoxious as a passenger. According to her, Gavin threw mashed potatoes at Jackson's sleeping doctor, tossed his backpack at her and complained endlessly about his food. His mother did not try to control him.

On the other hand, Bell found Jackson's two toddlers, Prince and Paris, "lovely" and well-disciplined. She said Jackson did prefer to have wine served to him in a Diet Coke can, but that many of her adult passengers routinely hid their drinking from their children. Bell also insisted that Jackson was never drunk on the flight, as had been suggested. She did recall that she served liquor to Gavin's sister, Davellin, who used a fake ID (she was sixteen). Bell said that at one point Gavin, who was belligerent from the moment he stepped on the plane, sat with his sister and her teenage friend, who was also drinking. The intent, it appeared, was to suggest that if the boy had any liquor, he got it from them and not from Jackson.

"This was a disaster for the prosecution," said legal analyst Jim Moret. "She ended up being a great witness for the defence."

There was one further witness who might have come to the rescue, boozewise. Jesus Salas, long-serving Neverland manager, testified that on two occasions he was asked to serve Jackson wine in his bedroom, once when Gavin and two other boys were present. Salas said he brought four drinking glasses and a bottle of wine to the room. But, in yet another catastrophe for the prosecution, he said the wine was not for the boys.

"Let me tell you something else," Salas said. "He ordered some sodas for them." So the boys had soft drinks! The prosecutor noted that when Salas testified before the grand jury he never mentioned soft drinks. Salas said he had just remembered it. He said the wine-cellar was always off-limits to kids and he also testified that the Arvizos were not forcibly kept at Neverland. Salas was scoring yet more own goals against the prosecution case.

By now, Tom Sneddon and his team had played all their cards as regards the sex 'n' booze allegations involving Gavin Arvizo, the only purported victim of child sex abuse in the trial; the Salas testimony marked the end of their case in this regard before they would move on to the alleged kidnap conspiracy. Witness after witness had been a disaster. Despite some important inconsistencies, Gavin's story might have had some lasting credibility with the jury, but much would depend on the testimony to be given later by his mother in the conspiracy part of the trial. If it looked as though Janet Arvizo was just a scheming liar out for money, as Mesereau had already suggested, it would be much harder to believe Gavin's own account.

Meanwhile, though, the prosecution had a humdinger of a trick up its sleeve in the shape of Section 1108 of the California Evidence Code, this being the section that would allow the introduction of a whole new class of accusers in relation to alleged "prior bad acts". This would breathe new life – and a lively controversy – into the prosecution case, and will be a major focus of the next chapter.

Before turning to this fresh phase of the case, we should note an important background element. By this time there were mounting stories of Jackson's financial difficulties surfacing in the media. Such stories had been a staple part of the celebrity gossip scene for years – but now they suddenly took on added urgency and even legal significance with the news that the star's cash flow had dried up so much that he had been forced to default on paying his Neverland bills, including his staff wages. The situation was rescued fairly quickly because Michael was still just about able to raise finance: lenders knew he had assets that could be realised if the worst came to the worst. There were persistent suggestions, for instance, that he might be forced to part with his share of the Beatles back catalogue of songs, said to be worth as much as $500 million. Even with the immediate cash crisis resolved, though, these intensified money worries could not have come at a worse time: Sneddon, it will be recalled, was claiming Jackson's motive in "kidnapping" the Arvizo family was partly financial.

On a lighter note, a writer with a British newspaper recounted an anecdote that would surely have given Michael heart. Euan Ferguson reported in the *Observer* overhearing two "smart girls in their twenties", discussing the star and his fate, saying one of them had tentatively asked the other a question:

> "Would you have let yourself be, you know, sort of fiddled with, just for a

minute or two, if you were fifteen, and it was safe and the rest, if the alternative was that Thriller had never existed?"

There was something of a pause and a sharpish intake of breath, quite possibly my own. And the answer which came back, after much heart-searching, was that yes, she probably would.[788]

CHAPTER SIXTEEN

The Trial, Part Three: 'Prior Bad Acts' and Conspiracy

Section 1108 of the California Evidence Code is not a fun read, especially for anyone facing sex charges in the state. It validates the use of evidence "of the defendant's commission of another sexual offence or offences". No mention is made of "prior bad acts" but the implication is that evidence can be dragged up from the past to bolster a current case.

It gets worse. The media made a big thing of 1108, but Section 1101 of the same code was arguably just as important and went virtually unmentioned in news reports. Whereas 1108 was confined to admitting evidence of actual crimes the defendant had allegedly committed in the past, 1101 went much further. This section admitted a whole range of prior evidence, if it was deemed relevant to showing the defendant's motive, opportunity or intent to commit the charged crime, or that he had in the past made preparations or plans to carry out a similar crime. Judge Melville said that under 1101 an "alleged pattern of grooming activities" would be examined – in other words all sorts of behaviour not necessarily illegal in itself. Prosecutors intended to bring testimony, for instance, that Jackson licked a child's head. Legal commentator Jonna Spilbor responded: "But so what? That act is about as illegal as sharing an ice cream cone."[789]

Section 1108 allows the presentation of evidence of previous acts of sexual abuse even if they were not reported at the time or prosecuted. The provision gives prosecutors the opportunity to demonstrate a propensity to commit sex crimes on the theory that most sex offenders, including "paedophiles", commit repeated acts in similar ways.

Introduced in 1995, the section is controversial. If a defendant had not previously been convicted of the alleged offence in question, how could he confidently be said to have committed it? The problem is reflected in the language used to describe these "offences". The prosecutor cannot talk about the defendant's "previous convictions" if there are none. Tom Sneddon cunningly and unobtrusively covered all bases by talking about "prior acts", as though *anything* an alleged sex offender might do was somehow reprehensible. Journalists and even legal commentators attempted to be a little more descriptive, speaking of "prior bad acts", but in doing so were reduced to the language of the kindergarten, with its regrettable lack of legal precision. As for "prior offences", that would wrongly give the impression of referring to convictions.

Controversial or not, however, Section 1108 was clearly part of the law of California and the judge in Michael Jackson's case ruled that prosecutors could take advantage of it. They would be allowed to present evidence to the jury that the performer previously molested five young boys: Jason Francia, Wade Robson, Macaulay Culkin, Jordan Chandler and Brett Barnes. These were immediately and inevitably dubbed "the Jackson Five" but only one prior "victim" – Jason Francia – testified against Michael. Macaulay Culkin, Wade Robson and Brett Barnes instead turned up as defence witnesses, insisting they had not been victims at all. Of the five, only Jordan Chandler played no part in the proceedings, though his mother would. The judge ruled that 1108 evidence would be limited to cases in which someone had claimed to have observed actual sexual conduct; witnessing sexual "grooming" activities would not be enough. On this basis, evidence relating to Michael's relationships with Jimmy Safechuck and Jonathan Spence was excluded.

Judge Rodney Melville's bombshell decision, which came after hours of intense and sometimes heated argument between the attorneys in the absence of the jury, was in legal terms a defining point in the proceedings. Precipitating a trial within a trial, it opened an enormous can of worms.

This is not a legal textbook but Section 1108 and the judge's ruling on it deserve some attention. Why? Because they provide a good illustration of how the odds are increasingly being stacked against alleged sex offenders these days, especially those perceived as "paedophiles". To start with, we may note that Section 1108 applies *only* to sex offenders. How come? Don't car thieves, or burglars, or drug dealers often have a discernible pattern of behaviour and criminal modus operandi? A similar measure was later introduced in California in connection with spousal abuse, but there can be no doubt that paedophilia is more often singled out for special treatment. Similarly selective measures targeting paedophiles are becoming ever more pervasive in jurisdictions far beyond California and the US.

Criminal appellate attorney Dallas Sacher has argued against the use of Section 1108, saying, "It completely distracts the jury from consideration of evidence about the charged offence". He told the *Los Angeles Times*, "It allows the government to substitute any weaknesses it has in its case by saying, 'Look – this dude has done it before.' Then you're convicting someone on who he is – not on what he did."[790] In other words, it allowed the possibility of a jury convicting Michael without ever believing he had molested Gavin – the only alleged victim in the case. What was worse, it allowed them to use evidence from cases too weak to bring to trial on their own but which, if a whole bunch of dodgy witnesses were paraded, might effectively smear the defendant's good name.

And if that were not prejudicial enough, the 1108 procedure allowed prosecutors to sneakily evade the high standard of proof usually needed to secure a criminal conviction – a justifiably high standard if the consequence is to blacken a defendant's name and wreck his life, possibly by way of a long prison term. The normal standard in criminal trials in common law jurisdictions throughout the world (broadly speaking the English-speaking nations) is the familiar one that guilt should be established "beyond a reasonable doubt". In the case of alleged "prior bad acts" under 1108 this is watered down: the jury is required to determine merely by *a preponderance of the evidence* whether those acts occurred.

Jurors were admittedly to be warned that they could not convict on the basis of the "prior bad acts" alone; they would be told they still had to prove the charged crime beyond a reasonable doubt. As Jonna Spilbor wrote:

> But that is cold comfort. If jurors believe it is indeed likely that Jackson molested earlier boys, their standards for finding him guilty "beyond a reasonable doubt" may, in effect, drop precipitously – whatever the jury instructions may say.[791]

Jackson was fortunate in getting a jury intelligent and scrupulous enough to pay attention to their instructions; other defendants may be less lucky. Spilbor also noted that Judge Melville was by no means obliged to admit 1108 evidence. She pointed out that Section 352 of the evidence code states that "the court in its discretion may exclude evidence if its probative value is substantially outweighed by the probability that its admission will (a) necessitate undue consumption of time or (b) create substantial danger of undue prejudice, of confusing the issues, or of misleading the jury." In her view this provision, especially on the issue of prejudice, "might as well have been written for the Jackson case".

In arguing for admission of prior evidence, Tom Sneddon said Jackson had long shown a proclivity for illicit behaviour with young boys the entertainer considered "special friends." He noted that Jackson's grooming of young boys often included the purchase of gifts for a child's mother, so as to keep the parent preoccupied, enabling him to spend quality time alone with the minor.

The fact that Sneddon had 1108 as a tool at his disposal was no accident. In 1994 he had been frustrated in his pursuit of Jackson by the settlement reached in the Chandler affair. The 1108 law was passed in the following year. James Rogan, an ex-prosecutor and former judge who sponsored the new law, told the *Los Angeles Times*, "The Jackson thing may have been on the back burner of my mind".[792]

As a result of Melville's decision to admit 1108 and 1101 evidence, jurors would also now weigh the 2003 molestation allegations in the light of two multimillion dollar settlement deals. While not admissions of guilt, details of these decade-old agreements – the Chandler deal and a $2 million settlement with Jason Francia – were a substantial embarrassment.

Tom Mesereau had argued that many of the third-party witnesses Sneddon would call to testify about the prior abuse were tabloid informants, disgruntled former employees, and money-hungry litigants. Tabloid deals were indisputably a salient feature, their significance explored in depth in the *Los Angeles Times*.[793] As regards employees, he specifically mentioned a group of former Neverland workers (the "Neverland Five") who had sued Jackson for wrongful dismissal and had lost in court (in fact, they lost a countersuit brought by Jackson and were hit with a seven-figure legal judgment, which drove some into bankruptcy). Diane Dimond has argued that these employees had been hampered in their initial court action by some key rulings. She said Judge Zel Canter ruled that the jury would hear nothing about prior allegations of child molesting by Jackson, including the Chandler case. Therefore, she said, the plaintiffs were not allowed to offer evidence that went to their main point: to show that they were drawn into the civil and criminal investigations of Michael Jackson as a result of what they knew, and that as a result of that knowledge they were harassed by the bodyguards of Jackson's Office of Special Services.[794]

If testimony by the Neverland Five could be trashed unfairly as the ill-motivated behaviour of beaten litigants, at least their stories managed to get an airing in Judge Melville's court. Potentially damning testimony from the earlier Hayvenhurst Five case failed to make it even that far. Abruptly sacked in February 1993, allegedly because they knew too much about Michael's behaviour with young boys, the five security guards were told they could only get their final pay and severance money by signing a second confidentiality agreement. Part of that new agreement's abstruse legal language was a clause barring them from suing any of the Jackson family. Accordingly, their case was thrown out by Judge Zel Canter (yes, the same one) before it started – a case which could have heard, as we saw in Chapter Three, testimony that one of the five, security guard Leroy Thomas, was ordered to destroy a Polaroid photo of a naked boy.[795] And as we also heard previously, another guard, Charli Michaels, who was not one of the five, had prepared a statement for the case. She could have disclosed details of the "sex dance" in which she reportedly saw Michael playing with little Wade Robson's genitals. Jackson must have felt he had something to hide. The single most important fact to emerge from the Hayvenhurst Five case was that he invoked the Fifth Amendment.[796]

But enough of Judge Canter's cases; we have plenty on our hands with Judge Melville's. In an unsuccessful bid to delay the 1108 ruling, Mesereau mentioned Gavin's mother, reminding the court that she had not yet given evidence. Once she had done so, he said, the prosecution case would be shown up as hopeless, and hence the purely prejudicial effect of introducing 1108 evidence would be apparent. He never said a truer word. But by that time the deed had been done.

The first, and in terms of credibility, the most damaging witness in the 1108 mini-trial would be Jason Francia, adult son of Michael Jackson's former maid Blanca Francia. The only witness in the entire trial who would give direct testimony as a "victim", apart from Gavin Arvizo, the 24-year-old Jason would say that as a child he had been sexually fondled three times by Michael. It was the first evidence presented to jurors of what prosecutors called a long pattern of predatory behaviour.

Jason said the first incident began when he was about seven years old, when he was sitting on Michael's lap watching cartoons on TV. The pop singer started tickling him, and the two playfully fell to the floor, where Jackson moved his hand to the boy's privates and fondled him for several minutes. "I'm tickling and he's tickling, and it eventually moved down to my little private region ... my crotch area," said Jason. "You're seven. I didn't think it was wrong."

The location was not Neverland but Jackson's apartment in Century City, Los Angeles, which he said his mother called "the hideout". Afterwards, Jackson gave him a $100 bill and he received the same amount the second time as well, when he was around eight years old. He said, "It was kind of don't-tell-your-mum money." On this second occasion, he remembered the two of them lying on top of a sleeping bag, with Michael "spooning" him from behind. Asked how long Michael's hand had been in his genital area this time, Jason said: "[It was] two cartoons worth, a cartoon and a half." The third incident occurred at Neverland two years later when he was about ten. Each time, said Jason, he had accompanied his mother to work and had been left alone with her boss. Asked by prosecution attorney Ron Zonen if Jackson had ever done anything to make him feel uncomfortable, Jason said: "I may not have felt uncomfortable at seven years old but when I think of it now I think that's wrong, that shouldn't have been done."

The adult Jason Francia had become a car parts salesman and was married. A *Los Angeles Times* report said of him: "Thin, handsome and dark-complexioned, the man shares several physical characteristics with Jackson's current accuser", a resemblance noted by other commentators. He was said to have appeared confident during early stages of the testimony and he smiled as he identified Jackson in the courtroom, saying, "Yes, he's right there. He's the light-complected gentleman".[797]

While describing the third incident he appeared to become emotional. He said he had been playing a video game – he thought it was Sega Genesis – in the loft of the amusement arcade when Michael started tickling him again. "Somehow" the two of them ended up on a couch. "This took a lot of counselling to get over, just so you know," he said, his voice quivering. He asked the judge for a break, took a drink of water and wiped his face with a tissue. After a moment, he said he was ready to carry on.

After playfully tickling him, he said, Jackson then slipped his hand inside his shorts and fondled his testicles for two or three minutes. It was the only time Jackson fondled him under his clothing.[798]

"Michael was pretty much behind me, like spooning me, again with the tickling. This time it was longer, but I wasn't laughing as much," the young man said. The prosecutor asked if Jackson touched his penis or his testicles. He said the latter. Asked what he was thinking at the time, he said "I should probably go".

It is important to note that a post-trial book endorsed by Tom Mesereau, and carrying a five-page foreword written by him, gave a false impression of Jason's account. In her book *Michael Jackson Conspiracy*, Aphrodite Jones wrote about "the curious testimony" jurors had heard from the young man, "who testified that he's been tickled by Jackson, that he's been tickled three times by Jackson, on the *outside* of his clothing. It was because of these tickling incidents, Jason Francia told the jury, that he decided to go into therapy".[799] Jones says nothing about Jason's testimony that Michael touched his testicles *under* his shorts in an incident lasting at least a couple of minutes. Some jurors would very reasonably make light of the "tickling", but what Jason was describing in this third incident would be hard to interpret honestly as merely playful or accidental.

Asked who the first person he told about it was, Jason said "probably God". The young man's piety would not have gone amiss, but the prosecutor had to find another way of putting the question. Zonen asked, "Who was the second person?" Second after God, claimed Jason, had been the rather more omniscient police who turned up to interview him: they did not need telling. (It would soon emerge in court that the police felt sure he had been molested, even though he initially denied it). He said he knew the interview would be about Michael Jackson because "it was on TV all the time" – a reference to the Chandler affair, then at the height of the public scandal.

At first, he had denied to the police that Jackson had done anything wrong. He had lied to detectives because it was a difficult subject to discuss. After meeting them, he spoke to two lawyers who helped the family obtain a monetary settlement from Jackson. Judge Melville had earlier ruled that prosecutors could not ask the amount of the settlement, but it was reportedly more than $2 million.

The witness said he spent five years in counselling, starting at about age thirteen, when he first told detectives about the molestation. Prosecutors were also interested in the Chandler allegations at this time. No criminal charges were filed in either case. As we know from earlier chapters, Tom Sneddon found himself stymied when Jordan Chandler stopped cooperating with police after the boy and his father had won a civil settlement. Why no action was taken in the Francia case is another matter – Tom Mesereau would soon have words on that subject.

In his cross-examination, Mesereau started by focusing most of his questions on Jason's initial denials to detectives that he had been sexually abused. In the 1993 interview with them he had said: "I'll just say this flat out: I don't remember anything except the tickling." Asked about that statement, he replied: "I didn't want to be embarrassed at school. I didn't want to be embarrassed anywhere. I was thirteen." The defence attorney suggested that the detectives had pressured him into talking about the allegations. Jason responded by saying the police had asked if Jackson had done something, and he had replied "No, I'm not gay".

The exchanges between defender and witness became increasingly confrontational. By the end of Jason Francia's first day on the stand, legal analyst and former prosecutor Jim Hammer said Francia appeared sincere and he rated him the most powerful witness in the trial to this point. It was a view all but universally shared among commentators – but there had not been much competition. Hammer also made the interesting point that Jason attended counselling for at least four years after he won a financial settlement from Jackson, saying, "If this is all about money, why did he keep going to counselling?"

The answer may actually have less to do with Michael Jackson than with California's counselling culture and the social status Jason in particular derived from it. One well-known book on sexual abuse details the case of a woman who confessed to lying about being an incest victim just so she could join an incest survivor group.[800] This was a story that highlighted the social value to some people of group therapy and counselling – people who had not necessarily been abused but who needed the *status* conferred by victimhood. For those who lack self-esteem for whatever reason, it can be immensely supportive to have their story listened to and validated as important; they can also expect to bask in the warmth of being told how *courageous* they are to tell their tale – though cowardly would be a more accurate word to describe such pathetic characters when, in their weakness, they wreck the lives of others by false accusations.

The news reports of Jason Francia's testimony concentrated on his allegations and the defence response to them. Understandably, Mesereau was not about to criticise Californian culture. He was, after all, addressing a Californian jury. So, although an important aspect of Jason's life emerged in early testimony, nothing was made of it by the defence and it never became a news story. After telling the court about his job selling auto parts, Jason had added: "And I run a mentoring programme for kind of like the probation department. Probation department refers kids to me, to my organisation, and we mentor them through them not being truants and not committing crimes again."

He described this mentoring programme as church-attached but with its own identity: Foursquare Programs. Jason's role was to run the programme and assign mentors to youngsters. He said his wife also helped with the programme. All this had begun when, at age eighteen – the same time as his years in counselling came to an end – he started an internship with Santa Maria Foursquare Church. His said his work as a youth pastor, was to "talk about ethics, God, morals and doing good."

All of this was manna from heaven to the prosecution. They were able to present Jason Francia as a young pillar of society. Unlike the problematic Gavin Arvizo, with his school discipline problems, Jason had every appearance of being a clean-living, God-fearing person, responsible and socially concerned. It made him look a reliable witness.

In general terms, we have no reason to believe this is a false image. He was probably a sincere and valued youth pastor, running a good mentoring programme – and perhaps still is. But his interest in this kind of work puts a big question mark over his motivation for spending five years in counselling following incidents which even by his own account seem quite minor – embarrassing, perhaps, and maybe distasteful. But traumatic? Sufficiently wounding to need five whole years of therapy? Significantly, no clinical evidence of psychological trauma was presented. The suspicion has to be that Jason spent so long in therapy because he *enjoyed* it – enjoyed it so much, in fact, that he continued the counselling process into adult life by becoming a species of counsellor himself.

If the defence did not pick up on these possibilities, it seems at least some jury members did – in sensational style. A report on Los Angeles radio station KFI was picked up by the widely followed Drudge Report news blog. Two jurors, KFI claimed, had been overheard during a break in the trial mocking Jason Francia. One of them was overheard by reporters saying, "Oh boo-hoo, Michael Jackson tickled me." Other jurors laughed. Evidently these jurors felt Jason's "trauma" was too trivial to be taken seriously. One of the reporters in question, Robert Cole of Sky News, later substantially verified the story, though he denied he had actually heard Michael's name mentioned.[801]

It was not the only time Jason would provoke unintended laughter. In cross-examination, Mesereau asked if he had told anyone he had been molested before the day the detectives came along to interview him in 1993. By this time he was thirteen and the last incident of alleged molestation was already three years into the past. Jason replied in the negative and the defender said: "They just kind of came one day and surprised you?" The young witness simply answered "Yes", provoking laughter in court – followed by a rebuke from the judge, who threatened to eject any further offenders.

The laughter showed a rich understanding of Mesereau's irony and the absurdity of the response: Why would detectives come to talk to Jason about Michael Jackson molesting him if he, Jason, had never said anything to anyone? Everyone in the courtroom was aware that at this time Jason's mother Blanca Francia had already been on TV, talking to the media about her anxieties over Jackson's contacts with young boys, including her own son. Mesereau's lead-up questions had been on this very point. It seemed inconceivable that she would have spoken to the whole world on the subject without her son having said anything to her about Jackson's behaviour.

Mesereau was driving at the money angle, as ever. He had already put to Jason that his mother had made $20,000 from the TV show *Hard Copy*. Jason claimed he knew nothing about the money. When the defender followed up with questions about Jason and his mother seeing lawyers, with the implication that his main interest was in making money from suing Michael, the young man became markedly hesitant and evasive in his answers. He claimed to know nothing about any lawyers.

But he was far from hesitant when Mesereau asked a question apparently referring to the $2 million settlement. Asked if he had ever got money from Jackson, Jason shot back: "Other than the money he put down my pants?" Even at age seventeen he had not known about his mother hiring lawyers who were threatening to sue Michael, he said. "Call me a stupid kid. I didn't know." He further claimed not to recall if he ever signed the settlement deal with Michael – an agreement which had been reached on condition of Jackson denying he had done anything wrong. He learned at age seventeen about getting money from the settlement but said he and his mother never talked much either about that or the issues giving rise to the deal.

One thing he did not talk about at all in court until Mesereau raised the matter was a socially acceptable reason for having Michael's money to tuck into his pants when he was a kid. Under questioning, Jason admitted that Michael would give him money – he remembered $20 a time – whenever he completed reading a book or getting an A for his schoolwork.

Jason stuck to his story that he did not initially tell even his mother of the alleged abuse. He had let God in on the secret, but no one else: "I never told her the specifics that I was molested. But I believe that I told her in counselling," he said, "…that was a crying time." Even his wife had not known, he claimed, right up until the start of his testimony, just the day before this cross-examination. He said he told no one until 1993, when detectives investigating the Chandler allegations came to him.

Even then, as he had already freely admitted, he denied to the police that he had been assaulted. Mesereau's line of attack was to suggest this denial had been truthful; Jason had only changed his story because the police had already made up their minds as to Michael's guilt and then bullied him into confirming their view. He confronted the witness with a statement he made during one of his interviews in which he said: "They made me come up with a lot more stuff. They kept pushing. I wanted to hit them in the head." Mesereau followed up:

> Q: Remember telling the police, "You guys are pushy?"
>
> A: Yeah, I remember telling the police that.
>
> Q: OK, and after they kept pushing you, you finally said "You know, I think he did tickle me", right?
>
> A: No.
>
> Q: Do you remember that? Do you remember at first saying you didn't know, and then after –
>
> A: Yeah, I remember saying at first, "I don't know".
>
> Q: And after telling the police "You guys are pushy", you eventually finally said, "Yes, he tickled me" right?
>
> A: I believe that's how it went.

Talk amongst the journalists "in the peanut gallery" was generally supportive of Francia's claims, according to local paper the *Santa Barbara Independent*, but some raised questions as to why Gavin Arvizo was able to recount his abuse in such a laid-back way as a teenager, while Jason Francia, a married man well into adulthood, "nearly broke to pieces on the stand".[802] Some reporters thought Jason's story was true but Gavin's might well be false. If the jury felt the same way and obeyed their instructions, they would be forced to acquit Jackson even while believing he was a child molester.

I go with the peanut gallery on this one: despite the money angle and the initial denials to the police, Jason was a largely credible witness. Admittedly, his mother, a poor Latino single parent on a maid's income, would be tempted by money from the media and a settlement with Jackson. That did not mean nothing illegal happened to Jason, only that a jury could not be sure it did. As for Jason's initial denials, what could be more natural for a teenager worried people might think he was gay? Nor was the counselling necessarily phoney, just because we cannot entirely take it at face value. While testicular tickling can hardly have been traumatic in the sense that a brutal, violent rape would be, it could conceivably have been troubling for a particularly religious young man, as Jason seemed to be. His tears, especially under the pressure of telling his story in public, may not have been entirely of the crocodile variety: for him, it would have been a matter of shame and humiliation.

The blame for such feelings lies firmly with the crazy negativity instilled in children towards sexuality by our society, and especially by conservative Christianity. While neither Michael nor any child-attracted adult can escape the moral responsibility for bringing about a potentially difficult situation for a child, society also ought to address a much larger responsibility for the beam in its own eye.

Jason's mother, Blanca Francia, also testified. Her name is a familiar one from earlier chapters, especially as a result of her appearance on the TV show *Hard Copy*, when she talked about Jackson's intimacy with young boys, including her own son. In court she told substantially the same story. She spoke specifically of seeing Jackson with the young Wade Robson, when he would have been seven or eight years old. She recalled going in to do some cleaning when she heard laughing and playing. "I came in and at first I thought they were playing in the bathtub or Jacuzzi and I didn't see them ... and I walked in and they were in the shower."

She said she could see two figures – Jackson's and the smaller figure of the boy – in the steamed up shower and saw two pairs of underwear on the floor. "Mr Jackson's, I knew, was white, and the boy's, I knew, was green like a neon colour, right by the shower." She said she was embarrassed and left without saying anything.

She also remembered Macaulay Culkin staying in Michael's bedroom when the *Home Alone* star had been about ten years old.

She said she had become concerned about her own son's relationship with Jackson after finding her child sitting in Jackson's lap and later seeing them lying together in a sleeping bag on the floor. Significantly, she said she had chastised her son on both occasions, ostensibly for being a nuisance to her boss. When Jason had been on Michael's lap, Michael had said there was no problem, he was reading to the boy, or encouraging him to read. That time, she pulled Jason away. When they had been in the sleeping bag together, though, Jason had refused to budge, saying he wanted to stay where he was. Blanca had been obliged to leave them and carry on with her cleaning elsewhere.

The testimony of the two Francias, mother and son, was all too credible. The young man's demeanour in the witness box and the relatively mild nature of the allegations alike tended to suggest their accounts were not just a by-product of some lurid tabloid yarn spun for money. The same could not be said of what was to follow.

Former Neverland security guard Ralph Chacon, told the jury he saw alleged sex abuse when he peeked through a bathroom window at the ranch one evening, probably in 1993. Chacon said he was doing his evening rounds when he saw the star and Jordie Chandler in a Jacuzzi in a building near the estate's amusement arcade. The pair then headed together to a shower room. The guard said he peeked through a window to see what was going on. After hearing them in the shower, he then saw Jackson and the boy standing naked together in the lighted bathroom. The jury then heard this astonishingly graphic exchange:

> A: I saw that Mr Jackson was caressing the boy's hair, he was kissing him on his head, and his face, his lips. He started kissing him on the shoulders and started going down to his nipples. Started sucking his nipples. Started going down to his penis and putting it in his mouth. And about that time I just – I left.
>
> Q: Okay. You say you saw him go down and do what?
>
> A: He put the little boy's penis in his mouth.
>
> Q: Did you actually see that?
>
> A: Yes, sir, I did.

Hearing this was all too much for Michael's mother, Katherine Jackson, who fled the courtroom. The guard also recalled another incident in which he claimed he saw Jackson kissing Jordie under the gaze of Peter Pan and Tinkerbell, featured in an illuminated window display behind the main house. The kissing was "not long, but passionate" and "Mr Jackson's hands went down to his crotch area, the boy's" where they stayed for ten to twenty seconds before the two returned to the main house, he said.

Chacon, who first mentioned the alleged incidents under oath when being questioned in 1994, said he did not go to the police as he did not think he would be believed – and what with the fairy tale locale of the second incident, it did seem a bit like being asked to believe in fairies. But plenty of people apparently did believe him, judging by the excited reaction to his sensational story. It was as though the court had been turned into a pantomime audience of spellbound children. Do you believe in fairies? Yes, oh yes! One legal commentator quoted in a report for the AFP news agency was so knocked out she got her terms in a twist, effectively calling it incredibly credible:

> "It was incredible, the testimony was very credible, stunning," said former prosecutor Ann Bremner. "We had an eye-witness describing fondling, oral sex, it is a huge turning point," she said.[803]

But only the incredibly credulous would have discerned such a "turning point" after Tom Mesereau's ferocious counter-attack on Jackson's behalf. He said Chacon, who worked for Jackson from 1991 to 1994, had lost a wrongful dismissal lawsuit against the star. Chacon was ordered to pay nearly $1.5 million in legal costs and other damages to Jackson after the star countersued, alleging the ex-guard had stolen from him. A jury found that Chacon and his co-plaintiffs acted with "fraud, oppression and malice" against Jackson. The defence lawyer portrayed Chacon's role in the present case as one of taking a chance to "get even" with Jackson. As Roger Friedman memorably wrote:

> "The jury said you stole and acted with malice," said Mesereau. "There was a judgment against you for fraud. Do you recall stipulating that you acted with fraud, oppression and malice?"
>
> Suddenly Chacon, who claimed to have a clear memory of seeing Jackson in an incriminating situation, could not remember a thing.
>
> He couldn't recall the exact amount each defendant in the dismissal case was ordered to pay Jackson ($1.4 million), or a judgment against Chacon in another case ($2,600), or his telling a doctor that he'd rather get $1 million than work again.
>
> Even when Mesereau, in a flamboyant but familiar lawyerly move, showed

> him his contradictory depositions from a year ago, Chacon was flummoxed.
>
> Did he remember his lawyer saying he wanted $16 million for the five former employees?
>
> "No," said Chacon. Mesereau showed him his deposition. The ex-security guard, now a substitute teacher, had an epiphany. "Now I see it," he declared.
>
> Did Chacon recall saying in his deposition that Jackson used to stare continuously at him? That he stared at no one else? The witness, in a rare moment of clarity, explained: "I said it just to say it."[804]

Mesereau destroyed Chacon's credibility by concentrating on the motives of the witness, including the fact that he had sold his story to a tabloid newspaper. But what went largely unremarked amidst the fireworks was that Mesereau did not dwell on Chacon's account of the oral sex incident itself, probing for any inconsistencies and contradictions between his accounts at different times; nor did he try to show that observation through the window would have been impossible, or in any other way discredit the guard's evidence directly.

This missing element from the defence case was not what caught the eye in the courtroom. Mesmerising Mesereau had once again pulled off the classic magician's tactic of diverting attention from his sleight of hand: the focus had been shifted away from his client and onto the hapless Chacon – a man of huge girth, a cropped-haired, bull-necked figure who was incongruously reduced to tears before the end of his tormentor's relentless onslaught, his distress brought on not by any sexual trauma inflicted by Michael but solely by the brutal shafting Michael's lawyer had given him.

Behind the scenes, Tom Sneddon was probably quietly weeping, too. At this point, his 1108 mini-trial had some way to run, but so far it was going badly and was destined to get worse. After the mini-trial had ended and attention had turned to the conspiracy aspect of the Arvizo case, Sneddon was so desperate he tried to persuade the judge to let him introduce another 1108 witness who he claimed could corroborate Chacon's story. Kassim Abdool, a colleague of Chacon's on Jackson's security staff, was potentially able not only to back up Chacon's testimony: the prosecution revealed he also had a further lurid tale of his own. The defence objected that Sneddon had already had his chance to present 1108 witnesses and that the new story would be unduly prejudicial. Judge Melville went half way. He would allow the corroboration, but nothing else.

Abdool duly told the court he had gone into the room where Chacon claimed he saw the oral sex and found two sets of wet swim trunks, one belonging to the boy and one to Jackson. Later, Abdool said, he saw Jackson and the boy heading inside the main house and locking the doors. Jackson "was bareback and he had a towel around his waist," and the boy had a bathrobe thrown over him. His account was similar to the one given by Chacon.

This corroboration did not help much, simply because Mesereau was able to take him apart on exactly the same basis as he had destroyed Chacon. Abdool had also been one of those who had sued Jackson and lost. He conceded that in 1994 he signed a statement saying he never witnessed any improper behaviour by the singer. Abdool also admitted that he and the other plaintiffs, who were ultimately ordered to pay Jackson more than $1 million in damages, sold their story to a tabloid newspaper for $15,000 in order to fund the lawsuit. "Obviously," Mesereau said in an aside, "that turned out to be a poor investment."

Of more interest to us is the part of Abdool's story he was not allowed to tell. Sneddon had written as follows in documents released by the court:

> Jackson called Abdool and asked him to go to Jackson's car and get a jar of Vaseline from the centre console of the vehicle and bring it to his bedroom. When Jackson opened the door to his bedroom, Jackson was wearing only his pyjama bottoms, appeared sweaty, aroused and Abdool observed Jackson to have an erection under his pyjama bottoms. There was a young boy, who he believed was Jordie Chandler, in the bedroom with Mr Jackson.[805]

It is just as well this stunning story was not admitted. As we know from the boy's own deposition for the impending civil suit in 1993, Jordie himself had not alleged that Michael had attempted anal intercourse with him, which was the likely inference to be drawn from the Vaseline. Nor had Gavin Arvizo or Jason Francia or any other boy said any such thing. The story was almost certainly fictitious, and beyond any doubt whatever would have been "unduly prejudicial".

But Vaseline and attempted anal sex *had* featured in Jordie's "secret diary", according to Victor Gutierrez. In this account, Jordie had shared a room with Michael in the Grand Floridian Hotel, Orlando, Florida, where the boy, his mother and half-sister were based for a visit to Disneyworld in late June 1993. Gutierrez cites what purports to be Jordie writing in his own words about Michael:

> He said that he had never done this before. He told me that he would put his penis in my ass. I told him that I didn't think it was a very good idea, that it would hurt. He put Vaseline on my ass and tried to insert his fingers, but it hurt. He stopped, and then put his penis between my ass cheeks, without penetrating…He told me that he would try to put my penis in his ass as he applied Vaseline, but I refused. So he put the Vaseline on his ass cheeks and excitedly moved and rubbed against my penis. He then grabbed my penis with his hand and passed it against his ass, but I never penetrated him.[806]

It is also worth noting that Abdool's Vaseline story, if true, would have disclosed a reckless lack of discretion by Jackson: this would have been the behaviour of a man who did not give a damn what anyone saw. But when Sneddon opened the prosecution case he had sought to portray Jackson as having a "pathological" obsession over the security of his bedroom suite. Much had been made of the password entry to the suite and the alarm to protect against unauthorised entry to the second-floor bedroom. The implication was that the star had much to hide in his sex life, though any number of rich and famous people use such systems to protect their personal security. What is abundantly clear is that the prosecution could not reasonably have it both ways: Jackson could not be both wildly indiscreet *and* obsessively cautious.

It is entirely possible that Abdool had read Gutierrez' book and thought that making a very similar allegation would give him credibility. Does it do so? From the timeline point of view it does. After Florida, Jordie and his family are said by Gutierrez to have gone straight to Neverland, where they would stay with Michael for the last few days of June, so if this chronology is correct there could well have been the opportunity for another go with the Vaseline shortly before Jordie's father intervened to end the relationship in July. It may or may not be significant that in his closing arguments prosecutor Ron Zonen would draw attention to the fact that a jar of Vaseline had been found by police in Michael's bathroom at Neverland in the same drawer as a pornographic magazine.[807]

So, two of Jackson's former security guards, Ralph Chacon and Kassim Abdool, had failed to make headway with their sexual stories. Another former guard, Charli Michaels, had been expected to testify but was never called. Perhaps the prosecution felt she would have just as much trouble on the stand as the others.

After Mesereau had disposed of Chacon in such fine style, in the 1108 hearing proper, he then turned the heat on another witness, Neverland maid Adrian McManus, who said she saw Michael kissing several boys, including Macaulay Culkin. In Jordie Chandler's case, she said, she saw Michael's hand on his crotch.

McManus initially gave her evidence confidently and forcefully, but was soon shot down in flames under cross-examination. She too had been a co-plaintiff in the failed unfair dismissal lawsuit against Jackson and was also deposed in 1993 for the grand jury investigation into the Chandler allegations.

In her deposition, McManus stated she never saw Jackson molesting any children. Now she testified that she had lied in her deposition, and attempted to explain this by saying she had feared repercussions from the Jackson camp. Mesereau attacked her as a disgruntled former employee for the wrongful dismissal suit, and as a perjurer for lying on oath to the grand jury.

"You said that you trusted Michael Jackson and would leave your own son alone with him, isn't that right?" Mesereau asked. She admitted she had said that.

Jackson's legal team had clearly done their homework on McManus, enabling Mesereau to show she had a gruesome skeleton in her cupboard. She and her husband had been sued by a sister-in-law, who won a judgment against them of over $30,000. The complaint? They had defrauded the woman's children for whom they had been guardians after her husband died.

McManus was also obliged to admit she used a "media broker" to sell stories to tabloids, including a totally baseless one claiming inside knowledge of Jackson's sex life with ex-wife Lisa Marie Presley. In court she confessed she had no genuine "sex secrets" to sell at all. And as if clear evidence of perjury, fraud and lying specifically about Michael's sex life were not enough to discredit her, McManus was even painted as a thief when Mesereau revealed McManus had stolen an ink drawing of Elvis Presley by Jackson and sold it. She claimed she found the drawing after it had been discarded as trash – a fate which would certainly befall her testimony. One has to wonder what on earth the prosecution hoped to achieve by relying on such people.

Yet still the flaky parade was not over. Next to appear was Philippe (by now anglicised to Phillip) LeMarque, another name we have encountered before in these pages. The former Neverland chef testified he saw the pop icon with his hand in the front of child movie star Macaulay Culkin's shorts. LeMarque told jurors he saw Jackson fondling Culkin, who was then ten or eleven, when he brought them French fries in the video game arcade in 1991.

"Michael was playing with Macaulay Culkin at one of the games," the chef said, explaining that the singer was holding up the young actor, who was too short to reach the controls.

"His left hand was inside the pants of the kid," he said. "It was in the crotch area." Then, in a classic remark that epitomised the lurid sensationalism of the 1108 mini-trial, he added: "I was shocked, I almost dropped the French fries."

But like so many of the other witnesses, his testimony also bore the taint of the tabloids. The chef acknowledged he once asked for $500,000 to tell a tabloid that he saw Jackson with a hand up Culkin's shorts, though he says he never actually received any money.

"Everybody was trying to sell our stories," said LeMarque, saying the competition to cash in on Jackson's fame divided the employees. "You couldn't have friends. Everyone was spying on each other."

One specific accusation levelled against the LeMarques by publicity agent Paul Barresi was that the chef made his original story more sensational in a bid to get more money for it. As Diane Dimond put it:

> Barresi told anyone who would listen, including the police, that when the LeMarques first told him the story about Macaulay Culkin being groped, Jackson's hand had been *outside* the boy's pants. When they felt they might get more money if their story was more salacious, the hand was suddenly *inside* the pants.[808]

Barresi's allegation was hugely damaging to the LeMarques and was exploited by Mesereau in his cross-questioning of Phillip LeMarque. But Barresi's own motives were questionable: after he had secured two tabloid bids for the couple's story, one for $100,000 and another for $150,000, the couple allegedly went behind his back to a lawyer who had convinced them he could get a deal for $500,000. A case, perhaps, of hell hath no fury like a publicity agent scorned? It may or may not be significant that Stella LeMarque had been dating Barresi before her marriage.[809]

The fact is that Phillip LeMarque did *not* change his story in response to tabloid temptation. On cross-examination, LeMarque was confronted with a statement he had written out for police in September, 1993, in which he had noted that he "couldn't distinguish what [Jackson] was really doing with his hand" while holding Macaulay, "but obviously it was more than fondling."

LeMarque agreed he had added a P.S. at the bottom of the page, saying "his left hand was in his pants under the shorts, left leg, all the way to the crotch". It is important that the P.S. is signed and dated: both the main statement and the P.S. were made on 10 September. So there was no intervening period of negotiation with the tabloids.[810] What appears to have happened is exactly what LeMarque told Mesereau under cross-examination: the P.S. was added for clarification. Read carefully, it can be seen that it does not sensationalise or contradict the primary account. Functionally, it serves to explain for someone who was not there at the time why the touching in question was "obviously…more than fondling". The witness could not see exactly what Jackson was doing with his hand precisely because it was under the pants, out of sight to him. But with the hand right inside the pants up to the crotch there could be no innocent explanation.

Under defence questioning, LeMarque said he and his wife, a cook, sued Jackson for unpaid overtime and received a settlement. LeMarque said he quit because his wife was asked to sign a false affidavit saying she saw a former maid go through people's purses. That ex-maid, he said, was none other than Blanca Francia, who had testified in the same week as himself, and who had been in a legal tussle with Jackson to win a financial settlement in respect of the star's alleged molestation of her son. The thought that Jackson or his aides might be so ruthless and dishonest in trying to blacken the character of a witness against him was as significant in its way as the more colourful French fries incident.

The last of Jackson's staff to testify to "prior bad acts" was his long-serving former publicist Bob Jones, the man who had coined the moniker "the King of Pop", and who still referred privately to his old boss as "the king". He was the "head-licking" witness briefly referred to earlier in the chapter. This particular "prior bad act", said to have taken place on a plane journey with Jackson, closely echoed anticipated testimony from Gavin Arvizo's mother, who was expected to say she had seen Jackson licking her own son's head, also during a flight. As such, the prosecution expected Jones to give important independent corroboration of a striking detail in Jackson's allegedly habitual intimacy with young boys.

The prosecution expected the witness to say he had seen Michael licking Jordie Chandler's head on a flight from Paris to Los Angeles in 1993. The incident had been described in draft material for a book about Jackson based on Jones' experiences. At the time of the trial, this was being written by

Jones and a co-author, Stacy Brown. When the book was published in 2005, soon after the trial was over, it included this passage:

> Michael and the young boy were hugging and very close on the plane. They held hands and Michael lovingly gazed into the boy's eyes much like a man would gaze into the eyes of a woman he's in love with. He'd kiss him on the cheek, rub his arms, pet him and inexplicably lick the boy's head.[811]

But on the witness stand Jones surprised prosecutor Gordon Auchincloss by saying he did not remember the licking. Shown an extract from the proposed book, he said he had not approved this part of the text. Only when confronted with an email he had written to his co-writer, in which he had clearly referred to the incident, did he reverse himself and decide it must have happened after all. Jones had written in the email: "Stacy: the licking is going to be important because he did this in this case too" – a reference to the Arvizo case.

Did Jones have a reason deliberately to "forget" the licking when giving evidence under oath? Could it be that Jackson or his aides had offered some sort of "carrot", perhaps financial, to induce his amnesia in court, just as once upon a time they had apparently tried to use "stick" to undermine possible testimony from Blanca Francia? The suggestion that Jones might at some stage try to hold over Michael's head what he knew about the Chandlers was made in court. Jones accepted that he had referred to this knowledge as an "insurance policy".

It is unlikely, though Jones would now be making a claim against the policy. It was too late. He had been sacked by Jackson a year before the trial and was a bitterly angry man. The dismissal, conveyed in a curt letter from a courier saying "Your services are no longer required", ended a 34-year relationship of loyal service to Jackson that began when the star was just twelve years old. Now he was being dumped without even a direct word from his boss. This is all explained on page one of his book, so it need surprise nobody that the text looks like an exercise in revenge. *Michael Jackson: The Man Behind The Mask* is highly critical of his old boss and packed with anecdotes guaranteed to embarrass him. It emerged in court that Jones was in some financial difficulties after his sacking but it hardly seems likely he would be in any mood to accept a bribe to tone down his testimony under oath.

On the other hand, what other explanation could there be? A genuine memory lapse is not impossible but is also highly unlikely, given that Jones had described the licking incident and its significance in not just one but two private emails to Stacy Brown. Later, when Brown was himself on the stand there was a further revelation proving beyond doubt that Jones not only remembered the licking but had thought about it quite a bit. Remember how, in the book, he had said Michael "inexplicably" licked the boy's head? The word "inexplicably" was there for a reason. It truly expressed Jones' private puzzlement. Brown told the court that Jones had talked to him about it. Jones had reportedly said:

> ...how strange it was, because Jordie had a head full of hair, and he said, "I thought maybe it would be... understandable if he had a bald head". But he just couldn't understand the licking of the head if he had a head full of hair.

One sees his point. Licking hair is something furry animals may do all the time but is not perhaps all that common among humans. Then again, licking bald-headed thirteen-year-olds may be an even rarer enthusiasm. But is all this just splitting hairs? As legal commentator Spilbor said, so what? The prosecution had laboriously made their tiny point, though Mesereau had the last laugh when, with a brilliant turn of rhetoric, he falsely, but effectively, managed to suggest the licking allegation was all about Jones' need to make money. Those playing close attention to the evidence could be certain this was not so.

By this point in the mini-trial, we had heard from an alleged victim of "prior bad acts", Jason Francia, and a whole parade of Jackson's former staff, including Francia's mother. As we have seen, the prosecution ended up not so much scraping the bottom of the 1108 barrel as licking out the dregs. Later on, though, with the mini-trial seemingly over and the jury once again concentrating on the Arvizo case rather than "prior bad acts", Sneddon came back for more of the stuff, out of the blue, like an alcoholic suddenly remembering an emergency reserve stashed away in a cupboard.

The evidence itself had been stashed away too – in a locked filing cabinet on the ground floor of Michael's bedroom suite at Neverland. It comprised two books of photographs seized from the cabinet in a 1993 police raid when the Jordie Chandler case was under investigation. One was titled *The Boy: A Photographic Essay* and the other *Boys Will Be Boys!* Both were credited to the same pair of editors, Georges St Martin and Ronald C Nelson.[812] Introducing them in the absence of the jury, when he was applying for them to be brought in as 1108 evidence, prosecutor Ron Zonen said 10% of the photos in one book were of naked boys, while in the other the proportion was 90%. They were lavishly produced coffee table volumes. *The Boy* is said to have included leisure-time on-location photographs of the boy actors in the classic 1963 Peter Brook film *Lord of the Flies*. The movie itself included scenes in which boys appeared nude. The two books were widely available in the 1960s and 70s. There was even a regular weekly advertisement for *The Boy* in the pages of the *Observer*, a newspaper generally held to be of impeccable respectability and one which has run its share of stories attacking child sex abuse, including child pornography.

There was no suggestion the books were illegal but it was claimed that they portrayed the singer's predilection towards young boys. Robert Sanger, defending, unsuccessfully argued that the books were irrelevant to the current case and would unfairly prejudice the jury. He said the books were kept in a locked cabinet and there was no evidence they were shown to anyone. Sanger asked the judge to look at an inscription in one of the books, apparently in Jackson's own hand, which read:

> Look at the true spirit of happiness and joy in these boys' faces. This is the spirit of boyhood — a life that I've never had and will always dream of. This is the life I want for my children.

Even the woman detective who had discovered the books on the raid did nothing to dispel this image when she described the books to the jury, saying the boys were depicted playing, swimming and jumping – "generally having a good time" as *a Los Angeles Times* report put it.[813] The other book had been inscribed "To Michael. From your fan Rhonda. XXXOOO." When the judge looked at this in the absence of the jury it inspired some light-hearted courtroom banter.

> *Judge*: I know what I mean when I put "XXXOOO".
> *Sanger*: "And I have noted Your Honour has never put that on any of your rulings in this case." (Laughter)
> *Judge*: "I can't top that".

There were to be many such humorous moments throughout the trial. I have no wish to be po-faced and critical about that, far from it, but I do find it interesting, and sad, that the court showed itself utterly unaware of the incongruity of the moment. Here we see "XXXOOO", or "love and kisses", as the subject of levity, a joke. Yet the entire, months-long proceedings of the court in this case were all about love and kisses being a matter of the utmost gravity, no laughing matter at all. The judge appeared to be saying love and kisses are fine, they have a positive part to play in his own personal life. So why not in the defendant's? Sitting there, silently, shut out of the joke, Michael must have felt very lonely as this jolly badinage beset his ears.

Before returning to the witnesses, a word is in order about the prosecution's seemingly ready acceptance of the view that Michael's books were legal. The California Penal Code forbids photographs depicting minors engaged in sexual conduct. There is no suggestion that the books showed anything that would come within widely accepted definitions of sexual conduct, such as coitus or fellatio. No one said the photos showed boys masturbating, or even with an erection. But there was evidence that some photos showed child nakedness which included "prominent display" of the genitals. In California law such a display can constitute sexual conduct. Section 311.3.(b) of the penal code states that sexual conduct includes "exhibition of the genitals or the pubic or rectal area of any person for the purpose of sexual stimulation of the viewer".

The photos in Jackson's books were not necessarily posed by the boys, nor taken, nor published, "for the purpose of sexual stimulation of the viewer", but they arguably *could* have been, depending how closely the photographer had zoomed in on the "privates" and whether the boy appeared to be provocatively presenting his "naughty" parts to the camera or sporting a "lascivious" facial expression. Such assessments are bound to be highly subjective, which means that it should not be beyond the wit of an imaginative prosecutor to detect such transgressions in any photo where there was a "prominent display" of a child's naked genitals.

Both *The Boy: A Photographic Essay* and *Boys Will Be Boys!* are described in website listings by online dealers in rare books. The latter appears to have been the one that featured a high percentage of nude images, to judge by the following online description:

> Photographs by various contributors. Edited with an Introduction by Georges St Martin and Ronald C Nelson. Presents photographs taken all over the Western world... of boys at their most uninhibited and exhibitionistic. It is disingenuous to say that this is simply a celebration of boyhood, then or today. Yes it is, and much more: A voyeuristic recollection

of such boyhood for adult consumption. Most of the photographs in the book show the boys outdoors, completely naked, swimming in the pond, camping, climbing mountains, playing games, and perhaps most disturbing today, simply posing for the camera...In the carefree Sixties, this book and its predecessor, *The Boy: A Photographic Essay*, were openly published, widely distributed, and very successfully sold.[814]

The writer of this piece then adds a philosophical comment:

> Can such voyeurism really be defended? The great cultural philosopher Roland Barthes thought so. He pointed out that looking arouses and ultimately suppresses, channels a human being's otherwise dangerous urges into viewing (instead of doing), making him a satisfied voyeur instead of a potential predator.[815]

In the mind of this particular bookseller, at least, there appears to be little doubt that the photographs were selected for their erotic appeal to the intended viewers. At another website we learn more about the photographers whose work is featured in *Boys Will Be Boys!* We read:

> Photographers include the legendary Hajo Ortil, Charles Egermeier, Carl Mansfield, Kurt Bingler, Jos Le Doare, Charles DuBois Hodges, Maurice Grosser, and many more. I can't find any information about Nelson, but "Georges St. Martin" is the pseudonym for Martin Swithinbank, a member of NAMBLA from New York who was jailed in 1981 for having sexual relations with boys; I am unaware whether he is still alive.[816]

All in all, we might ask ourselves whether the District Attorney would have been deterred from bringing a case if books such as Michael's had been in the possession of an ordinary Joe – someone lacking the means to mount a vigorous defence.

The final 1108 witness, like Blanca Francia, would be another alleged victim's mother, June Chandler. The Francia and Chandler families had one thing in common: both had agreed multi-million dollar civil settlements with Michael Jackson in the early 1990s.

In terms of the mothers' credibility in a criminal trial, these pay-offs were a problem for the prosecution in both cases. Sneddon would probably have sold his own grandchildren for spare parts surgery if it would have helped him drag the elusive "victim" himself, Jordie Chandler, into the witness box. That was not to be. As we have already noted, young Mr Chandler had deliberately made himself scarce, reportedly leaving the country for the duration of the trial. In the absence of the man in person, Sneddon would dearly have loved to put in evidence the deposition the boy had made in his civil case against Jackson. Jordie had, after all, made highly explicit sexual allegations written down in black and white in that solemn legal document. There had been other such formal documents, too, as we have seen copiously in this book: there had been his interview with psychiatrist Mathis Abrams, formally reported to the authorities on a mandatory basis. There had been a report by social worker Ann Rosato, and another frank and lengthy talk – this one audiotaped – with psychiatrist Richard Gardner. It must have been immensely frustrating to Sneddon that the rules of evidence did not allow him to use this material.

Compared to the dross that made up most of the 1108 evidence, this material was pure gold. The fact is, then, that readers of this book and other close students of Jackson's troubles in 1993-4 are in a much better position than the trial jury were to assess Michael Jackson's "prior bad acts". By comparison, June Chandler's evidence could only be indirect and circumstantial – as would Evan Chandler's have been, had he been called.

This did not mean June's story would be insignificant, far from it: one report would even refer to her "classic" testimony. In a sometimes emotional account, June told the court she deeply regretted trusting the pop icon at a time when she was separated from her second husband. She recounted how Jackson took an immediate shine to Jordie at their first encounter, engaging him in long telephone conversations and inviting the family to Neverland. She said Jordie asked several times to spend the night with Jackson and she refused until the singer came to her during a trip to Las Vegas – sobbing, shaking and begging her for a sleepover with the boy. She testified:

> Michael was trembling, saying, "We're a family. Jordie is having fun. Why can't he sleep in my bed? There's nothing wrong. There's nothing going on. Don't you trust me?"

June said she relented, and the next day, the singer presented her with a Cartier gold bracelet. That began a pattern in which Jackson spent many nights with her son, including about thirty in the boy's bedroom at the family's home in Los Angeles. June said she gradually lost control of Jordie as he spent more time with Michael, becoming withdrawn and ignoring other family members. During a trip to New York in the summer of 1993, she tried to intervene and Jackson again became distraught. "Why can't we be a family? Why are you objecting to Jordie staying with me? Why don't you trust me?" she recalled him saying. She said he was upset that she wanted her son back: "I didn't like the situation. It was getting out of hand," she said.

From St Grenadines in the Caribbean, and ethnically of mixed black and Chinese origin, June Chandler was described by one court observer as elegant, articulate and fashionable. She stood her ground as a prosecution witness. At one point in cross-examination she even made her own legal objection to a question, snapping out "Speculation!" before Sneddon could finish the more formal phrase "Calls for speculation". There was laughter in court as Judge Melville nodded at each of them in turn, saying "Sustained. Sustained."

She was hard-pressed, however, to explain why she let Jackson sleep in the same bed with her son up to fifty times in 1993. She was equally at a loss to rationalise taking expensive gifts from the pop star at the same time. She gave no evidence that she had seen anything sexual, but she had left a very clear impression that Jackson was desperate to be alone with her son. Her testimony made it clear that he would pay for that privilege by including her and her daughter in expensive trips just so he could be close to the boy. This all supported the prosecution case that Jackson would habitually "groom" young boys with a sexual purpose in mind.

Many commentators were unimpressed by June Chandler, concluding she had virtually sold her child to Jackson in exchange for expensive gifts and a few months of glamour. Jordie himself appears to have thought June was interested only in a glitzy lifestyle and not in him: June admitted in court that he had not spoken to her for the last eleven years, since shortly after the civil settlement. The jury probably took an equally dim view of other parents in the case too: as we shall see, these included a whole string of mothers who, like June Chandler, were effectively single mums at the time, and arguably very vulnerable to the persuasive power of a rich and famous man.

One of those mothers, Janet Arvizo, was destined to be the most important witness in the entire case, even more so than Gavin. Without her decision to go to lawyers and then to press her sons into revealing – or inventing – a story of sexual abuse, it is doubtful Gavin Arvizo would ever have become a complainant. The conspiracy aspect of the trial – the alleged kidnapping of her family – would also turn almost entirely on the strength or weakness of her testimony. Indeed, as we shall soon see, Gavin's own credibility, already in doubt, would be decisively bolstered or undermined by what his mother would have to say.

Having now heard all of the evidence on the alleged sexual abuse of Gavin Arvizo, and having completed the mini-trial into "past bad acts", the court could now turn its attention to the third and final phase of the prosecution case: the conspiracy aspect. It would be a long, complicated affair in court, with many witnesses and a great deal of tedious detail. Fortunately, we can bypass all of that with no loss of insight into the strength of the case against Michael Jackson. The main elements of the case were set out in the previous chapter in presenting Tom Sneddon's opening speech. Here it will be sufficient to focus on the evidence of Janet Arvizo. After reviewing her contribution, it will become clear why little more needs to be said.

Janet's testimony was dramatic from the start. In the absence of the jury, her very first move after being sworn in was to invoke the Fifth Amendment of the US Constitution, refusing to talk about claims that she had engaged in welfare fraud. Famously, "taking the Fifth" allows witnesses to avoid incriminating themselves during testimony. Janet had been legally advised to adopt this ploy, but the mere fact of announcing she had something to hide did not look good. The knowledge that she had a shady past would not play well with the jury; her credibility would be in doubt before she had uttered a single word about the case they were hearing.

The judge asked prosecutor Ron Zonen if the district attorney's office had considered giving the witness immunity from prosecution. This would then have allowed Janet to testify on all matters without inhibition. Zonen replied: "We're not terribly interested in giving this witness immunity." Soon after the trial she was in fact prosecuted for alleged welfare fraud. Appearing in court in September 2005, she agreed to pay restitution of around $18,000.

Arguing against allowing her testimony altogether, Jackson lawyer Robert Sanger said, "Michael Jackson, who has been accused by this witness, has a right under counsel to vigorously cross examine this witness to show that she has committed acts of perjury and acts of fraud and that she is not credible." The judge ruled that she could testify, but that jurors would be informed she has taken the Fifth over accusations of welfare fraud when she allegedly accepted state benefit payouts to which she was not entitled.

Dressed in a pink suit and spectacles, Janet "appeared girlish"[817] as she told a story that veered from heartbreaking to histrionic. A heavy-set woman with a pale, wide face, she had three children by the time she was twenty one, four by the time of the trial and a fifth due early in 2006. At the outset she was the picture of the struggling mother as she described her son's harrowing cancer and the family's life of poverty in a tiny, cramped apartment. But soon she was describing how she never asked questions or called the police after Michael Jackson and his aides told her killers were after her children. "I was just like a sponge, believing him, trusting him," she said.

She had claimed her children were being stalked by "killers" before the star allegedly kidnapped the family in a plot to force her and her children to help him restore his image after the Bashir documentary. She said Michael and three aides told her the lives of her three children were in danger after the documentary aired. She said she spoke with Jackson when he phoned Gavin following the broadcast in February 2003. "He told me that Gavin was in danger and there had to be a press conference because of this Bashir man," she said.

Jackson then flew the family from Los Angeles to Miami, ostensibly for a press conference, to refute suggestions of sexual abuse against her son. There he told her that the lives of her children were under threat. Jackson said "that he loves us, that he cares about us, that we're family ... that he's going to protect us from these killers," she told jurors. A few days later, Jackson returned the family to Neverland, where they were allegedly held prisoner until they agreed to make a video to clear Jackson's name. Janet said Jackson aides told her the video, in which the family praised Jackson, "would appease the killers."

"Appease the killers – I heard that so many times," she said. Referring to Jackson and his aides, she added with a flourish, "And you know what? *They* ended up being the killers." But who was dead? Where were the bodies? Apparently the evil conspirators hadn't got around to that bit.

Janet also claimed to have looked on in horror on the flight back to Neverland when she saw the star licking the side of her sleeping son's head. Anxious to justify the fact that she had done nothing to stop it, she turned to the jurors and pleaded in a choking whisper: "Please don't judge me. Please don't judge me." Gavin's younger brother, Star Arvizo, had also testified to the head licking, but a flight attendant said she saw no intimate contact between Jackson and the boy.

Given to gratuitous dramatic embellishments, at some moments Janet seemed sadly genuine, as when asked why she had so readily believed in Jackson and his people: "I wanted friends so badly, because David had always told me nobody loved me," she said sobbing, referring to her former husband, who had subjected her to domestic violence. She frequently heaved heavy sighs, sobbed at several points, and clearly had difficulty with the formal question and answer format, frequently jumping in to answer before she had understood an uncompleted question.

Observers felt her first day on the stand had been another terrible one for the prosecution. Lawyer Jim Moret told AFP news agency the damage had been done even before Janet started her testimony: "The jury has been told by the judge effectively she's accused of being a liar and a thief". As for her amazing story, "I think today we went from Neverland to Fantasyland. I think the jurors saw a woman who may believe what she's saying, but I don't think the jurors believe what she is saying".[818] At this early stage, though, with a crucial cross-examination to follow, some trial watchers doubted that Janet would be capable of concocting a complicated lie about Jackson and sustaining it over two years and numerous investigations – so maybe there had to be *some* truth in her story.

The doubts began to evaporate once Tom Mesereau got to work. In an explosive showdown, his cross-examination wrung out of the combative 37-year-old Janet Arvizo that she had succeeded – however improbably – in getting away with exceedingly tall stories before. Jackson's star lawyer forced her to concede she did not tell the truth in a sworn deposition she made while suing the JC Penney retail group in 2000.

"You lied under oath to increase the amount of money you could get, correct?" Mesereau asked, referring to her claim that she had been sexually assaulted when she and her children were detained on suspicion of shoplifting. Janet had claimed in the statement that she had never been abused by her then husband David – but she later reported him to the authorities for beating her and abusing their three children. He pleaded no contest to spousal abuse and child cruelty in 2001 and had not seen his children since. Mesereau suggested that Janet's claim against the JC Penney store that bruises on her body were caused by its security guards would have been weakened by the revelation of spousal abuse.

In her JC Penney deposition, Janet had alleged that guards knocked her down in the parking lot of a Los Angeles shopping centre and did belly flops on her body. Her breasts fell out of her bra, she said, and a guard squeezed one of her nipples ten to twenty five times. Yet she made no allegation at all of sexual abuse until a year after the car park incident.

"How many lies do you think you told in the JC Penney case?" Mesereau asked. She was reluctantly forced to concede she had lied about anything to do with her then husband until his subsequent arrest.

Confronted with questions about a report she made against her ex-husband accusing him of molesting her daughter, Janet refused to answer directly and instead turned to the jury and said, "No, he's wrong." But after a verbal tug-of-war between witness and lawyer, she agreed she had made such a report. "You reported him for falsely imprisoning your family?" asked Mesereau. "They investigated him," she said. The knowledge that Janet Arvizo's claim of false imprisonment against Michael Jackson was not the first time she had made such an allegation must have made an impression on the jury.

Mesereau walked her through the "rebuttal video". Even though all four members of the family had been perceived by media commentators as relaxed and spontaneous in that performance, Janet insisted over and over again it was scripted "word for word" – even the laughter – so that Jackson's people would be sure of the family saying exactly the right things. When Mesereau asked how long it took to memorise her lines or how long the script was, she could not answer. Her children had not mentioned any rehearsals or word-for-word scripts when they testified.

When this position became ludicrous to maintain, she refused to back down. Instead, she embellished the story, saying an aide named Dieter Wiesner had worked with her on it ten times a day so she would get her lines right. Wiesner, she said, wrote every word of it, despite the fact that he is German, has a poor command of English and, by her own admission, had no contact with her in the immediate run-up to shooting the video.

Observers were by now scoring the fight heavily in favour of the defence. In a series of tense exchanges with the defiant witness, Mesereau suggested the woman's stories of kidnapping were a tissue of lies and that she was in fact living in the lap of luxury as Jackson's guest at Neverland.

"You didn't escape from Neverland at all, did you?" he asked.

"Oh, yes I did," she retorted.

"How many times, in your mind, did you escape from that dungeon, Neverland?" Mesereau persisted, getting Janet to admit that she had left the ranch and then returned no fewer than three times during her "captivity".

The floundering witness was at times reduced to bickering over technicalities, sometimes to pitifully hilarious effect. A classic of the genre was triggered when Mesereau brought up a visit she made to a beauty salon in the town of Los Olivos, near Neverland, at the time when she was allegedly kidnapped. He claimed she had had a "body wax" there. She maintained it never happened. After some probing it emerged that the beauty treatment had been a leg wax. As though Mesereau had been caught out in a crucial lie – instead of herself, repeatedly – she protested: "I had a leg wax done. He keeps saying 'body wax'. There is no body wax." Her ill-judged crural hair-splitting did not please the court.

To make matters even worse, if that were possible, she foolishly insisted she had paid for the treatment out of her own money. In fact the "kidnap victim" had been making free with money from her "captor". Mesereau had the receipt for $140 to prove it, which showed multiple beauty treatments including leg, bikini and lip waxing, and a manicure. Janet refused to look at the receipt, claiming he had somehow changed it.

Among her ridiculous claims was that she had been limited to "one meal a day" during the "kidnapping". Restaurant receipts showed her dining out in style. She also claimed that she and her family were not allowed to leave the Calabasas Country Inn when they spent a week there at Michael's expense. Records showed they were hardly ever there and even went to the movies when they were not shopping or dining out. Of her allegation that Jackson's aides plotted to spirit the Arvizo family to Brazil to get them permanently out of the way, Mesereau noted that the airline tickets for the journey were round-trip, with a return flight scheduled a week later.

But why Brazil? The question is interesting not for any light the answer might shine on the Arvizo case but for evidence of a long-lasting association Michael had developed with that country, and one that might be seen as rather sinister. So, travelling faster than any jet plane on our own round trip, this narrative will now take off for a short diversion to South America, touching down shortly at Janet's testimony again. Fasten your safety belts!

Marc Schaffel, one of the aides accused of conspiring with Michael, brought up the Brazilian connection a year later when Schaffel successfully sued his former collaborator (but not co-conspirator) for money owed to him. Reporting on this lawsuit in his biography of Michael, Darwin Porter said Schaffel claimed he flew to Brazil on several occasions to try to find boys for Michael "to adopt". Schaffel claimed that these "boy searches" occurred twice a year between 1999 and 2001. According to an Associated Press report, though, he later modified the statement, claiming he had been sent for "children" to expand Michael's family.

In addition to the adoption scheme, Schaffel said, he had flown on a secret mission to Buenos Aires (in Argentina, of course, not Brazil) to pay hush money to prevent another child molestation scandal: this was allegedly because a certain Ruby Martinez and her son David "had knowledge of past abuse allegations against Jackson dating back to the 1990s". AP reported Schaffel as claiming that $300,000 was paid out, not to the mother but to a "Mr X". It seems likely that Ruby's son, presumably named David Martinez, was the alleged victim and that he had grown up to become Mr X.

Schaffel, incidentally, had been engaged by Michael on at least a couple of rather more high-profile projects than "the boys from Brazil" (and possibly girls), including producing TV specials to rebut the Bashir documentary. Jackson cut off contact with him supposedly because he discovered that Schaffel had a history as a producer of gay pornography, a history made much of in the media during Michael's criminal trial. In a videotaped deposition shown to jurors in Schaffel's civil case, in July 2006, just over a year after the criminal case ended, Michael said, "I just thought this association with Schaffel wouldn't vibe with the charitable work I've done". He also said, "I'm no fan of gay porn" – but hard-core gay porn seized by the police at Neverland would become a feature of the criminal case against Michael.

Of course, if Michael had known about Schaffel's gay porn history at the time when he was sending the guy to get boys (and maybe girls) for him to adopt and to deal with previous abuse allegations, that would hardly have vibed with his charity work either, or with any aspect of his career. Also noteworthy is the fact that despite all these trips to Brazil, not even one boy was ever actually adopted – not one girl either, though Michael had in the past indeed talked about wanting to adopt both boys and girls. Can it really be the case, one wonders, that this resourceful businessman was quite unable to find a single child among the teeming masses of needy Brazilian kids who was both available for adoption and acceptable to Michael? It begins to look as though either Schaffel was making the whole thing up or the purpose was not adoption. What is clear, if reporting of the judgment is accurate, is that the jury accepted Schaffel's claim that he did indeed spend $300,000 for Jackson on a secret mission to Argentina.[819]

As for why the Arvizo family had been offered a trip to Brazil, the issue is explained simply by the fact that Michael had initially planned around that time to go to Brazil to put on a concert in Rio's Maracana Stadium and create a video for the song "One More Chance". The plans failed to pan out, as did the Arvizos' Brazilian vacation. Marc Schaffel, according to testimony in Michael's criminal trial by travel agent Cynthia Montgomery, had been the aide whose instructions led to her ordering air tickets to Brazil for the Arvizos.

As promised, this brings my narrative back from its Brazilian diversion and allows us to continue with Janet Arvizo's testimony. One of her biggest problems with the kidnap story was how to explain why, when she had been able to "escape" from Neverland three times and visit such places as beauty salons, restaurants and movie theatres, she had been unable to get a message to the police about having been kidnapped. She had never phoned 911 for the police, nor did she tell her own lawyer. Instead, she insisted, she spoke to people, including friends, "in code," dropping hints so that her parents would not be murdered by Jackson's team. Mesereau pointed out that Janet spent the last two nights of this saga not trapped at Neverland, but with her fiancé in his apartment – and he happened to be a major in the US army. Sadly, it seems Janet's code was beyond even military decryption skills, otherwise the gallant officer could have led a squad to storm Neverland, cornering the evil Jackson and his hard-ball henchmen in a showdown fit for a James Bond movie.

In reality, *his* account was a great deal more prosaic. Major Jay Jackson (no relation to Michael) had testified as a sort of warm-up act before Janet (by now his wife) took the stand. He had failed to provide a solid foundation for the conspiracy allegations, while the defence scored points by forcing him to admit he had been negotiating a deal for a story with the British tabloid the *Daily Mail*.

Janet Arvizo's marriage to Jay Jackson of course fully entitled her to style herself Janet Jackson, and this was indeed the name she gave when she was sworn in. It is possible she enjoyed taking the same name as Michael's glamorous sister. It perhaps added a little lustre to a hitherto drab life, as did the social standing of her new husband. An army major was a good catch for Janet, but by a poignant irony it appears her capacity to enjoy her new life was blighted by her own limitations. In one of the saddest moments of the trial she began sobbing as she revealed she never went to army social functions with her husband because "I'm not smart enough to be with those people".

After five days on the witness stand, in which she had given fifteen hours of often bizarre, rambling and confused testimony, the court was finally through with Janet Jackson, formerly Janet Arvizo, née Janet Ventura. The end came not a minute too soon for many commentators, including Roger Friedman, then with the Fox network. He felt the time had come "to stop the madness and declare a mistrial". He thought child molestation was no longer the issue and that the D.A.'s office was "potentially guilty of exploiting a disturbed woman's condition to get a conviction". During the cross-examination, he noted, D.A. Tom Sneddon at times sat with his head in his hands, seemingly appalled at what he had wrought. After twelve years trying to proving Jackson is a child molester, said Friedman, "he chose the wrong case and the wrong people to close his deal".[820]

Michael Jackson himself appeared to agree. Leaving the court after Janet's confrontation with Tom Mesereau, he said simply, "It's going well". However, his biggest and most persistent detractor in the media, Diane Dimond, seemed determined to cling on to the conspiracy theory. Forced to admit Janet was a hopeless witness, Dimond insisted the kidnap story was corroborated by other evidence. She said, for instance, that "Team Jackson" had moved Janet out of her Los Angeles apartment against her will, "and there on the courtroom jumbo screen the jury saw the documents to prove it". Also, "This mother sounded ultra-paranoid when she described Jackson thugs conducting video surveillance of her and her family members. But prosecutors played several grainy videotapes showing it was true."[821]

As a news reporter, Dimond did not have the luxury of waiting until all the evidence was in before making her comments. Her documentary and taped so-called "proof" of the plot in fact proved nothing whatever against Michael Jackson. If his aides had done anything reprehensible they had acted alone, without his authority. There was some indication Michael had himself been a victim of dubious dealings behind his back by one or two of them, but there would be no credible evidence of a criminal plot against the Arvizos and not the slightest hint that their boss had masterminded any such plot, whether to kidnap or extort.

Not content with making a fool of herself by inventing non-existent "proof" of a plot, Dimond put her foot in it again immediately (along with many others, it has to be said) by forecasting that Michael's ex-wife Debbie Rowe was angry with him and would be "one of the prosecution's strongest conspiracy witnesses".[822]

In fact, like so many other prosecution witnesses, Debbie effectively became a superb witness for the defence. Identifying herself as "Deborah Rowe-Jackson", she smiled at the singer when she took the witness stand. She testified that Michael called her for help after the Bashir broadcast and that she agreed in the hope of seeing their family reunited. Totally contrary to prosecution assertions, she insisted she had not been bullied into giving an interview about her famous ex-husband. She had been offered a list of questions for the interview, so that she could give advance thought to her answers, but had declined to look at it. She had spoken spontaneously; there had been no script. Memorising such a script would have been a remarkable feat: Debbie said filming took place over nine hours, including a solid seven hours of interview conducted by *US Weekly* reporter Ian Drew. Drew had told her there would be 105 questions and her impression was that all of them were asked.

We also know from the range and kind of questions asked that Drew had his own agenda. He was an independent journalist busting a gut to get a real story out of Debbie, not some lackey of Michael's, paid to ask patsy questions. Material from this interview found its way onto *Entertainment Tonight*, as we saw in Chapter Thirteen. One of Drew's questions had been whether Debbie and Michael ever slept together, a question which forced her into an evasive answer. No interview scripted to make Michael look good would have skated on such thin ice.

Though prosecutors said taped interviews with Rowe and the Arvizo family were "highly scripted," she denied she was coached, saying she did not want to be later accused of giving rehearsed answers. "As Mr Jackson knows, no-one can tell me what to say," she said. "I tend to speak my own mind." She told jurors she saw the interview being edited down to a three-hour tape, on the same day it was shot. It was she who had instructed the videographer on the points she wanted included in the final edit: "That he's generous to a fault, giving and kind," she said tearfully. "A good father, great with kids ... a brilliant businessman."

This glowing tribute was paid on Debbie's second day of testimony. Many reports of the first day's proceedings had wrongly suggested she had admitted lying in the rebuttal interview when she had praised Michael's "parenting skills". In fact she readily conceded when asked by prosecutor Ron Zonen how she had dealt with "questions about Mr Jackson and his parenting of your two children" that she had not answered honestly. Parenting *skills* had not been mentioned at the point when she replied. Those of her answers which had been less than honest had not implicated Michael's talents as a parent at all: what Debbie may have had in mind, consistent with her claim on oath that Michael was a good father, was her evasiveness as to his sex life and the unorthodox method by which he had become a parent. Later, she was asked in court specifically about Michael's parenting skills and whether she really knew anything about them. She said before the divorce she spoke with the nannies about this and "I've seen him with the kids the whole time I've known him."

Later, sheriff's investigator Sergeant Steve Robel would testify that Deborah had privately described the pop star as a "sociopath" and that she had concerns over his parenting, but this undercurrent of doubt as to her real views was not a powerful one in the context of the trial: it would be her own clear testimony in court that really counted.

Debbie, appearing in a black pinstriped suit with shoulder-length blond hair, said that prior to the broadcast of *Living with Michael Jackson* in February 2003 she had not seen the superstar since their divorce four years earlier. Asked about what Michael had said on the phone to her, she said, "He told me there was a video coming out and it was full of lies and would I help. And I said, as always, yes." Her voice breaking with emotion, she said she asked to visit their two children, whom she had not seen in about two years, and Jackson agreed.

Prosecutors claimed that Rowe had been promised visiting rights with her children in exchange for defending Jackson, but she stopped short of saying this. When Jackson called, she said, she hoped to be reintroduced to the children "and to be reacquainted with their dad". Asked why, by Deputy District Attorney Ron Zonen, Debbie dabbed at a tear and said: "He's my friend."

She said she was not paid for the interview and could not take part until her divorce lawyer obtained a waiver of a confidentiality agreement with the pop star. Leaked legal documents showed that when they divorced, Debbie pledged never to talk about Jackson's alleged drug use, "sexual behaviour" and whether or how he fathered their children, in return for a multi-million-dollar settlement. Despite the waiver, Debbie did not reveal these details of her private life with Jackson in that marathon interview with Drew, and in court made it clear that she did not want to discuss such matters. "My personal life was my personal life and no one's business," she said when asked by the prosecution if she had talked completely truthfully on the video. The judge agreed her marriage secrets were a no-go area.

The worst she could have done, according to Roger Friedman, would have been to answer questions about her children's paternity. If she did, she would sensationally "have to concede that Jackson is not the father of Prince, eight, and Paris, seven". He claimed she acted as a surrogate twice and was artificially inseminated — and not with Jackson's sperm. He added that "this open secret" had been verified to friends by Debbie.[823]

Debbie signed away her parental rights entirely in 2001, but shortly after Jackson's arrest on child molestation charges in November 2003, she launched a legal battle to regain custody. To some it seemed a bit late in the day, and in court Debbie admitted that returning to the children as their mother would be "complicated." Under the title line "Won't somebody please think of the children?" one internet blogger wrote at the time:

> Another small pile of legal papers to add to the growing mountain of court stuff at Michael Jackson's house, as Debbie Rowe launches an action to reclaim custody of the kids. In a buy two, get one free deal, she's also offering to take on Prince Michael II, the third child that Jackson somehow has some sort of fatherly connection with.[824]

Debbie told the court that she had waived her rights in 2001 because of the difficulties imposed by a custody agreement which had limited her visits with the children to eight hours every forty five days. "The visitations were not comfortable," she said. "We were hooked up at a hotel. When I would bring things to do, like fingerpaints or colouring, the nanny was always very concerned they would get dirty." The visits were so tightly controlled that "it wasn't a quality relationship." But it was widely felt Debbie's real interest was in Michael, not the children, as we saw in Chapter Thirteen. Sadly for her, the feeling was not reciprocated. As she admitted, the real obstacle to her being reunited with her children – and thereby with Michael – was Jackson himself. "He's their father, ultimately it's his decision," she said.

Debbie said she had known Jackson for twenty years before they wed, but when asked about the marriage, she replied, "We never shared a home." Court observers said she "seemed to have a genuine affection for her ex-husband even as she testified for the prosecution".

As for Jackson's aides, Debbie denounced the singer's entourage as "opportunistic vultures" who were trying to make money out of him. Under defence questioning, she also recalled telling police investigators that Jackson was "very easily manipulated," especially when he was scared. Not much help for the prosecution there: according to Sneddon's version, Michael was supposed to be pulling all the strings himself, not some puppet manipulated by underlings. Her evidence bolstered the defence assertion that any wrongdoing connected with the conspiracy charges was carried out by maverick aides without Jackson's knowledge.

This was all a million miles from what the prosecution had expected. Sneddon needed her to say her responses in the interview with Drew had been heavily scripted. The idea was to bolster Janet Arvizo's testimony. Janet had claimed she had been kidnapped and coerced into mouthing a fully scripted paean of praise for Michael. Debbie had not been kidnapped, but Sneddon apparently thought she, too, had been asked to stick to an adulatory script. Evidence to this effect would have powerfully corroborated the conspiracy theory.

Legal analysts said Debbie had turned out, against expectations, to be a "dream witness" for the defence. "If this is the prosecution's bombshell witness she just blew up in their face," said one lawyer cited by the *Santa Barbara Independent,* a paper that felt she had "single-handedly destroyed any inkling that Jackson was a conspiratorial mastermind" and had left "Sneddon and his cohorts…flabbergasted and confused".[825]

It was a low point from which the prosecution case never recovered. The remaining week of testimony would be taken up with such tedious matters as the analysis of records of phone calls between Michael and his aides, and other hopeless would-be props to the collapsed conspiracy charges. Debbie had totally wrecked the conspiracy case, but thanks to Janet Arvizo's literally incredible testimony no one was going to believe it anyway. Janet had not only failed to make out any conspiracy, she had destroyed her own credibility across the board and in doing so made it harder for her children's testimony to be given the benefit of the doubt: for one thing, the whole family had now been implicated in lies over the JC Penney case.

In these circumstances, much would depend on the purely prejudicial effect of the 1108 evidence on "prior bad acts". Stan Goldman, professor at Loyola Marymount Law School in Los Angeles, said he did not feel the prosecution case was compelling, but, "What makes it a potentially winning prosecution case is that Jackson has been painted as a career paedophile. The jury has to decide two things: Is he a paedophile, and did he do this particular crime? If you bring in evidence of prior offences you've done two-thirds of the heavy lifting."

"That evidence is so radioactive that it doesn't just stand on its own; it infects everything else," said former San Francisco prosecutor Jim Hammer. "The case comes down to this: If the jury gives a lot of weight to the 1108 evidence, Jackson has a good chance of being convicted. If they don't and they just focus on the current case, the prosecution could be in trouble."

In a lengthy "half-time" analysis for the *Observer*, Paul Harris reported what he and others saw as a significant criminal pattern in Michael's behaviour, discernible in both the Arvizo case and the "prior bad acts" evidence. Referring to three mothers in these cases, June Chandler, Blanca Francia and Janet Arvizo, he wrote:

All three mothers described a similar pattern. It is, prosecutors argue, classic evidence of a predatory paedophile. They claim that Jackson uses Neverland, with its array of free amusement rides, endless supply of sweets and his own private bedroom as a honeypot into which to lure his victims. They are young boys whose fathers are usually absent. The mothers are then showered with gifts and pressured to allow their children to share Jackson's bedroom. Eventually the boys are abused. "There's a pattern here," said Steve Cron, a legal analyst and California defence attorney.

Whether juries make anything of such patterns can turn on the tone with which evidence is presented, and the emotional response it induces. The licking saga provides a good example. We heard one legal expert describe licking a child as no more illegal than licking an ice-cream cone. In Harris's report, though – and perhaps in the mind of some jurors – it assumed enormous significance. This is how Harris described Janet Arvizo's testimony:

> She theatrically recalled sitting on a plane and watching Jackson lick her child's forehead like a cat. "Like this, over and over," she told the court as she demonstrated by licking her own arm. That awful animalistic image, of the king of pop licking the head of a young boy, was just one of many direct hits on Jackson in the past two weeks.[826]

Could that "awful animalistic image" convict a man, along with comparably dubious "direct hits"? With another jury they might easily have done – yet no criminality had been disclosed by the licking. Incidentally, Janet had made no reference in her testimony to a cat or to any other animal. That appears to have been journalistic licence designed to bolster Harris's "animalistic" interpretation. Neither did Janet say Michael had licked Gavin's forehead. That must have been a careless error, because the star's behaviour, as described in court, *was* actually quite feline: he had licked the hair on the side of the boy's head. If there was one believable part of Janet's story this was it, because it was backed up by precisely the same detail in Bob Jones' email, which was surely intended as a purely private communication.

Months had now passed in the trial. February had been given over to jury selection; March and April had seen all but the dying embers of the prosecution case completed. To many, the case against Michael appeared so weak it looked hardly necessary to mount a defence at all. Arguably all that needed doing was to deal with matters of tone, to bring in witnesses who could burnish the image of the tarnished star. Star witnesses had been anticipated including Elizabeth Taylor and Stevie Wonder, who would come along just to say nice things about Michael. Such figures would have been irrelevant to the Arvizo charges but not perhaps to the 1108 case: with the prosecution allowed to bring evidence that Michael had a long-established propensity towards offences against boys, the defence had to be allowed to call witnesses who could rebut their claims. But superstars who could do no more than assert that Michael was a nice guy who would never harm a child were of doubtful value. Even a star-truck jury could soon become bored and turned off by a parade of big names all trotting out glowing testimonials. If the defence needed to burnish Michael's image, it had to do be done in a way that the judge and jury would agree was strictly to the point. The extent to which that was achieved will be seen in the next chapter.

CHAPTER SEVENTEEN

The Trial, Part Four: A Close Run Thing

If the likes of Elizabeth Taylor and Stevie Wonder were to be ruled out as witnesses, who else was there to play Michael's stay-out-of-jail card? The prosecution case had looked weak, but the nabob of Neverland still stood in the gravest peril. The mere fact of a middle-aged man admitting to sharing his life and bed with young boys was for many people quite enough evidence of his sexual inclinations and likely behaviour; many juries would surely have convicted on little more. With the matter standing on a knife-edge, who could Michael call upon to help him?

Boys, that's who. He had got himself into trouble over boys and now they would get him out of it. Specifically, several boys had been named by witnesses in connection with alleged "prior bad acts". Those boys, now young men, would be able to rebut that testimony directly. One of them, Macaulay Culkin, had been a superstar himself, and would be well placed to put Michael's eccentric life-style in a more favourable light. This would be the plan at least. Would it work?

Wade Robson, the first to appear, is a familiar name from earlier chapters who by this time had also become a considerable celebrity. A choreographer who has worked with Britney Spears and the band 'N Sync, and has hosted his own show, *The Wade Robson Project*, on MTV, he was once in a music video with Jackson.

Wade, and Brett Barnes, who would follow him on the stand the same day, both said they slept in the same bed with Jackson dozens of times when they were boys, and nothing sexual ever happened. Wade said he met Michael at age five after winning a Melbourne dance competition and later travelled to the United States, where he stayed overnight at Neverland numerous times, often sharing a bed with the singer. He acknowledged that Jackson helped him move from Australia to the United States in September 1991 and that he was grateful for the help.

This was the boy Jackson's maid Blanca Francia testified she once found in a shower with him. Robson, aged twenty two by the time of the trial, denied that he and Jackson had ever showered together. He said he visited Neverland more than twenty times, staying as long as a week or more and sleeping in Jackson's bed nearly every time. He said he and Jackson played together like children, riding golf carts around the ranch, holding pillow fights and once throwing pebbles at a napping lion to see if they could make it roar. He said Jackson occasionally kissed him on the cheek, but said the star often greeted children and adults with kisses and he thought nothing of it. However, he did the credibility of his testimony no good when he insisted Michael is attracted to women. As for the allegations that Jackson molested him, Robson said, "I think it's ridiculous."

Michael nodded at Wade when he took the witness stand and flashed him a thumb's-up sign during a court recess. This was something new. Jackson had sat still and stared blankly through much of the prosecution's nine weeks of testimony.

Ron Zonen, for the prosecution, asked Robson whether it was appropriate for an eight-year-old boy to sleep in bed with a man in his thirties. "I don't see any problem with it," he replied.

Zonen asked about the "sex dance" security guard Charli Michaels claimed to have seen – though she never appeared in court as a witness:

> Was there ever an occasion where you were on the dance floor with Mr Jackson, and he was showing you a routine and he grabbed your crotch in a manner similar to how he would grab his own crotch while doing those performances?

Wade flatly denied it.

The prosecutor brought out sexually explicit books and magazines detectives found in Jackson's home and asked the young man to examine them. One of the publications was the book *Boys Will Be Boys!*, while another showed two men engaged in overt homosexual acts – hard-core gay porn. Zonen began with the former:

> Q: Would you describe the picture on the right side?
> A: There's a young boy with his legs open and he's naked.
> Q: All right. The picture prominently displays his genitalia, does it not?
> A: Yes.
> Q: That boy looks, to you, to be approximately how old?
> A: Maybe eleven or twelve.
> Q: That's how old you were when you were sleeping with Michael Jackson; is that right?
> A: Yes.

When asked, Wade said he would have no concerns about a child sleeping with an adult male who read magazines such as *Playboy*. Zonen pounced on an opportunity to exploit any homophobia lurking in the jury. Referring to the gay hard-core book, which showed acts of masturbation, oral sex and what he called "sodomy", Zonen asked: "Would you have concerns about a person in possession of that book crawling into bed with a twelve-year-old boy?"

"Yes, I guess so," he answered.

With the dread word "sodomy" ringing in his ears, it would have taken a brave witness to give any other answer. It was an uncomfortable moment for Wade and the defence. Things got so bad that when the questioning returned to Mesereau, the defence lawyer actually pointed out Robson's girlfriend and said, "That's your fiancée right there, correct?" adding, "You are heterosexual, correct?" After affirmative answers, he continued: "If you saw ten years' worth of heterosexual material and one book of that nature, would that concern you?" Wade obligingly said it would not. The defender also elicited from Wade the point that Michael never showed him pornographic material and he was not aware that the pop star owned anything like that until Zonen produced the publications in court.

Between them, Zonen and Mesereau spent half an hour with Wade looking at and discussing Michael's pornography. The courtroom erupted in laughter as Wade said, "I never thought I'd be in a room with people watching me do this".

One point that could have been very significant for Michael's image in other circumstances was entirely ignored by most commentators. Understandably, they were focusing on the sexual issues and Wade's credibility and usefulness as a witness. But what are we to make of the curious incident of lion bating? How did this square with Michael's image as an animal lover? Here is how the exchange went:

> Q: Were there ever occasions where you and Mr Jackson were throwing stones at the lion in the zoo?
> A: Stones at the lion. Yeah, I think so.
> Q: That did happen, didn't it?
> A: Yeah.
> Q: Mr Jackson was throwing stones at the lion in your presence, is that right?
> A: Yes.
> Q: Was he encouraging you to do the same thing?
> A: Yeah, little pebbles, but yeah.
> Q: They weren't exactly pebbles. They were good-sized stones, weren't they?
> A: No, I remember small stones.
> Q: It was designed to irritate the lion, wasn't it?
> A: Yeah, we were trying to get him to make some noise.
> Q: Because it was entertaining to Mr Jackson and to you?
> A: Yeah.
> Q: How old were you at the time?
> A: I think I would have been seven or eight.

Mesereau later established from Wade that neither he nor Michael had intended to hurt the lion, but fans of Jackson's reputed kindness can take little comfort from this shameful lapse, in which a young and impressionable child was actively egged on to do something wrong. On the "How would you like it?" test, one wonders how well Michael would respond to having stones thrown at him – even small ones – to make him roar (or cry).

When it came to her turn on the witness stand, Wade's mother, Joy, put a credible spin on the incident – or at least it would have been credible coming from Wade himself – by saying the pair had been aiming for the lion's cage, not the lion itself. Just making a noise by rattling its cage, they hoped, would wake up the lion and make it roar.

Victor Gutierrez's book, published years before the trial, includes a version of a stone-throwing incident involving not Wade Robson but Brett Barnes and Jordie Chandler. Brett, in this rendering, had pleaded with

Michael to stop throwing stones after he had seen that the targeted lion, named as Kimba, had started bleeding. The story appeared within several pages alleging neglectful, abusive and even cruel treatment of the animals at Neverland.[827] But the author had been heavily reliant on dubious witnesses. Principally, these were security guards Kassim Abdool, Ralph Chacon and Melanie Bagnall, all members of the "Neverland Five" who had unsuccessfully sued Michael for unfair dismissal. It will be recalled that Michael had counter-sued, winning damages against the five for acting with "fraud, oppression and malice" against him. Clearly, they had a motive to badmouth Michael. It may be no coincidence that the worst allegations – those of deliberate cruelty – originated with Abdool. In the previous chapter we saw that he had been a witness in the "prior bad acts" phase of the trial when Mesereau had drastically undermined his credibility.

I expressed the view that Abdool had, in effect, over-egged the pudding with his "Vaseline" yarn. A similar tendency seems to have been at work when he told his lion-abuse story to Gutierrez. In his version, Michael told the boys to go and get fireworks from the house. They then threw firecrackers and fired rockets at Kimba. Fearful that the roof of the cage would catch fire, Abdool advised the fire department by radio to be prepared in case something happened.

If true, this could hardly be more appalling. But is it? It turns out yet another security guard has gone on the record: Robert Wegner. Wegner was never sacked or sued by Michael, whose service he left in December 1993 after an accident left him wheelchair-bound. In a book on his three years working for Michael, Wegner wrote:

> We were getting complaints that someone was throwing rocks at the lion. We were starting to hear the lion roaring at different times of the day. His cage was approximately 500 yards from the main house. We put on special patrols that would check the lion's cage at increased intervals to try and determine who was at fault. We got a report back that someone had seen Michael throwing medium size rocks at the lion. He liked to hear the lion roar. Naturally after that our special patrol was terminated.[828]

Wegner's account, with its "medium size rocks" and suggestion that stone throwing was becoming almost routine, is itself damning. But it may be significant that there is absolutely no mention of fireworks or calls to the fire department, something which, if true, he would surely at least have heard about and remarked upon even if he had not been on duty at the time of that particular incident.

Brett Barnes, whom we also met in earlier chapters, is a year older than Wade. He said he had been a five-year-old when he met Michael Jackson. Also Australian, Brett first encountered the star during a tour by the singer to his country. He said Jackson brought him and his family to California in 1991 when he was nine. In the years to follow, Barnes travelled the world with Jackson, often sleeping in his bed in hotel rooms and at the singer's Neverland ranch. He, too, said Michael never sexually molested him. "I can tell you...if he had I wouldn't be here right now," said Brett, who told the court he left his job as a roulette dealer in Melbourne to testify for Jackson.

Under cross-examination, Brett was vague on significant details, such as the duration of his visits to Neverland and whether or not these had been in his summer vacation. It would be "purely speculation," he said at one point, as though he were talking about some other person than himself, a complete stranger even. According to Roger Friedman, "Barnes presented himself as not the hottest shrimp on the barbie, especially when he revealed that he, his family and Robson and his family were all staying at Neverland during the trial."[829] It confirmed what the prosecution had tried to suggest with a number of questions, namely that both Robson and Barnes and their families had long been in Jackson's pocket, with the implication they might well say anything to keep on the right side of him.

It was a theme that played even more strongly when family members testified, especially the mothers, Joy Robson and Marie Lisbeth Barnes. Joy echoed Janet Arvizo in saying Michael was "like a member of my family" – but unlike the accuser's mother she insisted she never saw anything inappropriate or suspicious when Michael and Wade slept together. "I've known Michael a long time," she said. "I know him very well. I've spent many hours talking to him... I trust him with my children."

Under aggressive prosecution questioning, Joy admitted Michael had a habit of selecting favourites among his young visitors, and that her own son had been among these "special friends" from just eight years old. She said Michael would call all his favourites cousins, because "he didn't want them to be jealous of each other."

Joy was critical of Jordie Chandler's mother, whom she had encountered at Jackson's ranch. "My impression of June Chandler is she wanted to be mistress of Neverland," she said. "She would order the staff around like she owned it. My impression of June Chandler is she was a gold-digger." That drew audible gasps and murmurings around the courtroom. Some might have felt it was the pot calling the kettle black. Under cross-examination, Sneddon asked if Joy was jealous of the woman "because she replaced you."

"Absolutely not," she replied, also bristling at prosecution suggestions that she had wanted Jackson to propel her son's ambitions to become a professional dancer. But she admitted Jackson had assisted her family financially, organised a recording deal for Wade and helped legalise their situation in the United States. Legal analysts said the entertainer's significant support for the family would inevitably cast some doubts on their denials of any molestation. "There was a quid pro quo," said Jim Moret, a lawyer following the trial.

June's daughter, Chantal Robson, testified that she slept in Jackson's room with her brother four times as a child. She said she saw Michael hug children and kiss them on the cheek, but she never saw anything of a sexual nature.

Prosecutor Gordon Auchincloss was mercilessly personal with this witness. Pressing her about her decision to sleep in the same bed with the then 35-year-old Jackson when she was ten, he asked her if she slept with any other older men as a girl. Only her father, she said, with perhaps unfortunate ambiguity. She said she trusted Jackson totally, though she conceded she would "have to re-evaluate that" if she learned that he were plying a boy with alcohol and pornography.

Brett's mother, Marie Lisbeth, added to the ever-growing picture of mothers around Jackson who struck trial followers as overly star-struck, trusting and uncritically devoted to their idol and benefactor. She testified that she once wrote a letter to Jackson saying she would kill herself if she had upset him by an outburst she had in his presence.

But it was her daughter, Karlee, who would make a much bigger impression on the court. What she would reveal would be as significant as anything heard in the entire trial – and unlike the sensational allegations of oral sex in the shower room, the truth of her big disclosure would not be challenged. Her brother Brett had admitted sleeping with Michael – he and Wade had both done so on TV years before, back in 1993, when they went out to bat for their hero in the midst of his first great boy scandal. What we had never until now heard was the epic extent of those "sleepovers". Karlee told the court she estimated her then-ten-year-old brother shared a bed with Michael for a total of a full year during concert tours, and slept with him for eighty or ninety additional nights at Neverland.

"Didn't that ever seem odd to you?" prosecutor Gordon Auchincloss asked.

"No, not in the least," she declared unapologetically, "My brother wanted it".

She insisted she had no reason to believe anything illegal happened, but with that particular turn of phrase she might as well have said right out, "My brother wanted sex" – and it could be that is what she would have said, but for the fact that she was there to get Michael out of trouble, not drop him in it. The fact that Brett "wanted it", whatever "it" was, found further evidence in the young man's own testimony (allowing for his "speculative" memory) that he was no less than nineteen on the final occasion when he shared Michael's bed – positively geriatric in terms of Michael's preferences. One feels by this time the star may have been charitably doing Brett a favour.

Auchincloss put to Karlee that she was blinded by Michael's wealth and fame.

"You are positively thrilled to be friends with Michael Jackson," he said. "You seem to be almost giddy about it."

"I love him with all my heart," she said. It was hardly a denial.

Following the testimony of the Robson and Barnes families, Roger Friedman raised an interesting point about what we might call "Jackson moms". He noted that mothers regularly took their children out of school for months on end so they could spend time with Jackson on tour or at Neverland, but this had not been mentioned in their testimonies. "You wonder as you listen to these parents, what were they thinking?" he wrote. "And what did their children do all that time at Neverland? The steady refrain is: play video games, watch TV, stay up late, go on the carnival rides, visit the zoo... What no one has said at all yet: Michael read to us, or we learned about history, or nature or the stars. Not one Neverland visitor has mentioned a book as of yet, except for a collection of pornography."[830]

Friedman has a short memory: during Jason Francia's testimony it emerged that Michael had encouraged him to read, and rewarded him for each new book he managed to finish. But the gossip columnist had a point: Neverland was Liberty Hall, no doubt about that – or Pinocchio's Pleasure Island, as one witness put it. It was certainly no cramming college. For once, Michael's own difficult childhood gives him a pretty good excuse: all work and no play in his case made not a dull boy but a very troubled one. Some of his "special friends" at Neverland needed a break, too, especially from ambitious and sometimes over-controlling parents such as Evan Chandler and Kit Culkin, little Mac's father: a bit of freedom and wildness was not going to do them any harm and might actually have been beneficial.[831]

Friedman described Brett Barnes as unemployed, with no college background. Unfortunately, not everyone is hugely talented: wasn't it Friedman himself who witheringly dismissed poor Brett as "not the hottest shrimp on the barbie"? The remark was also unfair in deliberately ignoring the fact that Brett was only unemployed because he had given up his job as a croupier to attend the trial. As for Wade Robson, he was by now a rising star. Had this nothing to do with Michael's inspiration and encouragement?

However unjust Friedman's response had been, his reaction to the Robson and Barnes family witnesses reflected widespread unease with the pattern disclosed, of star-struck parents all but throwing their boys into Michael's bed, unconcerned (in the general estimation) for either their moral welfare or their orderly upbringing. To many people they just seemed plain irresponsible and, more importantly, none too credible in their denials of sexual abuse. Officially defence witnesses, they had ended up scoring points for the prosecution. By now, in a curiously consistent inversion of the usual pattern in a criminal trial, all the key witnesses for the prosecution had weakened the case Sneddon laid out in his opening speech, and all the defence witnesses so far had unwittingly helped revive it. If the pattern continued, Jackson could be in as much trouble by the end of the trial as at the beginning.

His next witnesses broke this pattern to a modest degree but by no stretch of the imagination were they key players. These were a number of Jackson's staff called on mainly to rebut evidence of both "prior bad acts" and conspiracy. Their task was a yawn-making one of saying things did *not* happen: they did *not* see improper behaviour with boys; the Arvizo family had *not* been kidnapped. As a bored reporter from the *Santa Barbara Independent* put it, "Proving a negative – or specifically, getting people to say that Jackson did nothing – is about as exciting as watching water boil, without the boiling part."[832]

The only one of any interest was ranch manager Joe Marcus. Testifying that the Arvizo family seemed "excited" to be at Neverland and had no complaints, he added that the boys, Gavin and Star, were "rambunctious and destructive" getting into trouble, crashing golf carts and trying to drive ranch vehicles. So far so good for Michael, but Marcus was forced to admit lying to police by telling them the singer never slept with children.

Even worse, he got himself tangled up in the gender issue:

"Mr. Jackson tends to form special bonds with some of these boys, true?" Auchincloss asked.

"Not just boys, but yes, I have seen bonds with children," Marcus said.

Prompted to name girls with whom Jackson had been close, Marcus appeared to struggle before naming Karlee Barnes and Marie Nicole Cascio, both sisters of boys who were "special friends". Asked whether Jackson had close female friends apart from his two wives, the witness again faltered before naming Elizabeth Taylor and Liza Minnelli.

"So, we're up to two?" said a sarcastic prosecutor.

The figure for boys was rather more impressive. Questioned over boys who had a "special bond" or friendship with Michael, Marcus admitted that all these boys fell into that category: Aldo Cascio, Brett Barnes, Jason Francia, Wade Robson, Jordie Chandler, Macaulay Culkin, Gavin Arvizo, Shane Brando (grandson of Marlon) and Omer Bhatti.

Five staff witnesses strutted, or rather struggled, their modest stuff while in the background another struggle was under way to get a more impressive figure onto the stand, the eagerly anticipated Macaulay Culkin. As one of Michael's former "special friends", he should logically have appeared in the same group of witnesses as the Robson and Barnes families but, with the timing of a true star, Little Mac (still not so big physically, even into his twenties) kept 'em waiting. After seemingly endless fanfares proclaiming his imminent arrival, the most celebrated child performer since Shirley Temple was in town, in court, and seriously in business.

Dressed in a black pinstriped suit and an open-necked shirt, the *Home Alone* star, now twenty four, soon showed he could perform confidently on this unfamiliar set, where a single fluffed or hesitant line might easily wreck the show. The allegations that Michael Jackson had molested him were "absolutely ridiculous", he declared, and he had never witnessed any improper behaviour by Jackson with anyone. He testified he had formed a bond with the entertainer in the early 1990s when the *Home Alone* movies made him rich and famous by the age of ten. Describing how he met the singer, he said, "He kind of called me up out of the blue at about the time of ...*Home Alone*."

Jackson, who started his own career at the age of five, understood the pressures of fame at a young age, Culkin said. "We had a really close relationship. We kind of understood each other," he told the jury, describing the fun of water-balloon fights and visiting toy stores after hours. Culkin, the godfather of two of Jackson's three children, said, "We're a part of a unique group of people...He'd been through that before, so he understood what it was like to be put in that position I was in, to be thrust into it...Anyone who was a child performer, we keep an eye out for each other."

That was the easy part. Sleeping with Jackson would take a little more explaining. He said he had occasionally shared a bed with Jackson during numerous visits to Neverland, but it was never planned: "I fell asleep basically everywhere on that ranch. I would basically flop down anywhere." When prosecutor Ron Zonen brought up the sexually explicit magazines that were found at Neverland, Culkin calmly pointed out, "Overall he's still a human being ... I don't find it inappropriate," He added that by the age of twelve he was keeping a copy of *Playboy* under his own bed. It was a reminder to the jury that Jackson is hardly the only guy in the world with "adult" material in his house. He also brushed off many attempts to make the fact that he "slept with" Jackson sound as though he had been molested. When Zonen suggested Culkin could have been molested by Jackson while he slept, the actor derisively replied: "I think I would have realized that."

His father, Kit Culkin, himself a former actor, had walked in at least once and found them in bed together, he said.[833] Referring to his parents, Mac said: "They never really thought it an issue. I knew they knew I was in that room. Sometimes my father would wake us up. He didn't really seem to have a problem with it from what I remember." He said neither of his parents had ever discussed if it was appropriate for him to be sleeping with a man of thirty five. He said the habit stopped when he was about fourteen. "You get older, you start enjoying your privacy," added the actor, who said he always slept fully clothed until he was seventeen. He corrected himself after referring to his "relationship" with Jackson – changing it to "friendship".

Despite this possibly Freudian slip, most commentators were impressed by a calm and convincing performance. Jackson junkie Roger Friedman gave a rave review: "Macaulay Culkin did more for Michael Jackson's defence in his child molestation trial yesterday than all the super-powered defence lawyers money could buy," he said. "He simply explained who Jackson is to a beleaguered, sceptical jury." By the end, Friedman felt, Culkin's hour or so on the stand "did a lot to erase the icky feelings associated with last week's Jackson defenders – Brett Barnes, Wade Robson and their respective mothers".[834]

Dan Glaister, of the *Guardian*, was harder to impress. He felt the prosecutors had scored points "in portraying a similar process of grooming that they allege Mr Jackson carried out with the boy in the current case".[835]

The jury may well have agreed with him, but in terms of generating "reasonable doubt" that Michael's interest in boys was necessarily sexual, Little Mac's rock solid testimony had undoubtedly scored a big, big triumph.

With such an unequivocal success in the bag, it may have been at this point that a definite decision was made not to put Michael on the witness stand. With the prosecution's conspiracy case already in ruins, and huge doubt cast over the sexual allegations, there was little to be gained and much to be lost by allowing the star to face tough questioning. He had been in enough trouble fielding embarrassing questions from Martin Bashir, even though the interviewer had needed to tread carefully in order to keep his subject talking. Tom Sneddon would have no such problem. He or his razor sharp fellow prosecutor Ron Zonen could be as fierce and persistent in their cross-examination as they wished. If Michael were to try getting away with his usual bland protestations of innocence, or bare-faced, obvious lies, he could easily come as badly unstuck as Janet Arvizo. So why bother? In an English court these days it would be a very different matter. The judge would be able to advise the jury that if a defendant was unwilling to go into the witness box, where he would have the opportunity to provide his own innocent explanation of events, they would be entitled to draw an adverse conclusion.[836] But this was California, where highly contentious evidence was allowed on "prior bad acts" but at least the important principle of the defendant's right to silence was respected.[837]

Consistent with a decision not to put Michael up for interrogation, the defence at this point in the trial decided to show the jury a video of out-takes from the Bashir documentary. This would allow jurors to listen at length to Michael talking about his feelings, views and behaviour without him having to take the stand or be cross-examined. These out-takes had been edited into a tape over two hours long taken by Michael's own videographer Hamid Moslehi. This included material not seen either on the Bashir programme or on the riposte later put out by the Fox Channel and hosted by Maury Povich (though this riposte included some of Moslehi's footage).

The footage portrayed a vulnerable, more compassionate man than Bashir's documentary had conveyed. "I would slit my wrists if I were to hurt children," he said. Of his charity work with children, Jackson said his reward had been "God's smile of approval" and the knowledge that he had brought some happiness into the lives of the disadvantaged. "Mother Teresa's not here, Lady Di is not here, Audrey Hepburn is not here... There is no voice for the voiceless," he said, portraying himself as an advocate for children around the world.

Part of this "soft" presentation showed Jackson talking about a bizarre fantasy of one day throwing a celebrity animal party for his beloved chimp, Bubbles. When Bashir asked how Bubbles was doing, Michael in all apparent seriousness said he had thought about giving his retired pet a party with guests such as Lassie, Benji and simian "Tarzan" sidekick Cheetah. Talking about chimps, he said, "They love snacks. They're very intelligent. Bubbles helps me clean up my room. He cleans the bathroom. He dusts."

It was all a long, long way from Gavin Arvizo's allegations, and that was the point. The video enabled the defence to explain Jackson's multitude of eccentricities in a sympathetic way. Said Roger Friedman: "Even though the Bashir outtakes were loopy, they will probably help more than hurt Jackson with the jury. He comes across as lonely, depressed and sympathetic."[838]

In keeping with this image of Michael as the innocent eccentric, two of the singer's former lawyers were next up in his defence, portraying him as a man more sinned against than sinning. David LeGrand, a corporate lawyer who worked for Jackson for about three months in early 2003, said he was so suspicious three of Jackson's close aides were trying to defraud the star that he hired a private detective to investigate them. He also had "grave concerns" about the singer's young accuser and his family and ordered them to be kept under surveillance because he suspected they were interested in scamming Michael.

Mark Geragos, the celebrity lawyer who defended actress Winona Ryder against shoplifting charges, greeted Jackson warmly as he came into court and hugged the performer as he left. He, too, was concerned about the Arvizos, saying "I thought they were going to shake him down". He insisted his client "was almost childlike in his love for kids". He said: "I didn't see anyone doing anything nefarious or criminal. I saw someone who was ripe as a target." He even felt that if anyone spent the night in Michael's room, "it was unconditional love". Not bad for a lawyer who had been sacked by Jackson.

Having easily popped the conspiracy case bubble and cast considerable doubt on the sexual allegations, what else could Michael's defence reasonably hope to achieve? The two lawyers had propped up their former client by attacking his aides and discrediting the Arvizo family; so far as the Arvizos were concerned it was a pattern that would continue to the very last defence witness.

A clutch of Michael's staff and a young cousin of his contributed a chorus of badmouthing against the Arvizo boys, Gavin and Star. Cleaner Maria Gomez said that while cleaning a guest room shared by Star and his sister Davellin she found a backpack full of pornographic magazines, which she assumed belonged to the boy. Star had testified he had never seen pornography until Jackson showed it to him. Security guard Shane Meredith said he caught the boys in the wine cellar laughing and giggling, with an open, half-empty "bottle of alcohol". Young assistant chef Angel Vivanco said Star once demanded a milkshake spiked with liquor, and threatened to get him fired if he did not make it – testimony that seems all the more remarkable when we learn that Angel and Davellin had struck up a romance during the family's "captivity" at Neverland. These witnesses all dented prosecution claims that Jackson exposed the boys to alcohol and adult materials by showing that they managed to get hold of such things on their own.

Safety officer Violet Silva added to the picture of the boys running wild and out of parental control. She described seeing the pair of them driving recklessly around the estate in golf carts, at one point crashing into a fountain. They would drop litter and generally behaved in a "pretty destructive" manner. Not exactly the most serious indictment since the Nazis were tried for war crimes. In Britain it might be worth an ASBO (anti-social behaviour order). But it was enough to shift the focus from Michael's behaviour to that of the Arvizos.

The star turn, though, in keeping with his pedigree, was Michael's twelve-year-old cousin Rijo Valdez Jackson, who lived in Lompoc, very close to Neverland. A striking figure with a ponytail almost down to his waist, he wore a grey suit and a pink tie to court. He was "a beautiful child" in Diane Dimond's estimation. Quietly spoken, often only nodding a yes, or shaking a no, he would nonetheless make quite an impact, depicting the Arvizo brothers as bad boys who stole wine, pilfered money from Neverland staff and masturbated while watching TV porn. He said that in 2003 he was with the brothers in a guest unit when they turned the TV to a channel showing naked women. They began masturbating and suggested he do the same. Rijo said he declined and instead went to Michael Jackson's room and told him what the boys were watching on TV.

"He didn't believe it," Rijo said. Under cross-examination he said he was scared to tell Michael about the masturbation.

He said he spent that night in bed with his cousin, admitting that was something he often did. Yet another boy on Michael's long list!

Rijo also testified he saw the boys steal wine, go through drawers in the house, and take money that belonged to a chef and another employee. According to Rijo, the wine incident occurred when an employee brought a bottle to the downstairs area of Jackson's bedroom suite while the singer was in the bathroom. He said the boys took it upstairs and the next time he saw it the cork was removed and some of the wine was gone. Rijo's sixteen-year-old sister, Simone, also claimed she saw the boys steal wine. Their grandmother, Michelle Jackson, testified briefly on the conspiracy side of the case.

How reliable was Rijo's testimony? He admitted under cross-examination that he did not know if Gavin and Star meant to steal or simply borrow some plastic crystals and a deck of cards that he saw them take from the ranch manager's office. As for the TV porn episode, Rijo's "butter wouldn't melt in my mouth" testimony had seemed suspect to some. He had said, "I saw them go to the TV, turn to a channel that had naked girls, and they did nasty stuff," a babyish turn of phrase implying that in his own childish innocence he had never been sullied by such things. When asked to describe what sort of "nasty stuff" he had seen, he said "jacking off" – a rather more earthy expression, suggesting the subject was familiar enough to him, verbally at least.

A curious footnote to the testimony of Rijo, his sister and his grandmother, is that by now there was a neat balance between Jacksons on the defence side and those for the prosecution. Rijo, Simone and Michelle Jackson had all been defence witnesses; Major Jay Jackson, his wife Janet (Arvizo) Jackson and Deborah (Rowe) Jackson had all appeared for the other side. Michael Jackson stayed firmly in the dock, but Debbie's role as the secret weapon of the defence had decisively tipped the balance of the Jackson witnesses in his favour.

Sandwiched between the staff and Jackson family witnesses was professional testimony of a rather different kind by two social workers, officers of the Los Angeles Department of Children and Family Services. These two, Irene Peters and Karen Walker, had interviewed Janet Arvizo and her three children on 20 February, 2003, right in the midst of Michael's post-Bashir public relations crisis and the so-called kidnapping saga. The interview, as explained in Chapter Fourteen, was the result of a call to their office's hotline from a complainant who thought Jackson's behaviour towards the Arvizo boys should be looked into in the light of the Bashir programme.

This was first revealed in a leaked memo about an investigation by the

Los Angeles Police Department and child welfare officials. It may be recalled that this probe had rejected the allegations as "unfounded", and that this put Tom Sneddon's nose out of joint. He had angrily dismissed the investigation as a mere interview. Much was at stake for the social workers, therefore, when they went in to bat for Michael. They had their professional judgment to defend and the honour of their department.

The brunt of this task fell to Irene Peters, who in Roger Friedman's words "toughed it out through gruelling…questioning". She stuck to her guns. She determined that there had been no abuse of any kind of the three Arvizo children. As of 20 February, 2003, they were in good shape. Their only complaint, Peters said, was that the Bashir documentary had been put out with their input but without their signed permission. Peters managed to get through her testimony, said Friedman, "like a champ, never once letting… Sneddon bait her".[839]

When Sneddon implied that despite three decades' experience, Peters was no expert on sexual abuse, she countered that she was not a therapist and had never claimed to be one. She simply knew what the signs of sexual abuse of children were, and were not. "There are indications," Peters said, such as "…if they're withdrawn or reluctant. Gavin appeared very open, eager to talk. He didn't seem uncomfortable. My observation at the time was he showed no indication of sexual abuse."

That was exactly right, though Peters probably did not know it. Gavin's demeanour was an indication he had not been sexually *abused*. He showed no sign of distress or a troubled mind. Whether he had been a willing, enthusiastic participant in non-abusive sexual intimacy with Michael was entirely another matter. The fact that the law under which Michael was charged makes no such distinction gave him an unseen advantage in this case. Had he been charged under something more like a "statutory rape" provision, in which the consent of the younger party is acknowledged, and if Peters had been allowed to consider the possibility of consensual activity between the pair, she would have found she lacked any firm basis for exonerating Michael other than the boy's flat denial – though if the law were based on common sense that should have been good enough.

Soundly based or not, the social workers' testimony had further strengthened Jackson's defence, which was now almost complete. The final plank in the defence platform would be to further discredit the Arvizo family by presenting witnesses who would show a pattern of behaviour on their part. The defence claim was that the family were lining up their ducks for multi-million dollar damages in a civil case against Jackson after a guilty verdict in the criminal one: they were scam-artists interested only in money. The aim was to demonstrate this in a final flourish, bringing on a clutch of big-name witnesses to do so. These would be other celebrities the Arvizos had tried to milk, just as they had Michael. What the defence would be showing, in effect, was the Arvizo family's "prior bad acts". This would not be 1108 evidence because the Arvizos were not on trial – but the defence would do everything they could to make it seem that way.

One of the biggest names, wisecracking TV chat show host Larry King, of CNN's top-rated *Larry King Live*, proved to be a damp squib. He made it as far as the courtroom, but the judge ruled out his testimony as irrelevant. Tom Mesereau and his team had better luck with fellow host Jay Leno, of NBC's *The Tonight Show*, who said he became suspicious of Gavin's effusive and improbable claims to being a big fan of his: "I'm a comedian in my mid-fifties. I'm not Batman," he said. He was referring to messages left by Gavin on his answering machine in 2000 when the boy was suffering from cancer; Leno thought they seemed scripted.

Unfortunately for Michael, this testimony was rather thin gruel compared to the negative impact Leno had on his image outside the courtroom, an impact that almost certainly filtered through to the jury. Michael had long been the butt of Leno's on-air jokes, and the comedian was not about to miss a new opportunity for laughs at the Gloved One's expense. "I was called by the defence. Apparently they've never seen this programme," he quipped, ahead of his testimony. Referring to a heat wave then gripping California, Leno said he had been "sweating like a Cub Scout at Neverland". Back in the Burbank, California, studio only hours after his court appearance, he came out with another gem: "Well, after, what, twelve weeks of trial, Michael Jackson's attorneys – they have finally admitted that Michael slept with children but it was about love, not sex. It just goes to prove that line works for all guys," Leno said.[840]

Jay Leno led the pack among American gag-meisters, but even Britain's staid BBC Radio 4 could not entirely resist the temptation to join in. Ned Sherrin, presenter of *Loose Ends*, introduced the programme with the news that Michael Jackson had "blown millions" in the last ten years. He reported a spokesman for Jackson saying, "it shouldn't be a problem as long as they don't all want to testify".[841]

If Jackson's two TV hosts had failed to hack it for him, one of their famous guests would make up the deficiency in fine style along with his equally impressive ex-fiancée. Film star and stand-up comic Chris Tucker had appeared on both King's show and Leno's, following success in his role as an abrasive, wise-cracking detective in the martial arts action comedy movie *Rush Hour*. His former girlfriend, and the mother of his six-year-old son, was "beautiful, articulate" casting assistant Azja Pryor.

The friendship between the pair and the Arvizos began when Tucker met the family at the Laugh Factory comedy club. The three children and their father, David, got closer to the couple when Gavin was diagnosed with cancer. Pryor, testifying first, said she quickly came to the family's aid, writing them a cheque for $600 for Christmas presents in 2001. But soon David Arvizo was usurped by his wife in the relationship with Pryor and Tucker. Until then, Pryor had seen David sleeping by his son's side in the hospital, never eating or leaving him alone. There was no sign of the mother. But when the boy's health improved, Janet Arvizo suddenly appeared on the scene. Her husband, whom she later divorced, had been painted by Sneddon as abusive and unfeeling. This new evidence suddenly cast Janet as the villain of the piece in her own right, as a callous opportunist. Janet claimed in the JC Penney case that store security guards had broken her son's arm. But she told Pryor the injury happened during a softball game – because the boy's mitt was worn out. Pryor immediately took the hint and bought him a new one.

Chris Tucker had met Michael Jackson through Gavin, and the two became good friends – Tucker stayed for lengthy periods at Neverland in 2001 and 2002. The final defence witness to take the stand, he said he had warned Michael about Janet Arvizo before the charges were brought.

He said he had befriended Gavin after meeting him in 2000 at a time when the boy was battling cancer. But he said he became concerned about the mother and about the boy's own wheedling, "cunning" ways. Relating an incident at Laugh Factory comedy club where he had helped in a fund raiser for Gavin, Tucker said the boy approached him and said the event had not raised enough money. "He was just real sad looking. He said they didn't raise any money and they really needed some money." Tucker added that he subsequently wired him $1,500. "He was really smart and he was cunning, but at the time I always overlooked it," Tucker said of the boy. "He was always saying stuff like, Chris, let me have this, let me have that. Come on, I'm not feeling good."

The defence rested at the end of Tucker's testimony after only three weeks, compared to ten weeks spent by the prosecution building its case.

Jackson's main defence strategist, Tom Mesereau, could legitimately have taken considerably longer by putting Michael on the stand but that, as we have seen, would probably have been unwise. Less legitimately, he could have tried to put up a parade of celebrity witnesses, but that would have run the risk of them humiliatingly being ruled irrelevant by Judge Melville, who showed from the start he would be running a tight ship. In any case, the jury had already been chained to their seats for an eternity: much as stars love to keep their audience waiting, this would have been ridiculous. In truth, the prosecution's case up to this point had been so weak that Mesereau did not need equal time, or anything like it.

That also explains why the prosecution decided their ten weeks had not been enough. For now, instead of proceeding directly to his closing speech, Tom Sneddon announced for the prosecution that he would be calling further witnesses in order to rebut evidence given in defence. A well established tactic in the United States, this procedure is practically unheard of in the English courts, where each side has one bite of the cherry and that's that. There are rare exceptions, but only where the line of defence in question could not reasonably have been anticipated. Sneddon, by contrast, piled in with a whole bunch of witnesses, in one instance to rebut a defence point which in general terms Mesereau had been megaphoning even before the start of the trial. Only two of these witnesses need detain us: Jesus Salas and Steve Robel, both of whom were brought back to the stand after giving evidence earlier in the case.

Salas, it will be recalled, had been a disaster for Sneddon first time round. Expected to say he had seen Jackson serve wine to boys in his bedroom, the Neverland manager actually testified Jackson had ordered soft drinks for them. Sneddon now recalled Salas not to rebut some obscure and devious defence point, but in some sense to get his own witness to self-rebut. Remarkably, he succeeded. Salas did not recant his evidence, but he did decant Jackson's alleged excessive boozing into the public arena. He testified that he had seen Jackson "intoxicated" on a number of occasions. That on its own would not have been so bad. The real killer was that he said he saw Jackson drunk in front of his own children, Prince, Paris and Blanket, no fewer than three times. Michael had been so far gone, Salas, said, that he thought the children were unsafe.

This point was such a killer to Michael's reputation, in fact, that after the trial was over one of his apologists airbrushed it out of the record, in a version of events endorsed by none other than his lawyer Tom Mesereau.

We saw in the previous chapter that Aphrodite Jones, in her post-trial book, falsely minimised Jason Francia's allegations to "tickling" over his shorts. Her neat performance in distorting Francia's evidence is outdone by the spin she put on Salas's. This time she would give an account of his testimony that would take the reader 180° in a misleading direction, making things look very good for Michael. She would then commend the witness for his honesty!

Specifically, she wrote: "In the twenty years that he served as Jackson's chief domestic worker, running Michael's home, Jesus Salas said that he had not witnessed the entertainer drinking alcohol in front of children – ever." True. Salas said he never saw Michael *drink* in front of children. But he also said he saw Michael *drunk* in front of his own kids. Jones makes no mention of this. After utterly misrepresenting the witness in this way, she said of Salas: "…the man was very sincere in his responses. He was being honest about things, as he recalled them…Jesus Salas was a credible witness". It is a pity she did not add, "and his honesty greatly exceeds my own."[842]

Is this unfair? Could Jones simply have made an honest mistake? I will not say it is impossible but the two "mistakes" described, in relation to key evidence by Francia and Salas, appear artfully constructed to deceive. It should also be understood that Jones had been a commentator for Fox News, "saying many things against Jackson" in "slanted news coverage" (her own confessional words) until the acquittal, after which she decided he might actually be innocent. She attended the trial; "media folks" were her "buddies", part of her "inner circle".[843] Even if she had personally misheard, or misconstrued the vital evidence, it is inconceivable that she missed the version all her colleagues were chewing over in the break periods and lunch intervals and, more significantly, what they published in their reports. While the news media frequently make errors, the testimony given by both Francia and Salas was accurately and widely reported in the main news accounts. Had she forgotten all that by the time she came to write up her book from her own perhaps faulty notes?

As for Mesereau endorsing her misleading account, it will be recalled that he wrote a foreword to her book. In it he wrote: "I have reviewed Ms Jones' book and commend her for her efforts. To anyone who wants to learn what happened in the Michael Jackson courtroom, this is the book to read." Readers may decide for themselves what this does for *his* credibility.[844]

Returning to what Salas said in court, he also testified that Jackson and Gavin Arvizo slept in the same bed 90% of the time and that the boy was present at Neverland between 7 February and 11 March 2003. So far, so good for Sneddon. Perhaps buoyed by this success, his next trick would be more ambitious. In the absence of any chance to tear Michael apart in the witness box, he tried to get the man's manhood presented as an exhibit!

Photographically, that is. What Sneddon wanted to bring in was the genitalia photographs from the 1993 molestation investigation of Jackson, which were still on file. Jordie Chandler, it will be recalled, had drawn a picture of Michael's penis and scrotum; prosecutors claimed it showed a blemish unique to Jackson's anatomy. Arguing for use of the pictures, Ron Zonen said the prosecution wanted to demonstrate to jurors that Jackson's relationships with boys were "not casual."

Judge Melville did not oblige, but Sneddon's team had better luck with another important ruling. The judge said prosecutors could play a videotape of a police interview with Gavin in July 2003, when the boy gave his first account to the authorities of Jackson's alleged sexual behaviour towards him. The prosecution said they wanted to counter a defence assertion that Gavin had been coached by his mother, and claimed the tape would show the boy had told a consistent story throughout. The defence position was that Gavin had been reluctantly goaded into fabricating the molestation claim by his mother in order to extort money from the pop icon. Judge Melville duly admitted the tape, in due course instructing the jury to watch it not for the truth of what Gavin was saying – they would have to go by what he had said under oath in court for that – but for his demeanour. In other words, did he seem like someone press-ganged into talking to the police, just going through the motions, or did he genuinely have his own complaint to make?

The tape was duly shown to the jury in conjunction with further evidence from Detective Sergeant Steve Robel, who had conducted the interview together with officer Paul Zelis, whom we met in Chapter Fifteen. The detectives' role in the interview was of some significance: rather than listening to Gavin in an objective way to see whether there was a valid case, it was as though they had made up their minds to get Jackson before they had heard a word. When defender Robert Sanger asked Robel in cross examination whether he had assumed the boy was a victim, the detective answered candidly that he had.

Incidentally, Robel played an unusually extended role in this case. Not only did he gently nurse Gavin through his interview, he also shepherded the boy and his siblings right through the trial: Davellin, Star and Gavin were house-guests of Steve Robel and his wife Nancy for the duration – no way were these young witnesses going to be lost to the prosecution. The psychological pressure on the kids to live up to their hosts' expectations must have been considerable. Gavin's testimony that he had begun to think about a career in law enforcement surely reflects the detective's influence.

Robel's role was small potatoes, though, compared to the dramatic sight and sound of Gavin on tape, which would suddenly wrench the case sharply back in favour of the prosecution after many weeks of little going right for Sneddon. Or at least, that was the general estimation reflected in the media, where the feeling seemed to be that Gavin had come across as a more sympathetic figure than he did in court, where his mixture of argumentative cockiness and bored indifference had not gone down well. He had seemed too tough and streetwise to be convincing as a badly hurt, innocent victim. On the interview tape, by contrast, he cut a very different figure, hesitant, clearly uncomfortable, often mumbling and avoiding eye contact. Wearing denim shorts and a blue shirt, he sat slumped in a chair. He occasionally smiled, scratched his arm and fumbled with a button on his shirt.

The interview had been conducted in the Santa Barbara County Sheriff's Department's Sexual Abuse Assault Response Team cottage in Santa Barbara on 6 July, 2003.

When asked by Detective Robel if Jackson had ever touched him in an inappropriate way, the young teen sat silently for some fifteen seconds before describing a night at Neverland that began with heavy drinking and ended with the singer masturbating him. "He put his hand in my pants," the boy said in a near whisper. "He started masturbating me. I told him I didn't want to do that. He kept saying he wants to teach me ... he said that it's OK, that there's nothing wrong with it, that it's natural."

Gavin said he slept in a bed with Jackson every night after the family returned from a trip to Florida with the superstar in February 2003, and that every night his younger brother was not in the bedroom, Jackson masturbated him. The recovering cancer patient said this happened four or five times in total, each time following bouts of drinking.

Legal observers pronounced the tape a devastating blow to Jackson. "Michael Jackson is right now at his greatest peril…throughout the entire trial," former San Francisco prosecutor Jim Hammer said. "In Tom Mesereau's worst nightmare he never wanted the trial to end like this, with that boy's voice ringing in the jury's ears." Several jurors appeared moved by the video. According to a Reuters report, "When the courtroom lights went on after it was shown, one female juror appeared to have red eyes and another was clutching a tissue."[845]

But Gavin had not broken down in tears in that interview, as might have been expected from a traumatised victim, and not every courtroom observer had been emotionally bowled over in judging the significance of that tape. Roger Friedman was among the sceptics. He pointed out that Gavin had seemed embarrassed, "but maybe more about selling out a friend than about being molested". He had seemed upset not over anything sexual but over Jackson having changed his phone numbers in the past so the boy could not reach him. After Gavin had finished telling his story, Friedman added, "one of the cops hands him a soft drink and a straw and his mood brightens immediately".[846]

In retrospect, it is easy to see how Gavin's hesitancy – that long, long pause before spilling the beans – might have convinced those who wanted to be convinced that that this was a child struggling to tell a harrowing story of sexual abuse for the first time. But, for those with eyes to see, there was a wealth of clues clearly pointing in another direction.

The most striking of these was that Gavin, at thirteen, told the detectives he had no idea what an erection was, or masturbation, and had not seen magazines like *Playboy* until they were introduced to him by Jackson. As Friedman wryly remarked, "This might be possible in a Merchant Ivory movie about a neurasthenic British lad, but hardly likely for a teen with battling parents in East Los Angeles." If Friedman had looked into his back files on the case he would also have been able to point out that this was the boy who admitted in a later police interview, in January 2004, that Jackson would "always, like, try to give me advice" about "the birds and the bees", but that Gavin knew more than Michael did!

In the interview the jury saw, the detectives questioned Gavin about his ideas of right and wrong. As examples of the latter, the boy mentioned staying up too late, fighting, breaking things and killing someone. But he did not mention sexual molestation. Was that not wrong? If Gavin had been sexually assaulted against his will, it would have been the first thing on his mind.

Such clues leave the strong suspicion that Gavin's hesitancy over telling his story had nothing whatever to do with injured innocence. We know that far from disliking Michael and being anxious to get away from Neverland, he had been crazy about the guy and bugged his family to get back there. Up to and including the police interview he had shown himself a reluctant witness. Was this was because of the supposed trauma of revealing sexual abuse? Or simply because he liked Michael and did not want to betray his friend? Does this possibility ring any bells? Jordie Chandler, maybe? He, too, found himself cornered into denouncing Michael. One might feel the only real difference is that in Jordie's case his father was the prime mover, pushing the kid behind the scenes; in Gavin's case it was his mother.

Once the prosecution had played the police video, it was widely assumed Mesereau would be forced to bring more evidence. He would have to do *something* to rebut that sensational rebuttal, so the jury would not start their discussions with "that boy's voice" ringing in their ears. But he did not. Instead, he stunned the court by resting his case once and for all. There would be no "surrebuttal", as the lawyers call it, and the judge was therefore able to tell the jury they would be hearing no more evidence in the case. Mesereau could have recalled Gavin and his mother to the stand in a bid to clarify the issues but decided the jury had already heard enough. It was a much criticised decision at the time but he would have no cause to regret it.

"At first blush, it looked like it would hurt us," Mesereau acknowledged in an interview with the *Los Angeles Times* when the trial was over.[847] But in his closing argument he was able to cite the tape as an example of the boy's changing story – a number of details given on oath in court were different from what he told the police. The point was not lost on the jurors, who viewed the tape with more detachment than the media, according to fellow defender Robert Sanger, in a different interview with the same paper.

So the evidence was over but there was still much work to be done before the jury could retire to consider their verdict. At the end of this long and complicated case the judge found himself obliged to spend an hour and a half going over ninety eight pages of instructions the jury would receive in written form (unusually), and he told them they would be hearing closing speeches of up to four hours each from the prosecution and the defence. Throughout it all, Michael Jackson sat impassively awaiting his fate.

Judge Melville told jurors they must make their decision without "pity for or prejudice toward" the defendant. There was also an instruction not to be swayed by public sympathy for him – an important factor given that some hundreds of fans were now rallying daily for colourful demonstrations outside the courtroom.

The judge listed the ten-count indictment against Jackson, including two counts of committing a lewd act on a minor as witnessed by the alleged victim and two counts of lewd acts on a minor as witnessed by his brother.

During testimony, Gavin described two molestation incidents and his brother Star said he twice saw Michael molesting Gavin while he was asleep. The indictment also alleged one count of an attempted lewd act (when Michael allegedly grabbed Gavin's hand with the apparent aim of getting the boy to masturbate him), one count of conspiracy involving child abduction, false imprisonment and extortion, and four counts of administering an intoxicating agent — alcohol — for the purpose of committing a felony, child molestation. The judge told the jurors they could also consider a "lesser charge" of "furnishing alcohol to a minor," a misdemeanour. In that case the jury would not have to relate the alcohol to the purpose of molestation.

By this stage the news reports were emphasising even more than usual the dire consequences for Jackson of a conviction on all ten counts. Typically, the phrase used was that he "faces more than twenty years in prison", tabloid-speak which slyly pandered to the sadism of its audience, misleadingly implying that the maximum term for each count would inevitably be imposed. In deciding the issues, the jury would have to consider the testimony of some fifty defence witnesses and ninety prosecution ones. The prosecution had taken up around ten weeks presenting their evidence, the defence three, without either side having gained a clear advantage, a fact that made the stakes extremely high for the lawyers' closing arguments.

It was a striking feature of Ron Zonen's performance for the prosecution that he was nearly two hours into his three-hour address to the jury before he even brought up child molestation. First, he was saddled with the unenviable task of defending the credibility of the Arvizo family, on which his entire case turned. This meant putting in a huge effort to shore up the badly undermined conspiracy allegations. Janet's wild tale about the family having been kidnapped was a disastrous burden for Zonen to carry, a monstrous albatross around his neck. Arguably, it would have been better to come clean with the jury and announce that the prosecution would be proceeding no further with the conspiracy count. A frank admission that Janet had been a hopelessly unreliable witness would have allowed Zonen to invest his time more credibly in the truth of her two sons' accounts.

But it was not to be, later leaving Tom Mesereau for the defence with an open goal: the credibility of the entire family, starting with the patently dishonest Janet. When it came to his turn to speak, he would tear into Zonen's claim that the boy's mother was not out for money, repeatedly returning to examples of how she had been so many times. He would cast her as a parasite who habitually lied and cheated to get by in life. "She'll say anything, absolutely anything," he said, reminding jurors that Janet said she escaped her "captivity" at Neverland three times, only to go back there twice.

Mesereau claimed the family had a history of making abuse allegations. He said Gavin once accused his mother of abusing him (the incident had been trivial but symbolically significant), his sister Davellin had accused her father of molesting her, and Janet had accused store security guards of beating and sexual assault. "These kids are being raised to make allegations," the defender said. "The biggest red flag in the case", he said was that Janet and her family went to lawyers months before seeing the police, indicating their interest in money rather than justice.

Zonen scoffed at Mesereau's portrayal of Janet as a criminal mastermind. "She's not the sophisticate he wants you to believe," Zonen said. "She can't string two consecutive sentences together that make sense." It was hardly the most ringing endorsement of his witness.

He was on much stronger ground when he at last felt free to go on the attack, turning to Michael Jackson's alleged pattern of predatory behaviour. He told the jury Jackson had a habit of going after susceptible boys, separating them from their parents and filling their days with candy, video games and other amusements. He followed the same "grooming process" with his accuser and the boy's brother, he said.

"At night they entered into the world of the forbidden. They went into Michael Jackson's room, which is a veritable fortress," Zonen said, adding that in that room the boys learned about human sexuality "from someone who is only too willing to be their teacher". The prosecutor referred to nights when both the boy and his brother stayed in Jackson's room and said the stage was set for molestation. "It began with discussions of masturbation and nudity. It began with simulating a sex act with a mannequin," Zonen said. He said Jackson carefully chose the kind of boys who were easiest to prey upon, especially those with fathers absent from their lives.

One highly significant but under-reported feature of the prosecution case is that Tom Sneddon and his team did not misrepresent the mutually affectionate nature of the bonds Michael had with his boys. There were no dark hints of coercion, except as regards the "softening up" effects of alcohol. Criticising one of Michael's security staff who had defended the propriety of the entertainer's friendship with Brett Barnes when the pair were on tour together and sharing a hotel room every night, Zonen said:

> That is not friendship. That is a relationship. Mr Jackson loved that child not as one loves a child, but as one loves a companion, an adult, a sexual relationship... You would be outraged if you were to find out there was somebody who lived in your neighbourhood who was taking young boys into his bedroom amidst a sea of pornography and alcohol. You'd be on the phone with the police in a second.

If we ignore, for the moment, the pornography and alcohol (of which there was no evidence in the Barnes case), we see that the jury is being invited to be outraged by love – both that of Michael for Brett, and Brett for Michael. Elsewhere, Zonen did not shy away from characterising Michael's relationship with Gavin as a mutual one. He mentioned having cross-examined defence expert witness Phillip Esplin about "the case of the consenting victim, the victim who's in a relationship with the offender".[848] His point was that in order to "get away with" molesting a child, an offender had to win the child's friendship and confidence. But in making that point he found it necessary to concede that the child might come to desire the relationship in all its aspects, including – as Zonen specifically mentioned – enjoyment of the sexual acts that were part of it. This was a rare and remarkable – even sensational – concession by authority to the existence of consent in mutually loving, sexually active paedophilic relationships. No wonder the mainstream news media turned a blind eye to it.

While Zonen had been forced for limited purposes to concede that Michael was no leap-out-of-the-bushes sex attacker, he was also adept at using language to make love seem dirty and disgusting. A classic example was his characterisation of the famous head-licking incident on the plane. Addressing the jury, he said: "You would no sooner lick the head of a thirteen-year-old boy than you would lick the bottom of their shoe, right?" From his position of authority, the prosecutor was in effect telling the jury what they ought to be feeling, implying there was something shameful, disgusting and repulsive to right-minded people in an affectionate act that was not even illegal. Some of the jurors might have blanched at the thought of loving intimacies with their own children being exposed to the censorious attention of this gentleman.

The nadir of Zonen's smear tactics came with his deployment of the pornography in the case. He projected on a large screen pages from books featuring adult homosexuality. Of one of them, he said, "This is a study of what two men are able to do with each other. The pictures are absolutely graphic. This is a publication you are not going to find on anyone's coffee table." He added, "Are you comfortable with a middle-aged man who possesses this book getting into bed with a thirteen-year-old boy?"

The prosecutor also showed again heterosexual adult material from Jackson's collection of magazines and said jurors should understand these were part of the scheme to get boys aroused. "These were not for him," he said. "These were for the boys."

Mesereau responded that Jackson had not been charged with possessing illegal pornography. Everything in his home was legal. No child pornography was found in Michael's home or computers (the books with some photographs of naked young boys were coffee table volumes), and prosecutors had used the adult magazines just to make the singer look bad. "They have dirtied him up because he's human. But they haven't proven their case because they can't," he said.

Visual material of another kind, videos, was a strong element in both the prosecution and defence presentations. Zonen showed a montage of images from the Bashir documentary, including a quote from the pop star: "I have slept in a bed with many children. I slept in a bed with all of them." People who saw that programme reacted with alarm, Zonen said, not least to a scene of Jackson holding hands with his accuser: "Their reaction is: Get that child out of there. Somebody take that child and get him away...And where are his parents?" The prosecutor also returned to the tape that had caused jaws to drop in court only days earlier, showing part of Gavin's police interview again. He told jurors they had witnessed "the worst seven minutes of this young man's life," and that no acting class could have taught the boy to imitate pain so convincingly. He may have been right about the pain, but why was Gavin suffering? Was it because he had been assaulted, or because he had been pushed by his mother into betraying a friend?

Mesereau showed the jury some of Hamid Moslehi's outtakes from the Bashir documentary, playing clips he felt were positive. Jackson was shown talking about seeing children as a reflection of God. "I love innocence," he said. "I'm a nut for innocence." At another point, he said he never had been "betrayed or deceived" by a child, adding, "It's adults who have let me down".

It was not the defender's strongest suit, but neither was it a mistake, He somehow had to bolster the image of Michael as a naïvely idealistic, eccentric artist, and having kept the star off the stand it was imperative to use material that might persuade at least a few jurors.

But he still had two other suits to play. One was the lack of any direct evidence in the case: no DNA samples or any other forensic evidence; and no witnesses to the alleged sexual assault on Gavin who were independent of the Arvizo family. He also pointed out that there had been no "pretext" phone call. He said that in molestation cases police may ask the alleged victim to phone the suspect, getting him or her to ask incriminating questions as police listen in. Gavin had in fact been asked to do this during a police interview but had refused. Why? Because, said Mesereau, Gavin knew if he did that, he would not get an incriminating statement, because nothing illegal had happened. An alternative explanation is that Gavin was a reluctant complainant, as we have seen from several indications. It was bad enough having to give a statement in a police station, well away from his famous friend. To betray that friend in a personal phone call, hearing his familiar voice yet fearful of saying something that would betray his own treachery, would have been emotionally just too much to endure.

Mesereau's other remaining suit seemed much stronger. He showed time-charts suggesting it was ridiculous to believe that in a period when Jackson was under international scrutiny he would choose to commit a sex crime.

But Zonen was able to trump this argument. The timing was not so crazy as first appeared, he said, or at least not after 20 February when Gavin had gone on tape in his interview with the child welfare authorities saying nothing untoward had happened. This must have given Michael confidence. But there was more (or less) to the psychology of the situation than that, said Zonen. Explaining further why Michael became sexually active at this time, he said:

> The answer simply is: Because he could...Because he had no restraints on his impulses...Because this child was in love with him. Because this child would do anything that he wanted him to do. Because this child was already in his bed and already sharing the intimacies of his affection...Because of porn and drink...Because Star had started leaving the room and was no longer there at that particular time. And his opportunity was there and the child was ripe.

Opportunity, in other words, made the thief. Had the jury been all male, rather than two thirds female, this argument might have been not just a trump card but the decisive ace of trumps. Why? Because men faced with imminent sexual temptation know how easily their own resistance can crumble, no matter how great the danger or dishonour of the situation. Women may *suspect* that guys are ruled by their dicks but plenty of guys *know* it.

But in the end it was Mesereau who held the aces. "Ladies and gentlemen," he said, "it only takes one lie under oath to throw this case out of court. You can't count the number of lies under oath by all of the Arvizo witnesses... They lie directly. They lie to your face. They lie under oath. They exaggerate. They give run-around answers to try to avoid the question. How many does it take to let you know this case is a fraud?"

In the closing stages of his presentation he returned to his strongest suit, the poor credibility of the Arvizo family and what it implied in terms of raising "reasonable doubt" – such doubt being all that was needed to prevent a valid conviction. That single phrase "reasonable doubt" would be hammered home time and again, driving nail after nail into the coffin of the prosecution case.

Not that this was at all obvious to observers at the time. When Judge Melville finally sent the jurors out to consider their verdict early in June, legal analysts and other media commentators were all agreed the case was too close to call. There was just no way of knowing what the jury had made of it all. Nor would that be revealed for what must have seemed an eternity to Michael Jackson.

His family had turned up in force for the last day. His parents, three sisters and three of his brothers, Randy, Jermaine and Tito, were all on hand as a sombre and gaunt Michael (reportedly down to ninety four pounds from an already slim 120 in November 2003 when he turned himself in to the authorities) began the long wait. More than 1,200 journalists and 300 fans had also descended on the court for the dramatic finale.

As hours, then days, slipped by with no indication that a decision was imminent, tension palpably built up outside the courtroom. After a fifth day of jury deliberations, heated exchanges began between Michael's fans, foes, and the media. Supporters clashed with several men who showed up, Bible and crucifix in hand, urging them to repent. One Jackson critic had a sign saying "Execute All Homosexual Paedophiles" – maybe he thought straight ones were OK. Another chanted "Queen of Pop." Meanwhile, fans hanged an effigy of Tom Sneddon from a tree and beat it with sticks.

Little was heard from the jury in these days except news in the first hours that they had sent a note to the judge, subject not revealed. After the verdicts it emerged that this has been a plea for an index to the copious evidence. The judge could not oblige, but he did send a court stenographer to the jury room to read out witness testimony to them. In another request, the jury asked for a clarification on "what child is referred to in count six", which alleged an attempted lewd act on a minor. Melville responded that all molestation allegations involved the same boy. It was astonishing they could still have been in doubt over such a fundamental point. Incongruously, loud, long laughter was heard from the jury room at the beginning of deliberations, which they may have intended as a sign to the world they were not in a hanging mood – unlike the Sneddon-baiters! And there was more merriment among the prosecution legal team, who celebrated with a night out together, reportedly in high spirits. Maybe they knew deep down it would be unwise to wait till the verdict before celebrating.

Finally, that verdict came, on the afternoon of Monday 13 June, 2005, after about thirty hours of deliberations over seven days. Not guilty on all counts. Jackson, and the lawyer lauded as "mesmerizing Mez", had pulled it off. Outside the court, the crowd erupted in cheers as each "not guilty" finding was read – no fewer than fourteen times in all, one for each of the ten felony counts and one for each of the four alternative misdemeanour counts relating to alcohol. A woman in the throng released one white dove each time an acquittal was read. While leaving the courthouse with his family, the triumphant King of Pop still looked shaken and grim, silent and unsmiling as supporters cheered him on. Notes from the jury to the judge, released later in response to a news media request, showed jurors had briefly been deadlocked on two of the misdemeanour charges of furnishing alcohol to a minor. They quickly broke that deadlock and agreed on an acquittal.

Jurors later gave a press conference, a deed which could have seen them all jailed for contempt of court following a trial in Britain – our jurors are strictly forbidden from discussing their deliberations publicly. At this and other media appearances, the Jackson jury were candid to a degree that must have stunned many in the UK and perhaps Michael, too, for it seemed to snatch victory from his hands.[849]

No sooner had the jury found him not guilty than several of their number began to backpeddle. One of them, Ray Hultman, told the Associated Press he was one of three people on the jury who voted to acquit only after the other nine persuaded them there was "reasonable doubt" specifically in the Arvizo case. He added that Jackson "probably has molested boys at some point". Referring to Jason Francia and Brett Barnes, he said he believed it was likely both boys had been molested. On the relationship with Brett, he said: "I can't believe that this man could sleep in the same bedroom for 365 straight days and not do something more than just watch television and eat popcorn. That does not make sense to me." He said he voted to acquit because he had doubts about Gavin Arvizo's credibility. The fact that his family had gone to lawyers before the police had been a factor, he said.[850]

Even jury foreman Paul Rodriguez, said on ABC's *Good Morning America* that Jackson may have molested other boys in the past. "It's possible," he said. Another juror on the same show, Eleanor Cook, said, "We had our suspicions, but we couldn't judge on that because it wasn't what we were there to do."

Doubtless mindful of what a close-run thing the trial had obviously been, Michael announced the big lifestyle concession he had always previously avoided, no matter what the pressure. His principal lawyer, Tom Mesereau, said on his behalf that Michael Jackson had learnt a lesson and would never sleep with young boys again. "He's not going to do that any more…He's not going to make himself vulnerable."

Whether Michael would keep this vow, and what the future might hold for him, were matters of intense media speculation: Would he emigrate, and if so where to? What would happen to Neverland? Could he shore up his shattered finances? What about a career comeback? Was it still possible, despite his tainted image?

Answers varied widely, but reaction to the acquittal itself saw something of a consensus: it was unwelcome. Predictably, the tabloid end of the market was more forthright: it stank. Michael got away with it thanks to smart lawyers and stupid jurors. His wealth, albeit depleted, had bought him out of trouble. A David Letterman joke reported in the *Sun* summed up the mood: "News just in: Saddam Hussein has requested his trial be moved to Santa Maria."[851]

Asked whether Michael really would alter his behaviour as Mesereau indicated, long-time Jackson watcher Maureen Orth said she had heard differently: as late as three weeks into the trial, she claimed, the man in the dock told one of his former aides he had no intention of changing his ways.[852]

At the posh end of the market, a writer for *Forbes* magazine ("for the world's business leaders") not surprisingly agreed on the importance of money and celebrity in securing a favourable verdict, providing some telling statistics to back the point. Columnist Dan Ackman demonstrated that in California acquittals after trial are rare events indeed: your average suspect without the money to invest in a top lawyer tends to accept a plea bargain, thus drastically cutting the number of cases that ever reach a jury. In 2002, the last year for which statistics were available, there were 236,471 felony charge dispositions and just 766 acquittals in the state – under 1% of all cases. There were also about 40,000 dismissals, where either the judge or the district attorney decided the case should be thrown out.

The overall conviction rate was about 83%. In Santa Barbara County, where Jackson was prosecuted, the district attorney wins even more consistently, about 87% of the time. In 2002, there were just three acquittals out of 2,407 felony cases. Ackman writes that assuming between 5% and 10% of the felony cases go to trial (with the rest resolved by plea bargain), the overall statewide post-trial acquittal rate is between 3% and 6%. In Santa Barbara County, the rate is between 1.3% and 2.6%. Those are the long odds Michael Jackson managed to beat. The figures are worthy of some attention not just to marvel at Michael's good fortune but also to emphasise that "justice" – if that is what he achieved – is far less readily available to most defendants.[853]

On a happier note, the *Daily Star* turned its attention to a post-trial Gavin Arvizo, who "looked relaxed yesterday as he chatted up two pretty classmates at his southern Californian school". An eyewitness is quoted as saying: "He showed no signs of being a boy who had just lost a child molestation case against perhaps the most famous pop star in the world. He was a real ladies' man and had the girls really cooing over him."[854]

The *Daily Star*'s improbably cheerful take found an interesting echo in a piece for the Canadian journal *Macleans* by maverick libertarian Barbara Amiel, well-known for her regular column in the UK's *Daily Telegraph*. Taking her courage in her hands, she dared to think the unthinkable, asking, "Where's the harm?" Her words make a fitting end to this chapter, and this book's review of Michael's trial:

> Is there really any doubt that he had children in his bed for his pleasure? And what was the damage to them? ...in the absence of violence, fear and physical coercion, in the total absence of penetration, what actual harm has he done? ... children have received millions for their moments in his bed. Before they were told it was a crime, they couldn't wait to get back to Neverland.[855]

CHAPTER EIGHTEEN

Never Again Land

If kids couldn't wait to get back to Neverland in its fun-packed heyday before the trial, in its aftermath Michael couldn't wait to get away. Within weeks he had abandoned the Ground Zero of his troubles and taken refuge in Bahrain with his family, under the patronage of Sheikh Abdullah bin Hamad al Khalifa. The significance of the move, and how long it would last, were inevitably the subject of intense speculation, as was Michael's future in music and generally.

Some of the earliest predictions were strikingly optimistic, even laughably so with the benefit of 20-20 hindsight. In Britain's staid *Daily Telegraph*, of all places, Neil McCormick wrote with the euphoric gusto of a relieved fan:

> Not guilty. I wonder at what point since the verdicts were read out did the pop tactician in Michael Jackson start thinking about those two words as a potential hookline with which to resurrect his incredible career. You can almost hear him screaming out the words in a breathless, hysterical falsetto, to swirling synths and a driving beat. Not guilty. Times ten. And if he is really daring, he could throw in a children's choir proclaiming his saintly victimhood.
>
> Jackson is among the greatest self-dramatists in the history of pop, and you can be sure that he is not going to let this moment pass unexploited. It represents not just his freedom, not merely his vindication by the courts, but

the possibility of that most American of dramatic scenarios: the comeback.[856]

For McCormick, the verdict looked like Michael's opportunity to reinvent himself by getting away from the freak show and back to the music. He almost made it seem easy. In a totally different and perhaps tongue-in-cheek way, so did Michael C Luckman, author of *Alien Rock: The Rock 'n' Roll Connection*, who claimed Michael was about to release a new album with a harder sound, portraying himself as a womanising hip-hop star. He reportedly said: "Soon you will see Jackson surrounded by beautiful women." Michael was pumping iron in Bahrain to make himself more macho and would be ditching his wigs and make-up. "Michael Jackson is headed to the stratosphere," he said. "Nothing can stop him now."[857]

Not since Iraqi regime spokesman "Comical Ali" proclaimed victory for Saddam Hussein even as US tanks rolled into Baghdad can there have been such a blast of baseless bombast. But Luckman was merely at the extreme end of widespread comeback talk. Roger Friedman, the most Jackson-focused of all gossip columnists, succumbed to the mood.[858] "Americans love a comeback," he wrote, "and in five years Jackson's child molestation scandal will be a distant blip on the radar" – but a year or so later he would be talking not about radar but the Geiger counter, with its rather more persistently alarming readings. All the signs after a couple of years were that in the music and showbiz worlds Michael was still regarded as highly radioactive.

But immediately after the trial even some big names in image management erred on the optimistic side. Brand consultant Morris Reid felt that Michael could make a successful comeback but only after showing an element of contrition. "The brand of Michael Jackson, the uber-entertainer, beloved all across the world – that's over," he said, but provided he apologised publicly for past excesses a comeback in America was still possible because "We're a forgiving society".[859] Try telling that to more than *two million* incarcerated in the country's notoriously vast penal estate, many of them for decades and sometimes for child-sex offences of a mild and consensual nature. Reid was arguably right in principle but, true to form, there was to be little sense of contrition from Michael, and hence commensurately little sense of forgiveness from America, or indeed anywhere else, except perhaps Japan.

On the other side of the Atlantic from Reid came somewhat similar advice from Christine Hamilton who, with her politician husband Neil, famously became a comeback couple in the UK after Neil's fall from grace in the so-called "cash for questions" scandal. A libel jury judged that Neil had taken illicit cash in return for agreeing to ask questions in parliament but a later Inland Revenue probe found nothing untoward. Not that the tax department's verdict did much for their rehabilitation, which, as Christine reports, was actually won (in popularity terms at least) in the court of public opinion, thanks to going on TV a lot and "being ourselves" in a way that could not be distorted through prejudiced journalism. Michael could do it too, she said, and her advice was brisk:

> Michael Jackson should not find it too hard to get his life back into order. Like us when we lost our political jobs, he just needs to implement an economical shopping policy and must rename his home "Never Again Land".[860]

As noted in the last chapter, Michael did promise after the trial never again to sleep with boys and there was no further controversy of that kind in the immediate post-trial years. As we shall see, though, he may have been finding it even harder to keep his hand out of his purse than out of boys' pants and ultimately his crazy spending proved more disastrous than any penile propensities. In the absence of any further sightings of Michael with fresh little pre-teens in tow, Roger Friedman was reduced to mentioning a somewhat older "personal guest/companion" during Jackson's stay at the Dorchester Hotel in London in October 2005. The columnist told us this was Anton Schleiter, twenty-year-old son of Sony executive Wolfgang Schleiter.[861] The sting, such as it was, came in a line or two of innuendo in which the young man was said to have been "a favourite" of the star "for years now". We were not told how many years, but left to wonder if it might have been ten or more – in which case Anton could have been among the long list of "special friends" we have heard so much about. Friedman added that when he spoke with Wolfgang Schleiter in 2004 he refused to defend Jackson and said he would not help him in his child molestation case. Also, Anton was placed firmly in the "mini-me" tradition long fostered by the star among his close boy companions: the youngster, it was noted, appeared in pictures to dress and wear his hair exactly like Michael.

One might suppose that the academic world, especially "cultural studies", with its remit to interpret the popular appeal of figures such as

Jackson in scholarly terms, would have come up with a rather more sober and realistic assessment of Michael's future prospects than we have seen thus far. Not entirely. Pulitzer Prize-winning academic Margo Jefferson came up with a book soon after the trial that could have been written for a fanzine: eloquent on what Jackson's music had meant to her and her generation, she appeared to have Michael's rehabilitation as her unspoken agenda but without demonstrating any convincing interest in the facts as to her hero's behaviour with boys. On the contrary, she dwelt on the social significance of Michael's art apparently as a means of deflecting attention from the inconvenient, embarrassing facts of his *life*.[862]

Seth Clark Silberman, co-organiser of a two-day Yale University conference on Michael Jackson in 2004, made what seemed a prophetic post-trial assessment: "I don't believe Michael is as washed up as his critics say," said Silberman. "I don't think anything is insurmountable in terms of his musical career."[863] That was at least half right: Michael's career would indeed take off again, but only posthumously: the singer himself would prove unable – precisely too "washed up", it would seem – to make a comeback on the basis of new music or concert performances. Silberman, incidentally, was one of a number of academic contributors to a special issue of the journal *Social Semiotics* in which the cultural significance of Michael's trial was among aspects of Jackson to be put under scholarly scrutiny.[864]

By far the most insightful prognosis I have been able to find was an article in *The Village Voice* by Richard Goldstein, written more than a year ahead of the trial and titled *I Believe I Can Open My Fly: Why Michael Jackson Is Damned and R Kelly Is the Man*. Beginning with the latter, he wrote:

> In a nation of bad Santas, why shouldn't an indicted child molester be the subject of an inspirational book for kids? Consider I Can Fly: The R Kelly Story, a tale for readers between the ages of six and nine. Its happiest illustration shows a passel of little girls beaming at the feet of the artist who calls himself "the Pied Piper of r&b". Quite an image for someone charged with 21 counts of child porn.
>
> Why does Jacko rate contempt while the Pied Piper gets a wink and nod? The answer lies in the widespread assumption that "awakening" a young lass is the mark of a potent man. When combined with the racist fantasy that black men are repositories of unbridled lust, sex with girls becomes the

> ultimate credential for a playa. But Jacko will never qualify as a stud. He's violated the rules of both racial and gender identity by transforming himself into an alabaster androgyne...
>
> Jackson's one reprieve came last month when he released a hit song co-written with Kelly. But not even that imprimatur can redeem him, because his emotional (if not erotic) object is a boy. The reaction to these two cases couldn't be more gendered. That's the way it often is with child abuse. Though the law makes no distinction between boys and girls or toddlers and teens, our sensibilities do – and our feelings about this crime vary enormously depending on the players.[865]

Obvious, really. Or at least that is how we may feel as a first response to the points Goldstein raises. On second thoughts deeper issues begin to surface: Why is it that a boy "awakened" by a woman would once have been regarded as a lucky young man, but is now increasingly seen as a victim of adult female abuse? Why is it that even a boy's sexual experiences at the hands of a scout leader, camp counsellor or priest might once have been made light of, but not any more? Times change. Nothing is forever or inevitable in the way society interprets sexual encounters. Michael's attachment to boys was thus not only illicit in the way Goldstein astutely describes but *additionally* ran against the current tide, which if present trends continue will soon leave no more sympathy for the R Kellys of this world than the Michael Jacksons.[866]

My hope at one time was that Michael's story would be the case that began to turn the tide. I had supposed that thanks to his immense global popularity it would be possible for people to see his love life as just that – a love life not just a lust life, a mixture of tenderness, affection and erotic passion like anyone else's and just as legitimate. He would of course be attacked by conservatives, and would suffer as a result, but opinion would eventually rally to him, as it did to Oscar Wilde, and like Oscar he would come to be seen as a martyr to irrationality and meanness of spirit. There is still time for a Wilde-like reappraisal, and there is some evidence my early optimism was not so wildly misplaced as might presently be supposed: in the early days of the Jordie Chandler revelations one British tabloid reported some fans saying they did not *care* whether he was innocent or not. They just loved Michael and his music, end of story.

This was presented in the paper as a scandalous, amoral indifference to the fate of child victims but there may be more to it. As reported in Chapter

Nine, I conducted my own survey. The polls in the newspapers were all asking simply whether people thought Michael was innocent or guilty. The precise language of the questions, assuming they were well designed by a specialised polling organisation, would not have appeared to favour either option over the other. It is usually very important to be scientifically neutral in this way. But I wanted to see what response I would get if I first made it clear that I would not be offended by *any* answers, now matter how libertarian or how conservative they were. So instead of asking just about innocence or guilt I asked where on a scale of goodness or badness they would place Michael's behaviour if – for instance – it turned out that a boy had been willingly involved in mutual masturbation with Michael. (I avoided asking about "sex" with him, because that would imply the highly taboo activity of anal intercourse with a child.) Respondents were invited to elaborate their answers if they wished.[867]

I will never forget one old gent who seemed so hostile to Michael I thought he would explode. "If he is guilty," I asked, "how do you think he should be punished?" I assumed he would say castration at the very least, probably followed by a gruesome form of execution. But no. Red-faced, the old boy spluttered: "He should get a very heavy fine!" Presumably the multi-million dollar settlement Michael eventually made in the Chandler case gave this senior citizen considerable satisfaction!

It will come as no surprise to learn that most respondents expressed disapproval of a hypothetically guilty Michael, even if the boy had been willingly involved in only relatively mild sexual activity. But, as I had surmised, there were others who were quite liberal once it became clear they had *permission* to be so: all it required was the understanding that I was not going to bite anyone's head off for expressing the "wrong" opinions. And once they had started on a tentatively tolerant note, the more liberally minded respondents tended to be even more forthcoming in response to an encouraging (and admittedly none too scientific!) nod or smile on my part. These included people who were not all Jackson fans, callously committed to his music no matter how much their idol had hurt a victim. There were also those who were genuinely unconvinced a Jacko-style love-life is really so terrible.

The thought that public opinion will not, inevitably and always, be against mutually desired adult-child sexual expression is admitted by a great many conservatives, too, not as a hope but as a fear: this is readily apparent from even the most cursory acquaintance with some of the numerous websites that scaremonger by presenting public acceptance of gay sexualities as a first step along the road to normalising paedophilia – no one would be scared if they felt the possibility did not exist.[868]

Why, then, were there so few signs, in the years after his acquittal, that Michael was achieving what I hoped for and what the conservatives fear? Why were Michael's relations with boys not being vigorously defended by his fans any more? Why were these fans not saying, as some did at the height of the Jordie Chandler case, that they didn't care whether Michael was actually "guilty"? Why had his fan-base apparently dwindled instead of grown in the wake of an acquittal that theoretically left Michael free to concentrate on re-building his career?

Sadly, the problem appeared to be largely down to Michael himself: whether through sheer emotional exhaustion and depression, or whatever else, he failed utterly in the wake of his trial to get a grip on key aspects of his life requiring urgent attention, most obviously his ruinous finances and stalled musical creativity. No one could seriously have expected him to pluck out of the air another megabucks record or advertising sponsorship deal, but *any* sign of life taking a new direction was desperately lacking: even busking in the streets with just one brand new song would have attracted a better press and better prospects than the tired, spluttering, half-assed "efforts" to which his long-suffering fans were subjected. Health correspondent Richard Ingham astutely noted after Michael's death that many stars find inspiration in new roles and new forms of music as they grow older, but that the Peter Pan of pop was cut off from this possibility. Other artists might have penned mellow reflections on the passage of time, past loves and watching their children grow up. But Michael had bought into the myth of Peter Pan quite literally as a boy who never grew up, going to desperate lengths to stay young in appearance. Even worse, he feared his fans would refuse to let him age. They would only buy concert tickets "to see the star of the 1980s. The singing, dancing, the moonwalk. They wanted the Jackson who was twenty five, not the Jackson who was fifty. They, too, demanded a piece of Peter Pan.[869] But all was not necessarily lost. As recently as 13 June 2007, *The Sun* carried the headline "Michael Jackson's a fan thriller" over a story saying "music league table Popscores has shown 82% of his fans would buy all the new material he releases, the highest score for any artist...Maybe Jacko's phone could start ringing again after all..."

Even worse than Michael's failure to pay attention to his own best interests was his seemingly utter indifference to people who served him well and who were owed a duty of consideration in return. It is a long list that includes close aides sacked on a whim – or as his surplus-to-requirements ex-manager Bob Jones would have it, for telling the boss unwelcome truths; there were also artistic collaborators (including Bruce Swedien, who recorded *Thriller* and much else), financial consultants, lawyers and numerous other providers of goods and services whom Michael neglected to pay for their work, sometimes for years; and as 2005 drew to a miserable close his staff at Neverland had a wretched Christmas wondering what the future would bring for them as they were left unpaid for weeks and months with no obvious sign of concern coming from Michael: thousands of miles away in Bahrain, he was well out of earshot to any complaints his staff might make.

It was even reported by Roger Friedman that Michael's zoo animals faced starvation, with food stocks at Neverland running low.[870] Hot on the heels of this report came news that animal rights group PETA (People for the Ethical Treatment of Animals) had written to the US Department of Agriculture asking it to investigate conditions at the zoo, claiming aerial photos revealed animals living in "bleak conditions".[871] By February, Friedman was telling us some of the animals had been moved out. He said Michael had a contract with local veterinarian Dr Martin Dinnes but that Dinnes was suing Michael for $91,000 in unpaid fees, leaving it unclear who was actually taking responsibility for the animals' welfare and rehousing.[872] As for press statements from Michael's people outlining a plan for closing down the zoo in an orderly fashion and finding new homes for the animals, there appeared to be nothing of that sort. On the contrary, Michael allowed the impression to develop, rightly or wrongly, that he had washed his hands of the situation.

Early in March 2006 the Neverland estate was closed down on the orders of California's State Labour Commissioner following Michael's failure to pay his employees or renew their insurance policies. One report said that the remaining animals, including elephants, tigers and a crocodile, "would be cared for by animal welfare officers", implying that the Department of Agriculture or another official agency had been obliged to step in to avert disaster.[873] There was at this time a steady drip, drip of negative stories such as this that went without comment or rebuttal. It was an indication of poor public relations across the board. Apparently, the only positive spin on these sad events, which came to my attention much later, was a Wikipedia entry recording that "a federal agency that inspected the menagerie after a complaint by an animal rights group" concluded that the animals "were not being mistreated".[874]

This PR shortfall was characterised most obviously by sins of omission of the kind just described but even Michael's more proactive efforts at rebuilding his image fell on stony ground – or, rather, on ground that had not been sufficiently well tilled. A classic example was his bid in September 2005 to show sympathy with the victims of Hurricane Katrina after the flooding of New Orleans. The idea, to bring out a single, with the proceeds going to help the victims, was fundamentally a good one. But the perceived need to have a galaxy of other stars working on the project with him, plus the mechanics of working with a new partner in the venture – Sheikh Abdullah of Bahrain – were hardly a recipe for the swift action that true concern for the homeless and dispossessed victims required. In the end Michael's response to Katrina was even more lumbering and ineffectual than the massively scorned efforts of President Bush and his administration.

This fiasco was all too typical, not just of Michael's poor PR record after the trial (and much earlier) but also of his musical creativity, or lack thereof. Rumours about his intended or suggested projects were actually a great deal more interesting than anything that had materialised before 2008 – which was simply nothing. *The New York Post*, for instance, reported in November 2005 that Michael was planning to record songs with his three children, by then eight, seven and three years old.[875]

For the youngest, "Blanket", it would have been an even earlier start to a singing career than Michael's own. A few months later, in February 2006, an Italian priest, Giuseppe Moscati, was trying to sign Michael up as one of several artists to perform songs with lyrics drawn from prayers by the late Pope John Paul II. As the idea needed Vatican approval and the Catholic Church is a tad sensitive these days about being associated with child abuse, this was clearly a project that never had a prayer.[876]

Michael long enjoyed a loyal following in Asia, especially in Japan, so when an Asian tour was mooted in 2006 it looked as though he might really "wanna be starting something". The reality, in March the following year, was merely a brief visit to Japan with a bit of glad-handing thrown in (including a party where guests paid $3,400 for the privilege of meeting Michael: in New York many would have paid that much to avoid him) but no singing whatever. Perhaps he was still too traumatised after his abortive rendering of "We are the world" at the World Music Awards in London just a few months earlier in November 2006 when, according to an Associated Press report, he sang fleetingly "among a group of swaying, clapping kids – until the musical accompaniment inexplicably stopped".[877] Another abortive effort, bruited just before the Japan trip, was the perennially discussed notion of a tour by Michael and his brothers, plus sister Janet. As usual, it never got off the drawing board.

By early 2008 Roger Friedman, ever the early riser, was telling Michael he had "better wake up and smell the coffee. He's got a real, solid, $1 million-a-night offer on the table to play London's Millennium Dome". He said the deal, from AEG Live, could total up to $30 million. There would be a $10 million guarantee for a minimum of ten nights, with a maximum of thirty nights, adding up to $30 million. He would just need to perform the songs from *Thriller*, plus encores from his other albums. Surely even megastar Michael would get out of bed for that. He would not even have had to introduce any new material.[878]

Yet just a couple of weeks later Friedman was telling us Michael had turned the deal down. Why? Perhaps because a twenty-fifth anniversary re-issue of *Thriller*, with remixed tracks from Akon, Fergie, Kanye West and will.i.am, had just come out, in mid-February, and following a good first week's sales was already flagging after its second. So the dismal prospect loomed of playing to embarrassing emptiness in the vastness of the O_2 Arena, as the once famously doom-laden Dome is now known.

By this time the original *Thriller* had reportedly sold a whopping 104 million copies. That was the figure given on the front page of *Ebony* in December 2007, which also carried a very flattering new head and shoulders photo of its begetter: the facial skin tone, an attractive, utterly unblemished, unlined pale tan rather than the alabaster white familiar from his usual pancake makeup, may have owed more to Photoshop than to nature, but it sure looked good. Clad in an elegant white jacket, Michael looked so young that one felt *Thriller* and he must have been born in the same year. Beneath the main headline, "Michael: 25 years after *Thriller*", ran the boast, "Exclusive: The King of Pop talks God, creativity, fatherhood and music". Claimed as his first major magazine interview in the US in a decade, this really was a fresh glimpse of the superstar. It may even have been the first significant media interview of any kind since the trial. At last he was tentatively peeping out of his shell, and allowing himself to be peeped at.[879]

Ebony, and its sister magazine *Jet*, aimed at a black American readership, had long been vehicles of choice for Michael's self-presentation. Their sympathies could be relied upon more than those of any other media outlet and this was to be no exception. So, was this the triumph of public relations that Michael so desperately needed post-trial?

Yes and no. It was a limited success. As a build up to the re-release of *Thriller* it served to put Michael back in the spotlight for the right reasons: there would be no Wacko Jacko stuff; this would be the star talking to his own agenda, with music and career issues to the fore, not scandal. So far so good. The only problem was that the piece looked backwards to *Thriller* without giving any credible prospects of a thrilling future. Promised "God, creativity, fatherhood and music", there would be too much of Michael's familiar God blather and nothing like enough on his future creativity and music. As for fatherhood, well, he told us he enjoys it and his kids are shy. And that was about it. It was a short article.

Perhaps this was because he had little to say. The best part – but that is hardly saying much – was probably when *Ebony*'s Bryan Monroe asked, "Can we expect more of Michael Jackson?" He replied:

> I'm writing a lot of stuff right now. I'm in the studio, like, every day. I think, like, the rap thing that is happening now, when it first came out, I always felt that it was gonna take more of a melodic structure to make it universal 'cause not everybody speak English. (Laughter) And you are limited to your country. But when you have a melody, and everybody can hum a melody, then that's when it became France, The Middle East, everywhere! All over the world now 'cause they put that melodic, linear thread in there. You have to be able to hum it, from the farmer in Ireland to the lady who scrubs toilets in Harlem to anybody who can whistle, to a child poppin' their fingers. You have to be able to hum it.

But nobody could hum it unless the artist released the song. Michael's band of loyal fans must have been tearing their hair out in frustration as they found themselves doing so often over the years. Their idol told them he was writing lots of stuff but gave no indication of when it would surface, if ever; nor did he hint at what *sort* of treat they might have been in for, except to say that melody was to be expected – which hardly gave a great deal away. The only significant clue to his state of mind was the grand ambition that he could once more get the whole world whistling and humming. Except where boys were concerned, he could never have been accused of thinking small.

Months before the new version of *Thriller*, Friedman had broken the news of its upcoming release, giving details of the re-mixed tracks. It proved to be a solid scoop for the gossip columnist, but nothing like as interesting as a possibly far less accurate story a few months earlier, when he was reporting that, "Jackson, according to insiders, is in perilous health right now. There is talk that his liver is damaged and that he's been seen vomiting blood. What has been confirmed is that Jackson is depressed, alone and mixing ingredients instead of making a new album or working."[880] Friedman later had to disown such claims when Michael put in a court appearance (no, not *that* sort: this was just a quickie, a cameo role when he was being sued by a creditor, as usual) and was clearly chipper, chirpy and apparently in the rudest of rude – or maybe the broodest of brood. Michael was able to enjoy his family life if nothing else: the kids doubtless played a huge part in encouraging him to stay physically in good shape and enable him to hang on to what remained of his sanity.

But if Friedman had erred it was surely excusable: starved of hard facts, it would have been remiss of him *not* to report increasingly credible rumours from insider sources that Michael was entering a dreadful terminal stage, like Elvis Presley and so many other burnt-out entertainers. Michael's long absences from the public arena did not help – absences which included failing to turn up when expected to the Black Entertainment Television Awards in Los Angeles just around the time when Friedman was speculating on his dire condition. The star's people reportedly said Michael was "too incapacitated to appear", thus appearing to confirm the rumours.

The word "rumours" in fact somewhat underplays the strength of the evidence. As we have seen, when Debbie Rowe testified at Michael's trial, she praised her ex-husband's role as a father but had nothing to say about her (apparently non-existent) intimate relations with Michael or how her children were conceived. However, in a court filing the following year, 2006, for her custody battle over the children, she said: "I have just been advised by Michael's inner circle that he is abusing drugs and I was even given the name of a physician prescribing all of Michael's medications, which I fear is dangerous not only to Michael but also to my children."[881]

A problem here for the credibility of Debbie's claim was that the "inner circle" could have included a multitude of sinners with their own dubious reasons for wanting to discredit Michael. The "inner circle" of earlier years had been a nest of fraudulent, conspiratorial vipers if some of the testimony at Michael's trial is to be believed and if the term "inner circle" is meant to include senior management aides as well as personal staff and friends. But one of those despised and vilified former senior aides, Marc Schaffel, was by now dishing the dirt on Jackson not in anonymous whispers but in sworn court testimony – and unlike the cases brought by the Hayvenhurst Five and

Neverland Five security guards, this was one Michael would lose. Schaffel alleged among other things that he loaned money to Michael that had not been repaid. He said Jackson's need to borrow money "accelerated when Jackson's increasingly more frequent and excessive use of drugs and alcohol impelled him into irrational demands for large amounts of money and extravagant possessions". In an interview with ABC News on *Good Morning America*, Schaffel went into considerable detail on this. One claim was that he was asked for $600,000 as a loan to buy Elizabeth Taylor a piece of jewellery in exchange for her appearing on Michael's behalf. This lent substance to long-standing rumours that he had been buying Taylor's public support for years.

In July 2006 a jury deliberated for nine hours after a ten-day case. They granted Schaffel $900,000, citing Michael's breach of contract. But there was a split verdict: Jackson, who had counter-sued, was awarded $200,000 against Schaffel in respect of money the producer was thought to have illicitly skimmed from the proceeds of the post-9/11 charity recording of "What more can I give?" It looks as though Schaffel's idea of charity may have been, "What more can I take?"[882]

Schaffel's portrayal of a dissolute Jackson seemingly found support even within the star's family. Brother Jermaine, in a book proposal he was said to be touting around this time, allegedly said Michael preferred Demerol, "his eternal favourite" but also used Vicodin, codeine, cocaine, Percocet, red wine and "good ol' Jack Daniel's". Jermaine would also claim that his most famous brother was "an out-of-control drug and booze abuser with a calculating mean streak and a thing for young children".[883]

Still on the theme of drink and drugs, there is one more story, a yarn I have been reluctant to include because *in itself* the source is dubious and I first encountered it in the relentlessly and often, it seems to me, unfairly, hostile pages of Diane Dimond's book.[884] Then it cropped up again in Darwin Porter's biography, *Jacko: His Rise and Fall*, a work definitely not for the squeamish, but not malicious or dishonest either, in my view. The essence can be stated briefly. Michael is said to have been at the Mirage Hotel, Las Vegas, in 2003 to shoot the video for R Kelly's *One More Chance*. Porter writes: "For nearly a month, Michael had been holed up at the hotel where a waiter reported that nearly three dozen boys, some of them 'German or Austrian' were seen coming and going at all hours of the day and night. Inside his lavish suite, Michael was said to be drunk or drugged and hadn't dressed for three weeks, appearing in a long dashiki robe dyed a deep, almost purplish scarlet."

Porter's account continues for a whole page with all sorts of apparently supporting detail. His main point is that on the morning of 18 November 2003 an assistant manager sent Michael a message asking him to vacate the premises as other guests had been complaining about the noise. When the manager saw inside the suite, the place had been trashed and "teenage boys were lounging about".[885]

While it seems likely that there was *some sort* of incident involving rowdy (and possibly drunken and/or drug-fuelled) behaviour that had angered guests and led to Michael's expulsion from the hotel, there is reason to believe the details have been exaggerated. For one thing, the manager reportedly entered the suite and was able to hear Michael speaking in his "whispery voice" on a telephone *in another room*. This might just have been physically possible if Michael had been alone in a quiet suite. But we are also asked to believe that with rowdy teenaged boys present this manager was able to stand there listening to what Michael was saying. Presumably the youngsters all conveniently maintained the silence of Trappist monks and none of them did anything to alert Michael to the manager's presence. If all this were not improbable enough, it is claimed that the phone conversation was not just a call to room service. Instead, the sensational message was coming through to Michael that Neverland had been raided by the police again. We are told he "appeared to be sobbing", and saying "Oh, God no!", though it is not clear how he could "appear" or even "seem" to be anything while he was in another room. Finally, "he raised his voice in a bellowing rage", shouting, "Not again!"

Just like the "I never hurt anyone" story recounted in Chapter One, this other story of Michael sobbing and ranting in a hotel room is highly plausible, but in the Mirage case the way in which it is said to have been witnessed is not. Readers can judge for themselves, but I am inclined to view elements of the Mirage scenario as, fittingly enough, a hallucination in the desert city.

So, with one PR disaster after another giving Michael an even worse image than that of Child Molester Who Got Lucky (and who would have thought he could sink lower than that, except by some District Attorney getting luckier one day than Sneddon had been?) and with no new music to satisfy the fans, what else could the one-time King of Pop do to foul up? Answer: plenty. One salient feature of Michael's life over the early post-trial years – the elephant that stubbornly stayed in the room after all his other animals had disappeared – was his continued disinclination to live within his means. The outrageous extravagance for which he had always been known simply continued in the absence of a commensurate income, leaving him running on empty.

By June 2005 he was already authoritatively reported as being in debt to the tune of $270 million, a figure next to which even the famously eye-watering Chandler settlement looked modest.[886] That expenditure, plus other settlements and gifts to boys and their parents was relatively rational compared to the long habit of waste and ostentation noted elsewhere in these pages. With so much debt, even a frugal lifestyle could not save him from massive interest payments. Michael had successfully played his stay-out-of-jail card but he was not out of the woods. In July 2005 a finance company sued him, claiming he owed it $48 million. The Prescient Acquisition Group said in court papers that it had been taken on by Jackson to provide him with financial advice and to help him refinance a $270 million loan. Prescient found the Fortress Investment Group, which agreed to buy out his loan and provide sufficient finance for Jackson to buy back his half of the all-important Beatles catalogue, jointly owned with Sony. The total amount provided was $537 million. Michael's brother Randy, then handling the star's business affairs, agreed that Prescient would receive a 9% commission, or $48 million. The lawsuit accused Jackson of breach of contract.[887]

A settlement was later reached in the Prescient case, but that was just one lawsuit among many as his creditors closed in. Perhaps the most revealing of these moves came in October 2007 when Michael was sued by his erstwhile patron, Sheikh Abdulla al-Khalifa of Bahrain, for $7 million plus damages. According to Roger Friedman's account of case papers he said had been sent to him, Jackson had an agreement with the sheikh to record two albums, write and produce a Broadway-type show with Jackson's music and a cast album, and to write and publish an autobiography. In other words, claimed Friedman, the skeikh "owns Michael outright" and was angry with Jackson skipping out on him around mid-2006.[888]

The sheikh stated in his claim that Michael moved to Bahrain in June 2005, just over two weeks after his acquittal at trial. For one year he underwrote Jackson's life in Bahrain – everything including living accommodation, guests, security and transportation, at a cost equivalent to millions of dollars. In April 2006, Jackson finally signed an agreement with the sheikh to create a record company and do many other things. Sheikh Abdullah built him a state-of-the-art recording studio and gave him a $7 million advance. But Michael left for Japan, and then Ireland. As Friedman put it:

> He exited Bahrain and never looked back. He took the money and moonwalked right out the door. This is the real Michael Jackson. He has never returned a phone call from the prince since he left Bahrain. The situation is not unlike those Michael put himself in with former manager Myung-Ho Lee or German concert promoter Marcel Avram. In those cases, Jackson signed complicated agreements, made promises for work in exchange for money and then left his partners high and dry. In both cases, he was sued and lost.

Later the same month Friedman reported that Michael had defaulted on a $23 million loan and that the holder had put him on notice. Jackson was given ninety days to pay the full amount plus interest on pain of losing the now unoccupied and boarded-up Neverland. The expired loan, with Fortress Music Trust, had been secured against the deeds for Neverland. This loan was separate from a (by this time) $300 million one secured by Jackson's stake in Sony/ATV Music Publishing.[889]

According to Friedman, no amount of wishing by Jackson fans nor spin from his much-diminished team could change what this all meant: "Jackson's financial house of cards is finally falling in."[890] While re-financing by another "white knight" was possible, it was clear Michael was nonetheless in the worst financial situation he had ever faced. By early 2008, and with the most offensive symbolism imaginable, Fortress had arranged for Neverland to be auctioned on the steps of the Santa Barbara Courthouse, albeit sale dates set first for March and later for May were each aborted as the auction drew near.[891]

What a mess! One farcical aspect of the whole sorry business was that practically all parties to Michael's business affairs ended up suing each other. Even Jackson's own lawyers sued him for non-payment, while he sued his accountant for failing to pay his bills for him![892] And in Michael's mind he was apparently not in any way to blame for this nightmare himself. Instead it was all the fault of Jewish "leeches". An anti-Semitic message from him on a former adviser's voicemail was broadcast on the news programme *Good Morning America*.[893] As well as calling Jews "leeches", he claimed he was the victim of a Jewish "conspiracy" targeting him because of his status as "the most popular person in the world." Even though Michael had once collaborated with Rabbi Shmuley Boteach, and been on good terms with many Jewish figures in entertainment, such as Steven Spielberg and Uri Geller, it was not Michael's first offence of this type: his 1995 song "They

Don't Care About Us" included the line "Jew me, sue me, everybody do me". Eventually, he was forced to apologise and change the lyrics to quell the inevitable controversy.

A charitable explanation is that such embarrassingly racist outbursts were merely a mood thing, the excusable reaction of a man at the end of his tether. Things had been going well for Michael when he was working with Boteach, but the "Jew me" lyrics had come after the immense pressure he had been under from Jordie Chandler's father Evan – who was, after all, Jewish. And in later years, when the huge debt burden finally morphed from a minor headache to a skull-crushing migraine, Michael just snapped: all those lawyers and finance people who were in his face all the time, well they *were* mostly Jewish, weren't they? Who wouldn't have gotten mad at them?

As anti-Semitism goes, this is at the innocent end of the spectrum: Michael was hardly a thuggish street Jew-baiter or a death-camp commandant, and it would be grotesquely unfair to present him as a closet supporter of such figures. His sentiments are of course distasteful, disgraceful and devoid of any insight into the real reasons for his financial problems, which were essentially of his own making – notwithstanding the allegedly "devilish" behaviour of Sony's Tommy Mottola (from a Catholic family but Jewish by conversion) and other music industry figures he accused of doing him down. What his voicemail vituperation reveals is not significant anti-Semitism but frustration, anger and dismay over his loss of status and any feeling of being in control of his destiny. That sense of control, no matter how illusory, is something we all crave, and for Michael it was in desperately short supply after a victory at trial that should have put him back in the driving seat.[894]

Quite contrary to the sense of invincibility that his successful disposal of the Chandler and Arvizo cases might have given him, unwonted insecurity had now become a feature of his life in a number of ways, not just financial. In a manner of speaking he became homeless as well as penniless. If Roger Friedman is to be believed, he bummed and freeloaded his way around the world, living in Bahrain, France, Ireland and (back in the US again) Las Vegas and Virginia, initially with Sheikh Abdullah picking up the tab and later dossing rent-free at dancer Michael Flatley's Irish castle for as many months as his welcome held good, and perhaps a few beyond.[895]

He still had a tenuous hold on the ownership of Neverland, but living there was out of the question: to do so would leave him within range of his old adversary Tom Sneddon, who showed every sign after the trial of being a bad loser intent on pursuing Michael in a never-ending vendetta, as long as he had breath in him. As an old man on the cusp of retirement, Sneddon alone might not have been too scary but the photos of Michael's genitals were still on file in California and use could yet be made of them: of all the states in the union, it would remain the most dangerous one for the waning star.

The sense that he might continue to be pursued and vilified in America was heightened soon after the trial with the news that the two publicly dissenting jurors would be writing books about the case, Eleanor Cook's to be titled *Guilty as Sin, Free as a Bird*, and Ray Hultman's *The Deliberator*. In the end neither of these projects came to anything but Michael could not have known how it would pan out. Ironically, he was called for jury service himself only weeks later – a tenuous confirmation of his officially restored status as a respectable citizen, but hardly a sufficient one to attract him back to the Sunshine State from even sunnier Bahrain.

Getting clear away from the whole of America had also allowed Michael to distance himself from yet another tiresome sexual abuse allegation, this time an entirely bogus one. A certain Joseph Bartucci accused Michael of sexually assaulting him as an eighteen-year-old during the 1984 World's Fair. In a federal civil lawsuit he claimed he had been kidnapped and sexually assaulted. Bartucci said he repressed the memories until 2003, when he saw the coverage of the child molestation charges against Jackson. Then the memories came flooding back to him in a sudden vision – a vision, clearly, of a big, fat damages cheque.

There was just one little hitch with Bartucci's ambitious get-rich-quick plan, even in a country all too prone to falling for "recovered memory" yarns: Michael had a cast-iron alibi. He was able to prove he was miles away from where the abduction allegedly occurred, and for that reason US District Judge Eldon Fallon threw the case out of his New Orleans court in April 2006. Bartucci had claimed he was forced into a white limousine on 19 May, 1984, during the New Orleans World's Fair, and driven to California while being molested, held at gunpoint and cut with steel wire and a razor blade. In a 2005 court filing, Michael's lawyers said Bartucci had been involved in eighteen civil and criminal suits over the previous seventeen years, including one raising allegations of sexual abuse against a minister.[896]

Bartucci's outrageous claim was just one of a number of opportunistic attempts by greedy or crazy people to jump on the bandwagon against Jackson. Pathetic stunts of this kind are doomed to be revealed as such under close scrutiny but unfortunately that does not mean they are completely insignificant. For one thing, a welter of bogus claims is bound to engender a dismissive attitude towards genuine ones, as with the boy who cried wolf. The exposure of these flaky falsities is bound to play all too well in key constituencies such as Jackson fans desperate to believe in Michael's "innocence" far beyond the legal meaning of that term, and "black pride" brothers and sisters shamed by the thought of a "guilty" Michael.

Readers who have stayed with me this far are unlikely to include those with a major psychological investment in denying Michael's sexual interest in boys, but that does not mean we should go to the other extreme and believe every allegation. And in sorting the wheat from the chaff it will help to be alert to a phenomenon that constantly bedevils the lives of those who spend their lives in the glare of publicity but is pretty much unknown to the rest of us: the more glamorous and high-profile you are, the more you inevitably attract not only packs of paparazzi but also plotters, fraudsters, stalkers, freaks and attention seekers of every imaginable and sometimes unimaginable type – even, as the case of John Lennon reminds us, assassins.

A more subtle example than Bartucci is to be found in the case of Eddie Reynoza, who claims to have been "drugged, dumbed down with alcohol and sexually assaulted at sixteen years of age" by Michael. At a time when he was struggling to make his name as a young actor, Reynoza first wiggled his sorry ass in public in 1993 making his allegations on the back of the Jordie Chandler story. Even in an atmosphere when the media were clamouring for stories from other "victims", Reynoza's story was not thought to stack up and the press attacked his credibility. According to a press release by an agency called PR Leap, "The negative publicity destroyed his vulnerable yet promising career." When were we told of this tragic outcome? Why, in February 2005, just ahead of Michael's trial, when Reynoza, now into his thirties, was about to make another "PR leap" into the abyss, having apparently not learnt his lesson the first time.[897] On 1 April that year – a date, it may be thought, of some significance and not just because it was in the middle of the trial – Reynoza's agent Jack Scagnetti put out a release reviving the original abuse claim, alleged to have occurred after "the young, innocent, somewhat naïve teen went to a music video dance audition where Michael Jackson spotted him and turned Eddie into his latest victim".[898]

Scagnetti pointed out that by this time in the trial the judge had ruled that "past allegations of sexual misconduct by Michael Jackson are fair game for the current trial", and that "if Eddie were to testify it could demolish any hope for Jackson to be found not guilty". The agent might have had a point, but for one thing: Reynoza, presented with a golden opportunity to take the stand and win justice at long last, did not do so! One will search in vain the list of ninety prosecution witnesses for the name Reynoza. More important to Reynoza, it seems, was putting out the news that he was now getting offers to act in movies again and that "There is also some talk of a television movie of Eddie's story. The rape by Michael Jackson would be the centre-piece of the film but the storyline would include the attacks by the press and Eddie's eventual success and redemption."

Bear in mind the atmosphere in which this press release was put out. Many people thought that Michael would be found guilty, irrespective of Reynoza's no-show. If that had happened, Reynoza could indeed have been back in business. His non-appearance as a witness could have been brushed aside as a non-issue. He and many other opportunists would have made it big-time. Worth a punt, no?

If Reynoza's claim could be described as more subtle than Bartucci's, then the opposite extreme is arguably best represented by a claim so preposterous it is hard to see any reason for its being advanced other than sick amusement – as the claimant was remaining anonymous, at least initially, it seemed he was not in it to make a name for himself. In January 2006 the man, aged twenty one, and later revealed as one Daniel Kapon, filed papers with Orange County Superior Court, California, charging that Michael Jackson had begun "repeatedly and forcefully" sexually molesting him from the age of *two*, saying that Jackson "plied me with drugs and alcohol and then molested me". Kapon also accused Michael of "burning and torturing" him, but even this was not the most extraordinary allegation. In addition, he claimed that Michael "forced me to undergo unnecessary plastic surgery". The young man's lawyer, Michael Mattern, said that surgical procedures performed on his client gave him "noticeably red lips, resembling the garish makeup Jackson often wears in public, and a pronounced cleft chin." Oh, yes, and Jackson had also stolen "music he composed as a toddler", according to the *New York Post* version, which also said the claimant had come forward after the Neverland raid in 2003 and was interviewed at length by the police who, unsurprisingly, did not believe the story.[899]

Leaving America had yet another advantage for Michael, apart from steering clear of crazy accusers. It gave him a bit of breathing space in respect of another key form of insecurity: while he stayed in the States he could have lost his two eldest children. Debbie Rowe, mother of Prince Michael and Paris, had been in a legal battle for custody and her hand had been strengthened by all the revelations at the trial, despite the verdict. Debbie had given up her parental rights in 2001 but went to court in 2004 to reverse the decision when Michael faced child abuse charges. Noting that Michael visited orphanages on his Japan trip in 2006, Friedman remarked with typical cynicism: "Jackson toured orphanages perhaps with a reason. I'm told he's looking for more kids to add to his current collection of three. He may be hedging his bets since his first wife, Debbie Rowe, wants hers back from him and is gaining ground in the courts."[900]

Friedman makes a sloppy factual error here by rubbing Lisa Marie Presley out of the historical record as Michael's actual first wife; but that is minor compared to the way in which he goes psychologically astray. His implicit contrast is between normal people who have "families" and Michael who has a "collection" of kids as though they are postage stamps or beer mats. But this forgets that quite a few people have progeny thanks to nothing nobler than a faulty condom. In reality it makes no sense whatever to portray Michael, of all people, as having a merely whimsical or trivial interest in his family: eccentric as his parenting style sometimes was, no one could seriously doubt the depth of his attachment to children. We may accordingly be sure that the outcome of this case was of passionate concern and anxiety to him: no issue could have been a source of greater insecurity until it was resolved. In the end that resolution came by a mutual agreement announced in September 2006; the precise terms were not disclosed, but the children continued to live with Michael.[901]

In May 2008 Michael even allowed them to be photographed without wearing masks, "to prove he really IS the daddy", according to a story in the *Daily Star*, which carried a spread of the pictures. Reporter Nigel Pauley opined, "There was no mistaking the resemblance between Wacko, forty nine, and his three kids…However, onlookers could not help wondering how they manage to resemble Jackson as he looks now, rather than before plastic surgery."[902] He had a point.

Another tabloid, the *Daily Mail*, marked the occasion by noting Michael's apparent closeness to the "stunningly attractive" Grace Rwaramba, "whose job title was nanny, but she was far more than that to Jackson and his children". Could the press have been falling, yet again, for a bogus "romantic" angle? So it seems. "The pair were so close," we were told, "that many insiders said they would marry." It is usual for journalists to be cast as cynical but in their dealings with Michael many of them appeared determined to be taken for serial suckers. In this case the romantic bubble had burst even before the end of the report: Grace, it had to be admitted, "has suddenly found herself surplus to requirements and has been frozen out." What a surprise![903]

Of all the tribulations that followed Michael's trial, there was one disaster he did *not* have to worry about: a claim for damages by the alleged victim Gavin Arvizo. Right up to the end of the trial and even after the acquittal, there was some speculation that a successful civil suit might yet conclusively trash what remained of the stumbling star's reputation. OJ Simpson had beaten a murder rap in the criminal court but lost a subsequent civil case and there were those who thought the Arvizo saga might play out the same way. Not a chance. It was the Arvizos' reputation that had crashed and burnt most spectacularly in the trial, not Michael's: their credibility as witnesses had been utterly destroyed. As part of the sad aftermath Gavin's mother Janet was convicted of welfare fraud in November 2006.[904]

As for Michael's feelings about the case, Taraborrelli offers a glimpse in the forth and presumably final edition of his biography, this time titled *Michael Jackson: The Magic, The Madness, The Whole Story, 1958-2009*. After the trial, we are told, Michael consulted a therapist for the first time in his life, as a result of which he apparently began to get in touch with emotions he would perhaps not otherwise have admitted, even to himself. He had always seen himself as a lover of children, but now he admitted to one of his inner circle that he had grown to hate Gavin Arvizo. Need we be surprised? Or shocked? Anyone who could entirely banish such "unworthy" sentiments towards a child after all Michael had been through might be thought scarcely human.[905]

So, in this final chapter we have reviewed the post-trial predictions for Michael's future and with the benefit of hindsight enjoyed a smugly superior laugh over their inaccuracy. Far less amusing has been all the evidence of a much diminished Michael Jackson, apparently going nowhere artistically and heading for financial catastrophe – yet also a man who was at least able to savour family life and unaccustomed domestic tranquillity even in the midst of his "homeless" wanderings.

And then, suddenly, we are into the awful, tragic, final chapter of his life. Ironically, it came at a time when his star appeared to be in the ascendant once more. A series of concerts had been lined up at the O_2 Arena in London, announced in March 2009 and due to start in the July. The public response was staggering. Within a matter of only days it was being reported that a *million* fans had already put their names down for tickets at £50-£75 a time. A profile in the *Observer* said it looked as though Jackson was set for "the biggest comeback since Lazarus".[906] Soon the projected number of concerts was being stretched into 2010 and it seemed Michael would have a real opportunity to get both his career and his finances back on track.

Provided, that is, the star was still capable of delivering the goods. As noted earlier in this chapter, there could be no guarantee that Michael, now into his fifties, would be able to sing and dance as he had in his *Thriller* days, no matter how much he practised. But the fans would expect no less, and letting them down by cancelling the concerts was not an option: the entertainer was inevitably under huge pressure not just from the fans but from everyone with a financial interest in the success of the comeback – the concert promoters, the wider music and merchandising industries and his numerous creditors. Michael reportedly kept his siblings and parents at a distance at this time, possibly to avoid the additional pressure of their expectations.

As now seems clear, it was all too much for him and he could not sleep. Long addicted to pain killing drugs, it was hardly surprising that he saw yet more drugs as the way to deal with his insomnia. When ordinary sleeping pills failed to do the trick he became desperate and looked for something stronger, paying doctors huge amounts of money so that they could be on call to obtain and administer a guaranteed knock-out punch. It has to be wondered whether the high pay was also designed to overcome any scruples the doctors might had felt about giving a patient dangerous drugs. As we now know, the knock-out was provided by a cocktail of drugs, including propofol, which is normally confined to hospital use as a surgical anaesthetic. This regime appears to have started in about March 2009 and within a few months it killed Michael, inducing a fatal cardiac arrest on 25 June. The Los Angeles Coroner ruled by the August that the case was being treated as homicide; Dr Conrad Murray, who reportedly admitted administering propofol to Michael, was said to be under investigation in connection with a possible manslaughter charge. The full toxicology report was withheld pending further police work.[907]

Shocking as the circumstances of Michael's death undoubtedly were, many fans were no doubt even more disturbed by a newspaper report some weeks later. It was claimed in the story that Michael had used a drug to control his sexual urges – something he might have felt the need to do if he had been worried those desires could lead to illegal behaviour. It was said he had been prescribed a "chemical castration" drug to suppress his sexual urges towards young boys.[908] That drug, Depo-Provera, had allegedly been administered to him by Dr Alimorad Farshchian, whom Michael first met at Neverland in 2001. Depo-Provera restricts men's flow of testosterone-producing brain hormones.

Dr Farshchian, an expert in arthritis pain relief who has written text books on orthopaedic medicine, unsurprisingly declined to confirm the story: patient confidentiality would no doubt have been a concern, especially on such a sensitive issue. The newspaper quoted Ian Barkley, described as Michael's official photographer from 2002 to 2006. Barkley reportedly said that Dr Farshchian became aware of the star's sleepovers with boys at Neverland and had tried to help him curb his urges. The doctor and Jackson grew apart following the TV airing of Michael's interview with Martin Bashir in 2003. An unnamed source reportedly said: "When the Bashir documentary came out Michael became severely depressed. He turned back to his old doctors who would prescribe him whatever he wanted and Dr Farshchian wouldn't do that. He was determined to do the right thing for Michael even if it meant disagreeing with him."

What does it all leave us with? As for where it leaves me, and you readers who have patiently followed me this far, I started this book with the aim of presenting an essentially sympathetic view of Michael's sexuality, while acknowledging his many faults, and going on from there to examine how his high-profile actions and trial might influence public understanding of his boy-love and of adult sexual attraction to children more generally. In truth, I am not now so convinced that public understanding is going to be as strongly influenced by Michael's life as I had supposed.

Why have I changed my mind? Partly it is a reluctant and belated admission that his "case" is so individual, so unique, that many people see him as having very little in common with the "pervert" teachers, sports coaches, priests and the rest who are so insistently vilified in the rogues' galleries of the media and who, unlike Michael, do end up in jail. This is a pity because so many of those figures are not rogues at all; the loving ones among them, those who respect children's feelings, do not deserve to be demonised any more than Michael. Despite Michael's undoubted uniqueness as a public figure, his kind of love life for children is by no means unparalleled. When pitching this book to publishers shortly before Michael's death, I referred to his narrow escape at trial:

> I will consider what, if anything, his narrow escape will mean for child-lovers. Will we see "the Jackson defence" successfully played out before courts around the globe, with defendants everywhere claiming they went to bed with boys or girls, but only with the purest of motives?

Er, no, actually, not much sign of that, although in fairness to myself the point was made slightly tongue in cheek. What I suppose I had actually hoped to see was defence lawyers in "consensual" cases willing to fight harder and to present their client's story with an element of pride, not shame. They could not of course argue in court that the law should permit such consensual acts: that would be a job for the political arena. So cases would still have to be fought on the deeply unsatisfactory basis that the client did not "do it". However, the emergence of an unashamed, triumphant Michael, a Michael giving millions to children's charities, wowing his fans with major hits, could have given lawyers around the globe the confidence to portray their child-loving clients as worthwhile human beings, in the expectation that juries would become more sympathetic and less eager to convict. In those circumstances, we might also have begun to see fewer cases given up without a fight in grovelling plea bargains or outright guilty pleas.

That is a lot of influence to hang on one figure, even such an iconic one as Michael Jackson. But it *could* have worked if the idol's feet of clay had not become so distressingly visible. My aim, as already noted, has been to take an essentially sympathetic view of Michael's sexuality. Readers of the foregoing chapters, especially those dealing most directly with Michael's undoubted rapport with children, and with the unquestionable mutuality of his most "celebrated" or notorious relationships, will know that this has been the easy part of my task: looked at purely as a "poster child" for child-love he has been an attractive figure – a lover, not a molester; socially at ease with kids and a genuine friend to them.

If only the rest of his behaviour had been half as attractive, I would be twice as happy about his long-term impact on the social acceptance of paedophilia. But honesty compels this author to tell it like it is, not as one might wish it to be. In a more generous and understanding age Michael may yet come to be seen as the Oscar Wilde of child-love and I would welcome that. To achieve it, though, the task of crafting his legend will one day need to pass to hands other than mine...perhaps Jordie's?

POSTSCRIPT

This book began with Michael's tragic sudden death. As it goes to press, comes news of another dramatic exit: it is reported that Jordie Chandler's father has taken a gun to his head and killed himself. Compared to the endless coverage of Michael's passing, often emotively told and speculative in content, the accounts of Evan Chandler's departure seem starkly terse and matter-of-fact: he is gone, and that's that.[909]

Evan will not be widely mourned, nor his life deeply scrutinised by millions. But it should not go unnoticed that his later years, passed in failing health and largely, it seems, in bitter isolation, were just as tragic as anything that happened to Michael, perhaps more so. Remember Evan's prediction, as the crisis loomed over his son's friendship with Michael?

"The facts," he said, "are so overwhelming that everyone will be destroyed..."

Evan was a talented screenwriter, a man of imagination. Sadly ironic, then – or poetic justice – that his prophetic vision of apocalypse evidently overlooked his own destruction. And it was all so preventable, so unnecessary. Without Evan there would have been no crisis: he was on the warpath; he was in control; he was writing the script. He could have just hit the delete key on a storyline that was never going to have a happy ending.

R.I.P. Michael

R.I.P. Evan

***

From tragedy to farce. In the same month as Evan's suicide, Michael's dermatologist Dr Arnold Klein gave a long, rambling interview to entertainment news website TMZ, in which he seemed eager to mouth off at breakneck speed on many aspects of Michael's life, and all too willing to blame other people for his client's problems while exonerating himself.[910]

Sensationally, we learned that Michael was not a paedophile but a pee-ophile. Asked about the detailed description Jordie Chandler had given to the police of the marks on Michael's genitals, Klein claimed the boy had seen the star's privates when Michael had been peeing into a cup – something he habitually did in public, according to Klein, including in front of children!

So that settles it then. Guess I have wasted my time writing this book, now that Jordie's evidence has been blown apart. Ho hum.

On the other hand, we were not told why all this public peeing had never been "leaked" to the media over the years, bearing in mind both its intrinsic Wacko Jacko interest and the huge evidential implications. Nor did we hear how Michael would have revealed his buttocks when peeing into a cup: are we to understand that he pulled his trousers and underpants right down for these "performances"? Evidently Klein had forgotten that Jordie's account included "brown patches on his ass, on his left glut". And perhaps Michael peed upwards, in an arc, so that his penis would be raised, enabling Jordie to see the mark that would otherwise have been hidden underneath it. In that case, catching the pee in the cup without spilling it on the carpet would have been a spectacle to match the moonwalk.

Perhaps the most telling aspect of Klein's whole spiel was that the dermatologist made no attempt to deny the accuracy of the boy's description.

***

The US Federal Bureau of Investigation (FBI) played Santa Claus to Jacksonologists with the release of three hundred pages of files on Michael Jackson just before Christmas 2009.[911] A looming press deadline prevented this author's personal trawl through the archive, but the scant news coverage that followed the release suggests there were no sensational new revelations.

However, Roger Friedman made one interesting discovery. He found that files in connection with the 1993-4 allegations against Michael included an FBI officer's note based on information from a Toronto woman who worked in children's services. She had allegedly been on the same train as Jackson and his entourage travelling to the Grand Canyon. Jordie Chandler, then aged twelve or thirteen, was in the party, travelling as Michael's cousin. The witness said the two seemed extremely close, and she was concerned about noises coming out of their compartment. "Jackson was very possessive of boy at night," wrote the officer. "(The witness) heard questionable noises through wall."[912]

***

The Michael Jackson Tapes, by Rabbi Shmuley Boteach[913] was published some three months after Michael's death. As it is said to be based on thirty hours, no less, of taped interview material, one might suppose it to be a work of such immense importance that our understanding of Michael must be considered seriously deficient until we have read it.

That is not the case. I found it an interesting read, especially on the perils and pitfalls, for stars and fans alike, of our obsessive celebrity culture. However, Boteach becomes so engrossed in this moral message that what we learn about Michael is rather limited – especially as regards his friendships with boys.

What Michael stood in need of, asserts the rabbi, was a wife – yes, a *third* one! Michael obligingly declared himself heterosexual and Schmuley felt, "it is not for me to question a man's sincerity when he firmly avows to me that he is attracted to women and is fully capable of a loving relationship with a woman."[914] At another point, he writes: "Was he heterosexual? Were his marriages real? Were they consummated? I would never have dared ask him any of these questions."[915]

This is not mere timidity, it is cautiousness on an heroic scale, as Schmuley gingerly skirts around the edges of inconvenient truths for hour after hour of conversation, on his epic voyage of resolute non-discovery.

It is not so much the questions that Schmuley fears as the answers. It suited his purpose to pretend Michael had an interest in women. It is a fiction that enables him to pootle along in his comfort zone, peddling, without fear of contradiction, his cosy, one-size-fits-all nostrum that every man needs a good woman.

But he cannot help little bits of truth breaking through here and there. When he asks Michael whether he likes modesty in women, one feels the reply is hardly what the rabbi was looking for:

> Yeah, I don't like women who are always saying, "My nails need to be done.

> I have to do my toes. I need a manicure." I hate all that. I like it when girls are a little bit more tomboyish. If they wrestle, climb a tree...I love that. It is sexier to me..."[916]

In other words, the closest a woman comes to being sexy is when she is behaving like a boy. So if Lisa Marie Presley or Debbie Rowe had climbed trees and wrestled, would that have done it for him? When Schmuley asked directly what sort of woman he liked, Michael replied:

> The ones who were classy and quiet and not into all the sex and all the craziness because I am not into that.[917]

He also explained to Schmuley that children were his real enthusiasm and that he did not need romantic love.[918]

So, let's see. He was not into sex with women or romantic love either. The only thing he found sexy was what boys do. Putting all that lot together it emerges from Schmuley's pages that getting Michael to mate conventionally was a challenge right up there with coaxing giant pandas to breed in captivity!

There is also the occasional reluctant admission by the rabbi that shows he knows the score, really. Referring to Jordie Chandler, for instance, he admits testimony by the boy's mother did seem to show, "that Michael was erotically obsessed with her son".[919] He also refers to Michael's "extremely questionable and perhaps even criminal sexual activities".[920]

To his credit, Schmuley does not condemn Michael outright on this basis, though he appears to think God might. The following passage, in which both blame and praise have their place, is perhaps a fit one upon which to end:

> He made me softer and gentler. He was highly imperfect and was perhaps guilty of serious, terrible sins for which there might not be any redemption... However, did that cancel out the good he tried to inspire in others?
> He used to watch me tell my children I loved them. He did not approve. "Schmuley, when you tell your children you luuuvve them, you have to look in their eyes. They have to know that you mean it. You have to focus only on them. You can't tell them and look somewhere else." And ever since then, I peer into their eyes.[921]

ACKNOWLEDGEMENTS

For their help, constructive criticism and encouragement, my thanks to: Leo Adamson, Paul Brangwyn, the late Prof Vern Bullough, Dr Peter Bremner, Marsaili Cameron, Dr Michael Carter, Floyd Conaway, Barry Cantor, Dr Joseph DeMasi, Rod Downey, Dr Frans Gieles, Prof Richard Green, Prof Thomas K Hubbard, Jim Jedson, Prof James R Kincaid, Peter Meltzer, Tom McGuire, Prof William Armstrong Percy III, Ricky Turner, Prof Donald J West, Dr Richard Yuill. Neither my views nor my errors should be imputed to any of them.

NOTES AND REFERENCES

1 "Michael Jackson's death 'second biggest story of century' ", *Daily Telegraph*, 9 July 2009

2 Including upmarket newspapers such as *The Guardian*, whose columnists joined in the hype with gusto. The most egregious excess was perhaps that achieved in the soaring prose of cultural guru and self-professedly boy-loving feminist Germaine Greer, who wrote: "Nijinsky may have been the greatest Spectre de la Rose, Nureyev the greatest Corsair, but these two candles pale in the light of Jackson's blazing star. The surprise is not that we have lost him, but that we ever had him at all." See: "Like Orpheus, Michael Jackson was destroyed by his fans", Germaine Greer, *The Guardian*, 26 June 2009

3 Andersen (1994)

4 Gutierrez (1997) and Chandler (2004)

5 "Michael Jackson's Victory", Joan Ryan, Associated Press, 10 April 1998, accessed at *http://www.eonline.com/News/Items/0,1,2828,00.html*

6 Taraborrelli (1992)

7 Guest (2006). At a much later point, on p131, Guest touches very obliquely on the evidence relating to Brett Barnes through the words of a member of the jury after the trial was over. This fleeting reference refers only to an unnamed person, of unspecified age, sleeping in Michael's bedroom, not his bed, "for 365 straight days".

8 This was Larry Feldman when he appeared as a witness at Michael's trial in 2005. Prosecutor Tom Sneddon showed Feldman a photo of the boy at the start of the following exchange:

> *Q:* Is that an accurate depiction of what Jordie Chandler looked like?
>
> *A:* He was much better looking, I can tell you, at that age. He was adorable. That's kind of blurry.
>
> *Mr Mesereau:* Objection; move to strike the gratuitous remarks.
>
> *The Court:* Stricken.

9 Andersen p.244

10 Taraborrelli p.447 (2004 edn)

11 The facts of the *Exorcist* sleepover and many others with Jordie and other boys were never contested by Michael. In this and other cases where the facts are not in dispute it would be tedious to keep citing my sources. In this case, though, now that I have raised the issue, I would just mention that when June was cross-examined in the 2005 trial the questioning focused not on the (admitted) facts of the sleepovers but on June's motives for allowing them to happen.

12 Taraborrelli cites a friend of Frank Dileo, p.415 (2004 edn)

13 A facsimile of the statement was leaked to The Smoking Gun website. Headed "Declaration of J. Chandler" it ends with the words "I declare under penalty of perjury that the foregoing is true and correct. Executed on December 28, 1993, at Santa Monica, California." It is signed in the name "J. Chandler" and on each of the four pages the name, address and phone number of the law firm handling Jordie's civil case appears at the side: Fogel, Feldman, Ostrov, Ringler.

14 *Today*, 27 August 1993. In general, and especially for references to newspaper stories from the 1990s, I have decided not to include headlines or the names of reporters unless they are of particular significance. These have generally been included for stories from 2000 onwards, though, as most of the news items in question can be found online using the additional information as search terms.

15 *The Sun*, 27 August 1993

16 Porter p.387. However, in Chandler's authoritative account the wording is more conservative. He says only that child abuse experts, including detectives, interviewed Jordie and found that the details of his story were "consistent" with those given to Rosato and, in an earlier interview, to psychiatrist Dr Mathis Abrams.(Chander p.123)

17 *The Times*, 28 August 1993

18 Randy Taraborrelli writes: "Jordie got the idea of a spoof of Kevin Costner's film, *Robin Hood, Prince of Thieves,* which he called *Robin Hood: Men in Tights*. For a twelve-year-old, he was amazingly creative. Jordie and his father, Evan, wrote the script (along with Evan's friend, JD Shapiro)". (Taraborrelli 2004, p.448) Raymond Chandler has a different version, in which Evan disputes the extent of his son's contribution. Evan and Jordie's mother, June, are depicted as quarrelling over the matter, with June complaining that Evan had gone back on a promise to give Jordie $5,000 from the sale of the screenplay. (Chandler p.55)

19 *Daily Mirror,* 26 August 1993

20 *The Observer* 29 August 1993

21 Raymond Chandler's book provides a detailed, at some points almost hour-by-hour and minute-by-minute account of events as seen from his family's side in the crucial months of April-December 1993, including a great deal on all the legal issues and manoeuvrings. While it is necessarily a partial account, it is clearly authoritative within its limitations. On matters such as the subject of this note, which has not been an issue of continuing dispute, it seems reasonable to accept Chandler's version of events – generally this version is strongly backed up by reference to specific legal documents, detailed discussion in specific times and

places between the named parties, and so forth. (Chandler 2004)

22 *The Sun,* 3 September 1993

23 *The Sun*, 25 August 1993

24 *News of the World,* 21 November 1993

25 *Today*, 28 August 1993

26 A good way to start is books dealing with children's sexuality and the perils of attempting to suppress it. See, for instance Levine (2002) and Yates (1979). A quick and interesting way of getting up to speed on historical and cross-cultural perspectives is via two articles in the July 2004 issue of the journal *Child and Adolescent Psychiatric Clinics of North America.* See Bullough (2004) and Nieto (2004). Indeed, this issue includes several other important articles, notably by Moser and others, Savin-Williams and others, and Yates. These various articles are scholarly but not dauntingly technical or "psychiatric", despite the title of the journal. Also, they all provide many pointers to further reading.

27 *The Sun,* 26 August 1993

28 Jones & Brown p.72

29 Taraborrelli p.396 (1994 edn)

30 Dimond p.22

31 Orth (1994)

32 *Today*, 13 September 1993

33 *The Sun*, 12 January 1994

34 My first thought was to speak of "paedophiles" rather than "child-lovers"; but then I realised this might seem incongruous. In popular usage these days "paedophiles" can only ever be bad guys. At one time, as readers who reached adulthood before about the mid-1970s may remember, paedophilia was a term little used outside medical circles. In clinical use it originally referred simply to adult sexual attraction towards children, whether or not any legal offence had been committed. Thus an entirely blameless adult who totally suppressed his or her sexual feelings for children could be diagnosed with paedophilia, or referred to as "a paedophile"; in theory, at least, this was a factual description, not a demonising term. Even to this day The International Statistical Classification of Diseases and Related Health Problems defines paedophilia as "a sexual preference for children, boys or girls or both, usually of prepubertal or early pubertal age". No behavioural component is required on this basis. The American Psychiatric Association's "Bible", the Diagnostic and Statistical Manual of Mental Disorders (4th edition, Text Revision) has a more complicated definition couched in terms of three diagnostic criteria. This definition – which is controversial within the profession – includes a behavioural component; but it is possible to be diagnosed with paedophilia on the basis of sexual feelings alone, if these feelings cause "distress or interpersonal difficulty". The three criteria are:

A. Over a period of at least 6 months, recurrent, intense sexually arousing fantasies, sexual urges, or behaviours involving sexual activity with a prepubescent child or children (generally age 13 years or younger);

B. The person has acted on these sexual urges, or the sexual urges or fantasies cause marked distress or interpersonal difficulty;
C. The person is at least age 16 years and at least 5 years older than the child or children in Criterion A.
Note the importance of the word "or" in criteria A and B, especially at the first occurrence in each case. Wikipedia has a well-referenced article on "Pedophilia" (US spelling) that describes the modern and historical clinical usage of the term.

35 The allegation has been made, as we shall see, that Michael used Vaseline in a sexual context with Jordie, but the two sources of this allegation are both dubious.

36 See, for instance, the *Daily Express*, 27 August 1993

37 Both from *Today*, 5 January 1994

38 *Daily Express*, 2 September 1993

39 A complete transcript of the tape was made available online by Raymond Chandler in connection with his book. The links, *www.AllThatGlittersbook.com* and *www.ATGbook.com* , were no longer displaying the relevant information at the time of going to press.

40 Allegedly! This is the version given by Chandler, p.68

41 The fact that everything short of thumbscrews was used to make Jordie talk will strike many as an odd form of child protection, but in reality ruthless tactics are an all too common feature of "saving" kids. Jackson's lawyer Bert Fields had occasion to take the Los Angeles Police Department to task for their "disgraceful" tactics in dealing with other boys they wanted to question in connection with Michael. Fields was particularly critical with regard to interviewing the boys without a parent being present. Indeed, the police in California have been known to go to extraordinary lengths to secure a child's "confession" to sexual involvement with adults, including dangling a boy by his legs over a cliff. No wonder it was rumoured Jordie had a nervous breakdown after these events and went into therapy – although, as we shall see, it was his father who experienced the more devastating mental problems in the long run.
The cliff incident, once dismissed as an urban legend, was actually confirmed on good authority at the time. James Grodin, the prosecutor in a subsequent trial (not of the police but of alleged "abusers"), is revealed to have conceded that one of the child prosecution witnesses may have been held over a cliff on Angeles Crest Drive north of the city of Los Angeles, and he astonishingly added, "you sometimes have to go to extremes because these kids are afraid to tell the truth". This was all a long time ago, back in the 1970s, but it is not misleading to quote it now as police and other law enforcement authorities in various parts of the US are still acting in the same no-holds-barred spirit. See Judith Levine's excellent *Harmful to Minors: The Perils of Protecting Children from Sex* (Levine, 2002) for recent and harrowing examples of children mangled by "the system". Extensive details of the-cliff dangling allegation and its history were posted on 27 October 2003 at this (now dead) URL: *http://www.paedosexualitaet.de/exp/*

Hollywood1973.html
This online account relates that the case was the subject of reports in 1974 (dates not given in full) in *The Advocate*, San Mateo, California.

42 Chandler p.96
43 *The Sun*, 4 September 1993
44 Chandler pp.104-111
45 *Daily Express*, 2 September 1993
46 Court transcript, 6 May 2005, p.9297
47 *National Enquirer*, 18 January 1994
48 *Today*, 5 October 1993
49 4641 Hayvenhurst, actually. "Hayvenhurst" is the name of the road where the house is located, but it appears to have been accidentally appropriated as a house name over the years, at least in the public mind.
50 *Today*, 3 December 1993
51 *News of the World*, 14 November 1993
52 *The Sun*, 18 November 1993
53 *Sunday Telegraph*, 29 August 1993
54 *Daily Mirror*, 24 November 1993
55 *The Sun*, 2 December 1993
56 *The Sun*, 17 November 1993
57 *The Sun*, 17 November 1993
58 *The People*, 14 November 1993. *The People* is a British tabloid Sunday newspaper, not to be confused with the American magazine *People*.
59 *The Sun*, 16 November 1993
60 *The Sun*, 16 November 1993
61 *The Sun*, 17 November 1993
62 *Today*, 17 November 1993
63 *News of the World*, 21 November 1993
64 *Daily Star*, 20 November 1993
65 *The People*, 14 November 1993
66 *The Sun*, 18 November 1993
67 *The People*, 14 November 1993
68 *Daily Mail*, 23 December 1993
69 *Daily Mail*, 23 December 1993
70 *Sunday Times*, 26 December 1993
71 *Today*, 24 December 1993
72 *Today*, 24 December 1993
73 *National Enquirer*, 11 January 1994
74 *News of the World*, 14 November 1993
75 *The People*, 14 November 1993
76 *Today*, 31 December 1993
77 *Today*, 15 November 1993
78 *Daily Mirror*, 24 November 1993; *News of the World*, 14 November 1993

79 *Wall Street Journal*, 27 December, 1995
80 Chandler p.190
81 Dimond p.103
82 *News of the World*, 14 November 1993
83 *Today*, 15 November 1993
84 *Today*, 31 December 1993. The figure of £6,500 is obviously an approximate rendering for readers of this British newspaper of what was originally an amount in US dollars. The same consideration applies to a good many other figures given in sterling throughout the book.
85 Dineen p.96
86 *Today*, 17 November 1993
87 *Today*, 10 December 1993
88 *The Sun*, 15 December 1993
89 *Today*, 31 December 1993
90 *Today*, 24 December 1993
91 *Today*, 21 January 1994
92 *Today*, 21 January 1994
93 Dimond pp.152-5
94 "Confession of judgment" meant that if Michael failed to make any of the scheduled payments that were part of the agreement the Chandlers would not have to start their case again from the beginning. If the case went back to court, the Chandlers would not need to re-plead their case; they would only need to show that Michael had failed to pay.
95 *Daily Mirror*, 26 January 1994
96 *The People*, 30 January 1994
97 " 'No angel' sex abuse case man jailed: Court of Appeal criticises judge for his unacceptable comment about girl, nine", Heather Mills, *The Independent*, 30 July 1993
98 *Today*, 4 March 1994
99 *Today*, 21 January 1994
100 See Chandler pp.127-167 for a very extensive account of how a legal strategy was developed on Jordie's behalf.
101 In December 1993, on his return to the US, Michael was served with a warrant for the strip search by the police. According to the order, any refusal to cooperate would be admissible in court and would be "an indication of his guilt". It was explained to his lawyers that in the event of a refusal Michael would probably be arrested anyway on "probable cause". (Taraborrelli p.534, 2004 edn)
102 *The Sun*, 18 November 1993
103 *Today*, 26 January 1994
104 Dimond pp.8-16 (Chapter One)
105 Taraborrelli p.536 (2004 edn
106 *National Enquirer*, 8 February 1994
107 *Daily Mirror*, 12 February 1994

108 Soon after Michael's death a book appeared by celebrity biographer Ian Halperin, in which Jordie's description of the penis markings was hastily dismissed on the basis of a single sentence from a news report appearing in *USA Today* and elsewhere in January 1994 which was later plastered all over the internet on Jackson fan sites. This snippet apparently confirmed from law enforcement sources that police photos of Michael Jackson's genitalia "do not match descriptions given by the boy". But if that was true, why did prosecutor Tom Sneddon attempt to get the photos admitted as evidence at Michael's trial in 2005?

Halperin made a number of other dubious claims in his book and in high profile press reports. His one great coup was that exactly six months before Michael died he publicly predicted that the star had only six months to live, saying he thought Michael was suffering from a genetic disorder affecting the lungs, Alpha-1 antitrypsin deficiency. The coroner's report of 28 August 2009 on Michael's death made no reference to a genetic disorder, fatal or otherwise, so far as I could tell from news coverage. Instead, the coroner confirmed the death as homicide primarily caused by administration of the powerful anaesthetic propofol. ("Jackson death ruled as homicide", BBC online news, 29 August 2009) Understandably, in the two months between Michael's death on 25 June and the coroner's report, Halperin's uncannily accurate prediction – accurate as to the timing at least – made him a very hot property in the media. But it appears he had just got lucky. (See Halperin p.56 as regards the penis markings and pp.210-1 on the genetic disorder.)

We learned considerably more a few weeks later. At the request of the Los Angeles Police Department and the city's District Attorney, the full autopsy had not been released; but the Associated Press soon got hold of a copy and published the details. The AP coverage revealed that, far from suffering from a fatal genetic disease, Jackson had been reasonably healthy for his age. However, he had been suffering from chronic inflammation of the lungs, a condition that was debilitating but not serious enough to be either a direct or a contributory cause of death in his case. ("Autopsy shocker: Jackson was healthy", Thomas Watkins, AP/Google, 1 October 2009)

109 *National Enquirer*, 7 June 1994

110 At Michael's trial, in the absence of the jury, King testified to the content of this conversation. The judge ruled King out as a witness on technical grounds unconnected to the accuracy of his account.

111 *National Enquirer*, 8 February 1994

112 Following the problems faced in getting "victims", including Jordie, to give criminal court testimony after a pay-off, the law in California was changed in a bid to compel them to do so, a subject that will be encountered again in Chapter Fourteen.

113 *The Sun*, 25 January 1994

114 *Daily Mirror*, 28 January 1994

115 *Today*, 22 January 1994

116 *Today*, 7 February 1994

117 Porter p.348

118 Little has surfaced publicly about these grand jury hearings. The most extensive account I have found is in Andersen (Andersen pp.315-7)

119 Andersen p.316

120 Porter p.204

121 Halperin pp.204-5. For completeness, it should be added that Jason Pfeiffer, an obese 35-year-old who worked for Michael's dermatologist Dr Arnold Klein, claimed after the star's death that he had had a love affair with him. The report does not include convincing details. ("Jacko 'gay lover': I lost a soulmate", Sean Hamilton, *The Sun*, 21 August 2009). Also, it seems unlikely Michael would have been physically attracted to anyone overweight. The boys who became his close friends, and with whom he shared his bed, were invariably lean. It is surely no coincidence that Michael became a bed-mate of his slim accuser Gavin Arvizo but not his massive younger brother, Star. Star reportedly weighed 225 lb at age fourteen when he appeared as a witness at Michael's trial; at the time of his arrest Michael was not much more than half that, at 120 lb. There was one rather stocky boy, to be sure, whom Michael was said to have admired and who had been invited to perform with him in his ill-fated *This Is It* concerts at the O_2 Arena in London. This was twelve-year-old Shaheen Jafargholi, a finalist in the TV talent contest *Britain's Got Talent*. Among the many acting and singing achievements in his young life was one that would certainly have appealed to Michael: he had toured on stage as a young Michael Jackson in *Thriller – Live*. Shaheen also sang for a TV audience of millions at Michael's memorial. However, there are doubtless those who admired the singing of outsize tenor Luciano Pavorotti without being sexually attracted to him. ("Fans and family remember Jackson", BBC news online, 7 July 2009; Wikipedia entry on Shaheen Jafargholi).

122 Tarraborreli p.316 (1992 edn). Lewis should not be confused – though he often is – with Gary Coleman, child star of TV's *Diff'rent Strokes*.

123 *Today*, 7 October 1993

124 Porter p. 178. Porter does not say when the picture was taken.

125 *Daily Express*, 26 August 1993]

126 Gold p.169

127 Dimond pp.130-1

128 Taraborrelli pp.306-7 (2004 edn)

129 Taraborrelli p.476 (1992 edn)

130 Taraborrelli p.476 (1994 edn)

131 A rare sympathetic view of "maternal men" with direct reference to Michael Jackson is to be found in a lucid and scholarly Master of Arts thesis undertaken by Kerry Mockler at Georgetown University (Mockler, 2004). Mockler's work will be considered in Chapter Nine.

132 Taraborrelli p.443 (1994 edn)

133 Jackson & Romanowski p.84

134 Jones & Brown pp.5-6

135 Porter p.359

136 *Daily Mail*, 27 August 1993

137 *Today*, 7 February 1993

138 *Today*, 26 February 1994

139 *Daily Mail*, 27 August 1994

140 *The Sun*, 28 August 1993

141 *The Daily Mirror*, 25 August 1993

142 *Sunday Times*, 29 August 1993

143 *Today*, 6 October 1993

144 Childhood "innocence", characterised by the complete absence of sexual feelings, fantasies, desires and overt sexual behaviours in children is a theme of popular and political discourse, but the professional literature across a range of disciplines, including psychology and sociology, tells a different story. The validity of Alfred Kinsey's pioneering statistical studies of children's sexual behaviour more than half a century ago (in Kinsey *et al.* 1948 and Kinsey *et al.* 1953) has been hotly contested, and since that time it has become increasingly difficult to conduct research in this area on account of ethical objections. Nevertheless, qualitative studies such as Floyd Martinson's *The Sexual Life of Children*, (Martinson,1994) and quantitative research such as that assembled and discussed in John Bancroft (ed), *Sexual Development in Childhood*, (Bancroft, 2003) leave little room for doubt that childhood sexuality is not an illusion, nor is it confined to abused children, as is sometimes claimed.

145 *Today*, 18 February 1994

146 Jackson (1988) pp.14-15

147 Levine (2002)

148 *Today*, 18 February 1994

149 O'Carroll (1980) p.157

150 *Today*, 6 October 1993

151 This can be seen on YouTube, here: *http://www.youtube.com/watch?v=T420qq9XY0Y*

152 Taraborrelli p.476 (1994 edn)

153 *The Sun*, 25 November 1993

154 Taraborrelli p.477 (1994 edn)

155 *Daily Express*, 26 August 1993

156 *Today*, 11 December 1993

157 Taraborrelli p.477 (1994 edn)

158 *Sunday Times*, 30 January 1994

159 *Today*, 11 December 1993

160 Leaked information that Jimmy's testimony had firmly backed Michael's "innocence" may well have reached reporters' ears. But that would surely have been judged a damp squib, a "non-story" not worth publishing.

161 Gilbey (1994)

162 Michael's leading trial lawyer, Tom Mesereau, would draw attention to this wedding in a question put in cross-examination to Neverland staff member Kiki Fournier.

163 "Would you let YOUR kids get so close to this weirdo?", Sharon Marshall, *Sunday People*, 18 April 1999.

164 *Mail on Sunday*, 29 August 1993

165 *Capital Gay*, 17 September 1993

166 Quoted by Porter without further attribution (Porter p.125).

167 Quoted by Porter (Porter pp.125-6).

168 *Daily Star*, 3 December 1993. No such controversy developed when Michael dedicated his 2001 album *Invincible* to the memory of fifteen-year-old Benjamin Hermansen. Benjamin, stabbed to death by neo-Nazis, had been a friend of Omer Bhatti, one of Michael's many "special friends". It appears that Michael never met Benjamin. As for Omer, we will be hearing considerably more about him later on ("Lovechild on the front row at memorial", Gary O'Shea, *The Sun*, 22 July 2009).

169 After a long hold-out, Michael had eventually been persuaded to let Bashir into his life in order to make the documentary over a period of several months in 2002. In these unusual circumstances it would have been foolish of the star not to put his best foot forward by allowing or inviting people such as David Rothenberg and young cancer victim Gavin Arvizo to tell their very positive stories. This was not so much "cashing in" as making sure the journalist could have no excuse for presenting an unbalanced account. In court in 2005 Gavin Arvizo testified to meeting at Neverland a "really badly burned" man he knew just as "David".

170 "Former Protégé Vouches for Jacko", Roger Friedman, Fox News, 7 April 2005. Except where otherwise stated, this and later citations of Friedman's work refer to his "Fox 411" column at Fox News online.

171 *News of the World*, 21 November 1993

172 Porter p.391

173 On the McMartin case see Eberle & Eberle (1986); on abuse panics in the UK see especially La Fontaine (1994) and Webster (1998, 2005).

174 Porter p.391

175 *Daily Express*, 26 August 1993

176 "Was There an Unknown Jacko Accuser?" Roger Friedman, Fox News, 25 March, 2005

177 *Daily Express*, 26 August 1993

178 *Ibid.*

179 Porter p.396, citing an unnamed journalist.

180 Porter p.92

181 Porter pp.111-2

182 Porter pp.350-1

183 Porter goes into considerable detail over several pages (Porter pp.280-4).

184 Jones & Brown p.127

185 Porter pp.442-3

186 Porter p.288. The *Daily Mirror* named Michael's housemaid Blanca Francia as a source regarding her boss's intensive interest in photos of child models. She reportedly said: "Michael Jackson trawled through hundreds of photos of boys to find special friends." (*Daily Mirror*, 18 December 1993)

187 Porter pp.442-3

188 Porter p.187

189 *The Sun*, 12 August, 1994

190 Wilson p.2

191 One exception to the rule, three-year-old Elbert Choi, will soon come into the picture.

192 Dimond pp.92-3

193 *Today*, 28 August 1993

194 *The Sun*,16 December 1993

195 Porter pp.348-9

196 Alert readers may have noticed a logical conundrum arising from the information so far given about Norma Staikos and Orietta Murdoch. In Chapter Three it was stated that Staikos had at some point during Murdoch's employment warned her never to leave her ten-year-old son alone with Michael. Why would she feel such a warning was necessary if Michael had no interest in black children? This could be explained if the boy was of relatively light complexion, like his mother, and could be taken for a Latino, or perhaps an Asian child. But if that were true, then, far from wanting to see Orietta sacked on racial grounds, Michael might have been expected to be keen on keeping her working at Neverland, in order to keep her son around as well – assuming, that is, that Michael was aware of the boy's existence and found him attractive! Logic, however, can only give us interesting speculations, not answers.

197 Jackson (1992) p.23

198 *Today*, 5 October 1993

199 Dimond p.36

200 *Mail on Sunday*, 29 August 1993

201 *News of the World*, 5 September 1993

202 Taraborrelli pp.461-2 (1994 edn)

203 *The People*, 29 August 1993

204 Taraborrelli p.462 (1994 edn)

205 *News of the World*, 5 September 1993

206 *Mail on Sunday*, 29 August 1993

207 *The Sun*, 6 September 1993

208 Although, in fairness, one has to admit the possibility that Quindoy had been referring to "creations" by the newspaper, not by himself.

209 *Today*, 25 September 1993

210 *Daily Mirror*, 22 September 1993

211 *Today*, 28 September 1993

212 *Today*, 16 September 1993

213 Taraborrelli p.473 (1994 edn)
214 *Ibid.* p.491
215 *Ibid.* p.505
216 *Ibid.* p.505
217 *News of the World*, 29 August 1993
218 Jackson & Romanowski p88-9
219 *News of the World*, 29 August 1993
220 *Today*, 5 October 1993
221 *The Sun*, 4 October 1993
222 *News of the World*, 12 September 1993
223 *Today*, 5 October 1993
224 *Sunday Mirror*, 29 August 1993
225 *Ibid.*
226 *The Sun*, 27 August 1993
227 *Daily Mirror*, 27 August 1993
228 *Daily Star*, 25 August 1993
229 *The Sun*, 25 August 1993
230 *Sunday Telegraph*, 29 August 1993
231 *The Sun*, 26 August 1993
232 Jones & Brown p.69
233 *Today*, 5 October 1993
234 *National Enquirer*, 5 April 1994
235 *Daily Mirror*, 27 August 1993
236 *Sunday Mirror*, 5 September 1993
237 *The Sun*, 4 October 1993
238 "Macaulay Culkin to Testify for Jacko", Roger Friedman, Fox News, 11 May 2005
239 At the time of the day-care panic, it was widely believed among those dealing with alleged abuse that children, who often live in a world of make-believe, would never make up stories about sexual abuse. Children, it was insisted, always tell the truth about such matters – except when they said there had been no abuse. When that happened, the prevailing dogma was that the child should be encouraged to "disclose". In practice what this often meant was that their interrogators were licensed to keep plugging away with leading questions, coercively repeated for as long as it took the child to produce the required story. In the UK children's homes panic, young adults were questioned about alleged abuse a decade or more earlier. Despite their by now mature years, they were still treated as "children" who would never tell lies – even though many of them had been assigned to state residential care in the first case following a background of delinquency and dishonesty. Others among them were highly suggestible, psychologically fragile people who struggled to distinguish fantasy from reality.

The evidence produced in the American day-care cases, and those of the British children's homes, was often so absurd it should have been laughed out of court. In the McMartin case the children produced colourful fantasies about their abusers building miles of secret tunnels under the school and whisking them away in hot-air balloons. Their adult British counterparts were at times almost as imaginative: one of them supposedly escaped from his children's home by jumping from a railway bridge onto a coal wagon of a train that took him over a hundred miles right across Wales. It was later discovered (but by then a wider investigation had been irrevocably prejudiced) that there were no coal trains going that way! Numerous allegations were made in which the abuse in question would have been impossible because the children's home resident and the accused staff member were not even at the same institution at the same time as each other. But those who were determined to "believe the children" managed to convince themselves that such inconsistencies and even impossibilities merely reflected the accuser's understandable confusion after the ordeal of abuse they had been through. As renowned abuse guru Roland Summit put it: "The more illogical and incredible the initiation scene might seem to adults, the more likely it is that the child's description is valid." As we shall see in Chapter Fifteen, a child psychologist schooled in such thinking, Anthony Urquiza, testified for the prosecution at Michael's trial. He would not be impressive under cross-examination. For the McMartin case see Eberle & Eberle; for the UK children's homes see Webster (1998 and 2005).

240 *Daily Mirror*, 24 November 1993

241 The statement is quoted in the same issue of the *Daily Mirror* just cited above i.e. 24 November 1993.

242 *Today*, 26 November 1993

243 *Ibid.*

244 *The Sun*, 30 November 1993

245 Gutierrez p.32

246 Porter p.191

247 *Daily Mirror*, 4 December 1993

248 *Today*, 6 January 1994

249 Unsurprisingly, Katherine's book, *The Jacksons: My Family*, does nothing to confirm any such awareness. On the contrary, she makes free with anecdotes about her son's strong interest in children apparently in all innocence, showing no awareness that eyebrows might be raised. Her book was published in 1990, three years before the first accusation of sexual abuse. She quotes her daughter Janet as saying that even as a teenager her brother was "crazy about younger children" (Jackson & Wiseman p.117). Remarkably, in what would be the ultimate embarrassing mum story for a man less used to public scrutiny, she says Michael's collection of family items included his nephew Taj's first diaper (Jackson & Wiseman p.207) – a detail later confirmed by Michael's sister La Toya, as we heard in Chapter Four.

250 Jackson & Romanowski p.164

251 Taraborrelli p.385 (1994 edn)

252 *Ibid.* p.386

253 *Ibid.* p.385
254 *Ibid.* p.385-6
255 *Ibid.* p.387
256 *Ibid.* p.386
257 *Ibid.* p.457
258 *Ibid.* p.389
259 Jackson & Romanowski p.165
260 Taraborrelli p.388 (1994 edn)
261 A couple of months after Weaver's story this police hype would be proven baseless. DeBarge reportedly appeared before a grand jury, but as a hostile witness. In other words, he was not willing to confirm a story that would be helpful to a prosecution case. (*Daily Express*, 25 March, 1994)
262 *Today*, 10 December 1993
263 *Today*, 4 February 1994
264 *Evening Standard*, 15 December 1993
265 *Ibid.*
266 *The Sun*, 15 December 1993
267 *Ibid.*
268 *The Sun*, 12 January 1994
269 Porter p.210 & p.354
270 Porter gives the address of this condominium as 10750 Wilshire Boulevard, locating it on the 14th floor. Jason would later confirm in his court testimony that it had been high up. His mother would testify, "I know it's on Wilshire. And I don't know the other street." Blanca would say she began working for Michael in 1986 at Hayvenhurst and he bought the hideout after she had been with him about a year, or somewhat less. Andersen and Taraborrelli both give the address as Galaxy Way, the latter being very specific, pinpointing it as 1101 Galaxy Way, #2247, Century City. Porter thickens the plot considerably by identifying another condominium as a locus of sleepovers by boys. In common with Taraborrelli, he says that in 1981 Michael purchased a condo at 5420 Lindley Avenue, Encino, at a time when reconstruction was going on at the Hayvenhurst family home. Taraborrelli says the place was purchased simply to provide temporary accommodation for the Jackson family and was later used by several of Michael's brothers at times when they had marital difficulties. Porter, though, says, "Since the condo afforded privacy, Michael would later share it with a series of very young boys he'd invite for sleepovers". This seems entirely possible, but Porter offers no evidence to back his claim. At the time when La Toya was denouncing Michael, she spoke of him bringing boys back to Hayvenhurst but made no mention of Lindley Avenue to the best of my knowledge. She may simply not have known what was going on but, according to Taraborrelli, she had a half-share in the Lindley Avenue property and would thus have been entitled to go there any time.
271 Gilbey (1994)

272 *The Sun*, 15 December 1993
273 *Today*, 7 February 1994
274 Gilbey (1994)
275 *Today*, 8 February 1994
276 *Today*, 7 & 8 February 1994
277 *Today*, 7 February 1994
278 Kincaid (1992) p.342
279 The McMartin case is examined in depth in Eberle & Eberle.
280 Eberle & Eberle p.10
281 "200 years not 'cruel and unusual punishment' in child porn case", Howard Fischer, *Arizona Daily Star*, 5 May 2006
282 "The Lies of Ashcroft", posting by Eric Cordian at internet group alt.activism.children; re-posted 15 August 2001 on the members' online forum of Ipce, *www.ipce.org* ; also "Child pornography: Buried by a pile of porn", *The Economist*, 16 January 2003.
283 Schuijer (1993)
284 *Ibid.*; O'Carroll (1980) pp.242-3
285 Schuijer; see also Sandfort, Brongersma & Naerssen (1991) p.206
286 These impediments to science were not confined to research on controversial topics such as child sexuality or paedophilia. In the late 1980s, when the AIDS epidemic made detailed knowledge of sexual behaviour an urgent public health concern, even the respected National Survey of Sexual Attitudes and Lifestyles in the UK found it had to watch its step. "Future historians", the authors noted, may wonder at the absence of information on the psychological and pleasurable nature of sexual relationships. The omissions must remain the responsibility of the researchers but, in mitigation…the sensitivities of funding bodies spending government money were made clear at a relatively early stage." Despite this cautious approach the expected government funding was eventually denied and a tightly constrained survey was able to go ahead only after securing the backing of the Wellcome Trust. See Wellings *et al.*, pp.7-11; also "Thatcher halts survey on sex", *Sunday Times*, 10 September 1989
287 Sandfort, Brongersma & Naerssen (1991), p.205
288 Schuijer p.15
289 Schuijer p.16. The radical new law of 1991 did not last long. Early in the new millennium the law was changed again, taking the age of consent effectively back to sixteen, the only exception being sex within wedlock, a provision which would accommodate the culture of certain immigrant communities within which a low age of marriage is traditional. In his paper *The Decline of Sexual Radicalism in the Netherlands*, Gert Hekma suggests that sexual radicalism across a range of issues ran out of steam for a variety of reasons. Interestingly, though, the retreat from permitting twelve-year-olds to have sex did not appear to have come about as a result of any specific problems with this liberal law. We are not told of evidence that children were being harmed by it. Hekma, a Dutch sociologist and

historian, tells us, rather, that the move appears to have been brought about by more diffuse concerns about the innocence of the young in the face of the increasingly visible sexualisation of society in general – as evidenced by an ever-growing amount of sex on television and elsewhere. See Hekma (2004), and Wikipedia entry on "Ages of consent in Europe".

290 O'Carroll (1980) pp.241-3

291 Associate Professor of Clinical Sociomedical Sciences (in Psychiatry) at Columbia University. Sandfort is also a past president of the International Academy of Sex Research.

292 Sandfort (1982) p.36. The research was published initially by a radical "alternative" imprint (Sandfort 1982) and later by an academic journal (Sandfort 1984)

293 Sandfort (1982)

294 The page references cited here are to Sandfort (1982), which is the text from which I worked. It may be, however, that Sandfort (1984), which is based on the same research, is now the more accessible source.

295 Sandfort (1982) p.48

296 *Ibid*. p.50

297 *Ibid*. p.47

298 *Ibid*. p.47

299 *Ibid*. p.52

300 *Ibid*. p.53

301 *Ibid*. p.54

302 *Ibid*. p.54

303 Carpenter pp.366-7

304 *Ibid*. p.368

305 Sandfort (1982) p.58

306 *Ibid*. p.65

307 *Ibid. p.67*

308 *Ibid*. p.69

309 *Ibid*. p.80

310 *Ibid*. p.81

311 *Ibid*. p.82

312 *Ibid*. pp.83-4

313 *Ibid*. p.85

314 *Ibid*. p.87

315 *Ibid*. p.100

316 *Ibid*. p.98

317 *Ibid*. p.98

318 *Ibid*. p.101

319 *Ibid*. p.102

320 *Evening Standard*, 25 August 1993; see also Chandler pp.22-3, where the reference is to a *National Enquirer* story in May 1993 about Michael's "new family".

321 Chandler p.159

322 Sandfort (1982) p.105

323 *Ibid.* p.105

324 *Ibid.* p.107

325 *Ibid.* p.108

326 Randall p.64

327 However, in 1982, thirty five years after Elwin's book, it was revealed to the surprise of the academic community that ghotuls continued to exist and even expand. This finding, by a scholar called Haimendorf (forename not given), is reported briefly in Nieto (2004).

328 Rind *et al.* (1998)

329 Coxell *et al.* (1999)

330 Sandfort (1982) p.117

331 *Ibid.* p.134

332 Taraborrelli p.559 (1992 edn). Taraborrelli also refers in his sources to sworn declarations in a lawsuit brought by Hazel Gordy Jackson: Taraborrelli p.581 (1992 edn)

333 Jackson & Romanowski p.257

334 *The Sun*, 21 February 1994

335 They may, however, all have become pleasanter and wiser people as the years have mellowed them. A documentary on Britain's Channel 4 TV in 2008 was particularly revealing in this respect. *The Jacksons Are Coming* was the story of a few weeks in which members of the Jackson family went property hunting in Devon. Present were Tito Jackson, his three sons, brother Jackie and mother Katherine. The family were subjected to a lot of media hassle and what seemed like cynical manipulation by a local opportunist. TV writer Lucy Mangan commented: "The Jacksons are odd. But on this showing, they are mostly oddly dignified and rather tolerant of a life that has evidently been strewn with betrayals, disloyalty and exploitation on all sides." I agree. The Jacksons came across as courteous and mature. ("Last Night's TV: On behalf of the whole country, I'd like to apologise wholeheartedly to the Jackson family", *The Guardian*, Lucy Mangan, 28 November 2008).

However, speaking after Michel's death, his brother Marlon made remarks that might be seen as giving a rather sinister explanation for the family's restraint. He was quoted as saying: "My father beat us a lot of times. I felt resentful. That sort of discipline wasn't abnormal in our neighbourhood but it doesn't mean it was right." He said he believed these beatings might have fatally damaged Michael's self-esteem and ability to fend for himself: "It does a couple of things to you – it forms you into this person who is not able to confront people when they're not satisfied with things. It also makes people able to take advantage of you. I found a lot of my siblings were that way." ("Michael Jackson to be buried in a gold casket – encased in cement – says brother Marlon", Kate Mansey, *Sunday Mirror*, 29 August 2009)

336 *Today*, 10 December 1993
337 *Sunday Mirror*, 6 February 1994
338 *The Times*, 10 December 1993
339 Gold pp.17-29
340 Taraborrelli p.107 (1994edn)
341 Nature is indeed awesomely cruel to the squeamish eye of civilised man. But we should not ignore the fact that rats packed into a cage behave more aggressively to each other than those that are not.
342 La Toya in discussion with Darcus Howe on *The Devil's Advocate*, Channel 4, 1993
343 Interview with Oprah Winfrey broadcast on 10 February, 1993. (Dineen p.93)
344 Taraborrelli p.12 (1994 edn); Jackson & Romanowski p.2
345 Taraborrelli p.21 (1994 edn)
346 Taraborrelli p8 (1992 edition)
347 *Ibid*. p.16
348 *Ibid*. p.187
349 *Ibid*. p.394
350 *Ibid*. p.199
351 TV miniseries, *The Jacksons: An American Dream*, first broadcast on ABC television in November, 1992
352 Taraborrelli p.187(1992edn)
353 *Ibid*. p.188
354 *Ibid*. p.188
355 *Ibid*. p.189
356 *Ibid*. p.143
357 *Ibid*. p.323
358 *Ibid*. p.210
359 *Ibid*. p111
360 *Ibid*. p.192
361 *Ibid*. pp.192-3
362 *Daily Star*, 15 July 1994
363 *The Sun*, 15 July 1994; *Today*, 12 July 1994
364 Barrie (1902) pp.229-30
365 Taraborrelli p.196 (1992edn)
366 *Ibid*. p.198
367 *Ibid*. p196
368 *National Enquirer*, 19 April 1994
369 Porter pp.345-6
370 *Ibid*. pp.267-8
371 *Ibid*. p.325
372 *Ibid*. p.275
373 Taraborrelli p.344 (1992edn)
374 Porter p.175

375 Taraborrelli p.344 (1992edn)

376 *Ibid.* p.347

377 *Ibid.* p.200; *News of the World*, 29 August 1993

378 A news release in support of Michael, issued by Jermaine and signed by the whole family was published in the *News of the World* of 29 August 1993. Interestingly, the statement does not spell out the family's belief in Michael's innocence in unequivocal terms despite using the word unequivocal. The key phrasing reads: "... we wish to state our collective, unequivocal belief that Michael has been made a victim of a cruel and obvious attempt to take advantage of his fame and success." That could be right, but it would not necessarily mean Michael was innocent. Is this ambivalence why La Toya's name appears on the fax along with all the others? By November, "the family appeared to water down their support" for Michael, according to the *Daily Mirror* of 19 November 1994, announcing that they would conduct their own "investigation" into his conduct. Soon after his civil settlement with Jordie he would be appearing with the rest of the family, minus La Toya, at the Jackson Family Honours concert in Las Vegas. Presumably he had survived their investigative scrutiny!

379 *News of the World*, 29 August 1993

380 *Daily Express*, 26 November 1993

381 Taraborrelli pp.78-9 (1992edn)

382 *Ibid.* p.45

383 Dineen p.96

384 Taraborrelli p.367 (1992edn)

385 *Ibid.* p.368

386 *Ibid.* p.374

387 *Ibid.* p.372

388 Marlon's twin brother Brandon died within twenty four hours of birth.

389 For an excellent neo-Darwinian view, see *Born To Rebel: Birth Order, Family Dynamics and Creative Lives*, by Frank Sulloway. The author provides extensive evidence to support the theory that a significant part of our personality is formed as a result of competition among siblings to win parental approval and attention. (Sulloway, 1996)

390 Taraborrelli p.52 (1992edn)

391 *Ibid.* p.174

392 *Ibid.* p.265

393 *Sunday Night Clive*, BBC1 TV, 27 February 1994

394 Taraborrelli p.262 (1992 edn)

395 *Ibid.* p.181 (1992 edn)

396 *Ibid.* p6. & p.84 (1992 edn)

397 "Gag on La Toya". Gerard Evans, *Sunday Mirror*, 6 February 1994

398 "La Toya threat to Jackson", *Today*, 10 February 1994

399 Dimond p.6. It may or may not be significant in this context that Rebbie reportedly "would not go anywhere near her father" at Michael's funeral. In order

to keep her distance, she, "ceded her monitoring of Michael's three kids. Janet Jackson shepherded the kids through the service." The children's grandmother, Katherine, had been granted guardianship of the children; with her approval, they were being cared for on a day-to-day basis by Rebbie at this time. ("Neverland NOT Sold, Certainly Not to Designer", Roger Friedman, *The Hollywood Reporter*, 6 September, 2009; "Katherine & Rebbie Jackson Jointly Raising Michael's Kids", *www.accesshollywood.com*, 5 September 2009)

400 See, for instance, Finkelhor (1980)

401 MacCarthy (1989). The index entry on p.335 for Gill's "sexual tendencies" has sub-headings for bestiality, casual liaisons, droit de seigneurism, homosexuality, incest, ménages à trois, New Women, phallic fixation, pubescent girls, uxoriousness, voyeurism, and women in uniform. And he still found time for his art!

402 Jones & Brown p.84

403 Porter p.530

404 This makes no sense, though, in terms of their age. When the boys' mother, Delores "Dee Dee" Martes, died in 1994, Tito's eldest son, Taj, was twenty one, middle son Taryll nineteen, and youngest of the boys, Tito Joe ("TJ"), sixteen.

405 Porter pp.530-1

406 *Ibid.* p.15

407 *Sunday Mirror*, 6 February 1994

408 Jackson & Romanowski p.133 & pp. 158-9

409 Taraborrelli pp.512-5 (1992 edn)

410 Jackson & Romanowski p.240

411 *Ibid.* p.17

412 *Ibid.* p.90

413 *Ibid.* p.129

414 *Sunday Night Clive*, BBC1, 27 February 1994

415 Taraborrelli p.486 (1992 edn)

416 Jackson & Romanowski p.178

417 *Ibid.* p.179

418 *Ibid.* p.258

419 Taraborrelli p.487 (1992 edn)

420 Jackson & Romanowski p.232

421 *Ibid.* pp.216-7

422 Maury Povich chat show, reported in *Today*, 14 December 1993

423 Taraborrelli p.487 (1992 edn)

424 *Ibid.* p.489

425 *Ibid.* pp.240-1

426 Jackson & Romanowski p.62

427 Taraborrelli p.241 (1992 edn)

428 *Ibid.* p.189

429 Bell *et al.* (1981) p.184

430 Jackson (1988) p.162
431 Taraborrelli p.257 (1992 edn)
432 Jackson (1988) p.164
433 Sky p.109
434 *Ibid.* p.108
435 Orth (2004)
436 Jones & Brown p.101
437 *Mail on Sunday*, 5 September 1993
438 Richard Matsuura also appeared in the documentary *Michael Jackson's Mind*, Channel 5, in October 2005. Footage was shown of Matsuura as a boy in Michael's company. In the Channel 5 programme Matsuura claimed the friendship had gone on for a while. He was wholly positive about the relationship and said nothing inappropriate had taken place. In passing, it might also be remarked that this post-trial programme featured a formidable line-up of figures: Randy Taraborrelli (almost inevitably), Diane Dimond, Stacy Brown, Ernie Rizzo, Carole Lieberman, Oliver James, Laurie Levenson, Shmuley Boteach, Philippe and Stella LeMarque, all of whom feature elsewhere in this volume, plus Jehovah's Witness Firpo Carr and Johnny Jackson (no relation), drummer with the Jackson Five, along with Geoffrey Beattie (behavioural psychologist), Dorothy Rowe (psychiatrist), and Gareth Smith (psychiatrist). Not even this stellar line-up, however, could make much sense of Michael's mind, except perhaps this highly technical contribution: "He's not schizophrenic, but he's pretty much away with the fairies."
439 This is not just an urban myth. A mutant allele of the ALDH2 gene, common in the east, causes the inability of the body to handle alcohol. See, for instance, Lin & Cheng (2002)
440 Sky p.106
441 Jackson (1988) p.272
442 Sky p.105
443 Taraborrelli p.534 (1992 edn)
444 Opinion of Dr Robert Kotler of UCLA Medical School, cited in *National Enquirer*, 22 March 1994
445 *Ibid.* p.257
446 Baudrillard (1990), p.147
447 Jones & Brown pp.45-6
448 *Ibid.* p.130
449 Sky p.105
450 *Ibid.* p.105
451 Taraborrelli pp.263-4 (1992 edn)
452 Ibid. p.399
453 Ibid. p.547
454 Green, cited in LeVay (1994) p.115
455 Jackson (1988) p.253

456 Jackson & Romanowski pp.82-3
457 Jackson (1988) p.254
458 Jackson & Romanowski p.89
459 The delightfully and, as we shall see, appropriately named cultural theorist Professor Awkward has suggested that Jackson's hand brings our attention to the symbolic domain of the "black phallus". For the professor, Jackson's crotch-grabbing is a "counterhegemonic act" that "seems intended effectively to problematise formulations of his asexuality" and "signifies resoundingly upon historical formulations of black masculinity that, through the ritualistic hanging, castrating, and burning of black male bodies, suggested white hypersensitivity to the perceived dangers of the black phallus." An awkward point Prof. Awkward hardly seems to have noticed is that Michael was not that black any more by the time his crotch-grabbing antics started, thanks to using the skin-bleaching cream Porcelana (see Porter p.259 and Taraborrelli p.351 (2004 edn)), and certainly not by the time the prof's work appeared in book form in 1995. As a culturalist, Awkward might have been expected to pay attention to the symbolic significance of Michael's changing complexion.
460 Taraborrelli p.222 (1992 edn)
461 Sky p.106
462 Jackson (1992) p.19
463 *Ibid.* p.50
464 *Ibid.* p.50
465 Taraborrelli p.475 (1992 edn)
466 *Ibid.* pp.125-7
467 Dineen p.38
468 *Ibid.* p.38
469 Taraborrelli pp.59-60 (1992 edn)
470 Jackson (1988) pp.158-9
471 Jackson (1992) pp.13-14
472 Quoted in Dineen p.30
473 Mecca (1997)
474 *King!* magazine, No. 11, April 1997. It should not be supposed that the market for Michael as a figure of spiritual significance was confined to the unsophisticated. Michael Dyson, when he was an assistant professor of American civilization and African-American Studies at Brown University, with a doctorate from Princeton University, authored a book published in 1993 called *Reflecting Black*, in which he devotes a chapter to what he calls Michael's "postmodern spirituality". Would his enthusiasm have survived the Chandler scandal later that year? It is a moot point. The "spiritual" inspiration Michael drew from children may suddenly have seemed a little too "postmodern".

Nevertheless, reading Dyson's eloquent testimony to a spiritual dimension in Jackson's work, it is very hard to be cynical. Dyson, like Michael, was born in 1958 and grew up as part of a large, black, working-class family. His father, a religious man, worked in a brake factory in Detroit. As a youngster, Dyson felt a "passionate identification" with the assassinated Martin Luther King, "this soldier of love". For him even to mention Michael's name in the same breath as King's is, to say the least, interesting. In one particularly committed, even enraptured passage, Dyson tells us that "perhaps the most poignant and powerfully explicit display of Jackson's brand of secular spirituality" was reserved for the 1988 Grammy Awards Show, at which he sang "The man in the mirror", with its message that if you want to make the world a better place, you first have to work on yourself. Joining in on the occasion, Dyson tells us, were Siedah Garrett, who wrote the song, and gospel singer Andrae Crouch. Dyson writes:

> As Jackson, Crouch, Garrett, and the others continued to sing, the choir from New York's New Hope Baptist Church emerged from the back of the stage, augmenting the vocal power of Jackson's message. The religious nature of Jackson's interpretation became visually apparent, and the implicitly religious sensibilities of his performance became explicitly captured in the religious symbols surrounding Jackson. Jackson spun and fell on his knees, dramatizing his message of the dialectical relationship between personal change and social transformation. Back on his feet, Jackson pleaded once more for the world to change. Again he fell to his knees, but this time he succumbed to the spirit and passion of the moment and remained there. Jackson was spontaneously touched by what was occurring, as if he were a spectator to the event, as if he were only a vehicle, an agent of a transcendent power. Jackson was as shaken by the power of the message as if he were hearing and delivering it for the first time, a lesson that great gospel singers and preachers have mastered. Andrae Crouch then moved over from the side of the stage, as if he were in a church service where someone was "slain in the spirit," and after wiping Jackson's brow, he helped him to his feet. Jackson, with new vitality breathed into him, "got happy" again, turning several times, spinning joyously, and spontaneously jumping up and down, shaking his hands, and doing a complex walk-skip-jump movement.
>
> Jackson's choreography of his religious joy, as he transformed the Grammy stage into a sanctuary, was infectious, and his audience, his faithful congregation, responded in the ecstatic glee of emotional abandon to his every move, groan, and gesture. Jackson exhorted them by telling them that everyone has to make a change, that the black man has to make a change, and that the white man has to make a change. As he dropped to his knees yet another time, the twenty-person choir moved ever closer to him, cutting off the stage and reducing it to a diamond, both in its shape and substance. It was priceless and invaluable because Jackson was projecting the power of African-American spirituality forward and having it rearticulated back to him in the reverberating emotion of the audience and the escalating ecstasy of his singers. Jackson went down, like a martyr figure delivering a messianic message, sinking to his knees

that his audience might, as he repeatedly implored them, "stand up, stand up, stand up." Jackson then resorted to his best exhortative deep-throated vocal to release a volcanic melisma and syllabic repetition of the word you, in "you-you-you-ou-ow-ow got to make a change," catalyzing a tumultuous response in the Grammy audience.

At the consummation of his homily in song, Jackson whispered, "Make that change," and his congregation came to their feet, thundering their applauded amen at Jackson, yielding their total love and trust to his expressed desire to change the world by their changing themselves. The camera displayed a felicitous complicity in the spirit of the moment and scouted the audience for the converted and the committed, finding them scattered throughout the auditorium's scene of pandemonium. (Dyson pp.56-7)

Dyson makes the extraordinary claim here that Michael had been "spontaneously touched by what was occurring". The professor's faith in his hero's – or idol's – sincerity is itself touching, but in showing that faith he implicitly gives the star too little credit for his abilities as a showman. It might be pertinent to ask whether, offstage, Michael was over the years as willing to face the man in the mirror as he was to urge his Grammy audience, or "congregation", to "make a change" in their lives.

475 Bach (1992) p.75

476 Taraborrelli p396 (1992edn)

477 As Stephen Hinerman, cultural studies academic and music critic has noted: "In the end, the authentic Michael Jackson remains ambiguous. He is painted as a mirror, one who simply reflects the world rather than creates it. Perhaps this is where postmodern stardom is ultimately most comfortable, where the 'authentic' star is whatever the audience is – devoid of motive, drive, or desire independent of that contained within the fans. In this sense, keeping one's image system a mass of contradictions which appear unresolvable is more than just a way to avoid getting caught in a career-ending scandal; it is the ultimate in postmodern marketing. There are always 'halls of mirrors' for the mass-mediated, postmodern star to be reflected in; if one mirror shatters, the star can always point to the 'real me, over there,' in another reflection, one that could itself shatter at any moment. We sometimes speak of criminals staying 'one step ahead of the law.' What Michael Jackson has shown is that for public figures, it is best to always stay one step ahead of having a singular authentic identity." (Hinerman, 1997, p.160)

478 Jackson (1992) p.63

479 *Ibid*. p.60

480 Jackson (1988) p.163

481 *The Observer*, 29 August 1993

482 Quoted in Dineen p.15

483 For an extensive discussion of sexual indeterminacy in the *Thriller* video, see Mercer (1994).

484 Smith (1994)
485 Dineen p.71
486 Smith (1994)
487 Jackson & Romanowski p.232
488 *Daily Telegraph*, 29 August 1994
489 *Daily Mirror*, 10 May 1994
490 I know of just one honourable exception, James R Kincaid. In two deeply insightful books (Kincaid 1992 & 1998) he explores adult attraction to children –including their erotic allure – as a mainstream cultural phenomenon rather than the preserve of a deviant minority. It will not be possible for me to comment on Kincaid's work in a way that would do justice to the sophistication of his ideas. I would simply urge readers to catch up on his books if they have not already done so. In the second of these, *Erotic Innocence: The Culture of Child Molesting*, he considers the allegations made against Michael Jackson in 1993-4. In common with other cultural studies scholars, he shows more concern with the cultural significance of the allegations than whether or not they were true, and he makes so light of them as to seem downright flippant. But, there is real depth to his work: his books need to be read in their entirety. He is also very hard to quote, because the potential "soundbites" tend to be deeply woven into their specific context, outside of which the meaning unravels. However, on the crotch-grabbing phenomenon, it seems just about possible to detach what Kincaid writes:

> Jackson's subtle abilities to woo his audience coexist with a defiance so blunt that young people everywhere respond immediately: Jackson looks the way he wants to look, dresses outrageously, adorns himself, and doesn't obey gravity, much less parental strictures: if you feel like it, he says, then grab your crotch and wave it right in Dad's face. (Kincaid 1998, p.237)

It is a comment which captures the subversiveness of the gesture even as it evades the overtly sexual implications of that subversion.

491 Fuchs (1995)
492 Jackson (1992) p.13. The reference is to Saint Teresa of Ávila
493 Barrie (1928) pp.9 & 25
494 *Ibid.* p103
495 *Evening Standard*, 11 October 1993
496 Taraborrelli p.283 (1992 edn)
497 *Ibid.* p328
498 Barrie (1928) p.118
499 Smith (1994)
500 *Ibid.*
501 Barrie (1928) p.140; Barrie (2007) p.136
502 Fraser (1976)
503 The part of Peter is usually played on stage by a woman, following the tradition

of the "leading boy" in pantomime. "Realism" is thus clearly sacrificed in favour of a purely symbolic representation of childhood. In the most popular screen versions, however, Peter appears as a pre-adolescent of eleven or twelve, giving an impression that Barrie cannot have intended if we bear in mind that children lose their baby teeth at a much earlier age. The novel, as well as the play, clearly specifies that Peter still had his first teeth (Barrie (2007) p.118)

504 Peter McKay, *Evening Standard*, 2 September 1993

505 Gilbey (1994)

506 Barrie (1928) p.178

507 *Ibid.* p.112

508 Smith (1994)

509 Barrie (1902) pp.227-8

510 Mockler (2004)

511 Barrie (2007) p.87

512 Barrie (1902) p.229

513 Mockler pp.32-3

514 See, for instance, Traina (1998) and Gabb (2004).

515 Mockler p.49

516 *Ibid.* pp.57-8

517 *The Sun*, 31 August 1993

518 O'Carroll (1994). I have adopted the name Carl Toms as a matter of branding strategy for the present volume, which is very different in character to my other work.

519 *Michael Jackson: What really happened*, A documentary by Jacques Peretti, Channel 4, 24 October 2007; see also Peretti's background article "The man who fell to earth", *The Guardian* (TV section, *The Guide*), 20-26 October 2007

520 Andrews & Taraborrelli p.1

521 Taraborrelli pp.592-3 (1994 edn)

522 *Ibid.* p.582

523 *The Sun*, 27 August 1994

524 Jon Pareles, *New York Times*, 6 February 1994

525 Jackson (1988) p.174

526 *Forbes*, quoted in the *Sunday Telegraph*, 29 August 1993; Taraborrelli (2004) p.442; *Daily Mail*, 25 August 1993.

527 *The Guardian*, 1 January 1994. Aphrodite Jones devotes several pages of her book on Michael's trial to a detailed description of an introductory video of Neverland shown to jurors by the prosecution. See Jones (2007) pp.51-5

528 And animals. His "influence" was nowhere more "extraordinary" than in the training of the chimps in his zoo if Victor Gutierrez is to be believed. He reports the following alleged account by Jordie Chandler: "Michael took us to the chimpanzee cage. Then he grabbed between his legs and called upon the monkeys to do the same. He told me they were trained. The chimpanzees held their penises and began to play with their penises in front of us. My little sister didn't

understand what was happening, so I got her out of there. For Michael, it was fun and he told us to watch." Gutierrez claims this story was backed up by Jackson's security guards, who told him children seeing this display were not amused. Specifically, he cites Ralph Chacon as saying some of the kids laughed at first but then they wanted to go. Said Chacon: "Michael asked them not to go and asked them if they knew what the animals were doing. The kids just shrugged their shoulders without knowing what was happening. We couldn't do anything." (Gutierrez pp.22-5) However, Chacon turned out to be a highly unreliable witness at Michael's trial. See Chapter Sixteen.

529 *Daily Express*, 1 September 1993

530 "Jackson: How the star was destroyed", Jamie Malanowski & Pete Clark, *Evening Standard* 20 December 1993

531 *Mail on Sunday* 10 April, 1994, *Night & Day* supplement

532 *The Sun*, 1 December 1993

533 *Today*, 5 January 1994

534 Hughes (2004) p.56

535 *Sunday Times*, 5 September 1993

536 *Today*, 7 February 1994

537 "The Pellicano Brief", Howard Blum & John Connolly, *Vanity Fair*, March 2004

538 *Today*, 26 January 1994

539 Dimond pp.171-82

540 Taraborrelli p.21 (1994 edn)

541 *Ibid.* pp.146-9

542 Taraborrelli pp.308-9 (1992 edn)

543 *Ibid.* p302

544 *Ibid.* p498-9

545 Gutierrez p.210

546 Andersen p.156

547 Testimony of Jesus Salas. Court transcript, 4 April 2005, p.4797

548 Orth (1994) p.137

549 "Michael Jackson at 40", Barney Hoskyns, *The Independent*, 29 August 1998

550 Andersen pp.105-6

551 *News of the World*, 2 December 1993

552 Jackson (1988) p.274

553 *Ibid.* p244

554 Skynner & Cleese (1993) p.140

555 Taraborrelli p.386 (1992 edn)

556 *Ibid.* p412

557 Oliver James in the *Sunday Express*, 25 February 1996

558 *King!* magazine tour special (1997) p.44

559 *The Guardian*, June 15, 2005

560 Hughes pp.171-6

561 Friedman wrote: "If you type healtheworld into the Internet, it automatically

takes you to a Web site for healthekids.net, which is hosted by Shmuley Boteach, the publicity hound/rabbi. On that site, it appears that Jackson and Boteach's charities have somehow merged. The phone number in New York for this group turns up an answering machine. Repeated calls were not returned." See: "Jacko No Longer Heals the World", Roger Friedman, Fox News, 18 February, 2002

562 Michael's flagship charity, the Heal the World Foundation, was launched in 1992. The Associated Press reported that with his career soaring thanks to the new album, *Dangerous*, and a lucrative Pepsi endorsement deal, the singer planned a world tour to help raise $100 million for his new children's charity and to "spread the message of global love." The organisation built playgrounds, provided immunisations and funded scores of children's causes around the world. It helped pay for a Hungarian boy's lifesaving liver transplant and co-sponsored an airlift of more than forty six tons of relief supplies to war-torn Bosnia-Herzegovina in 1992. Richard Fowler, director of the foundation from 1995 to 1997, is quoted by AP as saying that the lofty $100 million goal was never reached. Instead, the foundation doled out about $4 million in its first five years. By late 2002, however, it had net assets of just $3,542 and reported $2,585 in expenses, mostly for "management fees". The foundation no longer had a director, president or other top manager besides Jackson, who was listed as chairman. The foundation had been suspended in California from April 2002 for failing to file annual statements required of tax-exempt organizations. ("Jackson's foundation now virtually defunct", Associated Press, March 25, 2004; *http://msnbc.msn.com/id/4601265/*)

563 *Michael Jackson's Boys*, Channel 4, 26 January 2005

564 "How superstars spin out of control", Robert Sandall, *Sunday Times*, 30 January 1994

565 "Addiction" is a strong word but there is considerable evidence, including Michael's own testimony in court, to support the view that long before his sensational, anaesthetic-induced death, he continued to use drugs to the extent of impairing his mental faculties, even while conducting important legal business. In his Fox News column of 25 October 2007, Roger Friedman drew attention to a court deposition Jackson had given three months earlier, when "the beleaguered pop star 'fessed up for once about where his head's been at when he signs documents". The testimony, given on 25 July 2007, related to agreements he signed with former manager Dieter Wiesner. Jackson, "as usual", according to Friedman, claimed to have forgotten putting his signature on the dotted line. In the deposition, taken in London, an attorney for Wiesner asked if he had been impaired by the taking of prescription medications or "something else" at the time of signing documents in the case. Michael answered, "I could have been". Then there was the following exchange:

Q: How long in 2003 were you impaired because of the taking of prescription medication?

A: I don't know.

Q: Was it most of 2003?

A: I'm not sure.

Claims of mental impairment, especially memory lapses, can on occasion be very convenient to witnesses in court who wish to avoid taking responsibility for what they have done in the past. Was Michael merely pretending to drug-induced mental impairment for this reason? Evidence to be touched upon in Chapter Eighteen, especially claims made in legal contexts by Michael's second wife, Debbie Rowe, and another manager, Marc Schaffel, suggests there was more to it.

566 Taraborrelli pp.584-9 (1994 edn)

567 *Ibid.* p.585

568 Sandfort (1982) pp.81-2

569 Levine (2002)

570 Sandfort (1994)

571 *Ibid.* pp.52-3

572 O'Carroll (1980) p.173

573 Chandler p.45

574 *Ibid.* p.13

575 *Ibid.* p.41

576 A transcript of the taped conversation between Evan Chandler and Dave Schwartz, and other relevant documents, were put online by Raymond Chandler in 2004. The links were no longer working by the time this book was going to press.

577 Orth (1994) p.131

578 Chandler p.22. The text does not specify the date of the *National Enquirer* article but it would have been around mid-May

579 Chandler p.30

580 *Ibid.* p.48

581 *Ibid.* p.49

582 *Ibid.* p.54

583 National Institutes of Health *http://www.ninds.nih.gov/disorders/gauchers/gauchers.htm*

584 Chandler p.90

585 *Ibid.* p.91

586 Hughes p.46

587 Gutierrez (1997)

588 *Daily Mirror*, 10 May 1994

589 "Michael Jackson's Victory", Joal Ryan, Associated Press, 10 April 1998, accessed at *http://www.eonline.com/News/Items/0,1,2828,00.html*

590 See also "Who is Victor Gutierrez and why did Michael sue him?" *http://www.mjcafe.net/the%20legend%20speeches%20&%20faq/c13.htm*

591 "The Jackson Family's 'Jackie O' ", Roger Friedman, Fox News, 9 June, 2005

592 Orth (2003)

593 See "The Main Players in the Michael Jackson Case" *http://www.mj-case.net/players.html* (February 2005)

594 Eglinton 1971
595 Gutierrez p.77
596 Chandler pp.20-21
597 *Ibid.* p21
598 Gutierrez pp.52-3
599 The facsimiles and photographs in the book appear in a sequence of unnumbered pages.
600 Dimond pp.44-45
601 Gutierrez pp.108-9
602 Chandler p.102
603 Gutierrez p.112
604 *Ibid.* p.124
605 "Blasts From the Past", 28 March 2005. This online report cites "a British newspaper": *http://www.mj411.com/archives/2005/03/*
606 A transcript of the Gardner tape was among the documents made available online by Raymond Chandler at the now defunct *www.ATGbook.com*
607 Fischer (1994)
608 See Wikipedia entry on amobarbital.
609 Dimond pp.61-2. Raymond Chandler examined Fischer's claims in detail in one of the documents he put online in 2004. His article had been written soon after the Fischer piece appeared, in order to rebut it at the time; but there is also the following PS: "For many years Fischer's article has been hailed by Jackson's loyal fans as the definitive report on the 1993 scandal, and they have kept it posted on their Web site for all to see. It has, in effect, become their bible. On 1 September, 2004, I noticed that Fischer's article was gone. A note stated that Fischer had 'a change of heart' and her attorneys requested that the article be removed." The serially mistaken "investigator" Ian Halperin tried to revive the hoary old Amytal myth. Wrong about Jordie Chandler's description of Michael's genitals, wrong about Michael's "gay" orientation, wrong about the cause of Michael's death, he was wrong about this too: he relied on Mary Fischer's claim, blissfully unaware, it seems, that the claim had been withdrawn. (Halperin, 2009, pp.36-45)
610 Channel 4, 26 January 2005
611 Gutierrez p.203
612 "I want to see Jacko again says Jordie", Millicent Brown, *Daily Mirror*, 23 January 1995
613 "Divorce American Style", Barry Wigmore, *Today*, 8 March 1995. Wigmore's source is the US supermarket tabloid *Globe*.
614 *Globe,* 4 July 1995
615 *Entertainment Weekly* article quoted in Michael Jackson News International *Newsletter* No. 7, 9 July 1995
616 "Jordie: my ordeal", Mike Hamilton & Stephen Martin, *Sunday Mirror*, 9 February 2003
617 "Jackson's 1993 child sex accuser will not testify: uncle", AFP, 28 March 2005,

accessed on Yahoo.

618 Dimond p.268

619 *Ibid.* p160

620 Rutgers University Law Library has carried an online report of the case: *http://lawlibrary.rutgers.edu/decisions/appellate/a0422-05.opn.html*; see also "Ex-Jacko accuser in court against dad", Roger Friedman, Fox News, 19 August 2006

621 Wikipedia entry on "1993 child molestation allegations against Michael Jackson"

622 Michael could well have been sincere in his belief, and with good reason. When he was coming into adulthood, some thirty years ago, "dirty cop" methods towards gay men and boys were a reality he almost certainly heard about: in those days he hung out for a while in company that included quite a few gay celebrities. The police investigation described earlier, in note 41, for instance, in which boys were dangled by the legs from a cliff, also produced trial testimony that victims were indeed taken to juvenile hall. A report at the time stated: "The boys had been taken to juvenile hall after their mother refused to help [Detective] Martin extract testimony from the boys. The defendant said, 'Three days later – just to show you what a dirty cop can do – he convinced the juvenile authorities to have them taken from their mother and placed in a foster home. Then he called her up and said he could get them out if she would sign a complaint against me and order them to cooperate with him.' Their mother said 'The boys didn't want to testify against Rusty, and I didn't want them to. Rusty was like a father to the boys.' Eventually, the boys signed the blank deposition form." See *http://www.paedosexualitaet.de/exp/Hollywood1973.html*

623 "Four Elementary school students charged in sex case", Brett Norman, Pensacola News Journal, 13 February 2002

624 Gutierrez p.80

625 Andersen pp.263-4

626 See, for instance, Furedi (2001). Furedi was among the front-runners. At the time when his *Paranoid Parenting* appeared, his view that fears over children's safety are a bigger threat than paedophilia was highly controversial; but it appears steadily to be gaining ground.

627 See, for instance, O'Carroll (1980), Chapter Seven, "The philosophy of children's rights", in which I drew substantially on the work of the philosopher John Rawls and also that of Hillary Rodham (now better known as Hillary Clinton, US Secretary of State). As explained in an earlier footnote, I have adopted the name Carl Toms for the present volume.

628 Rind (2002) p.497

629 Jones & Brown p.5

630 Assiter & Carol (1993)

631 Personal correspondence, 28 December 1993

632 "Teachers' dismay at sex offences vote", Polly Curtis, *The Guardian*, 4 November 2003

633 Okami (2002) p.493

634 Hughes p.139
635 Chandler p.211
636 Andriette (1994) pp.18-20
637 Chandler p.150
638 Taraborrelli p.512 (2004 edn)
639 *Ibid.* p.552
640 Taraborrelli, in the *Sunday Times*, 14 April 1996
641 Taraborrelli p.506 (2004 edn)
642 *Ibid.* pp.507-8
643 *Daily Telegraph*, 3 August 1994
644 Taraborrelli pp.508-9 (2004 edn)
645 *National Enquirer*, 27 September 1994
646 Taraborrelli p.560 (2004 edn)
647 *The Sun*, 17 August 1994
648 *Hello!*, 20 August 1994
649 Taraborrelli p.510 (2004 edn)
650 *Ibid.* p.510
651 *Ibid.* p.551
652 *Ibid.* p.553
653 "Lisa Marie Presley on Scientology", *http://www.whatisscientology.org/html/part05/chp19/pg0310.html*
654 Edwards (1988)
655 In an interview with *Playboy* magazine, 30 July 2003. See: *http://www.elvis.com.au/presley/lisa_marie_playboy_interview.shtml*
656 *Ibid.* The quotation appears in the *Playboy* article. For details of the book see Edwards (1988).
657 Details taken from a variety of tabloid reports, notably the *National Enquirer*, 27 July 1994 and the *Daily Mirror*, 25 August 1994
658 *Today*, 14 July 1994
659 Taraborrelli p.556 (2004 edn)
660 *Ibid.* p.558
661 *King! News*, July 1995, citing a *Daily Mirror* story
662 Boteach (2009) p.217
663 Jackson & Hack (1996) pp.285-6
664 *Playboy*, 30 July 2003
665 Taraborrelli p.565 (2004 edn)
666 *Rolling Stone* interview with Chris Heath, 10 April, 2003
667 Taraborrelli p.567 (2004 edn)
668 *Ibid.* p.576
669 *Newsweek*, cited by Taraborrelli p.579 (2004 edn)
670 Porter p.432
671 Taraborrelli p.579 (2004 edn)
672 Jones & Brown p.89

673 Taraborrelli pp.570-1 (2004)

674 *National Enquirer*, 19 November 1996. More charitably, Brenna and his buddies may have been over-reliant on a dubious witness, such as Neverland maid Adrian McManus. As we shall see later, she would admit in court that she used a broker to sell bogus "sex secrets" of Michael's life with Lisa Marie to the tabloids.

675 *The People*, 10 November 1996

676 Taraborrelli p.462 (2004 edn)

677 *Ibid.* p.575

678 *Ibid.* p.584

679 *Ibid.* p.584

680 *The Sun*, 14 February 1997

681 The footage was from an extensive interview by Ian Drew, of *US Weekly*, shot in connection with "the Fox riposte": see below.

682 "Jackson 'Not The Father Of His Children' ", Yahoo News, 26 January 2004

683 Story credited to Carole Aye Maung, Matthew Drake & Sara Nuwar, *News of the World* online, 5 July 2009.

684 "Debbie Rowe: I won't see Jackson's children again", *The Age*, Melbourne, 29 June 2009

685 Taraborrelli p.585 (2004 edn)

686 After his death we learned that she had been cut out of his afterlife too. It was reported that, "The will includes language that expressly omits from his largesse Debbie Rowe". ("Debbie Rowe, Michael Jackson's ex-wife, cut out of will", Daniel Nasaw, *The Guardian*, 1 July 2009)

687 Taraborrelli p.586 (2004 edn)

688 Jones & Brown pp.96-8

689 Taraborrelli p.587 (2004 edn)

690 Adele Frittitta, *King!*, 10 February 1997

691 "Jacko's Ex May Prove Revealing", Roger Friedman, Fox News, 27 April, 2005

692 "Michael Jackson shared a bed with the child dubbed his", James Desborough, *News of the World*, 26 July 2009; " 'Michael Jackson was not my father', says man at centre of lovechild rumours", Will Payne, *Sunday Mirror*, 26 July 2009

693 Taraborrelli p.589 (2004 edn)

694 *Ibid.* p.590

695 "Michael Jackson prefers blondes!", *Asian News International*, 24 November 2004, citing *The Sun*

696 "Macaulay Culkin 'is the father of Michael Jackson's son Blanket' ", Urmee Khan, *Daily Telegraph*, 31 August 2009

697 "Jacko's kids: Mafia pal is dad", Nigel Pauley, *Daily Star*, 30 June 2009

698 "Jacko Doctor Klein Bans Debbie Rowe From Office", Roger Friedman, *The Hollywood Reporter*, 4 August 2009

699 "Jacko kids' real parents", Nigel Pauley, *Daily Star*, 10 July 2009

700 "Michael Jackson's doctor to stake custody claim on his kids saying: 'I'm the daddy' ", Adrian Butler, *Sunday Mirror*, 19 July 2009

701 "MJ could never be a dad", Tom Savage & Tom Hutchison, *Daily Star*, 17 July 2009; "Former Lover Of Jackson's Dermatologist Drops Bombshell; Says Michael Was Sterile From Abuse", radaronline.com, 16 July 2009. The Gohranson video was posted here: *http://link.brightcove.com/services/link/bcpid16157557001/bctid29635250001*

702 "Former Lover Of Jackson's Dermatologist Drops Bombshell; Says Klein Is Baby Daddy Of Jacko's 3 Kids", radaronline.com, 15 July 2009.

703 "Michael Jackson's dad Joe Jackson denies he hit his son", Jody Thompson, *Daily Mirror*, 21 July 2009

704 "Autopsy shocker: Jackson was healthy", Thomas Watkins, AP/Google, 1 October 2009

705 "Debbie Rowe's New Lawsuit: Kids' Paternity Revealed?", Roger Friedman, *The Hollywood Reporter*, 20 July 2009

706 Associated Press/Yahoo News, 30 June 2009

707 "The girl is mine", Guy Basnett, *News of the World*, 9 August 2009

708 "Mark Lester's ex on why he can't be the father of Michael Jackson's child", Adrian Butler, *Sunday Mirror*, 16 August 2009

709 Taraborrelli p.584 (2004 edn)

710 "The ga-ga world of Jacko Jill", David Jeffs, *News of the World*, 15 February 1998

711 For an extensive account of Mrs Everest's contribution to Churchill's early life, see Gathorne-Hardy (1993)

712 "The ga-ga world of Jacko Jill", David Jeffs, *News of the World*, 15 February 1998

713 *The Independent*, 23 May 1997

714 Taraborrelli pp.595-7 (2004 edn)

715 "Blanket's 'girl next door mum', Ryan Parry, *Daily Mirror*, 12 August 2009

716 Taraborrelli pp.615-6 (2004 edn)

717 "Jackson's tearful plea for the sanctity of childhood", David Lister, *The Independent*, 7 March 2001

718 *The Independent*, 13 March 2001

719 "We are all products of our childhood": extensive extracts from Michael Jackson's speech to the Oxford Union Society, in the *Independent*, 8 March 2001

720 Taraborrelli p.600 (2004 edn)

721 Blanket's 'girl next door' mum", Ryan Parry, *Daily Mirror*, 12 August 2009

722 "They stayed with Jacko's body for 30 minutes", James Desborough and Guy Basnett, *News of the World*, 12 July 2009

723 "Pia Bhatti: Mother of Omer Bhatti ... and Blanket?" *The Hollywood Gossip*, 27July 2009

724 Some news reports incorrectly said Michael held the baby over a balcony, rather than out of a window, and his more desperate defenders used this minor error in a grasping-at-straws effort to undermine the media's credibility in their characterisation of the event. Even years afterwards, those determined never to

credit anything negative about Michael were trying to spin the incident out of existence. It is only to be expected that fan magazines and websites would do this but such an important source as Wikipedia also went down the same route. Fans, it appears, have dominated the editing process. When I last read the complete entry on Michael Jackson in January 2010, it was clear that his achievements were dwelt on at great length but controversial aspects of his personal life and career were played down; biased attempts were made to minimise or discredit any allegations against him. Two years earlier, in January 2008, the entry contained the bizarre claim that "some perceived his actions as child endangerment although Jackson has vehemently denied these tabloid rumours, saying that he was holding the baby tightly". The entire world saw the pictures. It was a fact, not a rumour, that "some perceived his actions as child endangerment". To Wikipedia's credit, this claim was subsequently edited out and replaced by a version in which it was noted that Michael had apologised for his "terrible mistake".

But other major instances of exculpatory spin continue to go unchallenged and new ones made. For instance, Jordie Chandler's allegations are still being dubiously dismissed as having been made under the influence of the drug Amytal. And, as of November 2009, the new false claim has been advanced in Wikipedia that Michael did not come to a settlement in the Chandler case in January 1994. A statement correctly indicating that Jackson had agreed to a multi-million dollar settlement was replaced by wording saying his insurance company had done so. The implication, seized upon by Michael's defenders, was that the settlement had been made against his wishes, and he had never admitted any wrong doing. The fact remains that Michael and his lawyers signed the settlement document whether or not he paid the money personally.

725 "The kid's not alright", Rupert Smith, *The Guardian*, 4 February 2003

726 This may at first glance seem to contradict my observation in Chapter Nine that women's maternal feelings are often tinged with eroticism. For the public at large, though, this erotic response is not a salient factor in their evaluation of women's interest in children. We might also note that Michael's resort to dolls provides powerful support for Kerry Mockler's vision of Michael as a "maternal man". See Mockler (2004). This use of dolls in adulthood, however, does not carry the same implications as a young boy playing with dolls or engaging in other "gender atypical" behaviour: it does not mean Michael had always been "effeminate" or even that, as an adult, he was effeminate in any wider sense than that of "maternal" yearning. It certainly does not mean he was sexually attracted to adult males.

727 "Michael Jackson Mobbed in first London Appearance", MJJ Source; webpage created 8 October 2005

728 "Exclusive: Marc Schaffel Discusses Verdict", ABC News, 20 July 2006

729 From a transcript of Lieberman's complaint appearing on her website. The complaint was addressed to Randall Hudson, Santa Barbara Child Protective Services and was dated 11 February 2003

730 Taraborrelli p.625 (2004 edn)

731 *Ibid.* p.623

732 *Ibid.* p.624

733 Dimond is quoted in "Exclusive: Flight attendant describes 'odd' incident between Jackson and child", Harriet Ryan, Court TV online, 22 March 2005

734 Randy Taraborrelli's doomed efforts to bolster Michael's heterosexual image following the marriage to Lisa Marie were more than matched in their desperation by those of Aphrodite Jones in her book on the star's trial. Commenting on Lauren Wallace's contribution as a witness, she wrote: "As the gorgeous young woman was sworn in, staring over at Michael with adoring eyes, the pop star looked at her with a curious expression. It seemed like Michael was attracted to her on some level, but then he put on his wire-rimmed reading glasses and began glancing at notes from Mesereau. Apparently, Michael didn't want to be distracted by her beauty." For me, this was a laugh-out-loud moment. Aphrodite could have used some help from her son Eros, otherwise known as Cupid, the mischievous little guy with the Viagra-tipped arrows! (Jones p.137)

735 "Michael: 25 years after Thriller": interview with Bryan Monroe in *Ebony*, December 2007

736 Porter, pp.245-9

737 "Why my friend Michael is a fine father", Jonathan Margolis, *The Observer*, 9 February 2003. Of course, by far the most significant and well-known testimony to Michael's qualities as a father came from his daughter at the Staples Center memorial ceremony, long after Margolis was putting in his two penn'orth and also after this book was first being prepared to go to press. Famously, and movingly, her tear-choked words to the vast global audience were these: "Ever since I was born Daddy has been the best father you could ever imagine and I just wanted to say I love him so much". The emotional wallop of this brief microphone-moment from the tiny frame of that little girl was tremendous: the magnum, meltdown force of it was all the greater as this was the first utterance she or any of Michael's children had ever made to a public audience. ("Jacko daughter's tribute", Virginia Wheeler, *The Sun*, 8 July 2009) In private, the other children clearly also loved their father dearly. Taraborrelli told us that Prince once said: "If I could spend all my time with Daddy, I'd do it. He's the best daddy in the world." (Wacky world of Jacko's kids", Emma Wall, *Daily Star*, 3 July 2009)

Confirmatory information of a quite detailed sort emerged from several stories after Michael's death. *The Sun* reported that Michael had been working on a new song called "River Ripple" with his three young children and that they were calling themselves "The Jackson Four". A source "close to the family" said Michael had always wanted his children to be passionate about music and dance but he wanted them to love music for its own sake, not feel forced into performing, as he had been. This "insider" said, "Michael's oldest son Prince sings beautifully and all three children love to dance...I don't think he intended to bring the children on stage with him, but Michael wanted to announce to the crowds that his kids had helped him to write a song."

Nor were Michael's children cut off from having pals outside the family as was commonly supposed. *The Sun* ran photos showing the family's friendship with Al Malnik's family, in which "The Malniks' triplets are shown playing happily with Prince and Paris – destroying the myth that Jacko's kids have been leading a life in isolation that prevented them interacting with other children. ("Family were the Jackson 4", Virginia Wheeler, Dave Willetts & Pete Samson, *The Sun*, 29 June 2009) Another paper reproduced sketches and notes made by Michael's three children while he was in Britain and Ireland in 2006. Their reporters noted that most of the drawings were dedicated to "Daddy" with hearts and kisses. ("Jacko: The caring dad", Matthew Drake & Kevin Widdop, *News of the World*, 5 July 2009)

Even so, many among the millions watching the Staples Center memorial might have been puzzled by the demeanour of Michael's two sons, both of whom were to be seen chewing gum throughout the ceremony. Wasn't this a tad disrespectful? Even making allowances for their age, wasn't it at odds with feelings of grief? ("The King of Pops: Paris in tearful tribute to Daddy", Oliver Harvey, *The Sun*, 8 July 2009). Maybe this is just an old-fashioned, buttoned-up British sensibility. Michael's sister La Toya went on record after the event on how the kids had been feeling. She described the children as happy and well-behaved, and then added a few words about them as individuals: "Paris wants to be an entertainer. Prince Michael, the oldest, is assertive. I see such sadness there. He cried at the hospital but hasn't cried since. He has become the little man of the family. Blanket is the baby. He is very funny, a real prankster like his father." While this is not much to go on, it does offer some insight into how the children dealt with their grief in those difficult early days: the "little man", Prince Michael I, perhaps felt it was his job to be strong and not too publicly emotional – and it would not be surprising if his little brother took his cue from that. (La Toya Jackson: "Michael was murdered", Caroline Graham, *Mail on Sunday*, 12 July 2009) Indeed, seven-year-old Blanket may have been confused over exactly what had happened, although the solemnity and grief of those around him would have been all too apparent. Former child actor Mark Lester, godfather to Michael's three children, said that after the memorial ceremony Blanket asked "Where's Daddy gone? On holiday?" The question, said Lester, "broke my heart". ("Michael Jackson's son Blanket asks godfather heart-breaking question", Fiona Cummins, *Daily Mirror*, 21 July 2009. The *Daily Mirror* was citing an interview with Mark Lester in *Hello!* magazine)

738 Taraborrelli p.602 (2004 edn)

739 *Ibid.* p.602

740 "The kid's not alright", Rupert Smith, *The Guardian*, 4 February 2003

741 "Of course Jackson's odd – but his genius is what matters", Tom Utley, *Sunday Telegraph*, 9 February 2003

742 See Wikipedia on "Living with Michael Jackson"

743 Sneddon's reported remarks to the Santa Barbara newspaper are taken from an online report: "Jackson Will Not Face New Child Abuse Investigation", Ananova, 9 February 2003

744 "*Stogner v. California*: a collision between the ex post facto clause and California's interest in protecting child sex abuse victims", by Ashran Jen, *Journal of Criminal Law and Criminology,* March 2004. See: *http://www.findarticles.com/p/articles/mi_go2249/is_200403/ai_n6315618*

745 Chandler p.88. Ray Chandler may be right about what Abrams "believed" but what the psychiatrist actually wrote was somewhat more restrained. His report merely said that for a man to be regularly sleeping with a boy in the circumstances Evan Chandler had described to him gave grounds for "reasonable suspicion" that illegal sexual acts had taken place. Dr Abrams' entire report, including his legal opinion, is reproduced verbatim in Chandler (2004) pp.93-4.

746 "A nite with Jacko", Michelle Caruso, *New York Daily News*, 8 November 2004

747 "Jane Carter On Aaron's Night At Neverland", *Access Hollywood*, 8 November 2004, *http://www.accesshollywood.com/entertainment/3900596/detail.html*; "Aaron Carter Bashes Mom, Defends Jacko", Steve Helling and Marisa Wong, *People* magazine, 17 November 2004; "Carter Explains Jackson's Bentley Gift", *Contact Music*, 18 February 2005, *http://www.contactmusic.com/new/xmlfeed.nsf/mndwebpages/carter%20explains%20jacksons%20bentley%20gift*

748 "Inside Wacko's Weird Lair: I Saw Jacko's Secret Room: Singer slept in hidden den with six children at a time", By Lorna Hughes, *The Mail on Sunday*; report reproduced without original date at: *http://www.sundaymail.co.uk/news/content_objectid=13653231_method=full_siteid=86024_headline=-INSIDE-WACKO-S-WEIRD-LAIR—I-SAW-JACKO-S-SECRET-ROOM-name_page.html*

749 "Michael Jackson Expected to Surrender", Jeff Wilson, *Santa Maria Times*, 20 November 2003

750 "Man Behind Jackson Investigations Says He's Only After Justice", ABC News, 20 November 2003

751 Broadcast 28 December 2003

752 *PrimeTime Live*, ABC, 14 June 1995

753 "Michael Jackson booked on molestation charges", CNN, 20 November 2003

754 "Michael Jackson still doesn't get it", Michael Ventre, NBC, November 19, 2003

755 "Insanity caused by celebrity might be Michael Jackson's best defence", Mark Lawson, *The Guardian*, 22 November 2003

756 "Jackson charged with child abuse", Howard Breuer, Reuters, 18 December 2003

757 Harvey Levin, quoted by the Indian press agency ANI in a report dated 30 November 2003, *www.newindpress.com*

758 "Jacko in party mood after court date", Press Association, 16 January, 2004

759 Marina Hyde, *The Guardian*, 7 February 2004

760 Porter p.494

761 Soon after this leak Michael appeared as a guest on the TV chat show *Geraldo*. At the end of the interview host Geraldo Rivera announced, "Finally, we've studiously avoided the case and not talked at all about the case that's pending. You're under this gag order. I know that you have received permission from the judge to read a statement. I hate to end an interview that way, but if you'd like to

read that statement now, I think it's important." Michael then duly read a short statement which began, "In the last two weeks, a large amount of ugly, malicious information has been released into the media about me. Apparently, this information was leaked through transcripts in a grand jury proceeding where neither my lawyers nor I ever appeared. The information is disgusting and false..." It was the only dramatic note in a sympathetic and supportive interview. (Geraldo, Fox Channel, 2 February 2005)

762 "Subdued Jacko pleads innocent", Dan Whitcomb & Charles Feldman, Reuters report on Yahoo News, 30 April 2004

763 *Ibid.*

764 "Jackson 'seduced' boy at Neverland", Dan Whitcomb, Reuters report on Yahoo News, 28 July 2004

765 "Judge Wants Prosecutors to Stick to the Current Case", MJJ Source website, 12 January 2005

766 Roger Friedman, Fox News, 11 January 2005

767 During the trial itself one young man, Jason Francia, would indeed present himself as a true victim. As we will see, the jury appeared not to be greatly impressed by the extent of his victimhood even if they felt he was an honest witness.

768 "Jackson's 1993 child sex accuser will not testify: uncle", AFP/Yahoo, 28 March 2005

769 "Statement of Michael Jackson Regarding the Tsunami Disaster", MJJ Source website, 4 January 2005

770 It would be impractical and unhelpful to cite in detail my sources for the trial. Suffice it to say that I have made extensive use of the 13,055-page authorised court transcript, many hundreds of media reports and two books published after the trial by journalists who were present (Dimond 2005 and Jones 2007). From here on I will fully reference only sources of particularly distinct individuality or exceptional importance, plus any sources named in the text.

771 "The world's most famous defendant", Marcel Berlins, *The Guardian*, 1 February 2005

772 "Thriller? More like a lonely freak show", Charles Laurence in Los Angeles & Catherine Elsworth in Santa Maria, *Daily Telegraph*, 6 March 2005

773 "Day one of Jackson trial focuses on accuser, his family", CNN, 1 March 2005

774 If served consecutively, the maximum sentences on all the charges would have added up to fifty six years. However, it was possible for the sentences to be run concurrently, and Aphrodite Jones reports that legal experts were predicting a prison term of up to eighteen years eight months in the event of guilty verdicts on all counts. The four charges of committing a lewd act upon a child under the age of fourteen and the single charge of attempting to get a child under the age of fourteen to commit a lewd act (upon the defendant) were all punishable by a mandatory prison sentence of three to eight years. None of the other charges had a higher minimum sentence so a Jackson deemed guilty on all counts could

theoretically, albeit improbably, have been released after only three years. In Europe we are used to thinking of American sentencing as draconian, especially as regards sexual offences against minors. Partly under trans-Atlantic influence, though, UK law and practice have become increasingly harsh in this area in recent years. See Jones pp.291-2 for a full list of the penalties available in respect of each count of the Jackson indictment.

775 Court transcript, 28 February 2005, p.130, lines 15-27

776 Using a Google Scholar search for medical papers on the subject, I could find no mention of visualisation therapy, whether using US or UK spelling. The only papers on cancer that used the term "visualisation technique" referred to something utterly different. They were nothing to do with therapy for patients; they were technical papers describing a research technique. See, for example, Essmann (2000). On the other hand, a conventional Google search turned up plenty of alternative medicine books in which a "visualisation technique" was discussed.

777 "Jacko's icy glare of pure hatred", Antonella Lazzeri, *The Sun*, 2 March 2005

778 Sky News/Yahoo, 2 March 2005

779 "Michael Jackson's False Front?", Tina Brown, *Washington Post*, 10 March 2005

780 "Michael Jackson's courtroom fashion on trial", Dan Glaister, *The Guardian*, 19 March 2005

781 Coleman (1989)

782 Wikipedia entry on Stan Katz

783 For a summary of the Disney film version of the story see: *http:// faculty.washington.edu/kgb/film/pinocchio.html*

784 In the official court transcript, Dominick Cascio's first name ends with the letter k; his father is also a Dominic but without a k in the news reports and books I have seen.

785 Tariano (Taj) Jackson, son of Michael's brother Tito and his former wife Dolores; Austin (Auggie) Brown, son ofMichael's sister Maureen (Rebbie) and her husband Nathaniel Brown.

786 Fans claimed that, rather than a plot by Michael and his aides to keep the Arvizos captive, there had been a conspiracy *against* their idol. As Aphrodite Jones put it in her book, *Michael Jackson Conspiracy*, "There were fans who tried to convince the media that Michael was the victim of a conspiracy, that tabloids and money-grubbing people had conspired with Sony to destroy Jackson long before the trial in Santa Maria ever began." (Jones p.129) In some versions the plot even involved collusion between Sony Corporation and the prosecution. It was not just fans who promoted this conspiracy theory and perhaps in various degrees believed in it.

Lynton Guest, an expert on the music industry, and an historian of Sony, wrote a book which was sloppy, amateurish and half-hearted in its attention to evidence presented in the Santa Maria courtroom, but far more convincing on skulduggery in the field of artists' rights and contracts, particularly as those issues impacted on Michael. Guest gave a detailed account of Sony's interest in destroying

Jackson, and how the corporation allegedly went about doing so. What Sony wanted, he claimed, was to force Michael to part with immensely valuable music rights, including the star's share of the Sony/ATV music catalogue, which included most of the Beatles' oeuvre of songs. Sony Music, to which Michael had long been contracted, had been embarrassed by their relationship with him ever since the Jordie Chandler scandal: it did not fit with their carefully cultivated image of a family-friendly company.

From this time onwards, so the theory goes, Sony began to play a long game in which the corporation would monitor Jackson but keep him at arm's length, while failing to accord him either the "duty of care" he was owed as an artist or effective marketing of his work. (Guest pp.62-3) With Machiavellian cunning, Sony boss Norio Ogha oversaw and even encouraged the huge borrowings Jackson took out with the Bank of America in 1999 using the star's stock in Sony/ATV as collateral: if Michael defaulted, the bank would be a more reliable partner for Sony than a star even Guest admits was "wayward" and extravagant. (Guest p.64) The weightier Michael's debt, including predictably mounting interest payments, the more surely it could be used to topple him: the Japanese corporate boss, it appears, was going for an exquisitely slow-motion judo fall. The later prospect of Michael being tried, convicted and jailed would be an added bonus for Sony, making it even harder for him to keep control of his music rights.

Is Guest's case a strong one? Even Jackson's sober trial lawyer Tom Mesereau, a man more interested in hard evidence than wild speculation, agreed there could be something in the story, according to Jones. She quoted him as saying, "If Michael were in jail or in prison, how would he defend his ownership in the catalogue? How would he defend all these frivolous lawsuits? Sony had so much to gain if there was a conviction, and Sneddon would have gained celebrity status." However, in Jones' account, Mesereau admits he had no evidence of a plot and stops well short of accusing the prosecution of conspiracy. He said: "These people didn't have to actually sit down to conspire together. They might have helped each other on an unplanned level – because they had a common interest." (Jones p.13)

All this has few implications for the present volume, however. Just because Sony might have been out to get Michael, that does not mean he was innocent: after all, if there had been no Jordie Chandler affair to embarrass Sony in the first place the company's interests would have been best served by taking Michael to ever greater heights of artistic and sales success: they would have been helping to generate another *Thriller*, and the massive profits such success would bring them. My only reason for devoting so much as a footnote to the Sony saga is to avoid accusations that I am myself part of an evil conspiracy to suppress the truth about dark corporate deeds.

787 Porter pp.488-9

788 "Something evil's lurking in the dark ...", Euan Ferguson, *The Observer*, 17 April 2005

789 Spilbor (2005)

790 "Past Cases Loom Over Jackson", Steve Chawkins & Stuart Pfeifer, *Los Angeles Times*, 28 March 2005

791 Spilbor *op. cit.*

792 "Past Cases Loom Over Jackson", Steve Chawkins & Stuart Pfeifer, *Los Angeles Times*, 28 March 2005

793 Jackson Jurors Must Weigh Testimony of Tabloid Tattlers, *Los Angeles Times,* 18 April 2005

794 Dimond p.179

795 *Ibid.* p.114

796 "Judge Lets Jackson Plead 5th," Nicholas Riccardi, *Los Angeles Times*, 16 September 1994

797 "Maid's Son Testifies Jackson Molested Him", Stuart Pfeifer & Steve Chawkins, *Los Angeles Times*, 5 April 2005

798 For the sake of brevity and clarity, I present this as a straightforward narrative in much the same terms as the news reports of the time. In court the testimony was messier. Jason testified in his evidence-in-chief (direct evidence) that Michael touched his testicles, but his claim that this touching had been under his clothing rather than through it emerged later, under cross-examination by Mesereau. In evidence given on 4 April 2005, the relevant exchange on touching under the clothing is at page 4882 of the court transcript, lines 11-19.

799 Jones p.178

800 Elliott (1993). "Rachal", a woman suffering from depression, features in the Elliott book talking about her feelings in the mid-1980s when incest was coming to be a much talked about topic. She is quoted as saying: "One or two incest survivor groups were formed. More books appeared. I read them. I used to think, 'If only I had been sexually abused I could join these groups, I could get some help'." (p.151) A couple of pages later we find her going along to abuse groups. "Though deeply ashamed of doing this," she confesses, "I made up some stories about having been sexually abused by an uncle." (p.153) For many years it was an article of faith within survivor groups that all accounts of sexual abuse by alleged victims were true, including those induced by dubious "recovered memory" techniques in therapy. Every story was to be believed, no matter how improbable or even – as was often the case – downright absurd. So it is interesting to note that Laura Davis and Ellen Bass, key figures behind the mushrooming of survivor culture were later forced to acknowledge the problem of false accusations. See "Truth and reconciliation: Incest accusations of the recovered-memory craze tore families apart. Now one of its leaders wants to let bygones be bygones", Julia Gracen, *Salon*, 22 May 2002; *http://dir.salon.com/story/books/feature/2002/05/22/davis/index.html?pn=1*

801 The KFI and Drudge Report versions were reported in "Jackson jury rumours dismissed", Reuters/Yahoo, 7 April 2005; the Sky version, "Jacko jurors accused of mocking man" was carried by PA on Yahoo, also 7 April 2005

802 "Skeletons Come Out", Matt Kettmann & Svante Nilson, *Santa Barbara*

Independent, April 2005

803 "Jackson defense rocked by testimony from witness to alleged child sex", AFP/Yahoo, 7 April 2005

804 "Jacko: DA's Witnesses Admit Lying", Roger Friedman, Fox News, 8 April 2005

805 "What the Guards Saw: Two former Jackson employees are expected to provide more lurid details about events at the singer's ranch", Nomi Morri, *Newsweek* online, 29 April, 2005

806 Gutierrez p.86

807 Court transcript, 2 June 2005, page 12823, lines 5-8

808 Dimond, p.79

809 *Ibid.* p79

810 Court transcript for 8 April 2005, p.5496 line 3 to p.5499 line14 for the exchanges on the origins of the PS.

811 Jones & Brown p.71

812 St Martin & Nelson (eds) (1964 and 1966)

813 "Judge Bars Journalist's Testimony in Jackson Trial, but Allows Jurors to See 'Boy' Books", Steve Chawkins, *Los Angeles Times*, 30 April 2005

814 *www.vialibri.net/item_pg/257450-1966-martin-georges-nelson-ronald-boys-will-boys.htm* (accessed 21 Sept 2009)

815 There are some impressive figures to support this view, which is sometimes referred to as the cathartic theory of pornography. In a study of child sex abuse cases in the US, David Finkelhor, a doyen of child abuse research, discovered that substantiated cases of such abuse decreased from a national estimated peak of 149,800 cases in 1992 to 103,600 cases in 1998, a decline of 31%. (Finkelhor 2001) This was at the very time when the internet was coming into widespread public use and when its most enthusiastic early users included consumers of online child pornography. Those who claimed that the exponential growth in the availability of this material would inevitably lead to vastly more children being abused would thus appear to have a lot of explaining to do.

While it is always dangerous to leap from correlation to causation, the figures strongly suggest the possibility that many people who are sexually attracted to children have used such pornography "cathartically", as a substitute sexual outlet. In the free and easy years before law enforcement started to get a grip, online child pornography may well have helped to reduce sex crimes against children.

A sceptical reaction to the catharsis theory would be understandable if there were no further evidence of the negative correlation in question. But there is an abundance of such evidence, including studies from Denmark, Germany and Japan. These are discussed in Diamond (1999)

816 *http://dorianwrite.tripod.com/id1.html* (accessed 21 Sept 2009)

817 "Accuser's mother gives dramatic performance at Jackson trial", AFP/Yahoo, 14 April 2005

818 "Jackson said 'killers' were after my kids: accuser's mom", AFP/Yahoo, 14 April 2005

819 Porter pp.523-7; "Michael Jackson jury reaches split decision", AP/Yahoo, 16 July 2006. Many years earlier, Jordie Chandler's legal team had apparently suspected that Michael's efforts to adopt a child might not be entirely above board. They reportedly flew to Romania to interview a boy described in the press as a "street urchin" named Christian, who had been "adopted" by Michael during his 1992 European tour (*Daily Mirror*, 18 December 1993)

820 "Time to End the Jacko Trial", Roger Friedman, Fox News, 16 April 2005

821 "Jacko trial's gasbag", Diane Dimond, *New York Post*, 17 April 2005

822 "Wife no. 2 will zing the King of Pop", Diane Dimond, *New York Post*, 24 April 2005

823 Jacko's Ex May Prove Revealing, Roger Friedman, Fox News, 27 April 2005

824 "simon h b", Blogspot, 24 January, 2004 *http://xrrf.blogspot.com/ 2004_01_18_xrrf_archive.html*

825 "Blondie Bombshell as Prosecution Wraps", Matt Kettmann & Svante Nilson, *Santa Barbara Independent*, 5 May 2005

826 "Courting disaster", Paul Harris, *The Observer*, 17 April 2005

827 Gutierrez pp.22-5

828 Wegner (2002) p.35

829 "Jacko's Old Friends Can't Save Him", Roger Friedman, Fox News, 6 May 2005

830 "Culkin Still Undecided on Jacko Trial", Roger Friedman, Fox News, 6 May 2005

831 We have already heard a great deal about Evan Chandler's parenting style. As for Kit Culkin, columnist Jonathan Freedland dubbed him "one of the most loathed players in Hollywood" for his pushy-parent tactics, a man whose soaring ambition on his kids' behalf made him a "pain in the ass" to movie moguls; he allegedly demanded a role for his daughter Quinn in the film *The Good Son* even though she had failed two auditions and hated acting. ("Home alone with dad", Jonathan Freedland, *The Guardian*, 19 December 1994)

832 "The Art of Proving a Negative", Matt Kettmann, *Santa Barbara Independent*, 12 May 2005

833 Porter maintains that Kit once discovered Macaulay's younger brother Rory, two years old at the time, sitting on the floor with Michael, both of them drinking from baby bottles. (Porter p.317) Could it be that sharing a bed with a boy would have seemed relatively normal to the Culkin children's parents, once they had become inured to such bizarre but "innocent" behaviour as this?

834 "Mac Attack: Jacko's a 'Human Being' ", Roger Friedman, Fox News, 12 May 2005

835 "Child star shared bed with Jackson", Dan Glaister, *The Guardian*, 12 May 2005

836 Under Section 35 of the Criminal Justice and Public Order Act 1994

837 A number of important differences between trials in the US and the UK were discussed on Law In Action, BBC Radio 4, 3 June 2005, in a special programme on the Jackson trial. These included differences in media reporting, jury rules and the prosecutor's role. It was suggested that Tom Sneddon's position was unusual, even in US terms, as regards the high level of his personal commitment

to the case. Also, in the English system, a prosecutor would not seek out witnesses, visit the "crime scene", or hold press conferences as Sneddon did. Philip Katz QC said a barrister doing such things in the UK would be disciplined and indeed ridiculed.

838 "Mac Attack: Jacko's a 'Human Being' ", Roger Friedman, Fox News, 12 May 2005

839 "Jacko Bail Mystery Deepens", Roger Friedman, Fox News, 18 May 2005

840 There's a whole lot more where that came from. See: *http://politicalhumor.about.com/library/ blmichaeljacksonjokes.htm*

841 Ned Sherrin, BBC Radio 4, 7 May 2005

842 Jones p.167

843 *Ibid.* pp. ix-xi

844 *Ibid.* p.xix Music industry insider Lynton Guest was sceptical over Michael's drinking. In his book on Jackson he cited Paul Russell, a senior vice-president of Sony Music Entertainment, and before that an executive with CBS Records, who told Guest: "Look, I've been around Michael for years, decades. I've been with him at formal and informal occasions. I've been at private dinners with him when only four or five other people were present. I've flown across the Atlantic with him and Lisa Marie. In all those years I have never, ever seen him take one drop of alcohol." Unfortunately, this shows what such a high-flying (literally) executive can miss. He appears not to have noticed the testimony that in public, especially in front of children, Michael was discreet, even to the extent of using a soft drinks can when drinking wine. Even Michael's lawyer, Tom Mesereau, had no quarrel with a Passenger Profile prepared by Extrajet, and presented in evidence, showing that the singer's "Beverage Preferences" when travelling on that company's flights were as follows: "White wine in Diet Coke can on every flight. 7-UP, Orange Crush or fruit punch. * Will sometimes drink tequila, gin, or Crown Royal." The underlining appears in the original Extrajet document. Air stewardess Lauren Wallace answered in the affirmative when Mesereau said, "And was it your understanding that Mr Jackson wanted wine placed in cans because he gets nervous on flights?" In his later years Michael had good reason to get nervous about many things besides flying. However, in the light of Russell's comment it is hard to believe Michael was any kind of hell-raiser while under the influence. Guest p.2

845 "Testimony in Jackson case ends with accuser's tape", Reuters/Yahoo, 28 May 2005

846 Tape Tells a Story, Sort of", Roger Friedman, Fox News, 31 May 2005

847 "Jackson Defense Was Always Sure", Steve Chawkins & Andrew Blankstein, *Los Angeles Times*, 15 June 2005

848 Dr Esplin, a forensic psychologist, had been called to rebut a number of dubious assertions made by prosecution expert witness Anthony Urquiza, whose testimony had already proved weak under cross-examination, as we have seen.

849 For an explanation, focused on the Jackson case, of how US law differs from

British law with regard to jurors speaking to the media, see "Talk, don't talk", John Borger & Michael Evans, *The Guardian*, 20 June 2005

850 "I won't sleep with boys any more. My life will change, vows Jackson", Catherine Elsworth, *Daily Telegraph*, 16 June 2005

851 Telly Leno 'off to Disney!', *The Sun*, 15 June 2005

852 Maureen Orth interviewed by Kathryn Belgiornio, *Vanity Fair*, 13 June 2005

853 "Really Odd Facts About Michael Jackson", Dan Ackman, *Forbes* magazine, 14 June 2005

854 Photo caption, *Daily Star*, 16 June 2005, front page, with story, "JACKO: Give me my willy back!", Iain Burchell

855 "In the grip of predators: How a feeding frenzy consumed an oh-so-vulnerable Michael Jackson", Barbara Amiel, *Macleans*, 8 June 2005

856 "Jacko's journey from Neverland to comeback can now begin", Neil McCormick, *Daily Telegraph*, 16 June 2005

857 "Jacko to be more 'macho' ", 28 September 2005; *http://entertainment.iafrica.com/news/493800.htm*

858 "Jacko's Future: He'll Move to Europe", Roger Friedman, Fox News, 24 May 2005

859 "Jackson's post-trial future hinges on his past", Reuters/Yahoo, 5 June 2005

860 "Life after the verdict" Christine Hamilton, *The Independent on Sunday*, 19 June 2005

861 "Jacko: No Record Deal in Near Future", Roger Friedman, Fox News, 19 October 2005

862 Jefferson (2005); O'Carroll (2006)

863 "Michael Jackson: From 'King of Pop' to Court Jester", Bryan Robinson, ABC news review, 8 June 2005; "Scholars get Jacko-demic at Yale", Alex French, *The Hartford Advocate*, 30 September 2004

864 *Social Semiotics*, Volume 17, Issue 4, December 2007. See bibliography entries for Seth Clark Silberman, Debbie Epstein & Deborah Lynn Steinberg, Matt Hills, and Jenny Kitzinger & Sujata Moorti.

865 "I Believe I Can Open My Fly: Why Michael Jackson Is Damned and R Kelly Is the Man", Richard Goldstein, *Village Voice*, 14 January 2004

866 Though perhaps I should say "the alleged R Kellys" or something of the sort, as the man himself was eventually acquitted. He was finally tried in 2008 after years of delay.

867 The survey's findings appear in O'Carroll 1993. As explained in an earlier footnote, I have adopted the name Carl Toms for the present volume.

868 See, for instance, *www.narth.com*

869 "Jackson: The Dangers of the Peter Pan Complex", Richard Ingham, AFP/Yahoo, 30 June 2009

870 "Jacko: Financial Wipeout Imminent", Roger Friedman, Fox News, 17 December 2005

871 "Jackson accused of animal cruelty at Neverland ranch", *Irish Independent*, 17 January 2006

872 "Jacko: Llamas, Alpacas Are First to Go", Roger Friedman, Fox News, 22 February 2006

873 "Jackson's Neverland Ranch shut down", WENN (World Entertainment News Network) at Yahoo, 10 March 2006

874 Wikipedia entry on "Post trial lawsuits against Michael Jackson: Animal neglect", accessed 5 February 2008

875 The *New York Post* article is referred to without a date in this online report: "Michael Jackson planning an album with his kids!", *Hindustan Times*, 8 November 2005; *http://www.hindustantimes.com/news/181_1540472,0047.htm*

876 "Priest Wants Michael Jackson on Pope CD", AP/Yahoo, 6 February 2006

877 "Michael Jackson Sings Publicly for First Time Since Trial", AP/Yahoo, 16 November 2006

878 "Jacko: $30 Million Offer to Play London", Roger Friedman, Fox News, 14 February 2008

879 "Michael: 25 years after *Thriller*", *Ebony*, Vol. LX111 No. 2, December 2007

880 "Michael Jackson's Family Calls for Help", Roger Friedman, Fox News, 29 June 2007

881 Porter p.457

882 *Ibid.* pp.524-7

883 *Ibid.* p.531

884 Dimond pp.193-4

885 Porter pp.481-2

886 Forensic accountant John Duross O'Bryan testified at Michael's trial that the singer had been spending $20 million to $30 million annually more than he earned in the period leading up to the Bashir documentary. As noted in Chapter Fifteen, this financial testimony was an important element in the prosecution case. Sneddon claimed Jackson was so desperate for funds that he conspired to force the Arvizo family into taking part in a money-raising TV project. We reviewed other evidence that showed the conspiracy theory was absurd – but O'Bryan's testimony was not.

887 "Michael Jackson Settles Mega Lawsuit for $5 Million", Roger Friedman, Fox News, 18 June 2007. Jackson's financial and business affairs have been given extensive and authoritative attention in Guest (2006).

888 "Michael Jackson Gives Bahraini Prince Royal $$$ Pain", Roger Friedman, Fox News, 15 October, 2007

889 I am advised that the correct figure here should actually be $567 million and that Jackson's finances were in an even more desperate state than described in Friedman's analysis.

890 "Jackson Defaults on $23M Loan", Roger Friedman, Fox News, 26 October 2007

891 "Auction of Michael Jackson's Neverland cancelled", Roger Friedman, Fox News, 9 May 2008

892 "Michael Jackson Sues Accountants for Failing to Pay His Bills Properly", AP/Yahoo, 23 December 2006

893 "Jackson in trouble after anti-semitic phone rant", Gary Younge, *The Guardian*, 24 November 2005

894 Michael claimed rather unconvincingly to be a victim of racism rather than racist himself, alleging that Mottola failed to support Sony's African- American artists. Michael's main Wikipedia entry stated (when accessed in January 2008) that Jackson had referred to Mottola as a "devil" and a "racist" who used black artists for his own personal gain. He allegedly cited that Mottola called Jackson's colleague Irv Gotti a "fat nigger". The online encyclopaedia said Sony issued a statement stating that they found the allegations strange since Mottola was once married to biracial pop star Mariah Carey.

895 See two of Roger Friedman's Fox News columns: "Michael Jackson's Nanny Locks His Father Out", 31 January 2007; and "Michael Jackson's Neverland on Verge of Foreclosure", 11 January 2008.

896 "Judge Explains Why He Nixed Jacko Charges", AP/Yahoo, 18 April 2006

897 "Michael Jackson nightmare, Eddie Reynoza back again", 14 February 2005, *www.prleap.com/pr/4357/* . Even in the press release it is presciently conceded that "once again Eddie is risking the ridicule of the press by coming forth with his story".

898 "Michael Jackson raped 16-year-old Eddie Reynoza", Gary Revel, 1 June 2006. The text begins, "For immediate release April 1, 2005…" The text ends, "Agent: Jack Scagnetti". See: *http://article.maxlinks.org/index.php?CatID=18&ArtID=21298*

899 Porter pp.535-6; *New York Post*, 11 January 2006

900 "More adoptions could be in future", Roger Friedman, Fox News, 30 May 06

901 "Jackson child custody fight ends", BBC News online, 30 September 2006

902 "Jacko's brattos", Nigel Pauley, *Daily Star*, 28 May 2008

903 Jacko's children revealed", Alison Boshoff, *Daily Mail*, 29 May 2008

904 "Janet Arvizo accepts plea bargain", UPI, 14 November 2006. See: *http://www.upi.com/NewsTrack/Entertainment/2006/11/14/janet_arvizo_accepts_plea_bargain/*

905 Taraborrelli p.689 (2009 edn)

906 "Off the wall but still invincible", *The Observer*, 8 March 2009

907 "Jackson death ruled as homicide", BBC news online, 29 August 2009

908 "Michael Jackson had jab to curb sex urges for young boys", Kate Mansey, *Sunday Mirror*, 9 August 2009

909 "Father who accused Michael Jackson of molesting his son Jordan Chandler commits suicide", David Gardner, *Daily Mail*, 18 November 2009

910 Report: "Michael Jackson – The Urination Explanation", www.tmz.com, 4 November 2009; video interview with TMZ's Harvey Levin: *http://www.tmz.com/videos?autoplay=true&mediaKey=3e1cfd94-ae5f-48c0-8d5b-c372fc8c0d52*

911 See FBI website, here: *http://www.fbi.gov/page2/dec09/jackson_122209.html*

912 FBI Releases 300 Pages on Michael Jackson, Roger Friedman, *The Hollywood Reporter,* 22 December 2009

913 Boteach (2009)

914 *Ibid*. p.26
915 *Ibid*. p.191
916 *Ibid*. p.212
917 *Ibid*. p.198
918 *Ibid*. p.215
919 *Ibid*. p.53
920 *Ibid*. pp.7-8
921 *Ibid*. p.56

BIBLIOGRAPHY

Amiel, B, In the grip of predators: How a feeding frenzy consumed an oh-so-vulnerable Michael Jackson, *Macleans*, 8 June 2005

Andersen, C, Michael Jackson: Unauthorised, Michael Joseph, London, 1994

Andrews, B, & Taraborrelli, JR, Out of the Madness: The Strictly Unauthorised Biography of Janet Jackson, Headline, London, 1994

Andriette, Bill, Intergenerational sex: consent isn't the problem, NAMBLA Bulletin, 14(4):18-20, June 1994

Archives of Sexual Behavior, *Archives of Sexual Behavior*, 31(6): 465-510, Dec. 2002 Special section of the *Archives* on paedophilia with an introduction by Kenneth J Zucker, symposium papers by Richard Green and Gunter Schmidt, nineteen peer commentaries and closing replies by Green and Schmidt

Assiter, A & Carol, A, Bad Girls and Dirty Pictures: The Challenge to Reclaim Feminism, Pluto Press, London, 1993

Awkward, M, "A slave to the rhythm": Essential(ist) transmutations; or, The Curious Case of Michael Jackson. In Awkward M, Negotiating Difference: Race, Gender and the Politics of Positionality, University of Chicago Press, Chicago, 1995

Bach, R, Illusions: The Adventures of a Reluctant Messiah, Mandarin, London, 1992

Bach, R, Jonathan Livingston Seagull, HarperCollins, London, 1994

Bancroft, J (ed), Sexual Development in Childhood, Indiana University Press, Bloomington, Indiana, 2003

Barrie, JM, The Little White Bird, Hodder & Stoughton, London, 1902

Barrie, JM, Peter Pan, Hodder & Stoughton, London, 1928 [the play]

Barrie, JM, Peter Pan, Oxford University Press, Oxford, 2007 [the novel]

Baudrillard, J, Cool Memories, Verso, London, 1990

Bell, AP, Weinberg, MS, & Hammersmith, SK, Sexual Preference: Its Development in Men and Women, Indiana University Press,Bloomington, Indiana, 1981

Birkin, A, JM Barrie and the Lost Boys, Constable, London, 1979

Blum, H & Connolly, J, The Pellicano Brief, *Vanity Fair*, March 2004

Boteach, S, The Michael Jackson Tapes: A Tragic Icon Reveals His Soul in Intimate Conversation, Vanguard Press, New York, 2009

Brongersma, E, Loving Boys, Volumes 1 (1986) & 2 (1990), Global Academic Publishers, Elmhurst, New Jersey

Brongersma, E, Boy-lovers and their influence on boys: distorted research and anecdotal observations, *Journal of Homosexuality*, 20(1-2):145-73, 1990

Bruhm, S, "Dancing in Michael Jackson's Mouth", presented at a conference hosted by the Lesbian, Bisexual and Gay Studies Program, Cornell University, March 2004

Bullough, V, Children and adolescents as sexual beings: a historical overview, *Child and Adolescent Psychiatric Clinics of North America*, 13:447-459, 2004

Butler-Sloss, E, Report of the Inquiry into Child Abuse in Cleveland, Cm 412, HMSO, London, 1987

Campbell, L, Michael Jackson: The King of Pop's Darkest Hour, Branden Publishing, Boston, Massachusetts, 1994

Carpenter, H, Benjamin Britten, Faber, London, 1992

Carr, S, The Boys Are Back In Town, Arrow Books, London, 2000

Chandler, R, All That Glitters: The Crime and the Cover Up, Windsong Press, Las Vegas, 2004

Clegg, S, Studying child sexual abuse: morality or science? *Radical Philosophy*, 66:31-39, Spring 1994

Coleman, L, Learning From the McMartin Hoax, *Issues In Child Abuse Accusations*, 1(2), Spring 1989, *http://www.ipt-forensics.com/journal/volume1/j1_2_7.htm* (website of the Institute for Psychological Therapies)

Constantine, L & Martinson, F, (eds), Children and Sex: New Findings, New Perspectives, Little, Brown & Co, Boston, Massachusetts, 1981

Cook, M & Howells, K, Adult Sexual Interest in Children, Academic Press, London, 1981

Coxell A, King M, Mezey G, & Gordon, G, Lifetime prevalence, characteristics, and associated problems of non-consensual sex in men: cross-sectional survey, *BMJ*, 318:846-850, 1999 (27 March)

Dalrymple, T, Our Great, Societal Neverland, *National Review*, 22 Dec. 2003

Davenport, WH, Adult-child sexual relations in cross-cultural perspective, in O'Donohue, W & Geer, JH (eds), The sexual abuse of children: theory and research, Lawrence Erlbaum Associates, Hillsdale, New Jersey, 1992

Diamond, M, The effects of pornography: an international perspective, in Porn 101: Eroticism, Pornography and the First Amendment, Elias, J *et al.* (eds), Prometheus, New York, 1999

Dimond, D, Be Careful Who You Love: Inside the Michael Jackson Case, Atria Books, New York, 2005

Dineen, C, Michael Jackson: In His Own Words, Omnibus Press, London, 1993

Dover, KJ, Greek Homosexuality, Duckworth, London, 1978

Dyson, ME, Michael Jackson's Postmodern Spirituality, in Dyson, ME, Reflecting Black: African-American Cultural Criticism, University of Minnesota Press, Minneapolis, Minnesota, 1993

Eberle, P & Eberle, S, The Politics of Child Abuse, Lyle Stuart, Secaucus, New Jersey, 1986

Edwards, M, Priscilla, Elvis, and Me, St Martins Press, New York, 1988

Eglinton, JZ, Greek Love, Neville Spearman, London, 1971

Elliott, M (ed), Female Sexual Abuse of Children: The Ultimate Taboo, Longman, London, 1993

Epstein, D & Steinberg, D, The Face of Ruin: Evidentiary Spectacle and the Trial of Michael Jackson, *Social Semiotics*, 17(4): 441-458, 2007

Erni, JN, Queer configurations in the media: critical reflections on the Michael Jackson sex scandal, *Critical Studies in Mass Communication,* 15:158-180, 1998

Feierman, JR (ed), Pedophilia: Biosocial Dimensions, Springer-Verlag, New York, 1990

Fergusson DM & Mullen, PE, Childhood Sexual Abuse: An evidence-based perspective, *Developmental Clinical Psychology & Psychiatry*, 40, 1999

Finkelhor, D, What's wrong with sex between adults and children? Ethics and the problem of sexual abuse, *American Journal of Orthopsychiatry*, 49:692-697, 1979

Finkelhor, D, Sex Among Siblings: A Survey on Prevalence, Variety and Effects, *Archives of Sexual Behavior*, 9(3):171-194, June 1980

Finkelhor, D, Child Sexual Abuse: New Theory and Research, Free Press, New York, 1984

Finkelhor, D, The Decline in Child Sexual Abuse Cases, *Juvenile Justice Bulletin*, January 2001

Fischer, MA, Was Michael Jackson Framed? *GQ*, October 1994

Franklin, Bob, The Rights of Children, Basil Blackwell, Oxford, 1986

Fraser, M, The Death of Narcissus, Secker & Warburg, London, 1976

Frayser, S, Cultural dimensions of childhood sexuality in the United States, in Bancroft, J (ed), Sexual Development in Childhood, Indiana University Press, Bloomington, 2003

Frederiksen, A, Paedophilia, Science, and Self-deception: A Criticism of Sex Abuse Research, *www.ipce.org/* , 1999

Fuchs, C, Michael Jackson's Penis, in Case S, Brett P, & Foster SL (eds) Cruising the Performative: Interventions into the representation of ethnicity, nationality and sexuality, Indiana University Press, Indianapolis, 1995

Furedi, F, Paranoid Parenting: Abandon Your Anxieties And Be A Good Parent, Penguin, London, 2001

Gabb, J, "I Could Eat My Baby to Bits": passion and desire in lesbian mother-children love, *Gender, Place and Culture: A Journal of Feminist Geography*, 11(3), 2004

Gathorne-Hardy, J, The Rise and Fall of the British Nanny, Weidenfeld & Nicolson, London, 1993

Geraci, J (ed), Dares To Speak: Historical and Contemporary Perspectives on Boy-Love, Gay Men's Press, Swaffham, Norfolk, 1997

Gilbey, E, "Bad?", *Sunday Times* magazine, 30 January 1994
Gold, T, Michael Jackson: The Man in the Mirror, Pan, London, 1989
Grant, A, Michael Jackson: The Visual Documentary, Omnibus Press, London, 1994
Green, R, Is pedophilia a mental disorder? *Archives of Sexual Behavior*, 31(6):467-71, 2002
Greer, G, The Boy, Thames & Hudson, London, 2003
Groth, AN, Patterns of sexual assault against children and adolescents. In Burgess, SW, Groth, AN, Holmstrom, LL & Sgroi, SM (eds), Sexual Assault of Children and Adolescents, DC Heath, Boston, Massachusetts, 1978
Guest, L, The Trials of Michael Jackson, Aureus Publishing, Castle-upon-Alun, St Bride's Major, Glamorgan, 2006
Gutierrez, VM, Michael Jackson Was My Lover: The Secret Diary of Jordie Chandler, Victor M Gutierrez, Santiago, Chile, 1997 (2nd edition)
Halperin, I, Unmasked: The Final Years of Michael Jackson, Simon & Schuster, London, 2009
Haydock, G (ed), *Off the Wall*, issues 19-23, Reading, 1993-4
Haydock, G (ed), *King!*, issues 1-25, Bournemouth, 1994-2001
Haydock, G (ed), Michael Jackson News International *Newsletter*, issues 1-24, Bournemouth, 1994-7
Hekma, G, The Decline of Sexual Radicalism in the Netherlands. In: Hekma, G, (ed), Past and Present of Radical Sexual Politics, Mosse Foundation, Amsterdam, 2004
Hills, M, Michael Jackson Fans on Trial? "Documenting" Emotivism and Fandom in Wacko About Jacko, *Social Semiotics*, 17(4):459-477, 2007
Hinerman J, (Don't) leave me alone: tabloid narrative and the Michael Jackson child-abuse scandal, in Lull, J & Hinerman, J, (eds), Media scandal: Morality and desire in the popular culture marketplace, Polity Press, Oxford, 1997
Howitt, D, Paedophiles and Sexual Offences Against Children, Wiley, Chichester, 1995
Hubbard, TK, Greek Love Reconsidered, Wallace Hamilton Press, New York, 2000
Hubbard, TK (ed) Homosexuality in Greece and Rome: A Sourcebook of Basic Documents, University of California Press, Berkeley, 2003
Hughes, G, Redemption: The truth behind the Michael Jackson child abuse allegations, Branch & Vine Publications, Radford, Virginia, 2004
Jackson, K & Wiseman, R, The Jacksons: My Family, St Martins Press, New York, 1990
Jackson, La Toya & Romanowski, P, La Toya Jackson: The Shocking and Controversial Exposé of Life in the Jackson Family, Arrow, London, 1992
Jackson, M, Moonwalk, Mandarin, London, 1988
Jackson, M, Dancing the Dream, Doubleday, London, 1992
Jackson, MM & Hack, R, Jackson Family Values: Memories of Madness, Dove Books, West Hollywood, California, 1996
Jackson, S, Childhood and Sexuality, Basil Blackwell, Oxford, 1982

Jefferson, M, On Michael Jackson, Pantheon Books, New York, 2006
Jones, A, Michael Jackson Conspiracy, Aphrodite Jones Books, Lincoln, Nebraska, 2007
Jones, Bob & Brown, S, Michael Jackson: An Insider's Story of the King of Pop, SelectBooks, New York, 2005
Kincaid, JR, Child-Loving: The Erotic Child and Victorian Culture, Routledge, London, 1992
Kincaid, JR, Erotic Innocence: The Culture of Child Molesting, Duke University Press, London, 1998
Kinsey, A, *et al.*, Sexual Behavior in the Human Male, Saunders, Philadelphia, 1948
Kinsey, A, *et al.*, Sexual Behavior in the Human Female, Saunders, Philadelphia, 1953
Kitzinger, J & Moorti, S, Introduction to "Framing Michael Jackson: Celebrity on Trial", *Social Semiotics*, 17(4):413-415, 2007
La Fontaine, J, The Extent and Nature of Organised and Ritual Abuse, HMSO, London, 1994
Leahy, T, Positively experienced man/boy sex: The discourse of seduction and the social construction of masculinity. *ANZJS*, 28: 71-87, 1992
Leahy, T, Sex and the Age of Consent: The Ethical Issues. *Social Analysis*, 39, April 1996
LeVay, S, The Sexual Brain, MIT Press, London, 1994
Levine, J, Harmful to Minors: The Perils of Protecting Children from Sex, University of Minnesota Press, Minneapolis, Minnesota, 2002
Li CK, West DJ & Woodhouse TP, Children's Sexual Encounters with Adults, Duckworth, London, 1990
Lin, YP & Cheng, TJ, Why can't Chinese Han drink alcohol? Hepatitis B virus infection and the evolution of acetaldehyde dehydrogenase deficiency, *Med. Hypotheses*, 59: 204–207, 2002
MacCarthy, F, Eric Gill, Faber & Faber, London, 1989
Martinson, FM, Eroticism in infancy and childhood, in Constantine, L & Martinson, F (eds), Children and Sex: New Findings, New Perspectives, Little, Brown, Boston, Massachusetts, 1981
Martinson, FM, The sexual life of children, Bergin & Garvey, Westport, Connecticut, 1994
Mecca, C, Michael Jackson: American Master, CAM Co, Arvada, Colorado, 1997
Mercer, K, Monster Metaphors: Notes on Michael Jackson's *Thriller*, in Mercer, K, Welcome to the Jungle: New Positions in Black Cultural Studies, Routledge, London, 1994
Middleton, W (ed), The Betrayal of Youth: Radical Perspectives on Childhood Sexuality, Intergenerational Sex, and the Social Oppression of Children and Young People, CL Publications, London, 1987
Mockler, KB, M/others: JM Barrie, Michael Jackson and the frustration of maternal men, Georgetown University, OCLC: 58479383, 2004
Mohr, R, The pedophilia of everyday life, *The Guide*, pp.4-5, Sept. 1996

Nieto, J, Children and adolescents as sexual beings: cross-cultural perspectives, *Child and Adolescent Psychiatric Clinics of North America*, 13:461-477, 2004

Noonan, D, Michael Jackson, Orion Books, London, 1994

O'Carroll, T, Paedophilia: The Radical Case, Peter Owen, London, 1980. Online text: *www.ipce.org*

O'Carroll, T, A Jackson jury on the streets, NAMBLA Bulletin, 14(8):14-16, November 1993

O'Carroll, T, Is paedophilia violent? *www.icpe.org* World Congress of Sexology, Paris, 2001

O'Carroll, T, "A wasted opportunity", Review of Dimond (2005), *www.amazon.com* , 2006

O'Carroll, T, "Around Jackson, not 'on' him"; Review of Jefferson (2006), *www.amazon.com* , 2006

Okami, P, Self-reports of "positive" childhood and adolescent sexual contacts with older persons: an exploratory study, *Archives of sexual behavior*, 20(5):437-457, 1991

Okami, P, Muddy Waters, *Archives of Sexual Behavior*, 31(6):492-4, Dec. 2002

Orth, M, Nightmare in Neverland, *Vanity Fair*, Jan. 1994

Orth, M, The Jackson Jive, *Vanity Fair*, Sept. 1995

Orth, M, Losing His Grip, *Vanity Fair*, March 2003

Orth, M, Neverland's Lost Boys, *Vanity Fair*, March 2004

Pascal, Varieties of Man/Boy Love, Wallace Hamilton Press, New York, 1992

People for Children's Rights Collective, Who's Bad? An Analysis of Anglo-American child sex hysteria in the light of the Michael Jackson Saga, People for Children's Rights, London, 1994

Percy, W, Pederasty and Pedagogy in Archaic Greece, University of Illinois Press, Chicago, 1996

Porter, D, Jacko, His Rise and Fall: The Social and Sexual History of Michael Jackson, Blood Moon Productions Ltd, *www.BloodMoonProductions.com* , 2007

Powner, J, All things to all people: the universal appeal of Michael Jackson, *Off the Wall*, 19:20-23 (Part 1) Dec. 1992 – Jan. 1993 and 22:14-18 (Part 2) July – August 1993

Randall, JL, Childhood and Sexuality: A Radical Christian Approach, Dorrance, Pitsburgh, 1992

Riegel, DL, Pedophilia, pejoration, and prejudice: inquiry by insinuation, argument by accusation, *Sexuality & Culture*, 9(1):88-97, Winter 2005

Rind, B & Bauserman R, Biased terminology effects and biased information processing in research on adult-nonadult sexual interactions: an empirical investigation, *Journal of Sex Research*, 30(3):260-269, 1993

Rind, B *et al.*, A Meta-Analytic Examination of Assumed Properties of Child Sexual Abuse Using College Samples, *Psychological Bulletin*, 124:22-53, 1998

Rind, B, The problem with consensus morality, *Archives of Sexual Behavior*,

31(6):496-8, Dec. 2002
Rind, B, Adolescent Sexual Experiences with Adults: Pathological or Functional? *Journal of Psychology & Human Sexuality*, 15(1):5-22, 2003
Rose, J, The Case of Peter Pan, Macmillan, London, 1984
Rossman, P, Sexual Experience between Men & Boys, Maurice Temple Smith, London, 1979
St Martin, G, & Nelson, RC (eds), The Boy: A Photographic Essay, Arco Publishing, New York, 1964
St Martin, G, & Nelson, RC (eds), Boys Will Be Boys!, Book Horizons/Book Adventures, New York, 1966
Sandfort, T, The Sexual Aspect of Paedophile Relations: The experience of twenty-five boys, Pan/Spartacus, Amsterdam, 1982
Sandfort, T, Sex in Pedophilic Relationships: An Empirical Investigation Among a Non-Representative Group of Boys, *Journal of Sex Research*, 20(2):123-42, 1984
Sandfort, T, The Sexual Experiences of Children, *Paidika: The Journal of Paedophilia,* 3(1):20-54, 1993 and 3(2):59-74, 1994
Sandfort, TGM & Everaerd, WT, Male juvenile partners in pedophilia, in Perry, ME (ed), Handbook of Sexology, Vol.7, Elsevier, Amsterdam, 1990
Sandfort, T, Brongersma, E & Naerssen, A (eds), Male Intergenerational Intimacy, Harrington Park Press, London, 1991
Schmidt, G, The dilemma of the male pedophile, *Archives of Sexual Behavior*, 31(6):473-77, Dec. 2002
Schuijer, J, The Netherlands changes its age of consent law, *Paidika: The Journal of Paedophilia*, 3(1):13-20, 1993
Silberman, SC, Presenting Michael Jackson, *Social Semiotics*, 17(4):417-440, 2007
Sky, R, Michael Jackson: The Bad Year, Harper-Collins, London, 1994
Skynner, R & Cleese, J, Families and how to survive them, Cedar, London, 1993
Smith, J, Michael Jackson:The man we never saw, *The Guardian* (*Weekend* magazine section), 1 Jan. 1994
Spilbor, JM, The Michael Jackson case: Why the ruling on previous allegations is unfair to the defendant, CNN online, 31 March 2005, *http://www.cnn.com/2005/LAW/03/31/spilbor.jackson/*
Stone, BE, Abnormals, Freaks, and Michael Jackson: Foucault, Baldwin, and the Truth of the Grotesque. Presentation at University of Memphis alumni conference, May 2004 (*bstone@lmu.edu*)
Sulloway, FJ, Born To Rebel: Birth order, family dynamics, and creative lives, Little, Brown & Co, London, 1996
Taraborrelli, JR, Michael Jackson: The Magic & the Madness, Headline, London, 1992; also revised edition, 1994; plus a revised, expanded and updated edition, Pan, London, 2004; and finally, Michael Jackson: The Magic, The Madness, The Whole Story, 1958-2009, Hachette, New York, 2009
Taylor, B (ed), Perspectives on Paedophilia, Batsford, London, 1981

Traina, C, Passionate Mothering: Toward an Ethic of Appropriate Mother-Child Intimacy, in Kelsay, J (ed), The Annual of the Society of Christian Ethics, Vol. 18, DePaul University, Chicago, 1998

Tsang, D (ed), The Age Taboo: Gale Male Sexuality, Power and Consent, Alyson Publications, Boston, 1981

Webster, R, The Great Children's Home Panic, Orwell Press, Oxford, 1998

Webster, R, The Secret of Bryn Estyn, Orwell Press, Oxford, 2005

Wegner, RW, My Three Years Working for Michael Jackson, 1st Books, Bloomington, Indiana, 2002

Wellings, K *et al.*, Sexual Behaviour in Britain, Penguin, London, 1994

West, DJ, Boys and sexual abuse: an English opinion, *Archives of Sexual Behavior*, 27(6):539-559, Dec. 1998

Wilson, GD & Cox, DN, The Child-Lovers: A Study of Paedophiles in Society, Peter Owen, London, 1983

Wilson, P, The Man they called a Monster: Sexual Experiences Between Men and Boys, Cassell, Melbourne, 1981

Yates, A, Sex Without Shame: Encouraging the Child's Healthy Sexual Development, Temple Smith, London, 1979

Yuill, R & Evans, DT, Pedophilia, in Blackwell Encyclopedia of Sociology, Ritzer, G (ed), Blackwell, Oxford, 2007

Zucker, KJ, Introduction to the Special Section on Pedophilia: Concepts and Controversy, *Archives of Sexual Behavior*, 31(6):465, Dec. 2002

INDEX

3/7/2014

This fascinating, closely reasoned brief argues that Michael Jackson never harmed much less traumatized any of his favorites. He cuddled with, French kissed, and sometimes caused to ejaculate but never penetrated boys from eight to fourteen. Not one of them ever objected except when urged on by greedy parents. They were carefully groomed and dazzled by the King of Pop but never brutally dumped.
Professor William Armstrong Percy III, University of Massachusetts at Boston, author of Pederasty and Pedagogy in Archaic Greece

Michael Jackson's Dangerous Liaisons carefully sifts through the welter of tabloid gossip and conflicting statements by those involved with the late star to separate fact from fiction. The picture that emerges is one that confirms Jackson's sexual attraction and active involvement with pre-pubescent boys. However, what the book also shows is that the only real 'abuse' of children that occurred was not from Michael's bedroom horseplay, but parental manipulation of kids for financial gain. As such, this book gives us a profound cultural critique of received assumptions about childhood innocence, pedophilic 'power', and parental goodwill.
Professor Thomas K Hubbard, University of Texas at Austin, author of Homosexuality in Greece and Rome

Research shows that sex between men and boys ranges from murderous attacks, through all degrees of coercion and inducement, to enthusiastic participation by the boys. This exhaustive trail through the saga of Michael Jackson's eccentricities points to his obsession with boys being at the commoner, mild end of the pederasty range. The story of years of accusation and counter-accusation, culminating in final acquittal, shows criminal justice battling with the public's highly aroused sensitivity about children and sex, and with litigation marred by rewards in millions for particular verdicts. The author's sympathy lies with the children whose feelings are disregarded by adults in prosecutorial combat. His vivid and insightful commentary is a joy to read.
DJ West, Fellow of the Royal College of Psychiatrists, Emeritus Professor of Clinical Criminology, Cambridge University